The Internet for Everyone

J. Ranade Workstation Series

The Internet for Everyone

A Guide for Users and Providers

Richard W. Wiggins

McGraw-Hill, Inc.

New York   San   Francisco   Washington, D.C.   Auckland   Bogotá
Caracas   Lisbon   London   Madrid   Mexico City   Milan
Montreal   New Delhi   San Juan   Singapore
Sydney   Tokyo   Toronto

Library of Congress Cataloging-in-Publication Data

Wiggins, Richard W.
    The Internet for everyone : a guide for users and providers /
Richard W. Wiggins.
        p.   cm. — (Jay Ranade workstation series)
    Includes index.
    ISBN 0-07-067018-8   — ISBN 0-07-067019-6 (pbk.)
    1. Internet (Computer network)   I. Title.   II. Series: J. Ranade
workstation series.
TK5105.875.I57W54   1994
004.6'7—dc20   94-17608
                                                              CIP

1 2 3 4 5 6 7 8 9 0   DOH/DOH   9 0 9 8 7 6 5 4 (HC)
1 2 3 4 5 6 7 8 9 0   DOH/DOH   9 0 9 8 7 6 5 4 (PBK)

ISBN 0-07-067018-8 (HC)
ISBN 0-07-067019-6 (PBK)

*The sponsoring editor for this book was Jerry Papke, the editing
supervisor was Christine H. Furry, and the production supervisor was
Suzanne W. Babeuf. This book was set in Century Schoolbook by
North Market Street Graphics.*

Printed and bound by R. R. Donnelley & Sons Company.

To my father, for his perseverance, and to the memory of my mother, for her love of language

Contents

Preface

I suppose the folks at the National Geographic Society experience a similar mix of pleasure and frustration as I encountered in writing this book. They have the job of documenting and mapping a world whose political landscape has undergone massive change in the last few years. In my case, I've undertaken a project to write about a virtual landscape that is growing and changing even more rapidly—the Internet. Late in 1992, having written a chapter for a book in Jay Ranade's technical series at McGraw-Hill, I explored the idea of a book on campuswide information systems. Mr. Ranade, a wise editor and a best-selling author in his own right, suggested a more general text on the Internet, and this book is the result.

My thesis is that you will not merely want to passively partake of the many and varied information resources on the Internet—though surely you will want to do that. I believe that we are entering an era of online democracy in publishing, and I believe the Internet will be the place where the necessary tools will be forged. The early 1990s have seen the birth of the first of these tools—protocols and software such as Gopher, the World-Wide Web, and NCSA Mosaic. The democratization of Internet information publishing has already begun, with thousands of Gopher and Web servers online, and hundreds of new ones coming on stream each month. As this book goes to press, the most reliable estimate of the population of the Internet is 20 million people. Most users are consumers only. I believe the day will soon arrive when the vast majority of people with Internet access will also be information providers—offering to the world their résumés, papers they have written, sketches they have drawn, and so forth.

Does everyone in the world really need to be able to read everyone else's favorite poem? Of course not. The new world of Internet publishing allows individual readers to select those documents of interest on demand—your demand, not the wishes of the author or publisher.

Many readers of this book will undertake setting up a server as part of their job—as a way for their organization to offer information to potential customers or beneficiaries. Others will set up servers for more personal kinds of information. Whether you run your own server or employ the services of a proxy (in the form of an enlightened Internet service provider who offers individualized publishing services via Gopher or the World-Wide Web), this book will explain what it takes to get started as an Internet information provider.

The early chapters of this book cover the basic issues of what the Internet is all about, the basics of the Internet protocols, what the client/server model means in the Internet context, and how to connect to the Internet. Person-to-person communication is perhaps the most commonly used Internet service, so e-mail is covered next. Subsequent chapters explain group communications mechanisms—mailing list processors and Usenet News. Next, we cover the venerable File Transfer Protocol, still the number-one way people retrieve documents and software over the Internet. The chapter on FTP also offers detailed information on the multiplicity of file formats you will encounter on the net.

People don't just send e-mail and fetch files over the Internet—they also communicate in real time. A remarkable young information provider named Charles Henrich contributed the chapter on real-time communications. His boss, my old friend and colleague Charles Severance, contributed the next chapter, which explains how networked file systems can allow a user to access files on a remote computer across the Internet as if user and disk drive were adjacent.

Next, we cover the important new browsing tools of the Internet, Gopher and the World-Wide Web, including a discussion of a tool that has been called the "killer app of the Internet"—NCSA Mosaic. PC users will also want to consult App. A, which explains what it takes to install Mosaic under MS-Windows.

With the flood of documents and files available on the Internet, navigation has become a vital issue, so we devote a chapter to pioneering indexing and cataloging tools, such as Archie, Veronica, and a personal favorite of mine, John Doyle's Netlink. Next, we move from catalog tools to WAIS, a mechanism for indexing large document archives in their entirety. So far, WAIS trails Gopher and the World-Wide Web in its usage, but I predict that it is the sleeper application of the Internet.

Because Internet navigation can be such a challenge, Chap. 16 offers strategies and tactics for finding resources, people, and places on the Internet. Chapter 17, contributed by Judy Matthews, the physics-astronomy librarian at Michigan State University, offers insight into ways that professional librarians are exploiting (and cataloging) today's Internet.

Chapter 18 covers alternatives for electronic publishing, and explains the role of the Internet in the deployment of the digital library of the future. Chapter 19, contributed in part by my colleague Mark Riordan, covers security and privacy issues—information vital to both consumers and providers. (Mark is known internationally as the author of the RIPEM package.)

Chapter 20 explains what choices are available to you as a potential Internet information provider. The insights of Nat Torkington, a young Internet information provider from New Zealand, contribute to the discussion of providing documents via the World-Wide Web. Chapter 21 offers specific examples of how to install Unix-based Internet server software. The section on installing the Gn Gopher was written by a most able programmer here at Michigan State, Dennis Boone. Installation of WAIS is covered by Jim Fullton, well known in the WAIS and Internet engineering communities.

Chapter 22 covers some non-Unix options for Internet information delivery. One of these is the GopherSurfer program from the University of Minnesota—by far the easiest-to-install tool for Internet information publishing. If you don't want to wrestle with Unix, buy yourself a PowerPC Macintosh, get it connected to the Internet, and with a drag-and-drop or two you are an Internet information provider. (My thanks to Jeff Stuit of the University of Michigan, who alerted me to this Gopher server for the masses.) You will also learn how to install GoServe, a server for OS/2, thanks to the narrative contributed by David Singer of IBM's Almaden Research labs. Finally, thanks to the narrative of Chris McNeil, you will learn how to install the KA9Q Gopher server—a surprisingly easy way to run a server on a platform that was never intended for such purposes, MS-DOS.

Chapter 23 is entitled "Setting Up a Campus-Wide Information System," but don't be fooled by the title—many of the topics covered could be useful in corporate settings. With all the technical material in the preceding chapters, Chap. 24 is intended to show that Internet information providers include real human beings; it offers profiles of some of the pioneers on the electronic information frontier. Chapter 25 offers my speculations on the future of the Internet, and Chap. 26 provides a sampler of the many resources available online. With thousands of servers and millions of documents already online, no single catalog is comprehensive; do not believe anyone who says he or she has cataloged the whole Internet. The goal of my sampler is to whet your appetite; you will use the online navigation tools explained in earlier chapters as your real travelogue. Erik Larson helped prepare this chapter.

Much of this book is technical, and the epilogue was written by a political scientist who philosophizes about technology—Peter Lyman. Besides mulling over the meaning of the Internet, Dr. Lyman is the University Librarian at the University of Southern California (i.e., he's the director). He casts an appreciative but wary eye on technology, and his insights enrich this book.

Many of the tools covered in this book did not exist when I undertook the project; all of the tools are undergoing rapid change even as I type this preface. Therefore, the text offers many pointers to online resources that you can use to learn more and to obtain the most current information.

Looking to the future of electronic publishing, McGraw-Hill will use this book as a pioneering test case. Thanks to the initiative of Laura Fillmore and the Online BookStore, several chapters of this book will be available for personal viewing and printing over the Internet. Point your Gopher client at `market-place.com`, or your Web client at `http://marketplace.com/0/obs/obshome.html`. (If that suggestion appears to be written in Sanskrit, read Chaps. 12 and 13.) Thanks to Mark Cook for helping prepare the HTML.

The Michigan Engineering Television Network (a unit of the University of Michigan) is producing a series of video tapes that will serve as a companion to this book, in which your author will offer live demonstrations of tools such as Mosaic. Call METN for details (313-763-1233 voice, 313-936-3492 fax.)

Some portions of the text originally appeared in June 1993 in an electronic journal, the Public-Access Computer Systems Review 4, no. 2 (1993): 4–60. You can retrieve that article by sending the following e-mail messages to `list-serv@uhupvml.uh.edu`: `GET WIGGINS1 PRV4N2 F=MAIL` and `GET WIGGINS2 PRV4N2 F=MAIL`. My thanks go to editor Charles Bailey for his careful review of that document.

ACKNOWLEDGMENTS

There are many people I should thank for their encouragement, advice, and reviewing of draft material—so many that I fear I may omit someone. I apologize if this is the case. First, my deepest appreciation goes to Jay Ranade for endorsing the project, and to Jerry Papke and the staff at McGraw-Hill. Don't let anyone tell you about the ruthless New York publishing industry; Jerry and his staff have been models of civility in working with a first-time author who was hopelessly naive regarding the complexity of the job he was undertaking. Thanks, too, to the staff of North Market Street Graphics for coping with editing questions and the inevitable format issues.

Thanks go to another McGraw-Hill author, Sidnie Feit, for her technical review. Other reviewers of portions of the text include Jeff Mackie-Mason, Paul Wolberg, Jeremy Kargon, Hannah Kaufman, Nat Torkington, Mary Beth Meyer, Ben Hart, Marie-Christine Mahe, and Doug Nelson. Charles Henrich, while sometimes brutally candid, was an especially helpful reviewer.

The fine folks at CICNet—John Hankins, Paul Holbrook, Kim Shaffer, and others have been helpful on this and other projects, as have Jeff Ogden, Jo Ann Ward, Pat Smith, and others of Merit Inc. Thanks to an important Internaut, Ed Vielmetti, for sharing some of his wisdom with me, and to the other information providers who consented to being profiled.

Thanks to Gabe Goldberg and Donna Walker for their encouragement and for suggesting the title; special thanks to Hal Varian for giving an economist's counsel to a new author. And I was lucky to receive encouragement from my family—my father and brother, and various aunts, uncles, and cousins who knew about the project. My brother has tried every online information service and helped me figure out their Internet e-mail mechanisms. Thanks, too, go to my revered friends at the Peanut Barrel. And Chuck Severance—yes, it's finally in print, and your picture's in it. Thanks also to Gary Cosimini, John Cook, Gordy Thompson, Dan Gillmor, Mike Ammann, Margaret Wilson, Leigh Scherzer, John Klensin, Mark McCahill, Robin Marley, and my Computer Lab colleagues.

I would like to thank my management—my boss, Dr. Robert Wittick, my director, Dr. Lewis Greenberg, and our vice-provost, Dr. Paul Hunt for entrusting me with responsibility for coordinating MSU's effort in deploying a campuswide information system. That assignment, made in early 1992, afforded me the opportunity to observe and participate in the new world of Internet information delivery. I have been privileged to have met some of the leading technologists in this realm—the Minnesota Gopher team, Tim Berners-Lee, Alan Emtage and Peter Deutsch, and others—and through the magic of the net I've met many other toolsmiths and information providers. This has been the opportunity of a lifetime, and the ride is just beginning.

Finally, I would especially like to thank one very special person, Judy Matthews, for she not only contributed her own words in the form of one chapter of this book, she is also my sweetheart. Judy has been confident in the success of this effort from its inception, and her support has been unflagging despite many long nights of research and writing. Not only did Judy offer essential moral support, she also helped out with research, helping me locate many useful articles and online resources. Every author should be so lucky.

Whatever form your use of the Internet takes, I hope this book is helpful. Perhaps I'll see you on the net.

Rich Wiggins
wiggins@msu.edu

The Internet: An Overview

Computer networks are a popular topic these days, and the vision of a unified national or international network dominates much of the discussion. Major newspapers, popular magazines such as *Time* and *Newsweek,* professional journals, even radio and television are talking about "Information Highways," the "National Information Infrastructure," and "global virtual communities." Let's imagine what an international data superhighway might look like:

- Users from around the globe will be able to connect to the network. There will be high-speed access at universities, government agencies, and business installations worldwide. The public will be able to access the network via dial-up services, either as local calls or toll-free 800 services.

- The network will use standard communication protocols, providing access no matter what brand of computer one uses, no matter what operating system, no matter the size of the computer.

- Users on this global network will be able to exchange electronic mail with one another, with messages delivered instantaneously in many cases, or in a few seconds or minutes otherwise. The network will allow not just one-to-one communications, but will also provide tools to allow groups of individuals separated by distance and time to carry on discussions. Gateways will make it possible to exchange e-mail with private networks as well.

- The network will provide a simple, standard way for users to log into computers around the world. Individuals will take advantage of this not only from their homes or offices, but also will use the network when traveling so they can connect back home.

- Navigation tools will make it easy for individuals to cruise the network, glancing at information provided by universities, businesses, libraries, foundations, and individuals.

- Index tools will allow users to scan large databases, quickly locating documents of interest.

- Users will be able to retrieve and play back movies, sounds, and multimedia documents.

- The network will support real-time communications: people will be able to talk to one another online (by typing, or, with the right equipment, over audio links) and will even use the network to play real-time virtual reality games.

- Finally, the network will be a two-way highway. Users would not think of themselves exclusively as consumers; instead, tools will make it relatively easy for anyone to become an information provider. Individuals could publish résumés, papers they've written, photos of their families, samples of their artwork—any item they want to make accessible—and these items could be retrieved on demand by anyone with access to the network worldwide.

That list of features seems rather futuristic. One might speculate that we'd see it by the year 2000. In fact, *every feature listed above exists today*—on the Internet. Of course, we are a long way from having a network that is universally deployed, with simple appliances that the masses can use for connection and communication over high-speed links to every building in the land. Access to the Internet isn't as simple as signing up with your local phone company or cable company—though both kinds of companies are becoming extremely interested in the idea of serving as the on-ramp to the data highway. But right now—today—the Internet represents a real, functional, worldwide data network whose tools and technologies serve as the prototypes for the gigabit* data highways we're reading about.

THE INTERNET: AN INFORMATION TREASURE TROVE

The fastest, most capable network in the world wouldn't be very useful if it didn't have valuable information for people to retrieve. The Internet is not just a medium for person-to-person electronic mail; it's also a repository of all sorts of information, "published" by information providers worldwide. Here are some examples of how information is exchanged over the Internet:

---

* A "gigabit" is a thousand megabits, or 1,073,741,824 bits. A gigabit network can transfer that many bits in a second. Research projects are under way to build networks—both local and wide-area—that have that level of capacity. By comparison, today's local area networks commonly run at about 10 megabits per second, and networks that can run at 100 megabits per second are becoming somewhat common.

- Distributed discussion tools allow people who are separated by space and time to carry on discussions on topics of common interest over "mailing lists." One mailing list manager, Revised Listserv, supports over 800,000 users who subscribe to over 9000 such mailing lists. A similar global discussion medium called Usenet News delivers several megabytes per day of discussion, organized into 3500 "news groups." Topic areas in these two media range from very specific to very general; in either case, the audience can as easily be at one location or dispersed worldwide.*

- Many universities are building Campus-Wide Information Systems, or CWISes, as a way of consolidating campus information and computing services in one place. Most CWISes are accessible via the Internet. Users from around the world can search course catalogs, read about campus services, or examine the library's online catalog. At some schools, you can look at a campus map, view pictures of campus scenes, or read today's version of the student newspaper—all via the Internet.

- Individual scientists and scientific institutes are building collections of papers and databases and making them available for Internet access. Using tools such as Gopher, World-Wide Web, and WAIS (all of which are covered in detail in later chapters) users can retrieve information on everything from astronomy to biodiversity to the human genome project to epidemiology to zoology.

    In some scientific disciplines, the process of writing formal journal articles has taken on an Internet twist: "preprints" of articles to be submitted to print journals are made available for review by other scientists via the Internet. And in other cases, "electronic journals" are replacing print journals altogether. (These developments are discussed in detail in Chap. 16.)

- Commercial vendors have begun publishing current excerpts of "serious" books and magazines for open access on the Internet. You can read an article from the *New Republic* or the *New Yorker,* and decide if you want to buy a paper copy or get a subscription. Other vendors offer complete text issues of *USA Today,* the *Los Angeles Times, Forbes,* and other periodicals; for instance, a university in New Hampshire (or New Zealand) can subscribe to the *Los Angeles Times* on behalf of its students, and each day's issue will be delivered that day—via the Internet. The author Stephen King has made excerpts of his short story "Umney's Last Case" available initially over the Internet.†

---

* Note that both Revised Listserv and Usenet News largely have their roots in other networks: the former in Bitnet, the latter in the UUCP network. Today, much of the traffic for each is carried over the Internet. Other mailing list managers have evolved from pure Internet roots.

† The pioneering vendors of periodicals over the Internet are American Cybercasting and Clarinet; they offer full-text subscriptions, generally licensed for a campus or corporate network. A company called the Online Bookstore makes samples of books available freely on the Internet. Another firm, the Electronic Newsstand, offers samples from current periodicals.

- Classical works of literature are being made available freely on the Internet, through the efforts of a group called "Project Gutenberg." Titles online include the works of Shakespeare, the Bible, *Moby Dick,* the *Autobiography of Frederick Douglass,* and many more. Other Internet-resident text archives include collections of French literature and Irish literature, organized so as to help scholars do research.

- The written word isn't all you'll find; with the right equipment, you can listen to audio documents over the Internet. You can find snippets of historical voices, samples of music, and longer audio documents such as presidential debates and interviews delivered in a "radio" format. Already, some groups are demonstrating the delivery of real-time audio and moving images over the Internet.

- Current weather forecasts and weather maps are available from several sources on the Internet. You can even find motion-picture versions of weather maps, resembling the satellite loops seen on television. Earthquake reports are also made available daily. The Internet was even used to deliver advice to victims of the Mississippi River flood in mid-1993.

- Government agencies are discovering the value of the Internet as a way to disseminate information. Agencies with a scientific focus, such as NASA, are perhaps further along in publishing information via the Internet, but the day is not far off when every agency is an Internet information provider. Rather than stopping by the post office for a tax form (or spending $5.00 to fax it from the local newspaper), you might soon be able to retrieve the form over the Internet—and perhaps submit it after you've filled it out. If you're hoping to get money from the government, you can find information on federal grants on the Internet. And it's not only large agencies, and not only the U.S. government that are publishing on the Internet—you can read the city council minutes from Wellington, New Zealand if that suits your fancy.

In Chap. 2 we'll take a brief tour of the Internet, showing you some of these resources and an overview of what it takes to navigate the "net."*

WHO USES THE INTERNET?

As we will see, the Internet has historically been associated with the U.S. Department of Defense, and with research universities. While there are still many Internet users among those communities, the base of Internet users has become much broader over the last several years. Who uses the Internet?

- Teachers and students at universities, community colleges, and increasingly K–12 schools. They use the Internet as a virtual reference desk, as a way for

---

* Users often speak of "the net" when they mean the Internet. "I found some nifty software on the net today" or "You should ask about that on the net" are common expressions.

students and faculty to communicate with peers worldwide, and as a way to share lesson plans.

- Professors and other researchers at universities and in research divisions of corporations. These researchers are both consumers and producers of Internet-based information. Some universities are even teaching courses for credit over the Internet.*

- State and local government officials. Agencies from NASA to the National Institutes of Health to the Library of Congress to the Pima County Engineering and Geographic Information Services to the Metropolitan Toronto Police are on the Internet. Because the Internet is a two-way highway, officials at these agencies can mine the Internet for useful information, or they can provide information to the public or to peers at similar agencies worldwide.

- Professionals in businesses large and small. Many large corporations (and some small ones) have direct access to the Internet; other firms subscribe to dial-up access services for use by their staffs.

- Newspaper and other reporters, who use the Internet as a research tool as well as something that merits coverage in its own right.

- Increasingly, members of the public, accessing the Internet directly through specialized access providers, or indirectly via mass-market information vendors such as Delphi and CompuServe.

In recent years the visibility of the Internet has increased tremendously; even so, large numbers of users may benefit from the Internet without realizing it. Many users may not be aware of the role the Internet plays—for instance, allowing easy exchange of electronic mail with colleagues at other institutions. Each new user is a potential ambassador. One sign of the growing visibility of the Internet is the announcement of the address for sending electronic mail to the president and vice president.† (Senator Al Gore spent years promoting national computer networking before he assumed the vice presidency.)

Moreover, the Internet is now truly a global communications medium. The same sort of affinity groups listed above are plugging into the Internet around the world.

INTERNET ORIGINS

The Internet is often described as a "network of networks." The term is apt: there is no one authority that "owns" or administers the Internet; one could not draw a simple map of the Internet; there is not even a single authoritative list

---

* One example is Wright State University, which offers EDT 714, a one-credit course called Introduction to Online Communication. Other Internet-based online teaching pioneers include the University of Phoenix and Boise State.

of the millions of computers or users with access to the Internet. Instead the Internet is a sort of confederation—a worldwide collection of national, regional, campus, and corporate networks. In order to understand today's Internet, it will be helpful to consider its origins.*

The history of the Internet dates to the early days of computer networking in the 1960s. Today, when many workgroups have personal computers linked together in Local Area Networks (LANs), it's somewhat difficult to envision a world when mainframes dominated, and getting those mainframes to talk to one another was a bold new concept. But it's important to realize that the beginnings and growth of today's Internet parallel the evolution of computer networking itself.

An agency of the U.S. Department of Defense, the Advanced Research Projects Agency, issued a request for proposals to link together four initial sites in July 1968. ARPA chose Bolt Beranek and Newman's proposal in December 1968. To this day, BBN remains an important provider of Internet-related technologies and services (in fact, a division of BBN was named in July 1993 to operate the regional network NEARnet). The initial sites were the Stanford Research Institute, the University of California at Los Angeles, UC–Santa Barbara, and the University of Utah.

In today's terminology, we might call the network they were building a Wide Area Network, or WAN (albeit a rather small one). Just as there were no LANs and no PCs at the time, there were no interface cards to plug into the back of a computer in order to put it on the network. BBN built a set of Interface Message Processors, based on custom software and hardware on a minicomputer. The four sites were connected in the fall of 1969, marking the birth of the precursor to today's Internet. The new network became known as the ARPANET. During this early experimental phase, early versions of some of the core protocols† known to users today—including Telnet and the File Transfer Protocol—were born. A scheme called the Network Control Protocol managed the flow of data on the early ARPANET.

In these early days of the Internet, computers were much slower, communication lines were much slower—the fastest long-distance link was 50 kilobits per second, only about four times faster than what today's $200 dial-up modems achieve—and the number of computers on the network was small (only 200 hosts by 1981). But even in these early days, the ARPANET design community recognized that they needed to build a network not of computers, but a network of networks. Various competing networking technologies were

---

* The history of the Internet is covered in more detail in *The Internet System Handbook* (Addison-Wesley, 1993, ISBN 0-201-56741-5), David Lynch and Marshall Rose, eds. This book includes detailed technical descriptions of many aspects of Internet operations.

† A "protocol" is simply the language that is chosen for computers to use when communicating over a network. Just as there are numerous human languages, there are numerous computer communications protocols besides those used on the Internet.

evolving, and the ARPANET community wanted to be able to link these disparate networks together. The basic protocols that support communications on today's Internet—TCP/IP—were developed in the mid-1970s by Vinton Cerf of Stanford University and Robert Kahn of BBN.* TCP/IP coexisted with NCP until 1983, when it replaced the Network Control Program entirely.

The ARPANET grew as more installations—many of them defense department agencies, or research universities with ties to the defense department— became nodes on the network. While the ARPANET was growing into a national network, researchers at Xerox Corporation's Palo Alto Research Center were developing one of the technologies that would be used in local area networking—Ethernet. This approach to networking employed a scheme with a fancy name of "Carrier Sense Multiple Access with Collision Detection," which in a nutshell approximates what transpires around some conference tables: individuals speak whenever they please; when two speak at once, both back off for a second and try later; sometimes, everyone speaks at once and no one communicates.

Over time, Ethernet became one of the important standards for how to implement a local area network. In the meantime, DARPA (renamed from ARPA) funded the integration of TCP/IP support into the version of the UNIX operating system that the University of California at Berkeley was developing. When companies began marketing powerful, independent workstations that ran UNIX, TCP/IP was already built into the operating system software, and vendors such as Sun included an Ethernet port on the back. TCP/IP over Ethernet† became a common way for workstations to connect to one another.

Throughout the 1980s, the corporate and university worlds were busy installing personal computers on the desktops of many of their professional employees. The same technology that made personal computers and workstations possible—processors and memory on inexpensive, mass-market chips— made it possible for vendors to offer relatively inexpensive add-on cards to allow garden-variety PCs to connect to Ethernets. Enterprising software vendors took the TCP/IP software from Berkeley UNIX and "ported" it to the PC, making it possible for PCs and UNIX machines to talk the same language on the same network.

By the mid-1980s, the Internet TCP/IP protocols were in use for numerous campus-to-campus (wide area) links, and the same protocols were being used in many local area and campuswide networks. The stage was set for explosive growth.

---

* According to Cerf, much of the development of TCP/IP took place during 1973 through 1978; from 1978 to 1982 the protocols were implemented on a variety of hardware and software platforms, setting the stage for adoption of TCP/IP as a standard.

† Two closely related networking standards are often referred to as "Ethernet": "DIX Ethernet" and IEEE 802.3. Strictly speaking, this is not accurate; they are distinct protocols.

FROM ARPANET TO INTERNET

The term "Internet" appears in a planning document as early as 1974. But the network itself was called the ARPANET until the early 1980s. At that time, the U.S. Department of Defense decided to separate the military portion of the network into the "Milnet." The term "ARPANET" was still used for the portion of the network that was open to universities and corporate research divisions. At this point the ARPANET/Internet was still quite small, as the following chart shows:

Date	Hosts
Aug-81	213
May-82	235
Aug-83	562
Oct-84	1024
Oct-85	1961
Feb-86	2308
Nov-86	5089

A milestone in the history of the Internet also took place in the mid-1980s. In supporting five supercomputer data centers, the National Science Foundation (NSF) concluded it needed a high-performance network linking those computers to one another, and providing access to the machines for researchers across the country. In 1986 the NSF solicited proposals to create a network linking the supercomputer centers. In 1987, NSF proposed a newer NSFnet backbone, with much faster links between sites (1.5 megabits/second instead of 56 kilobits/second). The new backbone would link seven new regional networks with the supercomputer sites. NSF awarded a contract to build and manage the NSFnet to a partnership of IBM, MCI, and the Merit Computer Network.*

The creation of the NSFnet backbone and regional networks provided a milieu that encouraged Internet growth. A new data highway was in place, and many universities, keenly aware that leading research institutions had Internet access, wanted access for their own institutions. By the mid-1980s workstations either had built-in support for TCP/IP, or it could be added inexpensively. At the same time that the marketplace was delivering millions of computers begging to be connected into campus networks, along with hardware and software to connect them, the NSFnet backbone and regional networks came into existence. Numerous universities decided that they needed to be on the Internet in order to compete and cooperate with the leading academic institutions.

---

* Merit had operated a network connecting state universities in Michigan, and providing dial-up access around the state. Today that network is called Michnet.

Of course, the academy was not alone in its interest in the Internet. Business and government were also installing personal computers and local area networks throughout the 1980s. TCP/IP was less pervasive in those settings; proprietary networks such as Novell, Banyan, or Appletalk, or mainframe architectures such as IBM's SNA, were more common. Nonetheless, business and government represented pockets of growth in the Internet. Overall, the mid-1980s began a period of explosive Internet growth (see Fig. 1.1).

This is not simply a U.S. story, of course. Academic institutions in Canada, Europe, and the rest of the world were not immune to these trends. The Internet faced competition from other standards in Europe (notably one standard called X.25, part of a framework for computer communication called the OSI model) but TCP/IP-based local area networks and the global Internet were attractive, working alternatives. Growth of the Internet in the last couple of years has been especially strong.

The phenomenal growth in the size of the Internet, then, reflects these trends:

- The deployment of TCP/IP-based networks on thousands of campuses
- The deployment of TCP/IP-capable computers on millions of desktops
- The transition of the Internet from a relatively narrow base of U.S. defense department agencies and select U.S. universities into a truly international network with users in academe, government, business, and the general public.

There is every reason to believe this growth will continue. The number of hosts connected to the network appears to be growing at a rate in excess of 10

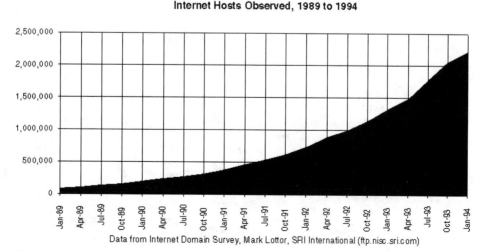

Internet Hosts Observed, 1989 to 1994

Data from Internet Domain Survey, Mark Lottor, SRI International (ftp.nisc.sri.com)

Figure 1.1 Data from Internet Domain Surveys, Mark Lottor, SRI Intl (ftp.nisc.sri.com)

percent per month. Estimates vary as to how many users this represents. In 1985, when most of the computers connected were minicomputers or mainframes, one could assume that a single host represented a few dozen or perhaps a few hundred users. Today, with one user per workstation a common scenario, that ratio is much lower. Still, the consensus in the Internet community is that 10 users per host is a conservative estimate. As we approach 2 million Internet hosts, that estimate translates into 20 million users with direct Internet access. Some number of additional users access the Internet via electronic mail gateways or through dial-up service providers.

The combination of the NSFnet backbone with the regional, or mid-level, networks, is an important part of the growth picture. These networks provide services to the institutions and individuals of their respective areas of the United States.* The idea of regional networks fits in nicely with the "network of networks" concept (see Fig. 1.2). The networks could be thought of as "mid-level" because in each case they themselves are networks of campus networks. The NSFnet backbone served as the high-speed link, connecting the supercomputer centers, other major research universities, and the regional networks. Figure 1.3 is a detailed map showing NSFnet-connected networks.

By 1990, the transition to the NSFnet-based Internet was complete, and the term ARPANET was phased out. The Defense Department remained a user of the Internet, with the Milnet carrying nonclassified traffic as a part of the Internet. (The Defense Department also continued to operate the Internet's Network Information Center, or NIC, until April 1993.)

---

* Strictly speaking, the term "mid-level" is more accurate, because the areas served by these networks don't always follow specific geographical boundaries.

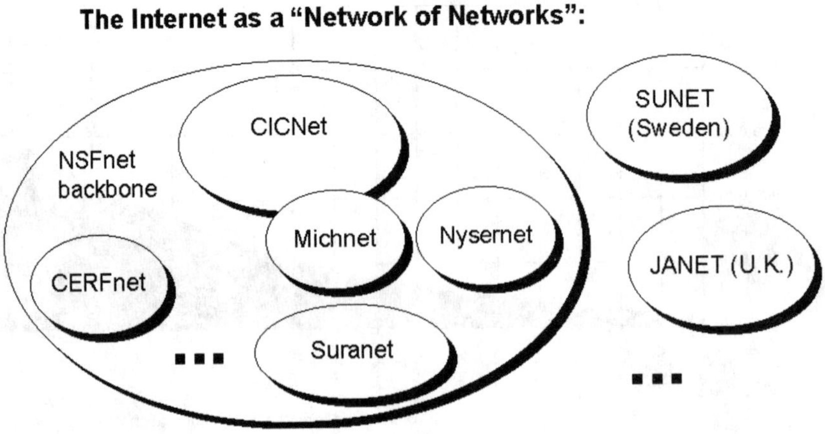

The Internet as a "Network of Networks":

Figure 1.2

Networks Connected to the NSFNET Backbone

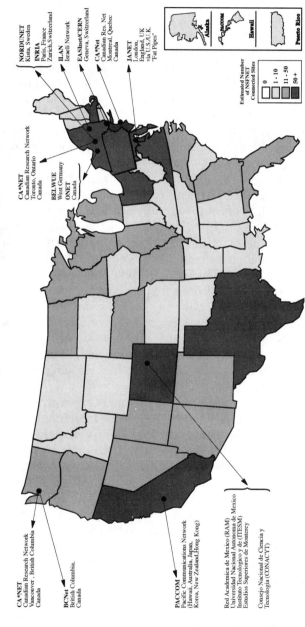

Figure 1.3

©1992 NNSC (NSF Network Service Center), BBN Systems and Technologies. Reproduction permitted provided this notice is retained.

THE SPEED OF INTERNET LINKS

As we have seen, campus and local area networks often carry the basic Internet protocols—TCP/IP—over Ethernet. Traditional Ethernet transfers data at a theoretical speed of 10 megabits per second. (Because of the way Ethernet shares its medium, actual peak transfer rates are somewhere around 80 percent of the rated speed of the medium.) In the last few years, many campuses have installed higher-speed fiber-optic networks, perhaps between a set of core buildings with need for higher network capacity. Current optical network technologies operate in the range of 100 megabits per second; one major standard now in use is FDDI (Fiber Distributed Data Interface). Newer Ethernet standards being developed allow these speeds over conventional copper cables. TCP/IP works well as a common communications method over all of these media, and more.

In order to form regional, national, and international networks, obviously there must be some sort of physical links among the various campus and corporate networks.* Most often these links are leased lines, obtained from the telephone company. The original NSFnet backbone, deployed in the mid-1980s, was based on leased lines running at the so-called "T1" rate, which means data moves at 1.544 megabits per second. In December 1992, the NSFnet backbone was improved to T3 rates, which translates to 45 megabits per second. (See Fig. 1.4.) Not surprisingly, T3 lines are considerably more expensive than T1 lines, and therefore are not widely used outside the NSFnet backbone at this time. Other intercampus links are commonly found at speeds varying from T1 speed down to 56 kilobits per second; the lowest-rate leased line commonly found moves data at 9600 bits per second. As one might expect, the slower lines are often used to connect small colleges or, in a growing application, elementary or secondary schools.

Internet links are not the exclusive province of governments or regional networks. In the United States, vendors such as PSInet and Alternet are building their own backbones as for-profit ventures. They, too, make use of leased lines, often at 56 kilobit or T1 speeds, to make up their networks.

In countries other than the United States, the story can be quite similar: for instance, JANET, the national network in the United Kingdom, supports a backbone connecting over 50 sites at 2 megabits per second. Just as the NSFnet has upgraded its national backbone in the United States, the new SuperJANET national backbone will carry data at 100 megabits per second.

Finally, we consider the communications links of users who do not have permanent connections to the Internet. They access the Internet by dialing into one of a number of Internet service providers, which could be private firms or,

---

* Or perhaps instead of a physical connection—a phone line—a microwave or satellite link might be used. Leased telephone lines are the most common type of link. The options for wide-area computer networks are discussed in Chap. 5.

NSFNET Backbone Service 1993

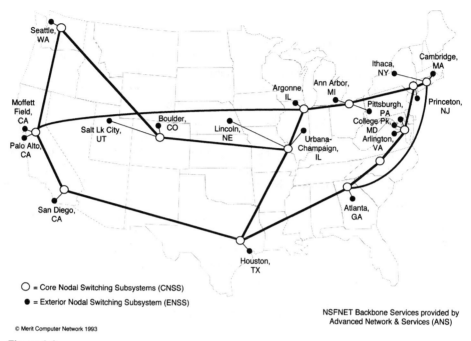

O = Core Nodal Switching Subsystems (CNSS)

● = Exterior Nodal Switching Subsystem (ENSS)

NSFNET Backbone Services provided by
Advanced Network & Services (ANS)

© Merit Computer Network 1993

Figure 1.4

in many cases, local universities or community colleges. Dial-up access speeds are determined by the speeds of the caller's and the provider's modems; obviously data moves only as fast as the lower of the two. Prices of 14,400 bit/second modems have become quite favorable for consumers, but many service providers still have modems that communicate no faster than 9600 or 2400 bits per second.

Why is the speed of links important? It is a measure of the kind of information and the number of active users a network can support. For instance, over a 9600 bit/second connection, it might take a minute to download a digitized photograph. If all of the communications links between the user and the data operate at the T1 speed of 1.5 megabits/second—and if the links aren't busy handling other people's traffic—the image could be downloaded in under a second. Users want higher speeds so that textual information can be retrieved quickly; they will demand higher speeds for quick access to multimedia documents. Of course, one shouldn't assume that access to the Internet is only useful at high speeds; many users derive great benefit from Internet access over 2400 bit/second dial-up modems. There is room for bicycles and Ferraris on the Internet.

THE INTERNET AND THE NEED FOR NAVIGATION TOOLS

In 1983, with several hundred hosts on the Internet, the challenge of navigation was relatively simple. As this book goes to press a decade later, the Internet will have reached the mark of two million hosts. A simple list of all the hosts on the network would occupy hundreds of megabytes of disk space. Of course, a given user is probably only interested in services on a fraction of the hosts on the network. But if each user had to maintain his or her own list of interesting services, there would be a lot of workstations with Post-It notes glued to the frames, and it would be virtually impossible to browse the network, looking for new resources of interest. The sheer scale of today's Internet dictates the need for tools for finding hosts and services available on the network. Mass-market information utilities such as Compuserve and Prodigy invest a lot of effort in making it easy for users to find their way through a maze of services. Their job is made easier by the centralized management of each service. With the Internet, there is no such centralized control. If such control existed it would be inimical to the spirit of experimentation that is an important feature of the Internet. This exacerbates the need for tools that allow users to discover useful resources on this disorganized global network.

Some of the most important tools have been developed only recently, starting in 1990 and 1991. Much of the story of the rest of this book revolves around such navigation tools. The main navigation aids we will learn about are:

- *Archie.*   Chapter 9 will describe how to retrieve files over the Internet using "anonymous FTP"—a process that allows use of the File Transfer Protocol without an account at the host offering the files. Thousands of computers offer more than two million files for this kind of access; this is an important avenue for obtaining public domain or sharing software on the Internet. Archie is a database that serves as an index to the holdings of some of the major anonymous FTP sites. Without Archie, one can hunt for hours without finding a desired title; with Archie, the search sometimes takes less than a minute. Archie is described in Chap. 14.

- *Gopher.*   The Internet Gopher is named for the mascot of its home, the University of Minnesota. The name is also an apt metaphor: picture a critter that burrows its way through the Internet, bringing useful things back to the user. Gopher is a simple tool, relatively easily implemented, but it has caught the Internet by storm. It is described as a document delivery tool; in fact, Gopher can deliver documents, lists of documents, and indexes. Thus, Gopher servers can offer not only textual information, but also organized "browsing lists" of resources on the Internet. Gopher is used for part of our tour of the Internet in Chap. 2, and is described fully in Chap. 12.

- *World-Wide Web.*   This tool is more ambitious in its model for delivering information on the Internet; rather than offering simple folders with one-line descriptions of documents, WWW offers *hypertext*. In a nutshell, this simply means that a document can have embedded links to other documents—anywhere within the text. A user clicks on such an embedded link, and voila, the other document appears on the screen.

In 1993, two new WWW "clients" have become available, greatly enhancing its usability and power. One tool, called Mosaic, is a multiplatform, multipurpose tool whose introduction has helped usher WWW from the hypertext mode into the hypermedia mode. Pioneering WWW administrators are delivering services no one dreamed of providing over the Internet until recently. WWW and Gopher are similar in some ways, and each tool has its adherents and detractors. Chapter 14 explains how to navigate the World-Wide Web, shows examples of some of the more interesting Web-based services, and contrasts WWW with Gopher.

- *Wide-Area Information Servers (WAIS).* Whether it is a pile of unread articles on one's desktop, or a virtual pile of unread documents scattered across the global Internet, users need a way to sift through large quantities of information. There are two sides to WAIS: it is a tool that allows an information provider to prepare indexes of such digital piles of unstructured documents, and it is a tool that lets users search these indexes with natural language questions. WAIS presents the user with a list of documents rank-ordered by how well they match the query. Although WAIS can't do anything about piles of paper, some versions of WAIS "clients" can also index local information on the user's workstation, such as a basket of electronic mail. WAIS is described in Chap. 15.

THE INTERNET AND OTHER NETWORKS

Without a doubt, the Internet is the most extensive network on the planet. It is uniquely suited for embracing other networks; no other network or network technology is growing as fast. But it is not the only large data network, or the only one of multinational scope; it is worthwhile to consider the Internet in contrast to other sorts of networks.

Figure 1.5 shows the worldwide scope of the Internet and some related networks.

Mass-market information services. Millions of subscribers belong to commercial information services such as Compuserve, America Online, Prodigy, Genie, Delphi, and so forth. These firms sell access to online discussion groups, up-to-the-minute news summaries, airline reservations and travel information, and so forth. Such vendors try to present their customers with seamless access to their various services—even though in fact services may be spread across multiple computers.

Historically, these services have been rather closed in their approach to service. They try to hide the details of the network from the user. This is laudable

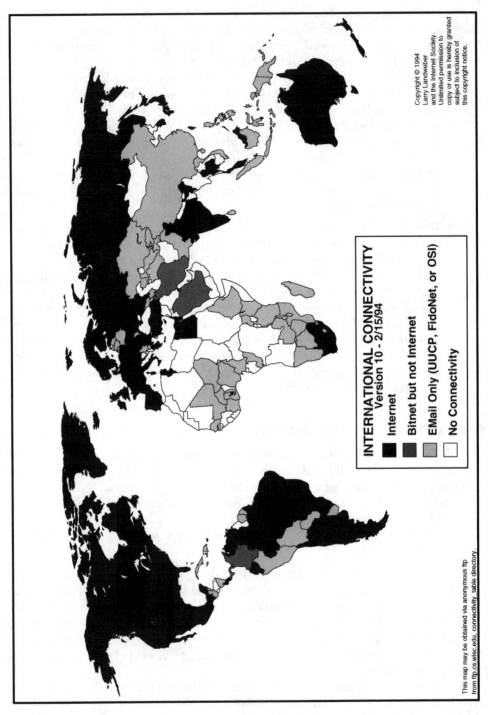

Figure 1.5

16

insofar as it makes the service easy to use; however, in some cases this makes it hard for users to exploit other networks such as the Internet. In some cases these vendors have also tended to view their services as a closed universe. For instance, each vendor offers its own scheme for electronic mail; historically, the emphasis has been on letting subscribers to the service communicate with fellow subscribers, with little thought to reaching out to the Internet at large.

There is tremendous pressure on these service vendors to open themselves to the Internet. Several vendors now provide gateways that make it easy for users to exchange e-mail to and from the Internet; examples include Compuserve and America Online. Delphi, one of the older information vendors for the public, now advertises more complete access to the Internet from their service, including remote login to Internet hosts, file transfer, and use of the Internet Gopher, in addition to e-mail.* And as of this writing, Prodigy is promising to provide the ability to exchange electronic mail with the Internet.

Over time, we can expect the commercial information providers to open up more Internet access, including perhaps access *into* the commercial services from the Internet. (It is already possible, for instance, to reach CompuServe from the Internet, via a gateway provided by Merit.†)

Because the Internet is not a single network or information provider, it isn't comparable to these mass-market information utilities. Information providers on the Internet are scattered across the millions of computers with Internet access. The global Internet can never present as unified a view to users as these vendors, but tools such as Gopher and World-Wide Web are providing some consistency and coherency to Internet navigation. And in its own way the Internet can serve as a unifying force for these services; for instance, encouraging electronic mail interoperability and perhaps eventually standard user interfaces that work across all services.

Specialized commercial data vendors. Vendors such as Mead Data Central with its Nexis/Lexis service, Lockheed's Dialog service, the Dow Jones Information service, and others, offer specialized data services. Subscribers include research libraries, information centers, and libraries in professional firms such as law offices and hospitals, and in some cases individuals. These data vendors may have huge compilations of material, indexed for online access. For instance, subscribers to Nexis can perform index searches of the full text of the *New York Times,* pulling up complete text of articles of interest. These specialized information vendors also offer access to some of their databases via the mass-market services discussed above.

---

* Indeed, Delphi's recent history shows the importance of the Internet to mass-market information services: in September 1993 it was acquired by the News Corporation, Rupert Murdoch's media conglomerate, and it is now called Delphi Internet. Another mass-market information utility, America Online, has announced plans to offer access to Internet services for its users, by means of the same graphical interface used to navigate other AOL services.

† To do so, one uses Telnet (explained in the next chapter) to reach hermes.merit.edu, and then simply types "compuserve" when asked which host to connect to.

In general, access to commercial data vendors entails more expensive hourly fees than the mass-market services. In many organizations, access to such online services is limited to information professionals, such as librarians, who have been trained to make efficient use of the services. This can minimize search charges.

As is the case for mass-market services, there is pressure on the specialized data vendors to provide access to information over the Internet. In many cases an organization with high-speed Internet links isn't able to exploit those links to get to a vendor; instead, they are forced to use a modem to dial into the information vendor over a connection as slow as 2400 bps. One vendor, Dialog, not only offers Internet access into its service, but also offers a discount for using that path.

Bitnet/CREN.   Bitnet (the Because It's Time Network) is an international network consisting mostly of universities and colleges. This network revolves around an IBM mainframe communications protocol called NJE, but non-IBM hosts (in particular Digital Equipment Corp. VAXes and various UNIX computers) outnumber the IBM mainframe hosts. Although the NJE protocol was intended as a mechanism for transferring batch jobs and print files, Bitnet is widely used for electronic mail. The Revised LISTSERV software, developed for VM/CMS mainframes and installed at hundreds of Bitnet sites, serves users who reside both on Bitnet and, through gateways, on the Internet.

Bitnet grew in popularity among academic institutions during the 1980s, and perhaps had a bit of a head start over the Internet in reaching smaller institutions. It grew to reach over 2000 nodes in 49 countries. In 1987, Bitnet merged with a smaller academic network, CSNET, forming CREN. Over time, many institutions found they were paying both for access to the Internet, and to Bitnet, and they began to ask why. Software developed at Princeton University allows Bitnet NJE traffic to be carried over Internet links. Thus in many cases sites have abandoned their dedicated Bitnet links while retaining membership and Bitnet services.

In the last two years or so, competitive pressure from the Internet has intensified, and some major Bitnet sites have withdrawn from the network. Although in some ways the NJE protocol used on Bitnet can outperform Internet delivery of large batches of electronic mail, Bitnet's lack of support for interactive communications renders it a poor competitor for the Internet. In areas where Bitnet has advantages—such as the ability to send an unsolicited file with arbitrary contents, such as a spreadsheet or an executable program—new Internet technologies are evolving to provide equivalent functionality. Today, the number of Bitnet hosts is stable or declining, while the Internet exhibits dramatic growth.

Commercial public data networks.   At the same time the Internet was growing, other packet-switched* data networks were evolving as well. These services

---

* A packet-switched network makes efficient use of expensive communications links by breaking traffic up into small packets that are sent over the most efficient (least congested) route to the destination. Each user has the illusion of a dedicated line to the destination. The "IP" of TCP/IP uses packet-switching; this is discussed in detail in Chap. 4.

allowed companies to send and receive data nationwide or worldwide without having to pay for expensive, leased phone lines of their own. During the late 1970s and 1980s, one standard for this type of network, X.25, was widely deployed in North America, Europe, and indeed worldwide. These networks provide customers with an economically attractive alternative to leasing their own long-distance telephone lines for data transmission: the cost of such leased lines is spread across many customers, each of whom pays for cheaper "virtual circuits." Commercial data networks continue to exist; examples include Sprintnet (based in the United States), Datapac (in Canada), and Datapak (in Sweden). Depending on the laws and customs of the countries involved, public data networks may be run by profit-making firms (as in the United States) or by a mixture of private firms and postal/telephone authorities in Europe and elsewhere.

Public data networks have evolved in parallel with the Internet. Historically, a company seeking to use a packet-switched network service would not have considered using the Internet; the Internet "belonged" to the Defense Department and a few universities, and didn't have the bandwidth* (capacity) to meet their needs. Over time the Internet may function more like a public data network. For now, commercial networks such as those that link banks together are built using leased telephone lines and/or public data networks; the Internet is not generally used for these purposes.

Private corporate networks. Many large corporations have built their own private data networks, to support data (and in some cases telephone) communications nationally or internationally. Corporations run their own networks in order to meet their demands for security, reliability, and performance, and also to comply with the rules of the constituent networks of the Internet, which up until recently have frowned upon purely commercial use of the Internet. Often these private networks have gateways to the Internet. For instance, IBM has an internal network called VNET that can exchange e-mail to and from the Internet.

Fidonet. Bulletin board systems, or BBSes, flourished in the mid-1980s, just as the Internet did; the personal computer and cheap modems made it possible for someone who was willing to dedicate some time, some electricity, and a phone line or two to become a bulletin board "sysop." Thousands of BBSes appeared in North America and elsewhere. Users access a BBS by using a modem and commonly available communications software and common communications protocols to dial into listed phone numbers.

Bulletin board systems have many features; the simplest among these is the ability for people to carry on a discussion electronically. Participants need not be located in the same place, and they need not log in at the same time. It's as

---

* Strictly speaking, "bandwidth" is a measure of the theoretical signaling capacity of a medium. The term is commonly used to refer to the actual speed of data transfer on a network or part of a network, which is usually considerably slower than the theoretical value.

if someone posted a large piece of paper on a public (physical) bulletin board, and passers-by wrote notes on the paper, one after the other. In its electronic form, the bulletin board can be a surprisingly effective discussion medium.

Fidonet endows dial-up BBSes with a special capability: to exchange electronic mail from one BBS site to another. Typically a Fidonet host calls one or more peers via modem and exchanges "echo mail" during hours when long-distance telephone rates are lowest. Fidonet has evolved from the grass roots into a formidable international network in its own right. Fidonet is not entirely distinct from the Internet: some of its traffic is carried over Internet paths, and electronic mail gateways allow Fidonet and Internet users to exchange mail with one another. Like the Internet, Fidonet is enjoying explosive growth; there are now over 20,000 Fidonet-linked BBSes.

Dial-up bulletin board systems complement the Internet. Fidonet and other systems provide electronic mail connectivity to people (and even countries) that otherwise would not have Internet access. Also, inspired by the success of dial-up BBSes in providing a way for people who are separated by distance and time to communicate, a number of Internet-accessible BBSes have arisen as well.

The UUCP network. Just as Fidonet hosts exchange mail with each other via dial-up lines, another network based on intermittent dial-up connections has evolved. The UUCP network has deep roots in the Unix operating system, which gives it its name: the command to copy files under Unix is CP, and this protocol supports *Unix to Unix CP* functions. The main use of this network is electronic mail and a medium of distributed discussion called Usenet News.*

NREN. Established as part of a 1991 act of Congress, the National Research and Education Network is not really a network at all; it is a program for enhancing the use of networking in research and education in the United States. In particular the NREN program is supposed to foster creation of a gigabit network for the research and education community. The NREN program also encourages the support of various federal agencies such as the NSF, NASA, and various Cabinet agencies. The NREN's status as an outgrowth of today's Internet is shown by the common use of the term "the Internet/NREN."

THE COST OF THE INTERNET

Economists constantly remind us "There is no such thing as a free lunch." This maxim is often invoked in discussions of the Internet, because in many cases there is the illusion that Internet access is "free." But someone pays for the leased telephone lines, networking hardware and software, and staff support that are required for Internet access.

---

* Usenet News is described in Chap. 8.

In the corporate and commercial settings, Internet access is often viewed as a fixed annual cost; there are no charges to users based on their utilization. The very idea of metered access evokes passionate defense of the right to universal access to information from some. Others argue that without some sort of charging, at least for high-volume consumption at peak times, individuals face no incentive to make efficient use of the network, and service providers receive no incentive to upgrade their facilities to meet demand. For the present, in the United States and in many other countries, users do have the luxury of not having to watch the meter as they browse the Internet.*

Individual users who access the Internet via service providers face fees that may in fact vary with usage levels—or the service provider may count on the fact that only so much data can be moved down a relatively slow phone line between the user and the provider's modem. Users of mass-market information utilities may pay a per-message fee to send or receive mail over the Internet.

Scarce Internet resources are also allocated through various forms of rationing. Some sites that provide files via anonymous FTP limit the times of day for access, as well as the number of concurrent users. Also, many sites limit the size of electronic mail messages that can be sent via their computers, so as to prevent flooding of the staging areas used in the mail delivery process.

RULES OF THE ROAD

As a decentralized network of networks, the Internet operates without any central agency or authority in charge. This is in sharp contrast to the commercial mass-market information services, which have centralized ownership and management. When asked "Who is in charge of the Internet?" Steve Wolff, the director of NSF's Networking Division, gives this retort: "Who's in charge of the national footpath and sidewalk system?"†

Without any one agency in charge, one might assume that anarchy prevails on the Internet. In fact the various constituent networks that make up the Internet each have adopted their own *Acceptable Use Policies* that govern traffic on their portion of the Internet. Users who make use of the Internet agree to abide by the policies of the constituent networks they traverse. Most networks make their AUPs readily available via standard Internet delivery tools such as Gopher or Anonymous FTP. Generally the rules are not very restrictive. Examples of common prohibitions include:

- Harrassing behavior toward other users
- Fraudulent use of others' accounts or identities; unauthorized access to systems or services

---

* See Chap. 24 for more discussion of these issues.

† From a comment posted to the mailing list `com-priv@psi.com`, reprinted with permission.

- Unsolicited advertisements (For instance, mass distribution of advertisements via e-mail is often prohibited; technical information and responses to
  questions about products are often explicitly allowed.)

Generally, the managers of networks on the Internet work with one another
to deal with problems. Violations of the policies of an Internet network can lead
to denial of access by the service provider that functions as the entry point for
the offender.

One gray area in the interpretation of Acceptable Use Policies has been the
use of the Internet for purely commercial activity. It has long been understood
that commercial firms may use the Internet to deliver information to their customers. Companies have not been allowed to use the Internet purely for their
own purposes. For instance, a company with offices in various major cities
could not use the Internet to send large computer-aided design datasets from
plant to plant over the Internet; they would be expected to form their own network, or use a public data network for this application.

With the explosion of interest in the Internet since the building of NSFnet,
use of the Internet to carry commercial traffic may become common. The
acceptable use policies (AUPs) of some of the networks that make up the Internet are being relaxed to allow more commercial uses as the Internet is transformed into a more broadly based data highway. Moreover, private network
providers (such as Uunet Technologies and Performance Systems International) are building their own Internet-connected backbones, allowing traffic to
be carried purely over private links.

As we've seen, the links connecting networks together into the Internet consist mostly of leased telephone lines; end users are not charged (in the United
States at least) for the traffic they generate. If commercial traffic is allowed,
the question arises: How will the agencies that run the various parts of the
Internet receive revenue to allow increases in capacity to meet demands generated by business uses? Proposals have arisen calling for charging by the
packet, at least during times of congestion. Some of the most contentious discussions in the Internet community revolve around how to make a national
(and international) network that serves all citizens—how to pay for it and
allow companies to use the network for private traffic while providing universal access.

Very little enforcement of rules on the Internet is done by formal action
taken by network authorities. Instead, peer pressure and the authority of local
system administrators are the main means of enforcement. Besides formal
rules, much of what is proper is defined by "network etiquette," or "netiquette."
In following chapters we will list some of the rules of netiquette appropriate to
each topic area.

Internet users and information providers should be aware that various laws
apply to them. Given the international scope of the network, multiple state/
provincial or national laws might be relevant. Laws restricting unauthorized

access, fraud, privacy, and copyright could all come into play. Although at times the Internet appears to be anarchic, users are advised to exercise caution and good judgment in their actions. If offensive actions cross the border from bad netiquette into illegality, prosecutions can and do occur.*

INTERNET-RELATED ORGANIZATIONS

Even though the Internet manages to operate without a central overseeing agency, there are numerous organizations involved with promoting, developing, and running the Internet. Given the worldwide reach of the Internet, a complete list of related organizations would take considerable space. Following are some of the key organizations.[†]

As the brief history of the Internet outlined above shows, U.S. government support has been a key part of its creation and growth. The role of the defense department, previously expressed through its ARPA organization, has diminished greatly since the splitoff of the Milnet. (However, various individual defense agencies remain active users and providers of information on the Internet.) The role of the National Science Foundation has risen tremendously; the explosive growth of the Internet probably would not have occurred without active NSF efforts and funding.

One important recent NSF action was the creation of a new Network Information Center structure that is separate from the military's network support organization, the DDN NIC. On April 1, 1993, three contractors took on the job of providing services to the Internet community under the common name of the InterNIC:

- *Information services.*   General user support is provided by a company called General Atomics. They provide access to information via FTP, Gopher, WAIS, and e-mail. Their offerings cover the gamut from information on getting connected to new resources on the Internet.

- *Registration services.*   Network Solutions, Inc. provides registration services to the Internet community. NSI works with the administrators responsible for naming Internet networks and hosts in order to provide a unified registration process.

- *Directory and database services.*   American Telephone and Telegraph has responsibility for providing directory and database services to the Internet community. In its InterNIC role, AT&T provides directories of Internet resources and of administrators of network resources.

---

* Perhaps the most notorious case was that of the Internet Worm, an attempt by a graduate student to dramatically reveal a flaw in UNIX security. The Worm proved more invasive than intended, and the perpetrator found himself convicted on Federal charges.

[†] A complete list of organizations, including postal and e-mail addresses, appears in App. B.

Taken together, these service organizations constitute the InterNIC, the integrated Network Information Center for the Internet.

Besides the NSF, numerous organizations are important in the support of the Internet. Since the Internet is a network of networks, whatever organizations are responsible for constituent networks are of vital importance to their users. Those organizations vary by type, by region, and by country. A few organizations are noteworthy for their scope of involvement in Internet affairs; here is a list of some of them:

- *The Internet Society.* This nonprofit organization promotes the Internet and its technologies. Membership is open to individuals and to other organizations. The current president is Vint Cerf, one of the developers of the Internet Protocol. The society's Internet Architecture Board has several constituent bodies. Of these, the Internet Engineering Task Force is the most visible. The IETF holds regular meetings that are open to anyone interested in furthering Internet standards developments; before and after each meeting, members carry on design efforts over electronic mail discussion groups. IETF members include vendor representatives, programmers, and engineers from regional networks and universities, and others. Whether it's the next generation of IP or the standard for multimedia electronic mail or the official specification for the Internet Gopher, the IETF is the key body where standards are defined.

- *The Coalition for Networked Information.* This joint endeavor is composed of organizations from academe: the Association of Research Libraries (whose members include leading research libraries), EDUCOM (an organization to promote information technology in higher education), and CAUSE (an organization of information technology administrators in higher education). CNI promotes networking in education "to enrich scholarship and enhance intellectual productivity." CNI meetings provide an important venue for research library and computing technology administrators to work together. CNI supports research projects in networked information and also seeks to shape policy and legislation.

- *The Federation of American Research Networks (FARNET).* This is not a computer network per se, but rather an umbrella organization of research networks. FARNET now includes profit and nonprofit network service providers, universities, and other organizations, both U.S. and international.

- *The Consortium for School Networking.* This group promotes Internet access for schools, from kindergarten through high school. It works closely with an IETF working group with a similar charter.

- *The Commercial Internet Exchange (CIX).* This is an association of commercial Internet access providers. It includes some of the leading Internet access providers in the United States as well as in Europe. CIX members interconnect their networks with one another, in effect creating a super-backbone that is free of any restrictions on commercial use.

- *The Electronic Frontier Foundation (EFF).*   Led by Mitch Kapor (one of the founders of Lotus Corp.), EFF promotes acceptance of computing and network technologies by the public. EFF is a major advocate for a national information highway, calling for rapid deployment of viable technology today rather than awaiting the day when every home and office is connected by a fiber-optic link.

- *Reseaux IP Europeans (RIPE).*   RIPE is a consortium of over 60 European IP service providers, representing over 300,000 computers on the Internet. RIPE's efforts constitute the IP activity of another European networking organization, RARE.

The preceding list is but a sample of the organizations that are involved with the Internet. Because the Internet reaches virtually every region of the globe, there are agencies and organizations too numerous to list here; see App. B for a more complete list.

An Introductory Tour of the Internet

Upon visiting an unfamiliar town, some people have the habit of taking out a map and driving around to get a feel for the lay of the landscape. Newcomers to the Internet often want to do the same thing. In the case of the Internet, the task is somewhat more complicated: there are no complete maps of the Internet. With millions of hosts and *resources*—services available to users—on the global Internet, it would be impossible to draw such a map. Moreover, new resources come and go on the Internet, and no central authority has the job of keeping track of what's new and what's gone.

Even though it may be challenging to tour this wonderfully anarchic network, there are enough well-known landmarks, signposts, and partial road maps for us to find our way. In this chapter we'll explore some of the better-known resources so as to introduce some Internet concepts and to give the reader a sense of the lay of the land. Even though the examples have been chosen with the belief that they will endure in their present locations, the reader should not despair if one of the services shown should seem to vanish; it may just be "down" at the time you try to connect to it, or it may have simply moved to another location.

For the purposes of this tour, we will use a couple of basic tools: Telnet, which allows users to log into remote computers on the Internet, and the Internet Gopher, the most popular document delivery and navigation tool on the Internet. We will assume the sort of text-oriented user interface that is available to all users, including those who use dial-up modems and "dumb terminal" emulators. Later chapters will explore retrieval of multimedia documents and use of tools that sport graphical user interfaces to navigate the Internet.

INTERNET HOST NAMES

Before we take a tour of the Internet, it is important to understand how hosts on the Internet are named. Every host* on the Internet is assigned an IP address, a numeric address that is in a sense the "real" address of the host. But for now we will just refer to hosts by somewhat friendlier host names. Internet host names correspond to IP addresses; a service called the Domain Name System relates host names to IP addresses.[†] Here are some examples of Internet host names:

Host name	What that name really refers to
mugwump.cl.msu.edu	A workstation in a department at Michigan State University
gopher.msu.edu	The main Gopher server at Michigan State University
msu.edu	The main host for electronic mail at Michigan State University
gopher.nd.edu	The main Gopher server at Notre Dame University
is.internic.net	The main host at InterNIC Information Services (providing information services for the Internet community)
spacelink.msfc.nasa.gov	A computer at the Marshall Space Flight Center in Alabama that provides interesting information on NASA programs
gopher.cs.nott.ac.uk	The Gopher server for the Communications Research Group at Nottingham University (England)
pinus.slu.se	Gopher server at the Swedish University of Agricultural Sciences

As you can see from the examples, domain names each consist of several parts; the parts of each name are separated by periods. When pronouncing a domain name, each period is pronounced "dot"—for instance, the second name would be pronounced "gopher dot msu dot edu."

Domain names read from left to right, going from the most specific part of the name to the most general. For instance, "mugwump" is one of several thousand computers on the campus of Michigan State University. It belongs to a department named "cl" which stands for "Computer Laboratory." In turn, the Computer Laboratory is one of numerous departments at Michigan State. The most general part of the name is "edu," which is the domain of institutions of higher education. Names are unique at each level; there is only one "msu" in the "edu" domain, only one "cl" at "msu," and only one "mugwump" in the "cl" department.[‡]

In each of these examples, and in domain names in general, the rightmost portion is chosen from a set of "top level" domains (see Fig. 2.1).

---

* A "host" is simply a computer that provides services to users over a network. A host might let remote users log into it over the network (as we'll see later in this chapter) or it might function as a "server" for remote users (as we'll see in Chap. 3).

[†] The Domain Name System is described in more detail in Chap. 4.

[‡] But there could be other "mugwumps" in other departments at MSU, or at other installations around the Internet. Mark Lottor of SRI International lists the most popular host names in his periodic surveys of the Internet; the top five are venus, pluto, cisco, mars, and gw.

Top-level Internet Domains:

Figure 2.1

As we've noted, "edu" refers to institutions of higher education. The other top-level domains in this example include:

com	Commercial firms
gov	Governmental agencies
mil	Military (U.S.)
org	General noncommercial organizations
net	Computer networks
int	International organizations
uk	United Kingdom
se	Sweden

It may appear from these examples that the names reflect a United States bias. In a sense, they do: U.S. networks are assigned to organizationally oriented top-level domains; elsewhere the top level is generally a country code. This situation arises because the roots of the Internet were in the U.S. defense and education communities. In fact, in recent years a "us" domain was defined and is being promoted as the politically correct style of name for future use. In practice, however, a large number of domain names have been assigned in the United States prior to the creation of the "us" domain.

A complete list of country codes appears in App. F. Chapter 4 tells more about how the Domain Name System works, including the relationship of "IP addresses" to domain names. For the purposes of our tour we will assume that your computer is "on the Internet," that it has access to a working Domain Name Server, and that it is capable of conducting Telnet sessions.

TELNET

We begin our tour by using a basic Internet tool, Telnet. Telnet is the name of the protocol that allows a user to log in to a host located elsewhere on the Internet. On most computer systems, the command that invokes Telnet is simply named "telnet."* For our tour we will tell the Telnet program what host to connect to as we invoke the command:

```
telnet hostname
```

---

* Telnet goes by other names on some systems. For instance, if you are using the TCP/IP package from FTP Software Inc., the command you'd type is "tn hostname".

When you log into a remote computer via Telnet, a great deal of work takes place behind the scenes to set up the connection and to move data to and from the remote host. We will leave the details of that behind-the-scenes work for later chapters.

The goal of Telnet is to allow a user to log into remote computers. Users often take advantage of Telnet to reach a computer they are authorized to log into. For instance, users visiting a site on the Internet can use Telnet to return to their regular computers back at their home sites in order to check electronic mail. Some professional conferences have begun offering an "Internet room," in which multiple terminals provide attendees with a means of staying in touch with the office.

In this tour, however, we will concentrate on services that allow the user to connect without worrying about who the user is. In order to do this, many services publicize generic user IDs. Members of the general public can specify such IDs, typically using well-known passwords (or no password at all). For obvious reasons, such generic user IDs usually are restricted in what they can do; typically they can only retrieve information, not update it.

Our first example service resides at the University of Washington; it provides information on current earthquakes. To connect to this service one would type:

```
telnet geophys.washington.edu
quake                                when asked for a user ID
quake                                when asked for a password
```

When you start a Telnet session, your computer informs you of connection progress:

```
Trying 128.95.16.50...
Connected to geophys.washington.edu.
Escape character is '^]'.
```

Once the connection is open, the remote computer responds, and the information it sends is displayed on your screen:

```
SunOS UNIX (gwiz)


login: quake
Password:
Earthquake Information account, NO LOGIN ALLOWED
Information about recent earthquakes are reported here for public use.
Catalogs are available by anonymous ftp in geophys.washington.edu:pub/seis-net
```

```
DATE-TIME is in Universal Standard Time which is PST + 8 hours, LAT and
LON are in decimal degrees, DEP is depth in kilometers, N-STA is number
of stations recording event, QUAL is location quality A-good, D-poor, Z-from
automatic system and may be in error.

Recent events reported by the USGS National Earthquake Information Center
DATE-TIME (UT)   LAT    LON    DEP  MAG              LOCATION AREA
94/01/15 17:03  20.4S  174.1W  33   5.6   TONGA ISLANDS
94/01/17 12:30  34.0N  118.7W  10   6.6   SOUTHERN CALIFORNIA
94/01/17 20:45  34.1N  118.7W  10   0.9   SOUTHERN CALIFORNIA. ML 5.1 (GS).
94/01/17 23:33  34.1N  118.8W  10   5.5   SOUTHERN CALIFORNIA
94/01/18 00:43  34.1N  118.9W  10   5.1   SOUTHERN CALIFORNIA

Recent earthquakes in the Northwest located by Univ. of Wash. (Mag > 2.0)
DATE-TIME (UT) LAT(N) LON(W) DEP  MAG N-STA QUAL
94/01/10 23:00  42.28  121.91  6.1  2.2   7   A  14.0 km WNW of Klamath Falls
94/01/11 06:53  42.28  121.90  5.6  2.0   6   A  12.5 km  NW of Klamath Falls
94/01/11 07:28  42.30  121.98  0.0  2.1   6   A  20.3 km WNW of Klamath Falls
94/01/12 01:37  42.26  121.91  6.2  2.4   7   A  13.3 km WNW of Klamath Falls
94/01/12 17:50  42.26  121.90  7.6  2.3   6   A  11.7 km WNW of Klamath Falls
94/01/12 22:38  42.26  121.91  7.9  2.2   7   A  13.2 km WNW of Klamath Falls
94/01/13 08:02  46.88  118.68  0.0  3.4  20   B  36.3 km   E of Othello
94/01/13 10:05  46.86  118.70  2.1  2.2  12   C  35.6 km   E of Othello
94/01/14 00:50  42.26  121.90  6.3  3.1   6   A  11.6 km WNW of Klamath Falls
94/01/14 02:13  42.26  121.93  9.6  2.0   6   A  14.1 km WNW of Klamath Falls
94/01/14 10:01  42.28  121.93  6.7  2.3   7   A  ...
94/01/14 17:58  42.26  121.90  6.5  2.8   7   A  ...
94/01/15 03:11  42.25  121.88  7.8  2.1   7   A  ...
94/01/15 05:15  42.26  121.90  3.8  2.0   6   A  ...
94/01/15 08:11  42.26  121.93  7.5  2.0   6   A  ...
94/01/16 00:21  42.26  121.90  6.6  2.2   7   A  ...
94/01/16 03:34  42.25  121.88  5.2  2.0   5   A  ...
94/01/16 03:35  42.26  121.88  5.1  2.1   7   A  ...
94/01/16 14:52  42.26  121.90  7.7  2.4   5   A  ...
94/01/17 20:56  47.66  120.06  7.1  2.3  16   A  ...
```

The designers of this particular service decided they didn't want to support a lengthy interactive terminal session; their goal is simply to deliver a list of recent earthquakes. Once that goal is accomplished, the earthquake computer closes the connection, and the following message is displayed on your workstation:

```
Connection closed by foreign host
```

After looking up recent earthquakes, let's assume you want to know more about one of the cities listed. You might connect to the geographic name server

provided by the University of Michigan. This simple service tells about cities in
the United States.* To reach the service one would use this Telnet command:

```
telnet martini.eecs.umich.edu 3000
```

The "3000" after the host name is a "port number," which is a way of identifying particular services on a computer that supplies services over TCP/IP. The
designers of the geographic name server have decided that if a connection
comes in on port 3000, that connection is intended for the geography service; it
is not, for instance, one of their colleagues connecting in order to log in and
read mail. Therefore this service doesn't even ask for a user ID or a password—
it immediately starts talking to the user:

```
# Geographic Name Server, Copyright 1992 Regents of the University
    of Michigan.
# Version 8/19/92.  Use "help" or "?" for assistance, "info" for
    hints.
.
help
...
Data came primarily from the US Geological Survey and the US Postal Service.
Coverage includes all US cities, counties, and states,
as well as some US mountains, rivers, lakes, national parks, etc.
A few international cities have also been included.
Unfortunately, some minor inaccuracies remain.  Send mail to
info@comsol.com for information regarding the data.

Queries should generally look like the last line of a postal
address, as in "Ann Arbor, MI 48103".

All these queries will also work:
1) ed(1)-style regular expression, like "[Bb]os.*n$"
2) A city name alone, like "Ann Arbor"
3) A ZIP or ZIP+4 code alone, like this: "46556", "48103-2112"
    NOTE: only the first 5 digits in a ZIP+4 code are used.
4) As in 1) or 2) but with a state name or abbreviation, like
    this: "Ann Arbor, MI", "Los Angeles, California"
5) As above but with optional nation name or abbreviation, like
    "Toronto, , Canada".  NOTE:  there are currently very few
    foreign cities.

Punctuation, white space, and upper/lower case are ignored.
Any reasonable state/nation abbreviations are recognized.
```

---

* The author of the service, Tom Libert, has stated plans to add Canadian and other international cities to the database.

Here are more example queries:

"Ann Arbor, Mich" "48103" "annarbor,mi" "Paris,,France"
"Mammoth Cave National Park" "mount mckinley" "lake michigan"

If a query fails, try expanding abbreviations (e.g. change "Mt."
to "Mount", etc.

Interpret server replies as follows:

0 <city name>
1 <county FIPS code> <county name>
2 <state/province abbreviation> <state/province name>
3 <nation abbreviation> <nation name>
A <telephone area code>
E <elevation in feet above mean sea level>
F <feature code> <feature name>
L <latitude DD MM SS X> <longitude DDD MM SS X>
P <1980 census population>
R <remark>
T <time zone>
Z <postal ("ZIP") code>

To exit the server, enter "stop", "end", "quit", "bye",
"exit", "logout", or "logoff".

Direct questions or comments to Tom Libert, libert@citi.umich.edu,
or phone (313) 936-0827. Please let me know if you write new clients.

The geography service waits for you to type a command after displaying a
period on a line by itself. Assuming we want more information on Walla Walla:

```
.
walla walla
0 Walla Walla
1 17035 Cumberland
2 IL Illinois
3 US United States
F 45 Populated place
L 39 12 03 N  88 11 32 W
E 585

0 Walla Walla
1 53071 Walla Walla
2 WA Washington
3 US United States
R county seat
```

```
F 45 Populated place
L 46 03 53 N 118 20 31 W
P 25618
E 926
Z 99362
```

It turns out that there are two cities named Walla Walla in the United States; in this case we want the one in Washington. Note that the latitude and longitude values match the ones in the earthquake report. The server allows the user to specify a state name to avoid listing extra cities. For instance, if you are interested in a particular town called Decatur out of the sixteen with that name in the United States, you might type:

```
decatur, al
0 Decatur
1 01103 Morgan
2 AL Alabama
3 US United States
R county seat
A 205
F 45 Populated place
L 34 36 21 N  86 59 00 W
P 42002
E 573
Z 35601 35602 35603 35699
```

Finally, we can verify the server is functioning properly by checking its ZIP code index:

```
90210
0 Beverly Hills
1 06037 Los Angeles
2 CA California
3 US United States
F 45 Populated place
L 34 04 25 N 118 23 58 W
P 32367
E 225
Z 90209 90210 90211 90212 90213
```

Fortunately, the server seems to know where Beverly Hills is located. Satisfied that the server answers our queries properly, we can sign off. When the remote computer closes the connection, the local Telnet program informs us:

```
bye
Connection closed by foreign host.
```

Universities offer more than these sorts of specialized databases over the Internet. Many universities now provide "Campus-Wide Information Systems"—systems that attempt to present a variety of information about the campus under one umbrella. North Carolina State University offers one such CWIS, accessible via Telnet:

```
telnet happenings.ncsu.edu

Connected to ccvs4.cc.ncsu.edu.
Escape character is '^]'.

        North Carolina State University Computing Center's VAXcluster

    *******************************************************************
    *         Happenings!, your campuswide information system         *
    *                                                                 *
    *     Access to Happenings! is available by typing INFO at the    *
    *     USERNAME: prompt following this message.                    *
    *                                                                 *
    *     Please make sure you are emulating a DEC VT100, 200 or 300  *
    *     style terminal; VT100 is the default.                       *
    *******************************************************************

Username: INFO

Please enter the type of terminal you are emulating:
            VT100 [default]
            VT200
            VT300

Enter EXIT to logoff

Enter terminal type: vt100
```

The user name "info" has been specially configured to operate as the campuswide information system. Several users can log in using this ID at once. The VT100 terminal type is commonly supported by most versions of Telnet in use today; it allows a program to present a "full-screen" view.* NCSU presents us with a menu of choices:

---

* The VT100 standard was defined by Digital Equipment Corporation as a standard for how video display terminals should communicate with DEC minicomputers. DEC terminals and clones became popular with many non-DEC host computers. Today the VT100 standard is commonly used by terminal emulators such as Kermit and Procomm for dial-up terminal sessions. The same VT100 standard has been implemented in most versions of Telnet as a standard way to "paint" a full screen of text.

```
NCSU's
        H a p p e n i n g s !
        H a p p e n i n g s !
                    Your campuswide information system
    1.  University Datebook            9.  Computing Information
    2.  NCSU Press Releases           10.  NCSU Libraries Information
    3.  Faculty/Staff Telephone Directory   11.  Visitor Information
    4.  Student Telephone Directory   12.  Newsstand
    5.  Jobs Jobs Jobs !!!            13.  Reach Out
    6.  Class/Course Listings         14.  Newsletters & Journals
    7.  Crime Beat                    15.  University Surplus Items
    8.  University Infobook

                    99.  Help Using Happenings!

        Suggestions? Contact Harry Nicholos, NCSU Computing Center,
            Harry_Nicholos@ncsu.edu, or (919) 515-5497.

Enter Menu Choice or Exit and press RETURN

NCSU>11
```

Deciding we want to learn more about the campus, we enter option 11, hit the Enter key, and the CWIS responds with this screen:

```
Visitor Information

    1.  Welcome to NCSU!!

    2.  Admissions Information and guided tours

    3.  NCSU Facts

    4.  The NCSU Campus: A Tour

    5.  Parking and Transportation Information

Enter Menu Choice or:    Main menu    Backup    Help    Exit


NCSU>1
```

Option 1 retrieves a brief description of the university:

```
                    Welcome to NCSU

North Carolina State University has had a remarkable century of
growth and service to the people of North Carolina. Today, it has
```

```
the largest student body in the state; it is the largest research
university in the state; and its extension programs provide
educational services and assistance to citizens and businesses
throughout the state. North Carolina State University is truly the
"People's University."
```

```
We hope you enjoy our campus and invite you to visit the points of
interest described in Happenings!. If you need assistance or
information while on campus, please call the Office of University
Relations at (919) 515-2850 or visit the office in Room 12,
Holladay Hall.
```

```
On behalf of Chancellor Larry K. Monteith, welcome to our campus and
thank you for your interest in North Carolina State University, home
of the Wolfpack.
```

```
 Information Provided by the NCSU Office of Undergraduate Admissions
```

```
NCSU>main
```

The command "main" returns you to the main menu. From there you can navigate the menus at will, obtaining information on admissions, enrollment, parking—you can even check to see what books are held by the library. Many services that allow Telnet over the Internet implement a similar easy-to-follow menu structure. To log off, you simply type "exit" and the NCSU system closes your connection to it.

You may have noticed a message `"Escape character is '^]"`. This is a notice from your Telnet program telling you that you can "escape" to Telnet "command mode" by entering the "Ctrl-]" key (i.e., by holding down the Ctrl key and striking "]"). This is necessary, for instance, when the remote host stops responding, or for some hosts that don't provide a graceful way to log out. Once you escape you'll see a prompt that will allow you a way to close the connection:

```
telnet> close
```

Universities are not the only providers of information on the Internet. Government agencies and private industry also use the Internet as a way to deliver information to citizens and customers. For instance, the Food and Drug Administration offers a bulletin board system to Internet users. Here is an example session:

```
telnet fdabbs.fda.gov
Trying...
Connected to fdabbs.fda.gov
Escape character is '^]'.
```

```
UNIX System V  R.3 (WINS) (FDABBS)

login: bbs


UNIX System V Release 3.2.3 AT&T 3B2
FDABBS
Copyright (c) 1984, 1986, 1987, 1988, 1989, 1990 AT&T
All Rights Reserved
Login last used: Tue Aug 24 01:52:29 1993

  @@@@@  @@@@@@    @
  @      @     @  @ @                    THE FDA
  @@@@@  @     @ @@@@@        ELECTRONIC BULLETIN BOARD
  @      @@@@ @ @      @

    Welcome to FDA's electronic bulletin board, a service of the Food
    and Drug Administration.

        UNAUTHORIZED USE IS PROHIBITED BY TITLE 18 OF U.S.C.

  Please enter your name (first and last) ==> Rich Wiggins

  Hello RICH WIGGINS
  Is this your correct name ? (Y/N): y

  Please enter your password ==>
```

This particular bulletin board requires you to identify yourself. The first time
you connect to it, you will be asked to give your name, address, and telephone
number. You then specify a password. Your full name and password allow you
to log in in the future without re-registering.

The warning about unauthorized use is common. It should not scare you away
from the service; the warning is used to make clear to those of a destructive bent
that they will be prosecuted. The system recognizes the returning user.

```
  Welcome Back! Your last login was: 08/22 20:40:42

  FOR LIST OF AVAILABLE TOPICS TYPE TOPICS
  OR ENTER THE TOPIC YOU DESIRE ==>topics

      TOPICS                          DESCRIPTION

  *   NEWS        News releases
  *   ENFORCE     Enforcement Report
  *   APPROVALS   Drug and Device Product Approvals list
  *   CDRH        Center for Devices and Radiological Health
```

```
*  BULLETIN    Text from Drug Bulletin
*  AIDS        Current Information on AIDS
*  CONSUMER    FDA Consumer magazine index and selected articles
*  SUBJ-REG    FDA Federal Register Summaries by Subject
*  ANSWERS     Summaries of FDA information
*  INDEX       Index of News Releases and Answers
*  DATE-REG    FDA Federal Register Summaries by Publication Date
*  CONGRESS    Text of Testimony at FDA Congressional Hearings
*  SPEECH      Speeches Given by FDA Commissioner and Deputy
*  VETNEWS     Veterinary Medicine News
*  MEETINGS    Upcoming FDA Meetings
*  IMPORT      Import Alerts
*  MANUAL      On-Line User's Manual
```

This simple bulletin board system has information on a variety of topics:

```
FOR LIST OF AVAILABLE TOPICS TYPE TOPICS
OR ENTER THE TOPIC YOU DESIRE ==>news

YOUR CURRENT TOPIC: NEWS
TYPE QUIT TO LOGOFF OR TYPE HELP FOR AVAILABLE BBS COMMANDS

PLEASE ENTER A BBS COMMAND ==>read

P93-34                          Food and Drug Administration
FOR IMMEDIATE RELEASE           Susan Cruzan -- (301) 443-3285
Aug. 16, 1993


     The Food and Drug Administration today announced that the
Warner-Lambert Co. has agreed to correct problems with manufacturing
and testing practices associated with its drug products, and to
bring its facilities into compliance with current Good Manufacturing
Practice regulations (GMPs).
     In a consent decree agreed to by FDA and Warner-Lambert, a U.S.
District Court Judge in New Jersey entered a permanent injunction
against the company and its officers. The decree requires the
company to hire independent experts to evaluate manufacturing
records and data for its products and submit written certifications
to FDA that drug products distributed from its six facilities in the
United States, including two in Puerto Rico, meet the applicable
manufacturing standards.
     The decree resulted from a series of plant inspections by FDA,

More? (yes or no): no
```

This bulletin board makes it easy to say good-bye:

```
YOUR CURRENT TOPIC: NEWS
TYPE QUIT TO LOGOFF OR TYPE HELP FOR AVAILABLE BBS COMMANDS
```

```
PLEASE ENTER A BBS COMMAND ==>quit

@@@@@  @@@@@    @
@      @     @ @ @                       THE FDA
@@@@@  @     @ @@@@@        ELECTRONIC BULLETIN BOARD
@      @@@ @ @      @

     Thank you for using the FDA's electronic bulletin board,
     a public service of the Food and Drug Administration.
```

These examples show some of the many services available for access on the Internet. By now you may wonder how to find a list of some of the many services available. One important answer is Gopher, which serves as both a document delivery tool and a way to browse the Internet. There are many ways to get started with Gopher. One way to connect is to use Telnet to reach a "public access" Gopher client. For instance:

```
telnet gopher.msu.edu
Trying 35.8.2.61...
Connected to gopher.cl.msu.edu.
Escape character is '^]'.

AIX telnet (burrow.cl.msu.edu)

Type   gopher   to log in

To report problems with this system send mail to
gopher@gopher.msu.edu

login: gopher
```

In this example, we are connecting to the "public Gopher client" at Michigan State University. Public clients allow you to run Gopher without installing any software on your computer (but there are powerful reasons why you should do so; the next chapter tells why). The method of connection in this example will give us a full-screen menu that looks like this:

```
            Internet Gopher Information Client v1.11

              Root gopher server: gopher.msu.edu

   -->  1.  Gopher at Michigan State University.
         2.  More About Gopher (Documentation & Other Gophers)/
         3.  Keyword Search of Titles in MSU's Gopher <?>
         4.  About Michigan State University/
         5.  MSU Campus Events/
         6.  News & Weather/
```

```
7.  Phone Books & Other Directories/
8.  Information for the MSU Community/
9.  Computing & Technology Services/
10. Libraries/
11. MSU Services & Facilities/
12. Outreach / Extension / Community Affairs/
13. Network & Database Resources/


Press ? for Help, q to Quit, u to go up a menu        Page: 1/1
```

This short menu lists documents offered by the host we've connected to. The menu is organized hierarchically, just as files on your computer are. Items ending with a period are documents; items whose titles end in the slash character ("/") are new menus.* The menus (or "folders" or "subdirectories" if you prefer) are organized into a hierarchy. Within that hierarchy we will find more documents offered by the local host, and links (pointers) to other documents and services from all over the global Internet. Before we navigate that hierarchy, let's examine the very first file. The arrow points to that file name to begin with; you simply need to press the Enter key to select the file. Then you will see:

```
About MSU Gopher
----------------


This is the Michigan State University root Gopher service. Here you
will find information about MSU, convenient reference items, and
easy access to campus and Internet services.

Gopher is a network based document browser. To view an item, move
the cursor to it and press Enter, or click it with your mouse. Some
items are files you can view; other items are directories containing
more items. As you travel through the menus, the system will keep
track of where you came from, allowing you to move "back up" the
hierarchy.

The best way to access Gopher is by installing a "client" program on
your workstation.

For more information on using Gopher clients, look in the "More
About Gopher" directory. While there you'll also find a "Guest Book"
where you can leave comments, as well as ways to look for and
connect to other Gopher servers. Also contained in this directory
are ways to perform keyword searches of Gopherspace.

(40%) Press space for more, h for help, u or q to quit
```

---

* Items ending in question marks are Search items, as we'll see later.

This particular item is simply a text file that describes the basics of Gopher. When you select a file for display, the public Gopher client uses an external tool, sometimes called a "browser," to display the file. The browser allows you to move up and down files that are too large to fit on one screen. In this case the entire file fits on a screen; when you're done reading it, you press the Enter key to go back to the menu from which you came.

A Gopher session differs from the sort of interactive conversation we saw in the NCSU and FDA examples: Gopher presents a similar style of menu navigation no matter what Gopher server you might connect to. The layout of the menus themselves will differ, but you use the same keystrokes to move through the menus no matter where you visit.* By contrast, hosts that offer Telnet sessions can vary quite a bit in what sort of commands they expect you to type.

The second choice is a menu that offers more Gopher documents, as well as ways to connect to other Gophers. To select an item, you can use the cursor (arrow) keys on your keyboard; each stroke of the up or down key moves the pointer one line. Or, you can type in the number corresponding to the item you want to select.

When the public Gopher client is busy accessing information for you, it shows you its progress by putting a message in the lower right corner of the screen. The message looks like this:

```
Retrieving Directory..\
```

The last character, shown as a backslash here, toggles among several characters so as to simulate a spinning wheel. When the wheel appears to move quickly, data is moving quickly. If the wheel stops spinning for a long time, something may have gone wrong in retrieving the document, and you may have to try again later.

Many universities use Gopher as their Campus-Wide Information System. This example is no exception. General information is offered under "About Michigan State University."

```
            Internet Gopher Information Client v1.11

                About Michigan State University


    --> 1.  A Brief History of MSU.
        2.  Michigan State University--Facts In Brief.
        3.  Things to do on Campus.
        4.  Common Phone Numbers.
```

---

* Note that the style of interaction with Gopher does change across various Gopher client programs. For instance you can have a mouse-oriented graphical interface to Gopher with the right software installed on your workstation. The use of specialized clients is explained in later chapters.

```
   5.  Mailing to Campus Addresses.
   6.  1992 Presidential Debate at MSU/
   7.  Michigan State University Online Photo Gallery/

Press ? for Help, q to Quit, u to go up a menu              Page: 1/1
```

One of Gopher's strengths is the ability for one Gopher to point to another; any Gopher document can in fact be a link to another Gopher server, which could be physically located anywhere on the global Internet. Most Gopher servers provide a list of other servers. The worldwide collection of Gopher servers and the information each contains is sometimes called "Gopherspace." A list of "other Gophers" can be found within the "More About Gopher" folder (along with other documents about Gopher):

```
            Internet Gopher Information Client v1.11


            More About Gopher (Documentation & Other Gophers)

      1.   About Gopher at MSU.
      2.   About Gopher: Overview and History.
      3.   About common Gopher clients.
      4.   More Gopher Documentation/
      5.   MSU Gopher Guest Book <TEL>
      6.   Road Map of MSU's Gopher.
      7.   Recent Changes In MSU's Gopher/
      8.   Featured Items/
      9.   MSU 1200/2400 baud dialin upgrade information.
      10.  Search Gopherspace/
  --> 11.  Other Gopher Servers/

Press ? for Help, q to Quit, u to go up a menu
```

Upon selecting "Other Gopher Servers" we are offered several different lists:

```
            Internet Gopher Information Client v1.11


                   Other Gopher Servers

  --> 1.   All the Gopher Servers in the World/
      2.   Other Gopher Servers in Michigan/
      3.   Keyword search of Gopher site names <?>
      4.   Search titles in Gopherspace using veronica <?>
      5.   Africa/
      6.   Asia/
      7.   Europe/
      8.   International Organizations/
```

```
 9.  Middle East/
10.  North America/
11.  Pacific/
12.  South America/
13.  Terminal Based Information/
14.  WAIS Based Information/

Press ? for Help, q to Quit, u to go up a menu
```

The list of all Gopher servers in the world is impressive—over 1400 servers have been registered as of this writing. You can select among any of the items on this list just as easily as we moved among documents on the MSU Gopher server. In fact, by selecting the list of all Gophers in the world, we have already moved to another Gopher server—the list itself resides at the home of Gopher's developers, the University of Minnesota.

```
          Internet Gopher Information Client v1.11

             All the Gopher Servers in the World

  --> 1.  Search Gopherspace using Veronica/
      2.  ACADEME THIS WEEK (Chronicle of Higher Education)/
      3.  ACM SIGGRAPH/
      4.  ACTLab (UT Austin, RTF Dept)/
      5.  AREA Science Park, Trieste, (IT)/
      6.  Academic Position Network/
      7.  Academy of Sciences, Bratislava (Slovakia)/
      8.  Alamo Community College District/
      9.  Albert Einstein College of Medicine/
     10.  American Mathematical Society /
     11.  American Physiological Society/
     12.  Anesthesiology Gopher /
     13.  Appalachian State University (experimental gopher)/
     14.  Apple Computer Higher Education gopher server/
     15.  Arabidopsis Research Companion, Mass Gen Hospital/Harvard/

Press ? for Help, q to Quit, u to go up a menu          Page: 1/53
```

Note that some of the Gopher servers listed may be much slower to respond than others; this depends on the speed of the communications links between you and the server you select, how much information you are trying to retrieve, and how busy that server is handling others' transactions. You cannot always predict which connections will be slow—overseas hops are sometimes slow, as you might expect, but sometimes are surprisingly responsive. The only sure guideline is that you must be patient at times.

A visit to "Gopher Central"—the main Gopher at the University of Minnesota—reveals some of the myriad useful resources on the Internet. Their root menu looks like this:

```
                    University of Minnesota

        1.  Information About Gopher/
        2.  Computer Information/
        3.  Discussion Groups/
        4.  Fun & Games/
        5.  Internet file server (ftp) sites/
   -->  6.  Libraries/
        7.  News/
        8.  Other Gopher and Information Servers/
        9.  Phone Books/
        10. Search Gopher Titles at the University of Minnesota <?>
        11. Search lots of places at the University of Minnesota  <?>
        12. University of Minnesota Campus Information/
```

"Libraries" presents several interesting-looking choices. For instance, the "Library Catalogs" option offers connections to hundreds of library catalogs available worldwide.* All of the items in this menu are worth exploring.†

```
                         Libraries

   -->  1.  Electronic Books/
        2.  Electronic Journal collection from CICnet/
        3.  Information from the U.S. Federal Government/
        4.  Library Catalogs via Telnet/
        5.  Library of Congress Records/
        6.  Newspapers, Magazines, and Newsletters/
        7.  Reference Works/
```

"Electronic Books" contains the complete text of a number of books in the public domain; many of them are classics, some are public domain reference works. Many online texts are made available on the Internet through the efforts of a collaborative undertaking called "Project Gutenberg" under the inspiration of Dr. Michael S. Hart. The title menu offers a glimpse of the texts already online:

---

* This example underscores the interconnectedness of Gophers—Minnesota can easily offer Yale's library catalog list as a document in their libraries menu.

† Once connected to the Internet, the reader would find a thorough exploration of the menus introduced here a valuable self-guided tour.

```
                              By Title

     1.   Search Electronic Books <?>
     2.   1990 USA Census Information/
     3.   Aesop's Fables/
     4.   Agrippa/
     5.   Aladdin and the Wonderful Lamp/
     6.   Alice's Adventures in Wonderland/
     7.   CIA World Factbook 1991/
     8.   Clinton's Inaugural Address/
     9.   Complete Works of Shakespeare/
     10.  Far From the Madding Crowd/
     11.  Federalist Papers, The/
     12.  Gift of the Magi, The/
     13.  Herland/
     14.  Historical Documents/
     15.  Hunting of the Snark, The/
```

The value of having such texts online may seem elusive; who would want to read Shakespeare on a computer terminal? But from a research and teaching perspective, this can be very valuable. For instance, a student working on a term paper can quickly scan through multiple texts, and could even cut and paste passages to be compared and analyzed.

The Electronic Books menu offers an option of searching the texts. The administrators of the Minnesota Gopher have set up an index of all the words in all the texts they have online. You could use this as a way to trace the use of a particular word among the classics. For instance, it is said that William Shakespeare invented the word "orb." You can quickly locate his uses of the word by selecting the search option. You will be asked what you want to look for in this manner:

```
           Internet Gopher Information Client v1.11

                        Electronic Books

        1.   By Author/
        2.   By Call Letter/
        3.   By Title/
   +--------------------Search Electronic Books--------------------+
   |                                                               |
   |                                                               |
   | Words to search for orb                                       |
   |                                                               |
   |                       [Cancel ^G] [Accept - Enter]            |
   |                                                               |
   |                                                               |
   +---------------------------------------------------------------+


   Press ? for Help, q to Quit, u to go up a menu      Searching..\
```

While the search takes place, the word "Searching" appears in the lower right corner of the screen; a simulated spinning character shows progress. This particular search yields an extensive number of places where Shakespeare used the word "orb":

```
             Search Electronic Books: orb

      1.  Lover's Complaint, A   /Gutenberg/shake/Poetry/.
      2.  ACT V   /Gutenberg/shake/Comedies/Merchant of Venice, The/.
 -->3.  ACT IV   /Gutenberg/shake/Comedies/Much Ado About Nothing/.
      4.  Chapter XXII.: THE PROCESSION   /Gutenberg/scarlet/.
      5.  ACT V   /Gutenberg/shake/Tragedies/Antony and Cleopatra/.
      6.  ACT V   /Gutenberg/shake/Histories/King Henry IV Part 1/.
      7.  ACT V   /Gutenberg/shake/Histories/King Henry VI Part 1/.
      8.  ACT IV   /Gutenberg/shake/Tragedies/Timon of Athens/.
      9.  ACT V   /Gutenberg/shake/Tragedies/Coriolanus/.
     10.  ACT II   /Gutenberg/shake/Tragedies/Romeo and Juliet/.
     11.  ACT III   /Gutenberg/shake/Comedies/Twelfth Night/.
     12.  ACT II   /Gutenberg/shake/Tragedies/Hamlet/.
     13.  BOOK I.   /Gutenberg/paradise/.
     14.  BOOK VI.    /Gutenberg/paradise/.
     15.  BOOK V.    /Gutenberg/paradise/.
  ...
```

You can move up and down among the documents listed just as you would in any Gopher menu. If you select a document (by hitting Return) the beginning of it will be displayed on your screen. Most public Gopher clients will let you search through a particular document you are viewing. The public client invokes a "file browser" on your behalf that allows such searches. For instance, if you select the second item listed, Act V of the Merchant of Venice, you would see on your screen:

```
ACT IV

SCENE I A church.

        [Enter DON PEDRO, DON JOHN, LEONATO, FRIAR FRANCIS,
        CLAUDIO, BENEDICK, HERO, BEATRICE, and Attendants]

LEONATO Come, Friar Francis, be brief; only to the plain
        form of marriage, and you shall recount their
        particular duties afterwards.

FRIAR FRANCIS You come hither, my lord, to marry this lady.

CLAUDIO No.

(1%) Press space for more, h for help, u or q to quit
```

On the last line of the screen, the browser asks you whether you want to page forward (signified by pressing the space bar), stop viewing the file, or get help. One option isn't listed but is present in most browsers: you can type a slash followed by a string of characters to search for. For example you might type:

```
/orb
```

The browser will search for that string of characters in the file you're looking at. Sure enough, the word "orb" does appear later on in the play:

```
CLAUDIO Out on thee! Seeming! I will write against it:
        You seem to me as Dian in her orb,
        As chaste as is the bud ere it be blown;
        But you are more intemperate in your blood
        Than Venus, or those pamper'd animals
        That rage in savage sensuality.
```

The Minnesota Gopher offers other online texts besides the Project Gutenberg books. Under "Newspapers, Magazines, and Newsletters" you'll find:

```
            **Directory of All Publications Here**

    1.  AIDSNews/
    2.  ALCTS Network News/
    3.  Aids Alert/
    4.  Athene-InterText/
    5.  Automatome/
    6.  CA*Net Newsletter/
    7.  CCNEWS/
    8.  Current Cites (Information and Library Studies)/
    9.  EFF/
   10.  EJournal/
   11.  Florida Sunflash/
   12.  Health Info-Com Network/
   13.  MSEN Internet Review/
   14.  Meckler Publishing/
-->  15.  Minnesota Daily/
```

Later in this list is a pointer to the student newspaper at the University of Texas:

```
-->  35. University of Texas--Austin Daily Texan/
```

A number of pioneering universities have begun offering their student newspapers over the Internet. Because most newspapers are prepared using computers these days, it is relatively easy to extract the text of each day's articles and deliver the information via Gopher. With today's tools it is not yet easy to offer a view of the paper that resembles the paper form, but even a "flat ASCII" view of a remote newspaper can be interesting and useful. For instance, a journalism class could do comparative analysis of how various newspapers around the world cover similar stories. Article titles look like this:

```
                 Today's Daily Texan Articles

     1.  astros.fri.txt.
     2.  bilds.fri.txt.
     3.  blaine.fri.txt.
     4.  briefs.fri.txt.
     5.  caps.fri.txt.
     6.  cyclegov.fri.txt.
     7.  ded4sure.fri.txt.
     8.  eco.fri.txt.
     9.  freaks.fri.txt.
    10.  gap.fri.txt.
    11.  hornjail.fri.txt.
    12.  junk.fri.txt.
    13.  loon.fri.txt.
    14.  marriage.fri.txt.
    15.  milehigh.fri.txt.
```

These Gopher titles are somewhat more succinct than headlines,* so it is necessary to skim articles to see what they are about: For instance, `blaine.fri.txt` contains:

```
File: :pi:Blaine2.fri
McDuff disrupts

murder trial

Tries to escape from deputies

deck has no subject-- Naka Nathaniel Daily Texan Staff

  Convicted killer Kenneth Allen McDuff was carried out of  a
county  courtroom  Thursday  by  six Travis County sheriff's
deputies after trying to escape from their custody.

  McDuff forced his way free  of  courtroom  officers  momen-
tarily  after  being thrown out of the courtroom by District
Judge Wilford Flowers at 4:15 p.m.

  . . .
```

---

* But this is not inherently true; the setup of the student newspaper software in use at Texas probably does not lend itself well to capturing the headlines along with the articles as the files are loaded into Gopher. Information providers face this sort of compromise daily; it is better to provide terse titles than to not provide the online daily paper at all.

The "Libraries" menu depicted previously offered a choice of "Reference Works." Those items include:

```
                        Reference Works

         1.  ACM SIGGRAPH Online Bibliography Project/
         2.  American English Dictionary (from the UK) <?>
   -->   3.  CIA World Fact Book 1991/
         4.  Current Contents/
         5.  ERIC-archive.
         6.  ERIC-archive Search <?>
         7.  Periodic Table of Elements/
         8.  Roget's Thesaurus (Published 1911)/
         9.  The Hacker's Dictionary/
         10. U.S. Geographic Names Database/
         11. U.S. Telephone Area Codes/
         12. US-State-Department-Travel-Advisories/
         13. Webster's Dictionary/
```

Many of these items are worth exploring. For instance, the CIA World Fact Book serves as a sort of online almanac of the countries of the world. The Libraries menu offered another option worth exploring: Library Catalogs via Telnet is a list of many of the Internet-accessible research library catalogs worldwide.

```
         Library catalogs beyond Yale (via the Internet)

         1.  About Library Catalogs.
   -->   2.  Catalogs Listed by Location/
         3.  Catalogs Search by Keyword <?>
         4.  Instructions for different catalog types/
         5.  Library Bulletin Boards/
         6.  Manuscript and Archives Repositories - at Johns Hopkins/
         7.  Paper List (BBarrons' Accessing Online Bib Dbases)/
         8.  Updates made recently to the list of libraries.
```

This list is maintained at Yale University. One form of the list is broken up by geographic area; alternatively, you can search for a specific institution whose name you know by selecting the Search item. If you do a search on "canberra" the following list will appear:

```
         Catalogs Search by Keyword: canberra

         1.  University of Canberra.
   -->   2.  University of Canberra <TEL>
         3.  National Library of Australia.
         4.  Australian National University.
         5.  Commonwealth Scientific and Industrial Research Organisation.
```

The first item is a file describing how to connect to the University of Canberra's catalog. The second item is an actual Telnet link to the catalog (as is indicated by the "TEL" notation). Gopher recognizes Telnet sessions among the types of documents it can handle. This is particularly useful in the list of library catalogs, as it allows users to search the list of libraries, then immediately open a connection to the catalog of choice over the Internet. If you pick a Telnet item, Gopher will warn you that it is about to run Telnet on your behalf. It may also give a hint such as

```
Use the account name "uclid" to log in
```

The following is a condensed log of a connection to the library catalog at the University of Canberra, Australia:

```
Connected to library.canberra.edu.au.
Escape character is '^]'.

WELCOME TO THE UNIVERSITY OF CANBERRA LIBRARY

From this point you can access:

1. UCLID - the Library's online catalogue
2. CWIS  - the University's campus wide information service

Please enter uclid or cwis (in lower case) at the login prompt.

If you need any assistance please contact the Library staff:
        telephone:  (06)201 2282
        fax:        (06)201 5068
        email:      helpdesk@libserver.canberra.edu.au

login: uclid
UNIX System V Release 3.2.0 i386
library
Copyright (c) 1984 AT&T    All Rights Reserved
Login last used: Sun Aug 29 13:34:43 1993
DYNIX/ptx(R) V1.4.0 #1 (): Mon Dec 14 11:06:08 EST 1992
Copyright 1988 Sequent Computer Systems, Inc.


        Welcome to:

        The University of Canberra Library's Information Database

Press the RETURN key to continue or type OFF to exit:
```

```
                    OPAC MAIN MENU

                1   Browsing

                2   Keyword Searching

                3   Other Enquiries

                4   Examine your Borrower Record

                5   Library News

To select an option, press a number from 1 to 5 then press the
  RETURN  key.
            To find out more about each option use the  ?   key.

 Please select 1


------------------------------------------------------------------
                 AUTHOR ALPHABETIC BROWSING
------------------------------------------------------------------
Please type in some text that you think may occur at the start of
the surname of the author of a work that you are attempting to find.

For example, you could type  ROBERTSON or
                             ROBERTS or
                             RO
Please enter your search text...
------------------------------------------------------------------


> tillich

Search text TILLICH]
Works found 1


-------------------- BRIEF BIBLIOGRAPHIC DETAILS --------------------

        TITLE Political expectation  / Paul Tillich ; edited by James
              Luther Adams.
       AUTHOR Tillich, Paul, 1886-1965.
  PUBLICATION Lanham, MD : University Press of America, [1983], c1971.

  Loc. Acc. No... Prefix/Call No........ Copy Desc.... Status......
  ML   8505562    BT738.T54 1983                       Available
```

Why is it worthwhile to be able to scan the catalogs of research libraries around the world? There are several reasons. It is sometimes useful to check on the practices of another library—for instance, to see what the strengths are of the collection. Many libraries have an interlibrary loan arrangement with nearby institutions; patrons of one facility can use the Internet to see if a book is available at a cooperating library, and can even see if the book is currently checked out.

The library catalogs list is also an example of the grassroots nature of Gopherspace in particular, and the Internet in general. No central authority mandated that library catalogs should be made available on the Internet. Instead, over the last decade or so, most major libraries completely replaced their card catalogs with online catalogs. Over the last several years, most major research universities joined the Internet. In just the last few years, visionaries have realized that a list of Internet-accessible library catalogs would be valuable. The first lists were circulated as textural reports. Then someone realized a database of library catalogs would be useful. Like many undertakings on the Internet, the list is kept up to date through a cooperative labor-of-love project.* With Gopher, it is possible for Internet users worldwide to access an up-to-date list; local Gopher administrators at each site can easily add a link to Yale's list, instead of trying to replicate the effort of building it themselves.

In order to see some of the other resources available on the Internet, let's return to the Gopher server at Michigan State University, and look at the Network and Database Resources menu:

```
                  Network & Database Resources

        1.   About Network and Database Resources.
        2.   Database Resources Located at MSU/
        3.   Information on the Internet and Networking/
  -->   4.   Internet Resources by Subject/
        5.   Internet Resources by Type/
        6.   Help With Telnet.
        7.   New Internet Resources (via Washington & Lee Law Lib)/
```

This menu offers lists of various resources available on the Internet. You will find a list of services organized by subject; you can use this list to find Internet resources from astronomy to weather.[†] Also available is a list of Internet resources organized by type of service:

---

* The library catalogs list is maintained by Marie-Christine Mahe of Yale University. Collaborators include Billy Barron of the University of Texas at Dallas, Lou Rosenfeld of the University of Michigan, and Peter Scott of the University of Saskatchewan. Scott is the author of a well-known database of Internet resources known as Hytelnet. The first Gopher version of the library list was created by Ed Symanzik of Michigan State University.

† More detail about the subject-oriented list of services, and more hints on Internet navigation, can be found in Chap. 16.

```
                    Internet Resources by Type

--->   1.  Archie Servers/
       2.  Bulletin Board Systems/
       3.  Campus Phone Books (other institutions)/
       4.  Campus Wide Information Systems (telnet-based)/
       5.  Free-Net Systems/
       6.  Gopher Servers/
       7.  Hytelnet Servers/
       8.  Miscellaneous Services (telnet-based)/
       9.  WAIS Servers/
      10.  World-Wide Web/
```

Later chapters will explain the various types of services available, and methods other than Telnet and Gopher for making the best use of these varied resources.

Many libraries offer "browsing shelves" so that patrons can quickly skim a collection of new and interesting titles. Although there is not now and never will be a single central virtual browsing shelf for the Internet, our tour shows how some Gopher administrators are trying to provide lists of Internet resources organized in useful ways. Later chapters will show how World-Wide Web and WAIS are also used as tools to organize Internet resources. Chapter 26 offers a smorgasbord of resources the reader may wish to explore as well.

DOWNLOADING FILES

A final example will complete our tour of the Internet and our introduction to the public Gopher client. Under the "About Michigan State University" folder is an "Online Photo Gallery" with various campus scenes. Many other sites around the Internet make images available for access via Gopher.

```
        Michigan State University Online Photo Gallery

       1.  About Online Photo Gallery.
       2.  Photo credits.
       3.  Administration Building in Spring (200 Kbytes) <Picture>
       4.  Aerial view of Administration Building surroundings (25.. <Picture>
       5.  Another winter view of Red Cedar River (250 Kbytes)   <Picture>
       6.  Beaumont Tower (240 Kbytes) <Picture>
--->   7.  Candidate Bill Clinton giving speech at M.S.U. (490 Kbyt.. <Picture>
       8.  Canoes at Red Cedar Yacht Club (225 Kbytes) <Picture>
       9.  Fall colors around Beaumont Tower (220 Kbytes) <Picture>
      10.  Fall shot of a residence hall (245 Kbytes) <Picture>
      11.  MSU's mascot at a football game (195 Kbytes) <Picture>
      12.  Main Library in Spring (390 Kbytes) <Picture>
      13.  Spartan Stadium on game day (170 Kbytes) <Picture>
      14.  Statue of Sparty (330 Kbytes) <Picture>
      15.  Students by Red Cedar in Spring (230 Kbytes) <Picture>
```

Gopher can deliver many different types of files—still images, moving images, even sounds. Retrieval is easiest when you have a Gopher "client" program installed on your workstation. In that case, you merely click on the title, and the file is retrieved and automatically displayed or played for you. If, instead, you are dialed into a public client, say over a telephone line using a program like Procomm or Kermit, you cannot retrieve non-text files by simply clicking on them. However, you may be able to download* such files. For instance, suppose you want to retrieve an image file from MSU's Online Photo Gallery. To do so, type a "D" with the arrow on screen pointing to the file you are interested in.† You'll be given a choice of what method of downloading to use (see Fig. 2.2). The file will be downloaded to your computer using the protocol you specify. In this case you would specify option 5 if you wished to use the Kermit protocol; binary transfer is required for image files. After the file is on your computer's disk, the public Gopher client will say:

---

* To "download" a file is to copy it from a remote computer to your desktop computer.

† Be sure you type a capital "D." A lower case "d" does something else. (Yes, that's not the best design choice on the part of the Gopher developers.)

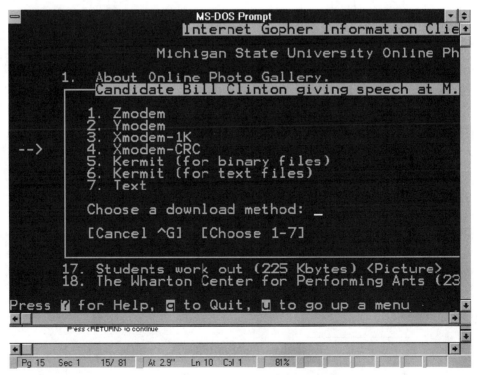

Figure 2.2

```
Download Complete. 493589 total bytes, 49358 bytes/sec
Press <RETURN> to continue
```

You can view the file later using your favorite image viewer.*

The ability to download is important for those who connect to their Internet service provider using conventional terminal programs over dial-up telephone connections. Much of the important information on the Internet resides in non-textual form: image files, sound files, even spreadsheets or executable programs. Users who have a "direct" Internet connection and who have installed specialized *client* software on their workstations are able to retrieve such files with even greater ease—you click on the title of the image file, and the image appears on your computer screen automatically. The advantages of direct client connection are explained in the next few chapters.

---

* Most Gopher image files are in the GIF format made popular by CompuServe. Image formats are explained in Chap. 9.

The Client/Server Model and the Internet

Today the term "client/server computing" is practically a part of the popular lexicon. Most of us think of a "client" as a customer in a law office or a real estate agency, and we think of "server" as a gender-neutral term for someone who waits tables in restaurants. But those words have taken on new meaning, as "client/server" has become the paradigm that defines how workstations and networks are used in the 1990s. Our discussion of Internet tools will require an understanding of the client/server computing model; therefore we devote a chapter to the concept. We introduce the concept by considering an example that long predates the era of online transactions.

Anyone old enough to remember the grand department stores that existed before shopping malls may recall how some sales transactions were handled. Each sales clerk's station had a pneumatic tube that ran under the floor and up the wall to a central area on a higher floor. Perhaps a dozen tubes met at this area, staffed by clerical personnel. If, for instance, a credit sale was made, the sales clerk would write up the information on a small form, place the form in a cylinder, and place the cylinder in the tube. Air pressure carried the cylinder to the upstairs area, where one of the credit clerks would open the cylinder, read the transaction, and check the books to see if credit could be extended. A receipt could be sent back down to the floor by tube as well.*

---

* To this day some banks use a similar pneumatic tube system to serve drive-up customers.

This model, based on paper and a mechanical network, is a physical manifestation of what client/server computing is all about. A sales clerk has a single transaction to complete—a charge to the customer's account. Rather than walking up to the credit department, the clerk fills out a form with the particulars of the transaction: who the customer is and the amount to be charged. In this context, the human customer is certainly a "client" from the store's point of view; from the point of view of the transaction, the client is the clerk filling out the debit form.

The credit department, with its bank of tubes and its staff of multiple accounting clerks, is the server in this model. Clerks take the transaction, which has been submitted in an agreed-upon format, and they do some database work: they see if the customer's account is in good standing, and if so, they debit the account and send the receipt back to the sales floor.

The pneumatic tube, of course, represents the network. Conceptually the job of the tube is the same as what we expect of today's computer networks: it is supposed to reliably deliver transaction data from one station to another. The pneumatic tube system was not fail-safe, of course; for instance, the mechanism pressurizing the tubes could fail. And the pneumatic network was far less flexible than today's computer networks—there was no tube connecting a sales clerk with a master database at the home office, and only a limited, defined set of paths within a store. But it will be useful to keep in mind this simplified view of networking as we analyze the services that today's networks in general, and the Internet in particular, supply on our behalf.

The term *client,* then, applies to the real human being who has a transaction to complete. But in the context of the client/server model, "client" refers to the side that initiates a transaction. Sometimes the term refers to the entire computer system, hardware and software, used by the human client; one also hears the word "client" applied to a particular piece of software for a particular Internet protocol (e.g., the TurboGopher client for the Macintosh). The primary job of the client is to serve as a user interface, letting the human who is initiating the transaction enter the request to be handled. The client software then prepares the request in an agreed-upon format, and ships it off to the server.

The *server* receives the request over the network, analyzes it, and usually does some sort of database lookup and/or update. The results of that database operation are sent back to the initiating client over the network. The client presents that information on the computer monitor (or perhaps on a printer; for instance, in the case of sales receipts) and the process is complete.

Some mass-market information utilities offer a form of client/server computing. Prodigy, CompuServe, and America Online each provide customers with software to run on their desktop computers. This provides a rich graphical interface that hides from the user the details of connection and navigation. In fact, Prodigy's "client" program is the only means of accessing the service; there is no option for using conventional terminal software. Note that these information utilities generally use dial-up telephone connections and public data networks, not Internet connections, as the path into their services.*

This simple division of labor—the client software performs the direct interaction with the human user, and it exchanges specific transactions in standard formats with the server—is the essence of the client/server model. There are far more complicated transaction scenarios than implied in the pneumatic tube example, of course, but in most cases this model holds. Given the global Internet, the client/server isn't limited to one building or one campus (see Fig. 3.1).

As implemented on the Internet, the client/server model requires no adjustments, whether the client and server are in the same building, on the same campus, on the same national network, or on separate continents. Of course, depending on the speed of links between client and server, the time it takes to send and receive transaction information can vary widely. But generally neither client nor server worries about the geography separating it from its partner.

FROM TERMINAL/MAINFRAME
TO CLIENT/SERVER

Another example will illustrate how the client/server model evolved with computer workstations and networks, and how it is replacing the traditional ter-

---

* But there is no reason why information utilities could not support Internet connections as an option, providing the same graphical view of their services by simply updating the client software to communicate using TCP/IP as an option.

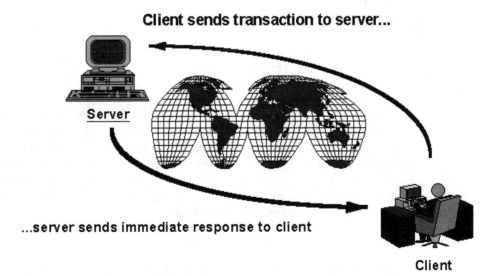

Client sends transaction to server...

Server

...server sends immediate response to client

Client

Figure 3.1

minal/mainframe mode of computer interactions. Let's imagine that the weather service offers an online computer service that provides historical climate information for selected cities.* First imagine what this might look like as a traditional terminal service. You'd connect over some sort of communications link—perhaps dial-up, perhaps Telnet—to the mainframe in question. Let's compare the traditional terminal/mainframe model to the client/server model, for the moment ignoring the details of how information is transmitted over the network. Let's assume that you dial in. Your terminal session might look like this (user typing is in bold):

```
Welcome to the Weather Service's Online Climate Database
Please tell me how many lines your screen can display? 24
Please tell me how wide your screen is? 80
Please enter your user name: bill

Weather Service notice:  System down on 6/5/94 from
0600 to 0800 for maintenance.

Do you want to read system news? (y/n) n

Do you want temperatures or precipitation? Enter t / p: t
Enter city's airport code: ORD
Enter date you want to look up: 9/19/56

Selected city: Chicago 9/19/56
The high temperature was 78 at 2:26 pm. The low was 54 at 4:12 am.

Look up another temperature? Y or N: n
Another request? Y or N: n

Thank you for using the Weather Service Climate Database.
Please dial in again soon.
```

This simple example shows what a typical conversational computer session might look like. This mode of interaction between a user and a database typified many computer applications throughout the history of online computing. Of course, there were many kinds of terminals, and other kinds of terminal sessions. For instance, rather than having a conversation with the remote computer, answering one question at a time, some computer terminals were designed to allow the user to fill out a form, answering a series of questions to be sent to the remote computer as a batch.

---

* This example is fictitious. It is possible to obtain weather information over the Internet, including from the National Oceanic and Atmospheric Administration; our example is a simplified case study. The domain names in the example are also fictitious.

Terminal sessions like the preceding one are intended to work with a human sitting at the terminal, and are not particularly well-suited to supporting communications between two computer programs. The climate database program asks the user several questions, one at a time. First the computer has to find out how big the user's terminal screen is so that it can format messages appropriately. Then it asks the user to sign in. A notice is posted about when the system will go down. The user is asked if more news is desired. Finally, the user is asked what kind of information is desired.

This process works well for humans; after all, for a large part of the history of computing, that was the goal. People logged into mainframes, whether local or afar, using specialized computer terminals, and they conversed with the computers using whatever ad hoc language had been defined by the designer of each particular program. But now let's say we have an intelligent computer on our side of the phone line—a personal computer or workstation—and we want to have an automated process—a program—dial into the climate database service and find out information on its own. Some of the friendly touches for humans could prove to be pitfalls for a program. A program might trip up on the system downtime notice. Also, the human eye probably doesn't notice it, but the conversation is inconsistent—at one point the user is asked to type "Y or N" but another time the question is "y / n." If the administrator of the system ever noticed that inconsistency—and fixed it—any automated query programs, trained to scan for specific text, might suddenly break.

In fact, to this very day, people still frequently use the traditional terminal model in order to look up this sort of information. And in some cases, people program computers to look up information that's only available via traditional terminal sessions. If the automated process breaks every once in a while, it can be adjusted to work again. But the client/server model offers an alternative.

Let's say the weather service decides to define a client/server protocol for handling this sort of query. First off, they would probably want to convene some sort of discussion among users of the service and the technical staff that supports the service. In standards parlance, they might call this committee a "working group." Then an effort would be made to define an acceptable protocol for communication between the client and the server. Computers are very literal, and although the protocol to meet this need could be very simple, the specifications would need to be exact.

One step would be to decide who is authorized to use the service. Let's assume that the weather service doesn't have secrets and doesn't need to bill for this service, so they decide to not worry about authorization and authentication. (Real Internet services often follow such an open model, though there are schemes for authentication of client/server interactions on the Internet.)

The next question would be what transactions to offer. So far, the climate database only has two kinds of data: temperature and precipitation. So those might be the initial transactions to be offered by the server. The other information the user types in is the airport code of the city and the date desired.

So a transaction might look like this:

```
temp-or-precip city-code date
```

Merely agreeing on these pieces of information is only half the battle. The designers of the new protocol have to be very specific as to what each element of the transaction can look like. Is it "temp" or will "t" or "temperature" be accepted? Is the case* of the transaction important? Are all city airport codes three characters long? Should the date be month/day/year or year/month/day?[†] Should the year be spelled out in four digits or will two suffice? Should there be exactly one blank (space character) between the parts of the transaction, or are multiple blanks acceptable? All of these details must be ironed out exactly, or someone will implement a client that won't be able to talk to the server.

It is sometimes surprising how relatively obscure questions can dominate the discussions of standards committees. In this case, let's assume that these questions are resolved to everyone's satisfaction. An example transaction might be:

```
TEMP ORD 1956/09/19
```

Now we have to define the sorts of response that the server will send back. Again, precise agreement is essential so that anyone who implements a client that talks to this server will be successful. Questions might include: Do we use Fahrenheit or Celsius for the temperature? Do we use local time or Greenwich (and what about daylight saving)? Is time shown in "a.m./p.m." or in 24-hour form? Do we return the original query or just the information that's been looked up? That last question might even prompt a religious dispute among our standards committee. Some might argue that the original query need not be returned because, after all, we have a reliable network and it's redundant and wasteful of bandwidth to send those characters back across the network.

Once again we assume that, after furious discussions, the standards committee agrees upon the precise format of the reply. The reply will look like this:

```
TEMP ORD 1956/09/19 HIGH 78 14:26 LOW 54 04:12
```

A transaction in our new client/server–based climate service might look like Fig. 3.2. Assuming our working group reaches a similar resolution for the precipitation transaction, it would seem we've got our protocol defined. Not quite: there must be provision for error conditions. Suppose the client submits a transaction

---

* "Case" refers to whether the text of the submitted transactions must be all uppercase ("TEMP") or all lowercase ("temp") or a mixture ("Temp"). Humans tend to see equivalent text despite differing case; computers need to be told whether case is significant.

† Actually, there is a standard, ISO 8601:1991 for "Data elements and interchange formats— Representation of Dates and Times" that the working group could use, instead of inventing its own scheme. Unfortunately, there are other standards that suggest how dates ought to be represented. It is sometimes said, "The nice thing about standards is there are so many to choose from."

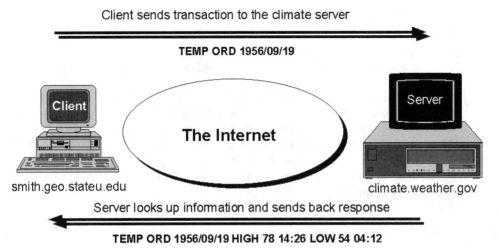

Client sends transaction to the climate server

TEMP ORD 1956/09/19

Client

The Internet

Server

smith.geo.stateu.edu   climate.weather.gov

Server looks up information and sends back response

TEMP ORD 1956/09/19 HIGH 78 14:26 LOW 54 04:12

Figure 3.2

for an airport code that doesn't exist. Or suppose the server is missing data for the days in question. Or suppose the client asks for data for a day in the future—since this is a historical climate data server, it doesn't do forecasts. Once all the error conditions have been identified, a scheme for identifying each error would be devised. One possible scheme would be to simply return the word "ERROR:" followed by some explanatory text. For instance, the server might return:

```
ERROR: City code requested doesn't exist
```

(In practice, some Internet applications protocols always return a numeric response code, for instance with numbers in a certain range indicating success, and other ranges indicating failure; the numeric code is optionally followed by explanatory text.)

It might seem that the next step would be to define what the user's workstation will actually display when information is fetched from the climate database. While it is true that someone will have to make those decisions, that isn't the job of the working group. Its task was to define a protocol—a standard—that others could implement. It is now up to one or more client writers to develop client software that follows the standard. Exactly how the information will be displayed on the screen is up to the developers of the client software (and their users). In fact, once a standard for weather database transactions exists, we could expect innovative client software programs to arise from a variety of programmers:

- One client might be relatively simple, answering queries in a textual form resembling the display that traditional interactive users observed.

- Another client program might be somewhat fancier, displaying temperatures as bar graphs.

- Still another client might be able to depict historical trends and perform statistical analysis.

- Yet another client program might be able to show high and low temperatures for major cities on a national map, or as color-coded temperature regions.

Although fictitious, this example is illustrative of what a simple Internet protocol might look like. Much more elaborate protocols are used for more sophisticated purposes, of course. In particular, many protocols require more extended negotiations between the client and server before real work can be completed. On the other hand, some of the most important applications on the Internet carry on client/server interactions that are no more complicated than our climate database example.

ADVANTAGES OF THE CLIENT/SERVER MODEL

So now we've defined the client/server model for the climate server. What are the advantages of this scheme?

- The model uses an efficient division of labor between the client and server computers. The client computer handles the problem of displaying the information. The server computer doesn't have to handle the overhead of supporting large numbers of logged-in users; this means the server can be a relatively inexpensive workstation-class machine itself, instead of an expensive mainframe. (Even if the server support does reside on a mainframe, client/server information delivery can still be more efficient than the traditional terminal model.)

- Because there is a simple, standard way to retrieve information, client developers can experiment with different implementations. The beauty of the client/server model is that all of these varied experiments in presenting the information to the user can be tried without any need to change the server or the communications protocol.

- Providers of information gain tremendous flexibility. For example, if the Weather Database is ever relocated to another computer system, programming language, or database, it will be relatively easy to move or even reimplement the server support. The client/server model is an important part of the industry trend away from proprietary systems toward open systems.

THE CLIENT/SERVER MODEL IN THE INTERNET CONTEXT

The client/server model is often touted as a feature of today's local area networks and high-end workstations and servers. But the term is actually not new; it is used in early Internet design documents. In fact, the Telnet process we saw in

Chap. 2 is an early example of the client/server model. Telnet's function is to allow a user to communicate with an application on a remote host, essentially exporting the traditional terminal/mainframe communications model over a network.

In the mid-1970s, there were many different models of computer terminal on the market, and variations in settings within a model. As more and more interactive services accepted remote logins on the ARPANET/Internet, it became obvious that there was a problem: If thousands of computers that accepted logins from remote terminals had to be endowed with the capacity to work with hundreds of different computer terminals, a great deal of programming effort would be wasted on terminal support. So the Telnet protocol was designed to provide a "network virtual terminal." The theory was that a computer offering a new interactive service would only have to support the one network virtual terminal, not every brand of physical terminal sold on the market.

Telnet, then, involves a user (or client) program that knows how to speak the protocol, and a server Telnet as well. In order for the two sides to work well, and to support the features of the user's real terminal, the two sides have to carry out negotiations. Most Telnet implementations will give you a simple glance into the workings of the protocol so you can see some of the negotiations that the Telnet client and server go through. An example:

```
# telnet
telnet> toggle options
Will show option processing.
telnet> open gopher.msu.edu
Trying...
Connected to gopher.cl.msu.edu.
Escape character is '^]'.
SENT do ECHO
SENT do SUPPRESS GO AHEAD
SENT will TERMINAL TYPE (reply)
SENT do SUPPORT SAK
SENT will SUPPORT SAK (reply)
RCVD do TERMINAL TYPE (don't reply)
RCVD will ECHO (don't reply)
RCVD will SUPPRESS GO AHEAD (don't reply)
RCVD wont SUPPORT SAK (reply)
SENT dont SUPPORT SAK (reply)
RCVD do SUPPORT SAK (don't reply)
SENT suboption TELOPT_NAWS Width 80, Height 43
RCVD suboption TELOPT_TTYPE SEND
SENT suboption TELOPT_TTYPE vt100
RCVD wont SUPPORT SAK (don't reply)
RCVD do ECHO (reply)
SENT wont ECHO (reply)

                              <--[remote host responses begin here]
AIX telnet (burrow.cl.msu.edu)
```

```
RCVD dont ECHO (don't reply)

Type  gopher  to log in

login:gopher
```

Without worrying about the details of what these negotiations are all about, you can see a bit of the behind-the-scenes work that takes place to allow you to log in to a computer across the Internet. The user (client) Telnet program you invoke was quite likely implemented by a different vendor than the server Telnet you log into. The two sides are able to carry out the negotiations, and provide your remote terminal session, because the implementers of the client and server Telnets followed the same standards. Obviously without careful agreement as to standards, the conversation couldn't take place.

Many of the other tools we will learn about in the rest of this book revolve around the client/server model. Gopher, World-Wide Web, WAIS, and Archie all embrace the client/server model. Even the world of electronic mail involves the use of client/server schemes in most cases.

The client/server model calls for the client software to be installed on your workstation—the computer on your desktop. However, in some cases you may exploit the client/server model indirectly. In Chap. 2 we saw examples of accessing Gopher via Telnet. Those examples involved use of the Gopher "public client" you connect to a computer that is running a client program on your behalf (see Fig. 3.3).

If you do not have a client installed on your workstation, but you do have access to Telnet, a public client service may be the only way you can exploit a

**A "Public Client" Allows Users without Client Programs
to Exploit Client/Server Systems**

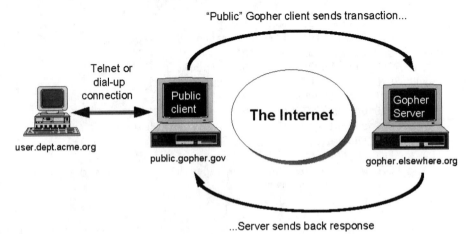

Figure 3.3

service on the Internet.* Usually, it is to your advantage to run a "real" client on your local workstation whenever possible. This provides the richest access to information, allowing much better use of the graphical capabilities of your workstation, and enhancing the presentation of information on your monitor and the ways in which you choose among options. The most elaborate client programs make it as easy for you to navigate among choices across the network as it is to use the graphical user interface found on Macintosh or Microsoft Windows. By contrast, when you use a public client via Telnet, you are usually limited to a fairly mundane character-oriented interface. But in those cases when you cannot install or run a local client on your workstation, a public client service is the next best thing.

MULTIPURPOSE CLIENTS

Historically, in most cases client developers thought of their job as implementing a specific client for a specific protocol. A multipurpose client developed in 1993 represents an important milestone in the evolution of the client/server model. The tool, Mosaic, comes from the National Center for Supercomputer Applications. The first implementation of NCSA Mosaic was delivered for the X Window environment popular on some Unix workstations; implementations for Microsoft Windows and the Macintosh became available in late 1993.

A multipurpose client allows a user to navigate different types of Internet information services without having to load different applications programs on the local workstation. This greatly enhances ease of use and the quality of the user's Internet experience; not only is the user freed from loading separate client programs, the user also may not be aware that different server technologies are being invoked at the other end of the network. Although Mosaic is intended as a multipurpose client, its first and greatest market penetration has come in the World-Wide Web community. We discuss Mosaic further in Chap. 13.

THE INTERNET STANDARDS PROCESS

Our example of how we might develop a client/server model for delivering climate information was modeled (in a simplified fashion) after the process used for the creation of new standards in the Internet community. The Internet is not static: new hosts, applications, and technologies become part of the Internet every day. New communications protocols are essential to the enhancement of the ways in which information is delivered over the Internet. The goal

---

* Note that public clients are sometimes called "curses" clients in honor of the Unix software tool used to implement them.

of the Internet standards process is to encourage the development of workable, functional new networking technologies.*

The Internet community encourages open discussion and experimentation before a new communications protocol is declared a standard. Often the discussion is quite heated, but usually the process produces workable standards. One of the important elements of the process is the acceptance of multiple rival protocols: in general the Internet standards community embraces any scheme that is technically viable and addresses a need. Before a protocol can be accepted as an Internet standard, it must have been implemented by more than one party. Alas, our client/server model for climate data is probably a little too narrow in focus and limited in design to become an Internet standard.

In order for all implementers and developers of Internet protocols to work from an agreed-upon base of knowledge, there is a set of official documents known as Request for Comments documents, or RFCs. RFCs are numbered sequentially from RFC 1. (As of this writing the number has reached 1500.) This name is somewhat misleading in that, by the time a document becomes an RFC, the author has probably circulated numerous draft copies of the document and received many comments. Some RFCs serve as instructional documents; some are general philosophical musings; some have been designated as Internet standards. Here are the titles of some selected RFC documents:

```
1492 I C. Finseth, "An Access Control Protocol, Sometimes Called
       TACACS", 07/23/1993. (Pages=21)

1491 I C. Weider, R. Wright, "A Survey of Advanced Usages of X.500,"
       07/26/1993. (Pages=18) ((FYI 21)

1489 I A. Chernov, "Registration of a Cyrillic Character Set",
       07/23/1993. (Pages=5)

...

1486 E M. Rose, C. Malamud, "An Experiment in Remote Printing",
       07/30/1993. (Pages=14)

...

1425 SMTP Service Extension. Klensin, J.; Freed, N.; Rose, M.T.;
       Stefferud, E.A.; Crocker, D. 1993 February; 10 p. (Format:
       TXT=20932 bytes)

1424 Privacy Enhancement for Internet Electronic Mail: Part IV: Key
       Certification and Related Services. Kaliski, B.S. 1993 February;
       9 p. (Format: TXT=17537 bytes)
```

---

* Strictly speaking, not all Internet standards relate to the client/server model per se. However, since much of the Internet standards corpus does concern client/server computing, we explain the standards process here. The details of the Internet standards process will be of greater interest to some readers than others.

```
...
1392 Internet Users' Glossary. Malkin, G.S.; Parker, T.L., eds. 1993
     January; 53 p. (Format: TXT=104624 bytes) (Also FYI 18)

1391 The Tao of IETF: A Guide for New Attendees of the Internet
     Engineering Task Force. Malkin, G.S. 1993 January; 19 p. (Format:
     TXT=23569 bytes) (Also FYI 17)

...
1386 The US Domain. Cooper, A.; Postel, J.B. 1992 December; 31 p.
     (Format: TXT=62310 bytes)

1385 EIP: The Extended Internet Protocol: A framework for
     maintaining background compatibility Wang, Z. 1992 November; 17
     p. (Format: TXT=39166 bytes)

...
822 Standard for the format of ARPA Internet text messages. Crocker,
    D. 1982 August 13; 47 p. (Format: TXT=109200 bytes) (Obsoletes
    RFC 733; Updated by RFC 1327)

821 Simple Mail Transfer Protocol. Postel, J.B. 1982 August; 58 p.
    (Format: TXT=124482 bytes) (Obsoletes RFC 788)
```

As you can see from the titles alone, the purposes of RFCs are varied. Some of the titles are deceptively modest. RFC 821, for instance, defines Simple Mail Transfer Protocol, which specifies the mechanics of how electronic mail is exchanged over the Internet. Most users of the Internet will never be interested in the particulars of how SMTP works. Other RFCs, however, are of broader interest, and might be documents that the general user would want to peruse; an example might be the Internet Glossary, RFC 1392.

Some RFCs define Internet standards. This happens when a proposal from the IETF to promote a draft document is approved by an organ of the Internet Architecture Board known as the IESG.* Those RFCs that are anointed as standards are each assigned a separate STD number. For instance, if a description of our weather database protocol were to be assigned RFC 1501, we might later submit the protocol as an Internet standard. STD documents define the core standards of the Internet; therefore, few have been assigned. If our protocol were to be designated a standard, a number, say STD-48, would be assigned. Later, if we modify the weather protocol, we might issue a new RFC for it, and at that time STD-48 would now refer to the new document. Here is a list of some Internet standards and the RFCs they correspond with:

---

* IESG is the IETF Engineering Steering Group. The reader will recall from Chap. 1 that the IETF is the Internet Engineering Task Force, which conducts the actual experiments and deliberations that lead to new standards.

Std	Protocol	Name	RFC
STD-01	--------	IAB Official Protocol Standards	RFC 1410
STD-02	--------	Assigned Numbers	RFC 1060
STD-03	--------	Host Requirements	RFC 1122, 1123
STD-04	--------	Gateway Requirements	RFC 1009
STD-05	IP	Internet Protocol	RFC 791
		as amended by:	
	--------	IP Subnet Extension	RFC 950
	--------	IP Broadcast Datagrams	RFC 919
	--------	IP Broadcast Datagrams with Subnets	RFC 922
	ICMP	Internet Control Message Protocol	RFC 792
	IGMP	Internet Group Multicast Protocol	RFC 1112
STD-06	UDP	User Datagram Protocol	RFC 768
STD-07	TCP	Transmission Control Protocol	RFC 793
STD-08	TELNET	Telnet Protocol	RFC 854, 855
STD-09	FTP	File Transfer Protocol	RFC 959
STD-10	SMTP	Simple Mail Transfer Protocol	RFC 821
STD-11	MAIL	Format of Electronic Mail Messages	RFC 822
	CONTENT	Content Type Header Field	RFC 1049
STD-12	NTP	Network Time Protocol	RFC 1119
STD-13	DOMAIN	Domain Name System	RFC 1034, 1035
STD-14	DNS-MX	Mail Routing and the Domain System	RFC 974
STD-15	SNMP	Simple Network Management Protocol	RFC 1157

Just as some RFCs are bestowed with the label "STD," other RFCs are assigned "FYI" numbers. These "For Your Information" documents provide general information intended for a wide audience. FYIs are a form of online documentation submitted for the benefit of the Internet community. Among the example RFCs listed above, RFC 1491 has been labeled FYI 21. The repositories for RFCs generally offer separate lists of FYIs and STDs for convenient retrieval.

This scheme for documentation may seem somewhat obtuse, but that is due to the character of its evolution. Of greatest importance to users of the Internet is not the exact nature of the standards process, but rather the simple fact that the process exists and that it works: it has served the Internet effectively from its inception through a period of spectacular growth, far beyond the dreams of its designers. In the remainder of this book, footnotes will list some of the RFCs that are relevant to various Internet protocols as they are described.

Because new RFCs are issued frequently, it is only appropriate that the official copies of RFCs are maintained online on the Internet. Several official repositories exist worldwide. Because the exact list of repositories varies, there is an official list of current ways to obtain RFCs. You can find this information on the InterNIC Gopher server that was shown in Chap. 2, or you can send an electronic mail message to rfc-info@isi.edu with the message:

```
help: ways_to_get_rfcs
```

. . . as the body of your message.*

The experimental nature of the Internet development process is an important reason why the Internet has been so successful. New tools such as Gopher are often developed in prototype before becoming part of the Internet standards process. Anyone can devise a new way of delivering information over the Internet and can experiment with it without securing the blessing of a standards committee. Of course, a new tool or protocol cannot violate the standards already in place. While some tools and standards are first deployed as prototypes, others may be designed collaboratively in Internet Engineering Task Force working groups before a prototype is developed.

Readers who choose to examine RFC documents should take note of one peculiarity of nomenclature: In common usage, the word "byte" is understood to mean an 8-bit chunk of data. Because in some obscure quarters the term has been used for chunks of different sizes, the Internet community tends to use the word "octet" in its deliberations and in standards documents. In this book we will use the term "byte," assuming its commonly used meaning.

In recent years, the Internet standards community has worked more closely with other standards efforts. In particular, the standards that fit into the Open Systems Interconnection model, defined primarily in Europe, are being examined and in some cases integrated into the TCP/IP family. One candidate for the "next generation" of the Internet Protocol, CLNP, comes from the OSI community. Chapter 25 discusses these developments in more detail.

---

* Note that the text of the message must match exactly what is shown here, with spacing and the use of underscores respected faithfully. Electronic mail is discussed in Chap. 6.

Internet Communications: The TCP/IP Protocol Family

In order for two computers to communicate, they must use a common language. The last chapter discussed how a protocol can be devised to support the client/server model of computer communications; we used the example of a tube carrying messages between a client and a server. The core protocols that provide that virtual tube on the Internet are TCP/IP. In this chapter we concentrate on how these core protocols allow basic communications to take place over the Internet. A basic understanding of how TCP/IP works is helpful in order to understand how to connect to the Internet and how to exploit network applications such as Telnet, electronic mail, file transfer, and Gopher.

THE DOMAIN NAME SYSTEM
AND IP ADDRESSES

Previous chapters showed examples of the host names that are assigned to computers on the Internet. In today's Internet these host names are the "handles" one uses to specify the names of computers whose services you wish to exploit. Recall, for instance, that `gopher.msu.edu` is the host name of the main Gopher server at Michigan State University. Each computer is also assigned an "IP address"—a numeric address that serves a role analogous to a telephone number. The computer named `gopher.msu.edu`, for instance, is assigned a number of `35.8.2.61`.

Why does a computer need two names? Because IP addresses are numeric, they can be easily understood and manipulated by the hardware and software that must move information over the Internet. Numeric addresses are not very palatable for human consumption, however; `gopher.msu.edu` is much more mnemonic than the corresponding IP address. So IP addresses are better-suited to computers, and domain addresses are better-suited to humans.

If both types of names are to be used, there must be a mechanism for translating from the domain-style host names to IP addresses. At the very beginning of the ARPANET, with only a handful of hosts to keep up with, each user on the fledgling network could keep up with all the "interesting" addresses that might be of use. Later, the ARPANET community began distributing a file that contained the host names and corresponding addresses. But the process of distributing this file grew geometrically more cumbersome as the Internet grew. In the words of Jon Postel*:

> Long ago and far away, there was an ARPANET, and it had a few hosts on it. People started keeping host names in a HOSTS.TXT file. At first it had about 20 names; then it had 200. When it got to have about 500 names, maintaining this file began to be a problem: because of the number of changes, it became an administrative load that was noticeable. So we went off and invented something called the Domain Name System. One major motivation was to divide the workload of maintaining this list of hosts, so there would be a higher-level structure of names that wouldn't change very often. The changes would take place down in the branches, and each of those would be fairly small, so the workload for any one person or any one site would also be small.

This notion of distributed control over Internet host naming led to the creation of the two-letter country codes as top-level domains:

> Another fact about the Domain Name System is that we started out with the idea of areas—commercial, education, government—but as the Internet became international, people in other countries said, "We'd rather have control over our part of the Domain Name System under our own countries," so this led to the development of country codes.

Today the trend is for domain names in the United States to conform to the geographically oriented scheme used in other countries. With the number of Internet hosts rising exponentially, there is a need for further delegation in naming of hosts. For instance, consider the plan for assigning domain-style host names to primary and secondary schools in the United States:

> This, in turn, has generated some pressure on the administrators of the Internet in the United States to move things under the `.us` domain. . . . Other schools [than universities] will be placed into the `.us` domain under individual states. This is a

---

* Dr. Postel is one of the leading architects of ARPANET/Internet protocols and services, including the Domain Name System. His comments here were transcribed at the March 1993 meeting of the Internet Engineering Task Force in Columbus, Ohio, and are quoted with permission.

major subdivision of the name space, breaking it into much more manageable sized units. Within each state we've established a branch for K–12 schools, which is a very fast growing area. Our suggestion is that within `.k12` delegations be made to school districts, and then to schools within districts. The long-term vision would be that each school district would have its own domain name server, and some larger schools might have their own domain servers within their schools too.

For K–12 schools in the United States, then, the preferred scheme is:

```
<computer-name>.<school-name>.<district-name>.k12.<state-code>.us
```

For example, one computer at a school in Los Angeles might be named:

```
alpha.washington.la-unified.k12.ca.us*
```

This geographic style of naming is also in use for organizations in the United States other than schools. For instance, the San Francisco–area community information service known as The Well has registered its Gopher server as `gopher.well.sf.ca.us`.

MORE ABOUT IP ADDRESSES

Here are some examples of how domain-style host names correspond to IP addresses:

Host name	IP address
mugwump.cl.msu.edu	35.8.1.212
gopher.msu.edu	35.8.2.61
msu.edu	35.8.2.2
gopher.nd.edu	129.74.250.103
is.internic.net	192.153.156.15
spacelink.msfc.nasa.gov	192.149.89.61
gopher.cs.nott.ac.uk	128.243.22.11
pinus.slu.se	130.238.98.11

As the examples show, IP addresses always consist of four numbers. For human consumption the numbers are often represented as shown: four decimal values separated by periods. Each part of an IP address is a value between 0 and 255; it is represented in one byte of computer memory. Thus IP addresses theoretically can range from 0.0.0.0 to 255.255.255.255.

---

* Note that host names are not case-sensitive. For instance, this name could also be typed as: `Alpha.Washington.LA-Unified.K12.Ca.US`

Domain-style names, by contrast, do not necessarily have four parts. They might have only two parts—a top-level domain such as "edu" or "com," preceded by a subdomain—or three, or four, or many. The only limitations are that a domain-style name cannot exceed 255 characters, and each part of the name cannot exceed 63 characters.

One misconception to avoid: Because many domain-style names happen to have four parts, it may appear that the parts of the host name correspond one-for-one with the parts of IP addresses. This is not the case. Once the top level of a domain is registered, it is up to the local network administrator to decide how to break up names within that space. For instance, within `msu.edu`, the campus Gopher server might be called `gopher.msu.edu` or `gopher.cl.msu.edu` or `gopher.server.cl.msu.edu`. No matter what domain-style host name is chosen, the IP address remains a four-token number, in this case `35.8.2.61`.

The job of the Domain Name System is to translate host names into IP addresses. When you ask a Gopher client program to connect to `boombox.micro.umn.edu`, the domain system translates that host name into the corresponding IP address. The process of looking up IP addresses on your behalf is transparent to you. Each constituent network on the Internet is required to provide a Domain Name System server for its local users. The job of keeping up with name changes is distributed throughout the Internet; local DNS servers keep up with the hosts in their subdomain, and the system is able to forward queries to the appropriate "authoritative" servers in order to complete a name lookup.*

Up until recently, some users continued to operate their workstation-class computers with a form of local domain name service, by maintaining a "local hosts" file. In today's Internet this is no longer practical. Whatever kind of connection you have to the Internet, whether through a LAN attached via a leased line, or over a dial-up service provider, you must have access to a Domain Name System server in order to make productive use of the Internet.

As you read an IP address, moving from left to right, you move from the most general part of the name to the most specific. By contrast, as you read a domain-style host name, you move from the most specific to the most general (see Fig. 4.1).

When should you use domain-style host names, and when should you use IP addresses? Whenever it is possible to use host names instead of IP addresses, you should do so. Besides being more mnemonic, host names tend to be more constant over time. The particular computer that provides a particular service may change over time; when that happens, the domain name for the service is

---

* In particular, your TCP/IP software must be configured with the address of a name server. When you try to connect to a particular host name, your computer asks that name server what IP address corresponds to the host name you're seeking. If your name server isn't responsible for the host you're looking for, it will refer your computer to another name server; this process is repeated until the address you're looking for can be "resolved" into an IP address.

Domain-style host names read from specific to general:

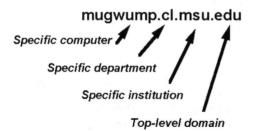

IP addresses read from general to specific:

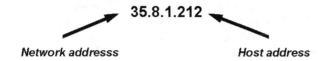

(The middle parts of the IP address can belong to the network address
  or to the host address depending on the "class" of the network)

Figure 4.1

likely to stay the same, even if the corresponding IP address of the new computer may differ.*

From time to time you will encounter lists of services on the Internet that provide IP addresses as well as host names. The best advice is to ignore the IP addresses and rely on the domain-style names, except in cases when it is essential to use the IP address.

When, then, will IP addresses be used? Generally you must specify IP addresses when setting up a computer for network access. You have to tell your TCP/IP software the IP address that has been assigned to your computer. You also have to tell it the IP address of the Domain Name System name server on your local network; it will perform the lookup of other host names on your behalf. And you may have to specify the IP addresses of a few other specialized services on your local network.

Note that it is possible for multiple domain-style names to be assigned to one computer. This is useful when an organization runs several services on one computer, and wants the flexibility to be able to tell users an address for each service. For instance, suppose Goethe University wants to run Gopher and World-Wide Web services on a single computer. They might choose to set up

---

* Therefore you should not assume that the IP addresses given as examples in this book will always connect you to the services listed.

gopher.goethe.de and www.goethe.de as separate host names pointing to a single IP address. Later, should they need to separate these services on two computers, the users of each service will not notice a change has been made.*

ASSIGNMENT OF IP ADDRESSES

Although in today's Internet it is wisest to use domain-style host names where possible, an understanding of how IP addresses are assigned can be useful as you set up your workstation for Internet access, and as you navigate the Internet.

We have seen that IP addresses are four-part numbers that uniquely refer to a computer on the Internet. IP addresses are assigned according to a scheme intended to allow large networks to manage large numbers of addresses, and small networks to manage small parts of the "IP address space." By analogy, imagine if the telephone company allowed very large organizations to assign telephone numbers within an area code, and allowed small organizations to assign numbers within a telephone exchange. Similarly, InterNIC Registration Services gives more control over IP addresses to certain large organizations, such as regional networks.

IP addresses are divided into classes. The leftmost part of the IP address determines the class; numbers from 0 through 127 are assigned to Class A networks. Class A networks can theoretically have 16,777,216 host computers. The next group of networks, Class B, are assigned IP addresses beginning with the numbers between 128 and 191; these networks can theoretically have 65,536 hosts. Class C addresses begin with 192 through 223, and can have up to 256 hosts each in each network.† Figure 4.2 shows how IP addresses are broken up differently in each class.

Recall that the Internet is a network of networks. Each constituent network has a network administrator whose job it is, among other things, to assign host addresses out of the block of IP addresses assigned to his or her network. In practice, the mechanics of how IP addresses are assigned is very important to the administrator, and of very little importance to end users. Once the network administrator has chosen an IP address for a new computer to be attached to the network, the job is not done; the administrator also must choose a domain-style host name. The administrator records both the IP address and the host

---

* It is also possible for a single computer to have more than one IP address. This is fairly common in the mainframe world, and rather uncommon in the world of desktop computers. If users refer to domain-style names, it generally isn't important to them what host—or which host interface out of several—they actually connect to.

† There are also Class D addresses, used for "multicasting," and experimental Class E addresses. In general use of the Internet you will not encounter these addresses.

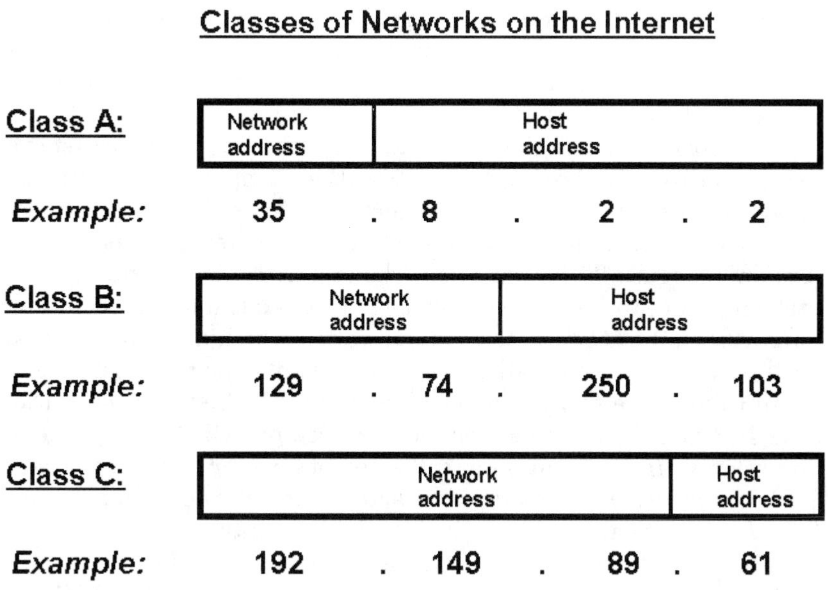

Classes of Networks on the Internet

Class A:

Network address	Host address

Example: 35   .   8   .   2   .   2

Class B:

Network address	Host address

Example: 129   .   74   .   250   .   103

Class C:

Network address	Host address

Example: 192   .   149   .   89   .   61

Figure 4.2

name (along with other pertinent information) in the local name server, and the user is ready to claim the addresses and start using TCP/IP.*

HOW TCP/IP TRANSFERS DATA
ON YOUR BEHALF

The process involved in moving data from your computer to another computer over a local network or over the Internet is rather elaborate. The details of how this process works may make it seem that actual communication would be more likely to succeed if you tied the message and its destination address to a helium balloon and released it into the air. Actually the process, though complicated, is quite reliable.

The core protocols used on the Internet are referred to as TCP/IP. In fact, TCP and IP are separate protocols with separate jobs. TCP's job is to provide a reliable mechanism for computers to send data back and forth; data must be delivered reliably, in sequence, completely, and with no duplication. IP's job is

---

* More information on how you as a user will use your IP address and host name appears in Chap. 5. The concepts of IP addresses, the domain name system, and TCP/IP functioning in general are explained in greater detail in *TCP/IP Architecture, Protocols, and Implementation* (McGraw-Hill, 1993, ISBN 0-07-020346-6) by Sidnie Feit. The definitive reference on TCP/IP (other than relevant Request for Comments documents) is *Internetworking with TCP/IP* (Prentice-Hall, 1991, vols. 1 and 2) by Douglas Comer.

to move chunks of data called "datagrams" over a complex web of networks (called "internetworks" appropriately enough) that sit between the computers that want to communicate. We'll look at IP in more detail later; for now we'll concentrate on how TCP works.

When one computer wants to establish a dialogue with another over the Internet, it opens a TCP connection to the other computer. More precisely, when an application program, such as a Telnet or Gopher client, wants to communicate with a corresponding process on a remote computer, such as a Telnet or Gopher server, it opens a TCP connection. The process could be compared to the way the telephone network operates—someone places a call to a specific address (phone number) on the network, some magic (called switching) takes place, and after the call is answered, information is exchanged until the parties decide to hang up.

In Chap. 2 we saw examples of how to use Telnet to reach various hosts on the Internet. Telnet relies on the services of TCP to carry out the dialogue between your workstation and the remote server. But a remote server could offer numerous services to users across the Internet—Telnet, Gopher, WAIS, etc. In order to allow calls to be identified with the service you want as a user, TCP calls include the "port" you want to connect to. Ports are roughly comparable to telephone extensions, except the "telephone number" (IP address) and "extension" (TCP port) are specified in one fell swoop. Different network tools such as Telnet and Gopher are assigned different port numbers. For instance, Telnet is assigned port 23, and Gopher is assigned port 70. Generally you don't have to worry about which port number will be used; the client program you run knows what it should do.

The connection that TCP provides between two cooperating computers allows data to move in both directions simultaneously.* You could envision the process as two streams of bytes, one flowing in each direction, from end to end. TCP also provides a way for one side to tell the other, "Hey! This is an important byte coming!" This is useful, for instance, so that the client Telnet program can tell the server Telnet program that you've struck the Enter key and you'd like for the server to process your command. TCP also provides "flow control" so that the receiving computer isn't overwhelmed with a flood of data from the sender.

TCP allows two computer programs to exchange information over a network or a group of networks—an internet.† It relies upon the services of IP to actually move the data across a series of network hops. Each message to be sent is broken up into one or more "datagrams." Each datagram may have to traverse multiple networks before reaching the destination. On each network along the way, a device called a "router" figures out if the destination address of each datagram it sees resides on a remote network; the router forwards datagrams accordingly. The division of labor between TCP and IP is depicted in Fig. 4.3.

---

* In other words, a TCP connection is "full duplex."

† With a small "i" the term internet refers to any cooperating network of networks.

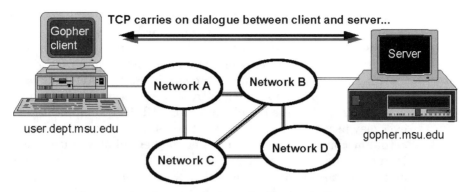

... IP routes the data across the web of networks between the two

Figure 4.3

Your data actually undergoes an impressive series of transformations in order to be delivered. For instance, when you select a document in Gopher, your client opens a TCP connection to the server and asks for the document to be transmitted back over that connection. Your request may follow one path over the Internet, and the document may be sent back over another path. In fact, IP may have to break the datagram up into smaller "fragments" for efficient delivery, and the various fragments may follow different paths along the way. IP doesn't guarantee that it will deliver datagrams in order. Perhaps, surprisingly, *IP doesn't even guarantee that the datagrams will get there at all;* it's TCP's job to figure out when one doesn't, and ask for a fresh copy.

Why is your data allowed to traverse multiple paths on its way to the destination? For one thing, this kind of networking, called "packet-switching," can be more efficient. If one path is congested, and there are other ways to get there, it makes sense to use a different road. Moreover, if one path becomes completely unusable, this scheme allows data to take an alternate route. These characteristics are especially appropriate to a network whose design was intended, you will recall, for military needs. The specialized computers whose job it is to decide how to move IP datagrams—routers—are very sophisticated contraptions.* The job of a router is to forward datagrams to other networks when a datagram isn't destined for the local network. When there are multiple possible paths to choose from, routers also may choose one path in preference to another based on relative speeds of the paths or according to administrative arrangements.

There is yet another layer of activity in the delivery of your data: the data has to actually go out over a physical medium, whether it is an Ethernet cable, a piece of fiber-optic cable, or even a telephone wire. IP relies upon the services

---

* Indeed, leading router vendors, such as Cisco and Wellfleet, have made a lot of money building faster and more sophisticated routers to keep up with growing demands of networks.

of "media access control" software to send and receive data over these physical media. The details of how these various media work are not important to our discussion. Conceptually, just as TCP relies on the services of IP to create and to route datagrams, IP relies on the services of the "lower layer" protocols, such as Ethernet, to physically move the data across the relevant communications link. This concept is often depicted as a "protocol stack," shown in Fig. 4.4. This is actually a simplified explanation of TCP/IP communication. Fortunately, everyday use of the Internet doesn't demand a thorough understanding of the actual mechanics. This overview may be helpful as you use the network—for instance, when you observe pauses in the delivery of information, you can visualize datagrams trying to wend their way through a maze of sometimes-busy links. This overview will also be helpful as you explore options for connecting to the Internet, discussed in the next chapter.

THE INTERNET APPLICATIONS FAMILY

The main applications that form the foundation of Internet services are Telnet, electronic mail, and file transfer. These core applications have existed since the early days of the Internet, and are supplemented by newer applications such as Gopher and WAIS. Those major new applications are covered in later chapters; following is a summary of the main applications plus some simple related tools.

We have already seen examples of Telnet in action. As you cruise the Internet, you will occasionally encounter services on IBM mainframes. (For instance, many online library catalogs are deployed on IBM mainframes.) You need a variant of Telnet in order to carry on full-screen communications with such "big iron." The full-screen communications standard for terminal sessions with IBM mainframes is referred to as the 3270 protocol; the variant of Telnet that emulates a 3270 session over TCP/IP is called TN3270. When an IBM mainframe offers TCP/IP connections, it generally can accept TN3270 sessions.

Some versions of Telnet are smart enough to recognize when they have connected to an IBM mainframe, and they communicate in TN3270 mode automatically. Other TCP/IP packages require the user to type in a different

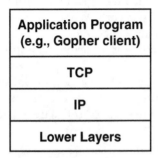

Figure 4.4

command (usually `tn3270`) when you make the connection. If the Telnet running on your computer isn't smart enough to negotiate a TN3270 session, you may find that the mainframe you're trying to talk to abruptly closes the connection, or it may allow the connection, but communications may be garbled.

The flip side of this situation involves connecting *from* an IBM mainframe to a non-mainframe TCP/IP host. The nature of the 3270 protocol makes it difficult to translate to the VT100-style Telnet that is commonly used on UNIX and other servers. Your outbound Telnets will not work to your satisfaction in this case. (On the other hand, when you Telnet from an IBM mainframe to another one, your 3270 communications will work wonderfully.) Consult your mainframe help staff for details on how to handle these situations.*

Electronic mail is the single most important application on the Internet; for many users, e-mail is their only access to the Internet. Electronic mail communications over the Internet are carried over a protocol known as the Simple Mail Transfer Protocol. A wide variety of e-mail packages are able to talk SMTP on your behalf. Chapter 6 has examples.

File transfer on the Internet is accomplished via the File Transfer Protocol, or FTP. Generally you invoke FTP with a command of the same name. Chapter 9 gives examples of using FTP to retrieve all sorts of information from across the Internet.

There are a variety of tools that are commonly provided with TCP/IP implementations. Some you might find useful include:

- *Ping.* This tool attempts to measure the speed at which data moves between you and another Internet host. For instance, you might type `ping rs.internic.net` and see how long it takes for packets to get between you and the InterNIC. Some versions of Ping will run until you interrupt them, and then present a report showing average performance. Don't let a Ping run more than a few seconds, as it consumes bandwidth to take its measurements. "PING" is said to stand for "Packet InterNet Groper."[†]

- *Finger.* This is a simple tool used to probe for information on the Internet. Originally intended as a way to find out about other computer users (for instance, when they last logged into their computers), Finger is used by some people as a simple way to deliver other kinds of information, from recipes to quotes of the day to useful small databases. The command is generally of the form `finger user@host`.

---

* Your mainframe may have a special version of Telnet that makes outbound connections to non-mainframe hosts viable. For instance, if you are a user of VM/CMS, your site may run a tool called TNVT100, written by Arty Ecock of the City University of New York, that will meet this need. Or, you might be able to open a Telnet connection directly from your workstation to the non-mainframe host, avoiding the mainframe as intermediary.

[†] According to RFC 1392, the Internet Users' Glossary.

- *Traceroute.*   This tool tries to discover the path packets generally follow between you and a remote host. You might use this tool to help understand the networks between you and your favorite hosts on the Internet. Traceroute is not included in all TCP/IP implementations; consult your manual.

- *rlogin etc.*   Most flavors of UNIX allow users to perform remote operations on other UNIX machines when authorized. There are commands for remote login (rlogin), for remote file copies (rcp), and other operations. In general you can only use these commands on computers where you have specific authorizations; they are not used for broadly offered Internet services.

TCP VERSUS THE USER DATAGRAM PROTOCOL

Recall that a TCP connection is analogous to a telephone call. It is said to be "connection-oriented." By contrast, IP is "connectionless"—it sends each datagram independently, without concern for the overall transaction taking place. From the point of view of the two computers talking to one another, TCP provides a continuous connection; IP helps TCP present the illusion of a continuous connection.

By contrast, a cousin of TCP known as the User Datagram Protocol is connectionless. There is a certain amount of overhead to setting up and maintaining a TCP connection, and there are some applications where the amount of data being transmitted is so small that the overhead isn't worth it. UDP allows such applications to send data to the remote host while avoiding the overhead. In essence, UDP is a way for an application program to send out an IP datagram. As is always the case with IP datagrams, there is no guarantee of delivery. Therefore a program using UDP must be willing to accept times when the message doesn't arrive, and cope accordingly. As a user you're generally not aware of whether an application uses UDP or TCP; that decision is made by the programmer, and is generally transparent to you.

Connecting to the Internet

Learning about the myriad resources on the Internet will only be useful for you if you can connect to the network and use navigation tools in order to locate and retrieve (and provide) information. This chapter describes the various types of Internet connections that are available, and details ways to exploit these various schemes.

There is a wide variety of styles of access for a variety of users. As an individual who wants to connect to the Internet for the first time, you don't need to understand all of these options in detail. You may want to start out with a connection option that you are comfortable with, such as dial-up access from a well-known service provider, and adopt another scheme after exploring for a while. No matter what category you fall into—a new user looking for access from a dial-up service provider, a student at a university that already has Internet access, or an employee of a firm that provides e-mail access—once you understand the range of options available, you can explore options in detail with your service provider or your network support staff.

STYLES OF INTERNET ACCESS

There are a variety of Internet connection schemes. Before exploring them in detail, let's look at the range of options in overview:

Electronic mail-only access. It is quite possible to take advantage of the Internet without having the ability to log into Internet hosts or to use tools such as FTP and Gopher. Many users have such e-mail-only access to the Internet. They may subscribe to a mass-market information utility like Compuserve or Prodigy that does not (as of this writing) offer other Internet services. Another class of users who have e-mail-only access may belong to a corporate network that supports e-mail to and from the Internet, but by choice does not allow other forms of access. Such limitations may exist for reasons of economy* or security.

An organization with e-mail-only access to the Internet can work with its service provider to obtain a domain-style host name of its own. For instance, Acme Corp. might have the address acme.com registered on its behalf by its Internet service provider. The service provider forwards mail to and from Acme, perhaps over dial-up sessions that exchange mail periodically. In this scenario, the customer appears to the world to be "on the Internet," with e-mail addresses that look like user@acme.com.†

Although this mode of access is rather limited compared to other options, e-mail is the most broadly-used service among all Internet applications. Moreover, there are some tools that allow e-mail-only users to exploit other Internet services, for instance to retrieve files.‡ Thus e-mail-only users can make productive use of Internet services.

Conventional dial-up. With this mode of access, the user dials into an interactive system offered by a service provider. The user workstation runs a conventional terminal program, such as Kermit or Procomm, usually using the VT100 terminal protocol.§ Upon login the user is greeted with a menu system, or in some cases with a simple UNIX prompt. (Services offering a UNIX prompt are said to offer a UNIX "shell" login.) The user is able to run application programs on the service provider's computer; often Telnet, FTP, electronic mail, Gopher, and other services are provided. The service provider may offer a way for the user to download files to his or her workstation; generally this is a two-step process—first the file must be transferred to the user's account on the service provider's machine, and then it is downloaded manually to the user's computer.

This mode of access is quite satisfying to a large group of users. Although it is primarily a text-oriented view of the Internet, it is possible on a VT100 terminal to use the cursor keys for point-and-choose navigation of menus, for instance using the public Gopher client we saw in the Internet tour. Moreover,

---

* False economy, in the minds of some Internet advocates.

† This type of e-mail-only access is sometimes referred to as "MX" access, after the special record that the service provider enters on Acme's behalf in the Domain Name System.

‡ These tools are discussed in later chapters.

§ Recall that the VT100 standard is a common standard for computer sessions that supports "full-screen" communications, which simply means that the user's computer screen can be updated at any point on the screen.

users are able to download multimedia files, though with some manual effort. On the other hand, this mode of access does not allow you to run client software on your own workstation.

Enhanced dial-up. A few service providers are exploring ways to provide some of the creature comforts of full Internet connectivity while having their users connect over otherwise conventional dial-up terminal sessions. One firm offering this approach is Performance Systems International, which offers software that runs on the user's workstation and handles the details of moving data over the telephone line. The software is called PSIlink for MS-DOS and Worldlink for the Macintosh environment.

This sort of scheme offers the user a more intimate connection than conventional dial-up, while freeing the user from having to cope with some of the complications of other modes of connection. The user needs only to know a user ID and password in order to connect, and is able to perform some functions as if directly connected to the Internet.

SLIP or PPP dial-up access. SLIP (Serial Line IP) and PPP (Point-to-Point Protocol) are alternate schemes that make it possible for IP to communicate over dial-up lines. With SLIP or PPP, you can conduct TCP/IP communications as if you were directly attached to the Internet. In order to use these options, you would install specialized SLIP or PPP drivers that work with TCP/IP software installed on your computer. That software allows your computer to be assigned a temporary IP address, lasting the duration of your telephone connection. (Or, in some cases, your service provider may offer you a permanent IP address which will always be used when you dial into a dedicated port.) There is some overhead to setting up such configurations, but the payoff is that you can run the same client software at home or on the road as you could over a corporate or campus network that is directly attached to the Internet.

SLIP is the older of the two schemes, and the simpler. The trend is away from SLIP and to PPP because the latter is more functional. In either case, a service provider may charge more for connecting using one of these protocols compared to conventional dial-up fees; sometimes the premium is substantial.

Direct permanent attachment. There are many different forms of direct attachment to the Internet, which we will explore later in this chapter. The most common configuration involves a local area network that is attached via a leased telephone line to an Internet service provider. The telephone line might run at speeds of 56 kilobits per second, up to "T1" speeds (1.544 megabytes per second) or even faster; or, instead of a leased telephone line, your network might be connected to the service provider over any of a range of newer, more exotic options. The service provider might be a midlevel (regional) network, or a private company offering direct Internet attachments, a telephone company, or even a cable television firm.

This mode of access generally provides the richest and fastest working environment for using the Internet.* It allows an organization to offer access to users on its local networks, sharing the leased line as a common path into the larger Internet. Each workstation is typically given its own IP address, and each user can install clients on the individual computers, providing each user a permanent spot "on the net."

If you are within a local area telephone call of your service provider, you may be able to simulate a direct permanent attachment by leasing a dedicated port from your service provider, and using PPP over a dial-up modem link, saving the cost of a leased telephone line.

INDIVIDUAL VERSUS ORGANIZATIONAL ACCESS

If you work at an organization that has Internet access, or in some cases if you attend school at an institution with Internet access, getting connected may be a simple matter of contacting your organization's computing information center for advice. In many cases your organization will have selected among the sometimes-bewildering array of connection options, and chosen a few options to support. Furthermore, your organization may offer setup services, freeing you from having to figure out how to configure hardware and software to access the local network and the Internet.

Even if you consider yourself highly computer-savvy, it is critical that you work with your organization's network support team when installing new local networks or networked workstations on the campus or corporate network. Very innocent mistakes can lead to highly visible outages for large parts of the network, providing the unfortunate new network user an unintended level of workplace visibility.† Moreover, some of your plans may conflict with standards set by your organization. In any event, you will need to work with your network support staff to receive your IP address and domain-style host name.

If you are an individual seeking Internet access on your own, you will need to choose a service provider and a style of access appropriate to your budget and your needs; obviously most individuals will invest less per month in Internet connectivity than large organizations might. Among the styles of access

---

* Your perceived speed of access is a function of the speed of the slowest link (often the leased line between you and the service provider) and how busy those links are servicing other users.

† One favorite episode in the author's experience: A user in a remote building was configuring a Sun workstation for use on the campus network, and supplied the IP address of the central academic mainframe as his own workstation's address. Hundreds of users logging into the mainframe to check mail (including the author) found themselves connected to a much smaller machine that had no idea who they were. Fortunately, the deployment of routers and bridges on large campus networks provides some isolation against such events.

listed above, e-mail-only access may suit your needs.* Or you may be satisfied with conventional dial-up access. Or you may want to try the enhanced dial-up services of providers like PSI. Finally, you may opt for SLIP or PPP access, in order to achieve the best connections possible over dial-up.

One style of access that is not viable for most individuals is permanent direct connection. The fees charged by the service provider and for a leased line will generally be prohibitive. Over time, this situation will change; the movement to provide national data highways may lead to mass availability of full-time Internet access at popular prices.†

If you seek Internet access on behalf of your organization, you generally will choose between providing an e-mail-only service versus some sort of permanent connection. While the latter provides full access to the Internet on behalf of everyone in your organization who has a computer on the network, the e-mail-only option can be very inexpensive by comparison. Companies are beginning to offer e-mail-only access that is especially marketed towards K–12 schools.

FINDING A SERVICE PROVIDER

Whatever style of access you want to obtain, you must first find a service provider that offers that style of access. The list of organizations offering Internet services changes frequently, so your best strategy is to look for a current list of providers in your area when you decide to get Internet access. First you need to be aware of the wide variety of service providers.

Types of Internet service providers include:

- Midlevel (regional) networks or statewide networks (In some countries, the national network offers access to end users wishing to obtain access.)

- Universities or community colleges that are "on the Internet"

- Specialized firms that offer Internet access as their main product

- Mass-market information utilities (As of this writing, these firms generally offer e-mail-only access; over time, more such services will probably follow the lead of Delphi Internet and America Online in providing more complete styles of access. See Fig. 5.1 for the America Online interface.)

- Telephone companies (or other information firms such as cable companies)

- Vendors of wireless access methods‡

---

* The author urges you to consider trying more complete Internet access, as it is likely to be rewarding. However, if e-mail-only access seems sufficient to you, a service like MCI Mail, which supports e-mail to and from the Internet with a simple addressing scheme, might be very attractive to you.

† Indeed, in August 1993, the service provider Performance Systems International and Continental Cablevision (a large U.S. cable TV company) announced plans to provide Internet access over cable TV by 1994. The exact style of access this will entail was not clear as of this writing.

‡ As of this writing this is a new form of access, not widely deployed, but its adherents say it will become an important way for people to connect using radio-equipped mobile devices.

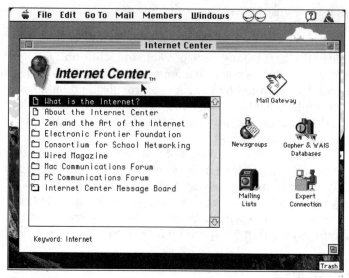

Figure 5.1

One strategy is to have a friend or colleague who already has Internet access help you search the lists of Internet service providers available online on the Internet. Or, you might choose to obtain Internet access from a well-known provider; then, hunt around for other options. After your survey, you may decide that the service provider you started out with has the best deal for you, or you may find a better option elsewhere. Once you have obtained some sort of access it is easy to pursue an up-to-date list of vendors in your area. There are several ways to look for service providers once you have some sort of Internet access.

Visit the Gopher server at the InterNIC and review its online list of service providers. With the list of service providers changing almost daily, an online list is much more apt to provide you with current information. As of this writing, the Information Services branch of the InterNIC has begun compiling a list of U.S. and international service providers, which it offers via its Gopher at is.internic.net. For example,

```
telnet is.internic.net
Trying 192.153.156.15...
Connected to is.internic.net.
Escape character is '^]'.

SunOS UNIX (is)

login: gopher
```

```
    Welcome to the InterNIC Information Service Gopher
    Please enter your terminal type

TERM = (vt100)

            Internet Gopher Information Client v1.11

            InterNIC Information Services InfoSource

        1.   Welcome to the InfoSource/
        2.   InfoSource Update <under construction>.
        3.   InfoSource Table of Contents.
  -->   4.   Getting Connected to the Internet/
        5.   InterNIC Store/
        6.   About InterNIC Information Services/
        7.   Getting Started on the Internet/
        8.   Internet Information for Everybody/
        9.   Just for NICs/
       10.   NSFNET, NREN, National Information Infrastructure
             Information/
       11.   Beyond InterNIC: Virtual Treasures of the Internet/
       12.   Searching the InfoSource by Keyword/


Press ? for Help, q to Quit, u to go up a menu
```

Follow the menus until you find the option listing the geographic area where you need service.

If you look at a file such as the provider list by using Telnet to access the InterNIC Gopher, the public Gopher client will offer to send you a copy via e-mail. This may be more convenient than reading the file online. Simply type in your e-mail address when asked.

If you do not currently have Telnet access to the Internet, but you do have the ability to send electronic mail to an Internet address, you can still retrieve the InterNIC's list of Internet service providers. To do so, you will send e-mail to a mail server at the InterNIC. A "mail server" is a sort of robot—an automated service that responds to commands included in e-mail.* To reach the InterNIC mail server, send mail to this address:

```
mailserv@is.internic.net
```

---

* Chapter 6 provides more information on electronic mail, including how to send mail to an Internet address from a mass-market information utility such as CompuServe. Chapter 7 provides more information on mail servers.

To retrieve the list of North American providers, send the following as the body of your e-mail message:

```
cwd getting-started/getting-connected/providers-na/
send internet-access-provider-list
```

To retrieve the list of international providers, send the following as the body of your e-mail message:

```
cwd getting-started/getting-connected/providers-international/
send providers-intl/inprov-overall
```

The list you ask for will be sent back by return mail.

Note that the InterNIC's list of access providers is relatively new, and may not include all providers. There are other lists of providers you might consult. One such list is called "PDIAL" and can be found online at various places (including the InterNIC Gopher, as an alternative to their list of providers). If you have e-mail-only access to the Internet, you can obtain a copy of the PDIAL list by sending electronic mail to this address:

```
info-deli-server@netcom.com
```

The subject line of your e-mail should consist entirely of the following:

```
send pdial
```

The body of your message will be ignored. The PDIAL list will be returned to you by e-mail.

Finally, another way to find a service provider is to post a public query looking for one. The Usenet newsgroup alt.internet.access.wanted is a good place to post such queries; many service providers watch this group carefully, and will respond to questions such as "Who is a good service provider in the 313 area code?" Users of these services also post their experiences, good and bad.

If it is not practical for you to obtain some sort of interim Internet access in order to search for a service provider, try the following steps:

- Consult with local computer user groups.

- Check to see if any professional organizations you belong to offer Internet access as a perquisite of membership. For instance, the Association for Computing Machinery makes such an offer. Various chapters of professional library groups do so as well. Over time, more professional associations will find Internet access a useful way to foster communications among their constituents. Access may be through a separate service provider, perhaps at a reduced fee.

- Call a local university or a regional network. Ask them if they offer Internet access, but also ask them who else does in the area.

- Look for magazines that cater to the dial-up user community. Two such magazines, *Online Access** and *Boardwatch,*† often carry advertisements from Internet service providers. Such advertisements are also beginning to appear in more general computer magazines such as *Byte, PC Magazine,* and *MacWorld.*

CHOOSING A DIAL-UP SERVICE PROVIDER

Once you've found a list of providers who offer service in your area, you then have to evaluate each in order to make an informed decision. Here are some questions to ask:

- What services are offered? (E-mail, Gopher, WAIS, World-Wide Web, Internet Relay Chat, etc.?)

- How much does the service cost? For dial-up access, is the charge by the hour alone, or are there additional charges based on volume? Are there off-peak rates at night? Are there charges for incoming or outgoing e-mail?

- Is there a limit to the amount of data you can retrieve? To the amount of data you can store on the remote system?

- What speed modems does the vendor support? Are there surcharges for using faster modems?

- How often are there busy signals when one tries to connect? What are the normal service hours?

- Does the vendor offer some sort of enhanced dial-up access? What software is needed? Do you obtain that software from the service provider, or from someone else? How much does it cost?

- If SLIP or PPP dial-up are being considered: Are they offering permanent IP assignment, or assignment by the session? What is the premium for this mode of access? Do they support a particular set of TCP/IP packages? Do they offer assistance in first-time configuration of this software?

- Does the vendor offer a special access package of its own, perhaps sporting its own graphical user interface, and "plug-and-play" ease of installation? Over time more services can be expected to offer packages that make it easy to install the software and to start accessing the Internet quickly.

- What are the payment options? Some services will charge only to a credit card. Others allow automatic debits from a checking account. Others allow you to prepay.

---

* *Online Access,* ISSN 0898-2015, 920 N. Franklin Street, Suite 203, Chicago, IL 60610.

† *Boardwatch,* ISSN 1054-2760, 8500 West Bowles Ave., Littleton, CO 80123.

One major consideration in choosing a dial-up access vendor is how they expect you to connect. A big part of the access question is finding a way to call a service provider without paying long-distance charges. Some vendors are large enough to offer dial-up access to local numbers in major cities. Other vendors may offer toll-free access via 800 numbers. Yet another scheme uses local telephone numbers that trunk to remotely located modem pools (so-called 950 exchanges are used for this purpose in the United States). Be sure to compare all of the costs, including any measured-rate or long-distance charges you may have to pay.

If you are looking for Internet access as an individual for the first time, it would be wise to start with conventional dial-up access, or with an enhanced dial-up option. This will give you access to most Internet services with a minimum amount of setup on your behalf. If a service provider offers SLIP or PPP access, and you wish to avail yourself of that option, be prepared for a somewhat complicated setup procedure. Ask your would-be service provider what sort of documentation and technical assistance will be offered to you in configuring your system.*

If a service provider offers SLIP or PPP access, and you wish to avail yourself of that option, be prepared for a somewhat complicated setup procedure. Ask your would-be service provider what sort of documentation and technical assistance they will offer you in configuring your system.

A list of Internet service providers appears in Appendix D.

DIAL-UP ACCESS ON THE ROAD

Many Internet service providers offer dial-up access only in certain localities or regions. Many Internet users are highly mobile, often carrying modem-equipped laptop computers with them. There are several ways to obtain Internet access when you are on the road:

- You can subscribe to an Internet service provider that offers local access in most major cities.

- You can dial your Internet service provider back home using a long distance call. Today's error-correcting modems should work well except over the most noisy of lines. Obviously this option can grow expensive; you would use this only for short periods.

- You can subscribe to an Internet service provider that offers nationwide service, for use only when on the road. While at home you would continue to use

---

* If you are new to the use of modems for dial-up services, you may want to obtain a book on that subject. One such book is the *PC Magazine Guide to Modem Communications,* by Les Freed and Frank T. Derfler, Jr. (Ziff-Davis, 1992, ISBN 1-56276-937-8).

your local provider. For instance, you might subscribe to Delphi Internet and use its local numbers as a way to Telnet back to your local provider.

■ You can subscribe to an Internet service provider that offers toll-free dial-up service. Such services are available for well below $10 per hour. They may also offer less expensive local dial-up access in certain cities, providing you a combination of low-cost local access and easy-to-remember access when you are traveling.

■ If you attend conferences or trade shows, you can often find a terminal room that provides Internet access. If your professional conference does not offer this service, you might want to urge them to adopt it.*

Vendors are already offering various radio-based connectivity services, some with Internet access. Over time this may become an attractive way for large numbers of users of hand-held computers to maintain Internet access.

CHOOSING A DIRECT-CONNECTION SERVICE PROVIDER

Picking a permanent service provider is generally a much more weighty decision than is the selection of a dial-up service for an individual. There is a lot more at stake: the costs are significantly higher, and the number of users affected is higher. Questions to ask include:

■ What kind of connection do they propose for you to use? (Some of the options are explored below.) What is the monthly cost? Is there a variable cost based on usage? Is this connection yours alone, or will it be shared with other organizations?

■ Will the service provider assist you in obtaining a block of IP addresses (normally Class C) and in registering your organization in the Domain Name System?

■ What devices need to reside on your premises, and who will purchase them? Who will maintain them? (At a minimum, a router will generally be installed on your premises, along with a telephone line and a modem or codec.)

■ Is the provider offering simple IP connectivity, or will other services be provided? For instance, will they deliver Usenet News to your site?

■ What setup and maintenance services will be the responsibility of the service provider, and what will be your responsibility? Is the vendor offering to

---

* Enterprising hotel chains should consider offering Internet access—in meeting rooms or even in individual guest rooms—as a marketing advantage.

obtain the link between your site and the vendor's—whether a leased telephone line or another option—or is that your responsibility?

- What level of service reliability is promised? How often does the provider's service go down, whether due to power outage, telephone trouble, or other problems? Is the service provider's operation monitored 24 hours a day? Are there rebates after extended outages?

- What is the duration of the agreement? What provisions are there for accommodating any new Internet access options that may become available during that time?

- Is the proposed type of connection suited to your organization becoming an information provider in its own right? (Some newer connection technologies are able to deliver data faster in one direction than the other.) Will the provider offer advice or setup assistance as you become an information provider (e.g., in setting up a Gopher server)?

Organizations that seek permanent Internet access vary widely in their level of expertise. Some already run internal networks and therefore have staff with at least some expertise; others may be relatively new to networking and may require more assistance from the service provider. It is important to understand what is and is not offered before you sign a contract.

This sort of decision suits itself well to the Request for Proposal process. After identifying Internet service providers in your area, and after discussing what they can do for you in general terms, prepare a list of required services as an RFP. As with any proposal process, the quality of the responses will depend in part on how carefully you prepare the RFP. Done right, the process can yield the best service offering at the lowest price.

PHYSICAL CONNECTION SCHEMES FOR LOCAL/CAMPUS NETWORKS

Many corporate or university networks are based on Ethernet. Such networks are well-suited to running TCP/IP, and are suited for easy connection to the Internet via a service provider. An Ethernet port is commonly included as a standard feature of high-end workstations. Increasingly, vendors of personal computers are offering Ethernet as an optional feature (and in some cases as a standard feature.) In cases where an Ethernet port is not provided, it is easy to acquire an Ethernet Network Interface Card for PC compatibles and other computers; over 100 vendors market such cards.

There are three types of physical cabling used in Ethernet LANs today:

- *Thick Ethernet.* This is an older style of cable whose use in new networks is declining.

- *Thin Ethernet.*   This newer type of Ethernet cable is relatively popular and somewhat easier to wire. Thick and thin Ethernet cables both resemble the coaxial cable used for cable TV.

- *Unshielded twisted pair.*   This type of cable is the easiest to physically wire, and is becoming increasingly popular. The connector is from the same family of standards used for modular telephone connections.

You may encounter terms such as "10base2" and 10baseT" in discussions of wiring options. This notation expresses the data rate of the medium (10 megabits per second), whether the medium is baseband or broadband,* and the cable's maximum length or type. (For instance, the 10base2 designation, which corresponds to thin Ethernet, has a maximum length of 200 meters; the 10baseT designation refers to the twisted pair cables, resembling telephone cords.)

Examples of the different kinds of Ethernet cables and adapters are included in the photographs section of this book.

For our purposes, Ethernet is a "lower layer" protocol whose exact functioning isn't directly important to use of the Internet. It may be useful for you to keep in mind a few points about how Ethernet functions:

- Ethernet is a shared "broadcast" medium; every computer on an Ethernet "sees" every packet sent by other stations. The nominal speed of an Ethernet cable is 10 megabits per second. That is plenty fast for most users for most applications, but as workstations become more powerful and as we rely on the network for more and more services, you or your colleagues can use up that bandwidth. When you get slow response on the Internet, the problem may be local, not global.

- Large campuses often connect multiple Ethernets together into campus networks. Otherwise, there would be problems with congestion and with physical limits of Ethernets. Campus "backbones" carry traffic from building to building, often over broadband cable or fiber-optics links. Within a building, routers and bridges isolate traffic to that building's local Ethernet. All the users of TCP/IP on a campus can generally ignore what kinds of cable they are communicating over.

- Networking vendors are trying to develop ways to extend the capacity of Ethernet. One development is the invention of the Ethernet "hub." This device makes it possible to easily run several Ethernets in a building at a relatively low cost, isolating high-volume users from one another. Another recent development is the movement to extend Ethernet from its current speed of 10 megabits per second to 100 megabits per second.

---

* A "baseband" cable carries one "channel" of information at once; a "broadband" cable carries more than one. Thin Ethernet cables are baseband; coaxial cable TV cables are broadband.

Ethernet is not the only kind of local area network. The other commonly used local area network standard is Token Ring. Originally developed by IBM, Token Ring LANs are a fairly common alternative to Ethernet. Most vendors of TCP/IP software offer Token Ring support as an option. Over time, high-end workstations may expect direct fiber-optic connections instead of one form of copper cabling or another.

TCP/IP SOFTWARE OPTIONS FOR VARIOUS WORKSTATIONS

In order to run Internet applications on your workstation, you will need to have TCP/IP hardware and software installed. Hardware connection options are discussed in the next section. This section gives you an overview of what is required to connect to a TCP/IP network on various computer platforms.

Most UNIX workstations come with built-in TCP/IP software and with an Ethernet adapter. You simply plug in the adapter, configure the software with your IP address and some additional information, and you're up and running.

Most IBM PC-compatibles do not come with built-in network interfaces. You will need to acquire a Network Interface Card and install it in your PC. Another option is a parallel port Ethernet adapter, which can be very useful for laptop computers and for other situations where you want to move your adapter among various computers.*

One pioneering vendor of TCP/IP software for the PC family is a company called FTP Software, which markets a package called PC/TCP. In recent years many other vendors have entered this market, including Frontier Technologies with its SuperTCP package, NetManage with its Chameleon product, Novell with TCP/IP support in its LAN Workplace (LWP) product, and others. Over time these vendors are offering more functionality in their products. Improvements include vastly simplified installation procedures, support for operation under MS-DOS and under MS-Windows, and support for the Network File System and X Window standards. These developments allow PCs to participate fully in TCP/IP networking, both locally and over the Internet at large.

There are several terms and concepts that come up in discussions of TCP/IP networking on the PC. Here is an explanation of some of the more commonly used terms:

- *Packet drivers.* Packet drivers are software that allow multiple network software packages use the same Network Interface Card at once. This is useful, for instance, when a single computer needs to communicate using Novell's proprietary standard, IPX, and TCP/IP at various times.

---

* For instance, the author used a Xircom parallel port adapter on an 80486 laptop in preparing examples for this book.

Packet drivers are also used to run a particular vendor's TCP/IP software package over a SLIP or PPP connection; you load a specific SLIP or PPP packet driver to work with the generic TCP/IP software from your vendor. Vendors such as FTP Software provide supported SLIP and PPP drivers with their TCP/IP packages.

There are two proprietary standards, NDIS and ODI, that share the basic function of packet drivers. In some complicated environments, you may encounter "shims," whose function is to convert between packet driver format and ODI or NDIS.

- *NDIS.* This is the Network Driver Interface Specification, a standard that allows multiple protocols to share a Network Interface Card; NDIS driver software is often shipped with your interface card. By using NDIS you can, for instance, run FTP Software's PC/TCP and Microsoft's LAN Manager at the same time.

- *ODI.* The Open Data Link Interface is a Novell standard that allows NetWare to coexist with TCP/IP or other protocols. A Novell user would install the Novell ODI driver to work "underneath" the TCP/IP package of choice.

- *Winsock.* Winsock is a standard "sockets" interface for applications programs. It is gaining wide acceptance, meaning that new applications are likely to work with any TCP/IP package that is Winsock-compatible. Once you've installed a TCP/IP package that supports the Winsock standard, installing various applications such as Gopher or WAIS clients is easy.

  Most developers of Internet applications for MS Windows are writing to the Winsock standard first. If you are in the market for a TCP/IP package for MS-Windows, be sure it supports the Winsock standard.

- *NCSA Telnet.* This is a public domain implementation of TCP/IP for the PC. It comes from the National Center for Supercomputer Applications.

- *KA9Q.* This is a shareware TCP/IP package that also includes a kind of multitasking that allows a PC running MS-DOS to be used as a server. For instance, there is a KA9Q Gopher server, described in Chap. 22.

- *Clarkson / Crynwr Packet Drivers.* Originally developed at Clarkson University, the Crynwr drivers are a family of packet drivers that support a variety of network interface cards. Users often run NCSA Telnet with Crynwr drivers.

As an alternative to MS-DOS and Windows, some IBM PCs run the OS/2 operating system. TCP/IP support is available as a separately priced product from IBM. Other vendors, such as FTP Software, also offer TCP/IP packages for OS/2.

Finally in the PC category, there is Windows NT. That new Microsoft operating system comes with TCP/IP support built in. You will need to install the hardware driver for your Network Interface Card and configure specific options such as your IP address.

The Apple Macintosh comes with built-in support for Apple's proprietary networking standard, AppleTalk. The built-in hardware over which AppleTalk is normally carried is LocalTalk. Increasingly Macintosh networks are using Ethernet instead of LocalTalk as the physical medium. Apple offers a MacTCP product that supports TCP/IP over Ethernet, or "encapsulated" over an AppleTalk link.

WIDE AREA NETWORK CONNECTION SCHEMES

Earlier we discussed the model of using a leased telephone line to connect a local area network or a campus network to the Internet. Several variations of connection schemes are becoming available; here is an overview of the options you may confront:

- *Leased line.*   This is the oldest, most conventional scheme for permanent connections. You lease a line from the telephone company (directly or perhaps through your service provider). You may need to install a "channel service unit" (CSU) to connect to the T1 circuit and a "digital service unit" (DSU) to connect to your primary host or network interface.

- *ISDN.*   The Integrated Services Digital Network has been discussed for years, deployed in some cases in Europe and Japan, and appears to be gaining acceptance in the United States. With ISDN you have a digital telephone line instead of an analog one. The basic ISDN scheme provides two digital links that run 56 kilobits per second, and one "control" channel that runs 16 kilobits per second. Because ISDN is digital, you do not use a modem to connect to the line; instead, you use a device called a "codec." As of this writing ISDN appears to be gaining momentum, but some skeptics point out that, with modems capable of running at 14.4 kilobits per second (up to 3 or 4 times that rate with compression) costing $100 or less, basic ISDN may not compete well with other dial-up options.

  ISDN could be affordable for both individuals and for organizations. Organizations may also be interested in a higher-capacity ISDN option (the "primary" ISDN) whose total capacity equals the 1.544 megabits per second of a leased T1 line. Whatever flavor of ISDN you might use, keep in mind that some tariffs call for charging by time, some by the amount of data you move, and some for both; caveat emptor.

- *CATV links.*   Your local cable TV company may be able to lease you "space" on their cable at prices more attractive than leased telephone lines. You will want to find out what equipment you need on your premises and how much bandwidth you are being offered, as well as how the channel is to be shared with other customers.

A more exotic type of "hybrid" network has been announced, where a CATV channel is used for traffic in one direction, and an ISDN line or a dial-up is used for return traffic. If you expect to provide information on the Internet, you will want to be sure that your "back channel" has enough capacity to serve the needs of consumers of your information.

- *Frame relay.*   Frame relay is one of several ways that a telephone company can offer a wide-area connection that is somewhat more flexible than a dedicated leased line. Customers leasing a frame relay link can purchase a certain level of service—a "Committed Information Rate" (CIR). If your demands on the network are very "bursty"—for instance, if your users will make high demands on the line during certain times of the day, and little or no demand at night—frame relay might be more economical than leasing a full T1 (or T3) line. Your telephone company or service provider may also offer a similar scheme, Switched Multimegabit Data Service, as an alternative.

- *Asynchronous transfer mode.*   ATM is a relatively new scheme, the first to promise the same technology for local and wide area networks. ATM uses very small packets called "cells," and very fast switching. ATM is suited to delivery of real-time multimedia along with conventional data. It promises to be a big part of the future of networking.

- *Microwave links.*   If you need a permanent connection to your service provider but find that leased line and other options are too expensive, you might consider microwave as an option. You don't have to pay for expensive right-of-way with microwave; however, you will have to invest more money up front, and you must consider hazards such as lightning bringing down your network.

- *Satellite links.*   If you need to be able to move large amounts of data, especially to remote locations, satellite links might be an answer. Such links tend to be quite expensive. The distance of geosynchronous satellites from the planet Earth also adds a delay (or "latency") that is perceptible to Telnet users.

No matter what style of link you use, Fig. 5.2 shows a general view of connecting your network to the Internet.

As you can see, the range of options open to you as you connect your network to the Internet is quite varied. With technology changing rapidly, you may want to be sure you don't lock yourself into one technology for too long a period. You may want to choose a simple option over an exotic one as you begin. You may also want to read other books and trade journals to learn more about these evolving connectivity options.*

---

* A book devoted to these issues is the *PC Magazine Guide to Linking LANs* (Ziff-Davis, 1992, ISBN 1-56276-031-9) by Frank Derfler, Jr.

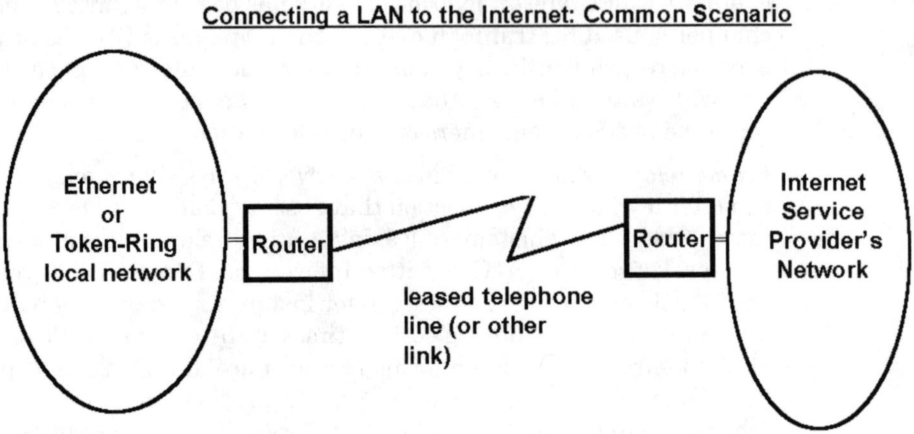

<u>Connecting a LAN to the Internet: Common Scenario</u>

Figure 5.2

CONNECTING AN EXISTING NETWORK TO THE INTERNET

Once you choose a link between your existing network and the Internet, you will need to integrate the Internet protocols into your network. Among the local area networks in common use today:

- In the PC-compatible world: Novell's Netware, Microsoft's LAN Manager, and Banyan's Vines

- In the Macintosh environment: A combination of AppleTalk/LocalTalk, and Ethernet

- In the UNIX environment: TCP/IP

In order to connect your network to the Internet, you need to be able to bring a TCP/IP link on site, and to provide access from your existing network to the TCP/IP services. Generally you will need to run some sort of router, which has the job of forwarding IP packets to and from the Internet link as appropriate. You can buy a stand-alone router,[*] or, in some cases, you may be able to install router software on an existing server.[†]

Organizations that already run TCP/IP obviously have the easiest job of connecting; they already run the Internet protocols. This is not limited to Unix sites; some PC and Macintosh shops have adopted TCP/IP as their internal

---

[*] There are more than 50 vendors of routers, including Cisco, Wellfleet, Proteon, Chipcom, 3Com, and Telebit.

[†] For instance, if you are connecting a Novell network to the Internet, you may be able to save several thousand dollars by installing Novell's Multiprotocol Router software in lieu of a separate router box.

standard for networking. Among sites that run proprietary networks, one option is to install TCP/IP software on the workstations on the existing LAN; most TCP/IP packages are able to coexist with the proprietary standards mentioned above. Another option is to provide some sort of gateway service so that your users continue to use the proprietary networking standard, but can make use of Internet services via the gateway.

It is very common for organizations to run Novell Netware in order to network IBM PC compatibles (as well as other machines). In the K–12 school arena in the United States alone, Novell estimates there are over 40,000 installed Novell networks. Novell's native communications scheme, IPX, differs from TCP/IP, but it is possible to have IPX and IP coexist on one Ethernet network. There is some overhead to this process; you need to install separate TCP/IP software to run alongside your Novell network software.

Another option enables you to run TCP/IP applications on an existing Novell network without installing TCP/IP support on your individual Novell-attached workstations. Software known as Novix* makes this feat possible. This can be a very attractive option; some Novell networks are quite large, and Novix allows you to save the effort and complexity of installing TCP/IP support on hundreds or thousands of workstations. Novix allows users to connect to their Novell server using IPX, and the server opens the TCP/IP sessions on behalf of each user. Firefox is planning support for the Winsock standard, which should make it possible to run TCP/IP clients on each station in the Novell network. The clients behave as if they are connected directly to the Internet; full client functionality is available.

In the Apple world, a variety of vendors sell routers that allow AppleTalk/ LocalTalk users to connect to the Internet; these include Cayman's GatorBox and Shiva's FastPath. If your Macintoshes already speak Ethernet directly, a conventional router will do the job.

---

* Novix is marketed by Firefox Inc., PO Box 8165, Kirkland WA 98034. Phone 206-827-9066.

Internet Electronic Mail

ELECTRONIC MAIL: AN OVERVIEW

Some moments in the history of communication approach the status of legend. For instance, children are taught in school about Alexander Graham Bell's cry "Come here, Watson, I need you!" There is no such mythical moment in the history of electronic mail; various electronic mail systems evolved at about the same time in different computing environments. One of the earliest electronic mail systems was created in the early days of the ARPANET, when two developers began sending notes to each other using the nascent network.

Since those days, electronic mail, or e-mail, has become a familiar concept. It has been deployed on large mainframe platforms such as the IBM PROFS* system made famous when Oliver North's old messages were recovered from backup tapes and used as evidence. E-mail is provided on various local area networks as a way for members of a work group to communicate with one another. And e-mail is one of the popular offerings on mass-market information utilities such as Compuserve. Significantly, all of these environments can also offer gateways that make it possible to exchange mail over the Internet.

---

* PROFS was a mainframe-based system that is no longer marketed.

The appearance of electronic mail systems is as varied as the platforms they run on. Even though they vary widely in features and appearance, most e-mail systems afford similar advantages:

- You can send e-mail at your convenience, just as you would with postal mail. Delivery usually occurs within a few minutes or a few hours.

- Your recipient can read your message at his or her leisure as well. Telephone tag is eliminated. Most e-mail packages make it easy to reply to a message, even including the sender's note (or relevant pieces of it) to provide context. And most systems make it easy to forward a message to another interested party.

- E-mail can as easily be sent to one person, to several, or to many. Most e-mail software provides a mechanism for you to maintain personal mailing lists so that you can send notes to various groups of correspondents by using simple group nicknames.

- Correspondents can retain old messages from friends, colleagues, or supervisors, using them as reminders of things to do or agreements previously reached.

Users of e-mail systems may encounter certain common hazards:

- Mail can get lost. This can happen due to a slight error in addressing on the part of a human, or a software or hardware failure as a message traverses various network links.

- Mail can be misdirected. Again, this could be due to a subtle problem with addressing, or it might be because your notion of who you are "replying" to may differ from your software's view of the matter. The result can be embarrassment or hurt feelings.

- Internet mail can be forged. Fortunately this is relatively uncommon but it does occur.*

- Sometimes e-mail is delivered flawlessly but the intended message is not; e-mail is easily misunderstood due to the absence of cues such as vocal inflection and facial expression that we take for granted in face-to-face communications.

This chapter will explain how to partake of the benefits of electronic mail while minimizing some of the hazards.

Until recently, e-mail has been primarily textual in nature; you send and receive words, not images, sounds, or spreadsheets. But recent developments

---

* We do not supply detailed instructions for obvious reasons. Of course, forging of messages violates most networks' policies and may violate the law.

in Internet standards and in workstation technology make it likely that a rich world of multimedia e-mail is coming. We will examine some of these possibilities at the end of this chapter. To begin with, we'll concentrate on sending and receiving textual messages.

Because of the wide variety of electronic mail systems in existence, we cannot cover each specific system in detail. Instead, in this chapter we will introduce some of the general concepts of Internet e-mail, and give some specific examples with a few of the more common packages.

Internet e-mail systems employ a division of labor among the programs that cause mail to be delivered on your behalf. To send e-mail or to view incoming mail, you use some sort of electronic mail package on your computer; such packages are referred to as *user agents*. Think of the user agent as helping you to type up the message and address the envelope. Your e-mail package then relies on the services of one or more *message transfer agents* to actually move the mail across the networks that lie between you and your recipient. Think of the transfer agents as the workers who sort and move paper mail through one or more postal service offices in order to deliver it; just as postal services worldwide cooperate to deliver paper mail, transfer agents on the Internet cooperate to deliver mail to far-flung Internet correspondents. (See Fig. 6.1.)

You and your Internet correspondents need not use the same e-mail software; indeed, it is often the case that your recipient uses a different tool than you do. Just as we've seen with other Internet services, standard protocols enable this use of a variety of tools. The principal standard for how mail is addressed and structured is Request For Comments 822; due to its importance to the vital function of supporting electronic mail, this document is probably the best known of all the Internet RFCs. A companion, RFC 821, specifies the protocol used as mail is exchanged between message transfer agents; that scheme is known as the Simple Mail Transfer Protocol, or SMTP.

User agents help users prepare, send, and view electronic mail; *message transfer agents* forward the mail across intervening networks

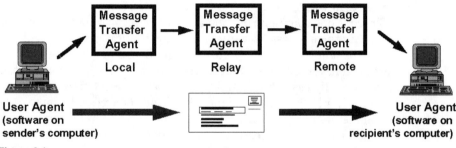

Figure 6.1

ADDRESSING INTERNET E-MAIL

Just as you can use Telnet or Gopher without knowing the exact mechanics of their underlying protocols, you can send and receive Internet e-mail without knowing the details of how SMTP works. However, it is helpful for you to understand the formats of Internet addresses so that you can maximize the chances that mail will be delivered and so you can understand what went wrong when it isn't.

In order to send an electronic mail message across the Internet, you have to identify whom you wish to send mail to and where that person is located on the Internet. The simplest form of addressing looks like this:

```
user@host
```

The `user` name is often a login name used by your recipient. The `host` name often is simply the familiar Domain Name System host name. For example, the author's e-mail address is:

```
wiggins@msu.edu
```

In practice, this is one of the simpler-looking Internet e-mail addresses you'll confront. As we've seen, host names are often longer (e.g., `ibm.cl.msu.edu`). If your mail has to traverse a gateway to be delivered, you may have to specify a more complicated "path" instead of a simple host name, as we'll see in examples later. And many systems assign user names that are less mnemonic than this example (e.g., `smith964` or `12345ABC`).

Some sites use e-mail software that allows their users to be addressed by friendly "real" names instead of computer-specific user names. For instance, you might be able to address mail to `John_Doe@msu.edu` or `Jane_A.Roe@msu.edu` rather than using a hard-to-remember login name. Because this capability depends on the particular e-mail software in use, you can rely on this form of addressing only when you know it works for particular correspondents.

Note that the case of user names (unlike host names) can be significant. That is, if you're given `bob` as someone's e-mail name, and you address the mail to `BOB`, your mail may not be delivered. Under Unix you often will encounter complete devotion to names that are all lowercase.

There is one common rule about formats for user names: You generally have to specify the address literally and accurately, or your mail will go astray.

The host names used in Internet mail are generally similar to the host names that you specify when using Telnet, Gopher, and other tools—that is, they generally resemble domain-style host names. Often the host name will be the same for both e-mail and for other kinds of access. In some cases, however, the name of an organization's main computer for handling e-mail isn't one of the well-known computers at that site. In order to deliver mail, message transfer agents rely on the Domain Name System to identify the actual hosts that serve as "mail exchangers" on behalf of various institutions. The bottom line is that you can't assume that a particular host name you happen to know at a particular site is the place to which you should send e-mail.

Here are some examples of host names seen in Internet mail:

vm.marist.edu	Marist College, Poughkeepsie, New York
weizmann.weizmann.ac.il	Weizmann Institute in Israel
ricevm1.rice.edu	Rice University (Dallas, Texas)
access.digex.net	Digex (an Internet service provider)
holonet.net	Holonet (another Internet service provider)
msen.com	MSEN Incorporated (another Internet service provider)
wais.com	WAIS Incorporated
eff.org	The Electronic Frontier Foundation
umichum.bitnet	The Bitnet gateway to/from the University of Michigan
econ.lsa.umich.edu	The economics department at the University of Michigan
techcn.msk.su	A university institute in Moscow

If user names can take various formats, and if host names can't be inferred from the names of computers you know about, then how can you address mail to a particular individual at a particular organization without knowing their complete e-mail address in advance? Unfortunately, the answer is you cannot. Imprecisely addressed postal mail usually finds its way to its recipient (grumblings about the postal service notwithstanding); by contrast, imprecisely addressed e-mail usually doesn't arrive.

So how do you find the exact e-mail address of someone you want to correspond with? At this point, there is no single answer to that question; there are several kinds of directory services in use on the Internet, none of which is comprehensive. Techniques for using these various directory services are covered in Chap. 16.

The safest way to find your correspondents' e-mail addresses is to obtain them directly. More and more people are placing their Internet e-mail addresses on their business cards.* If you don't have an address in written form, you might call your correspondent on the telephone to ask for it. One time-honored technique is to give your correspondent your address so that he or she can send mail to you first; when that mail is delivered to you, take note of the address from which it came, and use that address to send other messages to your correspondent.†

---

* If you intend to have your e-mail address printed on your business card, it's a good idea to have it reviewed by your network support staff. Some sites have rather complex e-mail configurations; even if your address is functional, there may be a form of address that is simpler and more long-lasting.

† This trick is especially helpful if your correspondent is not directly on the Internet, and you cannot figure out the required path through various e-mail gateways. If your correspondent knows how to send to the Internet, it may be easier for him or her to initiate e-mail communication.

INTERNET E-MAIL HEADERS

Each e-mail message on the Internet contains a set of "headers" followed by the body of the message itself. The headers include some expected information such as whom the message is from, whom it is addressed to, the date and time it was written, and the subject. For example:

```
Date:      Sat, 25 Sep 93 19:37:51 EDT
From:      Alastair Smythe <smythe@msu.edu>
Subject:   My next masterpiece
To:        Rich Wiggins <wiggins@msu.edu>

I've got a great idea for a new TV series....
```

The fields shown in boldface are standard Internet e-mail headers whose meanings are obvious. Note that different e-mail programs use different formats for the "from" and "to" addresses. Some programs might use the form:

```
smythe@msu.edu (Alastair Smythe)
```

The "real" name of Alastair Smythe is provided for human consumption. Whichever form is used, the e-mail address—shown underscored in these examples—is what the computers pay attention to.

Note that it is legal to have more than one recipient listed in the "To:" header; in fact it is quite common. Commas separate the addresses in this case.

The date header is provided by the e-mail program (the user agent) that the sender users; it reflects the date and time when the message was composed.

The subject header contains whatever brief summary of the contents of the message that the sender wishes to supply. Subject headers are optional; you can omit the subject altogether. It's helpful to your correspondents if you use meaningful subject lines—they help your reader sort among multiple incoming messages. A subject like "Here is the draft for the fall sales report" is more meaningful than "Draft" or "Fall" (or no subject line at all).

There are many other header fields that may be supplied by the sending user agent or by any of the message transfer agents along the way. One common header is the "Received:" line:

```
Received: from watson.ibm.com by garnet.msen.com with smtp
        (Smail3.1.28.1 #11) id m0oX9HF-000EbCC; Mon, 30 Aug 93 09:28 EDT
Received: from WATSON by watson.ibm.com (IBM VM SMTP V2R3) with BSMTP
id 4853;
    Mon, 30 Aug 93 09:28:09 EDT
Received: from YKTVMH by watson.vnet.ibm.com with "VAGENT.V1.0"
        id 3837; Mon, 30 Aug 1993 09:27:57 EDT
Received: from earth.watson.ibm.com by yktvmh.watson.ibm.com (IBM VM
SMTP V2R3)
```

```
        with TCP; Mon, 30 Aug 93 09:27:54 EDT
Received: by earth.watson.ibm.com (IBM OS/2 SENDMAIL 1.2.10/)
        id AA0808; Mon, 30 Aug 93 09:27:43 -0700
```

As a message traverses the network, one of these lines is added by each message transfer agent along the way. These lines serve as a log of the path followed by the message. They appear with the most recent at the top (but many e-mail packages suppress their display.)

Here are some of the other header fields you may see as part of your Internet e-mail:

- `cc:`   This specifies names of additional recipients, i.e., those who should receive "carbon copies."

- `bcc:`   "Blind carbon copy."

- `Message-Id:`   This field is followed by a unique identifier for the message, supplied by the sending user agent.

- `Reply-To:`   This header lists the e-mail address to which any replies to this message should be sent. Some e-mail programs honor this header; others do not.

- `Sender:`   The "sender" of a message may differ from the "From:" header when a program sends mail on behalf of someone else. An example of this is mail from automated mailing list processors such as LISTSERV.

- `X-xxxxxx:`   Headers that begin with "X-" are provided for uses that aren't defined as Internet e-mail standards. You may see such headers used for new, experimental uses of e-mail.

Note that some e-mail programs suppress the display of some header information. This can lead to confusion at times. For instance, some messages may arrive with a `Resent-From` header; if your mail program only shows the `From` header, you may confuse the original author for the forwarder of a message. Some e-mail programs give you the option of displaying extended header information when you want to do so.

Following all of the headers of an e-mail message is the actual body of the message.

EXAMPLES OF SENDING AND RECEIVING E-MAIL

Because numerous e-mail packages, both commercial and public domain, exist on many different computer platforms, it is not possible for us to review examples of sending and receiving mail for each of them. There is an especially large group of packages on Unix systems, including programs such as mh, mush, and Z-mail (now a commercial product), not to mention many systems whose mail program is simply named `mail`. Popular LAN-based programs such as Microsoft Mail and Lotus Corporation's cc:Mail support gateways that allow users on the local network to send and receive Internet mail (assuming the local network is attached to the Internet, of course). Virtually every computing platform is blessed with an array of e-mail options from which to choose. Although the user interfaces vary from package to package, the concepts are similar across all.

Following are examples using a popular, easy-to-use package called Pine.* Pine is in use at over 2000 sites in over 30 countries. Versions of Pine are supported under Unix and MS-DOS. Many users find Pine and its text editor to be friendlier than other mail programs found on Unix systems; Pine is especially suited for use over the conventional dial-up style of Internet access. On most systems you invoke it by simply typing "`pine`". The main menu looks like this:

```
PINE 3.07      MAIN MENU                    Folder:inbox  5 Messages

?    HELP         - Get help using Pine

C    COMPOSE      - Compose and send a message

I    MAIL INDEX   - Read mail in current folder

F    FOLDERS      - Open a different mail folder

A    ADDRESSES    - Update your address book

O    OTHER        - Use other functions

Q    QUIT         - Exit the Pine mail program

? Help      Q Quit    F Folders    O Other
C Compose   I Mail Index A Addresses
```

Next let's look at how incoming mail looks in Pine. Each Pine command is a single keystroke, either a letter of the alphabet or a control character; if you type "I," you'll see all your incoming mail:

```
PINE 3.07     MAIL INDEX     Folder:inbox  Message 7 of 7

1   Jul 30 Internet-Drafts@CN  (4,158) ID ACTION:draft-ietf-tn3270e-
                                       luname-p
```

---

* These examples were generated courtesy of the Internet service provider MSEN and its vice president, Ed Vielmetti.

```
     2   Aug 22 Network Mailer      (1,840) mail delivery error
     3   Aug 30 leiba@watson.ibm.c (61,734) Test MIME note from MultiMail
     4   Sep 21 jayne levin          (1,512) Re: Infoworld article
     5   Sep 23 Judy.Matthews          (928) gopher
     6   Sep 21 Gabriel Goldberg     (1,810) DC User Group Internet happenings
   N 7   Sep 23 Dennis Boone         (2,356) USENET News Interface for Gopher


     [New mail! From Dennis Boone regarding USENET News Interface for Gopher]
   ? Help        M Main Menu  P Prev Msg    - Prev Page  F Forward     D Delete
   O OTHER CMDS  V View Mail  N Next Msg SPACE Next Page  R Reply       S Save
```

Pine signifies which line in the mail index is the "current" line by showing it in inverse video. You can use cursor keys to move from line to line. To view a message you strike "v" with the cursor on the appropriate index line*:

```
        PINE 3.07      VIEW MAIL      Folder:inbox  Message 7 of 7  58%


   Date: Thu, 23 Sep 93 15:17:52 EDT
   From: Dennis Boone <DRBMAINT@msu.edu>
   To: Richard Wiggins <RWWMAINT@msu.edu>
   Subject: USENET News Interface for Gopher


   ------------------------------Original message------------------------------
   A couple of months ago I developed a gateway (Mercury) in an attempt to
   provide more efficient (i.e., doesn't eat my entire machine) news service.
   The first concept, a single-thread server, didn't work out well.  The code is
   in pieces awaiting reassembly in some other form, and isn't at all ready for
   distribution.  If you're still interested, I'll be happy to share it when
   I get it working properly.  I don't have any time estimate yet.  I may pursue
   using NFS-mounted NOV databases, instead of attempting transactions through
   NNTP.

   Dennis

   ? Help        M Main Menu  P Prev Msg    - Prev Page  F Forward     D Delete
   O OTHER CMDS  I Mail Index N Next Msg SPACE Next Page  R Reply       S Save
```

As you view mail, you have several options, shown at the bottom of the screen. Options include forwarding the message to another person, deleting the message from your mailbox, and saving the message in a mnemonically named folder.

---

* Pine interprets upper- and lowercase commands as the same.

To send mail in Pine, you select "c" for "compose" from the main menu:

```
     PINE 3.07       COMPOSE MESSAGE       Folder:inbox  7 Messages

To     : helen@access.digex.net
Cc     :
Attchmnt:
Subject : Second issue of "The Internet Letter"
----- Message Text -----
Jayne,

How's the second issue coming?  Learn any good scoop
re National Information Infrastructure?

/rich

^G Get Help ^C Cancel   ^R Read File^Y Prev Pg  ^K Del Line ^O
Postpone
^X Send       ^J Justify  ^W Where is ^V Next Pg  ^U UnDel Lin^T To
Spell
```

Pine offers help at every screen. Inside the Compose menu, for instance, Ctrl-G will yield assistance. Editing in Pine is straightforward; you can use cursor keys to move to any point in the message at any time; Pine will scroll the display up or down if need be. Notice the options to justify your text (that is, reformat it for smooth margins) and to invoke a spelling checker.

In order to send mail, you will need to supply the proper Internet address for your recipient. Like most e-mail packages, Pine provides an address book in which you can record addresses of people you correspond with frequently. You can also build distribution lists that hold addresses of groups, such as a list of office mates. The Attachment line allows you to specify files that you want to send along with the message; we discuss e-mail attachment options below. When you're done composing the message, Ctrl-X will cause Pine to send it.

These examples should give you an idea of the general flavor of Internet e-mail. Whatever e-mail package your service provider offers, you will want to read the user documentation that goes with it.

WHEN MAIL ISN'T DELIVERED

Most organizations that make substantial use of e-mail have one or more employees who serve as "postmasters." The postmaster has the job of dealing with lost e-mail, and with helping users solve problems with getting mail to their correspondents. When mail goes awry, sometimes it will be "bounced" back to the sender by the message transfer agent that detects a problem. On other occasions the mail may end up at a postmaster's mailbox, and it may take a few days before you learn of the nondelivery. When important messages don't get answered, your best strategy is to pick up the phone and call your recipient. If it turns out that your correspondent has received the mail but is choosing not to reply, a phone call may be a better means of communication to use anyhow.

When the postmaster receives lost mail, he or she will forward the message back to the sender, sometimes with a note diagnosing the problem. A common canon of postmasters calls for them to avoid reading the content of wayward messages they deal with, but this is not always possible. Some experienced Internet users advise that you compose each message as if there's a chance unintended eyes will see it.

Postmasters can be helpful before mail is lost, as well. If you've exhausted other methods for trying to find someone's e-mail address, sometimes a postmaster can help. If you know the host name used by an organization for its e-mail—perhaps from another piece of mail from that site—you can usually send mail to the postmaster at that same host. The postmaster usually goes by a name of `postmaster` (e.g., `postmaster@umich.edu`*), or in cases where user names are limited in length, `postmast`.

COMPLEX ADDRESSES

From time to time you will encounter addresses that don't follow the simple user@host model we've seen so far. Usually these addresses are required because the mail is traversing non-Internet links. One example is of the following form:

`doe%ricevml@cunyvm.cuny.edu`

In this example the mail is being routed through the Bitnet-Internet gateway at the City University of New York; we are using the gateway to send to a user at a Bitnet host named ricevml.† That service will take the initial portion of the address and replace the % with an @, yielding a regular Internet address of `rww@mugwump.cl.msu.edu`. From there the mail is delivered normally. If you as an Internet user need to send mail to someone on a Bitnet host, you can usually take their Bitnet address and tuck ".bitnet" on the end of it, and the mail will be delivered automatically via a gateway. (For example, if you're trying to

---

* This is the address of the Postmaster group at the University of Michigan; it is included as an example. You should use this address only for problems with delivery of mail to that institution; send to the Postmaster at the location to which you are having problems sending mail. Be sure to exhaust other means of finding someone's e-mail address, including the telephone, before you resort to Postmasters.

† That is a host at Rice University. Because `ricevml` is also on the Internet (as `ricevml.rice.edu`) it is not necessary for Internet users to send mail to this host via a gateway.

send mail to someone whose Bitnet address is `franklin@greenvm`, you can try the address `franklin@greenvm.bitnet`.) If this trick does not work, contact your network service provider for advice on using a gateway. (Chapter 7 describes a way of obtaining a list of sites that offer Bitnet-Internet gateway services.)

You may encounter addresses of the form

```
red!orange!yellow!green
```

This style of addressing is used in the uucp network. Originally this form was actually a relative address, which is to say the address varied depending on the location of the sender relative to the recipient. If you encounter uucp addresses at all, they will probably be a more modern, absolute form. In order to correspond with someone on the uucp network, your best bet may be to follow the trick of having your correspondent mail to you first.

Do not be deterred by the complexity of these examples. Most of your correspondents will either have straightforward Internet addresses, or will know what form of address you should use to get your mail delivered.*

X.400 ADDRESSES

If you encounter an e-mail address that looks like this:

```
"JGJG-5321-1234/56"*/PN=EDWARD.R.MURROW/o=US.SPRINT/ADMD=TELEMAIL/C=US/
```

then you've seen an example of an X.400 address. X.400 is an international standard for a sophisticated, hierarchical scheme for e-mail addressing, formatting, and delivery; the standard is popular in Europe and in some corporate e-mail environments in the United States and elsewhere. There are gateways that allow users on X.400 networks to exchange mail with users of traditional SMTP mail on the Internet.

Over time, the Internet community may move towards X.400 as the common standard for e-mail. Do not despair about having to type or read X.400-style addresses; the theory is that a directory service will look up addresses for you, and your e-mail package will be able to use the X.400 address as appropriate without your having to handle them.

CONTEXT IN REPLIES

Many e-mail packages provide a scheme for including the sender's remarks in your reply. This provides context. Often the context is flagged with a ">" as follows:

---

* More complete coverage of various mail addressing schemes and gateways can be found in *A Directory of Electronic Mail Addressing and Networks* (O'Reilly & Associates, Third Edition, 1993), by Donnalyn Frey and Rick Adams (ISBN 0-937175-15-3).

```
> What do you think of the President's health care proposals?
> Do you think managed care will work best?

Well, I prefer the single-payer model that they have in Canada.
...
```

When you invoke this function, called "reply text" on some systems, the sender's entire message appears in your to-be-delivered message, with the greater-than-sign prefixes. You can intersperse your comments point by point within the message, or you can put all of your comments in a block at the end. You may want to delete lines in the original message that aren't necessary to the reply. (If you and a correspondent reply back and forth multiple times, you may end up with several layers of context, causing the original message to shift off to the right due to the ">>>>>" prefixes. Delete the oldest parts of the message in your next reply.)

SIGNATURES

Many mail programs provide a mechanism for you to "sign" your e-mail automatically. You record a standard "sig" to be tacked onto the end of every message you send. Often people provide via their sig the same information they'd put on a business card. This affords easy access to information such as your phone number for recipients who may not know you personally.

Frequent senders of Internet e-mail sometimes use sig lines to include a favorite quotation, slogan, or verse of Scripture with their messages. Some use sigs as a subtle form of advertising (e.g., "author of the book *Yet Another Internet Guide.*") Others concoct imaginative sigs, complete with small drawings of their company logo or their state outline. It is impressive to see the creations people devise, even when limited to an ASCII palette. When sig lines grow beyond four or five lines in length, they tend to attract complaints from readers who'd rather get substance instead of artwork in their correspondence.

LIMITATIONS ON LENGTH OF MAIL

Many sites impose limits on the length of e-mail files that they will accept or relay. In many cases the limit is 100,000 characters. In some cases the limit is even lower. This is especially true when you send mail to or from mass-market information utilities; for instance, Prodigy has announced a limit of 60,000 characters for mail into its Internet gateway. Some systems will reject your mail if it exceeds the limit; others will split your message into several parts and allow delivery to continue. Over time, as communications links get faster and disks get cheaper, we can expect sites to relax these limits. Unfortunately, the advent of multimedia mail tools means people will want to send ever-larger files via e-mail, so the limits may always be a concern.

GATEWAYS TO AND FROM
OTHER NETWORKS

Earlier we discussed examples of e-mail gateways to and from the Internet. These gateways make it possible to send mail from a non-Internet user to a recipient on the Internet, or vice versa. From your point of view the operation is often quite simple. For instance, Fig. 6.2 shows an example of sending a message from the information utility America Online to an Internet address.

The American Online sender need do nothing special to address the mail for the Internet; the standard Internet address is used. When the message in Fig. 6.2 arrived, it looked like this:

```
Received: from MSU by MSU.BITNET (Mailer R2.08 PTF008) with BSMTP id
 3073; Tue, 06 Jul 93 01:50:06 EDT
Received: from jlev.hp.aol.net by msu.edu (IBM VM SMTP V2R2) with TCP;
   Tue, 06 Jul 93 01:50:06 EDT
Received: by jlev.hp.aol.net
 (1.37.109.4/16.2) id AA10380; Tue, 6 Jul 93 01:49:47 -0400
```

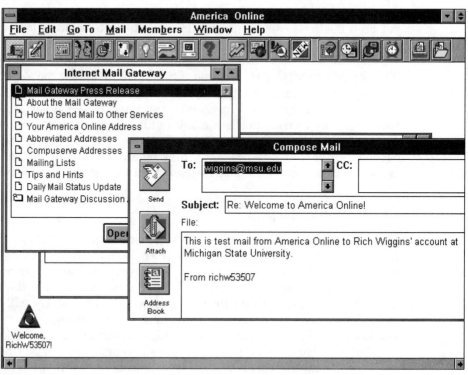

Figure 6.2

```
From: richw53507@aol.com
X-Mailer: America Online Mailer
To: wiggins@msu.edu
Sender: <richw53507@aol.com>
Errors-To: <richw53507@aol.com>
Reply-To: <richw53507@aol.com>
Subject: Re: Welcome to America Online!
Date: Tue, 06 Jul 93 01:48:20 EDT
Message-Id: <9307060148.tn24416@aol.com>

This is test mail from America Online to Rich Wiggins' account at
Michigan State University.
```

Sending from a non-Internet mailbox may require a tad more effort; Compuserve has you prefix the Internet address with "internet:" as shown in Fig. 6.3.

Once you know the rules for sending via a gateway, the process is similar for other users of the same services. Here is a set of examples showing how various gateways work. In each case assume the Internet recipient is Annie Chat, whose address is annie@feline.edu.

Service/Network	To the Internet	From the Internet
America Online	annie@feline.edu	soph53157@aol.com
ATT Mail (EasyLink)	internet!feline.edu!annie	user@attmail.com*
CompuServe	internet:annie@feline.edu	76543.2101@compuserve.com (A period replaces the comma normally used in Compuserve addresses.)
Delphi Internet	annie@feline.edu	user@delphi.com
GEnie (General Electric service)	annie@feline.edu	user@genie.geis.com
Fidonet	annie@feline.edu	John.Doe@f555.n125.z1.fidonet.org ("f" followed by the Fidonet node, "n" followed by the net; "z" followed by the zone)
MCI Mail	Annie Chat EMS [at To: prompt] Internet [at EMS prompt] annie@feline.edu [at Mbx: prompt]	472-0000@mcimail.com
Prodigy	annie@feline.edu (use menu choice for Internet under separately downloadable Mail Manager Desktop)	abcd12a@prodigy.com (where abcd12a is the Prodigy user ID)

* Some EasyLink users may have their own host names. If John Doe at Acme Corp. subscribes in this manner, the address might be doe@acme.attmail.com.

Note that you cannot assume that mass-market information services with Internet gateways will necessarily be able to exchange e-mail with one another.

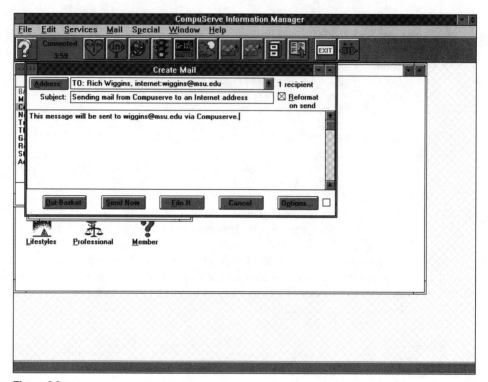

Figure 6.3

In some cases, thanks to reciprocal agreements between a pair of services, delivery may succeed; in the absence of such agreements, it probably will not. The best way to find about Internet e-mail support in general, and cross-vendor support in particular, is to read documentation provided by the information utility, or consult with their help desk.

POP AND IMAP E-MAIL SERVERS

Because many Internet users don't have direct, permanent access, there is a need for users to be able to retrieve mail over transient connections from a variety of locations. There are two schemes addressing this need: the Post Office Protocol, or POP, and the Interactive Mail Access Protocol.* These two protocols differ in their capabilities and functions, but they share the notion of providing an intermediate mail server on behalf of the user. This sort of approach is useful not only for the intermittent user; it also allows an organization to offer cen-

---

* Actually two flavors of POP are currently in use, POP 2 and POP 3. Your POP client software will need to match the server's flavor.

POP server queues mail for later delivery to users of
temporary connections (dialup or intermittent TCP/IP access):

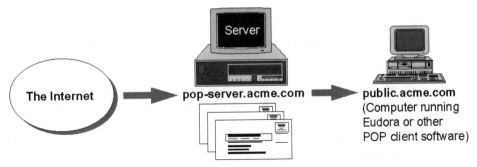

Figure 6.4

tralized e-mail services for distributed users. This can provide the reliability of
staffed central operations while giving the user the benefit of a workstation-
based mail user agent. Figure 6.4 shows this concept in graphic form.

Implementations of POP include programs such as Nupop and Eudora. The
latter is a graphically oriented e-mail package that has become quite popular.
Originally released as public domain software, Eudora is now marketed as
commercial software by a company known as Qualcomm. Packages like
Eudora inform the user of progress while retrieving messages from a POP
server (see Fig. 6.5).

In order to use an e-mail package with POP or IMAP, you will need to have
your service provider tell you how to connect to the relevant server.

E-MAIL ATTACHMENTS AND MULTIMEDIA

We've seen how Pine offers to "attach" a file to send along with textual e-mail.
This sort of capability greatly enhances the medium; with the right tools, you
can send any sort of file you might wish to correspondents. Examples could

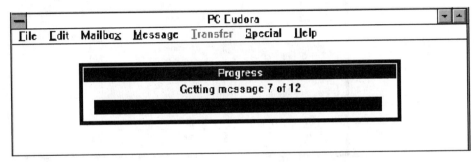

Figure 6.5

include spreadsheets, image files, or even executable programs. Eudora includes this sort of functionality, making it easy for Macintosh and PC users to share information. This becomes especially useful as a way to bridge the dissimilar environments when both parties use tools such as Microsoft Word and Excel, whose files are compatible across the two platforms. Figure 6.6 shows an example of Eudora offering to save a file mailed from a Macintosh to a Windows session.

Multimedia mail offers the promise of attaching voice annotations to textual documents. This could be useful in many contexts: A teacher might have students submit their term papers as electronic mail, and the teacher could return the paper with spoken comments in place of red ink scribbled in the margins. Or, colleagues who are located at opposite ends of the earth could work on a monograph jointly, using voice annotations to convey questions and new ideas far more richly than the spoken word would allow. Or a professor might add voice annotations to a transcript of a debate or a political speech, inviting further analysis by students. Figure 6.7 shows an example of what a voice commentary might look like in NextMail.*

---

* This example is genuine; the sender, Jeff Mackie-Mason, used NextMail and a microphone-equipped workstation to send comments on a monograph describing Gopher. Printed with permission.

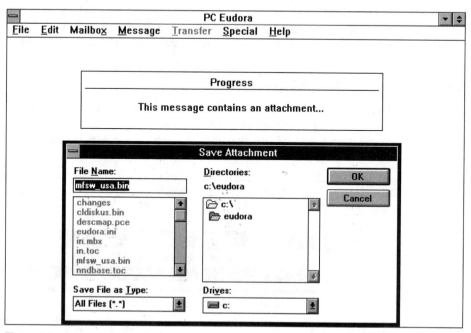

Figure 6.6

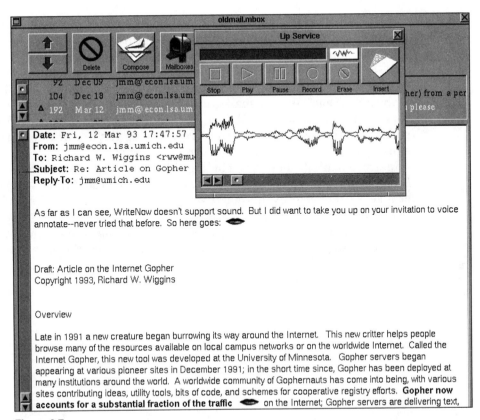

Figure 6.7

This form of attachment is especially useful. The attached voice snippets are placed in-line among the words of the written document, allowing the recipient to click on the lips icon corresponding to a particular passage.

In order for these sorts of exchanges of arbitrary documents to take place, all users must use e-mail software that handles attachments in the same way. NextMail uses a common encoding scheme internally for its attachments, but the method is not standard across all platforms; the above example was only possible because both parties happened to work with Next workstations.

In 1992 a standard was defined for delivering arbitrary files as attachments to Internet e-mail. This scheme is known as MIME (for Multipurpose Internet Mail Extensions). MIME not only defines a way for correspondents to share nontextual information in a standard way, it also defines encoding schemes that allow the messages to survive transit over a variety of intervening network paths paths. This is important because the original SMTP standard only requires hosts to provide a data path for 7-bit ASCII characters, which is to say that the topmost bit of each byte is not guaranteed to be preserved across all

Internet e-mail paths. MIME overcomes this by employing a "Base-64" encoding scheme that uses additional bytes as needed to represent all 8 bits. The MIME standard extends standard RFC 822 headers with two new fields— MIME-version: and Content-Type:—and defines the structure by which the body of a message can hold the various binary components to be sent as part of a given message. Many e-mail packages, including Pine and the commercial version of Eudora, support MIME. More can be expected to do so. MIME support should be a key part of your evaluation if you are in the market for an e-mail package to use in Internet communications.

Many e-mail packages, including Pine and the commercial version of Eudora, support MIME. More can be expected to do so. MIME support should be a key part of your evaluation if you are in the market for an e-mail package to use in Internet communications.

Figure 6.8 is an example mail message sent using IBM's MIME-compatible mail package, UltiMail/2.* The image of the planet Earth was sent as an

---

* This example was provided courtesy of Barry Leiba of IBM's Advanced Commercial Applications group.

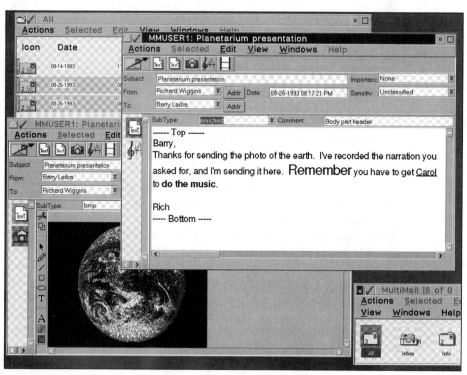

Figure 6.8

attachment to a textual message, and the pending reply refers to an attachment of an audio document. Note that the message in the example refers to the
image of the planet Earth, which was attached as part of the message, and to
a sound document that was also attached.

In order to take advantage of MIME, your e-mail program must be MIME-
capable. More and more e-mail packages are being endowed with MIME support. This promises to make it possible for Internet users to share multimedia
and other complex files easily. If you receive a MIME-encoded message, but
your e-mail package cannot handle MIME, you will at least be able to read the
straight text in the message, as this example shows:

```
Message-Id: <9308301627.AA0808@earth.watson.ibm.com>
Mime-Version: 1.0
Date: Mon, 30 Aug 93 09:18:35 -0500
From: leiba@watson.ibm.com
To: rww@msen.com
Subject: Test MIME note from MultiMail
X-Mailer: MultiMail, IBM T. J. Watson Research Center
          Coming September 1993...
          For more info call: 1-800-954-0144
Content-Type: multipart/mixed;
      boundary="PART.BOUNDARY.807.6D"
Status: RO
X-Status:

> THIS IS A MESSAGE IN 'MIME' FORMAT.  Your mail reader does not
support MIME.
> Some parts of this will be readable as plain text.
> To see the rest, you will need to upgrade your mail reader.

--PART.BOUNDARY.807.6D
Content-ID: <799_109_746716828_1_leiba@LOCAL>
Content-type: text/plain
Content-Description: A plain text part.

Rich,
This is a two-part MIME note, with a plan text part and an
image (BMP) part.  Please let me know (1) if you get this and
(2) if you can view the image. Thanks,

Barry
```

HINTS AND NETIQUETTE

We've already covered some of the pitfalls of Internet e-mail and how to avoid
them. Here are some other tips that may be useful:

- It is axiomatic that e-mail doesn't carry all the information of verbal communications, but even experienced e-mail users sometimes forget this. When communication is breaking down, consider a phone call or a face-to-face visit.

- If you and your correspondent are unable to agree on something, agree to disagree. If your correspondent asks you to stop sending e-mail, do so.

- Exercise caution when forwarding e-mail to others. In sending private e-mail, people sometimes assume, without explicitly saying so, that "this is just between you and me." There are no hard-and-fast rules to follow, but it is especially advisable to think twice before forwarding a message to a mailing list or to someone in authority over your correspondent.

- Note also that the writer of a document is considered to own his or her words even after mailing it; use attribution when quoting others, and get permission before reusing substantial amounts of writing.

- From time to time chain letters appear over the Internet. Although this may be an apt extension of the paper mail metaphor, this practice is harmful to networks and is forbidden by most use policies. The only person to whom you should forward a chain letter is the postmaster, for appropriate action.

- Unsolicited e-mail per se is allowed. Unsolicited e-mail for advertising is often forbidden by acceptable use policies.

Mailing List Processors
and E-mail Servers

Electronic mail plays a vital part in communications on the Internet. It is primarily a one-to-one medium; one person at a time decides to send a message to another individual recipient. At times, through the use of personalized mailing lists, e-mail can become a one-to-many medium—for instance, someone can send e-mail to a list of colleagues. Most e-mail packages provide a way for individuals to maintain such personalized mailing lists. Mailing list processors carry the personal mailing list to another level, allowing people to organize themselves into Internet-wide discussion groups. In this chapter we will discuss one popular mailing list tool in some detail, and then look at some other packages with similar functions.

The mailing list processor that delivers the most mail on the Internet was born on another network. Eric Thomas' LISTSERV tool was initially deployed on VM/CMS mainframes and primarily served users on Bitnet. The interoperability of e-mail between Bitnet and the Internet makes LISTSERV equally accessible to Internet users, and LISTSERV increasingly has become an important tool for group communications on the Internet. As of this writing there exist almost 10,000 LISTSERV mailing lists serving almost one million subscribers; subscriptions are growing at a 67 percent annual rate. LISTSERV delivers from two to six million messages per day. Here are some examples of some of the mailing lists managed by LISTSERV:

LISTSERV list name	Topic
CARR-L@ulkyvm.louisville.edu	Computer-Assisted Reporting and Research
EDTECH@msu.edu	Educational Technology
E-EUROPE@pucc.princeton.edu	Eastern Europe Business Network
EUDORA@vmd.cso.uiuc.edu	Eudora e-mail package mailing list
PACS-L@uhupvm1.edu	Public-Access Computer Systems (vis-à-vis libraries)
WPCORP-L@ubvm.cc.buffalo.edu	WordPerfect Corporation Products Discussions

Note that a user name ending in "-L" is often used, so that the name is obviously that of a mailing list; note also that this convention is not always observed.

The basic idea behind LISTSERV is very simple: someone decides to start a discussion group, and works with a LISTSERV administrator to set it up. For instance, suppose a researcher wants to discuss the problem of nematodes with other interested parties worldwide. A mailing list named nema-1 might be created. Next, the owner of the mailing list will want to recruit subscribers by sending private e-mail to them, announcing the new mailing list's existence. At the owner's discretion, new list members can be allowed to subscribe on their own, or the owner may reserve control over membership. Once the mailing list has been set up and subscribers have been registered, any subscriber can send a message to the mailing list—and that message will be automatically forwarded to all other subscribers. The process is depicted in Fig. 7.1.

Mailing list processors forward mail to those who "subscribe" to a given mailing list

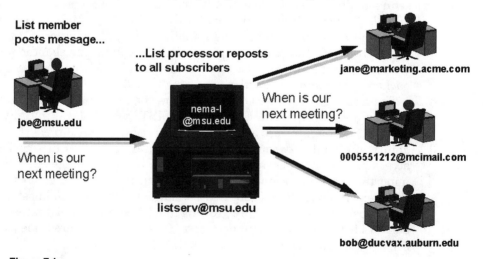

Figure 7.1

It may seem surprising that this relatively simple process has evolved into such an important discussion medium—but it has. Of course, LISTSERV has many features that enhance its basic operation; there are options for obtaining lists of subscribers to a given mailing list, for obtaining log files of previous discussions, and for searching through many log files for specific past postings. Before exploring those options, let's look at the process of subscribing to a mailing list of interest.

As of this writing, there is no client program you can use to interact with LISTSERV. Instead, you use e-mail in order to subscribe to mailing lists, to change various options related to your subscription, and to send correspondence to other subscribers.* If a mailing list is set up for open subscription, you can subscribe to it via e-mail without need for any human intervention. To do so, you send mail to the user named `listserv` at the computer hosting the mailing list. For instance, there is a mailing list that covers topics relating to Southeast Asia; it is located at msu.edu and it is called `seasia-1`.† If your name is Elizabeth Windsor and you want to subscribe to this mailing list, you might send e-mail as follows:

```
To:       listserv@msu.edu
From:     windsor@castle.ucl.ac.uk

subscribe seasia-1 Liz Windsor
```

Note that no Subject line is necessary. Also note that Elizabeth chooses to subscribe to the mailing list under the name of Liz Windsor. This is perfectly acceptable; LISTSERV goes by the name you supply on the "subscribe" command, ignoring your given name (if present) on the "To:" line.‡

Once your subscription request has been processed, LISTSERV itself will send you back a short e-mail message telling you that you have been accepted. Some mailing lists are "closed," meaning that only the owner of the mailing list can act on your subscription request. If you try to join a closed list, LISTSERV will so inform you.

If you decide that a LISTSERV mailing list is not your cup of tea, leaving it is as easy as joining. Simply send a message of the following form:

---

* Users running under VM/CMS on Bitnet can also "talk" to LISTSERV servers by using the CMS TELL command. And a type of client software for searching databases runs under CMS; it is called LDBASE EXEC.

† The founder and guiding force of this mailing list is Elliot Parker, a professor at Central Michigan University.

‡ Actually, if the LISTSERV you are corresponding with already knows what name is associated with your e-mail address, you can omit specifying your full name. It's usually simpler just to include your full name with your e-mail address on all subscription requests.

```
To:        listserv@msu.edu
From:      windsor@castle.ucl.ac.uk

unsubscribe seasia-1
```

It is very important that you send subscription requests to the LISTSERV address, and that you send actual correspondence to the user name that is associated with the mailing list. Quite frequently one sees "subscribe" messages sent to the mailing list itself, where it may be read by hundreds or thousands of members of the mailing list—and the would-be subscriber still doesn't get added to the list. In fact, LISTSERV tries to intercept such messages; when it does it will send an explanatory note back to the user with the proper procedure to follow. Figure 7.2 depicts this important distinction.

Another pitfall to avoid: Some LISTSERV mailing lists—and many mailing lists managed by other list-processing software—are configured so that mail comes from a user name of the form "owner-listname." For instance, if the Southeast Asia mailing list were set up that way, mail would be sent by owner-seasia-1. One reason behind this is to force undeliverable message notifications to go to a user other than the mailing list itself; users often let their mailing list subscriptions live on even though their computer accounts are expiring, which means extra work for mailing list owners. When you post to a mailing list, you do not want to send to the "owner-" address, but rather directly to the list name.

MAILING LIST CORRESPONDENCE

Once you subscribe to a mailing list, correspondence from other subscribers will be sent to you automatically as it is posted. Different subscribers use dif-

Subscription-related requests go to "`listserv`" address:

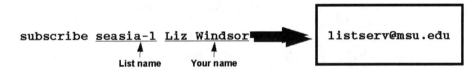

Messages to other members go to the mailing list by its name:

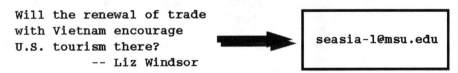

Figure 7.2

ferent terms for messages on mailing lists; they are referred to as "articles" or "letters" or "messages." Some mailing lists are extremely active, generating dozens of messages per day; other mailing lists may go for dozens of days with no postings. Your mailing list correspondence will be sent to you just as any other e-mail would be delivered, and you can use your normal e-mail package to read discussions and post replies.*

Here is an example of a few messages that might be sent on the SEASIA-L mailing list in response to the example message from Liz Windsor:

```
Sender:     Southeast Asia Discussion List <SEASIA-L@msu.edu>
From:       Charles Wales <wales@acme.com>
Subject:    Normalization of U.S. - Vietnam Trade

There would be political opposition to this in the U.S., with veterans'
groups wanting more of an accounting of missing-in-action status.

Sender:     Southeast Asia Discussion List <SEASIA-L@msu.edu>
From:       Diana Spence <di@nadir.org>
Subject:    Normalization of U.S. - Vietnam Trade

Yes, but it would be in the interest of both countries to resume relations.
The current situation only penalizes American workers.
```

As long as discussion continues on the same "thread," it's useful for subscribers posting replies to use the same subject line. This allows those reading the mailing list to keep up with multiple conversational threads at once.

Depending on your location and how congested your link to the Internet is, there may be some delay in the delivery of mailing list mail to you. Other subscribers also face variable delays. Therefore, you may not see a given set of mailing list messages in the same order in which they were posted. Sometimes, you may respond to a posting on a mailing list, only to receive five minutes later a "better" reply from someone else that was posted prior to your submission! This is a natural occurrence, and it shouldn't discourage participation.

Note that when you post a message to a LISTSERV mailing list you normally do not receive a copy of the message back in your own in-basket. Your message will be sent to the other subscribers, but by default LISTSERV assumes you don't need to receive another copy. (By contrast, some of the non-LISTSERV mailing lists processors will in fact mail you back a copy of your own posting.)

---

* In fact, because LISTSERV messages are delivered as normal e-mail, this discussion medium is very accessible to a wide audience, including those who have e-mail-only access to the Internet, and those who have Internet access but who have not yet explored other client-oriented tools.

Note also that some LISTSERV mailing lists are moderated, meaning that postings are sent to the owner of the list for review; he or she allows messages deemed germane to the list's focus to be sent on to all subscribers. If you post a message to such a mailing list, LISTSERV will tell you that it has forwarded the message to the list owner for consideration.

Sometimes it is useful to see a list of all subscribers to a mailing list. This gives you an idea of who your potential audience is. The Review command provides such a list:

```
To:       listserv@msu.edu
From:     windsor@castle.ucl.ac.uk

review seasia-l
```

SETTING LISTSERV OPTIONS

Because mailing list mail is intermixed with your other e-mail, and because many e-mail packages send you an announcement when new messages arrive, you may find the steady flow of messages from busy mailing lists to be a burden. LISTSERV offers an option that can help: you can ask it to send you a day's worth of messages from for a given mailing list in a bundle known as a "digest." This is one of many options you can set for a mailing list. For instance, if Liz Windsor decides she wants this option for the Seasia-L mailing list, she could send this message:

```
To:       listserv@msu.edu
From:     windsor@castle.ucl.ac.uk

set seasia-l digest
```

LISTSERV will send a day's messages in a single e-mail message, with a nice table of contents at the beginning. (The table of contents is constructed from the Subject lines each correspondent supplied when posting each message.)

This is one of several options that you can set for a LISTSERV mailing list. To query this current setting of various subscription options, use the Query command:

```
To:       listserv@msu.edu
From:     windsor@castle.ucl.ac.uk

query seasia-l
```

You will receive a message with the current setting of various options. The meaning of these options is detailed in LISTSERV documentation, retrieval of which is explained below.

THE INTERCONNECTEDNESS
OF LISTSERVS

LISTSERV servers know how to talk to one another. If you are looking for a particular mailing list whose name you know but whose location you do not, you may be able to subscribe anyhow. Just use the name of a LISTSERV server near you; if you're not aware of the relative geography, just pick a server that you've used before. Send your subscription request to that server, and it will forward the request to the LISTSERV where the list actually resides—all on your behalf.

Some LISTSERV mailing lists are "peered"—that is, the workload for the list is divided up among several servers. This is usually done with large, active mailing lists that have a worldwide audience. You can contribute to efficiency by subscribing to the mailing list that's closest to you; if the geography isn't clear to you, just pick a host located on the same continent where your computer service is located.

LOCATING LISTSERV MAILING LISTS

Usually you learn about a mailing list from a colleague, via another mailing list, or perhaps in a brochure or a directory. Sometimes you may want to go looking for a list in a more purposeful manner. Given the large number of mailing lists in existence, how does one find a list that covers a particular topic? LISTSERV has a LIST GLOBAL command that can be used to retrieve lists of mailing lists. You can send mail to any LISTSERV in order to retrieve these lists; if the LISTSERV you pick cannot satisfy the request, it will suggest the name of a LISTSERV that can. Because of the large number of extant mailing lists, you might want to hone your search a bit. You can specify a string search with your request. For example:

```
To:  listserv@listserv.net

list global /photo
```

You will receive a list like this:

```
Excerpt from the LISTSERV lists known to LISTSERV@SEARN on 2 Oct
1993 08:06
Search string: PHOTO

Network-wide ID  Full address     List title
---------------  ------------     ----------
MAPS-L           MAPS-L@UGA       Maps and Air Photo Systems Forum
PHOTO-L          PHOTO-L@BUACCA   Photography Phorum
PHOTOSYN         PHOTOSYN@TAUNIVM Photosynthesis Researchers' List
```

```
PHOTREAC          PHOTREAC@JPNTUVMO Electro- and Photo-Nuclear
                  Reaction Discussi+
```

Chapter 16 contains other hints on locating mailing lists of interest.

FINDING THE INTERNET ADDRESS FOR A BITNET HOST

Because of the Bitnet heritage of many LISTSERV hosts, you may encounter instructions on subscribing to a mailing list listing the Bitnet address, not the Internet address, of the host in question. You could use a Bitnet gateway (as we saw in the last chapter) but this could prove inefficient; subsequent exchanges would go through that gateway when you might have a faster, more direct Internet link. Because most hosts that run LISTSERV do have direct Internet links, you might want to find and use the corresponding Internet address. LISTSERV provides a mechanism for you to do so: simply send mail to any LISTSERV and ask it. For example, there is a mailing list for journalists called CARR-L at the University of Louisville. Suppose you are told that this list is called CARR-L@ULKYVM—which is correct for Bitnet subscribers, but you want to subscribe directly over the Internet. To find out the Internet address of ULKYVM, you could post the following e-mail:

```
To:  listserv@listserv.bitnet*

show alias ulkyvm
```

You will receive a message with the Internet address of that host, or a note telling you there is no corresponding Internet address. In this example, ulkyvm has an Internet address of ulkyvm.louisville.edu. By sending your subscription request to listserv at that address, you'll ensure that articles are mailed to you over an Internet path.

If the LISTSERV server you seek is only on Bitnet, and if you cannot reach it by using the address listserv@host.bitnet, you may need to explicitly specify a Bitnet gateway. An example of gateway addressing was shown in Chap. 6; the addresses would be of the form listserv%bitnode@gateway. For instance, the Bitnet host waynest1 could be reached through the gateway at the City University of New York by addressing it as:

```
listserv%waynest1@cunyvm.cuny.edu†
```

---

* This is a special address that will reach a LISTSERV server with up-to-date information. In theory you could send this request to any LISTSERV server.

† This is only an example of using the gateway; for this particular host, you normally would want to use the Internet address of msu.edu instead of forcing your subscription or other e-mail to follow a Bitnet path.

You can even obtain a list of Bitnet-Internet–e-mail gateways through List-serv. To do so, send e-mail as follows:

```
To:  listserv@bitnic.educom.edu

get bitnet gates
```

This list of gateways is updated monthly. (You will have to use the `show alias` command depicted previously to find the Internet address of a gateway you want to use; this list is prepared for the benefit of the Bitnet community.)

LISTSERV AS A DATABASE FACILITY

LISTSERV can store files associated with a mailing list for retrieval on demand. For instance, if you had a mailing list called recipe-1, you might pick some of the favorite recipes of all time as separate files. LISTSERV file names have two 8-character parts; an example file might be `recipe-1 curry`. LIST-SERV even offers an option for users to register for automatic delivery of a file every time it is updated; see the online documentation for the Automatic File Distribution command.

LISTSERV can be configured to keep archival copies of communications gone by. This can be useful for subscribers (new or old) who want to review previous discussions on a given topic. Log files are generally organized by month, with busy mailing lists having four or five log files per month. You can list the log files for a given mailing list, along with other files associated with that list, by using the INDEX command:

```
To:  listserv@msu.edu

index seasia-1
```

Log files are of the form:

```
listname LOGmmyya
```

For instance, the first log file for the Southeast Asia list for October 1993 would be:

```
seasia-1 log9310a
```

(The second file would be log9310b, then log9310c, and so forth.)

Wading through a long collection of old log files to find something of interest would be time-consuming at best. LISTSERV provides a search mechanism to make the job easier. You mail it a sort of batch job containing commands, and it performs the search and sends back results. Suppose you want to find out about use of liquid crystal display projectors that work with IBM PC compatible VGA output. The Ed Tech mailing list might be a good place to look for old discussions on this topic. An example of a database search job might look like this:

```
To:         listserv@msu.edu
From:       windsor@castle.ucl.ac.uk

//listsrch job echo o
database search dd=rules
//rules dd *
select projector and VGA in edtech
index date.8 sender.30 subject.40
/*
// EOJ
```

In a nutshell, this job tells LISTSERV at `msu.edu` to do this: "Retrieve all the articles in the Ed Tech mailing list that contain both the words "projector" and "VGA" and show me the date of posting, the sender's e-mail address, and the subject (limiting display of those fields to 8 characters, 30 characters, and 40 characters respectively). By return mail you would receive a file that looks like this:

```
From:       BITNET list server at MSU (1.7f) <LISTSERV@msu.edu>
Subject:    File: "DATABASE OUTPUT"

> select projector and VGA in edtech
--> Database EDTECH, 5 hits.
> index date.8 sender.30 subject.40
DATE      SENDER                      SUBJECT
----      ------                      -------
92/08/04 cismike@uhunix.BITNET        Video/data projector installations
92/08/09 CCSCOTTY@MIZZOU1.BITNET      LCD panels for overhead projectors
92/10/12 TMILLS@UCONNVM.BITNET        RE: LCD panels
92/11/18 WIGNALL@VALPO.BITNET         A new LCD panel
93/08/28 WIGNALL@EXODUS.VALPO.EDU     Re: Color Notebooks & Video
                                      Projection
```

Your commands are listed interwoven with the results. As requested, you are shown the date of the posting, the e-mail address of the poster, and the subject line that was used with the message. Your search can produce a few hits or many, depending on what you're looking for and the pattern of word usage in the mailing list. You can refine your search by adding more search words (separated by "and") to narrow the search; or you could broaden the search by removing search terms or by using "or" to separate your choices.*

---

* This is an example of a "Boolean" search, similar to the method used with many online databases. LISTSERV supports more complicated Boolean searches; the LDBASE MEMO file, available on all LISTSERVs, explains more.

Once you get back a list of items that looks promising—neither too narrow nor too broad—you can resubmit the job with a line that says "`print`" immediately after the "`index`" line. This will cause LISTSERV to send back the entire original messages that match your criteria.

OBTAINING LISTSERV DOCUMENTATION

We have explored only a few of the options of this powerful package. You may want to read more about LISTSERV's facilities in order to make full use of the package. LISTSERV will send you documentation about itself if you ask it. To get a brief summary of options, simply send e-mail to any LISTSERV server with the following line:

```
help
```

In order to get more complete documentation, you would use the GET command. There are several different files you can retrieve. For instance, if you want to learn more about LDBASE searches, send any LISTSERV this command:

```
get listdb memo
```

To get a list of all files that comprise the online documentation on LISTSERV, send this command:

```
get listserv filelist
```

Once you receive the list, use GET once again to retrieve the files of interest to you.

UNIX LIST PROCESSOR

LISTSERV has inspired a variety of servers that aspire to provide the same sort of function. Some of these tools have gone by the same name, but their developers now tend to use more unique names to minimize confusion. Many of these tools work under Unix, allowing their deployment on inexpensive workstations with built-in Internet networking capacity.*

One such tool was developed by Anastasios Kotsikonas. Known as the Unix List Processor, it is in use at numerous sites, including the Coalition for Networked Information (`cni.org`). This tool supports many of the same commands as LISTSERV. The user subscribes to a List Processor discussion group

---

* L-Soft International, Inc. now markets a Unix version of the original LISTSERV. Logika, Inc. is developing a graphical user interface for LISTSERV; see Fig. 7.3.

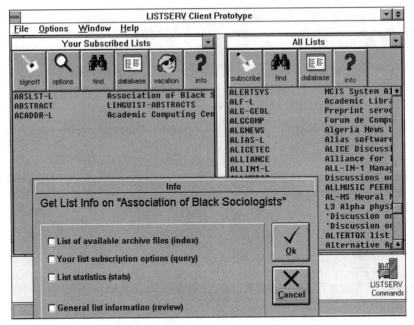

Figure 7.3

using the same procedure; for instance, to subscribe to a recipe mailing list one might send this e-mail:

```
To:  listproc@cookware.com*

subscribe recipe-1 Robert Gourmet
```

In order to retrieve online documentation about the Unix Listprocessor, send the following e-mail:

```
To:  listproc@avs.com

help
```

MAJORDOMO

Majordomo is a Unix-based mailing list processor written by Brent Chapman. Its command set is similar to LISTSERV (although not identical) and is relatively simple. To sign up for a Majordomo list, send a command of the form:

---

* Note that some Unix List Processor sites still use "listserv" as the user name for the tool.

```
subscribe list
```

or

```
subscribe list address
```

Note that address is an optional e-mail address, not your full name. To learn more about Majordomo send the following e-mail:

```
To:  majordomo@msen.com

help
```

MAIL REFLECTORS

Some mailing lists are maintained using relatively simply schemes, without the services of more sophisticated tools such as LISTSERV or the Unix List Processor. These tools are often referred to as "mail reflectors"—they simply reflect incoming mail to a specified list of users, without providing digest, log, or database functions. In some cases archives for such mailing lists be offered in another medium—for instance, on a Gopher server.

Typically in order to subscribe to a mailing list that is managed by a mail reflector, you send a note to a human being, not to an automated process. Often the subscription mailbox consists of the name of the mailing list followed by "-request." For instance, if you want to subscribe to the mailing list com-priv, which holds discussions on commercialization and privatization of the Internet, you would send the following mail:

```
To:       com-priv-request@psi.com
From:     christopher@access.digex.net

Please add me to the com-priv mailing list. My name is Anna
Christopher. Thank you.
```

Because of the need for human intervention, there can be a delay of several days before you are added (or deleted) from such mailing lists.

Note that mail reflectors, unlike LISTSERV mailing lists, are often configured so that they will mail you a copy of each posting you send to the mailing list.

MAILBASE

Mailbase is a tool that originated in the United Kingdom for use on their JANET network. It is a project of the UK Networked Information Services Project located at the University of Newcastle upon Tyne. Commands in Mailbase generally follow the format of LISTSERV commands; subscription requests are sent to a Mailbase address:

```
mailbase@mailbase.ac.uk
```

Mailbase uses the verb "join" where LISTSERV uses "subscribe." Actual postings for Mailbase mailing lists are sent to:

```
listname@mailbase.ac.uk
```

Mailbase uses the convention of listname-request for all its mailing list owners; you can send e-mail to the human who owns eng-lit by addressing it to:

```
eng-lit-request@mailbase.ac.uk
```

Mailbase also offers an interactive service. This service allows you to browse various Mailbase mailing lists over Telnet. For more information on this service, you can retrieve online documentation by sending the following e-mail:

```
To:  mailbase@mailbase.ac.uk

send mailbase on-line-guide
```

Note: Because the United Kingdom historically has followed a host name convention that is the reverse of standard Internet practice, you may encounter documentation that shows uk.ac.mailbase as the address for the Mailbase server. From some starting points inside the United Kingdom, this may be the proper address form to use; non–U.K. users can normally follow the standard format, with the "uk" country code at the end.

MAIL-SERVER AT MIT

A useful repository of information resides at the Massachusetts Institute of Technology. This server offers a variety of information files. In particular, it serves an archive of useful postings to various Usenet News discussion groups (a medium which we will discuss in the next chapter) and other helpful documents on the Internet and computing. For instance, to retrieve a guide to Internet services that is periodically posted to Usenet, send the following e-mail:

```
To:      mail-server@rtfm.mit.edu
From:    wiggins@msu.edu

send usenet/alt.internet.services
```

In order to retrieve online documentation about the MIT mail server, send e-mail to the previous address with the command "help" by itself as the body of the text. The files stored by this server are organized hierarchically; send the command "index" to receive the top-level index. The help file explains more about the mail-server and its offerings.

USDA ALMANAC

Almanac is a server developed by the U.S. Department of Agriculture. Almanac supports the delivery of documents as well as providing LISTSERV-like discussion groups.

To receive the general online help file for Almanac, send the following e-mail:

```
To:       almanac@esusda.gov

send guide
```

Subscriptions to Almanac-managed mailing lists follow the familiar "subscribe" format; however, there is no option for including your full name. For example:

```
To:       almanac@esusda.gov

subscribe usda.farmbill
```

HINTS AND NETIQUETTE

- *Be very careful subscribing to mailing lists.* Try to find out the correct procedure for subscribing, making sure you send mail to the appropriate user name, so that your mail won't be sent to the entire group by mistake.

- *Be very careful responding to mailing list messages.* Depending on the interaction of the mailing list processor and your e-mail package, you can easily "reply" to a message, thinking you are sending a private note, and have the reply go to the entire mailing list. Be especially cautious as you reply to a message that started on a mailing list but then was forwarded to you.

- If you subscribe to a mailing list under a particular e-mail address, and then you move to another address, the mailing list manager software will probably not recognize that the two addresses represent a single human being. If possible, unsubscribe from all mailing lists before you abandon the old e-mail account. Otherwise, you will have to contact the owner of the mailing list for manual removal of your old address.

- Be patient when subscribing (or unsubscribing) to mailing lists that are manually administered (as is the case with mail reflectors and limited-enrollment LISTSERV lists). For busy lists your request could take a week or more. If you post a note of exasperation to the discussion group, you'll likely see exasperated replies from folks who want to stay on topic.

- Be very discreet in posting private messages to a mailing list. Try to work out private disputes privately. Taking a private disagreement public often leads to escalating tensions.

- Conversely, consider taking public disputes private when it's clear that further discussion on the mailing list would not be fruitful. If nothing else, private mail can be used as a way to "agree to disagree."

- It is possible to carry on quite vigorous discussions over mailing lists with no ill feelings. However it is easy for ad hominems to slip into discussion, poisoning any subsequent remarks. Consider saying "That argument doesn't hold water if you consider . . ." instead of "You sound like a 13-year-old."*

- Don't repost an offer of service from people unless you know they intend a broadly available service. For instance if someone sends you a helpful document, don't assume that he or she is willing to provide copies to hundreds or thousands of others.

- Be cautious in reposting others' words. This is an area in which netiquette and copyright considerations apply. It is common practice to repost general announcements that someone broadcasts to several mailing lists. On the other hand, people are becoming increasingly cautious about reposting a long, specific treatise that someone posts to a focused mailing list. When in doubt ask the author for permission to repost. In all cases, repost with attribution.

- Keep postings relatively brief. If you are reposting a general announcement—say, a press release about a new laptop computer—to a mailing list with a specific focus, consider posting a brief summary, or skipping the posting altogether.

- There is a great deal of overlap among the many mailing lists in existence. This leads to the practice of "cross-posting" messages to multiple lists. Keep this practice to a minimum; instead, pick one or two mailing lists that seem to represent your topic best for your posting. Avoid the temptation to post "help wanted" advertisements to every mailing list you can think of; instead, use a mailing list in the field that specifically welcomes such traffic.

- Try to be aware of the focus and culture of each mailing list. These qualities vary based on the membership, the moderator, and the topic area. If you suggest changes to that culture, (for instance, asking that items you consider

---

* Besides insulting your partner in discussion, that particular ad hominem also insults 13-year-olds. One of the joys of the net is that from time to time you "meet" young people whose articulateness belies their youth.

not to be topical belong elsewhere) you may find your views are in the minority. Conversely, if you send nontopical mail to a highly focused mailing list, you will definitely incur the wrath of other participants. Be especially cautious not to violate conventions and rules against advertising.

- Many Internet users are students or faculty at universities, and the Internet is an ideal source of many kinds of information. It is very tempting to send out surveys as a part of course work or research. Unfortunately, many other folks may have the same idea. Be sure that a survey fits in with the mission of your target mailing list and that others haven't overmined that forum before you. Resist the temptation to cross-post your survey to dozens of mailing lists you don't normally follow.

- If you become a moderator of a mailing list—i.e., if it is your job to review messages, filtering out ones that you feel are nontopical or not of general interest—you will have the opportunity to shape the flow of discussion. Successful moderators use minimal intervention and are consistent. For instance, don't censor someone because you think their posting contains wrong information; instead, add an editorial note that offers your view and solicits others' input.

- When you will be disconnected from e-mail access, say during a vacation, consider unsubscribing from mailing lists that have a lot of activity. That will save you from wading through large quantities of mail or an overflowed mailbox.

- Your e-mail environment might include an auto-reply robot—a tool that serves as a sort of answering machine, telling correspondents you are not in to accept mail. If that is the case, be sure your robot is smart enough not to respond to mailing list mail. Otherwise you could be sending a note to thousands of readers of mailing lists, most of whom probably are more interested in the mailing list's topic than your vacation plans.

Usenet News

Over 350 years ago, the French mathematician Pierre de Fermat conceived a theorem, and then challenged posterity by writing in the margin of a notebook that he had proved the theorem correct, but he didn't have enough space to write down the solution.* On June 23, 1993, at a conference at Cambridge University, Dr. Andrew Wiles announced he had developed a proof of this theorem. Professor Richard Borcherds of Cambridge sent an e-mail note to his colleague John McKay of Concordia University in Montreal; Dr. McKay decided that mathematicians worldwide would be keenly interested in the news. He chose Usenet News as his medium, posting the following message:

```
Newsgroups: sci.math.research
Path:newsflash.concordia.ca!utcsri!utnut!torn!howland.reston.ans.net!
ux1.cso.uiuc.edu!news.cso.uiuc.edu!dan
From: mckay@alcor.concordia.ca (John McKay)
Subject: Fermat's Last Theorem has been proved
Approved: Daniel Grayson <dan@math.uiuc.edu>
Date: Wed, 23 Jun 1993 11:00:27 GMT
Message-ID: <C92MKs.8F2@newsflash.concordia.ca>
Sender: Daniel Grayson <dan@math.uiuc.edu>
Originator: dan@symcom.math.uiuc.edu
```

---

* Fermat's theorem holds that the equation $x^n + y^n = z^n$, where n is an integer greater than 2, has no solution in positive integers.

```
Organization: Concordia University, Montreal, Quebec
Lines: 8
```

```
I have heard that an announcement to this effect has been
made in Cambridge by Andrew Wiles today, June 23rd. 1993.
```

Mathematicians around the world who follow this news group received the message within minutes or hours. Subsequent postings from others who follow `sci.math.research` elaborated on the method of the proof and discussed its significance.*

Usenet News (sometimes called Network News, Netnews, or just Usenet) is a worldwide discussion medium. Estimates are that over 1.5 million readers look at Usenet articles daily. `Sci.math.research` is but one of thousands of Usenet News groups; many megabytes of information are transmitted over Usenet each day. In some ways, Usenet's role is similar to that of LISTSERV-style mailing lists. However, unlike mailing list discussions, which are sent via e-mail to far-flung individual subscribers, Usenet News traffic is sent en masse to each of thousands of computer installations in the form of "news feeds." Most of these installations offer their users a majority of the news groups available. Users at each site use a type of client program called a "news reader" to browse news groups of interest and to submit postings of their own. The process can be envisioned as shown in Fig. 8.1.

News groups in the Usenet News world are organized hierarchically. For instance, the "sci" category contains several subgroups, including "math"; the math subgroup, in turn, contains a subgroup of "research." You use one of a variety of news reader packages to skim the thousands of news groups for articles that interest you. Figure 8.2 shows an example screen from one such tool.

This newsreader, NewsGrazer,† works under the NextStep operating system; the example shows graphically the hierarchical organization of Usenet News. The user has selected a particular posting to the `comp.infosystems.gopher` news group. Each of the columns in the panels shown in gray represents one level of the hierarchy; the rightmost columns shows the subject lines of current postings. Selected items are highlighted. The white text panel shows the actual text of the currently selected posting.

Usenet news groups are divided into "mainstream" and "alternative" categories. Groups in the mainstream categories are established under a "call for votes" process; for example, `comp.infosystems.gopher` was created after a vote of Usenet participants from around the world. The top level of mainstream groups are `comp`, `misc`, `news`, `rec`, `sci`, `soc`, and `talk`. By convention, groups

---

* Dr. Wiles' proof is still under scrutiny as of this writing.

† NewsGrazer was written by Jayson Adams and updated by Bryce Jasmer. NextStep is the graphically-oriented version of Unix pioneered on Next workstations and now marketed for IBM PC compatibles.

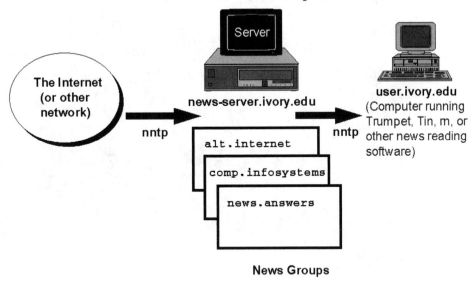

A local news server receives a "news feed" from a cooperating upstream site. Local users fetch articles of interest using "news readers"

Figure 8.1

can be created in the alternative categories without need for the call-for-votes process. However, system administrators at a given site often choose not to carry some of the alternative groups. The top-level alternative groups include alt, bit, gnu, and k12; the alt category contains most of the alternate news groups. Alternative groups may host discussions that are relatively serious—before there was a mainstream Gopher group, there was `alt.gopher`. Other alternative groups include `alt.sex`, `alt.tasteless.jokes`, and `rec.humor`.

Some of the more popular Usenet news groups include:

News group	Topic
`alt.bbs.internet`	Lists of Internet-accessible bulletin boards
`alt.internet.access.wanted`	Internet access options by location
`alt.rush.limbaugh`	An opinionated American radio talk show host
`alt.tv.seinfeld`	A television comedy
`comp.os.ms-windows.misc`	Microsoft Windows
`news.answers`	Frequently Asked Questions documents (see below)
`rec.arts.tv.soaps`	Television soap operas
`sci.space.news`	NASA and other space news
`soc.culture.indian`	Culture of India
`talk.politics.mideast`	Discussion & debate over the Middle East

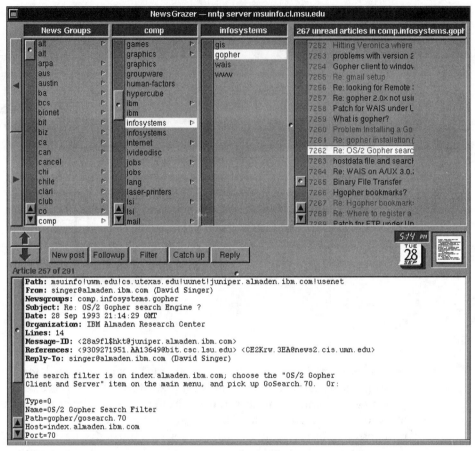

Figure 8.2

As you can see, the topic areas are as varied as they can be for mailing lists. A site can also set up one or more "local" news groups, to hold discussions of interest to the local computing community.

News-reading software provides your window into the world of Usenet. If your workstation is directly connected to the Internet, you should consider running a news reader locally. Examples of such programs include Trumpet for the PC, and Nuntius for the Macintosh. Some developers are endowing e-mail packages with news-reading capability; Pine and Eudora are examples. There are even Usenet readers for mainframes, such as the NNR tool that runs under VM/CMS.

If you use a Unix workstation, either via direct Internet attachment or by dial-up into a service provider, you might use a program such as nn or rn. These tools provide a great deal of flexibility and power as you navigate through the news. Experienced users of nn and rn are able to move from group to group extremely quickly, separating wheat from chaff with multiple one-keystroke commands. Rn and nn have dozens of command options each; the manual for nn is about 70 pages long.

READING NEWS WITH TIN

Some Unix systems offer another newsreader known as Tin. This tool is a "threaded" newsreader—that is, within news groups, Tin uses Subject lines to locate and present articles that cover the same "thread." Because Usenet mail (like LISTSERV mail) often contains intermingled subjects, this feature allows you to read related postings together.

Here are some examples of reading news using Tin.

```
<rww@garnet>
<rww@garnet> tin
tin 1.1 PL9 (c) Copyright 1991-93 Iain Lea.
Connecting to news.msen.com...
Reading news active file...
Subscribe to new group bit.listserv.gophern (y/n/q) [n]: n
Subscribe to new group bit.listserv.down-syn (y/n/q) [n]: n
Subscribe to new group comp.unix.user-friendly (y/n/q) [n]: y
Subscribe to new group alt.med.ems (y/n/q) [n]: n
Subscribe to new group alt.bbs.majorbbs (y/n/q) [n]: y
Reading attributes file...
Reading newsgroups file...
```

Usenet News readers feature a concept of "subscribing" to news groups of interest. This is analogous to subscribing to a mailing list, but the mechanics are different. With a mailing list, your subscription is registered at the mailing list processor, which might be on a computer halfway around the world. By contrast, your Usenet News reader records your "subscriptions" locally, on your workstation or in a file associated with your user ID. News groups are delivered to your site's news service regardless of whether you are subscribed to them; by subscribing, you simply tell your news reader "These are the news groups I want to see by default."

At startup, Tin offers to let you subscribe to any news groups that might have been created since your last session. The list can be lengthy; "q" stops the prompting. Then, Tin shows you the news groups you have subscribed to, and the number of postings in each that you have not read. In this example we had previously subscribed to nine news groups, and at the start of session we added two new groups:

```
 1        alt.binaries.pictures.fractals For postings of fractal pictures
 2        clari.news                     ClariNet UPI general news wiregrou
 3    23  clari.news.top
 4  1792  news.answers                   Repository for periodic USENET art
 5    44  rec.sport.volleyball           Discussion about volleyball.
 6   164  rec.travel.air                 Airline travel around the world.
 7   348  comp.infosystems.gopher        Discussion of the gopher informati
 8    71  comp.os.linux.announce         Announcements important to the Lin
 9   645  comp.infosystems.www           The World Wide Web information sys
10   110  comp.unix.user-friendly        Discussion of Unix user-friendline
11        alt.bbs.majorbbs
```

```
    <n>=set current to n, TAB ext unread, /=search pattern, c)atchup,
  g)oto, j=line down, k=line up, h)elp, m)ove, q)uit, r oggle all/unread,
   s)ubscribe, S)ub pattern, u)nsubscribe, U)nsub pattern, y)ank in/out
```

If you want to see the names of all the news groups available at your site, Tin allows you to do so easily. By typing "y" you ask it to "yank" in all the available groups. (If you type "y" again, Tin will toggle back to the news groups you've subscribed to.)

```
    <n>=set current to n, TAB ext unread, /=search pattern, c)atchup,
  g)oto, j=line down, k=line up, h)elp, m)ove, q)uit, r oggle all/unread,
   s)ubscribe, S)ub pattern, u)nsubscribe, U)nsub pattern, y)ank in/out
```

```
[user types "y"]

Yanking in all groups...
```

With some 5600 news groups, the list of all groups is quite formidable. (Note that "u" appears in the list to the left of each group name—that is because we have not subscribed to any of these groups.)

```
                Group Selection (news.msen.com 5691)                h=help

u   1        3b.config
u   2        3b.misc
u   3        3b.tech
u   4        3b.test
u   5    45  alt.3d                      Three-dimensiona
u   6   268  alt.abortion.inequity       Paternal obligat
u   7  1520  alt.activism                Activities for a
u   8    51  alt.activism.d              A place to discu
u   9    15  alt.aeffle.und.pferdle      German TV cartoo
u  10   406  alt.alien.visitors          Space Aliens on
u  11        alt.als
```

```
u  12      8   alt.amiga.demos
u  13    180   alt.angst                        Anxiety in the m
u  14          alt.angst.xibo.sex
u  15    107   alt.aquaria                      The aquarium & r
u  16    138   alt.archery                      Robin Hood had t
u  17     51   alt.artcom                       Artistic Communi
```

```
    <n>=set current to n, TAB ext unread, /=search pattern, c)atchup,
g)oto, j=line down, k=line up, h)elp, m)ove, q)uit, r oggle all/unread,
  s)ubscribe, S)ub pattern, u)nsubscribe, U)nsub pattern, y)ank in/out
```

Most news readers provide a mechanism for easily moving through the list of all news groups; Tin is no exception. You can use the arrow keys to move a highlighted cursor from group to group. After you hit the end of the list, Tin will scroll forward one page. Instead of scrolling down to a group of interest, you can strike the "g" key and type in the name of the group you want. Or, if you want to search for a news group, you can type a slash ("/") and enter a string of characters you believe appear in the name of the group you want.

Let's assume we moved forward using one of these methods to comp.info-systems.gopher, so as to read current discussions on the Internet Gopher. A list like this will appear:

```
            comp.infosystems.gopher (129T 181A OK OH R)

 1  +      Problem locating Veronica server           Peter S. Fillmore
 2  + 2    curses client trouble                      E. Hagberg
 3  + 2    PC Gopher III and command line arguments   Alan J Flavell
 4  + 2    looking for Remote Sensing Info-board      Carsten Juergens (t3
 5         Need client for use with LAN Workplace for DOS  Tim Shaw
 6         Need Help with Scripted Telnet Code        John Doyle
 7  +      What happen to mail option?                Chris Shenton
 8  +      Gopher client to windows                   newsmgr@dec.ciemat.e
 9  +      gmail setup                                Prentiss Riddle
10  +      Root-Server Duplication with Gopher -b     uh..Clem
11         OS/2 Gopher search Engine ?                Daniel Torrey
12  +      problems with version 2.06 server          Rob McDonald
13  + 3    gopher 2.0x not using $PAGER?              Roberto Mazzoni
14  +      Problem Installing a Gopher Server         Charles Bailey, Univ
15  +      gopher installation (fwd)                  dittrich@cac.washing
16  +      Patch for WAIS under Unix gopher 2.07      Peter J Wilcoxn
17  + 2    Gopher mail server                         James Meritt
```

```
    <n>=set current to n, TAB ext unread, /=search pattern, ^K)ill/select,
a)author search, c)atchup, j=line down, k=line up, K ark read, l)ist thread,
   |=pipe, m)ail, o=print, q)uit, r oggle all/unread, s)ave, t)ag, w=post
```

Now let's assume that we want to read more about item 17, whose subject is the Gopher mail server. So we move the cursor to that line on the screen. The "+" sign indicates we have not yet read a given item. If we wanted to read this particular posting, we could do so by simply hitting the Enter key. Or, we could take note of the "2" after the plus sign, which tells us that there are two articles on this subject (or "thread"). We can ask to see a list of those two articles by striking "l" for "list." The resulting screens:

```
                    Thread (Gopher mail server)                    h=help


0  +  James Merritt (m23364@mwunix.mitre.org)
1  +  Edward Vielmetti (emv@garnet.msen.com)



       <n>=set current to n, TAB ext unread, c)atchup, d)isplay toggle,
          h)elp, j=line down, k=line up, q)uit, t)ag, z ark unread
```

This shows the ability of Tin to group articles into a logical sequence for reading. You can select a subject of interest, then quickly skim through all the related articles. When you select one of the articles in a thread, Tin shows you the text of the article. You can then use the Tab key to move from one article to the next:

```
Tue, 28 Sep 1993 15:14:44      comp.infosystems.gopher    Thread   17 of  130
Article 7275                   Gopher mail server                  1 Response
m23364@mwunix.mitre.org            James Meritt at MITRE Corporation, McLean VA

Is there a gopher mail server except the one at Calvin.edu?


  --

James W. Meritt:  m23364@mwunix.mitre.org - or - jmeritt@mitre.org
The opinions above are mine. If anyone else wants to share them, fine.
They may say so if they wish. The facts "belong" to noone and simply are.


       <n>=set current to n, TAB ext unread, /=search pattern, ^K)ill/select,
        a)uthor search, c)atchup, f)ollowup, j=line down, k=line up, K ark read,
          |=pipe, m)ail, o=print, q)uit, r)eply mail, s)ave, t)ag, w=post
```

Now, upon a strike of the Tab key, Tin shows you the next related article:

```
Thu, 30 Sep 1993 01:43:37      comp.infosystems.gopher    Thread   17 of  130
Article 7276                   Re: Gopher mail server      Respno   1 of   1
emv@garnet.msen.com Edward Vielmetti at Msen, Inc. -- Ann Arbor, MI (account info
```

James Meritt (m23364@mwunix.mitre.org) wrote:

: Is there a gopher mail server except the one at Calvin.edu?

Try

       To: gophermail@ncc.go.jp
       Subject: help

              <n>=set current to n, TAB ext unread, /=search pattern, ^K)ill/select,
         a)uthor search, c)atchup, f)ollowup, j=line down, k=line up, K ark read,
            |=pipe, m)ail, o=print, q)uit, r)eply mail, s)ave, t)ag, w=post

News readers like Tin make it easy to join in on a discussion. If you want to send a note to the author of a particular posting, a "reply" function allows you to send private e-mail. If you want to join the discussion publicly, then a "follow-up" request is in order. For instance, let's suppose we want to learn more about who actually uses a Gopher mail server. If you specify "f," Tin will inform you the news groups you are about to post to:

       Responses have been directed to the following newsgroups

alt.gopher
comp.infosystems.gopher

You can post a message to several news groups if you think its content applies to the focus of each group. In this example, alt.gopher is an older group, where discussions about Gopher took place before the mainstream group comp.infosystems.gopher was formed. After showing you where the posting will go, Tin will use a text editor to display the text of the original message—so that your posting will have context. You can delete portions of the original postings that seem extraneous, and then type in your comment:

   PICO 1.8   File: /usr/guest/rww/.article   Modified

: Try
:
:   To: gophermail@ncc.go.jp
:   Subject: help

: --Ed
Out of curiosity, how would you use a mail server for Gopher? Is
it correct to assume this would be to repeatedly fetch a file
(such as a weather map) as opposed to navigating the menus? It
seems like any sort of hierarchy hopping would be painfully slow.
/rich

When composition is complete, you close the editing session (with Ctrl-W if the editor is Pico), and Tin informs you:

```
                        Article posted
```

If we revisit the Gopher news group listing after a few moments, the entry for the Gopher mail server will reflect that there is a new posting:

```
    14 + 3 Gopher mail server                      James Meritt
```

And sure enough, the last item in the thread is the article we posted:

```
Tue,  05 Oct 1993 17:49:08    comp.infosystems.gopher   Thread   17 of  130
Article 7276                   Re: Gopher mail server    Respno   1 of   1
rww@garnet.msen.com Rich WIggins at Msen, Inc. -- Ann Arbor, MI (account info

: Try
:           To: gophermail@ncc.go.jp
:           Subject: help

: --Ed
Out of curiosity, how would you use a mail server for Gopher? Is
it correct to assume this would be to repeatedly fetch a file
(such as a weather map) as opposed to navigating the menus? It
seems like any sort of hierarchy hopping would be painfully slow.
/rich

    <n>=set current to n, TAB ext unread, /=search pattern, ^K)ill/select,
   a)uthor search, c)atchup, f)ollowup, j=line down, k=line up, K  ark read,
      |=pipe, m)ail, o=print, q)uit, r)eply mail, s)ave, t)ag, w=post
```

Note that Tin, and most news readers, keep track of which articles you've read already. By default, those articles are not listed in subsequent sessions. If you do want to review all articles, including those previously read, the "r" key commands Tin to add them to the list.

Usenet news readers offer a plethora of other options that make it easier to cope with the vast quantities of information served daily over this remarkable medium. Most readers provide ways to export an article to disk, or to send it to someone via e-mail. One useful option is the "kill" feature, which allows you to automatically eliminate the display of articles matching certain characteristics. The simplest option is to specify that postings from a certain user's e-mail address should be suppressed. If you find a particular person's postings annoying, this feature can help. Tin offers a menu of choices if you ask it to kill by typing Ctrl-K.

Tin makes it easy to configure various settings that affect how articles are displayed. For instance, you may prefer to have articles sorted by their subject lines instead of the posting dates. By typing "M" (capital M, as lowercase "m" invokes mail) you cause a list of such options to be displayed. Option settings are stored in a file under your user name and therefore persist after you leave Tin and log out.

This overview of using Tin should serve as an example of the kind of features you'll find in all news readers. After exploring how to perform the same functions using the package offered by your service provider, you can then graduate to more advance options.

One word of caution about Tin (and other news readers in particular and Unix-based programs in general): the case of commands is often significant. Note, for instance, that the letter "k" causes Tin to move the cursor up one line in a list of articles; the letter "K" marks an item as read. If a command isn't doing what you want, you may need to hit the shift key.

RETENTION OF ARTICLES IN NEWS GROUPS

Each Usenet News administrator decides how long news groups should be kept online. Sites that serve a majority of news groups to their users have to deal with 50 megabytes of incoming news flow daily—or more. This means that most sites cannot afford to leave discussions online for long periods. Most Usenet administrators choose a period of a week or two. It is also possible for the administrator to tailor the retention period by news group, so that groups of particular local interest remain online for longer periods. (Note that the administrator may choose not to carry some news groups at all, based on local interest, cost of disk space, and other considerations.)

Some news groups are archived indefinitely, often in other media. For instance, the University of Minnesota keeps an archive of comp.infosystems.gopher (under "Information About Gopher"). Other archives may be stored under anonymous FTP or other media.

One company is offering Usenet archives in a personal format: CD Publishing Corporation offers complete archives of Usenet traffic on CD-ROM discs. One series is offered for general (mostly mainstream) news groups, and another for specialized/regional groups. Each disc holds two to four weeks of traffic. For further information on these products, send e-mail to info@cdpublishing.com.*

USENET NEWS AS INFORMATION REPOSITORY

Usenet is much more than a discussion medium. It has evolved into a significant repository of useful information. This evolution had humble beginnings:

---

* Or call the company in Vancouver, British Columbia at 604-874-1430.

with a constant flow of new users into Usenet, the cognoscenti grew tired of responding to the same beginners' questions time and time again. Such questions came to be known as Frequently Asked Questions, or FAQs, and old-timers began composing answers to some of these questions. They kept the answers in files so that it would be convenient to repost a standard set of answers as new users ask the same old questions.

Today there is a news group that is dedicated to holding these FAQ documents for easy retrieval and reference. Called news.answers, this group holds an astonishing amount of information about the Internet, computing, and topics from amateur radio to the works to Douglas Adams to the other roles played by actors in Star Trek. Here are some sample titles as listed by Tin:

```
                    news.answers (619T 622A OK OH R)

511  +   Space FAQ 10/13 - Controversial Questions          Jon Leech
512  +   Space FAQ 11/13 - Interest Groups & Publicatio      Jon Leech
513  +   Space FAQ 12/13 - How to Become an Astronaut        Jon Leech
514  +   Space FAQ 13/13 - Orbital and Planetary Launch      Jon Leech
515  +   JPEG image compression: Frequently Asked Quest      Tom Lane
516  +   Introduction to comp.editors (July 29 1993)         Ove Ruben R Olsen
517  +   RIPEM Frequently Asked Questions                    Marc VanHeyningen
518  +   RIPEM Frequently Noted Vulnerabilities              Marc VanHeyningen
519  +   rec.scouting FAQ #2: Scouting around the Worl       Danny Schwendener
520  +   Astro/Space Frequently Seen Acronyms                Mark Bradford
521  +   Unix - Frequently Asked Questions (Contents) [      Ted M A Timar
522  +   Welcome to comp.unix.shell [Frequent posting]       Ted M A Timar
523  +   Welcome to comp.unix.questions [Frequent posting]   Ted M A Timar
524  +   Unix - Frequently Asked Questions (5/7) Digest      Ted M A Timar
525  +   Unix - Frequently Asked Questions (7/7) Digest      Ted M A Timar
526  +   Unix - Frequently Asked Questions (1/7) Digest      Ted M A Timar
527  +   Unix - Frequently Asked Questions (3/7) Digest      Ted M A Timar
```

Note that some of the documents are split into multiple parts. This makes the information more accessible than it would be if the information were posted as one large file—the user can fetch the parts desired, which can be an advantage over slow communications links.

Here is an example of an FAQ document that describes a format for still-image files known as JPEG:

```
From: tgl+@cs.cmu.edu (Tom Lane)
Subject: JPEG image compression: Frequently Asked Questions
Message-ID: <jpeg-faq_749699923@g.gp.cs.cmu.edu>
Followup-To: alt.binaries.pictures.d
Summary: Useful info about JPEG (JPG) image files and programs
Keywords: JPEG, image compression, FAQ
Sender: news@cs.cmu.edu (Usenet News System)
```

Supersedes: <jpeg-faq_748473687@g.gp.cs.cmu.edu>
Reply-To: jpeg-info@uunet.uu.net
Organization: School of Computer Science, Carnegie Mellon
Date: Mon, 4 Oct 1993 01:59:02 GMT
Approved: news-answers-request@MIT.Edu
Expires: Mon, 1 Nov 1993 01:58:43 GMT
Lines: 1082

Archive-name: jpeg-faq
Last-modified: 3 October 1993

This article discusses JPEG image compression. Suggestions for additions
and clarifications are welcome.

New since version of 19 September 1993:
  * New version of LView (3.1).
  * More info about converting Mac PICT files to standard JPEG (section 11).
  * Simtel20 is history, sad to say. FTP archiving arrangements for DOS and
    Windows programs are changing, but no details yet.

This article includes the following sections:

[1]   What is JPEG?
[2]   Why use JPEG?
[3]   When should I use JPEG, and when should I stick with GIF?
[4]   How well does JPEG compress images?
[5]   What are good "quality" settings for JPEG?
[6]   Where can I get JPEG software?
      [6A] viewers, application programs, etc.
      [6B] source code
[7]   What's all this hoopla about color quantization?
[8]   What are some rules of thumb for converting GIF images to JPEG?
[9]   Does loss accumulate with repeated compression/decompression?
[10] Why all the argument about file formats?
[11] How do I recognize which file format I have, and what do I do about it?
[12] How does JPEG work?
[13] Isn't there a lossless JPEG?
[14] What about arithmetic coding?
[15] Could an FPU speed up JPEG? How about a DSP chip?

Sections 1-6 are basic info that every JPEG user needs to know;
sections 7-15 are more advanced info.

...

[1]   What is JPEG?

JPEG (pronounced "jay-peg") is a standardized image compression mechanism.
JPEG stands for Joint Photographic Experts Group, the original name of the
committee that wrote the standard.

```
JPEG is designed for compressing either full-color or gray-scale images
of natural, real-world scenes. It works well on photographs, naturalistic
artwork, and similar material; not so well on lettering, simple cartoons,
or line drawings. JPEG handles only still images, but there is a related
standard called MPEG for motion pictures. ....
```

Following the usual convention for FAQ files, this document lists all the questions it will answer in a question-and-answer format. Then, the document proceeds to answer the questions, one at a time. FAQ files like this are usually a labor of love for the author. Often the author has assistance from a variety of fellow travelers around the net; those who make significant contributions are usually given credit in the file itself. New versions of FAQ files are posted periodically, incorporating corrections and new information. Usenet FAQ files can be a very valuable way of keeping up with changing computer technology (and myriad other subjects). Most FAQ files are reposted periodically—every two weeks or so. Many FAQs are posted to several news groups whose readers would find the document of interest. News.answers serves as an overall repository for all FAQs, no matter the topic.

As we saw in Chap. 7, a service at MIT can provide copies of FAQ files via e-mail. This file could be fetched by sending e-mail to `mail-server@rtfm.mit.edu` with send `usenet/news.answers/jpeg-faq` as the body of the message.*

POSTING TO USENET VIA ELECTRONIC MAIL

In order to get the most out of Usenet News, you should run a good newsreader program, like Tin, that makes it easy both to read news online, and to post submissions of your own to news groups. Some Internet service providers may provide a way to peruse Usenet articles—for instance via a Gopher gateway—but they may not allow you to post directly. You may be able to find a gateway that enables you to post via e-mail. One such gateway resides at the University of Texas.† To use it, send mail to:

```
groupname@cs.utexas.edu
```

In this case, groupname is the Usenet News group name, with the periods in the name replaced by dashes. For instance, to submit a posting to comp.infosystems.gopher, you would mail to:

```
comp-infosystems-gopher@cs.utexas.edu
```

---

* MIT also offers these files via anonymous FTP from `rtfm.mit.edu`; this FAQ file is named `/pub/usenet/news.answers/jpeg-faq`. Chapter 9 describes retrieval of files via anonymous FTP.

† This service was implemented by Fletcher Mattox of the computer science department at the University of Texas.

You should submit such postings from a mail service that correctly identifies your real name.

THE LANGUAGES OF USENET

Most Usenet News groups conduct their discussions in English. Because literacy in English is widespread even in countries with different native tongues, postings to such groups come from all over the world. One study found that per capita access to the Internet is higher in Finland than in the United States, and informal glances at the countries of origin of Usenet traffic seem to bear out the notion that Finnish participation is high.

Some news groups are conducted in languages other than English; naturally enough, this is especially true for news groups local to a particular country or that specifically pertain to its language.

Several news groups intended for students and faculty of primary and secondary schools are oriented towards language instruction. For instance, `k12.lang.deutsch-eng` conducts conversations in German and sometimes English. The old idea of the pen pal becomes a worldwide group discussion thanks to Usenet; students whose native tongue is English can correspond with native German speakers, leading to rich discussions for both. Not only is language instruction enhanced, understanding of other cultures can reach beyond the level of textbooks.*

MULTIMEDIA AND BINARY DOCUMENTS
VIA USENET

Several news groups are devoted to the delivery of images and sounds over Usenet. One example is the group `alt.binaries.pictures`, where participants post photographs. Image files are usually sent in JPEG or GIF format. Often the files are broken into several separate postings because of their length. Many news readers' programs are able to group such files together by sorting on the title lines, which are usually of the form:

```
Mendenhall Glacier (GIF) Part 01 of 06
```

Many news readers allow you to select such a group of files, and have the files decoded and placed on your hard disk. (For instance, in the above example, the news reader might leave on disk a file named `menden.gif`.) Common encoding schemes are "uuencode" and, less frequently, the Unix "shar" format.

---

* Not all multinational dialogue is profound; recently students in a computer laboratory at Michigan State were overheard discussing an argument with a German correspondent. It seems each side thought the beer of the other country was superior. Perhaps Usenet and the Internet can promote bilateral respect.

Once the file is on your hard disk, you use an external tool to view it (or listen to it in the case of sounds). Chapter 9 details file formats and tools for coping with them.

Usenet is also used to deliver executable computer programs. Newsgroups such as `comp.binaries.mac` offer software in ready-to-run form for various computer platforms, including the Macintosh, PCs running MS-DOS, OS/2, and other systems. You will also want to explore other forms of archives, such as anonymous FTP sites.

SMILEY FACES

Smiley faces are a form of shorthand for telling a reader "The adjoining remark is made in jest" without having to say so in that many words.* The simplest smiley face looks like this:

```
:-)
```

The idea is to look at the characters as an icon by tilting your head to the left; imagine, quite literally, a smiley face.† There are numerous variations on this theme; occasionally you see articles in Usenet offering large collections of smiley faces and their interpretations. Reportedly someone has even published a book with a collection of choice smileys.

Opinions vary on the use of smileys. Used sparingly they can be a helpful way to inject some expression into a textual medium and perhaps avert hurt feelings from time to time.

HINTS AND NETIQUETTE

Many of the general hints and netiquette pointers shown in Chap. 7 apply equally to Usenet as they do to mailing lists; you may want to review the list of items at the end of that chapter.

- Because Usenet has no central governing authority, and because news groups (unlike mailing lists) have no owners,‡ peer pressure is the main enforcement mechanism for handling behavior that is considered a violation of netiquette. If you violate the norms of a news group you may find yourself

---

* Smiley faces are often used not only on Usenet but in private e-mail and mailing lists. We mention them here because Usenet seems to be the environment where they were invented.

† Readers who grew up after the smiley face craze of the 1970s may be at a disadvantage in this exercise.

‡ But like some mailing lists, some Usenet news groups are moderated; it is up to the moderator's discretion whether a given posting is topical.

receiving large quantities of mail (private and public) advising you of the error of your ways.

■ Postings should be considered the private opinions of individuals, not the official statements of their employers, unless the comments are identified as official. Of course, readers are likely to impute official status to the remarks of high-ranking officials in any organization. Some Usenet posters include standard signatures explicitly stating that their opinions are their own.

■ Usenet groups that deliver images or other binary files (e.g., `alt.binaries.pictures`) often have corresponding discussion groups (e.g., `alt.binaries.pictures.d`). It's considered bad form to post textual queries to the groups that are intended to deliver binary files; use the discussion group.

■ You will encounter various bits of shorthand in the Usenet world (and elsewhere on the Internet). Examples include:

BTW	By the way
FWIW	For what it's worth
IMHO	In my humble opinion (often used to convey that you are not claiming your argument to be the absolute last word on a subject)
RTFM	[Loosely translated] "The answer to your question appears in the documentation"

■ "Flames"—postings that reflect a venomous reaction to a previous article—are both an art form and a nuisance on Usenet. Some news groups are known for their frequent flame fests; others display high levels of comity. In some cases, flames become part of the norm. The most extreme example is the group `alt.flame`, which exists as a sort of Hyde Park forum in which participants try to out-insult one another.

■ Many Usenet users prefer not to have to deal with extremely long articles. The conventions for maximum length of articles are not universally standardized. If you are posting a new article that's part of a thread of discussion, a limit of a few screenfuls is a good idea; longer postings may not be read by anyone. For news groups that accept documents, a length of several hundred lines is a good number. If your article is longer than that, break it up into several separate messages, with subject lines that describe each part. (Some news readers will take care of splitting long articles on your behalf.) If you have a long document you want to offer to members of several news groups, consider putting the document itself on a Gopher server or an FTP server, which makes it possible for you to post to relevant Usenet groups a relatively short announcement that your document exists and how readers can retrieve it. (Later chapters give hints on providing information through such vehicles.)

■ Sometimes you will encounter postings that include the string "rot13" in the subject line. This means the message will be encoded using a simple transformation of characters* so as to obscure the text. The goal is to render the text illegible to the casual viewer, not to securely encrypt it. Some newsreading programs offer a command to decode or encode according to this scheme. The theory is that a user who affirmatively decodes a message waives the right to be offended by it.

---

* Specifically, each letter of the alphabet is substituted by the letter that is 13 characters "later" in the alphabet; i.e., "N" replaces "A," "O" replaces "B," and so forth.

Transferring Files with FTP: Methods and Formats

One of the most popular services provided by mass-market information utilities such as CompuServe and America Online is the ability to download files. All sorts of files are provided: ready-to-run software for various types of computers, libraries of still images, and even videos with moving images and sounds. The Internet offers similar repositories. You can exploit such services by using one of the core applications of the TCP/IP family: the File Transfer Protocol, or FTP. In this chapter we will explore how FTP can be used to fetch files from the variety of servers online, and we'll also examine how you can use FTP to move your own files over the Internet.

FTP was devised to fill a basic need identified early in the history of the Internet: to move files from one computer to another. The process is conceptually simple: You want to fetch a file that resides on a machine located elsewhere on the Internet—or, conversely, you want to copy a file from your local computer to a remote one.

As an example, assume you want to retrieve a file called `manual.txt` via FTP. The process you would use can be envisioned as in Figure 9.1.

On most systems, the File Transfer Protocol is implemented as a command of the name `ftp`. Once you invoke FTP, you must log into the remote server. If you have been given an account on a remote machine through a cooperative arrangement, you specify a user ID and password as if you were logging into a

FTP Allows Copying of Files to or from Remote Servers

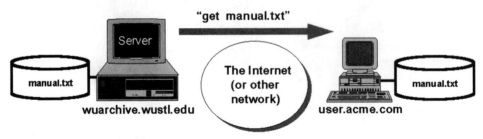

Figure 9.1

Telnet session. Or, in the case of software repositories offered openly to the general public, you can log in using a generic name, and no password checking is performed. Suppose you wanted to retrieve a file called "index.txt" that you know resides on server archive.probono.org:

```
ftp archive.probono.org
Connected to archive.probono.org.
220-Welcome to the Archive service of the Probono Organization.
Name (archive.probono.org:rww) anonymous
331-Guest login ok, send e-mail address as password.
Password: doe@user.acme.com
331-Guest login ok, access restrictions apply
ftp> cd pub
ftp> get index.txt
200-PORT command successful
150-Opening ASCII mode data connection for /pub/index.txt (1234 bytes)
226-Transfer complete
local: index.txt remote: index.txt
ftp> quit
221-Goodbye
```

Note that you are prompted for a user ID; in this case we use "anonymous," which by convention is the pseudo ID you specify for FTP services open to the general public.* You will be asked to specify a password; in practice, you can specify anything you want for anonymous FTP services, but many sites request that you specify your e-mail address for their records. The remote server sends you some informative messages, which are prefixed with standard numeric codes. The get command tells the remote server what file you want to retrieve. Files are shipped to you in "ASCII" mode by default; we'll explore the alternative, "binary" mode, later. The FTP process informs you of the file name used

---

* Many anonymous FTP servers will accept the name "ftp" as an alternative to "anonymous."

on your workstation and on the remote server; the name can differ because of different file-naming conventions on different computer systems.* Once the file has been delivered over the network and placed on your hard disk by your local FTP client program, you can either fetch another file, or close the connection by typing "quit."

Following is a real-world example, fetching the Gopher client for MS-DOS offered by the University of Minnesota:

```
C: ftp boombox.micro.umn.edu
Connected to boombox.micro.umn.edu.
220 boombox FTP server (Version 4.1 Tue Apr 10 05:15:32 PDT 1990) ready.
Name (boombox.micro.umn.edu:rww): anonymous
331 Guest login ok, send ident as password.
Password: wiggins@msu.edu
230 Guest login ok, access restrictions apply.
```

The login process follows the pattern of the previous example. In this case, let's assume we do not know the specific file name we are looking for. The FTP command dir will cause a list of files to be displayed:

```
ftp> dir
200 PORT command successful.
150 Opening ASCII mode data connection for /bin/ls (0 bytes).
total 6
drwxr-xr-x   2 root      512 Oct  6  1992 bin
drwxr-xr-x   2 root      512 Oct  6  1992 etc
drwxr-xr-x  18 bin       512 Oct 14 20:55 pub
226 Transfer complete.
159 bytes received in 0.02 seconds (9.86 Kbytes/s)
```

Most anonymous FTP servers run on Unix hosts, and this one is no exception. The directory listing resembles the listing you would see if you were a local user of that host and you typed a command to display the directory on that machine; the list of files is similar to the results of the "ls -1" command under Unix. The key elements of an FTP directory listing are shown in Fig. 9.2.

The three lines displayed on the Minnesota server correspond to subdirectories, as is denoted by the "d" at the beginning of each. This server follows the

---

* For instance, Unix machines allow very long file names, and MS-DOS limits you to eight-character names with optional three-character extensions. If you transfer a file with a long name to an MS-DOS machine, the name will have to be truncated. You can also specify a different local name for a file on the get command. In this case, for instance, you could say:

```
get index.txt probono.ind
```

and the name probono.ind would be used for the copy on your hard disk. Some FTP clients will, by default, prompt you for an alternate name; you can type in a different name or press Enter if you want the names to match.

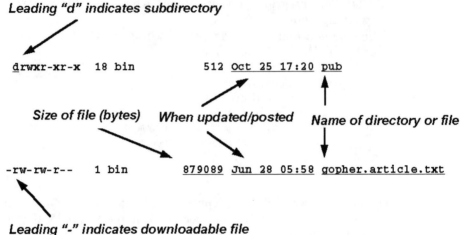

Elements of an FTP Directory Listing (Unix Server Example)

Leading "d" indicates subdirectory

drwxr-xr-x   18 bin   512 Oct 25 17:20 pub

Size of file (bytes)   *When updated/posted*   *Name of directory or file*

-rw-rw-r--   1 bin   879089 Jun 28 05:58 gopher.article.txt

Leading "-" indicates downloadable file

Figure 9.2

convention of offering a `pub` directory. Again, as if we were working on a local hard disk, we can "change directory" easily:

```
ftp> cd pub
250 CWD command successful.
```

Another `dir` command reveals a number of files and directories under `/pub`:

```
ftp> dir
200 PORT command successful.
150 Opening ASCII mode data connection for /bin/ls (0 bytes).
total 350
drwxr-xr-x    2 bin              512 Sep 23 04:08 CAP
drwxr-xr-x    2 bin              512 Sep 23 05:22 Japanese
drwxr-xr-x    4 bin              512 Sep 23 16:10 POPmail
drwxr-xr-x    4 bin              512 Sep 23 04:52 VSL
drwxr-xr-x    2 bin              512 Sep 23 11:27 addfinder
drwxr-xr-x    4 bin              512 Sep 23 11:22 binhex
lrwxrwxrwx    1 bin                4 Oct  6   1992 chronos -> ietf
-rw-rw-rw-    1 bin           155648 Oct 22 03:43 core
drwxr-xr-x    2 bin              512 Sep 26 02:50 customcf
drwxr-xr-x   19 bin              512 Sep 24 17:03 gopher
...
```

We're interested in a Gopher-related file, so that directory looks like a good candidate.

```
ftp> cd gopher
250 CWD command successful.
ftp> dir
200 PORT command successful.
150 Opening ASCII mode data connection for /bin/ls (0 bytes).
total 50
-rw-r--r--   1 bin          1483 Aug 10 17:21 00README
drwxr-xr-x   2 bin           512 Oct 14 21:08 GopherMoo
drwxr-xr-x   3 bin           512 Oct  7 01:56 Mac_server
drwxr-xr-x   4 bin           512 Oct 19 13:53 Macintosh-TurboGopher
drwxr-xr-x   3 bin           512 Sep 23 22:41 NeXT
drwxr-xr-x   5 bin           512 Sep 23 03:52 PC_client
drwxr-xr-x   5 bin           512 Sep 23 03:52 PC_server
drwxr-xr-x   4 bin           512 Sep 24 14:08 Rice_CMS
drwxr-xr-x   9 bin          1024 Oct 20 05:03 Unix
...
```

Since we're pursuing a PC Gopher client, we select the appropriately named directory:

```
ftp> cd PC_client
250 CWD command successful.
ftp> dir
200 PORT command successful.
150 Opening ASCII mode data connection for /bin/ls (0 bytes).
total 1614
-rw-r--r--   1 bin           559 Aug  9 15:03 00readme
-rw-r--r--   1 bin             0 Mar 22  1993 FTP_THESE_FILES_IN_BINARY_MODE
-rw-r--r--   1 bin             0 Sep 13 16:56 Latest_version_is_1.1.2
drwxr-xr-x   2 bin           512 Oct 15 15:12 icky_old_client
drwxr-xr-x   2 bin           512 Sep 23 06:02 packet_drivers
-rw-r--r--   1 bin        343353 Aug  9 15:03 pcg3bin.zip
-rw-r--r--   1 bin        359123 Aug  9 15:03 pcg3binx.exe
-rw-r--r--   1 bin         44926 Aug  9 15:03 pcg3doc.zip
-rw-r--r--   1 bin         60696 Aug  9 15:03 pcg3docx.exe
```

When downloading software, you usually will want to perform the transfer in "binary" mode, which preserves the exact format of the file during the transmission. In this case, that is the mode we want. To conclude the example:

```
ftp> binary
200 Type set to I.
ftp> get pcg3bin.zip
200 PORT command successful.
150 Opening BINARY mode data connection for pcg3bin.zip (343353 bytes).
226 Transfer complete.
local: pcg3bin.zip remote: pcg3bin.zip
```

```
343353 bytes received in 5.59 seconds (59.96 Kbytes/s)
ftp> quit
221 Goodbye.
C:
```

In this case, the Gopher client software we want to download is stored in a "ZIP" file, which means the file actually contains a bundle of files encapsulated in a special format. To open the ZIP envelope and reveal all the files inside, you would use a tool called PKUNZIP, discussed later.

So far our examples have shown "line mode" FTP. This is still a common way to invoke the FTP protocol. But in this world of graphical interfaces, users demand a graphical FTP option, and vendors are beginning to answer. On the Macintosh, for instance, a tool called Fetch makes it possible for the user to scroll through a list of files on a remote FTP server just as one would scroll through a list of local files. Vendors of TCP/IP packages for the PC world are offering similar functionality. For instance, FTP Software's PC/TCP package now includes such an interface. If we were fetching the same file using that tool, the transfer would look like Fig. 9.3.

Tools sporting this sort of graphical interface use the same underlying FTP protocol as line-mode FTP, while providing services in a manner many users

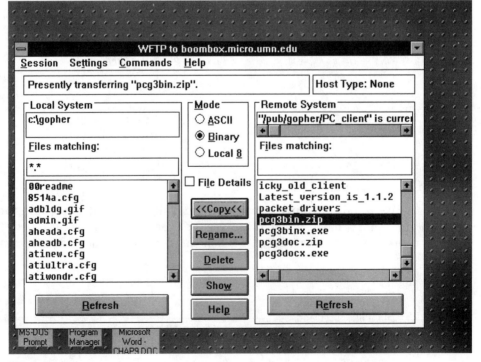

Figure 9.3

find far friendlier. With a graphical FTP client, you use mouse clicks to select the functions to perform and the files you want transferred. You are prompted to type in information such as the name of the server to connect to, and option-ally a different file name to use on your local disk. An advantage of this scheme is that the scroll bars allow you to review long lists of files easily; with the line-mode interface, a long list may not fit on your screen and you may have to type repeated "dir" commands to find the file you're looking for.

NOTES ON FILE NAMES

Both line-mode FTP and graphical interfaces allow you to limit the display of files using wildcards. In line mode, you might type:

```
dir gopher*
```

to limit the display to all files beginning with the string "gopher". Similarly, under the graphical interface, you can limit the display by entering `gopher*` in the dialog box labeled "Files matching."

Just as you can use wildcards to display file names matching a particular pattern, most FTP clients also allow you to retrieve multiple files based on such patterns. If you want to retrieve all the .XLS files in a directory, for instance, you might type:

```
mget *.xls
```

Note that file names on some systems are always uppercase, and on other systems may appear in mixed-case. If you are transferring a file named `read.me` but you type the command `get READ.ME` you will be told the file doesn't exist. You will have to retype the command using the name with case matching exactly. If you are moving mixed-case file names to an MS-DOS machine, the names will be translated to upper case as the transfer takes place—but you still have to type the correct mixed-case file name on the get command.

For unknown reasons, some FTP administrators like to use very long file names and odd mixes of case. You might see a file name like:

```
Comparison_of_Features_of_NeXTStep_and_SunOS_and_AIX
```

If you want to fetch such a file, you've got to type the name exactly correctly, including capitalization and placement of underscore characters. If you are using a graphical FTP client, you can point to the file name instead of typing it. Or, if you are able to cut and paste text on the screen, one easy answer is to paste the file name as displayed by `dir` into your command instead of typing it all out. Another trick is to use the `mget` command, typing enough of the file name to be unique, followed by the asterisk wild card.

Also note that the forward slash—"/"—is used to separate parts of hierarchical file names under Unix, which is the operating system used on most FTP servers. Microsoft chose the back slash—"\"—for this purpose in MS-DOS and in Windows. In FTP sessions, you will usually use the forward slash as a separator, even when fetching files to an MS-DOS computer. Of course, once files reside on your computer, you will use the Microsoft naming convention to work with them locally.

MAJOR FTP ARCHIVES

A large number of sites serve as archive sites on the Internet. Files offered can include software (both public domain and shareware), still images, data files, etc. Often a site's collection may be especially strong for a certain operating system or functional area. Here is a list of a few of the well-known archive sites.

Host name of FTP server	Name of institution	Strengths
wuarchive.wustl.edu	Washington University in St. Louis	Very complete collection of MS-DOS and Macintosh tools.
mac.archive.umich.edu	University of Michigan	Large collection of Macintosh tools
oak.oakland.edu	Oakland University	Large collections of Mac and PC tools, including mirrors of other FTP sites
sumex.stanford.edu	Stanford University	Very large Mac collection
nic.funet.fi	Finnish University network	Wide variety of tools, esp. image tools
archie.au	Australian Academic & Research Network	Mirrors of FTP collections for various computer platforms

Note that because these services are offered at no charge to an ever-growing universe of Internet users, limitations are sometimes placed on access. Some anonymous FTP servers refuse off-campus connections during prime business hours. Others limit the number of concurrent users that can connect; even when the limit is 400 or more, you may encounter times when that many others are already signed on.

Archive sites are increasingly offering services known as "mirrors." This simply means that they offer a verbatim copy of the files offered by another archive site.* This practice helps balance the load on network links and on archive server computers. It also provides redundancy, which is to say a backup option when a server or link is down. In many cases the entire directory structure of the mirrored site is preserved. For instance, if a site were to mirror the fictitious archive archive.probono.com they might place the entire directory tree of Probono's files online under the subdirectory /pub/mirrors/probono.

---

* Indeed, the site listed at Oakland University began as an archive of a venerable Internet FTP archive known as Simtel20. As of this writing that archive had lost its funding and its organizers were seeking a new home.

Some FTP archive sites also offer the same set of files via other media. For instance, the Sumex archive is available via Gopher. This can be more convenient for users of the archive, and actually presents a lower resource burden on the server, which in turn makes it possible to support more connecting users at once. You will want to read more about using Gopher in Chap. 12 to exploit this option.

FTP archive sites are appearing all over the world. Because international data links tend to be slower and busier than domestic ones, it's a good idea to locate an archive site in your own country and region whenever possible. Chapter 14 describes how a tool called Archie can be extremely useful in finding a particular file offered by a wide number of servers on the Internet; after using Archie for a while you will notice certain FTP sites that tend to offer the kinds of files you look for most commonly.

Various lists of anonymous FTP archive sites are posted in the Usenet News group `news.answers` and in the various Usenet subject areas. These documents, such as the `rec.music.info` FTP list, can be your index to a gold mine of information offered via this medium. Occasionally a more general list of FTP sites is also posted to `news.answers`.

REQUIREMENTS FOR USING FTP

The examples of using FTP shown thus far assume you are "on the Internet"— that you either have a direct connection to a local area network that is in turn connected to the Internet, or you are using SLIP or PPP to dial into an Internet service provider. Assuming you enjoy one of those styles of access, you can make use of the FTP client program provided with your TCP/IP software package; virtually all include FTP as one of the basic applications. With direct Internet access, you can use FTP to move files directly from a remote server to your workstation.

If you are not directly "on the Internet" you may be able to use FTP indirectly. For instance, a service provider offering conventional dial-up access may support FTP on the service's computer. You might be able to use a two-stage process, first using FTP to move files to your account on the service's computer, and then using a protocol such as Kermit or Xmodem to download the files over the telephone connection to your workstation. Although less convenient than direct exploitation of FTP, this two-step process allows you to avail yourself of the many anonymous FTP repositories on the Internet. This process is depicted in Fig. 9.4.

Some software and data files offered for anonymous FTP can be quite large; you obviously must have enough spare disk on your workstation to hold the files you download. Because many files are delivered in compressed archive formats such as ZIP, you may need considerably more spare space than the size reported for the original file in a `dir` display.

Using FTP over a Conventional Dial-Up Service

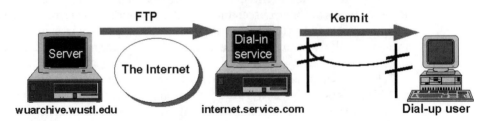

Figure 9.4

Note that many of the tools described in the remainder of this chapter are themselves available for retrieval via anonymous FTP. If your Internet service provider does not offer a local FTP archive, or if a particular tool you need isn't on that service, you will want to go to one of the well-known FTP sites, or use Archie to locate a nearby repository. Many of these tools will also be available on the software archives of dial-up bulletin board systems or mass-market information utilities; depending on the quality and cost of your Internet access, you might want to explore one of those avenues first.

USING FTP TO MOVE YOUR OWN FILES

Examples so far have shown how to retrieve files using anonymous FTP. You can use FTP to move your own files as well, either submitting files to anonymous FTP servers, or copying files of your own between computers on which you have appropriate authorization.

Anonymous FTP servers that accept submissions from the public often maintain a special directory called /incoming. To submit files to such servers, you sign onto the server in the usual way, whereupon you issue the command cd /incoming. For instance, if you are on the faculty of Mythical State University, and you want to submit a document for inclusion on the FTP service there, you might do so as follows:

```
ftp ftp.mythical.edu
Connected to ftp.mythical.edu.
220-Welcome to the FTP service at Mythical State University
Name (ftp.mythical.edu:rww) anonymous
331-Guest login ok, send e-mail address as password.
Password: bernoulli@boyle.physics.mythical.edu
331-Guest login ok, access restrictions apply
ftp> cd incoming
ftp> put physics.seminar.txt
200-PORT command successful
150-Opening ASCII mode data connection for /pub/index.txt (1234 bytes)
226-Transfer complete
local: physics.seminar.txt remote: physics.seminar.txt
```

```
1859 bytes sent in 0.08 seconds (20.07 Kbytes/s)
ftp> quit
221-Goodbye
```

The administrator of the FTP service might expect you to also send an e-mail message announcing your submission.

If you have your own account on two computers on the Internet, and you want to move files between them, FTP makes the job easy. For instance, a professor on sabbatical from Mythical State might want to retrieve a spreadsheet from his or her computer back home. If the computer is a multitasking server such as a Unix workstation—and if it is still running properly back in the home office—the user would simply open an FTP session and use the get command to retrieve the file. Similarly, the professor could use FTP to fetch files from the university mainframe (assuming the mainframe is connected to the Internet). For a user ID and password, the professor would specify the same ID and password normally used for work on that computer. All files that belong to that user name would become available once the FTP session is established.

If the professor's computer at Mythical State is running MS-DOS, the professor probably will have to get someone back at the home office to place the machine in a mode where it can function as an FTP server. For instance, under the PC/TCP package from FTP Software Inc., the user can invoke the ftpsrv command to accomplish this. Here is a session log from a machine acting as such a server:

```
C:\SHEET>ftpsrv
FTP Software PC/TCP FTPSRV Version 2.2 02/25/93 18:05
Copyright (c) 1986-1993 by FTP Software, Inc. All rights reserved.
Type `q' to abort; `?' for other commands.
debugging logging on                    [Enabled by typing "d"]
write-protect mode is enabled           [Enabled by typing "w"]
#1: Connection from 35.8.1.212, port 3181
#1:>>> USER wiggins
#1: User wiggins logged in at C:\SHEET
#1:>>> TYPE I
#1:>>> PORT 35,8,1,212,12,110
scanned port, got 35.8.1.212:12/110
port(): Got ip address 35.8.1.212, port 3182
#1:>>> RETR netgrow.xls
ftp_open_data(35.8.1.212, 3182)
active open on 35.8.1.212:3182
ftp_open_data() returns 0008
#1: Data connection closed
#1:>>> QUIT
#1: Closing connection to 35.8.1.212
Cleaning connection 1
Connection 1 cleaned
FTPSRV aborting at user request...        [Session closed by typing "q"]
C:\SHEET>
```

Note that in this example the operator immediately typed "d" to turn on "debug" logging of transactions, and then "w" to protect the local hard disk from unscrupulous users who might connect via FTP and store unwanted files or remove files maliciously.* The session log shows the activity of the remote user connecting to retrieve a file called "netgrow.xls". Here is the dialog from the point of view of the client side of the connection:

```
ftp wiggins.mythical.edu
Connected to wiggins.mythical.edu.
220-wiggins.mythical.edu PC/TCP FTP Server Version 2.2 by FTP Software ready
220 Connection is automatically closed if idle for 5 minutes
Name (wiggins.mythical.edu:wiggins): wiggins
230 User OK, no password, directory is C:\SHEET
ftp> bin
200 Using data type IMAGE
ftp> get netgrow.xls
200 Port OK
150 Opening data connection
226 Transfer successful. Closing data connection
local: netgrow.xls remote: netgrow.xls
3024 bytes received in 0.01 seconds (4.04e+02 Kbytes/s)
ftp> quit
221 Closing connection, Bye!
```

We have seen examples of how to move files between machines on which you are an authorized user, and how to retrieve files from and submit files to anonymous FTP servers. Chapter 21 provides an overview of setting up your own anonymous FTP server so that you can use this time-honored technology to serve information to other users on the Internet.

TEXT VERSUS BINARY-MODE TRANSFERS

In the example of retrieving a spreadsheet, the user typed the command binary, and the server responded that the file would be transferred in "image" mode. There are two basic modes of transfer for files sent via FTP: ASCII[†] ver-

---

* The FTPSRV option of PC/TCP also supports a password scheme. You should either disable writing to the hard disk, or invoke the password scheme, whenever invoking FTPSRV. If your machine is left open as an FTP server with no protection, eventually someone will compromise your data files. See your TCP/IP software documentation to find out how to secure your data while your computer is operating as an FTP server.

[†] ASCII stands for "American Standard Code for Information Interchange." The ASCII character set is pervasive on many types of computers, including personal computers, Unix computers, the DEC VMS operating system, etc. FTP implementations on IBM mainframes offer an EBCDIC mode, to specify that a transfer should take place in IBM's mainframe character set. Use EBCDIC when transferring between IBM mainframes; the default mode of ASCII will cause text files to be translated to/from EBCDIC when moving between an IBM mainframe and an ASCII host.

sus binary. In ASCII mode, sometimes known as text mode, the file is assumed to be simple text file. Because different computers represent text files differently, ASCII mode allows certain translations to take place as the data is transmitted. For instance, MS-DOS, Unix, and the Macintosh operating systems all treat the end of a line differently.* When you transfer a file in ASCII mode, the end-of-line is translated so that it will be understood by programs on a dissimilar receiving computer. By contrast, if you transfer a text file in binary mode between machines running different operating systems, you will probably find that the text appears to be one extremely long line of information.

You can specify that you want a file transferred in binary mode by the command `binary`; many implementations accept `bin` as an abbreviation. Alternatively, you can issue the command:

`type i`   for "image" or binary mode

or

`type a`   for "ASCII" or text mode

Binary-mode transfers are used to preserve the exact contents of a file, byte by byte. You would use binary transfer to move an executable version of a program from one MS-DOS machine to another, or even between machines running dissimilar operating systems if you know that the file can be understood on your machine. For instance, a software archive might well employ a Unix server but offer programs in .EXE format for MS-DOS users. Because the files are copied to the server in binary mode, and from the server to your MS-DOS computer in binary mode, the files are preserved exactly as they were created on the originating MS-DOS machine.

Binary transfer is appropriate for files such as spreadsheets because the internal layout of data in the file remains the same regardless of computer platform. Such files can be moved even between dissimilar computers. For example, it is possible to transfer and use a Microsoft Word document—or an Excel spreadsheet—between a PC and a Macintosh, because Microsoft has carefully adhered to the same internal formats for these files on either platform. Just as you could copy a .DOC file or a .XLS file to a floppy on your DOS computer for someone to read on a Macintosh, you and a colleague can share these files via binary-mode FTP.†

---

* Specifically, under MS-DOS both a carriage return (CR) and a line feed (LF) denote the end of line; under the Macintosh operating system a CR alone does so; and under Unix an LF alone does the job.

† Macintosh users should note that the special "Macbinary" option available to them should *only* be used among Macintosh users. This transfer mode causes a special "header" to be prepended to each file sent; a receiving Macintosh uses this header to determine information about the file transmitted. If you send, say, an Excel spreadsheet to an MS-DOS user with this header, the file will not be recognizable by Excel on the PC. Use generic binary transfer, not Macbinary, for such transfers.

Examples of files that normally ought to be transmitted in binary mode include:

File extension	Description
.XLS	Excel spreadsheet
.WK*	Lotus 123 spreadsheet
.DBF	Foxpro or Dbase database files
.DOC†	Microsoft Word documents
.EXE	MS-DOS executable files

† Unfortunately, Microsoft chose an extension for Word documents that is also commonly used for documentation text files on the PC. If you do not know whether a file you are downloading is in Word format, you will have to experiment (i.e., download the file in binary and feed it to Word; if Word rejects the file, try again by downloading in ASCII mode and viewing the file using a text editor).

In general, various image (picture) file formats call for binary-mode transfer, as do various formats for archive and compression; examples of these kinds of files appear in the following section. Perhaps surprisingly, files in the PostScript printer language generally should be transferred in ASCII mode. (PostScript is the highly popular language developed by Adobe Corporation and used on many laser printers.) Even though PostScript files can contain elaborate images, the PostScript language represents information in a textual sort of layout. Similarly, the Portable Document Format for PostScript, supported by Adobe's Acrobat family of products, was designed to survive ASCII mode transmission, whether via FTP or Internet mail.*

A MULTIPLICITY OF FILE FORMATS

Files are offered on Internet FTP sites (and on other archives on other networks) in a wide variety of formats. There are several different layers of formats to consider:

- The *internal format,* or type of the actual file(s) you want to retrieve. This defines what sort of file you are dealing with, whether it be a simple text file, an executable program, an image file, a sound file, etc.

- The type of *archive / compression* software that may be used to package a set of files into a compact bundle for transmission. In order to make files easy to transmit as a logical group, as well as to minimize transmission time through compression, a variety of file archiving schemes might be used. We have already mentioned the example of PKZIP, used in the PC world; other schemes include tar, common on Unix systems, and Stuffit, common on Macintoshes.

- The *encoding scheme* that may be used to allow a file to survive network transmission. The most commonly used scheme, derived from Unix practice,

* PostScript and the Portable Document Format are discussed in greater detail in Chap. 18.

is called uuencoding. Because FTP allows exact binary transmission, use of such encoding schemes isn't essential for FTP users. But you will encounter uuencoded files on some FTP archives, as you will when binary files are delivered via Usenet newsgroups or from some mail servers. Other common encoding schemes include BinHex (popular in the Macintosh world) and Base64 (adopted as the standard for MIME transmissions).*

All three of these file characteristics—the file's internal format, the archive compression type, and the encoding scheme—tend to imply file extensions that serve as mnemonics. Users of MS-DOS and numerous other operating systems are familiar with the use of extensions to describe file types—`.exe` means an executable program, `.bat` is a batch file, `.xls` is an Excel spreadsheet, etc. Extensions are also used to denote archive types—`.zip` refers to the PKZIP format, and `.sit` refers to the Stuffit format used on Macintoshes, and `.tar` refers to the Unix `tar` format. Finally, the encoding scheme is also often represented by mnemonic extensions—`.uue` for uuencoding, `.hqx` for BinHex encoding.

The concept of an archival program is quite simple: rather than forcing the user to download a large collection of separate files, a set of related files is gathered together and stored in a standard archive format. A user receiving the bundled file invokes the archive tool (sometimes a separately named program) to restore the original files on the local workstation. Use of such archival software is by no means limited to the Internet; other networks take advantage of such schemes, and in fact software vendors use archival/compression tools to save expenditures on floppy disks in software packages. Figure 9.5 depicts the file archiving concept.

An advantage of the use of archiving tools is that the creation dates of the component files are generally preserved as they are extracted from the archive. By contrast, when you use FTP to move files across the Internet, the date shown on the downloaded files is the date of the FTP transfer. It can be useful to be able to track the creation date of programs, for instance when trying to determine if you have a recent version of a tool.

In many cases, a file may go through both an archival/compression step and a subsequent encoding before it is made available for retrieval (whether by FTP or other means). Thus if you encounter a file whose name is:

```
image.sit.hqx
```

this means that the file has been compressed using the Stuffit program, and then encoded using BinHex.[†] You will need to invoke Binhex to decode the file, and Stuffit to extract the files stored in that archive format.

---

* The uuencode scheme is very widely used but it does not always create files that can accomplish their purpose: to survive transmission over Internet mail. This is because some of the characters used by uuencode can at times undergo irreversible translations as mail traverses a variety of hosts. Other schemes such as xxencode have arisen as a result. The growing popularity of MIME may in turn make Base64, which does not share this shortcoming, equally popular.

[†] It also probably means that the file was intended for use on a Macintosh (or if not, the provider has a Macintosh-centric view of the universe).

File Archiving Tools Allow Bundling of Multiple Files

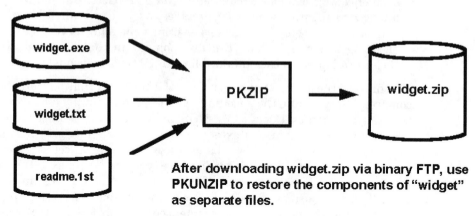

After downloading widget.zip via binary FTP, use
PKUNZIP to restore the components of "widget"
as separate files.

Figure 9.5

The Unix practice is to use separate programs for file archiving and for compression. Appropriately enough, compression is accomplished using a separate `compress` program, which labels the resulting files as `.z` files. If a file then is to be sent in text (ASCII) mode (for instance via e-mail) the file may also be uuencoded. For instance you might see a file name of the form:

```
next-gopher-client.tar.Z.uue
```

Here, a group of files that constitute a Gopher client package have been bundled into the tar format. The tar file has been compressed, adding the .Z suffix to the name; finally, the file has been uuencoded to allow it to survive text-mode transmission. Upon receipt, you would use `uudecode`, then `uncompress`, then the `tar` command (for instance `tar -xf next-gopher-client.tar`).

Usually files that are uuencoded will carry the .uue suffix, so the format will be obvious. Sometimes you will encounter files without such names, or you may receive a uuencoded document via e-mail or Usenet News. Here is an example of what a uuencoded file looks like:

```
begin 644 test.txt
M3$$@@+TPZ,#LQ++#OR,S@T("]3($,,Z77$$1/4UQ334%25$$125BY%6$$4-"D!%0TA/-
M($$&1@T*4*4T54($$))5$9!6%U#.EQ"251&05@@-"E!23TU05"`D<"1G#OI0051(H
[...lines omitted...]
M5$%,3"!!1$11%1"!,24Y%%$$,("T@14Y$$("HH#$$J*B$$H4!F5M(%1U$<FX@;9V9FW
M($$-A<',@3&]JC:RP@4VQU$$V0$$08VLL($$YU;2;!L;V,;V@:5Y<R`M+9+R96O9UOW
L=F4@@&\@3&==7=E-$$('!A9',-$$+%4FME=]6$@08V@4$!!-%%5%04UX4$14#OI4W
``
end
```

If you receive such a file as a part of an e-mail message, you should be able to take the parts between the "begin" and "end" lines (inclusive) and paste them into a separate file using a text editor. You then can decode the file using the uudecode tool available for your computer system.*

In the PC world, the PKZIP program[†] enjoys widespread use. Some archives use other formats for PC file archives, including ZOO, LZH, and even PC implementations of the Unix tar command. Copies of the nonregistered versions of such tools can be found on many anonymous FTP servers that offer MS-DOS utilities. PKZIP itself is shipped as a "self-extracting archive"—a program that, upon execution, extracts internally embedded files onto your hard disk. Thus you do not face the catch-22 of needing PKZIP to unlock PKZIP.[‡]

The permutations and combinations of internal file formats, archival schemes, and encoding formats may appear daunting. Fortunately, the range of options faced by any one user is quite a bit smaller than the full set of choices. When you encounter a document describing a program or data file available for FTP, the document will often include explicit instructions on how to fetch the program and complete the installation process. Also, most archives of files will contain a READ.ME or INSTALL.TXT file that includes hints on the detailed installation process. For instance, if you have downloaded the NCSA Mosaic for Windows package, you may want to examine the list of files before you unwrap the whole bundle. Here is the PKUNZIP command to list its contents:

```
C:\MOSAIC>pkunzip -v wmos20a4.zip

PKUNZIP (R)    FAST!    Extract Utility    Version 2.04g  02-01-93
Copr. 1989-1993 PKWARE Inc. All Rights Reserved. Shareware Version
PKUNZIP Reg. U.S. Pat. and Tm. Off.

_ 80486 CPU detected.
_ XMS version 2.00 detected.
_ DPMI version 0.90 detected.

Searching ZIP: WMOS20A4.ZIP

Length  Method  Size    Ratio   Date      Time    CRC-32    Attr  Name
------  ------  -----   -----   ----      ----    ------    ----  ----
  5525  Implode  2689   52%    09-28-93  17:33   cd86a2c1  --w-  INSTALL.TXT
  7392  Implode  2423   68%    10-17-93  18:23   b5f79d98  --w-  WMOSAIC.INI
1955076 Implode 909572 54%    10-17-93  17:58   c6491477  --w-  WMOSAIC.EXE
```

---

* Large files are often broken into parts when distributed in uuencoded form. If you reassemble them into a single file in order, you should be able to decode the entire package using a decoder.

† PKZIP is a shareware offering of PKWARE, Inc., 9025 N. Deerwood Drive, Brown Deer, WI 53223.

‡ The name of the self-extracting archive for PKZIP is of the form pkz204g.exe—the name changes with the version number.

```
    10880  Implode  5192  53%  10-17-93  17:45  7c64faec  --w-  WMOSAIC.WRI
   ------            ------  ---                                          -------
  1978873            919876  54%                                                4
```

After noticing that a file called INSTALL.TXT is present, you might want to extract that file by itself and read it before proceeding further. PKUNZIP allows you to extract a single file from the archive; for instance by issuing the command:

```
pkunzip wmos204a.zip install.txt
```

In order to extract all of the files stored within a ZIP archive, simply specify the name of the archive on the PKZIP command, omitting the second parameter.

The following table shows some of the common formats you may encounter at Internet file archive sites, and some of the tools that help you cope with them:

Extension	Name of scheme	Common tools (system)	Comments
.arc	ARC	ARC (MS-DOS)	Older scheme, less commonly used now
.arj	ARJ	ARJ (MS-DOS)	Fairly new, fairly common. Author: Robert Jung (Email: robjung@world.std.com)
.Z	Compress	compress (Unix) MacCompress (Macintosh) compress (MS-DOS)	Standard Unix tool
.lzh	LHarc	LHarc (Amiga) LHA (MS-DOS) MacLHarc (Macintosh) lharc (Unix)	Free of license limitations of many other schemes.
.shar	Shell Archive	shar (Unix) shar/unshar (MS-DOS) Shar/UnShar (Macintosh)	Unix Shell Archive format (actually both an encoding scheme and an archive scheme)
.zoo	ZOO	ZOO (MS-DOS)	Moderately popular tool. Author: Rahul Dhesi
.zip	ZIP	PKZIP (MS-DOS)	Extremely popular shareware tool Author: Phil Katz
.GZ (formerly .z)	GNU zip	GZIP (Unix, MS-DOS)	GNU project compression/archive tool. Becoming more commonly used. Naming convention caused confusion due to .z extension; .GZ is unique to GZIP

MULTIMEDIA FORMATS

When you turn on your television, you can tune to any channel without worrying about what format the channel will carry.* Someday we may see a ratio-

---

* Of course, even television standards are not universal—as tourists find when they bring home a PAL-encoded tape and try to play it on an NTSC television. The advent of High Definition Television will introduce new incompatibilities.

nalization of the multiplicity of formats used for still images, sounds, and motion pictures on various computer platforms. For now, to view a given file on your workstation, you either must have software that is capable of dealing with that file's format, or you must have a tool that can translate the data into a format that your computer can in fact handle.

The following table shows some of the formats for documents that you may encounter. There are many other formats besides the ones shown, some of which are proprietary to particular operating systems. Over time, old formats evolve and new formats are devised; refer to current FAQ documents for the latest information.

Name of format	Common extension	Comments
GIF	.GIF	Compuserve's Graphics Interchange Format™. Very Vpopular on various computers and operating systems. Includes a moderately effective compression scheme.
JPEG/JFIF	.JPG	A "lossy" compression scheme for still images; very effective with photographs; compression of 4:1 or even 10:1 is possible. Named for "Joint Photographic Experts Group."
Targa	TGA (also VDA, ICB, VST)	Format devised by Truevision for use with their video board, one of the first 24-bit (16 million colors) boards; now used to exchange high-resolution graphics among several packages.
Tagged Image File Format	TIFF	Implemented on numerous computers; supported by many image viewers. 24-bit format.* Files are large compared to other formats. Not all TIFF dialects work with all viewers.
Windows Bitmap	.BMP	A format native to MS-Windows. OS/2 supports a similar BMP file. "Wallpaper" files are exchanged in this format. Files tend to be large compared to other formats.
Windows RLE	.RLE	A compressed variant of Windows BMP.
Zsoft Image format	PCX	An image format developed by Zsoft Inc and used by a variety of graphics and desktop publishing packages.
X-Window Bitmap	.XBM	Image bitmap for X-Window.
PostScript	.PS	Adobe's printer language; commonly used with laser printers. Commonly used to deliver documents with layout, font changes, and diagrams/photographs over the Internet.
Encapsulated PostScript	.EPS	A form of PostScript file intended to be embedded ("placed") within other PostScript files.
Portable Document Format	.PDF	Adobe's format for exchanging PostScript across multiple platforms; created/manipulated/viewed via Acrobat tools.
WordPerfect Graphics	.WPG	The format for graphics files used by WordPerfect products.
Kodak Photo CD	.PCD	Kodak's format for storing photographs on Compact Disc ROMs.

Name of format	Common extension	Comments
MPEG	.MPG	A full-motion video standard using a frame format similar to JPEG with compression based on similarities across frames.
Audio Video Interleaved	.AVI	Microsoft's format for motion videos under their Video for WIndows standard; found on some CD ROMs (dialects of AVI include IBM's Ultimedia and Intel's Indeo).
Digital Video Interactive	.DVI	Another motion video format, also used on some CD ROMs.
Quicktime		Apple Computer's format for motion video, including sound. Popular in Macintosh world; also available for MS-Windows.
FLI	.FLI	Another motion video format (originated with Autodesk Animator).
GL	.GL	Another motion video format.
DL	.DL	Another motion video format.
Microsoft Waveform	.WAV	A sound format used in Microsoft Windows for event signals.
Sound Blaster Instrument	.SBI	Format used for a single instrument with Sound Blaster sound cards for the PC (multi-instrument format is .IBK).
8 KHz μlaw ("mulaw")	.SND, .AU	8-kilohertz (voice-grade) sound format commonly supported on workstation-class machines (Sun workstations, Nextstep, etc.).

* If an image file is "24 bit" it is capable of representing 16 million colors, which, combined with a high resolution display can produce high quality rendering of photographs on screen. That level of color "depth" is supported on some workstation-class machines and on newer video cards for PCs and Macintoshes. Such image files can be displayed on 16- or 8-bit displays but at a loss of quality.

The following chart lists some of the tools for viewing and manipulating various multimedia formats. Unless a tool is offered to the net as a public domain offering, you are generally expected to pay a shareware fee after a trial period.

Example viewers	Operating system(s)	Formats	Comments
Compushow (CSHOW)	MS-DOS	GIF, JPEG, TIFF, Macpaint, etc.	Good support for variety of PC video cards; better with some formats (GIF) than others (JPEG); shareware.
giffer	Macintosh	GIF	One of several shareware GIF viewers for the Macintosh.
xv	Unix/ X-Window	Wide variety	Very powerful tool for viewing and converting among formats; shareware.
Graphic Workshop	MS-Windows	Wide variety	Shareware viewer/format converter (Alchemy Mindworks).
Paint Shop Pro	MS-Windows	Wide variety	Shareware viewer/format converter (JASC Inc.).

Example viewers	Operating system(s)	Formats	Comments
DVPEG	MS-DOS	JPEG	Good JPEG viewer.
Xing MPEG	MS-Windows	MPEG	Works best with 24-bit video cards (shareware).
vfwrun	MS-Windows	AVI	Standard Microsoft tool.
Quicktime View	Macintosh, MS-Windows	Quicktime	Bundled with Macs, available commercially for Windows since mid 1993.
AAPLAY	MS-DOS	FLI	
GRASPRT	MS-DOS	GL	
DL-VIEW	MS-DOS	DL	Shareware from Italy; supports English & Italian command modes.
Sox	MS-DOS, Unix, Amiga	.snd, .au, .wav, etc.	Tool for converting among a variety of sound formats.

As you can see, some tools can handle multiple formats, and some tools are able to perform translations among various formats. If you intend to become an information provider, you may need to be able to view and manipulate a wide variety of image formats. Besides the tools listed above, you may want to obtain a family of tools called PBMPlus. Written by Jef Poskanzer, this package supports a wide variety of format transformations. Or, you may want to obtain a commercial image manipulation product; examples include Adobe's Photoshop and Aldus' Photostyler. Commercial drawing packages such as CorelDraw also have the ability to import and manipulate various image formats; a drawing package also provides powerful features for making diagrams, schematics, and artwork. Before you invest in an expensive commercial package, be sure it can import and export the formats you need to support.

Sound editors and multimedia authoring software are a rapidly advancing marketplace. Powerful tools are marketed for the experimenter and the professional. Multimedia software may also require an investment in specialized hardware if your computer was not delivered with such capabilities. You will want to survey current offerings before investing in such tools; sources of information include popular magazines such as *Byte,* specialty multimedia magazines, and online discussions in Usenet News.

FURTHER READING ON MULTIMEDIA

The set of tools available for handling multimedia is constantly changing, and the multimedia formats themselves also change over time. Fortunately you can find good information on multimedia formats in documents posted periodically to various Usenet News groups. You can find out very detailed information on formats and on available tools in these postings. Some documents to look for especially include:

Title	Author	Topics covered	News group*
Pictures FAQ	Jim Howard	Variety of picture formats	alt.binaries.pictures.d
JPEG FAQ	Tom Lane	JPEG/JFIF (still image format with efficient compression)	alt.binaries.pictures.d
MPEG FAQ	Frank Gadegast	MPEG (motion picture format)	alt.binaries.pictures.d
Audio File Formats	Guido van Rossum	Various audio schemes	alt.binaries.sounds.d

* Like most FAQ documents, these are generally posted periodically to the group `news.answers` as well; they are also often cross-posted to other news groups besides the ones listed.

Besides the Usenet News articles mentioned previously, you can track the evolving world of multimedia file formats by following the news groups `alt.binaries.pictures.d`, `alt.binaries.multimedia`, and `comp.multimedia`. The group `alt.graphics.pixutils` hosts discussions on picture manipulation tools. Trends in compression schemes are discussed in `comp.compression`, which also periodically carries a Compression FAQ file. The Usenet News groups that discuss various operating systems may also have relevant advice from time to time. The scientific community has some specialized formats of interest to scholars who exchange data over the Internet; see `sci.data.formats` for further information.

FTP MAIL SERVERS

A few organizations offer services that simulate the use of FTP for users who have e-mail-only access to the Internet. Princeton University offers such a service. Primarily intended for users residing on Bitnet, the service can be helpful for others who lack direct Internet access. To learn more about this service send e-mail to the automated mail server at:

`bitftp@pucc.princeton.edu`

The body of your message should be the word "help." You will receive instructions on how to submit batches of FTP commands as the body of subsequent e-mail messages. The BITFTP server will conduct an FTP session on your behalf and will send you the files by return mail, using the encoding scheme you specify. Large files will be split into several parts for your reassembly prior to decoding. A new master server is being deployed to allow sharing of load across multiple BITFTP services; it will accept the commands described in the help file and forward them to the server closest to you. The master server's address is:

`bitftp@bitftp.bitnet`

Digital Equipment Corporation offers a similar service. To learn more about it, send e-mail to:

`ftpmail@gatekeeper.dec.com`

The body of your message should be the word "help."

Note that these servers, like all Internet servers, are subject to occasional backlogs. If you do not receive a quick reply, be patient.

HINTS AND NETIQUETTE

- Be careful downloading files. Many versions of FTP will allow you to overwrite existing files without warning. It's best to use a new, empty subdirectory.

- Be careful extracting files. Some archive programs will warn you if you are about to overwrite existing files; some don't. Again, a clean slate is safest.

- Watch for viruses. Download from sites that are familiar. Periodically use virus detection software to make sure your files do not contain unwanted hazards. Be especially wary when you download executable programs from sites you aren't very familiar with.

- Where possible use an FTP server close to you—e.g., don't FTP from California to New Zealand when you know you can find a file closer to home. Overseas links tend to get saturated.

- Use your Gopher or World-Wide Web client program to download files instead of FTP, in cases where software repositories support this option. This approach can present less load to the site offering the service, and a better user interface for you.

- Don't use an e-mail FTP gateway if you have a more direct connection to the Internet. This will minimize load on such services and generally will provide you with faster results.

- If you are submitting large quantities of material to an FTP archive be sure you know what file format, archive scheme, and encoding scheme the site prefers. Also check with the site administrator before submitting large files; the disk space allotted for incoming files is often limited.

Real-Time Communication on the Internet*

Charles Henrich

The popularity of e-mail, mailing lists, and Usenet News shows that people want to communicate over the Internet. These media all operate on a store-and-forward principle; messages are sent via batch delivery mechanisms. In contrast, another mode of delivery, real-time communication, is not only possible, it is already being done on today's Internet. As direct access to the Internet has spread to many people, the ability to interact with other users in real time has become much more readily available. This chapter will explore some of the tools that support real-time communications on the Internet.

INTERACTIVE COMMUNICATION
AND THE INTERNET

The most basic example of real-time interaction is the Unix "talk" program. This program allows a user on one computer system to open a split screen session with a user on another computer system. Each person involved in the talk (maximum of two) can see what the other types. While talk is great for private

---

conversations and the like, no group discussions are possible. To establish a talk connection, a user on a Unix system would type:

```
talk username@internet.host.name
```

In order for the call to go through, the host being called must support the Talk service, and the user being called must be logged in. A user is notified that someone wishes to talk interactively with a message like the following:

```
Message from Talk_Daemon@crs.cl.msu.edu at 18:00 ...
talk: connection requested by henrich@smurfy.cs.berkeley.edu.
talk: respond with:  talk henrich@smurfy.cs.berkeley.edu
```

After the connection is established, a screen similar to that in Fig. 10.1 will appear on both users' computers. As each user types, text is displayed in separate parts of each user's screen: The remote user's text will appear in the bottom half of the window. The top half of the window displays text as typed by the local user. If you and a remote colleague are communicating via Talk, both of you can type simultaneously without fear of disrupting the other's messages.

Although a very basic form of communication, Talk can be a quite effective way to converse using text with someone who may be located hundreds of miles away or on another continent. Because the speed of discussion is limited to the rate at which humans type, the bandwidth requirements are extremely low.

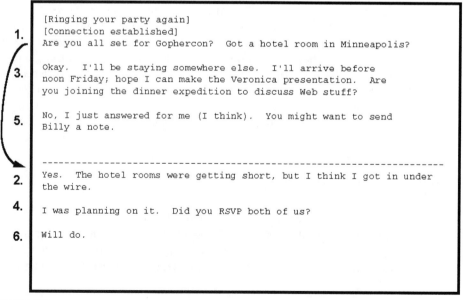

```
     [Ringing your party again]
1.   [Connection established]
     Are you all set for Gophercon?  Got a hotel room in Minneapolis?

3.   Okay.  I'll be staying somewhere else.  I'll arrive before
     noon Friday; hope I can make the Veronica presentation.  Are
     you joining the dinner expedition to discuss Web stuff?

5.   No, I just answered for me (I think).  You might want to send
     Billy a note.

     ---------------------------------------------------------------------
2.   Yes.  The hotel rooms were getting short, but I think I got in under
     the wire.

4.   I was planning on it.  Did you RSVP both of us?

6.   Will do.
```

Figure 10.1

INTERNET RELAY CHAT: WORLDWIDE
ELECTRONIC CB

The next step of real-time communication is made available with client-server programs such as Internet Relay Chat (IRC). IRC allows many people from around the world to communicate in a manner similar to Citizen's Band radio. IRC is divided into channels; conventions have evolved as to what topic of conversation corresponds to what channel. Because IRC can be rather anarchic, these conventions are not always honored. When you first start up an IRC client, you are asked what nickname you would like to use. From then on everything you say is prefixed by that nickname. To prevent people from "stealing" others' nicknames, there is a nickname server that stores a nickname, and a password for that name. So when someone tries to use that nickname, before it is issued, the user is prompted for a password. If the given password is incorrect, the nickname will not be granted, and the user will have to choose another.

When a user joins a channel, anything that is typed (excepting control commands) is displayed to all the other users who have also joined that channel. Channels are created when someone joins a channel that doesn't exist, and channels are destroyed when everyone has left the channel. Channels can be one of three basic types: public, private, and secret. Public channels are the most common, and are just that: public. Public channels show up in the channel list, and anyone can join and converse on them. Private channels, on the other hand, only show up on the channel list as "private" with no associated name. Unless you know the name of the channel, you cannot join it. Finally, there are secret channels. Secret channels do not show up on any list, nor do the users in the secret channels. Several other characteristics can be associated with IRC channels. Channels can be moderated; that is, only channel operators can talk on moderated channels. Channels can also be limited to a certain number of users. Finally, channels can be made "invite only"; that is, no one can join unless someone on the channel issues an invite command for you.

The first person to join a new channel is designated the "channel operator." The channel operator has several privileges made available. Channel operators can change all the parameters associated with a channel, such as the type, or whether or not the channel is moderated. Operators can also kick any user out of their channel.

IRC also makes available to its users the ability to send short, one-line messages to any other user who is connected to IRC.

Figure 10.2 is an example of an IRC conversation. The text window shows conversation between two Russian émigrés to the United States.

IRC is a very popular communications medium. At any given moment there are typically over one thousand people using IRC. Although IRC offers users the ability to talk in real time, it lacks an environmental context to promote sustained, meaningful dialogs. Conversation on IRC is equivalent to a CB conversation, where everyone speaks in monotone.

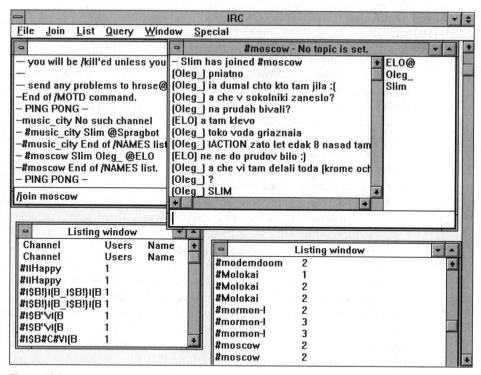

Figure 10.2

IRC documentation is offered locally by many Internet service providers. An IRC documentation archive is available for anonymous FTP from cs.bu.edu under /pub/irc. Look for the IRC Primer, and for the IRC Frequently Asked Questions document. The Usenet News group alt.irc carries relevant discussions.

MULTI-USER DUNGEONS

MUDs or Multi-User Dungeons* were created as a sort of automated dungeons-and-dragons game. A MUD can be viewed as a very low tech, mostly text only, virtual reality game. MUD has roots in various text-oriented games including the Adventure game that was popularized in the 1970s, as well as the Infocom games. In all of these games, when you enter a room you are presented with a textual description of the room and its contents, and a list of exits. However, while in your standard Infocom game there was only one

---

* The exact meaning of the acronym is not universally agreed upon; some claim the term is "Multi-User Dimension."

player (e.g., you), a MUD has tens of players interacting from all over the world in real time. MUDs serve as a way for users around the global Internet to play games; they also can provide some of the conversational environment missing in IRC.

There are several different varieties of MUDs with all sorts of funny names, from TinyMUDs to FurryMUCK's to Diku's to LPMuds. While each is very different, they all share common elements. The most basic of these common elements is the virtual environment. That is, when you first connect to a MUD you are standing in a virtual room. A room can contain other items, from players to bulletin boards to various objects. Rooms typically have descriptions and exits associated with them. For example when you first connect you might see:

```
The Diag
You are standing on the Diag of Metadelphia Universitat.
A holographic clock pulses in the air above you.
A small sign reads: Orientation -- 'press button' for guided tour.

Obvious exits: northwest, northeast, southwest, southeast, south, west

Crity the utter frosh is standing here.
```

This was the start room of Hero MUD, a MUD whose rooms were based on the campus of the University of Michigan. The beginning areas were laid out exactly as the campus. As a MUD user you have a variety of commands available to you; one of them is look. It does the predictable: it shows the rooms' description. However there may not be enough light to see by, in which case, typing look would get you something like "It's too dark to see." That could be remedied by finding a lantern, or other illuminating device. As well as look, you could type any of the standard directions to move to the next room. A powerful feature of MUDs is their ability to give users a feel for the surrounding environment, as well as giving users more than just a textual voice. For example, along with the standard command say, there are a variety of emotion commands. So a typical dialog could look something like:

```
>say Hiya Crity
You say: Hiya Crity
Crity asks: Hows it going?
>say Not bad, doing well in classes?
You ask: Not bad, doing well in classes?
Crity grins evilly.
Crity exclaims: Classes are just wonderful!
Crity rolls his eyes.
>say That good eh?
You ask: That good eh?
Crity nods.
```

and so on. So as well as the standard textual information, emotional information can be conveyed as well. This allows users to express various nuances of speech that would be much harder to convey with other communication media such as IRC. There are typically hundreds and hundreds of emotion commands available to the typical user. As well as that, some MUDs allow users to issue feelings that aren't normally available. For example, a user might type

```
emote runs up to you and shouts HI!
```

which would display "Crity runs up to you and shouts HI!" to everyone in the room. Usually these commands force your name into the message so that users cannot forge others' speech. As well as the ability to converse in real time, most MUDs provide bulletin boards and e-mail. Messages can then be left for others in both public and private forums.

MUDs fill a variety of roles on the net. There are MUDs that are set up exclusively as a place for folks to get together and chat, while others are set up for the serious gamer. An example of the more socially oriented MUDs is Tiny-MUD; a combat-oriented MUD is LPmud. These are server archetypes; for instance, there may be dozens of TinyMud servers at once. Other MUDs have the loftier goal of offering some sort of educational experience.

Gaming MUDs usually have real-time combat systems, skills, powers, weapons, armor, and other tools of conflict. Some Gaming MUDs aim to emulate realistic, strategic, combat-style board games where each player enters an action, which in turn leads to reactions on the parts of the monsters and other players. Other MUDs involve real-time combat. In real-time combat systems if you just stand there and don't do anything, the computer players and other players can continue to attack and kill you.

In some MUDs, such as LPmud, the ultimate goal is to reach the level where you are given the power to create new areas in the game. At this point you are titled a wizard, and are usually not allowed to interact with players in any way. Moving from novice* to wizard status grows progressively more difficult. As you kill other monsters, you gain experience; however, when you are killed you lose typically 25 percent or more of what you had gained, and are also penalized in other ways. To the beginning player that is not a serious concern, but as you reach the higher and higher levels, losing 25 percent can be an enormous setback. It can take as little as a day or two to reach wizard level, or as many as 10 or 14 days depending on how cruel the game administrators are.† So if you have been playing for 10 days of game time, and you die, you can lose 2.5 days of work. When you are at a point where 2.5 days of your life are at stake,

---

* A less diplomatic term for a novice is a "clueless newbie."

† Some players of these games do participate in sessions that last days on end; "day" in this context can mean 24 hours of active connect time.

adrenaline starts pumping. Dying is painful. As you fight and become hurt, you must heal. Healing in MUDs usually comes by getting drunk, and eating, and waiting to heal. Of course you must purchase the food and drink to consume. Like real life, in a MUD, money is obtained by chance, theft, murder, or hard work. Of course in some MUDs there are instant healing methods—such as going to a hospital—but these methods (as in real life) are usually expensive.

The best way to really get a good feel for a MUD is to use one. Most MUD players are extremely helpful to new players and will take a fair bit of time-out to show you around. A warning to all considering playing a MUD: MUDS are incredibly addictive. They take an enormous amount of time to play, and once entrapped it is mighty hard to stop playing.

The programs behind MUDs are becoming more and more complex. For example, the vast majority of MUDs out there allow users to utilize the standard Internet services of e-mail, FTP, Finger, Talk, Gopher, World-Wide Web, Usenet news, and so on. It is possible today to utilize these various Internet tools entirely from the comfortable MUD environment.

MUDs can be accessed via Telnet; but, as is the case with many Internet services, the best interaction is obtained when running a MUD client. To read more about MUDs, see the MUD hierarchy in Usenet News, including `rec.games.mud` and `rec.games.mud.announce`.

OTHER REAL-TIME RECREATION ON THE INTERNET

The Internet is the world's greatest sandbox, where everyone gets together and plays. From batch communications media such as recreational news groups to real-time gaming environments such as MUDs, the network is used extensively for fun. There are many other text and graphical games available to Internet users.

Empire. An incredibly complex, strategic warfare game played in real time over the Internet. If you like games of world domination and conquest, you will love Empire. The goal of Empire is total world domination. As a ruler of an empire you have total control over who produces what, who researches what, what your military does, and so forth. While the game affords you a sense of control over an empire, your fellow players want to see you killed. Interaction with Empire is via special client programs. The game is broken into turns, with a turn lasting as long as the update period. Depending on the pace of the game, updates can occur very frequently, as is the case with a "Blitz" game, or can occur only daily. There are both text-based and graphic-based clients for Empire. Empire is so complex that there is an abundance of clients that have automatic computer assistance of game play. Some clients even allow multiple people to play one empire, with each player managing only portions of the empire. Although some players take part without any form of computer assistance, this is incredibly difficult. Learning to play Empire is a daunting task that can take many, many hours of time.

The Internet Chess Server (ICS). A MUD that has been modified exclusively for chess playing. Two people on the net can meet in this MUD and set up and play a game of chess, while others can watch games in progress. Players are rated on how well they play. Games can be timed or not, penalties can be assessed for not moving within time periods, and the like. It implements a full regulation game of chess. ICS can display its output in one of two ways. The first is text-based, where a crude chess board is displayed on the screen using ASCII characters. In the second, a graphical client is used that has a graphical chess board, and manipulations can be done with the mouse instead of via the keyboard. Besides allowing chess games, the LPmud say and tell commands are also available.

Nettrek. A classic X Window fast-paced action game. In this game up to 16 players come together to battle it out over universe domination. The game starts off with up to eight players on each side. The game universe is divided into four quadrants with the Federation, Romulans, Klingons, and Orions each controlling a portion. To conquer a portion of the universe all the planets must be taken over by the attacking team. This is done by beaming down friendly forces onto the planet; of course before this can be done, all enemies must first be removed. There are many different options available to players, from the type of ship to use to the type of weapon. Statistics are kept on each player. As players get better and better ratings, they climb the ranks from lieutenant to admiral. The game is highly graphical, and is the doom of any mouse.

Xpilot. Another X Window action shoot-em-up type game. Players in Xpilot fly a classic Asteroids spaceship around the game world, while trying to avoid being shot down by players, robots, cannon, etc. This game also offers the peril of gravity: you might round a corner in the game world and be sucked into a wall. As well as offering the standard single-shot cannon, various weapons and other devices appear in the game world for players to enhance their spacecraft. One notable comment on this game is that the networking code has been extremely well written, so it is possible to play on servers located halfway around the world without too much penalty. This game is a definite must for fans of shoot-'em-up games. Figure 10.3 is an example screen from Xpilot.

Crossfire. Another highly graphical game that was originally designed for players on a local system. Recently it has been turned into a client-server game, where folks from all over the Internet can play simultaneously. Crossfire originally appeared somewhat similar to the arcade game Gauntlet where players run around and kill monsters with weapons that can be found or bought, or with magic that has to be learned. However, as the game matures, it is evolving from a free-for-all into a more sophisticated adventure game.

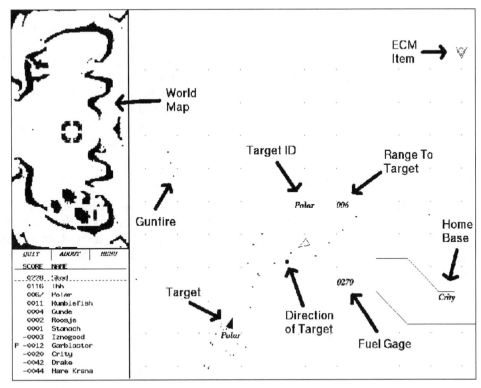

Figure 10.3

WHITEBOARD ENVIRONMENTS

In many corporate conference rooms and in some university classrooms, the melamine whiteboard has replaced the chalkboard as a medium for jotting down ideas in a group conversation. As the number of workstations capable of running and displaying graphical applications increases, so does the proliferation of whiteboard products. Whiteboard products attempt to simulate over the Internet the environment of whiteboard discussion in a real conference room. When you invoke a whiteboard application, typically you are asked the name of a whiteboard server to connect to. Once a connection is established you are presented with a whiteboard window. Each participant in the virtual meeting can use the mouse to draw sketches in the whiteboard. As each user draws, every other user connected to the server sees the updates almost instantly. In the whiteboard environment the user typically has the ability to draw arrows, lines, boxes, and circles by just clicking on the appropriate tool. The user also has the capability to draw freehand, and even type text into the whiteboard. Most whiteboard programs also have a "chat" window where collaborating members can type messages to each other.

The National Center for Supercomputer Applications (NCSA) has developed a product named Collage that provides whiteboard support for Internet users. Collage was initially developed to provide researchers with an easy-to-use data analysis tool. As part of this goal, NCSA added the ability for researches to collaborate on the analysis of data objects by allowing Collage group sessions. The primary collaborative features are a whiteboard where users can draw rudimentary pictures with a mouse or other input device, a Chat window for textual collaboration, and a text editor for textual composition collaboration. Figure 10.4 shows an example of a Collage session.

THE MULTICAST BACKBONE

The Mbone was developed by the IETF (Internet Engineering Task Force) to experiment with multicast transmissions of all sorts of data. The initial use of the multicast backbone was to broadcast live audio and slow-scan video of the IETF meetings around the world. The transmissions enable those interested in Internet engineering issues to observe meetings in progress in real time using the Internet as the delivery medium. The Mbone experiment

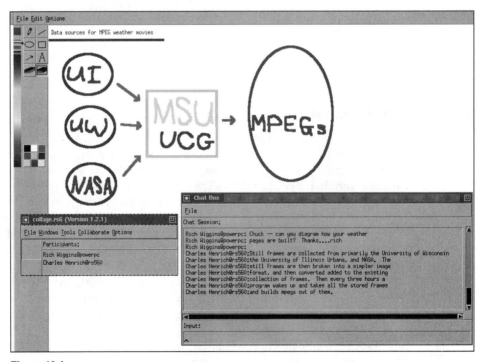

Figure 10.4

began in 1992, and continues to serve as a way to test the concept of audio/video transmissions over the Internet while accomplishing a useful broadcast function.

Audio is broadcast in a voice-quality resolution (8-kilohertz sampling) and video is broadcast with frame updates several times per second. One strategy used in Mbone broadcasts is to include two slow-scan subchannels along with the audio feed. By aiming one camera at the speaker, and another at the overhead projector or whiteboard, the Mbone broadcasters can convey a live meeting in a surprisingly effectively manner.*

Figure 10.5 shows one of the two video channels in an Mbone broadcast from an IETF meeting. In the background of the photograph you can see the meeting room and the participants whose images appear on the computer monitor.†

To view Mbone broadcasts you need to install a modified operating system on your workstation, and run special software developed by various folks from around the net. The necessary operating system modifications are available for Sun, Silicon Graphics, and some other workstations. The Mbone is a "multicast" medium: special routing software provides a mechanism for Mbone data to be "tunneled" over the Internet for delivery to those places where users have "tuned in" for Mbone multicasts. Because of the highly specialized nature of the Mbone, you should contact your Internet service provider for information as to how and whether you can receive broadcasts. An Mbone Frequently Asked Questions document and archives of an Mbone mailing list can be found via FTP to `venera.isi.edu` in the `/mbone` directory.

AUDIO ON DEMAND OVER THE INTERNET

Numerous sites have offered audio documents over the Internet. One of the most prominent is the Internet Talk Radio (ITR) project of the Internet Multicasting Service. ITR seeks to bring professional quality radio to listeners with appropriately equipped workstations over Internet links. Programming has included interviews with leading Internet technology figures, rebroadcast of National Press Club luncheons and various public radio programs, and, most recently, a series of voices of historical figures through a joint arrangement with the publisher HarperCollins. Listeners can use Mosaic or other client pro-

---

* In a live presentation, most of the time it is the case that neither the speaker nor the presentation materials changes very much. A human stands and makes occasional gestures; an overhead transparency usually stays on the screen for quite some time before it is changed.

† This photograph was taken in the general session meeting room of the IETF in Columbus, Ohio, on April 1, 1993. The speakers shown are representatives of the organizations that make up the InterNIC, announcing its operations commencing as of that date. Photograph by Richard Wiggins.

Figure 10.5

grams to fetch documents, which are normally offered in an 8-kilohertz μlaw format (commonly associated with .au or .snd files). ITR began "broadcasting" in March of 1993.

Generally speaking, ITR is not a real-time medium; instead, the listener fetches files from one of several mirror sites when the user wants to listen.

Depending on the client program and audio browsing software, the audio files are either staged on the client workstation's disk, or played in real time as they come across the network. Program segments are often 20 to 30 minutes long, and the resulting audio files take about one-half megabyte per minute. Listeners may start a program playing on the workstation, then move on to other work as if listening to a local radio broadcast in real time.

Although ITR generally offers prerecorded material instead of real-time broadcasts, its founder, Carl Malamud, has arranged various demonstration projects that make use of the Mbone network in order to simultaneously multicast in real time. These demonstrations take place under the Internet Town Hall and Internet Talk Radio rubrics. On May 21, 1993, ITR offered a simulcast of National Public Radio's "Talk of the Nation" program. The program was heard by NPR listeners across the United States, and also was heard by listeners endowed with Mbone access around the world. Files were also archived for "regular" ITR listeners to retrieve later. This demonstration proved the concept of offering real-time audio over the Internet.

Another pioneer in bringing radio to the Internet is the Canadian Broadcasting Corporation. Working with partner agencies in Canadian government and industry, the CBC is offering samples of its radio programming for retrieval over the Internet. As with ITR, most of CBC's offerings to date have not consisted of real-time applications, but technology such as the Mbone would allow them to undertake real-time programming as ITR has done. Figure 10.6 shows the beginning of an online description of the CBC service; connect to this page over the World-Wide Web for more information.*

VIDEO ON DEMAND OVER THE INTERNET

The alliances of various cable television companies with telephone companies in the United States has sparked discussion of the idea of "video on demand" services. Rather than offering a fixed number of channels, and expecting viewers to pick among the programs that happen to be scheduled at any given instant, video on demand would allow the viewer to select what program he or she wants to see at any given time. Visionaries expect that cable companies will operate vast automated movie libraries, using robots and optical disks. When a user makes a selection, the program of choice is loaded for playback, and the audio and video are sent in digital form over fiber and/or coaxial cable to the viewer's house.

---

* See Chap. 13 for information on using the World-Wide Web to fetch such documents. You will use the "Document URL" shown here to specify that you want to retrieve this document.

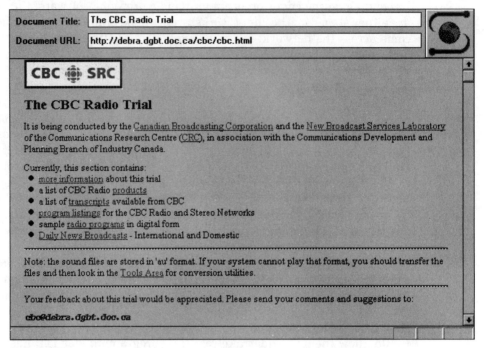

Figure 10.6

In today's Internet, there is a growing amount of multimedia material available for viewing on demand. In contrast to the bandwidth required for television (especially for high-definition television), most of these multimedia documents are offered at relatively low resolution with small image sizes. Information providers who offer multimedia demonstration projects over the Internet are generally sensitive to the possible logjams that delivery of multimedia images might cause, so they limit the size, resolution, and duration of the video images they offer. However, as available bandwidth increases, multimedia applications will arise to exploit it.

The Telemedia, Networks, and Systems Group at the Massachusetts Institute of Technology is offering an example of a multimedia demonstration project that shows how video on demand could be ordered via World-Wide Web. They offer snippets of live television as being displayed on several television monitors on the MIT campus. The number of simultaneous connections is limited so as to minimize network bandwidth consumed. The video and audio are captured and delivered in real time. Images are delivered via X Window drawing operations; therefore, viewers must use X terminals or X-capable workstations. A Web client such as Mosaic is used to "order" the video feed desired; the

A MOTHER'S FACE
APPEARS ON A TELEPHONE

Control Panel   Program

Dismiss

Figure 10.7

television server then writes directly to the user's X server screen using X primitives. Resolution is relatively low, and frequency of update can be tailored by the user to an appropriate value given the speed of intervening network links. Figure 10.7 is a window showing a frame from a Cable News Network television program as delivered by the MIT service, reprinted with permission.

Pioneering audio-on-demand and video-on-demand projects have paved the way for audio/video teleconferencing via the Internet. In early 1994 Cornell University released a tool, called CU-SeeMe, that allows Windows and Mac users to engage in such conversations. (For details, FTP to `gated.cornell.edu`.)

Network and Internetwork File Systems*

Charles R. Severance

This chapter deals with network and internetwork file systems which allow data to be read and written with appropriate security across the Internet. Most of the network services discussed thus far, including Gopher, World-Wide Web, FTP, and others, allow you to share data with others on the Internet in a read-only fashion or read-write with very simple security controls. In addition, to access the data across the network the user must use a special client program such as FTP, Mosaic, or Gopher.

Networked and internetworked file systems allow data from a remote system to be read and written across a network using the same interface as data which is stored on the local system. The purpose of a networked file system is to make the fact that the data must be accessed across a network transparent to the user.

The difference between a network file system and an internetworked file system is the type of network interconnection between the clients and the servers. Typically the interconnection for a networked file system is a local area network (LAN) and covers a limited geographic area. The interconnection for an internetworked (or distributed) file system is a metropolitan area network (MAN), wide area network (WAN), or the Internet.

With an effective distributed file system you could begin working on a demonstration using a desktop workstation in one location, get on a plane and continue working on the demonstration on a portable computer, and when you land at your destination actually perform the demonstration using customer equipment. (See Fig. 11.1.) Using an effective internetworked file system, it would not be necessary to use a floppy disk or explicitly transfer any data over a modem or network.

Another advantage of a worldwide distributed file system is the ease of exchanging data with other users. An example of sharing data using an internetworked file system might be the following mail message:

```
To: peter@rice.edu
From: crs@msu.edu
Subject: The visualization Data

I stored the results of the visualization run in the file

/afs/msu.edu/user/crs/vis/data4

Give it a try and let me know if this is what you want
/crs
```

If the remote users were on a Unix system, they could use a simple command to copy the data on their systems across the Internet to their home directories, such as:

```
cp /afs/msu.edu/user/crs/vis/data4 ~/data4
```

An MS-DOS user might access the same data using:

Figure 11.1 Internetworked file system.

```
copy e:\afs\msu.edu\user\crs\vis\data4 c:data4
```

A user with a Macintosh computer could open the folder labeled "AFS Data," enter the appropriate subfolders, and use the mouse to drag the data4 folder onto their desktop.

While these seem like fanciful concepts, distributed file systems currently exist which allow these types of operations across worldwide networks.

CHALLENGES OF INTERNETWORKED FILE SYSTEMS

There are many network file systems, ranging from very simple to very complex. To be a true internetworked file system, the following problems must be addressed:

- The data transport protocol must be able to use a wide-area network protocol (e.g., TCP/IP, OSI TP4, X.25) efficiently.

- The management and security of the file system must be distributed and must be scaled to millions of users and millions of servers. A single central management and security scheme is unacceptable.

- The system must have robust security and be protected from hacker attacks.

Many networked file systems can be internetworked to varying degrees, but all have limitations in these areas.

The remainder of this chapter will cover networked file systems ranging from extendable LAN-based systems to the current best technologies for internetworked file systems. In addition, the future directions of internetworked file systems will be discussed.

LOCAL AREA NETWORK FILE SYSTEMS

When people talk about network file systems, they typically are referring to local area network file systems. These local area network file systems include products such as:

- NOVELL Netware
- Apple Filing Protocol (AFP)
- Banyan Vines
- LANTastic

These file systems evolved in a truly local-area-networked environment. The typical environment was a small number of personal computers with a few servers at a single location. Security features were simple or nonexistent because the network was not accessible to anyone except the people with physical access to the systems. The network was never shared with 100,000 undergraduate computer science students bent on gaining access to the data. When security features were provided in these products, they were typically designed based on a work-group model.

These local area network file systems tend to have limited application as internetworked file systems because of shortcomings in all three areas mentioned previously. The basic transport protocol used by these networked file systems is not a wide area network transport protocol. Each of the vendors evolved their own proprietary transport protocol (e.g., Novell's IPX). Most internetworks do not route any of these protocols across the internetwork.

Figure 11.2 shows how user workstations share resources such as servers and printers on a typical LAN.

The solution that allows LAN file systems to use Internet connectivity is a technique called tunneling. Tunneling allows two or more local area networks to be connected using virtual point-to-point connections across the internetwork. The server's proprietary packets are encapsulated in a packet that can be used on the Internet and forwarded across the Internet to another server which removes the Internet headers and places the packet on a local area network.

Tunneling can be done with most local area network protocols. A large number of servers can be linked together using tunneling to form a wide area file system made up of multiple, geographically distributed file servers.

Even with the tunneling ability, the configuration and management of the clients and servers must be coordinated. It is hard to imagine that all of the users in the world would be willing to participate in a large Novell network with accounts and configuration managed by some central authority. The system administration and security do not scale to internetwork sizes.

An example setup of the configuration shown in Fig. 11.3 might use the following Novell commands on server 128.7.14.3:

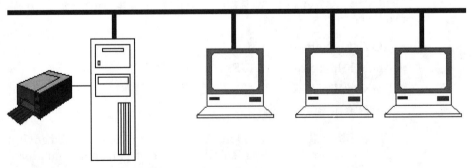

Figure 11.2 Typical Networked File System.

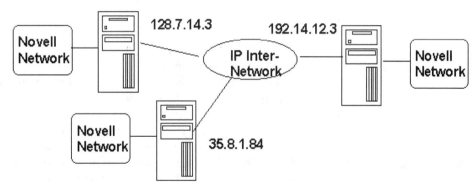

Figure 11.3 Typical Tunneling Setup (Novell over IP).

```
LOAD IPTUNNELL PEER=35.8.1.84 LOCAL=128.7.14.3
LOAD IPTUNNELL PEER=192.14.12.3
```

The reason that these Internet links must be set up explicitly for each pair of servers is that the Novell IPX protocol relies on "broadcast" packets. IP does not support true broadcast packets. (If it did, it would probably be unusable as an internetworking protocol.) When server 128.7.14.2 receives a broadcast packet on the IPX network, it must send the packet through each IP tunnel to the remote server which rebroadcasts the packet on their respective local IPX networks.

An important aspect of these local area network file systems which use tunneling to cross the internetwork is that individual clients do not typically exchange data across the internetwork. Data from one workstation is routed to its local server which forwards it to a remote server across the net. The remote server may forward the request to yet another server.

NETWORK FILE SYSTEM (NFS)

NFS is a network file system which was developed in the late 1980s by SUN Microsystems and added to its SUNOS operating system (a version of Unix). NFS was initially designed and is still primarily used as a local area network file system. NFS has one advantage over the other local area network file systems: NFS uses IP as its transport protocol. Because of this, tunneling is unnecessary, and NFS traffic can be routed directly across the IP-based internetworks. Using IP for the NFS protocol allows NFS clients to communicate with NFS servers directly across the Internet without having to pass through intermediate servers.

SUN Microsystems published a standard describing the protocol used for NFS and placed the standard in the public domain (RFC-1094). Publishing the protocol specification has allowed other vendors to easily implement compatible versions of NFS which could interoperate with the SUN version of NFS. By making NFS readily available to other vendors, SUN insured that there would be a wide range of implementations from multiple vendors.

NFS is well-integrated into most Unix-based systems. On most Unix systems, NFS is delivered as part of the base operating system. Some Unix systems will automatically install and configure NFS for a client-server network. Many users of Unix are using NFS without being aware of it.

Any system can be used as an NFS client or server or both with simple configuration changes. To configure a system as a server, the system administrator indicates the areas of the disks which are to be accessible to the network attached clients. The configuration of the data "exported" from the server is typically stored in the file /etc/exports. An example exports file is as follows:

```
/usr/man      -ro
/home/steve  -access=bongo.stfs.com
```

Different portions of the disk can be exported with different access controls. In the previous example the data in /usr/man (and all the data in directories below /usr/man) is exported read-only to the world. The directory tree /home/steve is exported to the system bongo.stfs.com with read-write access.

To access the data in /home/steve on the system ibis.stfs.com, the system administrator would have to type the following commands:

```
mkdir /usr/usrs/steve
mount ibis.stfs.com:/home/steve /usr/usrs/steve
```

Figure 11.4 shows how a file system can be shared under NFS. The mount command associates a network file system with a local path. Note that it is not necessary for the local name to be the same as the remote name. Network mounts which the system administrator wants to occur at system restart time are typically placed in a file such as /etc/fstab. Once the mount has completed successfully, the data in /usr/usrs/steve can be accessed on the client system just as if it were a local disk.

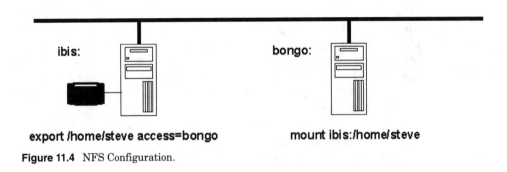

export /home/steve access=bongo   mount ibis:/home/steve

Figure 11.4 NFS Configuration.

While NFS is well-integrated and easy to use, it was still designed as a local area network file system and has problems scaling into an internetworked file system. These problems are in the area of data security, data protocols, and system administration.

NFS security is a simple extension of the Unix file system security. In Unix each file is owned by a single user. The file system tracks the ownership of a file based on an integer number called the user identification number or UID. Although this number is often displayed as a symbolic name, it is still stored internally as a number. This mapping between the internal UID number and symbolic name is typically stored in the file /etc/passwd on Unix systems.

When system A exports a file to system B, the UID numbers on system B are used to control the access to the files stored on system A. On most Unix systems the system administrator (root) can set the UID to any number, allowing system administrators of a client system to access any file across NFS which has been exported read-write to their system.

Exporting data through NFS allowing read-write access to a system which cannot be trusted is a possible security hole. In an internetworked environment, it is dangerous to trust the administrator of a remote system. NFS is not effective for broad sharing of read-write data in an internetworked environment. Secure NFS adds additional authentication which solves this particular security problem. Even with Secure NFS, significant coordination between clients and servers is still necessary for sharing read-write data.

The security configuration of NFS for multiple systems can be coordinated centrally using the Network Information Services (NIS). An earlier version of NIS was called "yellow pages" or "YP." NIS allows multiple systems to share a common security configuration. Unfortunately, NIS requires cooperation among all the systems in a network to trust a central security authority.

While NFS does not have sufficient security to operate in a general internetworked environment using read-write data, it can be very effective in an enterprisewide environment where a central security authority may be less of a problem.

Even though the NFS protocols are based on IP transport protocol, NFS data protocols are not well suited for internetworked environments. A number of messages must be exchanged between the client and the server each time a file is accessed or a block of data is read. Because so many packets are exchanged between the client and the server, the longer latencies of an internetworked environment can significantly impact the perceived response time of an NFS file system in an internetworked environment. Compared to other schemes, NFS can be relatively slow over busy, long-haul Internet links.

INTERNETWORKING WITH NFS

NFS has been used with some success to provide publicly readable information on the Internet. For instance, the University of Wisconsin makes its public domain archives available via NFS in addition to FTP. Using NFS is much more convenient than FTP because you can simply access data from the server using standard commands normally used to access local data on your system. However, unless your system has excellent network connectivity to the University of Wisconsin, NFS transfers may not work well.

The following is an example of a file system entry for a typical Unix system to access these archives using NFS:

```
wuarchive.wustl.edu: /archive /archive nfs ro,noquota,soft,intr,bg,noexec 0 0
```

Because of the security limitations of NFS, this kind of internetworking is effectively impossible with read-write data.

DISTRIBUTED FILE SYSTEMS

In a sense, the largest problem for true internetworked file systems is one of security. For an internetworked file system to be acceptable the security must have the following attributes:

- The security must not require central administration.

- Each administrative organization must be able to completely control its own security configuration. The security administrators must not be required to trust any services which are not under the complete control of the organization.

- The security must scale to millions of users without any changes in architecture.

- The security must be robust enough that it can withstand hacker attacks.

ANDREW FILE SYSTEM (AFS)

AFS is the first true distributed file system. AFS provides full file system semantics transparently across an internetwork. Unlike NFS, AFS security is based on individual users rather than on systems and system administrators.

History of AFS

The Andrew File System was developed at Carnegie Mellon University starting in 1984. The idea was to provide a campuswide file system for home directories which would run effectively using a limited bandwidth campus backbone network.

In 1989 the Transarc company was formed to evolve the Andrew File System into a commercial product. Transarc renamed the product from Andrew File System to AFS. In 1990 the Open Software Foundation (OSF) chose AFS from

Transarc as its Distributed File System (DFS) component of its Distributed Computing Environment (DCE).

AFS architecture

When a user logs into a client system and begins to access the data, AFS copies the user data from the server disks to local client disks. Further reads and writes access the copy of the data stored on the local disk. Using local disk whenever possible minimizes the number of accesses to the data which have to travel across the network. This local caching of the data also allows a single server to support many more clients because many data accesses never need to contact the server at all.

The AFS file system allows data from many different security domains to be integrated into a single distributed file system. Unlike NFS, AFS does not require a single point of control for security.

The AFS file system is broken into security domains called "cells." Each cell can consist of one or more servers. Within a cell, the security configuration is controlled by the administrator of the cell. Each client system can access data on as many cells as it has access to. A client may choose to associate itself with one particular cell as its default cell. (See Fig. 11.5.)

Configuring an AFS server

In AFS the servers are typically dedicated systems which do not allow general user access. The setup of a server is somewhat complicated and the user should refer to the AFS installation documentation.

Configuring an AFS client

One problem with setting up an AFS client is that AFS does not typically come preinstalled on any operating systems. The steps in installing the AFS client soft-

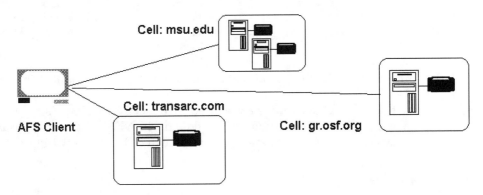

Figure 11.5 AFS cell architecture.

ware are described in the Transarc documentation. Some sites have site licenses for the AFS clients and those sites may have a special installation procedure.

When you are setting up an AFS client, you must configure the client with a list of the cells which will be accessed by the client. This configuration is typically done in a file such as `/usr/vice/etc/CellServDB`. An excerpt of this file might look as follows:

```
>citi.umich.edu          #Univ. of Mich - IFS Development
141.211.128.99           #babble.citi.umich.edu
>math.lsa.umich.edu      #University of Michigan - Math Cell
141.211.60.13            #bull.math.lsa.umich.edu
>gr.osf.org              #OSF Research Institute, Grenoble
130.105.64.9             #barere.gr.osf.org
>transarc.com            #Transarc Corporation
158.98.3.2               #ernie.transarc.com
>msu.edu                 #Mich. State Univ. home cell
35.8.2.70                #afs0
35.8.2.71                #afs1
```

When a cell has more than one server, the client will attempt to contact the other servers when contact is lost for one of the servers in the cell. CellServDB controls which cells appear as part of the client file system hierarchy and the names which are used by those cells. File names in AFS typically start with the path `/afs/` followed by the cell name. For example, to see the root-level directories at the `osf.gr.org cell`, one would type the command on any client system.

```
% ls -l /afs/gr.osf.org
drwxrwxrwx   3 agent        2048 Nov 13  1992 /afs/gr.osf.org/common/
drwxrwxrwx   3 root         2048 Jul  9 08:20 /afs/gr.osf.org/i386_osf10/
drwxr-xr-x   2 agent        2048 Feb 24  1993 /afs/gr.osf.org/library/
drwxrwxrwx210 root          4096 Aug 12  1991 /afs/gr.osf.org/localroot/
drwxrwxrwx210 root          4096 Aug 12  1991 /afs/gr.osf.org/release/
drwxrwxrwx210 root          4096 Aug 12  1991 /afs/gr.osf.org/tools/
drwxr-xr-x   2 root         2048 Jun 15 05:12 /afs/gr.osf.org/users/
drwxrwxrwx210 root          4096 Aug 12  1991 /afs/gr.osf.org/vice/
%
```

In addition, the client sets the default cell using the file named `/usr/vice/etc/ThisCell`.

Even though a client is associated with a cell by default (similar to a client associating with a particular NIS domain in NFS), the security relationship between the AFS client and AFS server can either be very tight or very loose.

AFS security

In order for a user to access read-write data on the servers which make up a cell, an account is required. The account name, number, and password of the server may be completely different from the account name, number, and password on the client system. In addition, a single user may have accounts in several cells. There is no need to coordinate the user names, numbers, or passwords between cells. Each cell can create or delete users independently.

Basic AFS access

In the simplest case (the typical case will be described later), when users log in, they have no access to any nonpublic AFS data on any cell. For each cell they want to access, they must provide authentication for that cell using the `klog` command. In the following example, the users will log into a client system and then `klog` into several cells.

```
login: crs
Password:                       <- Local client password
You have new mail.
Coming in as vt100
% klog severanc -cell msu.edu
Password:                       <- msu.edu cell password
% klog msuacc -cell transarc.com
Password:                       <- transarc.com password
%
```

At this point, the users can access the data that belongs to them in the cells `msu.edu` and `transarc.com`. Without the `klog` commands, the servers would not allow access to the data in those cells. With these `klog` commands and proper passwords, the servers will allow access to data from any network-connected client.

The tokens command shows which cells you currently have authenticated:

```
% tokens

Tokens held by the Cache Manager:

User's (AFS ID 103) tokens for afs@msu.edu [Expires Sep  3  11:12]
User's (AFS ID 993) tokens for afs@transarc.com [Expires Sep  2 14:16]
%
```

An AFS token is a security key which is used to ensure that the proper user is accessing the data. In addition to the token, a time stamp is also transmitted to the server. Both the token and time stamp are encrypted before they are sent to the server. Thus an intruder cannot copy a message from the network and "replay" it at a later time because the time stamp in the copied message would be incorrect and the message would be rejected. These security tokens are only valid for a certain length of time (typically 25 hours).

The client stores the authentication token for each cell and uses the appropriate authentication token when communicating with each cell.

Typical AFS access

Typically, when a client is configured, the users will have a local cell which they use regularly. It would be inconvenient to have to klog every time the users log in to their client system so the system can be configured to perform the klog automatically as part of the standard log in process. In this case the account name on the client must match the account name on the local AFS server. At login, the users type their client/server account name, followed by their server password. If the server password is correct, then the user is both logged in and authenticated for the local cell automatically. For example:

```
login: severanc                        <- client/msu.edu cell account
Password:                              <- msu.edu cell password
You have new mail.
Coming in as vt100
% tokens
Tokens held by the Cache Manager:
User's (AFS ID 103) tokens for afs@msu.edu [Expires Sep  3 11:12]
% klog msuacc -cell transarc.com
Password:                              <- transarc.com password
% tokens
Tokens held by the Cache Manager:
User's (AFS ID 103) tokens for afs@msu.edu [Expires Sep  3 11:12]
User's (AFS ID 993) tokens for afs@transarc.com [Expires Sep  2 14:16]
%
```

Once the user has logged in and been authenticated to the local server, additional cells can be authenticated manually using klog. When the client is configured in this fashion it behaves much more like a traditional Unix system.

While the tight integration of the client and server is very convenient, using the server password to log into the client has the disadvantage that the security administrator can change a user's server password and gain access to the client system. The local server administrator is one of the least likely persons to attempt to break into a client system. Sites with high security requirements can configure their clients to have separate login passwords from their AFS passwords as in the first example.

AFS protocols

The AFS data protocols use IP so AFS packets can be routed directly over many internetworks. There are many features of the higher-level protocols of AFS which make AFS a much better system for a distributed file system in an internetworked environment.

These features include:

- File-oriented transfers with variable block sizes
- Client caching of directories and data

- Server tracking of client cached data
- Distributed administration and security

In most networked file systems, data is transferred across the network whenever an application reads the data or opens a file.

In AFS, when an application on a client system opens a file, AFS copies a relatively large portion of the file from the server to the local client disk. Further reads and writes of the data are done using local disk rather than to the server. It is quite common to get many complete files into the client cache and not require any network traffic for simple operations. If a file is modified, the changes are sent back to the server when the file is closed or when the local cache fills up.

The AFS server maintains a list of which files each client has cached to maintain file consistency. For example, if one host opened a file and read it completely, it would be completely stored in the client cache (assuming reasonable sizes). Once the file is closed, the file remains in the local cache until the client runs out of space. However, if another client wants to open the file for write, the server will "call back" the first client and instruct it to discard the cached copy of the file.

In this way, a client can keep data cached for long periods of time and be assured that unless it has been notified by the server, the cached copy is correct.

Given that most data on a typical server is not being modified continuously from many clients, this caching technique with server callback results in less network bandwidth when a client has a reasonably sized cache. A good example is when "home directory" data is used regularly on a single workstation day after day and is accessed from no other systems. After some time, nearly all of the active data will be resident in the local cache of the workstation. Because the data can be accessed locally, network accesses will be minimized and the file access will be effectively the same performance as locally attached disk.

Experiments have been performed with modified versions of AFS where a portable workstation connected to a network accesses all of the data in some directory, loading it into the cache on the workstation. Then the workstation is disconnected from the network and the data is used, modified, and edited using the cached versions with no network connection at all. At some later time, the portable workstation is reconnected to the network and any file updates are sent back to the server.

AFS administration

In a worldwide file system with thousands of servers, each administered by a different organization, and hundreds of thousands of clients, system administration is a very important issue. AFS has some features that begin to address these issues.

The most important system administration feature that AFS has is that the physical location of data is transparent to the user and the client configuration.

Each cell has a server called the volume location server. When a client wants to open a portion of AFS space, it contacts the volume location server and the volume location server tells the clients which server and which disk on that server hold the data.

The advantage of this technique is that data can be moved transparently among servers within the same cell. Data can be moved from one physical disk to another even while it is being accessed by the clients.

AFS allows the system administration to add new servers, add new disks, or reorganize existing disks and servers with no impact on the client configuration or users.

AFS shortcomings

A shortcoming of AFS is the inability of AFS security to permit access to a file directly to an individual user of a different cell. Each user will need an account on each cell the user wants to access secured data as in the previous examples. While AFS security has some limitations, it is sufficient to provide a reasonable security environment for an internetworked file system.

Also while the distributed authentication for AFS is very secure the data is transferred without encryption. Data encryption was not included because it would have a significant impact on AFS performance.

In addition, because AFS was designed for an internetworked environment, there are some applications which are better suited for a LAN-based network file system. These are applications which have one or more of the following features:

- Multiple simultaneous clients writing data in a single file
- Multiple clients reading large files randomly

AFS works best when only one client has write access to a file because of its caching techniques. While this is seldom a problem with user "home directory" data, database applications require this type of access.

Database applications will also generate a lot of small read operations on a large file. AFS will often transfer too much information to the cache for these small reads. In addition, this data will seldom be reused, so the additional step of copying it onto a cache disk is unnecessary.

For LAN-wide database applications, a network file system like NFS or Novell should be used.

An internetwork-wide database application with access to read-write data is a very difficult problem to be solved. It is unrealistic to expect that an effective solution for an internetwork file system would also solve the problem of an internetwork database system.

OPEN SOFTWARE FOUNDATION DISTRIBUTED COMPUTING ENVIRONMENT (OSF-DCE)

In the implementation of several of these networked file systems, the developers created a number of general distributed computing tools including:

- Remote Procedure Calls
- Distributed Security
- Accurate Distributed Time Services
- Multithreaded Application Support

These distributed computing services were produced to solve the problem of implementing a networked file system. However, many distributed applications (such as database) need these services much like a distributed file system. Unfortunately, the developers of these file system products did not make these services available to other application developers. A notable exception is Sun Microsystems which made the Remote Procedure Call (RPC) services used to implement the NFS file system available to application developers.

The goal of the Distributed Computing Environment (DCE) from Open Software Foundation (OSF) is to develop these distributed computing tools with standardized interfaces.

The Distributed Computing Environment (DCE) has been completed for some time and is widely available on a number of platforms ranging from OS/2 to Unix to IBM MVS.

OPEN SOFTWARE FOUNDATION DISTRIBUTED FILE SYSTEM (OSF-DFS)

In addition to the distributed computing tools, the Open Software Foundation is using these tools to implement a distributed file system (DFS).

DFS is based on AFS with a few extensions. The primary improvement of DFS over AFS is the use of the standardized Distributed Computing services. DCE/DFS will also have security improvements over AFS such as finer grain security, cross-cell authentication, and data encryption.

The Distributed File System (DFS) portion of the project is nearing completion and some people expect that it will be widely available sometime in 1994.

CONCLUSION

Many different technologies can be used to create wide area networked file systems. They offer the user the ability to access files across networks like the Internet as if the user and his or her data were physically adjacent. The challenges of building a truly distributed file system are very difficult. The AFS file system is an example of the potential of a distributed file system but there are improvements which need to be made. Distributed file systems and distributed computing are still evolving. In the next several years the Open Software Foundation Distributed Computing Environment and Distributed File System products should advance the quality and usability of distributed file systems.

# Chapter 12

Gopher: Internet Browser and Document Delivery Tool

The Internet Gopher was conceived at the University of Minnesota in 1991. In less than two years, Gopher moved from conception to prototype to Internet-wide deployment. As of this writing the number of registered Gopher servers exceeds 1000 and continues to grow rapidly. Our tour of the Internet in Chap. 2 featured the basic use of Gopher; this chapter will explore the history of Gopher, how to use client programs to enhance your experience with Gopher, and some of the inner workings of the Gopher protocol.

GOPHER'S ORIGINS

Computer center staff at the University of Minnesota began discussing the need for something like Gopher in early 1991. They wanted an online mechanism for "publishing" hints on computing services at the university. Mark McCahill, project leader for the group that developed Gopher, says the goal was to find a scheme that was more efficient than one-to-one consulting or conventional handouts and short courses. At the time, another group at the university was proposing a mainframe-based solution for campus document delivery. The group designing Gopher wanted a simple, network-based scheme that supported browsing of available documents. They also wanted to build a service that was fun to use so that a critical mass of users would develop.

The developers' earliest discussions produced a goal of a simple protocol—easy to understand, describe, and implement. They decided upon a client/server model: a client would open a TCP connection to the server, request specific information, receive and display the information, and disconnect. The initial model called for only two document types: text files and folders (subdirectories). Thus, from the beginning, the developers envisioned a mechanism that would deliver lists of files and directories upon request. The client/server model would provide for sessions lasting only long enough to deliver that list to the user's client software. These aspects of the Gopher model have endured.

The design team held their first serious meetings during the first week of April 1991.* The goal was to build a working prototype that could readily be discarded; the team assumed that whatever they produced might be replaced by something better within a year. By late April, prototype Gopher clients and servers were working. Initially, there was a Macintosh client and server, a Unix client and server, and a PC client. The developers decided that some sort of search mechanism was also needed. They also decided Gopher should support telephone directory searches, and they settled upon the CSO telephone directory search protocol, already in use at numerous universities, as the best way to implement online phone books.

These different document types—text, folders, and CSO and other index searches—would be sufficient to define a Gopher that could deliver documents stored on a single server. But, from the start, the protocol allowed a server to point to another server as the physical home of a given document. This allows a Gopher to include services that may be scattered across the Internet all in one list. It also makes possible a directory of other Gophers, any of which is a keystroke or a mouse click away. But the developers thought about providing ways to connect to existing external database servers on campus, such as a university's online library catalog. They decided to include a document type that was itself a Telnet session to another host computer. To round out the collection, a document type for transferring Macintosh or PC binary files was included. The original protocol was designed to be extensible; the one-byte, data-type field could potentially support 255 different data types. A draft Gopher protocol specification was released in spring 1991.

Delivery of sound via Gopher was born during the early development phase. One weekend the team member doing most of the server code, Paul Lindner, wanted to hear some music in his office, which is several rooms away from the

---

* The original Gopher team included Farhad Anklesaria, Paul Lindner, Daniel Torrey, Bob Alberti, and Mark McCahill. Torrey implemented the MS-DOS client, and Bob Alberti wrote the first Unix curses client. Anklesaria wrote the initial server and the Macintosh client. Lindner developed the initial Unix server code. McCahill set up the first index server using the Nextstep Digital Librarian tool on the Next and assisted with early development of the Macintosh client. Recent work on TurboGopher (the Macintosh client) has been done by Dave Johnson; additions include foreign language support.

communal CD player. His Next workstation was capable of playing sounds, and there was a CD player available on a workstation in another room. A few hours later he had implemented the sound data type, and Gopher was capable of playing music across a real-time Internet link.

The first production Gopher services were in place at Minnesota by late summer of 1991. Gopher was announced to the world via the campuswide information systems mailing list (`cwis-1@msu.edu`). A Usenet news group, `alt.gopher`,* was started. Computer system administrators from around the Internet began to learn about Gopher. The code was made available for others to try, and Gopher servers began popping up in various places. By early 1992, Gopher was no longer a prototype but was becoming a tool of choice as universities sought ways to implement campuswide information systems.

GOPHER CLIENTS

The example Gopher sessions in Chap. 2 used the "public" client, which provides a simple full-screen, nongraphical interface for incoming Telnet users. When you run a Gopher client program on your workstation, you benefit from a superior user interface and often from enhanced ability to access nontextual documents such as image files. Gopher clients have been implemented on a variety of platforms. Common clients include:

- *PC Gopher III.*   The University of Minnesota's PC client which was written using Borland's TurboVision. It provides a quasi-graphical interface complete with mouse support. PC Gopher is a relatively large program; more recent releases have used memory more efficiently. A multipurpose client, Minuet, has supplanted PC Gopher.

- *UGOPHER.*   A PC client from the University of Texas Medical School at Houston. It is a port of the Unix curses client. It provides a very simple interface, but it demands little memory. It supports special data types such as TN3270, still-image files, and sound files.

- *Novell LWP client.*   A PC client from the University of Michigan Medical School. This client works with Novell's LAN Work Place for DOS. It supports images and audio as well as TN3270. It sports a friendly graphical interface with more options than the standard client.

- *TurboGopher for the Macintosh.*   A Macintosh client from the University of Minnesota. Various Mac Gopher clients have been developed independently but TurboGopher appears to be efficient and robust. TurboGopher handles a variety of document types. TurboGopher was the first client to implement the Gopher+ extensions described later in this chapter.

---

* Since supplanted by `comp.infosystems.gopher`.

- *WinSock Gopher.*   Another client for MS-Windows, WinSock Gopher was written by Dave Brooks of the Idaho National Engineering Laboratory. Unlike HGopher, WinSock Gopher opens a new window for each new document or menu. A pull-down menu option called "Recent" allows you to quickly jump to previous points of your journey. HGopher and WinSock Gopher require a TCP/IP implementation that supports the WinSock standard.

- *HGopher.*   A Windows client by Martyn Hampson of Imperial College in the United Kingdom. This client supports the Gopher+ extensions, increasing its ability to cope with a wide variety of file formats.

- *Curses client.*   A generic client for Unix workstations. It is also used at many Gopher sites to provide Telnet access to the Gopher world for users who haven't yet obtained client software for their workstations. Users installing the curses client on their Unix workstations must build the client from source code on the target machine (as is commonly true with Unix software offerings). A version of this client can also be compiled for use under the DEC VMS operating system.

- *Nextstep Gopher Client.*   A Nextstep client from the University of Minnesota and the University of St. Thomas. This client makes good use of large windows: it leaves the last two or more menus on the screen, providing useful context as to where you are in the Gopher hierarchy.

- *Xgopher.*   A client from the University of Illinois* that runs under X-based Unix systems. (The X release must be later than X11 Release 3.) Xgopher supports multiple active items and an easy-to-use graphical user interface. It is highly configurable.

- *Rice University CMS Client.*   A client that allows users of VM/CMS mainframes to connect to Gopher servers.† The host must be connected to the Internet and must have outbound VT-100 Telnet to function well when connecting to Unix-based services. (The IBM 3270 terminal protocol does not lend itself well to outbound connections to byte-oriented hosts; check with local support personnel to determine if such access is available at your site.)

- *MVS Gopher Client.*   A client from Draper Laboratory for TSO users on MVS mainframes.‡ Like the CMS client, his client can provide users connecting to mainframes via 3270 terminals with access to Gopher services.

- *OS/2 client.*   This client runs under IBM's OS/2 operating system.§

---

* Written by Allan Tuchman.

† Written by Rick Troth.

‡ Written by Steve Bacher.

§ Written by David Singer of IBM Almaden.

Figure 12.1 is an example of what a Gopher menu looks like with a graphical Gopher client. The client in this case is HGopher, which runs under MS-Windows. As you can see, each document's title is shown on a line by itself. An icon at the beginning of each title line depicts the type of the document; in this example, the first document is a text file, the second is a subdirectory (i.e., it is another menu of documents), and the third is an index search document. Most Gopher clients offer some sort of "item information" option, allowing you to look up the specific location information for a given document. HGopher will display such information if you point the mouse at the document's icon and invoke the "info" option; in this example, the dialog box at the bottom of the screen shows the location information for the last document, "Network and Database Resources."

Figure 12.2 is an example of what the same Gopher menu looks like as presented by TurboGopher, the Macintosh client from the University of Minnesota. Below the root menu is a panel showing the text of the first item in the menu, which the user has selected by pointing the mouse at the title and clicking.

Figure 12.3 shows the interface presented by IBM's OS/2 Gopher client. The basic ideas are the same, but the icons used are somewhat different.

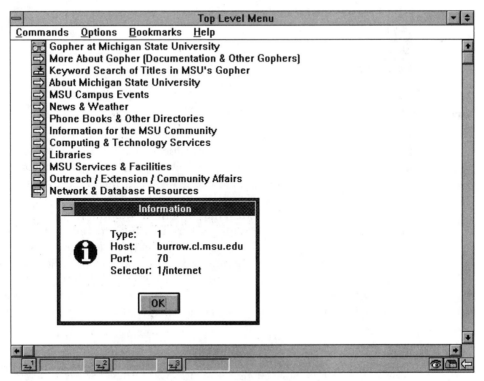

Figure 12.1

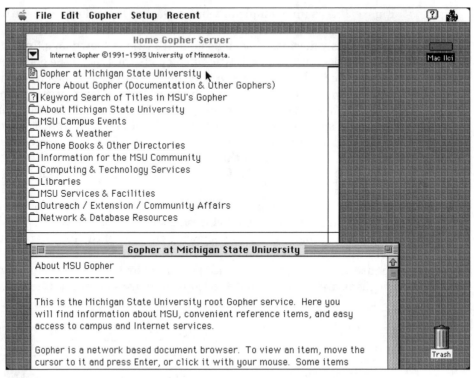

Figure 12.2

Common features of Gopher client programs

Gopher clients vary in appearance and features, but their basic tasks are similar: to present to the user the hierarchical menu of documents, and to fetch and display documents as the user selects them. Among the various client programs and the computer platforms, the form in which a document is displayed may vary considerably. Ultimately, the information is the same, even though the display format varies. (Marshall McLuhan would have a field day.) Besides display variations, there are also differences in features among clients. Most clients allow the user to save a selected file to local disk for external purposes; this makes it possible for Gopher to deliver complex documents or even executable computer programs.* Some clients allow the user to print an entire document. With the PC client, the document goes to a locally attached printer; a Unix client might assume its printer is a PostScript device, which might be

---

* At least one software archive encourages its users to obtain software via Gopher instead of anonymous FTP. (The Stanford University Macintosh archive, Sumex, suggests users choose Gopher over FTP or other methods.)

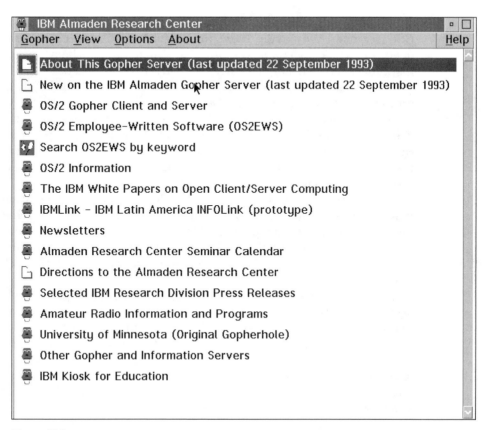

Figure 12.3

connected over the local Ethernet. Finally, some clients allow the user to send a document via e-mail to the destination of choice.

Gopher clients need a way to display files on the user's screen. Some clients may contain such capabilities as an embedded part of the client program. Alternatively, the client may launch an external tool, often called a "viewer" or a "pager." For instance, UGOPHER has a relatively limited built-in viewer. The user can install a superior file display tool, such as the popular shareware tool LIST from Vernon D. Buerg, and tell UGOPHER to use it instead. Windows clients are likely to use the Notepad to display text files. If you want to view a GIF image, display a PostScript document, or listen to an audio document, it's likely that your client will have to rely on an external tool appropriate to the task.*

---

* The advantage of this division of labor is that the Gopher client need not incorporate all the possible viewers for all the possible document types. This would make the client program unacceptably large and cumbersome to maintain. Moreover, as new document types evolve, you can easily upgrade external viewers as needed.

Similarly, clients may launch separate programs to open Telnet sessions, do CSO searches, play audio files, and so forth. The user must install all the needed external tools and configure the client to use them. Instructions on installing such external tools are provided with every client.

Many Gopher clients sport the useful feature of "bookmarks." Upon finding an item of particular interest, the user sets a bookmark. The client software stores the bookmark on the client workstation's disk. In a later session, the user can call up the list of bookmarks and immediately jump to items of particular interest without having to navigate the menus. Because resources of interest could be buried deep within Gopher servers, the bookmark option lets the user build a customized view of Gopherspace.

The HGopher client for Microsoft Windows supports the creation of bookmarks; it even allows you to organize your bookmark files hierarchically. This allows you to create your personal view of Gopherspace, organized as you see fit. For the Gopher user this ability to customize is almost like running one's own Gopher server.* Figure 12.4 shows an example of creating a bookmark entry under HGopher.

As is the case with many Internet applications, the original Gopher design assumed that the user's workstation would be connected directly to the Internet, with a permanently assigned IP address, and client software would reside on each workstation. This model does not always provide dial-up users (users dialing in over a phone line using asynchronous ASCII terminal emulators) with the same level of service as on-campus users receive. Many Internet service providers are experimenting with schemes to allow dial-up users to appear to be directly connected, using protocols such as SLIP (Serial Line IP) and PPP (Point-to Point Protocol).[†]

Under SLIP or PPP, the user can run a standard Gopher client, which works as if it were on a local TCP/IP network. Of course, data is delivered more slowly; even today's high-speed modems don't match local area network speeds. Because these dynamic IP assignment schemes are relatively new and they are not widely used, traditional dial-up users must usually rely on the public curses client.

Obtaining a Gopher client via FTP

Most of these clients are offered for anonymous FTP at `boombox.micro.umn.edu`. If you cannot locate one of these clients at that location, you may want to consult

---

* Some Gopher users have chosen to run local Gopher servers merely to allow themselves to have their own customized view of Gopherspace. Running one's own server has the advantage of making it possible for others to connect to your server to see your "bookmarks" as well as any original files you might have stored on the server. If your server is a workstation that allows inbound Telnet, you can also access your personal Gopher hierarchy over the Internet when you are away from your workstation. See Chap. 21 for details on setting up your own Gopher server.

† In fact, the University of Minnesota itself has been an aggressive leader in deploying SLIP service for its campus community.

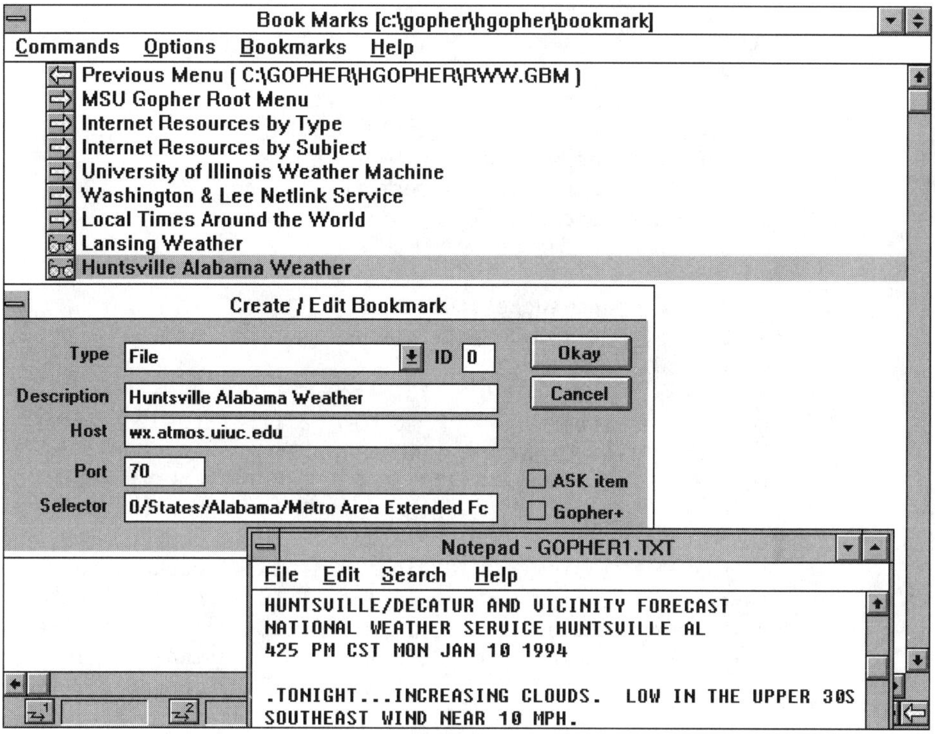

```
┌─────────────────────────────────────────────────────────────────┐
│ ─        Book Marks [c:\gopher\hgopher\bookmark]          ▼  ▲   │
│ Commands   Options   Bookmarks   Help                            │
│    ⇦ Previous Menu ( C:\GOPHER\HGOPHER\RWW.GBM )              ▲  │
│    ⇨ MSU Gopher Root Menu                                        │
│    ⇨ Internet Resources by Type                                  │
│    ⇨ Internet Resources by Subject                               │
│    ⇨ University of Illinois Weather Machine                      │
│    ⇨ Washington & Lee Netlink Service                            │
│    ⇨ Local Times Around the World                                │
│    ◙ Lansing Weather                                             │
│    ◙ Huntsville Alabama Weather                                  │
│ ┌────────────────────────────────────────────────────────┐      │
│ │ ─               Create / Edit Bookmark                  │      │
│ │                                                         │      │
│ │      Type │File                     ▼│ ID │0│  ┌─Okay─┐ │      │
│ │                                                │      │ │      │
│ │ Description │Huntsville Alabama Weather    │   ┌Cancel┐ │      │
│ │                                                │      │ │      │
│ │      Host │wx.atmos.uiuc.edu             │            │      │
│ │                                                         │      │
│ │      Port │70      │                  □ ASK item        │      │
│ │                                                         │      │
│ │  Selector │0/States/Alabama/Metro Area Extended Fc│ □ Gopher+ │
│ │ ┌────────────┬──────────────────────────────────────────┐    │
│ │ │            │ ─      Notepad - GOPHER1.TXT       ▼  ▲   │    │
│ │ │            │ File  Edit  Search  Help                  │    │
│ │ │            │ HUNTSVILLE/DECATUR AND VICINITY FORECAST ▲│    │
│ │ │            │ NATIONAL WEATHER SERVICE HUNTSVILLE AL    │    │
│ │ │            │ 425 PM CST MON JAN 10 1994               ▼│    │
│ │ ┌─┬──────────┤                                           │    │
│ │ │←│          │ .TONIGHT...INCREASING CLOUDS.  LOW IN THE UPPER 30S │
│ │ │⌐1│   ⌐2│   │ SOUTHEAST WIND NEAR 10 MPH.            ⇦  │    │
└─────────────────────────────────────────────────────────────────┘
```

Figure 12.4

the Usenet news group `comp.infosystems.gopher`, or the archive of that group, available via Minnesota's Gopher service (`consultant.tc.umn.edu`, port 70). Most Gopher clients are offered freely to the Internet community; at least one commercial product, WinGopher, has been announced by Notis Systems Inc.

Note that many organizations offer their own archives of Gopher clients, in many cases configured appropriately for local use. For instance, the client might be preconfigured to point to the local Gopher server rather than connecting by default to "Gopher Central" at the University of Minnesota. Local network support staff at your site should be able to advise as to the best archive location for you to use.

The following is an example of obtaining the University of Minnesota's client for MS-DOS. It assumes that the user has a copy of the PKZIP file compression tool.

Example FTP session to download
a Gopher client

```
C:\GOPHER: ftp boombox.micro.umn.edu
Connected to boombox.micro.umn.edu.
```

```
Connected to boombox.micro.umn.edu.
220 boombox FTP server (Version 4.1 Tue Apr 10 05:15:32 PDT 1990)
ready.
Name (boombox.micro.umn.edu:rww): ftp
331 Guest login ok, send ident as password.
Password:wiggins@msu.edu
230 Guest login ok, access restrictions apply.
ftp> cd pub/gopher/PC_client
250 CWD command successful.
ftp> dir
200 PORT command successful.
150 Opening ASCII mode data connection for /bin/ls (0 bytes).
total 1352
-rw-r--r--   1 bin           385 Apr  1 15:43 00readme
-rw-r--r--   1 bin             0 Mar 22 17:22
FTP_THESE_FILES_IN_BINARY_MODE
-rw-r--r--   1 bin         75376 Apr  1 15:43 bmkcvt.exe
-rw-r--r--   1 bin          2151 Apr  1 15:43 bmkcvt.txt
-rw-r--r--   1 bin           370 Apr  1 15:43 gopher.bmk
-rw-r--r--   1 bin        182910 Apr  1 15:43 gopher.exe
-rw-r--r--   1 bin         75711 Apr  1 15:43 gopher.ovr
drwxr-xr-x   2 bin           512 Mar 22 17:29 icky_old_client
-rw-r--r--   1 bin           643 Apr  1 15:43 manifest.101
drwxr-xr-x   2 bin           512 Mar 22 17:29 packet_drivers
-rw-r--r--   1 bin         41929 Apr  1 15:43 pcg3.txt
-rw-r--r--   1 bin         62341 Apr  1 15:43 pcg3.worddoc
-rw-r--r--   1 bin        211699 Apr  1 15:43 pcg3.zip
-rw-r--r--   1 bin          2999 Apr  1 15:43 release.101
226 Transfer complete.
838 bytes received in 0.31 seconds (2.66 Kbytes/s)
ftp> bin
200 Type set to I.
ftp> get pcg3.zip
200 PORT command successful.
150 Opening BINARY mode data connection for pcg3.zip (211699 bytes).
226 Transfer complete.
local: pcg3.zip remote: pcg3.zip
211699 bytes received in 6 seconds (34.47 Kbytes/s)
ftp> quit
221 Goodbye.
C  gopher: pkunzip pcg3
```

At this point, the client software is on your PC's disk. Your copy of the client program may require some configuration before you can make use of it. At a minimum, you may want to supply the address of your local Gopher server as the primary host to connect to. Depending on the client program and on what sort of TCP/IP package you are running, you may also need to provide the client with other information, such as the address of the local Domain Name System server. If the correct answers for these values are not obvious to you after reading the documentation, ask your Internet service provider for assistance. In the case of the Minnesota PC client, you can run the client with both commercial TCP/IP packages (such as FTP Software's PC/TCP) or with public domain packages. You invoke the Minnesota PC client by typing "gopher"; configuration options are specified via a pull-down menu. Future sessions do not require configuration (unless you want to change a setting, for instance to choose a different default Gopher server).

USING YOUR GOPHER CLIENT

Once the client is installed, you can use it to navigate Gopherspace just as we used the public "curses" client during our tour in Chap. 2. Graphically oriented clients will let you select documents with the mouse if you prefer that over use of the cursor key. The hierarchy of each Gopher server works the same way no matter what sort of client access you have.

Besides offering friendlier user interfaces, Gopher client programs also make it possible for you to deal with a wide variety of document types. Most client programs offer a way for you to configure the program that will be used for each document type you might encounter in your online travels. For instance, the HGopher client lets you configure a viewer with a panel such as in Fig. 12.5, selected by pulling down "Options," then "Viewer Setup."

Note that some operating systems allow you to specify what program to launch when a given file type is encountered. For instance, in this case, we are using a Shareware tool called Cshow when GIF image files are fetched. Microsoft Windows allows you to "associate" a given program with a file extension, but in the case of HGopher, we explicitly tell the Gopher client what program to use, rather than relying on the operating system to make the connection for us.*

Once you have installed and configured the viewer, you can select a document of that type by pointing and clicking. The viewer will be launched automatically, and the image will be displayed on your screen without any further work on your behalf. Many image archives are offered via Gopher; for example, see Fig. 12.6.

If your client and image viewer are configured appropriately, the server will download a selected image, and your client will launch the external viewer to display it. Both the downloading and the display phases can take time, depending on the speed of your network connection, the speed of your workstation,

---

* Windows users who need to use the "associate" option with other clients will find the option under the File Manager window. Consult the documentation that comes with your Gopher client to learn whether you will use a configuration menu in the client or the native association feature of your operating system to handle the launching of external viewers.

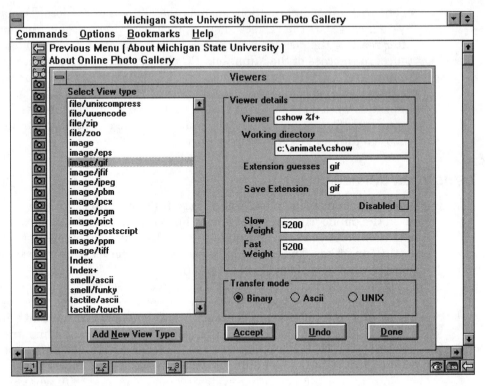

Figure 12.5

and the efficiency of the image viewing software. Generally the Gopher client will place the downloaded file into a scratch area using a temporary file name for viewing; the client program or the viewer may allow you to save the image as a permanent file. If you were to select the highlighted image in the above screen, you would see the photograph shown in Fig. 12.7.*

Besides image display, sounds and video images are becoming popular formats for downloading, especially as personal computers and other workstations are endowed with ever-improving multimedia hardware. As we saw in Chap. 9, there is a proliferation of formats in these areas, and it will probably be a while before sound and video formats are agreed upon across the wide range of computing platforms. In the sound arena, the 8-kilohertz μlaw format popularized on Sun, Next, and other workstations is commonly used. If your computer hardware and software can handle that format, it may be possible to configure your Gopher client to play sounds. In the video realm, the mpeg for-

---

* Photograph taken by Bruce Fox of Michigan State University, University Relations. Reproduced with permission.

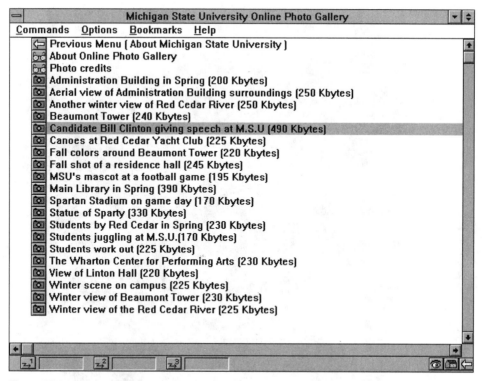

Figure 12.6

mat is commonly used for video images to be transmitted over the network; also used is Apple's Quicktime format. Until a rationalization of these competing formats takes place, networked delivery of multimedia documents will remain frustrating for users and providers alike.

HOW THE GOPHER PROTOCOL WORKS

The Gopher protocol rests on a metaphor of a file system. As we've seen, a Gopher client presents a menu in the form of a list of document titles. When a Gopher client connects to a server, it opens a TCP connection to a specified "well-known port"—typically port 70. Once the connection is established, the client then transmits a "selector string" that specifies what you, the user, want to see. Upon initial connection to a Gopher server, the client sends a null selector string.* This tells the server to deliver the highest level, or root, menu to

---

* A null selector is simply an ASCII Carriage Return character with no preceding data.

Figure 12.7

the client. Once the server has finished sending the list of items, the connection is closed. The client then displays the document titles on the user's console, and the user is free to click on items of choice.

The information sent by the server includes the following fields:

<u>Type</u> <u>Document</u> <u>Title</u> <u>Selector string</u> <u>Server domain name</u> <u>Server port number</u>

One line of this form is delivered for each document. The initial field is a one-byte document type identifier. The type field is concatenated with the beginning of the title field; other fields are separated by the ASCII tab character. The Document Title field is the descriptive text that the client should display for each item. The "selector string" is a string of characters, usually derived from the location of the document in the server's file system, that can be used to uniquely identify the document for retrieval. The server domain name is simply the domain address of the server. The port number is the TCP port common in TCP/IP server nomenclature; generally, the Gopher server "listens" on port 70 for transactions.*

A series of item descriptors is returned for all the items in a given menu. A specific item descriptor might look like this (with the Tab character depicted as =›):

```
0Gopher at Michigan State University=>0/about burrow.cl.msu.edu=>70
1More About Gopher=>1/more_about=>burrow.cl.msu.edu=>70
7Keyword Search of Titles in MSU's Gopher=>7/ts=>burrow.cl.msu.edu=>70
```

For each document descriptor delivered by the server, the client inspects the one-byte type designation. If a document is of a type the client can't handle, many clients simply omit that document from the list of titles. For instance, audio files are not currently supported via PC Gopher III. If a user points PC Gopher III at a directory that contains such files, those titles will not be shown to the user. Since the user can't select it, there's no frustration with impossible requests. (Although the protocol specification calls for this behavior, some clients, such as the public curses client, do not in fact omit such items. This may be useful in some cases. For instance, the user may want to download an item via the public client for later use outside the Gopher session.)

The Gopher client/server interaction is depicted in Fig. 12.8. The selector string tells the server which document the user wants to retrieve. Once the server has delivered a document (whether it be folder, plain text, or otherwise), it has done its job for this transaction; so it disconnects. The Gopher server does not retain any information about the client across transactions—it is said to be "stateless." This aspect of the Gopher design is the key to Gopher's efficiency—the server is only connected to the user long enough to serve a particular request, and it does not pay the high overhead cost of having hundreds or thousands of users "logged in" at once. This highly efficient model allows rela-

---

* The Internet Assigned Numbers Authority, or IANA, which concerns itself with such issues, has assigned port 70 as the standard Gopher port, though a given server may use another port—or ports, if a single machine runs multiple Gopher services.

tively small workstations to function as Gopher servers, handling perhaps millions of requests per week from thousands of users across the Internet.*

The Gopher document types that were defined as part of the original Gopher protocol are:

Document type code	Meaning
0	File
1	Directory
2	CSO phone-book server
3	Error
4	BinHexed Macintosh file
5	DOS binary archive
6	Item is a Unix unencoded file
7	Index-Search server
8	Text-based Telnet session
9	Binary file
+	Redundant server
T	Text-based TN3270 session
g	GIF format graphics file
I	Image file

The term *document* is used broadly to include any type of resource that can be accessed by a Gopher client program. The directory type, type 1, is essential to Gopher's nature as a hierarchical menu system. Type 3 is returned by some servers when an error condition occurs.

SOURCE: Internet Request For Comments document, RFC 1436.

In practice, other document types have also been adopted (e.g., "i" has been used by the University of Iowa as a menu annotation pseudo document, a convention the Minnesota team will reportedly embrace). The term "document" is used broadly to include any type of resource that can be accessed by the Gopher. Here is a more detailed explanation of some of the important document types:

- *File.* This is a simple ASCII text file, which is displayed on the user's workstation using some sort of file viewer.

- *Directory.* This is a list of documents that is used to construct a Gopher menu. When a directory item is selected, the server sends the client the list of items in that directory. Included with each item is the information that the client will need in order to fetch the document when the user requests it.

---

* Actually, the benefit of "statelessness" does not accrue uniquely to Gopher; other client/server protocols may have the same attribute. For example, the protocols underlying the World-Wide Web also call for the client to disconnect from the server once a document is delivered.

Gopher client program sends "selector string" to server via TCP port 70

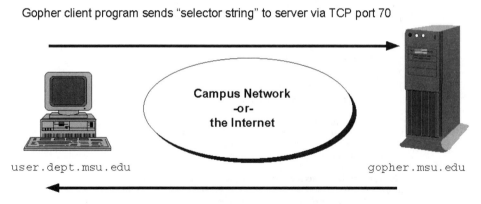

user.dept.msu.edu   gopher.msu.edu

...server delivers requested document, then disconnects

Figure 12.8

- *CSO phone book server.*   Named after the Computing Services Organization at the University of Illinois, CSO provides a client/server protocol for searching a phone database. Gopher recognizes this protocol and lets the user interact with a CSO server in order to look up information.

- *Text-based Telnet session.*   This document type allows a Gopher to present a list of host services that accept Telnet as a remote access protocol (for instance, a list of Internet-accessible online catalogs).

- *Text-based TN3270 session.*   A variant of Telnet, TN3270 is required to connect to IBM mainframe hosts. Support for this form of connection was incomplete early in the life of Gopher but has become pervasive.*

There are also document types for PC (DOS binary archive), Macintosh (Bin-Hex file), and Unix (unencoded file) files; graphic files (GIF); searchable databases (index-search server); and backup Gopher servers (redundant server).

Note that the case of the document type identifier is significant. Because each document descriptor line contains the name of the server where that document is located, it is easy for a Gopher server to point to documents stored far and wide. For instance, a Gopher server at Mythical State University might set up the document types for a root menu as shown below:

---

* Some Telnet implementations will function in TN3270 mode automatically upon connection to an IBM mainframe. If your workstation's Telnet has this capacity, you would configure the same command (probably "telnet") to be invoked for both mainframe (Gopher type "T") and nonmainframe (Gopher type "8") terminal sessions.

Type	Document title	Selector	Server	Port
0	About this Gopher	0/about_MSU	gopher.mythical.edu	70
1	Fun & Games	1/fun	gopher.tc.umn.edu	70
1	MSU Campus Events	1/events	events.mythical.edu	70
2	MSU Telephone Directory	[blank]*	cso.mythical.edu	105
7	Search MSU Gopher titles	7/ts†	gopher.mythical.edu	70
7	Veronica search via PSInet	[blank]	gopher.psi.com	2347

* Gopher embraces the "CSO" telephone book protocol; your Gopher client knows it should launch an external CSO query tool, commonly called Ph, on your behalf, when it encounters the CSO document type. Your client program may depict a CSO search document using a telephone icon. In this case, rather than sending a selector to the Gopher server, the external CSO client program will transmit your query to the CSO server.

† A Type 7 Index-Search can connect you to a variety of search engines. This example shows two Type 7 documents. The first of these uses a tool for indexing document titles local to a Gopher called ts/tb; in this case, the administrator has chosen a selector of 7/ts as the string to identify a title search request.

Note that the Document Title is the only field that clients display by default, along with some sort of icon to flag the type of the document. Users normally do not care to find out where a document resides or what the client program must transmit in order to fetch a selected document. In those cases where you do want to find out the specifics for a given document—for instance, if you want to add a pointer to that document to a Gopher server you are building— you can invoke the Item Info option on your client to have it displayed.

The combination of Selector, Server, and Port describes each document uniquely. Note that the selector string consists of whatever text the server wants to receive in order to deliver a document.‡ For Unix-based servers, this string is typically prefixed by the type of the document and a slash. Also note the variety of servers shown in this example. Often a Gopher administrator will store items peculiar to his or her domain on the same server machine as the Gopher server, but this is not essential. It is common for documents of local interest to reside on several servers, as shown above. Theoretically, a server could offer *only* documents that reside on other Gopher servers.

Because the Gopher design calls for a simple protocol built on TCP/IP, it is possible to observe the Gopher client/server interaction without even using a client program. You might want to try connecting to a Gopher server "manually" to see how this works. For instance, you might open a Telnet session as follows:

```
telnet gopher.tc.umn.edu 70
```
[Hit the Enter key without typing any other characters.]

---

‡ In other words, the selector string is said to be "opaque." As a user you are not supposed to make any assumptions about the actual file name used by the server based on what you see in the selector string; indeed, you should never need to do so. The protocol merely specifies that if a client sends that selector string to the specified server, it will respond with the corresponding document.

In this case you would see the initial menu for the main University of Minnesota server displayed in raw form.* For index searches, the string of characters you are looking for appears after the selector string, separated by an ASCII tab. For instance, to manually invoke the title search of document titles at the central Gopher at Michigan State University, searching for the string "vincent":

```
telnet gopher.msu.edu 70
7/ts [tab] vincent
```

You might want to compare the results of these "manual" Gopher sessions with the behavior of real clients in order to fully understand how the Gopher protocol works. This could be especially useful if you intend to build your own Gopher service.

GOPHER+

In August 1992, the regional computer network CICNet sponsored a Gopher Workshop in Ann Arbor, Michigan. Invited attendees included Gopher implementers at the various CICNet institutions as well as other pioneering Gopher sites. Mark McCahill and Farhad Anklesaria attended from the University of Minnesota. The University of Minnesota developers presented Gopher+, their vision for how to extend Gopher beyond its original design.

The original Gopher design, with its one-byte document type, was adequate to meet many of the needs of the community. But there were many demands for additions to the protocol, to handle everything from PostScript files and various image files (e.g., GIF and JPEG) to global document attributes, such as author name and document expiration date. Rather than embed each and every requested extension in the protocol, the University of Minnesota team devised a mechanism to support general ways to add them to the protocol.

Gopher+ adds new, named fields to the simple 1-byte item descriptor in basic Gopher.[†] If a client sends a special form of a selector string, the Gopher server is expected to deliver a series of Attribute Information blocks describing the document in detail. The first named block, +INFO, is required; it resembles the descriptive line sent by the old protocol. Optional fields include the +ADMIN block, which identifies the name of the owner of the document; and +DATE,

---

* Most Telnet programs allow you to specify a TCP port number as an optional parameter after the host name; we want to specify port 70, the default port for Gopher servers. Some Telnet implementations may provide a different way to specify port numbers. Also recall that some Telnet implementations use a different command name; in particular, FTP Software Inc.'s PC/TCP package uses the command tn.

† The term "Gopher0" is sometimes used in discussions to refer to the original Gopher protocol, to distinguish it from the Gopher+ extensions.

which would be the date the document was last modified. These global document attributes are intended to help administrators maintain and describe documents, and, after Gopher clients generally support Gopher+, to help users select documents of interest.

Another block that has been defined for Gopher+ is +ABSTRACT, which would be a textual abstract describing the document.

Besides providing a mechanism for supporting global document attributes, Gopher+ is intended to support alternate views of a document. For instance, an attribute information block called +VIEWS describes alternate formats for a document. With +VIEWS a document could be offered in a variety of formats, from flat ASCII to PostScript; it would even be possible to list alternate languages for a document.

Gopher+ servers identify those documents that possess Gopher+ attributes by appending extra information to the standard Gopher item description:

```
Original Gopher Item Descriptor=>Gopher+ Information
```

In other words, the Gopher+ information is added to the end of the old item descriptor, with a tab separating the new from the old. The purpose of this design is to allow old Gopher clients to work with the new-style descriptor, ignoring the Gopher+ information. An item list can include a mixture of descriptors with and without Gopher+ information.

When a client wants to retrieve Gopher+ attribute information, it appends a Tab and a "+" character to the end of the selector string. Optionally, a client can append a "$" character in lieu of the "+" in order to fetch all of the Gopher+ attributes for a given directory. If a client requests a document from a Gopher+ server in the original style of query, the server will respond with an old-style descriptor list; this allows old clients to fetch information from new servers.

With the original Gopher protocol, the expected basic behavior of clients is fairly obvious. Different clients vary as to their look and feel, but the underlying function is generally similar. By contrast, the design for Gopher+ assumes that different clients may take radically different approaches as to how they handle Gopher+ fields. For instance, one client program might allow the user to specify his or her preferred views of a document. That client program might always fetch a PostScript version of a document, if one were available, instead of a flat text version of the same document. Another client might offer the user the choice of the various formats available, expecting the user to always make the decision as to which version to fetch. Both clients would comply with the Gopher+ specification, despite the variation in capabilities.

In fact, Gopher+ is intended to serve as a framework for highly sophisticated clients. One could envision, for instance, a client that searches the abstracts of documents, displaying only those titles that match the user's search criteria. (To date, no such client exists.)

Details of the interactions between Gopher+ clients and servers can be found on the main University of Minnesota Gopher server.

Other Gopher+ capabilities

Beyond the global attributes and alternate views functions, Gopher+ also provides a mechanism for interactive queries. A Gopher+ server can interrogate a user for specific information such as a password, or it could even serve as an interface between a user and an interactive process on another host. This feature, referred to as +ASK support includes options for prompting for file names or for the user to make a choice among a range of options.

This +ASK scheme could be used to implement a variety of functions in which the server polls the user for specific information. However, in a sense, the very concept of the +ASK mechanism runs counter to the "stateless" nature of Gopher; the basic function of Gopher involves delivering documents to a widespread audience of anonymous users, with no need for the server to worry about who an individual is, and with TCP sessions that close as soon as a document is delivered. But many of the functions of any organization—from updating the telephone book to filling out a purchase order to signing up for the office picnic—require filling out of simple forms, and Gopher seems a natural place to put the online forms query mechanism.

Along with the +ASK extensions, a mechanism for allowing "lightweight" authentication of users for access to protected documents was announced with Gopher+. For instance, some vendors may insist that their documents can only be read when users have typed in a unique password assigned to them. The AdmitOne Authentication scheme lets a user obtain a "ticket" that allows access to restricted documents. The AdmitOne scheme uses encryption to avoid sending passwords over the network. It also provides a way that a client can reuse a ticket for subsequent transactions. Critics of AdmitOne have pointed out schemes for defeating the security of AdmitOne, some rather elaborate. One claim is that security cannot be provided by a client and a server alone—a trusted third party is required. It seems likely that for many applications, such as providing access to copyrighted material licensed to an entire campus, AdmitOne would provide a level of security that would satisfy most database vendors.

Registry of Gopher+ data types

Initially the Minnesota team announced that they would register all Gopher+ data types. However, members of the Internet standards community in general, and those Gophernauts familiar with the Multipurpose Internet Mail Extensions (MIME) in particular, prevailed upon the team to use the MIME-type registry for the majority of data types. This eliminates some duplication in standards setting. As of this writing, however, while the

MIME registry is established, not all of the Gopher+ attributes are defined in that registry.*

Other Internet standards efforts also overlap the Gopher+ effort. The Minnesota team has announced its intention to adopt the Internet Assigned Fields Authority standard when it is deployed. This could lead to an overlap with the functionality of Archie; see Chap. 14 for details.

Prospects for Gopher+

Gopher+ has been somewhat slow in its acceptance, especially compared to the original Gopher protocol. The University of Minnesota announced a Gopher+ capable version of its Unix server in early 1993, followed by Gopher+ capable versions of the Macintosh client (TurboGopher) and the Unix client A Gopher+ capable client for Windows appeared in fall 1993 in the form of HGopher.

Gopher+ offers a potential framework for numerous advanced applications. As of this writing relatively few Gopher+ servers are in production around the world. Related functions such as AdmitOne are also not widely deployed. The Gopher+ protocol itself has generated some criticism for its complexity. Moreover, Gopher+ faces competition from developments in other Internet tools such as World-Wide Web and WAIS.

GOPHER INDEXES

As we saw earlier, one of the Gopher document types is a searchable index. The Gopher server software is flexible enough to support a variety of indexing schemes. With the Unix server from Minnesota, the most common index uses a version of the search tool delivered with an early public domain version of the Wide Area Information Server (WAIS). If a site is running a standalone WAIS database, Gopher can point to the WAIS server as a searchable index; the client prompts you for a string to look for, and the Gopher server acts as an intermediary between you and the WAIS server, eventually delivering the results to your client for display.

It is also possible for a Gopher administrator to set up various sorts of ad hoc search mechanisms that appear to you as a user to be simple searchable indexes. This makes it possible for an administrator to present a similar look and feel for a variety of database searches. (It also can lead to confusion, when different underlying search engines behave differently.)

The standard release with the WAIS engine does not provide for boolean or proximity searches. In November 1992, Don Gilbert of Indiana University

---

* MIME data types are listed in a document called `mime-types` at the anonymous FTP site `venera.isi.edu` in the directory `/in-notes/mime`.

announced modifications to the WAIS indexing engine normally used with Gopher servers. His enhancements include boolean, partial word search, and literal phrase searching. These enhancements have been adopted by numerous other sites—but not all—so that boolean search capability is not universally available.[†] His biology-oriented Gopher (located at `ftp.bio.indiana.edu`, port 70) allows testing of these search features. Examples of the kinds of searches possible include:

Boolean: red and green, not blue	*Result:* just those records with both the words "red" and "green," excluding all records with the word "blue"
Partial words: hum*	*Result:* all records with "hum" (e.g., "humming-bird," "human," and "humbug")
Literal phrases: red rooster-39	*Result:* only those records with the full string "red rooster-39" will be retrieved

Gopher provides an effective mechanism to allow an administrator to provide a hierarchical browsing list—for a campus, for the Internet, or both. But the organizational scheme carefully designed during months of deliberation by a campus menu design team may bear no relation whatsoever to the organization of a given user's brain.

Some Gopher sites offer tools to make it easier for you to find items within a Gopher server—tools such as indexes of local titles, or "road maps" to show you the way to your documents. These tools are described in Chap. 20.

When you want to search across many Gophers—i.e., across Gopherspace—you will want to use a service like Veronica. A user connecting to Veronica specifies a keyword to search for, say for the word "biology," and gets a list of document titles from throughout Gopherspace that match. More information on Veronica is provided in Chap. 14.

When you encounter a document labeled as an "index" on a Gopher server, you need to keep in mind what sort of index it is, as its scope can vary:

- It might be an index of document titles on the local Gopher server.

- It might be an index of the full text of documents within that server.

- It might be an index of titles, or of full text, across many Gopher servers.

The scope of a given Gopher index is determined by the administrator. The administrator can choose to index one file, all files in a subdirectory, or all files in a directory and its subdirectories. Often a large file is broken up into a series of small files so that it can be loaded into Gopher. This will allow the user to selectively retrieve sections of interest. Usually, the wording of the Gopher

---

[†] Up-to-date details on deployment of this feature (and others) can be found in the archive of the `comp.infosystems.gopher` newsgroup at the University of Minnesota main Gopher.

menu item makes it clear what the scope of a given index is. It's the administrator's job to make sure this is the case.*

SPECIALIZED GOPHER CLIENT TECHNOLOGIES

We saw earlier that Gopher is best utilized when the user takes advantage of specialized client software. Recent developments in the area of specialized Gopher client technology are worth noting.

Not all clients have the straightforward goal of simple retrieval of documents for the user to read. In May 1992, Steve Ludtke of Rice University announced a 3-D Gopher client for NeXT workstations. Dubbed "A Gopher in a Forest," the client presents a 3-D rendering of IP address space, and it updates the image in real time as the user moves from server to server or down the menu hierarchy. This tool generated considerable excitement, but no one was able to identify a practical use for it. Because IP address space doesn't correspond to geography, it was not a way to visualize where in the world documents were coming from, but it did inspire the idea of a client that could depict a geographical view of Gopherspace. Late in 1993, Ludtke enhanced his tool to serve as a Gopher+ client and has rechristened it Gopherspace.† Figure 12.9 is a sample screen showing the sort of nontraditional view a creative client program might offer.

Perhaps the most exotic alternative Gopher client is the MOO Gopher. The Xerox Palo Alto Research Center has created a variant of MUD called MOO, which provides an object-oriented language for MUD. MOO is rich enough to support implementation of a Gopher client, and this has been done. In some MOO games, the player uses the MOO Gopher to browse the Internet for answers to questions in order to advance in play. Opinion is divided as to whether this is of research/educational value or a waste of time and bandwidth.

READING MORE ABOUT GOPHER

You can best learn more about Gopher by browsing through various servers: connect to "Gopher Central" (`gopher.tc.umn.edu`, port 70) and follow its list of servers. (Of course, most Gopher servers offer some sort of list of "Other Gophers" in their menu hierarchy; you need not connect to Minnesota explicitly to find such lists.)

Under Minnesota's "Information About Gopher" folder you will find a great deal of online information about Gopher, including detailed client descriptions.

---

* Tools used to build such indexes include the WAIS support native to Gopher, the Digital Librarian included with the Nextstep operating system, the ts/tb mechanism mentioned above, and a title index tool called Jughead, implemented by Rhett Jones of the University of Utah.

† The Gopherspace client is available for FTP from `ion.rice.edu`. Versions for platforms other than Nextstep are anticipated.

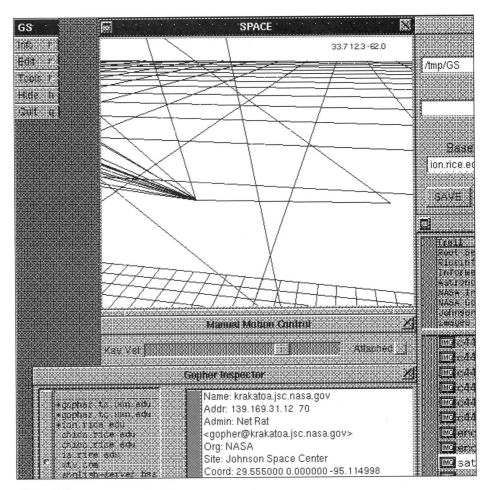

Figure 12.9

Also you will find there an archive of past discussions in the Gopher news groups. You may want to review the archives before you post a new question to the news group. Of course, the news group itself (`comp.infosystems.gopher`) can be a valuable way to get answers from the worldwide community of Gophernauts.

If you have a specific question or suggestion about how Gopher works, you can mail it to the Minnesota team at `gopher@boombox.micro.umn.edu`. They receive a large volume of mail and may not be able to answer each inquiry.

Networked Hypermedia:
The World-Wide Web and NCSA Mosaic

As we saw in Chap. 12, the Internet Gopher offers documents organized in a hierarchical view. Compared to other ways of delivering information, such as anonymous FTP, Gopher offers a much friendlier way of finding information. In contrast to Gopher's hierarchical organization, an alternative scheme known as the World-Wide Web offers documents under a hypertext model. Put simply, a hypertext system allows documents to contain embedded links to other documents. The author of a hypertext document can insert "hot links" to other documents of interest, giving the reader the choice of moving from topic to topic at will. In this chapter we will explore how to navigate the World-Wide Web, and we will see how a client program deployed in 1993, NCSA Mosaic, has transformed the World-Wide Web from a hypertext system into a rich hypermedia universe.

   To understand the difference between a hierarchical menu system and a hypertext one, consider the example of an online travel guide. If you created such a document under Gopher, you would organize the various parts of the guide into a tree structure, or hierarchy. Gopher distinguishes between menu-type documents and documents that actually contain text; only menu-type documents contain pointers to other items. By contrast, under the World-Wide Web, any document can contain links to other documents. For example, see Fig. 13.1.

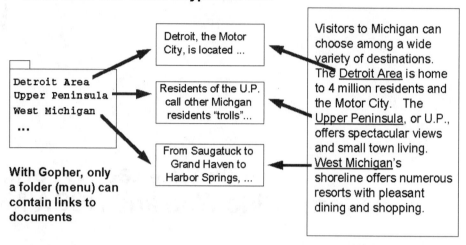

**Gopher offers a hierarchical view of documents;
World-Wide Web offers a hypertext view**

Detroit, the Motor City, is located ...

Residents of the U.P. call other Michgan residents "trolls"...

From Saugatuck to Grand Haven to Harbor Springs, ...

Detroit Area
Upper Peninsula
West Michigan
...

With Gopher, only a folder (menu) can contain links to documents

Visitors to Michigan can choose among a wide variety of destinations. The Detroit Area is home to 4 million residents and the Motor City. The Upper Peninsula, or U.P., offers spectacular views and small town living. West Michigan's shoreline offers numerous resorts with pleasant dining and shopping.

**Any World-Wide Web document
can contain links to other documents
as part of the narrative text**

Figure 13.1

An author can use annotation sparingly within a hypertext, so that the ratio of hyperlinks to text is high. For example, an author might use brief annotation to enhance the reader's understanding of the titles listed in a menu. By contrast, an author might write prose as dense as a Ph.D. thesis, with relatively few or no hypertext links to be found within the document. An example of using hypertext for brief annotation of an online document is shown in Fig. 13.2. This is a sample screen from the central World-Wide Web server at Michigan State University. As you can see, the view of text is quite different than one would expect with Gopher; in fact, this section is an annotated version of the root menu on MSU's Gopher. The annotation expands on the words in the title of each document, giving the reader more clues as to what's within each document.

This screen comes from a client program known as Mosaic. Developed by the National Center for Supercomputer Applications at the University of Illinois, Mosaic is not only one of the best client programs for navigating the Web, it also is a multiprotocol client, able to work with many different Internet services. We will explore its multilingual capabilities later in this chapter; for now we will concentrate on its considerable power as a Web client.

A client like Mosaic knows how to connect to World-Wide Web servers and allow the user to navigate the links embedded within Web documents. Versions

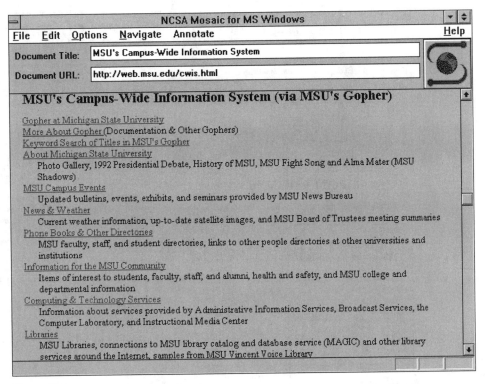

Figure 13.2

of Mosaic are available for Microsoft Windows, for the Macintosh, and for the X Window system under Unix. On all of these platforms, Mosaic is not only able to fetch and display documents, but also offers rich features such as inline graphics. For instance, if we looked at the beginning of MSU's home page* we would see the screen shown in Fig. 13.3. The block logo is actually delivered as an inline GIF image. The various versions of Mosaic have built-in image decoders and are able to offer images in context. We also see on the screen the beginning of another inline image; you could use the scroll bar to bring that part of the page onto your screen. Note also as you look at this page that bold-facing and font size changes are used for different parts of a document. Later we will see how the language one uses to prepare documents for the Web, the Hypertext Markup Language, enables clients like Mosaic to understand the

---

* Note the position of the scroll bar to the right of each Mosaic screen. In the first example, the scroll bar is partway down the scale, showing that we are viewing the middle portion of this page. The second example shows the scroll bar positioned at the top of the page. More often than not, pages delivered via the Web will not fit entirely on your screen. All versions of Mosaic allow you to resize the window, up to the maximum allowed on your monitor.

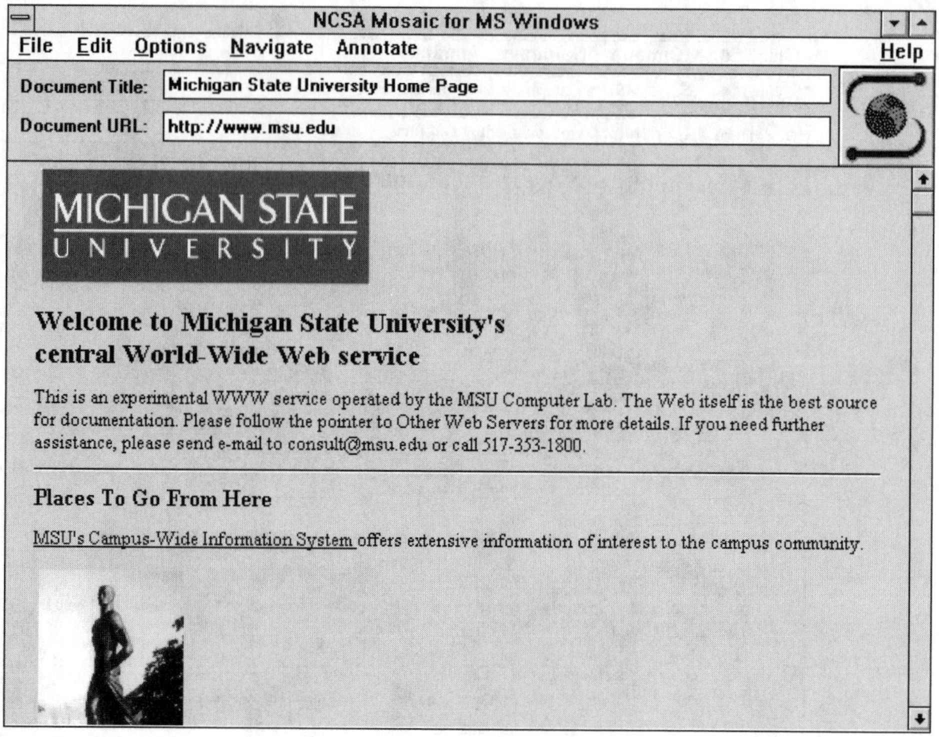

Figure 13.3

different parts of a document; for now, note that this document looks much more similar to a professional print document than one might expect from an online medium.

Consider the example of an archive of documents made available by the Library of Congress during 1993. The Vatican Archive was offered for access via anonymous FTP as a pioneering example of the potential for electronic document delivery over the Internet. FTP access presents a rather dull view of the documents:

```
C:\ ftp seq1.loc.gov
220 seq1 FTP server ($Header: ftpd.c 2.5 89/12/15 $) ready.
Userid for logging in on seq1.loc.gov (rww)? ftp
331 Guest login ok, send ident as password.
Password for logging in as ftp on seq1.loc.gov?
230 Guest login ok, access restrictions apply.
ftp:seq1.loc.gov> cd pub/vatican.exhibit
250 CWD command successful.
ftp:seq1.loc.gov> dir
total 173
```

```
-rw-r--r--  1 kell        ftpsu         733 Jan  7  1993 Bibliog.txt
-rw-r--r--  1 kell        ftpsu        1509 Apr 12  1993 Catalog.txt
-rw-r--r--  1 kell        ftpsu        4756 Mar 17  1993 Events.txt
-rw-r--r--  1 kell        ftpsu       16302 Jul 30 15:05 FILELIST
-rw-r--r--  1 kell        ftpsu        6445 Mar 10  1993 History.txt
-rw-r--r--  1 kell        ftpsu       54960 Jan 28  1993 Intro.txt
-rw-r--r--  1 kell        ftpsu       12775 Mar  9  1993 Master_list
-rw-r--r--  1 kell        ftpsu        5058 Aug 23 16:56 NEWFILES
-rw-r--r--  1 kell        ftpsu       58531 Feb 26  1993 Object_index
-rw-r--r--  1 kell        ftpsu        7395 Jul 30 15:02 README
-rw-r--r--  1 kell        ftpsu        1480 Jan  7  1993 WARNING
drwxr-xr-x 11 kell        ftpsu         512 Jul 30 15:01 exhibit
drwxr-xr-x  2 kell        ftpsu        1024 Dec 14 23:19 viewers
Transferred 857 bytes in 0 seconds
226 Transfer complete.
ftp:seq1.loc.gov> ...
```

Navigating through files on an FTP server is not very rewarding; the titles are Unix file names, and the screen is cluttered with noise of little use to the reader. Recognizing the value of the archive but seeking to advance the quality of the reader's experience, an enterprising Gopher administrator, John Price-Wilkin of the University of Virginia, decided to create a Gopher version of the same collection.* The reader is presented with a more accessible view in Fig. 13.4. By any measure, this is a more civilized way for the online reader to access the information. Instead of Unix file names, the reader confronts carefully chosen titles. Instead of manually fetching files, the reader can use the point-and-click interface of a Gopher client to select documents of interest. With the right sort of client, such as HGopher in this example, the reader can pull down image files at will, for display online with an installed image viewing program.

A pioneering Web wizard from the Netherlands, Frans van Hoesel, also discovered the Vatican FTP archive, and felt that this collection was a good candidate for delivery via the Web. Figure 13.5 is a sample page from his handiwork.

These samples from three different realizations of the same archive demonstrate the progression from anonymous FTP to Gopher to the World-Wide Web and Mosaic.† The combination of inline graphics and the use of different fonts

---

* The Gopher archive can be found at gopher.lib.virginia.edu (port 70) under the Library GWIS Collection menus (or under selector string 1/alpha/vat).

† The various realizations of the Vatican Archive also demonstrate how publishing documents on the Internet can lead to worthwhile international collaborations. Much of Van Hoesel's development work was done with him connecting over a relatively slow (9600 bps) link. NCSA and the University of North Carolina have supported his efforts by providing access to servers and disk space.

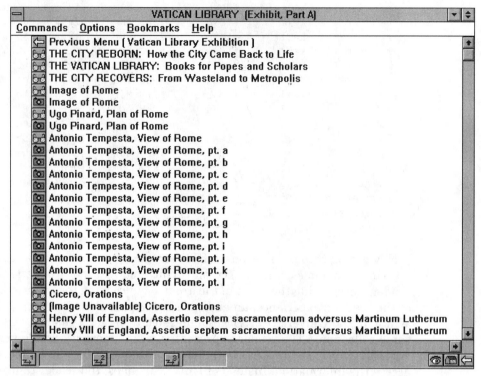

Figure 13.4

for different parts of the image make for a rich, journal-like presentation. Text appears on the screen next to the image to which it refers. Since the introduction of Mosaic in early 1993, more and more sites have begun deploying online exhibits, some quite elaborately constructed. One example is the Australian National Botanical Gardens, which offers detailed information about the gardens, lovely scanned images, and, in a nice use of multimedia, descriptions of native birds along with images and sounds of the calls made by those birds (see Fig. 13.6).

Hypertext links make it possible to offer introductory information in an initial page of a document, with more detailed information offered as selectable links. If an entire book were offered as hypertext, one could concoct a table of contents consisting entirely of links. But hypertext allows an author to embed links subtly, woven into the flow of the narrative. Notice how this document suggests "Listen to a recording of the *bird call*." Assuming you have the right hardware and software setup, you can choose to pause and listen to those calls you find interesting, or you can continue to skim the document, at your dis-

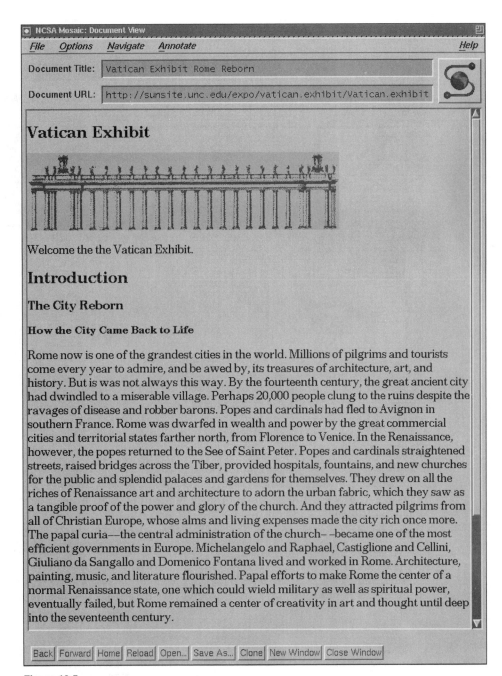

Figure 13.5

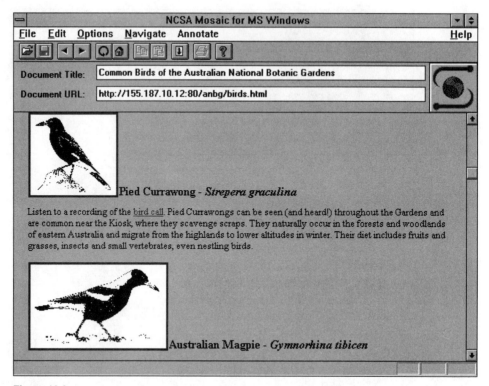

Figure 13.6

cretion. Many authors avail themselves of this capacity to offer elaboration in context.

Moreover, Mosaic enables even more elaborate applications. For instance, consider the possibility of including moving images in a document delivered over the Internet. For example, in Fig. 13.7 you can view a video by clicking on its corresponding still image. The video is downloaded to the Mosaic client running on your workstation, which invokes an external MPEG viewer to display the moving images.*

Mosaic and the World-Wide Web offer an even higher level of interactivity; they make it possible for a user to click on a particular spot on a map and

---

* This service, implemented by Charles Henrich of the Unix Supercomputing Group in the Michigan State University Computer Laboratory, offers current real-time weather movies. Henrich harvests weather information and still images from a variety of sources on the Internet in order to offer this unique service. The U.S. movie is a composite of infrared satellite images and radar maps, showing both cloud formations and precipitation at once. The source images for the movies shown come from the Space Science and Engineering Center at the University of Wisconsin. See the online narrative for details.

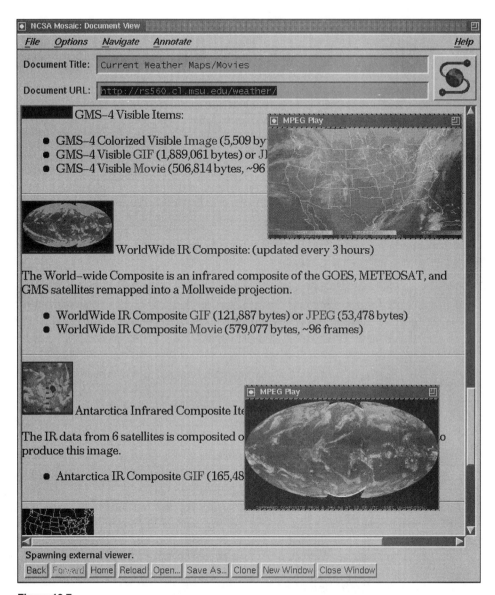

Figure 13.7

have the server deliver information that pertains to that location. This sort of function might be useful for a map service, allowing, for instance, a user to click on a building on a map and find out what offices are located in that building. Or it might be useful for letting a user obtain weather information for a specific location by pointing and clicking at that location on a map. As an example, look at the screen in Fig. 13.8 from an interactive weather browser.*

When you click on a location on the map, the interactive weather browser will present you with a new image, zooming in on the area around the spot you've selected, including the text of the local forecast (see Fig. 13.9).

Another example of the use of the interactive map technology made possible by Mosaic and the Web resides at Xerox Corporation's Palo Alto Research Center. They offer an interactive world map that allows the user to zoom into points of interest by pointing the mouse and clicking (see Fig. 13.10).

The interactive capability of Mosaic and an intelligent World-Wide Web server enable Internet delivery of the sort of highly interactive, highly graphical multimedia documents that one expects to see on a desktop CD-ROM system.

WORLD-WIDE WEB CONCEPTS

At the top of each sample shown above is a field labeled "Document URL." "URL" stands for "Uniform Resource Locator," a term invented to describe a sort of "handle" by which one retrieves a document that resides somewhere in the World-Wide Web. The parts of a URL consist of:

```
Components of a Uniform Resource Locator

http:        //web.msu.edu          /vincent/index.html
Protocol     Location (domain       Specific document on
             address of server)     server (path name)
```

This is a somewhat simplified view of URLs; they can contain other sorts of information as we will see in later examples.

All the URLs we have seen so far represent "native" Web documents; such URLs begin with the prefix http:. "HTTP" is an abbreviation for Hypertext Transfer Protocol, which is the communications protocol defined for the Web. However, the Web is designed to embrace all Internet protocols, and URLs might begin with other prefixes. For instance, the URL for the root menu of a Gopher server might be:

```
gopher://gopher.msu.edu/†
```

---

* The interactive weather browser is also the handiwork of Charles Henrich.

† This URL assumes that gopher.msu.edu listens on the standard port for Gopher (70). If port 7000 were the port for this server, the URL would be gopher://gopher.msu.edu:7000/.

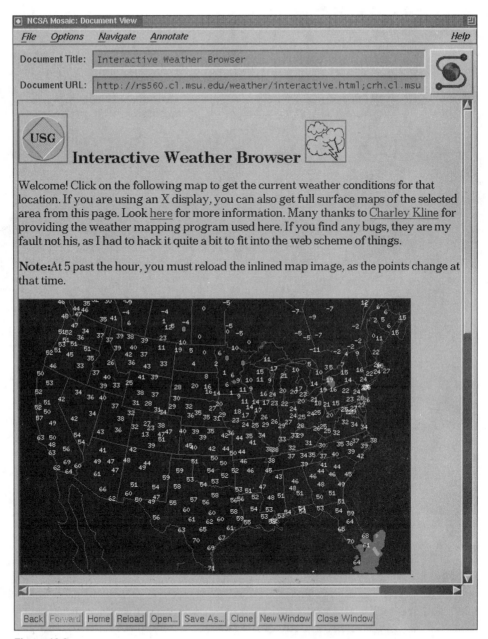

Figure 13.8

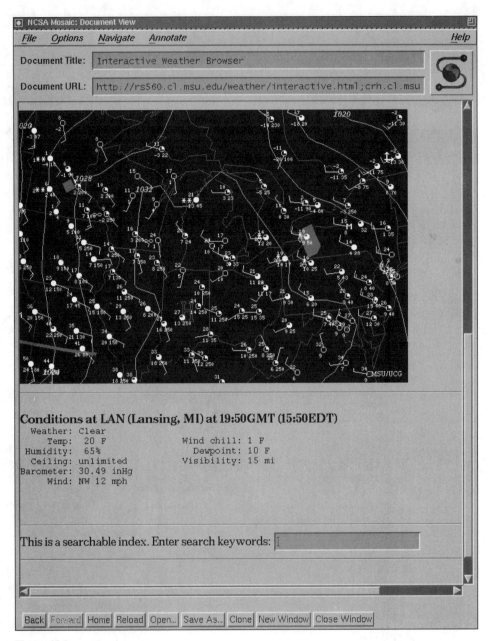

Figure 13.9

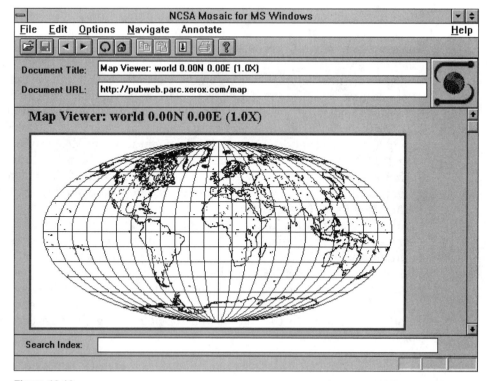

Figure 13.10

Similarly, a URL has been defined for FTP servers. For instance, Mosaic is offered for anonymous FTP at `ftp.ncsa.uiuc.edu`.* The URL for that service is:

```
ftp://ftp.ncsa.uiuc.edu/
```

The `ftp` tag is used to refer to an anonymous FTP server. (Alternatively, a URL beginning with `file` can refer to a file local to the user's system; if the file is not present locally, the client will fetch it via anonymous FTP from the named site.) Other protocols that are supported include `WAIS` (Wide Area Information Server) and `news` (Usenet news).

Mosaic displays links to other documents using color, highlighting, or underscores, depending on the options you select. As the cursor passes over each doc-

---

* If you already had Mosaic installed on a workstation, you could use it to fetch a newer version of the software. You would want to be careful to install it in a different location on your hard disk until you verified its correct function.

ument title, Mosaic will display the corresponding URL in the Document URL area. When you click on a document link of interest, Mosaic connects to the server whose name is encoded in the URL, and retrieves the document from that server.

Once you have begun a journey on the World-Wide Web, it is possible to skip from document to document, and from place to place, using the interconnected links established by the author of each document. If you have encountered a URL of interest, for instance in e-mail or in a journal article, you need a way to jump directly to that document. All implementations of Mosaic offer an option labeled "Open URL." This is simply a way to jump to a given document on a given server. The URL may not list a specific document, in which case the "home page" of that server will be delivered and displayed. Figure 13.11 is an example of using Open URL.

Mosaic maintains a history of the places you've visited, and even is smart enough to vary the display of links—for instance, changing the color—so that as you reread a document it is clear to you which links you've already selected. Mosaic also lets you keep a "hotlist"—a list of interesting documents and servers you've encountered on the net, similar to Gopher's bookmark option. The different flavors of Mosaic use slightly different pull-down menus for adding to the hotlist and for navigating through the history of prior selections.

MOSAIC: A MULTIPROTOCOL CLIENT

We saw earlier that Uniform Resource Locators can refer to the Web protocol, HTTP, as well as other common Internet protocols. Mosaic understands these forms of URL and the corresponding protocols. For instance, if we ask Mosaic to open the Uniform Resource Locator `gopher://gopher.msu.edu` it will con-

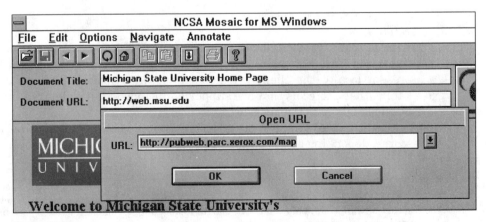

Figure 13.11

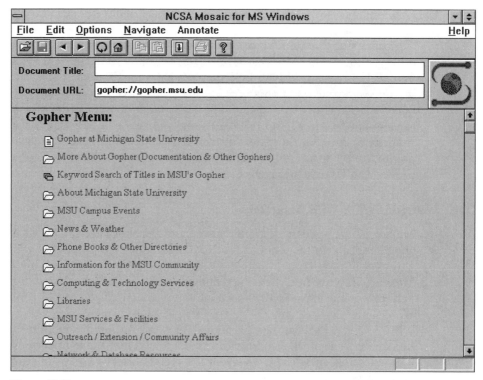

Figure 13.12

nect to the Gopher server in question and display that server's root menu (see Fig. 13.12).

In this case Mosaic is connecting directly to the Gopher server at gopher.msu.edu and speaking the Gopher protocol; Mosaic displays the fetched document titles with icons depicting the document type, just as a native Gopher client would do.* Whereas a Gopher client stores the item descriptor for each document internally, Mosaic stores the same information internally in URL form.† Although this distinction is not important for Mosaic users, it is noteworthy because it allows Mosaic to completely navigate

---

* Compare this menu with the annotated menu that is part of the MSU web service; the latter is an example of a document that has been rewritten in HTML. The version on the Web page uses HTML to enable the annotation shown. Mosaic fetches a Web home page using HTTP; it fetches a Gopher menu using the basic Gopher protocol.

† For instance, the first document on gopher.msu.edu has a URL of gopher://gopher.msu. edu:70/00/about. The :70 specifies the Gopher TCP port number; the 00/about represents the Gopher document type (0, for a text file) and the selector string (0/about).

Gopherspace, fetching any selected document using its standard URL interpretation mechanism.

Mosaic shines as a Web browser, but it is also quite capable as a client for other protocols. In some cases, however, you may find that you are more satisfied with a client that is intended specifically for the tool you want to use. For instance, Mosaic as of this writing does not have Gopher+ support; you will need to run a client that specifically has that support in order to avail yourself of Gopher+ features. Similarly, although Mosaic can serve as a Usenet newsreader, its function is generally limited to fetching specific news groups as pointed to by documents on the Web; Mosaic does not serve as a good way to browse the Usenet hierarchy.

OTHER WORLD-WIDE WEB CLIENTS

Mosaic is by no means the only Web client. Earlier clients include a line-mode client and a graphical client for Next workstations. As of this writing, those users who have true Internet access from workstations capable of running Mosaic will often find it the best choice.*

If you do not have a Mosaic-capable environment you can still navigate the Web. A client called Lynx does a very respectable job of offering Web access to the VT100 user.† Lynx can be run on a Unix workstation or via Telnet to a public Lynx client. (As of this writing a PC version of Lynx is also under development.)

Here is an example of the view of the Web offered by Lynx. It is the beginning of the Vatican Exhibit page shown in Fig. 3.5.

```
Vatican Exhibit Rome Reborn (p1 of 3)
VATICAN EXHIBIT


[IMAGE]

Welcome to the Vatican Exhibit.

INTRODUCTION

The City Reborn

HOW THE CITY CAME BACK TO LIFE
Rome now is one of the grandest cities in the world. Millions of
```

---

* Recommended machines would be a high-end 80386 processor or better in the PC world, or a Macintosh of recent vintage, or an X Window-capable workstation. Slower machines can run Mosaic but handling of inline images might be painfully slow.

† Lynx was developed by Lou Montulli of the University of Kansas.

```
pilgrims and tourists come every year to admire, and be awed by, its
treasures of architecture, art, and history. But is was not always
this way. By the fourteenth century, the great ancient city had
dwindled to a miserable village. Perhaps 20,000 people clung to the
Arrow keys: Up and Down to move. Right to follow a link; Left to go back.
   S)earch P)rint M)ain menu O)ptions G)o Q)uit [delete]=history list
Type a command or ? for help:     Press space for next page
                    ukanaix.cc.ukans.edu 20:05:55
```

Lynx lets you use cursor keys to navigate quickly through the Web. Lynx displays links* in highlighted letters. The down arrow key moves to the next highlighted topic; the up arrow moves up to the previous one in the current menu. The left arrow key goes to the previously selected topic (i.e., back to the page you visited before the current one). The right arrow key (or Return) jumps to the document the cursor currently points to. The question mark offers help, including a complete map of single-key commands.

As you can see from the example, Lynx lets you know where inline images appear in the text. A future version may offer options for downloading. Although the VT100 realm does not offer the richness that a native client can present, Lynx does make it quite possible for users to experience the Web without running Mosaic on their workstations.

Several public Lynx services are available; to try Lynx yourself, do this:

```
telnet www.cc.ukans.edu
www         [Log in as 'www'; no password required]
```

Lynx offers the equivalent of "Open URL"—simply type "g" for "go to" and enter the URL. However, public Lynx clients generally disable this feature; you need to run Lynx locally or on a host that knows your identity.

A user's guide for Lynx is available via the Web. The Uniform Resource Locator for that document is: `http://www.cc.ukans.edu/lynx_help/Lynx_users_guide.html`. Lynx itself is available for anonymous FTP from `ftp2.cc.ukans.edu`. As of this writing a version of Lynx intended for MS-DOS users is under development.

There is another Web client for Microsoft Windows as well. Created at Cornell University's law school, the tool is known as Cello. Cello was written explicitly for Windows; it does not have versions for other platforms.[†] As of this writing Cello has some performance and functional advantages over the Windows version of Mosaic. If you plan to navigate the Web extensively from the Windows environment you might want to evaluate Cello as well as Mosaic as candidate clients. Cello can be found at `ftp.law.cornell.edu`.

---

* Pun intended, no doubt.

[†] Cello was written by Thomas R. Bruce.

You can read more about available Web clients by connecting to the server at CERN. (The client overview begins at `http://info.cern.ch/hypertext/WWW/Clients.html`.)

INSTALLING MOSAIC

Mosaic is available for anonymous FTP from `ftp.ncsa.uiuc.edu`. Versions for all three supported platforms reside there. For the Macintosh and for Windows, only executable binaries are available. For Unix systems, source code for Mosaic is available; in addition, executable versions are available for several platforms as well. The Unix version works under the X Window graphical environment with the Motif library from the Open Software Foundation. Contact your network support staff for details as to whether your site has a Motif license.

AN OVERVIEW OF HTML—THE HYPERTEXT MARKUP LANGUAGE

Imagine you are writing a script for a multimedia document. In sketching your design for the document you might use a different color ink or make use of uppercase to flag places where, for instance, audio or video clips are to be included within the text. Such markup might look like this:

```
<INSERT FOOTAGE OF ARMSTRONG STEPPING ON MOON>
```

You might mark up the entire document in this manner; humans involved in the project would be able to read and understand the multimedia elements called for in the script.

Now suppose we are looking for a way to distribute such scripts over a network for use by client software on behalf of human readers. We would need some sort of language that allows authors of hypermedia documents to embed links to other documents in a standard way—a standard form of "markup" that is understood by authors and client programs.

The rich functionality offered by the Web and tools like Mosaic demand such a language—a standard way of identifying the various components of a document. A "markup" language called HTML was devised for this purpose. HTML is an example of a language that complies with a general standard for markup called SGML.* A basic understanding of HTML will give insight into how authors prepare documents for delivery over the Web. The best way to envision how HTML works is to look at an example. Figure 13.13 is the home page for a particular document as displayed by Mosaic.†

---

* For "Standard Generalized Markup Language." See Chap. 18.

† This is the home page for the University of Kansas' campuswide information system.

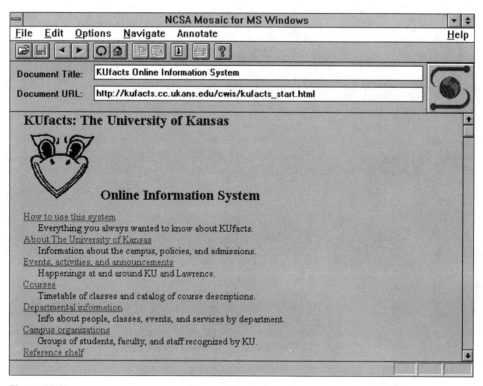

Figure 13.13

Following is the actual HTML text that corresponds to this document as shown by Mosaic. If you glance through the text you will see all of the words that appear on the screen somewhere on the page:

```
<base href="http://kufacts.cc.ukans.edu/cwis/kufacts_start.html">
<HTML>
<HEAD>
<TITLE>KUfacts Online Information System</TITLE>
<!-- OWNER_NAME="Charles Rezac, Academic Computing Services"-->
<LINK rev  ade href="mailto:rezac@ukanaix.cc.ukans.edu ">
<!-- OWNER_INFO="University of Kansas, Consulting (913) 864-0410" -->

</HEAD>
<BODY>
<H1>KUfacts: The University of Kansas<br>
<IMG ALT="" ALIGN="bottom" SRC="hawk_face.xbm">
Online Information System
</H1>
```

```
<dl compact>
<dt><A HREF="how_to.html">How to use this system</A>
<dd>Everything you always wanted to know about KUfacts.

<dt><A HREF="about_ku/about_ku_main.html">About The University of Kansas</a>
<dd>Information about the campus, policies, and admissions.

<dt><A HREF="events/events_main.html">Events, activities, and announcements</A>
<dd>Happenings at and around KU and Lawrence.

<dt><A HREF="courses/courses_main.html">Courses</a>
<dd>Timetable of classes and catalog of course descriptions.

<dt><A HREF="units/units_main.html">Departmental information</a>
<dd>Info about people, classes, events, and services by department.

<dt><A HREF="student_services/student_services_main.html">Campus organizations</a>
<dd>Groups of students, faculty, and staff recognized by KU.

<dt><A HREF="reference/Reference_main.html">Reference shelf</A>
<dd>Reference materials, phonebooks, and worldwide resources.

<dt><A HREF="Index.html">Index</A>
</dl>
</BODY>
</HTML>
```

As a "markup" language, HTML expects authors to embed "tags," or markup, that identify the different elements of the text. The special fields such as <HEAD> constitute the document's tags; the <HEAD> tag identifies the beginning part of the document.* Figure 13.14 depicts how some of these tags correspond to the parts of the document that you see on the screen. The <TITLE> tag establishes the title of the document, which is displayed by Mosaic in the Document Title area as long as this document remains open. The author also wants a nice title to appear in the text area on the user's screen; the <h1> header serves this function. HTML defines up to six layers of "headers"; the <h1> tag is the most prominent of these six levels. In a more

---

* The <HEAD> section makes up the beginning of the document, as opposed to the main body. The HTML specification divides a document into these parts so that, for instance, it is possible for a client to request that the server deliver only the "front matter" instead of the entire text. The rest of the document is marked by the <BODY> tag.

Hypertext Markup Language is used to "mark up" text,
allowing the author to describe hypermedia documents
to be rendered by clients like Mosaic:

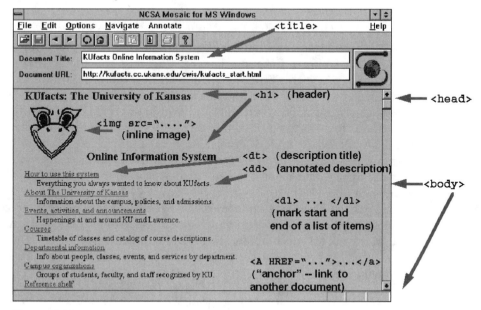

Figure 13.14

complex document an author might use several levels of headers reflecting different subsection levels.

The `<img alt=...src=...>` tag points to an inline image; in this case, that inline image is the logo shown at the beginning of the document. The image is not delivered concurrently with the HTML; instead, the Uniform Resource Locator of the image is sent, and it is up to the client to fetch the image. The image might reside on a different server than the document that points to it.*

Note that many HTML tags require explicit termination of a block of text. The tag for the end of such a block has a slash in front of the name of the tag; see for instance `</HEAD>` at the end of the header text, and `</TITLE>` after title text.

HTML accepts tags in upper or lower case; `<HEAD>` and `<Head>` and `<hEaD>` are all equivalent. All HTML tags begin with a "less than" sign and end with a "greater than" sign.

---

* In this case, the image does reside on the same server as the rest of the page. In fact, a "relative reference" is used to specify the image: the part of the tag SRC="hawk_face.xbm" does not begin with a slash which means the reference is relative; the file is located in the same folder on the same server as the rest of the page we are reading.

Hypertext links in HTML are referred to as "anchors."* The preceding example HTML shows a common form of an anchor; i.e.,

```
<A HREF="UniformResourceLocator"> Title to appear on user screen </A>
```

HREF= is a common attribute that appears in an anchor; it simply is a way of specifying a Uniform Resource Locator that tells the client where to get the document to which this link refers. Immediately following that URL is the text that will appear on the user's screen as the selectable link for this document.

Note that not all of the text that is shown in the HTML document appears on the screen. Text that is intended to be used as a comment is flagged by the <!— tag. The "OWNER_NAME" information is supplied as a special convention within the comment tag; it is understood by the Lynx browser, which will display the owner data when the user requests "item information" by hitting the equal sign.

This particular page is an example of a relatively simple home page; in fact, the document consists of titles and annotated lists of links, with no running text. Many HTML documents are of course much more verbose; the conciseness in this case was a deliberate choice by the author, who wanted an easy-to-skim home page.

Here is the beginning of the HTML text that describes the Vatican Exhibit's home page, shown earlier in this chapter:

```
<base href="http://www.ncsa.uiuc.edu/SDG/Experimental/vatican.
    exhibit/Vatican.exhibit.html">
<title>Vatican Exhibit--Rome Reborn</title>
<h1>Vatican Exhibit</h1>
<p><img src="exhibit/gifs/hall.gif"><p>
Welcome to the Library of Congress Vatican Exhibit.
<h1>Introduction</h1>
<h2>The City Reborn</h2>
<h3>How the City Came Back to Life</h3>

Rome now is one of the grandest cities in the world. Millions of
pilgrims and tourists come every year to admire, and be awed by,
its treasures of architecture, art, and history. But it was not
always this way. <P>

By the fourteenth century, the great ancient city had dwindled to a
miserable village. Perhaps 20,000 people clung to the ruins despite
```

---

* Anchors can also be used to identify named sections within a document, so that another document can link to any of those named sections.

```
the ravages of disease and robber barons. Popes and cardinals had
fled to Avignon in southern France. Rome was dwarfed in wealth and
power by the great commercial cities and territorial states farther
north, from Florence to Venice. <P>   ....
```

This document contains somewhat more verbiage than the Kansas page. The <P> tag denotes the end of each paragraph. This is the signal to the client that it should depict the break between paragraphs—however it is configured to do so. In the World-Wide Web universe, control over the exact rendering of a document on the user's screen is up to the user and to the client software (for instance, Mosaic). This allows Web documents to be adapted to a variety of monitors and window sizes. Very little control is given to the author of the document or the administrator of the Web server delivering the document. A client might offer the user the choice of whether a new paragraph is to have one blank line before it—or none, or two. This user/client control over how a document appears extends to other areas: the user configures options as to what font, character size, use of boldfacing, etc., is to be used for the different elements of a document. If the user wants H1 headers to appear in 24-point Helvetica, and H2 headers to appear in 10-point Courier, that is the user's choice.*

HTML defines some tags that provide the author with a modicum of control over rendering, however. For instance, a <br> tag explicitly specifies a line break exactly where the author wants it. Without this option, large headlines might be displayed with odd breaks, depending on the user's font choice and window size. Another item offering some authorial control is the <hr> tag, which tells the Web client to insert a "horizontal rule" in the document. An author might denote various sections of a document by using the <hr> tag.

Another tag to note is the <address> tag, which is used to show the address of the owner or author of a document. Clients like Mosaic by default render the text associated with this tag in a different font than other text so that the information appears as a distinct line, analogous to the signature at the end of a letter. It's also a common practice in the Web for document authors to include links to a short online biography of themselves.

This overview shows the highlights of HTML; the purpose is to explain the basic concepts of how markup is used by Web authors to deliver the rich hypertext documents their readers expect. For users, it is not necessary to understand HTML in detail; a user can point Mosaic (or another Web client) at a starting point on the Web and cruise with abandon without ever seeing the

---

* Of course, documents will be easier to read if the fonts chosen for various headers and other special text items are chosen rationally. Note that HTML does afford authors the opportunity to specify whether text is to appear in boldface, italics, or underlined (respectively, with <b>, <i>, and <u> tags).

underlying HTML that makes the magic possible. Users who decide to become information providers on the Web will need to learn more about how HTML works; more pointers are provided in Chap. 20.

As we've seen, HTML is the language used for markup within Web documents. A related set of rules governs the transmission of documents over the Web. Known as the Hypertext Transfer Protocol, or HTTP, this protocol specifies how Web clients fetch documents, and provides ways for "meta-information"—information about a document that is not part of the document, such as the date it was last modified—to be exchanged. HTTP allows servers to offer different document types, based on the MIME model.* Design documents also call for HTTP to offer a framework for features such as authorization and charging; these features are not yet solidified.

Here is an example of the most common dialog in HTTP, whereby a client fetches the page from the Kansas Web server shown previously. This is analogous to the "manual" fetching of a root Gopher menu shown in Chap. 12:

```
telnet kufacts.cc.ukans.edu 80
Trying 129.237.33.1...
Connected to ukanaix.cc.ukans.edu.
Escape character is '^]'.
GET /cwis/kufacts_start.html HTTP/1.0
```

[Followed by the HTML document shown previously; the connection is then closed.]

You can use this manual mode of connection to observe the behavior of HTTP servers. Note that HTTP servers expect commands such as GET to appear in capital letters. If you want to save a document in HTML in order to examine it, there is a more direct approach: Mosaic offers options to save a document as HTML (or as PostScript or raw text); alternatively, you can send a copy of a document to yourself via e-mail. Examining existing HTML documents can be a fruitful way to learn more about how HTML works.

Nomenclature may be the greatest enemy of the Web. It is important to distinguish carefully between HTML and HTTP. As we've seen, HTML is the language that enables authors to write hypertext (or hypermedia) documents that can be interpreted by clients for presentation to users. HTTP is the communications protocol that governs the dialog between client and server; it is the set of requests and responses that allows a client to fetch HTML documents. Both specifications are essential to defining the World-Wide Web. Note that you will often see Web servers referred to as HTTP servers. Generally speaking, HTTP and HTML go hand in hand.[†]

---

* Thus HTTP incorporates some of the design goals of Gopher+.

[†] Many World-Wide Web enthusiasts define the Web as all-encompassing, subsuming other technologies such as Gopher and WAIS. For our purposes in this book we use the term more narrowly, to refer specifically to the use of HTTP and HTML to provide networked hypertext.

ORIGINS OF THE WORLD-WIDE WEB

The World-Wide Web is the brainchild of Tim Berners-Lee, who works at the European particle physics research facility known as CERN. Berners-Lee experimented with hypertext-like systems as early as 1980. In 1989, Berners-Lee conceived of a hypertext-oriented, networked document delivery system to serve as a way to integrate a large collection of documents to serve the needs of the researchers using CERN facilities. The idea was to overcome the incompatibilities of numerous document formats, and offer text over the network with a client/server interface. At the beginning, Berners-Lee recognized the possibility of incorporating sound and images (thus yielding hypermedia) but his initial focus was text. Berners-Lee and collaborator Robert Cailliau issued early design memoranda in March 1989 and October 1990.

Berners-Lee developed a prototype tool for the Next workstation in November 1990, and a line mode browser was developed that month as well. Development work continued over the next several months, and the term World-Wide Web came to be used to describe the project. In August 1991 the World-Wide Web was announced on the `alt.hypertext` news group. Much of the early penetration of the Web took place in the worldwide high-energy physics community.

In January 1993, two clients became available for the X Window platform. At that time there were about 50 servers online worldwide. NCSA released the X version of Mosaic in March 1993; awareness of this tool spread throughout the year. The lead developers were Marc Andreessen and Eric Bina. The Macintosh and Windows versions became available in fall 1993. The Lynx client was announced in spring 1993. Throughout 1993 numerous Web servers appeared worldwide; there were over 700 servers worldwide by the end of that year.

Several alternatives to the CERN server became available in 1993; see Chap. 20 (and CERN's online documentation at the address shown above) for more details.

Much of the corpus of the World-Wide Web effort exists in the form of `libwww`. This is a standard library of program code that is used by various Web clients (including Mosaic) and by HTTP servers. Much of the early code in the library was written by Berners-Lee and collaborators at CERN; in recent months the World-Wide Web community has submitted improvements that have found their way into the library.

NAVIGATING THE WEB

The philosophy of the Web implicitly rejects the idea of a "top node" or "mother of all Webs," but CERN serves as one logical starting point; point your client at

```
http://info.cern.ch/hypertext/WWW/TheProject.html
```

There you will find connections to other Web servers, categorized by type and by subject, as well as comprehensive information on Web clients and servers, and the history of the Web.

Another good starting point is NCSA, which offers information on Mosaic and the NCSA HTTP server, as well as their own list of interesting sites on the Web. A good starting document is `http://www.ncsa.uiuc.edu/SDG/Software/Mosaic/Docs/mosaic.docs.html`. NCSA offers good online descriptions of Mosaic, a "What's New" page that is a good source for new Web services, and a description of HTML that explains the basic capabilities while offering online examples of text as rendered. Also see the NCSA Mosaic Demonstration at `http://www.ncsa.uiuc.edu/demoweb/demo.html`.

Many sites offer pointers to these sites, and to other sites that have undertaken their own efforts to provide indexes of the Web.

Navigating the Web can be frustrating at times—for some users more so than Gopher navigation. Some argue that networked hypertext is indeed a Web—something that ensnares the hapless user. It is certainly possible for an author of a Web document to build in so many cross-links that it becomes impossible for the user to recognize any structure to the space being navigated. On the other hand, it is possible for a Web author to construct links that are highly organized—even to the point of building a hierarchy as rigid as that imposed by Gopher. Thus, one can use the hypertext model even if one's design philosophy calls for spare menus. Web advocates argue that the greater flexibility of hypertext offers flexibility for the reader.

Web advocates also point out that too many Gopher documents include sentences like "Look under the About Mythical State University folder, then go to the Photo Gallery menu, then look . . ." No Web document would contain such indirect hints to the user; the link would be on the screen, and the document would be one click away.

Regardless of the relative merits of Gopher and the Web, both tools seem likely to endure for quite a while, and navigation will remain a key issue for users of both. We will discuss some of the solutions being devised to aid navigation in subsequent chapters.

# Chapter 14

Internet Index Tools: Archie, Veronica, and Friends

During the early 1990s users came to view the Internet not merely as a series of autonomous hosts on autonomous networks, but also as a worldwide collection of shared resources. Tools like Gopher and World-Wide Web have provided users with ways to browse lists of resources on the Internet, and have provided information providers with new ways to deliver documents to a worldwide audience. In any given excursion, the documents you look at might all be resident on a single server, or they might be scattered across the global Internet.

Quickly, however, it has become apparent that the browsing model has its limitations. Few users will have the time or patience to scan for documents across a wide range of hosts, visiting each service one at a time, scanning each server for items of interest. For instance, suppose you want to find documents relating to weather on Gopher servers worldwide. To do so manually, scanning every Gopher server on the Internet, would take days. One alternative might be to find a good list of such servers by connecting to one of the many subject catalogs now in existence. Even though subject-oriented lists require a great deal of human effort to create and maintain, numerous attempts at building such catalogs have been undertaken. In contrast to manually maintained subject catalogs, there are also resource indexes that are maintained by automated processes. In this chapter we will explore some of the tools that allow users to search for items by file name or document title. In Chap. 15, we will examine a different tool, WAIS, which allows searching for documents based on the entire text *within* each of a set of documents. Chapter 16 offers strategies for searching the Internet using all of these tools, and provides more information on subject catalogs now in existence.

We have seen examples of title indexes that enable a user of a particular service to find all the documents whose titles contain a certain string of text. For instance, a Gopher server might offer a local index that lets you quickly locate all documents related to "athletics." Internet index tools allow you to perform this sort of search *across* a set of servers dispersed around the global Internet. For instance, a tool that indexes titles found on Gopher servers accessible worldwide might help you find all the Gopher servers with documents whose titles include the word "weather" (see Fig. 14.1).

Internet toolsmiths have forged index servers that allow users to search for resources in this manner, freeing them from this burdensome server-by-server search. The first of these to gain prominence was Archie.

ARCHIE

One of the first tools providing an Internet-wide index facility is known as Archie. Developed by a team at McGill University,* Archie's initial goal was to provide an index of anonymous FTP archives. Suppose you are looking for a particular file, whether it be a public domain computer program, a NASA photograph, or a monograph someone has written. Suppose further that you know the name of the file, but not which FTP services might hold a copy. Without Archie, you would face a most tedious search process. With Archie, you can locate such files quickly.

Like many of the other tools we have seen, Archie operates on the client/server model. There are a number of well-known Archie servers around the world. Periodically, through a cooperative effort among these index servers, anonymous FTP servers around the world are polled as to their current collections. An index of all the holdings on all of these FTP servers is built and propagated among the Archie servers. Users can interrogate an Archie server, which consults this index and lists all anonymous FTP sites that hold the sought files.

Services like Archie may give the impression that they are searching in real time across the global sea of anonymous FTP servers, and reporting back what they find. This is a misconception. To do such a search in response to every query would be enormously expensive in terms of real time and computer and network resources. Instead, Archie follows a strategy of periodically polling its list of known FTP servers; newly discovered files are added to its database.

---

* The main developers of Archie were Peter Deutsch and Alan Emtage. Deutsch and Emtage have formed a corporation, Bunyip Information Systems, that is centered around the commercial development of Archie.

Using an Internet Index Server

"List all the documents in Gopherspace with 'weather' in their titles"

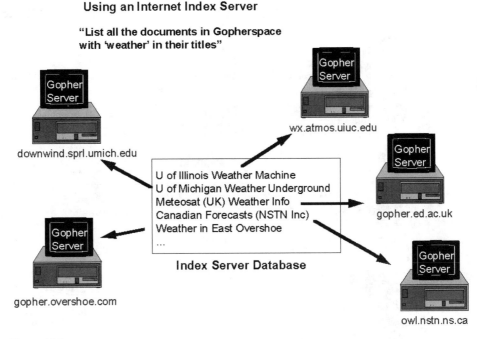

Figure 14.1

Because there are several Archie servers distributed worldwide, the Archie developers have invested some effort in distributing this information-gathering task among the servers. Figure 14.2 shows a simplified view of what the process looks like.

Although there are Archie client programs for various computer platforms, deployment of these clients isn't quite as common as one sees with, for instance, Gopher clients. Many users take advantage of the public Archie clients available on the Internet. A list of these public clients can be found via Gopher. For instance, the Gopher server at Michigan State University offers the list of public Archie services shown in Fig. 14.3.*

As denoted by the terminal icon, each of these documents points to a Telnet session on the named host. Upon selecting any of these hosts, you would log in under the user name `archie` with no password required.

Unfortunately, due to popularity, you may find the server you've chosen is busy. One of the first commands you might type to an Archie server is `servers`, which will provide an up-to-date list of all known servers. (Gopher-based lists should be fairly complete but in some cases may not have the most recent addi-

---

* At `gopher.msu.edu`, look under `Network and Database Resources`, then `Internet Resources by Type`. You can find similar lists of Archie servers at many Gopher and World-Wide Web servers.

How Archie Works: Indexing FTP Servers Internet-Wide

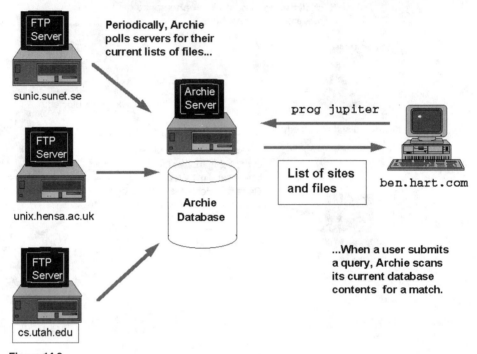

Periodically, Archie polls servers for their current lists of files...

sunic.sunet.se

unix.hensa.ac.uk

cs.utah.edu

Archie Server

Archie Database

prog jupiter

List of sites and files

ben.hart.com

...When a user submits a query, Archie scans its current database contents for a match.

Figure 14.2

tions.) If your chosen server is often busy, pick another one from the list. As a rule it is a good idea to try a server that is close to you geographically.

Here is an example session using the Telnet-accessible version of Archie:

```
telnet archie.sura.net
Trying 128.167.254.195
Connected to yog.sothoth.sura.net
Escape character is '^]'.
```

The public Archie service accepts a number of commands. For information about command options, type help. For our demonstration purposes, we want to limit the number of "hits," or items returned in response to our search, to six:

```
archie> set maxhits 6
```

Archie was originally a tool for finding programs; today it is used to look for all sorts of files, but the command prog is used to initiate a search. For instance, if we want to find photographs of Jupiter, we might issue the command:

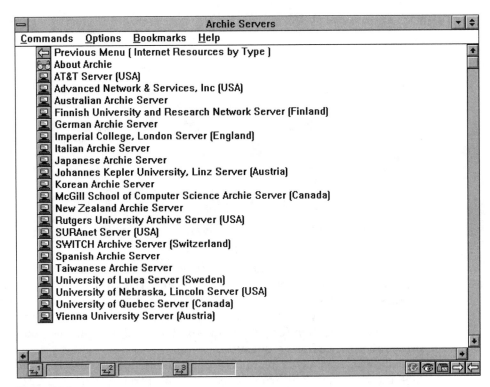

Figure 14.3

```
archie> prog jupiter
```

Results might look like this:

```
# matches / % database searched:    6 /   4%
Host xanth.cs.odu.edu    (128.82.4.1)
Last updated 05:28 17 Jan 1994

    Location: /pub/tccas-gif/nasa-color
       FILE      rwxr-xr-x    357376  Apr 17  1992   jupiter.gif

Host plaza.aarnet.edu.au    (139.130.4.6)
Last updated 07:05 15 Jan 1994

    Location: /micros/pc/garbo/pc/gif-astro
       FILE       r--r--r--    74011  Mar 16  1993   jupiter.gif

Host ftp.germany.eu.net    (192.76.144.75)
Last updated 22:17  6 Jan 1994
```

```
        Location: /pub/comp/msdos/mirror.garbo/gif-astro
           FILE        rw-r--r--      74011  Mar 16  1993     jupiter.gif

Host cnam.cnam.fr    (163.173.128.6)
Last updated 04:23  4 Jan 1994

        Location: /pub/Astro/jupiter
           FILE        rw-r--r--      74011  Oct  2 12:56     jupiter.gif

Host ee.lbl.gov    (128.3.112.20)
Last updated 07:38  5 Jan 1994

        Location: /poskbitmaps/j
           FILE        rw-r--r--      77901  Jan  6  1993     jupiter1.gif
           FILE        rw-r--r--      97708  Jan  6  1993     jupiter2.gif
```

An Archie search can take a number of seconds or perhaps much longer, depending on how busy the server is and the nature of your search. As requested, this search was terminated after six hits—six files matching our search request—were found. Archie displays the name of the anonymous FTP site, and the location (or path name) under which the file was found, and the full names of the files in question.

Archie can perform several different kinds of searches of its database. By default, the search pattern you specify is interpreted as a "regular expression." This is a term commonly used in Unix to describe patterns that can be used for sophisticated kinds of matching. In its simplest case, as we saw in the example above, the Archie regular expression search will match any file name containing the substring "jupiter." Regular expressions are analogous to the use of wildcards in filenames under operating systems like MS-DOS, but the language is more powerful and somewhat more obscure. To find out more about regular expressions as used in Archie searches, type `help regex` while connected to an Archie server (or consult a Unix how-to manual).

You can choose among the different types of Archie searches by using the command:

```
set search [type]
```

The types of Archie searches are as follows:

regex   The regular expression search described previously (default).

exact   The file or directory name must match exactly the string you type, character by character. This search is fastest because it requires the least work by the server.

sub   The string you type matches a file name if it appears anywhere within the name, regardless of case. For instance, "Chive" matches "archive."

subcase   The string you type matches a file name if it appears within the name, and if the case matches. For instance, "Chive" does not match "archive" but it does match "arChive."

There are Archie clients for various computer platforms. Some clients offer little more than the interface you see when you log into a public client; interaction is textual and via keyboard commands. Other clients, such as the X Window client and the Nextstep client, are more graphical and powerful. For instance, the Nextstep client will not only search the database for you, it will also retrieve files from the chosen host and path name, conducting the FTP session on your behalf. Figure 14.4 is an example of how that client lets you choose from among a list of files the one you wish to retrieve.

If your style of Internet access is e-mail-only, you can still make use of Archie. An Archie e-mail server resides at `archie@sura.net`. You can send e-mail to the server containing your Archie commands and you will receive responses by mail. For more details on the e-mail server, send a message to its address with the word `help` as the body of the message. Note that as an e-mail-only user you can combine the use of the Archie mail server with the use of mail servers for anonymous FTP. This empowers you as an e-mail-only user both to search for files residing on the various anonymous FTP archives around the globe and to retrieve the files that interest you. As we saw in Chap.

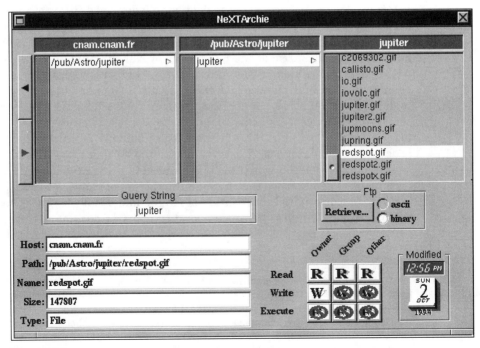

Figure 14.4

9, thanks to encoding schemes used by the FTP mail servers, you can even retrieve binary files such as programs or images via e-mail.

While connected to a public Archie service over Telnet you can also request that the output of your last command be sent to you via e-mail. This can be useful if the list of files is rather large and you want to digest the information later. For instance, you could do an Archie search while dialed in on a slow connection from home, and have the results mailed to your e-mail address at work for later use. For details on this option, type `help mail` while connected to an Archie service.

In addition to the options of using Telnet to access a public Archie client, or running an Archie client locally on your workstation, or using the e-mail interface, there is one more mode of access to Archie: a gateway from another service. For instance, a couple of attempts have been made to offer Archie gateways from World-Wide Web. One of these, developed by a programmer in the United Kingdom named Martijn Koster, uses Mosaic forms support to provide a simple fill-in-the-blank interface to Archie. If you wish to experiment with this service, point your Mosaic client at `http://web.nexor.co.uk/archie.html`.

VERONICA

Anonymous FTP is one of the oldest ways that information is offered on the Internet; Archie, in turn, was the first widely deployed Internet index scheme. As Gopher gained popularity throughout 1992, it became obvious that there was a need for an analogous tool in Gopherspace. In November 1992, Steven Foster and Fred Barrie of the University of Nevada announced a service that could search document titles across many Gopher servers. Other tools had been developed that allowed searching within a Gopher's hierarchy; their new tool could search across Gopher servers worldwide.* Foster and Barrie christened their service Veronica.[†] Just as Archie surveys anonymous FTP servers for their list of holdings, Veronica must periodically poll its target servers in order to build a database. A user connecting to Veronica specifies a keyword to search for, say for the word "biology," and gets a list of document titles from throughout Gopherspace that include that string of characters.

Whereas the original incarnation of Archie had the basic goal of searching a database of file names, Veronica searches a list of document titles. Veronica

---

* For instance, in summer 1992 Dennis Boone of Michigan State University offered a pair of tools known as Gophertree and `ts/tb` that produced a "road map" of a single Gopher server and a means for doing a keyword search of a server's document titles.

† The Nevada team says the name Veronica is an acronym for "Very Easy Rodent-Oriented Netwide Index to Computerized Archives." More than one observer has noticed the association of the names Archie and Veronica in the famous comic strip.

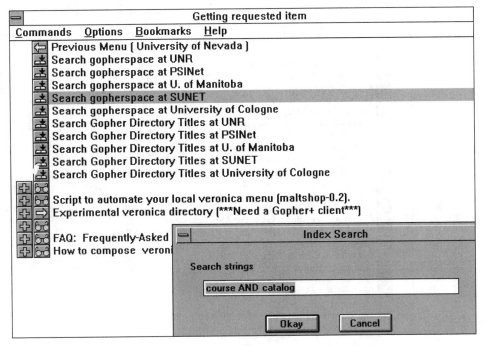

Figure 14.5

supports a different set of search options than Archie. In particular, it allows boolean searches of its title database. For instance, if you wanted to find titles on Gopher servers that relate to university course catalogs, you might do a search as shown in Fig. 14.5.

Most Gopher servers offer a list of Veronica servers such as the one seen here.* When you select a title that points to a Veronica server, your Gopher client will ask you for the string of text you want to search for. It then submits the query to the Veronica server you have chosen, and that server scans its database. The search might take several seconds, or perhaps a minute or more. This particular search asks for a list of all titles with "course" and "catalog" in the title. If only one of the two words appears in a given title, that title does not match. (However, the title would match if "course" and "catalog" are not adjacent, or even if they appear in reverse order, potentially leading to false hits.) The results of this sort of search might look like Fig. 14.6.

Veronica returns a list of document titles in Gopher form, and your Gopher client displays that list of titles as if it were any other list of Gopher docu-

---

* As of this writing the Veronica team is implementing a scheme to allow a Gopher server to pick the least-busy Veronica service for you automatically.

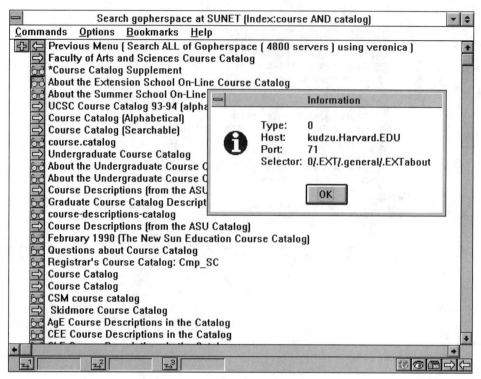

Figure 14.6

ments. You can select any of the titles and jump off to the document in question. Therefore Veronica provides the user a somewhat more intimate linkage to the Gopher documents it indexes than Archie can provide for anonymous FTP.

One problem becomes obvious when you look at Fig. 14.6: the various titles are yanked out of their hierarchical context and presented on the screen with no clues as to their normal surroundings. For instance, we do not know if "About the Extension School On-line Course Catalog" comes from Auburn University, the University of Wisconsin, or the University of California at Davis. In this case the answer becomes clear if we use the "Item Info" option of our Gopher client; that particular title happens to reside at Harvard University. Virtually every Veronica search using common terms may suffer from this sort of loss of context. This is purely an artifact of pulling each title out of its place in a Gopher hierarchy; it would not make sense for Harvard (and every other organization offering a Gopher service) to include the name of the institution in every title served by their Gopher.

A related form of context loss becomes apparent with these sorts of searches: the same word may have radically different meanings in different places. If you do a Veronica search looking for information on the Wharton School of Economics, you will find many documents that relate to that institution, but you will also find documents on the Wharton Center for the Performing Arts at Michigan State University.

But these are mere quibbles compared to the alternative of not having a tool like Veronica. Without this sort of tool, one would have to manually search the directory trees at each of the thousands of servers on the network. Many of those Gopher servers offer no local indexes of their own documents, so you would have to manually traverse each part of the hierarchy. Veronica can help you find a document searching all of Gopherspace in less time than it might take you to find it manually hunting through *one* Gopher server.

Another advantage that Veronica has over manual searches is its handling of duplicate pointers to the same resource. Many of the titles in Gopherspace are pointers to popular resources elsewhere in Gopherspace. This is a natural evolution—when a popular document or service becomes known to a server administrator, the natural tendency is to add a pointer to it in the local Gopher server. If one were manually searching across a number of Gopher servers, one would encounter many such duplicate pointers. Veronica tries to collapse these duplicates down to a single pointer, favoring if possible the "parent" pointer on the same server that owns the document.*

Proof of the utility of Veronica comes from the results of recent Internet Hunts. These monthly quizzes, issued by Rick Gates, a librarian and Internet enthusiast, challenge users to find answers to arcane questions using only Internet resources, and to report where the information was found. (For example, "Who is the author of the only book held by Victoria University of Wellington on the training of sheep dogs?") Increasingly, the winners of the Hunt have exploited the power of Veronica to enhance their burrowing through Gopherspace.†

REFINED SEARCHES USING VERONICA

The Veronica menu shown previously offers two basic kinds of searches: searches for titles generally, or searches restricted to Gopher directory titles. The latter kind of search can return a much shorter list of candidate documents, which may let you hone in on the information you are looking for quickly. Of course, for this tactic to succeed, the document in question must be a directory name as such. You will want to experiment with both kinds of

---

* But it does not always succeed in collapsing duplicate document pointers. For example, the same Gopher server may be listed under different host names, making it hard for Veronica to recognize the identity between two pointers.

† The Internet Hunt is posted monthly to numerous mailing lists and Usenet News groups. Archives of the Hunt can be found on the CICnet Gopher server, `gopher.cic.net`.

Figure 14.7

searches. (For instance, you might try looking for "course and catalog" using both search options.)

It is important that you not accidentally select the directory search when you want the general one (labeled "Search gopherspace"). If you do so you will often miss many or all of the items you are looking for. If all of your searches are coming back with little or no information, you may be choosing the directory-titles-only search by accident.

You can refine the general title search by type of document. The -t parameter allows you to limit the search by Gopher document type. For instance, if you are looking for images of towers stored on Gopher servers, you might submit the search shown in Fig. 14.7.

This search might yield a list looking like Fig. 14.8.

This search succeeds because the type "I" is used to identify all of these documents. Any Gopher type may be used, and if you want to search for more than one type at once, you can concatenate the types.* For instance, if you want to search for Telnet links or documents that might refer to course catalogs, your query might look like this:

```
course and catalog -t18
```

By default, Veronica servers limit the number of titles returned in any given search to 200. You can request a different limit by specifying a -m parameter on the search. For instance if you want to find up to 1000 titles with the word "manufacturing" you would type:

```
manufacturing -m1000
```

Veronica allows you to search for partial words as well. To catch titles with "manufacture" or "manufacturing" you might submit the search:

```
manufactur*
```

---

* See the list of Gopher types in Chap. 12. As Gopher+ is deployed, Veronica may adapt to allowing searches of Gopher+ types; see the online documentation for Veronica for details.

eiffel_tower.gif
tower.gif
tower_of_jewels.gif
tower.gif
tower.jpg
Bell Tower.gif [14Oct93, 133kb]
Bell Tower color.gif [18Oct93, 223kb]
Ivory tower (640×480; 39991)

Figure 14.8

These various search options can be combined in very powerful ways. One caveat to note as you begin to invoke complex Veronica searches is that sometimes there are artifacts of the use of WAIS as the underlying search engine that may cause searches to behave a little differently than you would expect from a strict boolean index.* Generally, however, you will get the results you expect.

You can read more about Veronica by connecting to the Gopher server at the University of Nevada at Reno: `veronica.scs.unr.edu`, port 70, under the Veronica directory.†

In March 1993, carrying on in the Archie vein, Rhett Jones of the University of Utah announced a Gopher title search tool called "Jughead." Jughead is used by a number of Gopher administrators as a tool for indexing their local Gopher hierarchies. Generally if a site is using Jughead as an index, this fact is transparent to you. You can find more information on Jughead in the Gopher news archives available via the Minnesota Gopher service; the software is available for FTP from Minnesota's archive server (`boombox.micro.umn.edu`).

WORLD-WIDE WEB INDEX SERVERS

The World-Wide Web enjoyed dramatic growth in 1993, and that growth made it obvious that a tool analogous to Veronica was needed. Indexing the Web is a bit more complicated than indexing Gopher servers, however. An HTML document is considerably more verbose than a list of titles in a Gopher menu. The "titles" associated with a hyperlink may be a paragraph or more of text—or they may be "titles" as terse as the word "here," as in "Click *here* for a map of Australia."

---

* For instance, you cannot currently search for all the titles that begin with "t" and are of type I; you have to specify a longer root word, like "tower," to feed the index engine.

† The selector string for retrieving Veronica at this Gopher site is `1/veronica`.

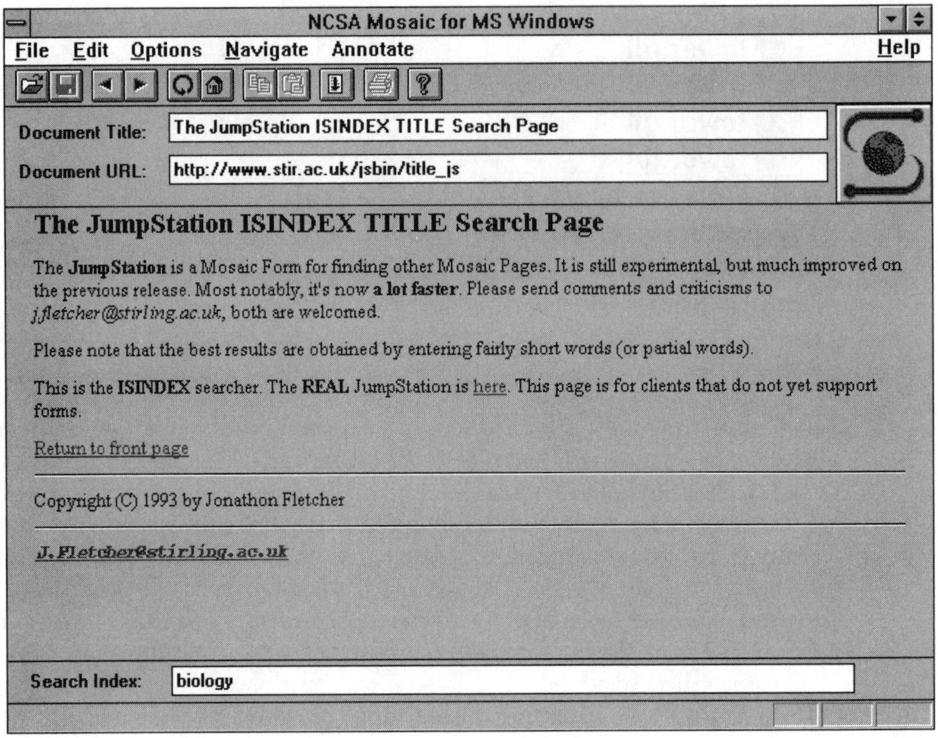

The JumpStation ISINDEX TITLE Search Page

Document Title: The JumpStation ISINDEX TITLE Search Page

Document URL: http://www.stir.ac.uk/jsbin/title_js

The JumpStation ISINDEX TITLE Search Page

The **JumpStation** is a Mosaic Form for finding other Mosaic Pages. It is still experimental, but much improved on the previous release. Most notably, it's now **a lot faster**. Please send comments and criticisms to *j.fletcher@stirling.ac.uk*, both are welcomed.

Please note that the best results are obtained by entering fairly short words (or partial words).

This is the **ISINDEX** searcher. The **REAL** JumpStation is here. This page is for clients that do not yet support forms.

Return to front page

Copyright (C) 1993 by Jonathon Fletcher

J.Fletcher@stirling.ac.uk

Search Index: biology

Figure 14.9

Indexing the Uniform Resource Locators would not be a satisfying alternative; these names are intended for consumption by client and server, not humans.

Despite these challenges, as of this writing there have been several efforts to build automated Web index tools. One of these is called the JumpStation.* This tool indexes the titles or headers associated with each page offered on the Web. Figure 14.9 shows an example of submitting a search to JumpStation.

Figure 14.10 shows the results one might see from this sort of search using the JumpStation.

We can expect more attempts to catalog the Web to appear over time. You can find a current list of indexing efforts, both automated and otherwise, on the Web server at CERN.† See Chap. 16 for a discussion of other kinds of Web indexes such as subject and geographical lists.

---

* JumpStation was implemented by Jonathon Fletcher of Stirling University in the United Kingdom. Examples shown by permission.

† See

http://info.cern.ch/hypertext/DataSources/bySubject/Virtual_libraries/Overview.html

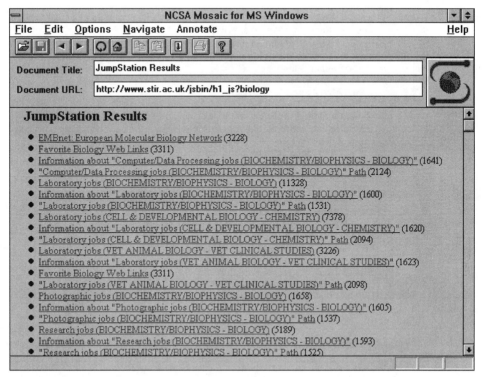

Figure 14.10

NETLINK

John Doyle of Washington and Lee University has used Veronica data, Jughead software, and his own programming to create an index service that strives to provide a comprehensive view across Internet information services, while limiting the depth of searches. Called Netlink, Doyle's service offers access to a variety of services organized by type of service. Netlink is perhaps the first Internet index tool that combines various Internet resources into a single index, allowing searches across these varied types of tools. The service combines automatic and manual efforts, and records the date of the addition of a service as a searchable field.

Netlink can be accessed via Telnet at `netlink.wlu.edu`. (Log in as `netlink` with no password required.) Gopher-based and World-Wide Web views of the service are also available.* The root menu, as viewed via Gopher, looks like Fig. 14.11.

---

* The Gopher link is hot `liberty.uc.wlu.edu`, port 1020, null selector. The Uniform Resource Locator for access via the World-Wide Web is:

`http://netlink.wlu.edu:1020/`

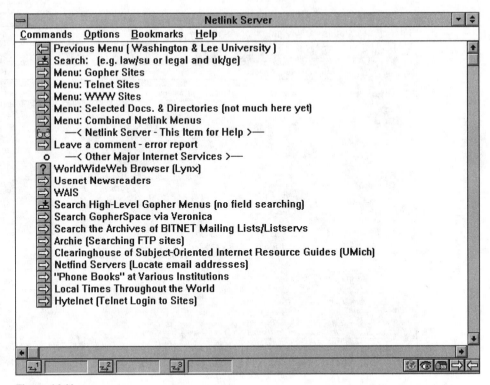

Figure 14.11

The Netlink option "Search High-Level Gopher Menus" offers a variant on the Veronica theme; it only traverses several layers deep in each Gopher server rather than "walking" the entire hierarchy. This service enhances each title by appending the name of the host on which the document resides, partially addressing the loss of context experienced in Veronica searches. A search of Netlink's high-level Gopher menus index for "weather" yields results like those shown in Fig. 14.12.

Netlink offers both a menu-oriented view of resources, and a sophisticated search facility that is more structured than that of Archie or Veronica. You can specify search options for the following fields:

Field	Code	Example
Date added to Netlink database	da	9312*/da (added in December 1993)
Subject	su	humanities/su
Domain-style Host name	ho	msu/ho (host name contains "msu")
Document/Resource Name	na	michigan/na (host name contains "Michigan")
Document Type	ty	I/ty (Gopher type "I"); x/ty (WWW executable)
Geographic	ge	au/ge (resources located in Australia)

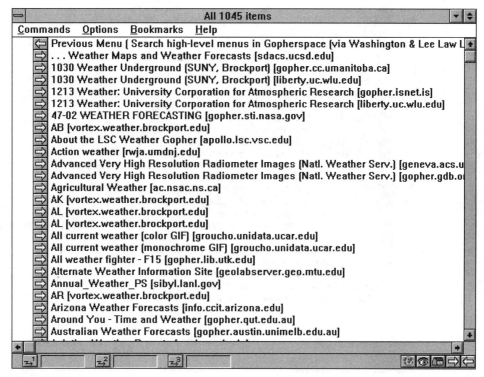

Figure 14.12

Suppose, for instance, that we want to find a list of Gopher servers whose titles include the word "biology." We might submit the query `biology/na` to Netlink; the result would look like Fig. 14.13.

The menus listed are broken down by type of service, or you can select the combined list of services. Figure 14.14 is the list of Gopher services offered as a result of our "biology" query. The last title listed in this example—"Text copy of links"—is another useful special feature of Netlink. This list of links includes the host name, port number, and selector string for each item listed in the accompanying menu. You could use this document to build a list of book-

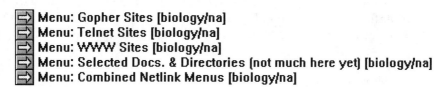

Figure 14.13

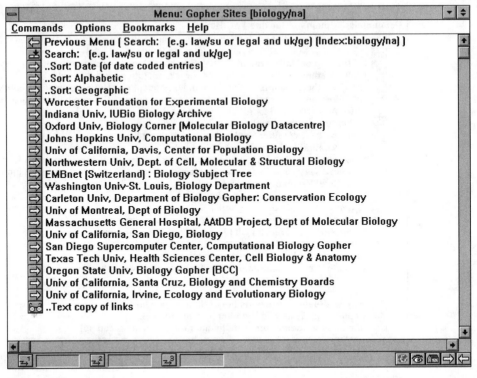

Figure 14.14

marks for your Gopher client by simply cutting and pasting the specific information for each entry. Or, if you run a Gopher server, the file could help you build a custom menu on behalf of your users. You could use Netlink's search options to locate items of interest in Gopherspace, and the text copy of links to help build your own Gopher menus.

You can combine search requests with Netlink in powerful ways. If you want to find any information servers on the Internet with "Russia" in their name that were added in January 1994, you would submit this search:

```
russia/na 9401*/da
```

Netlink is unusual in its use of dynamic menus. If you want a different sort order for the list shown in Fig. 14.14, you merely select a special document title listed at the top of the menu.* As with Veronica, you can select any title and

---

* This is accomplished by encoding the sort request into the selector string. This somewhat arcane scheme may interest future Internet service administrators or software developers; it allows the Gopher administrator to offer customized documents, storing necessary information in the client workstation. For instance, the selector for the "Sort by date" option for this search is:
`-in gop biology/na -sd`.

jump directly to it. As an additional service, Netlink offers at the end of the list a text document containing the complete "item info" for all the titles; this makes it easy for you to cut and paste pointers for resources into bookmark files—or into a Gopher or Web server you might be building.

Netlink even offers a better window into Veronica. As an alternative to having the user embed cryptic search options in the search string, Netlink offers a variety of "canned" search choices. Figure 14.15 is an example.

By choosing among different menu choices, you can select a type of service and a maximum number of "hits" you are willing to have listed. Netlink submits your request to Veronica with the necessary options automatically appended. This menu-oriented mechanism should prove more convenient and intuitive than having the user specify use of options such as -t in the search string.

THE USEFULNESS
OF INTERNET INDEX TOOLS

Considering the recent advent of advanced Internet information delivery tools, and the disorganized nature of the Internet, index tools do a remarkable job of indexing the wonderful chaos of the Internet. Tools like Archie and Veronica

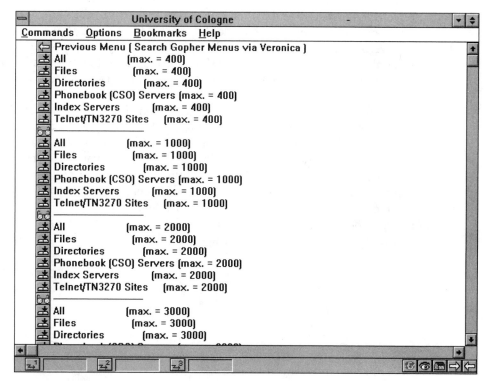

Figure 14.15

Figure 14.16

are relatively new, but they are enjoying considerable popularity. Archie developers estimate that over 2.5 million files appear in their indexes. (Many of these files are duplicates; for instance, a popular image or piece of public domain software might appear at dozens of anonymous FTP sites.) As of this writing, Veronica indexes documents residing on almost 5000 Gopher servers worldwide. The Veronica team estimates that about one million searches per month are requested by users of the various Veronica servers in existence. The Veronica index alone takes up over 1.3 gigabytes of space on the server's disk.

Not surprisingly this level of usage means that these services are busy. From time to time a server will reject your call, either politely or otherwise. For instance, you may receive the message shown in Fig. 14.16. When this happens you can either retry the request on this server, or pick a different server that might be less loaded.

Netlink sets the standard for the next wave of Internet index tools. Its ability to support combinations of field-oriented searches, and its use of dynamically created menus, place Netlink in the league of professional database tools and online commercial search services—the sorts of tools that allow an information professional like a librarian to hone in on results quickly. Yet Netlink shows that such power can be packaged with a friendly user interface.

We can also expect to see greater integration of items indexed by these tools. Bunyip Information Systems has announced that they will extend the scope of Archie to include indexing of Gopherspace. Effectively, Archie and the new tool will become a unified index of Gopherspace and the world of anonymous FTP. Similarly, a tool like Netlink or the JumpStation could embrace indexing of titles in Gopherspace *and* the World-Wide Web, not just one or the other. Integration of multiple kinds of indexes under one index service would free Internet searchers from the artificial distinction imposed by having to negotiate the different types of servers separately.

15

WAIS: Wide Area Information Servers

Online databases have become important elements of everyday life—from airline reservation systems to prescription databases at the pharmacy to computerized inventory control at the grocery store to online library catalogs. Most of these databases are "structured" databases; for instance, a library catalog has a particular field for the name of the author, another field for the call number, another field for the abstract, another field for the name of the person currently borrowing the book, etc. WAIS, by contrast, is an example of an "unstructured" database facility—its goal is to allow a user to quickly perform keyword searches of the full text of a large collection of documents. The queries are not field-oriented; each query is a search of all the words in a document, not particular words in the context of a field such as "author."

We've seen other tools, such as Gopher and World-Wide Web, that could fairly be described as "wide area information servers." How does WAIS compare? The following analogy, attributed to WAIS designer Brewster Kahle, underscores the differences. If the Internet is a book, then:

- Gopher provides the table of contents.
- World-Wide Web delivers the text.
- WAIS serves as the index at the back of the book.

Like most analogies, this one is instructive but not entirely accurate in its implications. Both Gopher and Web servers primarily are browsing-oriented—

the user browses a list of document titles, then reads through documents of interest. Both Gopher and the Web can deliver documents—but it is indeed true that Gopher's hierarchical menu system resembles a table of contents. The Web, of course, offers more than just text: it offers a hypertext view of text. As examples will make clear, WAIS has a different orientation: all searching begins as a keyword query handled by a set of information servers selected by the user. And although Archie and Veronica are keyword-oriented, client-server search mechanisms, WAIS differs from those tools as well:

- First, one connects only to *one* Archie or Veronica server, each of which searches a database that is global in scope. With WAIS, a large set of servers is distributed across the global Internet; each tends to be associated with a specific topic area, and it is common for a client to query several servers to satisfy a given search.

- Second, Archie and Veronica are title indexes; they do not index the text within documents. By contrast, WAIS is primarily used as a way to index and to search the full text of each document in one or more document databases. It is in this sense that WAIS is analogous to the index at the back of a book.

PERFORMING A SEARCH WITH WAIS

The worldwide WAIS community relies upon a "directory of servers" that points to the actual repositories of documents that users might search. From your point of view as a user, performing a WAIS search involves two steps:

- selecting one or more WAIS servers that might hold documents of interest

- submitting the search to those servers using a WAIS client

Before you can choose among a set of servers, you must supply your WAIS client program with a list of servers from which to choose. A master index called the Directory of Servers holds the list of all registered WAIS servers. In order to obtain information about a server from the Directory of Servers, you actually perform a WAIS search of that database. The resulting set of "documents" is a list of WAIS servers. In WAIS parlance, each of these servers—including the Directory of Servers—is a "source."

The process of doing a WAIS search could be compared to searching among a number of reference works at a library. Your first step is to choose the books and journals you want to probe for information on a given subject. You might gather these books and journals on a nearby shelf before you open a single title. This is analogous to selecting titles from the Directory of Servers. Then, you begin searching for the desired information among the titles you've selected. If that search comes up short, you might return some items and fetch additional

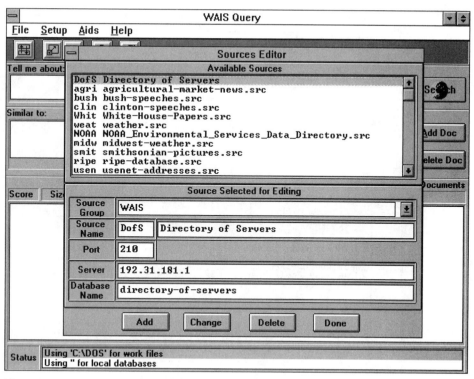

Figure 15.1

ones. Similarly, WAIS will allow you to update the list of WAIS sources against which you perform searches.

The Directory of Servers is located at `quake.think.com`, which is a server residing at Thinking Machines Corporation. Many WAIS clients are delivered with a pointer to this "master server" already installed in the list of possible candidate sources.

Figure 15.1 is a list of sources as displayed by one WAIS client program, the WinWAIS client from the United States Geological Survey.* The highlighted source is the Directory of Servers. The edit panel at the bottom of the screen shows the characteristics associated with that server, including its name, its Internet address, and its TCP port. (The default port for WAIS is 210, and that default applies to the Directory of Servers.†)

---

* WinWAIS was written by Tim Gauslin.

† Actually, TCP port 210 has been assigned to the Z39.50 protocol, of which WAIS is one implementation; see the discussion on WAIS origins later in this chapter.

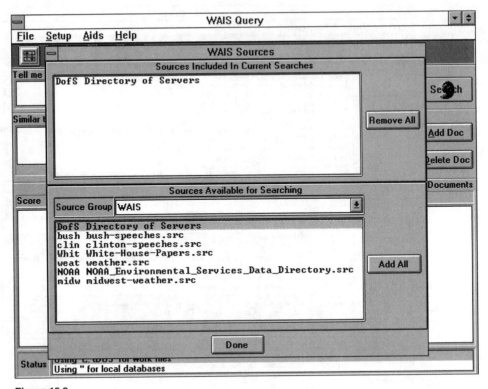

Figure 15.2

In order to search for a new source, you perform a query against the Directory of Servers with one or more keywords that describe what you are looking for. First you tell your client that the Directory of Servers is the database you want to search (see Fig. 15.2).

The icon shown directly beneath the "File" menu item is a shortcut for telling WinWAIS you want to select a source to search.* This opens a panel with a list of all the sources your client currently knows about. In this case we want to select *only* the Directory of Servers; if we were to select other databases we would be hunting for documents, not WAIS sources, which would lead to false hits and a waste of our time and server resources.

Once you have selected your source, you then type in a query. A query might be a quite complicated list of keywords, perhaps even expressed in a sentence. In this case let's suppose we kept the query simple, as in Fig. 15.3. The "Resulting Documents" panel shows the list of documents found that best matches the

---

* Or, if you pull down the "File" menu item, you will see a "Select Sources" option that invokes the same window.

search query, shown in descending order of the strength of the match. We'll see an example of what that list looks like later in this chapter. For now, let's assume the top document was entitled "Agricultural Market News." WinWAIS understands that the "documents" listed as a result of a search of the Directory of Servers are themselves descriptions of WAIS databases. If you double-click on a listed server, WinWAIS will display the panel shown in Fig. 15.4. The "Add This Source" button at the lower right allows you to add this source to the list of candidate sources known by your client. This does *not* mean that this source will be used in all future searches; it merely means this source is now known to your client, and will be listed as an *available* server for any searches you might perform in the future. (To use our library analogy, it means this source is available as a possible source of information, sitting on your virtual reference shelf, but not necessarily on your study desk.)

Once the sources you need have been "installed" in your client you're ready to perform a search. Let's say you want to learn about the political rhetoric that preceded the passing of the North American Free Trade Agreement. If you used the WinWAIS client to perform this search, you would pull up the

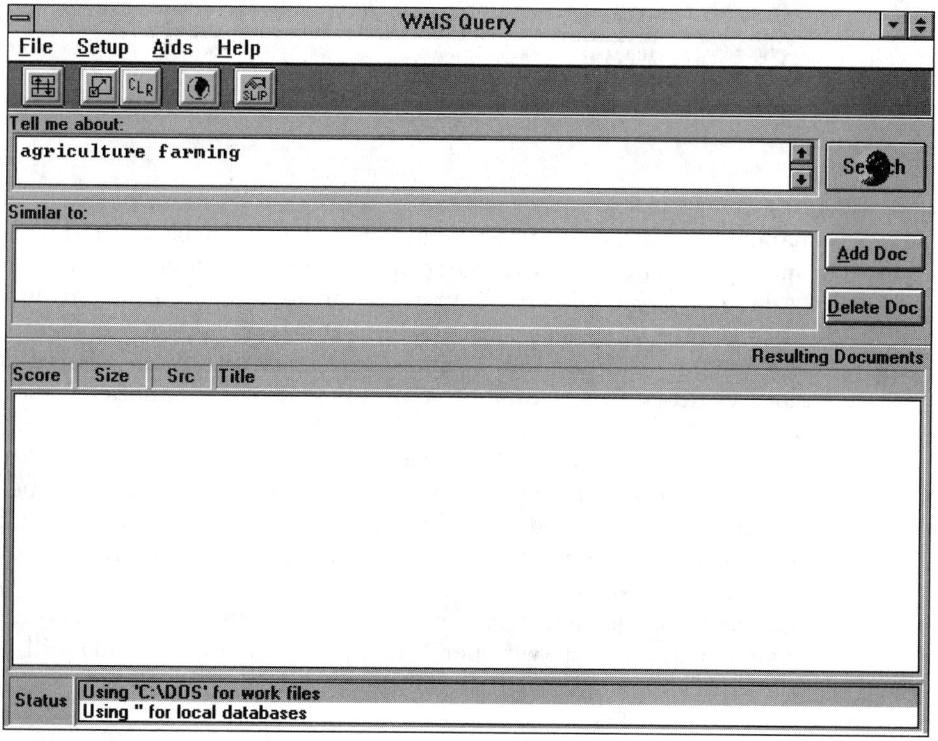

Figure 15.3

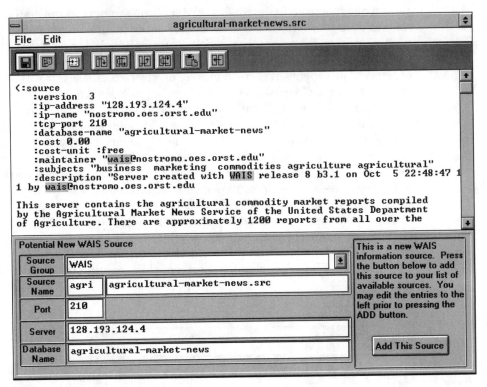

Figure 15.4

panel of available sources (again with the icon beneath the "File" menu option) and click on each source that looks promising; then you would select "Add Doc" to include each source for the search you're preparing to do. Let's say we want to look at speeches from the 1992 presidential campaigns from the Bush and Clinton camps, and at papers issued by the Clinton administration. Sources are available with all these documents online for WAIS searches.* (See Fig. 15.5.)

Once you have selected the sources you want searched, you can close the source selection window and proceed with your search. Simply type in the keywords you're interested in, and click on the Search button. WinWAIS will open a connection to each of the servers you have listed and send your query to the server. The server will return a list of documents and a weighted score indicating how well the search matched your keywords. Once all servers have been searched, the client (whether WinWAIS or another client) will display the

---

* These particular WAIS databases are provided by the University of North Carolina.

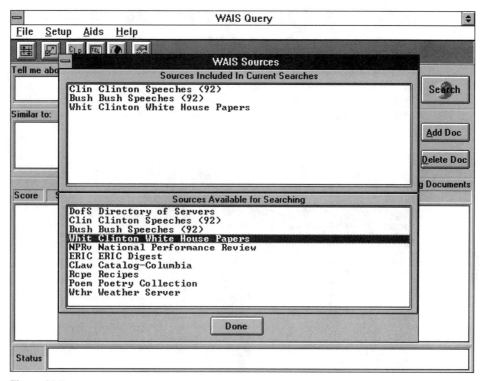

Figure 15.5

results for you in the form of a rank-ordered list of documents (see Fig. 15.6). At the bottom of the screen is a Status panel, in which WinWAIS apprises you of its progress. Note that the final status message in this case is "Found 75 references." In this case we have limited WinWAIS to that many possible documents, by pulling down "Setup" and selecting the "Max Documents" option. This can be useful when you expect to have a large number of documents and you only want to browse among the top-scoring titles.

Note the bar graphs at the left of each document title. These give at a glance a rough idea of each document's relative score. Next in each title appears the size of the document. If you double-click on any of these document titles, the client will reconnect to the server that owns that document and fetch the full text of the document for your review.

Merely by looking at the titles of these documents—without even examining the complete text of any document—one has the definite impression that WAIS has done a pretty good job of sifting through the candidate texts for us. But let's look at another example, wherein we add a poetry database to the sources for documents. We'll leave the three sources used in Fig. 15.6 in the mix, and resubmit the same search (see Fig. 15.7). The top document listed—and therefore the

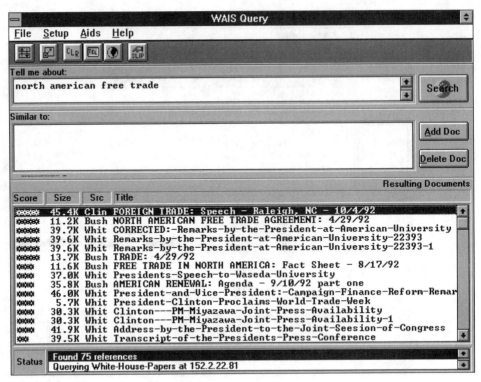

Figure 15.6

highest-scoring document—is a poem. In this case it is a work by Yeats. If we were to retrieve this poem and examine it, we would find that the phrase "North American Free Trade" does not appear anywhere within the poem.* We would find that those words do not even appear in close proximity to one another. In fact, many versions of WAIS work on a very simple algorithm that counts the number of times each of the keywords sought is found in the candidate document; WAIS does not give higher weight to proximity or to context.

It might seem that such a simple-minded searching tool would not be very useful in the real world. As a matter of fact, assuming you do not test WAIS by giving it source databases that are not germane to your query, it can be very useful. The goal of WAIS is not to find exactly *the* set of documents that matches your query. Instead, its goal is to help you sort among a large set of candidate documents, spread far and wide, and come up with a "browsing list"

---

* And note that several other poems appeared fairly high on the list as well. Readers of a literary persuasion may wish to look up these works and see how the sought keywords appear in each.

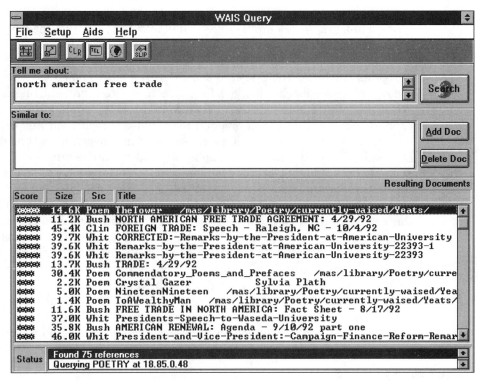

Figure 15.7

that is short enough to be workable. From there, it is up to you to determine which documents are actually useful for your purposes.*

RELEVANCE FEEDBACK

WAIS also provides a mechanism to find more documents that are "like" the documents you found most useful. The fancy term "relevance feedback" is the name of this feature; in plain English it's a way of saying, "Hey, that document is close to what I want. Find me more that are just like it." After an initial round of searching has resulted in a list of candidate documents, you skim those documents to determine which ones are the best matches. Then you tell your WAIS client that those are examples of the sort of document you are looking for. For instance, with the WinWAIS client you would click on a title that was an especially good match, then click on the "Add Doc" button. The title

---

* Some users report that with very large source databases—say over 25,000 candidate documents—the WAIS algorithm breaks down due to excessive false hits. There are relatively few databases with this many documents, and therefore relatively little experience in this regard.

would be added to the "Similar to" panel. Once you've selected all these proto-type documents, a click on "Search" will invoke the relevance feedback feature. After all the databases in your search list have been queried, you'll receive a new list of matching documents.

Just as the basic WAIS search scheme turns out to be surprisingly simple, the relevance feedback scheme is far less complicated than one might surmise. What actually happens is that every word in each "similar to" document is used as a keyword in the new search. WAIS users report varying experiences with this feature. Some find it extremely useful; others report that it leads to numerous false hits. Results probably depend upon the number of candidate documents, the length of the documents selected for relevance feedback, and the nature of the text being searched. For instance, in searching biology sources, feeding a short document with a number of specific terms of art into the relevance feedback loop might be very productive; by contrast, if you selected a Shakespearean sonnet as the seed for a relevance feedback search against a poetry source, the resulting set of documents might have little in common with one another. In the former case, the ratio of unique target words to "noise" words would be higher than in the latter.*

As in all endeavors on the Internet, your mileage may vary based on your driving habits. You may want to experiment with WAIS searching in general, and relevance feedback in particular, searching disciplines of interest to you.

OTHER WAIS CLIENTS

WAIS clients exist to support most common computing platforms.

One of the most powerful WAIS clients is a tool called WAISstation, initially implemented for Next workstations. This client is able to index local resources such as an individual's e-mail folders and Usenet News article archives. The user can then invoke the WAIS search engine locally, in order to quickly locate documents in those virtual piles of paper. For instance, a user might ask WAISstation "Who did I have lunch with at the economics conference last Thursday?" and the top-ranked document might be a saved e-mail message that says, "Would you like to have lunch at the economics conference next Thursday?"†

WAIS can be used for interesting nontextual applications. For instance, François Schiettecatte has implemented a browser on the Macintosh that is

---

* On the other hand, precisely that sort of search might turn out to be useful, if, for instance, you are trying to trace the use of words invented by Shakespeare in other works. The example should not discourage you from trying relevance feedback on all sorts of topic areas.

† In fact, this is a real example demonstrated to the author by Hal Varian, a professor of eco-nomics at the University of Michigan; Hal is known for his thorough exploitation of computer-based support tools.

able to fetch and display documents with text, thumbnail images, and full-sized images. An initial demonstration of this application works with a photography archive at the Smithsonian Institution; the corresponding WAIS source is `smithsonian-pictures.src`. Figure 15.8 is an example of this client in action.

You can read more about WAIS clients, servers, and the WAIS protocol in general by connecting to the Gopher service at `gopher.wais.com` (port 70). (The same information is available for anonymous FTP at `ftp.wais.com`.)

ACCESS TO WAIS WITHOUT A CLIENT

If you don't have a WAIS client program you can still use WAIS. There are two basic approaches: you can either use a line-mode client called SWAIS, which is made available at some sites via Telnet, or you can use a Gopher or World-Wide Web gateway. The Gopher server at Michigan State University (`gopher.msu.edu`) offers both forms of access via one menu, located under Network and Database Resources / By Type. Sites offering public SWAIS services include:

Figure 15.8

```
                              Public clients

    1.  American Mathematical Society SWAIS Preprints Demo <TEL>
    2.  NISSWAIS <TEL>
    3.  NNSC.NSF.NET <TEL>
--> 4.  SUNSITE at University of North Carolina <TEL>
    5.  THINK.COM (Thinking Machines) <TEL>
```

The Sunsite server offers several kinds of services besides the SWAIS service; you can select SWAIS by logging in under that name. You will be presented with a list of WAIS sources. Simple one-keystroke commands, shown at the bottom of the screen, allow you to select a source and to enter a keyword search. Selected sources are flagged with an asterisk:

```
SWAIS                          Source Selection            Sources: 631
   #            Server                        Source              Cost
  001              archie.au]  aarnet-resource-guide              Free
  002   ndadsb.gsfc.nasa.gov]  AAS_jobs                           Free
  003:  [ndadsb.gsfc.nasa.gov] AAS_meeting                        Free
  004    weeds.mgh.harvard.ed] AAtDB                              Free
  005        munin.ub2.lu.se]  academic_email_ nf                 Free
  006: * [wraith.cs.uow.edu.au] acronyms                         Free
  007         archive.orst.edu] aeronautics                      Free
  008      bloat.media.mit.edu] Aesop-Fables                     Free
  009      bloat.media.mit.edu] aesop                            Free
  010       ftp.cs.colorado.edu] aftp-cs-colorado-edu            Free
  011:  [nostromo.oes.orst.ed] agricultural-market-news          Free
  012        sunsite.un .edu]  alt-sys-sun                        Free
  013        archive.orst.edu] alt.drugs                          Free
  014       wais.oit.un .edu]  alt.gopher                         Free
  015           sunsite        alt.sys.sun                        Free
  016       wais.oit.unc.edu]  alt.wais                           Free
  017    alfred.ccs.carleton.] amiga-slip                        Free
  018        munin.ub2.lu.se]  amiga_fish_contents               Free

Keywords: ndis


<space> selects, w for keywords, arrows move, <return> searches, q quits, or ?
```

In this case we search a database of acronyms and enter "NDIS" as our search item. This is an example of a special-purpose WAIS database; its goal is simply to offer short definitions of acronyms. The underlying documents contain no additional text beyond that conveyed in the title. Fortunately, the keyword we submit has a perfect match with the "document" that offers its definition*:

---

* But someone skeptical as to the WAIS algorithm might note the relatively high scores achieved by other documents that do not have anything to do with NDIS.

```
SWAIS                                 Search Results                     Item
    #    Score       Source                       Title                 Lines
  001:  [1000] (          acronyms)  NDIS  - Network Driver Interface Specific
  002:  [ 715] (          acronyms)  CAPTAIN      - Character And Pattern Telephon
  1
  003:  [ 715] (          acronyms)  BCC     - Block Check Character      1
  004:  [ 715] (          acronyms)  CHARGEN      - CHARacter GENerator
  005:  [ 715] (          acronyms)  COP     - Character-Oriented Protocol
  006:  [ 715] (          acronyms)  CRC     - Cyclical Redundancy Character
  007:  [ 715] (          acronyms)  LF     - Line Feed Character
  008:  [ 715] (          acronyms)  LRC     - Longitudinal Redundancy Character
```

Besides using Telnet to connect to a public SWAIS service, you can use a Gopher or World-Wide Web gateway into the WAIS world. The same menu at Michigan State also offers a Gopherized list of WAIS servers*:

```
                    WAIS sources via Gopher
  --> 1.  Directory of Servers <?>
      2.  ANU-Aboriginal-Studies.src <?>
      3.  ANU-Asian-Computing.src <?>
      4.  ANU-Asian-Religions.src <?>
      5.  ANU-CAUT-Projects.src <?>
      6.  ANU-French-Databanks.src <?>
      7.  ANU-Local-Waiservers.src <?>
      8.  ANU-Pacific-Linguistics.src <?>
      9.  ANU-Pacific-Manuscripts.src <?>
     10.  ANU-Pacific-Relations.src <?>
     11.  ANU-SSDA-Catalogues.src <?>
     12.  ANU-SocSci-Netlore.src <?>
     13.  ANU-Thai-Yunnan.src <?>
     14.  ANU-Theses-Abstracts.src <?>
     15.  ASK-SISY-Software-Information.src <?>
     16.  AVS_TXT_FILES.src <?>
     17.  Applications-Navigator.src <?>
     18.  Arabidopsis-BioSci.src <?>
```

Let's say we want to find recent magazine and newspaper articles that concern the national information infrastructure. Current Cites, a service of the library of the University of California at Berkeley with collaborators around the Internet, offers a periodic summary of articles that pertain to online information issues. The Current Cites WAIS source offers an indexed database of back issues of this valuable summary of the literature. To search the database via Gopher, simply select the title in question, and you'll be prompted for a

---

* Various other Gopher servers also offer lists of WAIS sources accessible via Gopher gateways; similar gateways are offered by several World-Wide Web sites as well.

search string as you would for any Gopher index. Enter the keywords you are interested in:

```
Internet Gopher Information Client v1.11

         WAIS sources via Gopher

  199. cool-net.src <?>
  200. cool-ref.src <?>
  201. cool.src <?>
  202. cosmic-abstracts.src <?>
                current.cites.src


Words to search for national information infrastructure


                            [Cancel ^G] [Accept - Enter]

  210. ddbs-info.src <?>
  211. directory-irit-fr.src <?>
  212. directory-zenon-inria-fr.src <?>
  213. disco-mm-zenon-inria-fr.src <?>
  214. disi-catalog.src <?>
  215. dit-library.src <?>
  216. domain-contacts.src <?>


Press ? for Help, q to Quit, u to go up a menu Page: 12/24
```

The resulting list of articles might look like this:

```
       current.cites.src: national information infrastructure

-->1. Kahn, Robert "National Information Infrastructure Components" Seri...
   2. Roberts, Michael M. "Positioning the National Research and Educati...
   3. Love, James P.  "Internet Access to Federal Information" posting o...
   4. Kahin, Brian "Publication of Building Information Inferase" Posted...
   5. Love, James P.  "Internet Access to Federal Information" posting o...
   6. Kahin, Brian "Publication of Building Information Inferase" Posted...
   7. The National Public Telecomputing Network "Infosphere Report"  .
   8. The National Public Telecomputing Network "Infosphere Report"  .
   9. "Questions and Answers with Jane Ryland and Peter Young" Informati...
  10. "Questions and Answers with Jane Ryland and Peter Young" Informati...
  11. Kirk, Thomas G. and Noreen S. Alldredge "Coalition for Networked .
  12. Kirk, Thomas G. and Noreen S. Alldredge "Coalition for Networked .
  13. Garcia, Linda.  "Information Exchange: The Impact of Scholarly  .
  14. Garcia, Linda.  "Information Exchange: The Impact of Scholarly  .
  15. Braunstein, Yale M. "Resolving Conflicts between Information  .
  16. Kahle, Brewster and Art Medlar "An Information System for  .
  17. Citizens Rights and Access to Electronic Information; A Collection...
  18. Braunstein, Yale M. "Resolving Conflicts between Information  .
```

Note that in general Gopher searches of WAIS sources operate on only one source at a time; you lose the ability to search across multiple sources at once.

THE ORIGINS OF WAIS

Most of the Internet tools we've seen—Gopher, World-Wide Web, Archie, Veronica—have been developed by small teams, often under the leadership of one or two Internet visionaries. The same could be said of WAIS, but it evolved in the milieu of a community of librarians and information scientists who have been working on standards for online information delivery using the client/server model. An NISO standard, Z39.50, serves as the underlying protocol used by WAIS. Actually, there are two flavors of the Z39.50 protocol, a 1988 and a 1992 version; WAIS is an implementation of a subset of the 1988 standard.

The person most associated with WAIS development is Brewster Kahle. He has pursued an interest in the WAIS concept while working at Apple Computer, at Thinking Machines Corporation (a vendor of massively parallel supercomputers), and now at a firm he heads by the name of WAIS Inc. Besides a general interest in the problem of network-based document delivery, Kahle and Thinking Machines colleagues worked on a specific project on behalf of Dow Jones that led to a product called DowQuest that was released in 1988. Kahle and colleagues wanted to extend the DowQuest functionality to a general product. They became active in the Z39.50 standards effort, and began working to create functional Z39.50 code. They released a working version of WAIS (a Unix server and a Macintosh client) in spring of 1991.

In summer 1992 Kahle left Thinking Machines to form WAIS Inc. His new firm sells commercial WAIS products, initially in the form of a commercial Unix-based server. In 1993, the Clearinghouse for Networked Information Discovery and Retrieval (CNIDR) developed a FreeWAIS, a public domain WAIS server based upon the earlier, freely available WAIS corpus. Information providers who choose WAIS as their delivery mechanism thus have a choice between a supported commercial product and a public domain tool.

WAIS has enjoyed pockets of extreme enthusiasm but in terms of the amount of information delivered has lagged behind Gopher and World-Wide Web. Over time, as the number of documents and services offered on the global Internet increases, WAIS may well enjoy a resurgence of interest, when a tool like it becomes essential for the most basic kinds of navigation.

16

Internet Search Strategies

At times navigating the Internet can be frustrating. There are so many resources to exploit, and so many paths to take, that the poor traveler may give up in despair. At such times you can draw some consolation from the fact that this worldwide network of networks has over 2 million hosts, many thousands of which offer information in one form or another, as well as millions of people communicating via e-mail, mailing lists, and Usenet. Due to the decentralized nature of the Internet, there are no comprehensive user-friendly indexes of places, people, or resources. But there is some hope; there are tools that provide at least a measure of organization to the wonderful chaos of the Internet. This chapter will offer some search strategies and tactics to employ in your pursuit of an elusive Internet target. We will explore some additional tools of the trade that, combined with the devices described in previous chapters, will help you in your searching. Grab your magnifying glass and meerschaum pipe.

LOCAL RESOURCES VERSUS
THE GLOBAL INTERNET

The Internet can be a wonderful resource for answering all sorts of research questions, but it is not a replacement for more traditional kinds of resources.*

---

* Not yet, anyhow.

The most important starting point for many research questions remains the local library—either a research library at a major university, or a corporate library, or a public library. The library has access to traditional print documents—conventional books, magazines, and journals—that contain information simply not accessible over the Internet. Moreover, many libraries have subscriptions to online commercial databases. You may be able to access such commercial databases as Nexis/Lexis or Dialog at little or no charge through a visit or telephone call to your library. Finally, many libraries have CD-ROM databases that are in many cases far richer than Internet resources.

Most importantly, libraries have trained information professionals who can assist in searching for particular pieces of information. These professionals are known as "librarians." Not only are librarians well-versed in the traditional research armamentarium, they are becoming increasingly adept at assisting in Internet searches as well.

It is especially advisable to use some discretion when posting questions to mailing lists. As more and more people gain access to the Internet, there are more and more extremely broad queries posted to general mailing lists and Usenet News groups. Examples of such questions might be:

- I'm doing a term paper on rockets. Where can I learn more about rockets?

- Is St. Petersburg in Russia or in Ukraine?

- I'm new to the Internet. What's out there?

There are places on the Internet where one can find answers to all of these questions. There are even some mailing lists and Usenet News groups that would probably gladly entertain such queries. In fact, in Chap. 17 we will explore some of the ways that specialized mailing lists serve specific research needs. The general rule is to respect the purpose of each mailing list to which you belong. A moment's reflection shows that the explosion of access to the Internet will lead to an infusion of such questions; part of good network etiquette is to find the right forum for your questions, and to do basic research using familiar reference tools first. The Net can be an amazingly effective medium for getting answers to questions, but friendly Internauts may not take the time to answer questions that the researcher could easily nail down with a small expenditure of his or her own effort.

The rest of this chapter is divided into three main areas: finding resources, finding people, and finding places.

FINDING RESOURCES

We have seen many of the different kinds of information technologies used on the Internet. You may want to refer back to the chapters corresponding to each technology for general information on getting started with that tool. Enterprising Internauts have established various kinds of organizing resources—for instance, Gopher servers whose main purpose is to categorize other resources in a chosen discipline.

There is a basic distinction among these Internet organizing resources:

- Some are oriented toward browsing; you navigate by selecting menu choices. You will find "lists of lists" and even "lists of lists of lists" that allow you to browse for resources on the Internet.

- Some are index-oriented; you navigate by entering one or more keywords, as with Archie or Veronica, and you select among matching items.

Still other navigation aids offer both browsing and index features.

In the next few sections we will explore some of the organizing resources available on the Internet. Keep in mind that newer cataloging efforts will appear over time; the compleat Internet angler will take note of new tools as they are announced.

Subject catalogs

In Chap. 14 we saw examples of title indexes such as Archie, Veronica, and the Web JumpStation. These tools let you type in a search term you think is likely to appear in the titles of documents you are seeking; you are presented with a list of matching document titles, and you then can browse that list. As we saw in Chap. 15, WAIS combines the concept of a subject catalog and a full-text index in one tool: it employs the use of an index to help the user find the right databases (via the Directory of Servers search) and the same indexing mechanism for the actual search for particular information.

Browsable subject catalogs are an alternative to searchable indexes. There are numerous efforts to offer such subject catalogs, which allow you to browse a list of servers (or documents within servers) that has been organized in advance. Many World-Wide Web servers offer pointers to such subject lists. One highly visible subject list is offered at the home of the Web, CERN. Figure 16.1 is what the beginning of CERN's list looks like.

Here are pointers to other attempts at building Web-based subject catalogs:

- O'Reilly and Associates, a publisher of various computer texts, offers a subject catalog as part of their Global Network Navigator server; the Uniform Resource Locator* is:

    `http://nearnet.gnn.com/wic/newrescat.toc.html`

- An organization called EINet, associated with Microelectronics and Computer Technology Corporation in Texas, offers a service that combines a

---

* Recall from Chap. 13 that a Uniform Resource Locator, or URL, is the "handle" you feed a World-Wide Web client such as Mosaic in order to access a particular Internet resource.

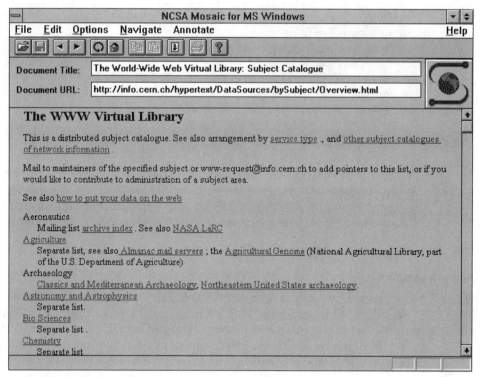

Figure 16.1

browsable subject catalog with a keyword-searchable index. Their service is called EINet Galaxy. The URL is:

```
http://www.einet.net/galaxy.html
```

- The School of Library and Information Science at the University of Michigan has a Clearinghouse for Subject-Oriented Research Guides. This catalog combines the efforts of library professionals and library science students with those of various subject catalogers around the Internet. You can reach the Clearinghouse via this URL*:

```
http://http2.sils.umich.edu/~lou/chhome.html
```

Some Web indexes encompass more than a title index like the JumpStation described in Chap. 14. One example is called W3 Catalog.† It differs from JumpStation in that it offers more contextual verbiage about each item, draw-

---

* Gopher access to the Clearinghouse is available at `una.hh.lib.umich.edu`, port 70, with the selector `1/netdirs`.

† The W3 Catalog was developed by Oscar Nierstrasz of the University of Geneva.

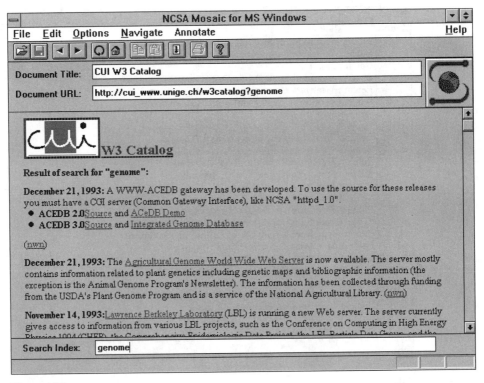

Figure 16.2

ing that information from sources such as the online announcements of new Web services. Figure 16.2 is an example of W3 Catalog reporting results of a search for the word "genome."

Gopher-based subject catalogs

Numerous attempts have been made by members of the Gopher community to create subject-oriented catalogs. Figure 16.3 is a list of such attempts from the Michigan State University central Gopher service.* One of the items listed here, the subject tree from the Library of Congress's Marvel service, may over time become one of the more complete lists online. As of this writing, another subject catalog, the compendium online at Rice University, is one of the more complete efforts.† The Rice catalog is actually a composite of several subject

---

* This "list of lists of resources" is available via `gopher.msu.edu` (port 70) under the selector `1/internet/subject`.

† The Rice subject catalog was implemented by Prentiss Riddle. See the online documentation for details as to how Riddle's Linkmerge program is used to automatically merge subject catalogs from around the world.

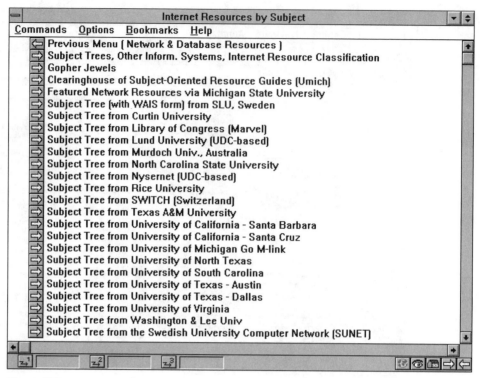

Figure 16.3

cataloging efforts; in librarian parlance, it might be referred to as a "union catalog." Figure 16.4 shows the beginning of the list of topics.

Specialized catalogs

Besides the examples of subject catalogs we have seen so far, there are some other specialized catalogs that might be useful. One of these is the Hytelnet database. This catalog, conceived and maintained by Peter Scott of the University of Saskatchewan, is a single database offering access to a number of Internet resources. Hytelnet offers a list of Internet resources in a simple, easy-to-navigate menu system. With Hytelnet, you can install an application program and a corresponding list of Internet resources; in effect, you download both a program and a database. Of course, this means that you must periodically download a new version of the database in order to stay current. You can find versions of Hytelnet for MS-DOS, Unix, and for VAX VMS. The standalone versions of Hytelnet are available for download from `ftp.usask.ca` under `pub/hytelnet`.

You can also connect to an online version of Hytelnet:

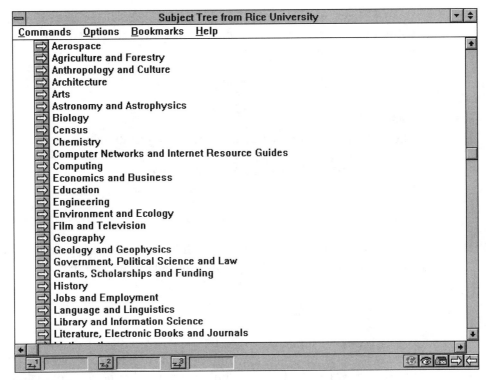

Figure 16.4

```
telnet access.usask.ca
```

Log in as `hytelnet`—no password is required. The interface is a simple hierarchical menu scheme; the feel is somewhat similar to that of the public Gopher client. When you have the cursor on a resource of interest, simply hit the Enter key to jump to that resource. In addition to this direct Telnet path into Hytelnet, you may also encounter gateways to Hytelnet as you cruise Gopherspace or the Web.

There is also a World-Wide Web version of the Hytelnet database, available at this URL:

```
http://www.cc.ukans.edu/hytelnet_html/START.TXT.html
```

There are several other efforts to organize Internet resources in a centrally maintained database. One of the better known is the "Yanoff list" produced by Scott Yanoff of the University of Wisconsin at Milwaukee. Yanoff's list is a succinct summary of many of the most useful resources on the Internet. It is updated frequently—as often as biweekly. This list is periodically posted to the

Usenet News group `alt.internet.services`. There are several other ways of obtaining the current edition of the list; to find a method convenient for you, issue the following command:

```
finger yanoff@csd4.csd.uwm.edu
```

New Internet services

The National Center for Supercomputer Applications list of new Mosaic/Web resources is a good place to learn about newly announced Web services. The list is maintained in reverse chronological order for ease of access. The URL for this document is:

```
http://www.ncsa.uiuc.edu/SDG/Software/Mosaic/Docs/whats-new.html
```

The Netlink service at Washington and Lee University, described in detail in Chap. 14, has a very good list of new resources, as well as ways to search the list. The URL is:

```
http://netlink.wlu.edu:1020/
```

The InterNIC maintains a Net Resources mailing list that describes new resources on the Internet. The mailing list is archived on the InterNIC Gopher; the first file gives instructions on subscribing to the mailing list, should you wish to receive announcements as they are made. You can find this list archive on the InterNIC Gopher; select:

```
InterNIC Information Services (General Atomics)
    About InterNIC Information Services
        InterNIC Lists (Archives)
```

This Gopher is located at `is.internic.net`, port 70.

The Usenet News group `comp.infosystems.announce` is also dedicated to announcements of new Internet resources.

You may notice overlap among these lists, as many new resources will be announced multiple places. Over time there will probably be some sort of merging of these efforts.

Geographical listings

In Chap. 2 we saw how the University of Minnesota's Gopher server offers a list of all Gopher servers in the world. Virtually all Gopher servers contain a pointer to this master list. You can pull down a list of all servers, or you can browse the list by geographical location. Similarly, in the Web you will find pointers to CERN's list of all Web servers (see Fig. 16.5).

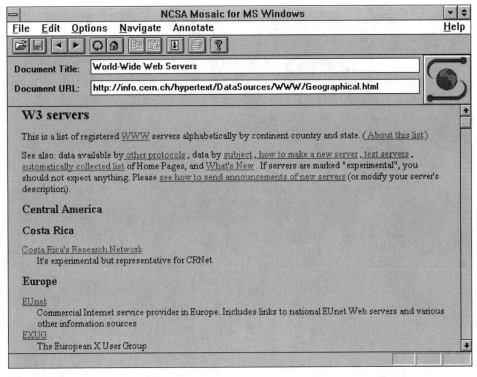

Figure 16.5

If you are looking for a copy of the latest Stephen King novel, you usually do not worry about where you find the book, but rather are more interested in convenient access (and perhaps the price). Similarly, when you look for online information you are usually more interested in the document itself than in the place where you found it.

Sometimes, however, geography may play a role in where you want to look for information. You may assume, for instance, that a Gopher server in Michigan or Ontario is more likely to have information about the Great Lakes than one in Arizona or Zambia. When geography is one of the filters you have in mind for a particular search, you may want to look for information resources via a map, not by scanning a list of servers. The WAIS protocol provides a framework for limiting searches based on the location of the servers; the United States Geological Survey has begun exploring ways to exploit this feature with online maps. Pioneering Web publishers are also beginning to offer map-based tools. One such early effort, from the University of Buffalo, makes it possible to pick a spot on a map and thereby connect to an associated server. Figure 16.6 is an example of a Web page offering such searches.

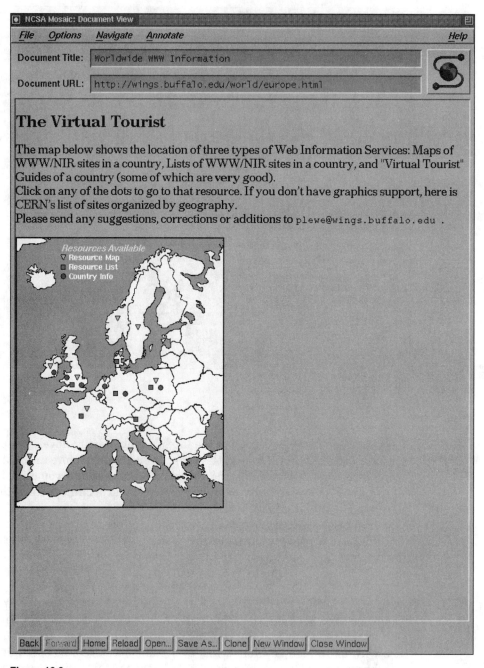

Figure 16.6

Special Gopher hints

No matter how much effort went into the design of a particular Gopher's menu structure, as a user you will sometimes find yourself at a loss to understand its organization. You will find on some Gopher servers tools to make it easier to find your way. One such tool is a Road Map; here is an example:

```
LUC Gopher Road Map                      Host: gopher.luc.edu
Last Update: 10/12/93


Lev Name                                 Type    Destination
--- ------------------------------------ ------  ------------------
  1 Loyola University Chicago (LUC) Internet G File  gopher.luc.edu
  1 Using Gopher                         Dir     gopher.luc.edu
  2    About Gopher (from University of Minneso Dir  gopher.tc.umn.edu
  2    How to display Gopher document    File    gopher.luc.edu
  2    Moving through the Gopher menu    File    gopher.luc.edu
  2    How to send documents via e-mail  File    gopher.luc.edu
  2    How to save documents             File    gopher.luc.edu
  2    How to add information to Gopher   File    gopher.luc.edu
  2    Frequently Asked Questions about Gopher  File  gopher.luc.edu
  1 About Loyola University Chicago      Dir     gopher.luc.edu
  2    Course Schedules                  File    gopher.luc.edu
  1 LUC Computing Services and Resources Dir     gopher.luc.edu
  2    Division of Information Technologies (IT Dir  gopher.luc.edu
  3      Offices                         File    gopher.luc.edu
  3      Staff List                      File    gopher.luc.edu
  2    Help Desk                         File    gopher.luc.edu
  2    Hours and Locations of Campus Computing  Dir  gopher.luc.edu
  ...
```

You will often find maps like this in the root menu of a Gopher hierarchy, or perhaps in a folder with a name like "More About Gopher." By browsing the map you can find specific titles in the hierarchy quickly, while at the same time getting a feel for the general layout of documents within the Gopher service.

Many Gopher servers will offer you a title search option, often in the root menu. The title search is similar to Veronica, only its scope is limited to the document titles within the Gopher you are currently browsing. (Veronica, of course, is the title search concept writ large; it is an index of all of Gopherspace.) When using a local title index, you simply type in a word that is likely to appear in the title you want, and all the titles within that Gopher that contain that word are displayed. You can then jump to the document that appears to be most promising, regardless of its location in the hierarchy.

Some Gopher menus can run to hundreds or even thousands of items. It can be difficult to locate a particular item in such a long list. Some Gopher clients allow you to do a keyword search of a menu in order to locate a particular entry or set of entries. For instance, the public Gopher client has this feature. Suppose you want to find a server at Johns Hopkins University and you do not happen to know that that institution is located in Maryland. You can select the list of all Gopher servers in the world (offered by the Minnesota server and pointed to by virtually all other servers) and then type a slash ("/"). You will be prompted for a search string; type the word you are looking for, and the public client will move the cursor to the next title that includes that string.

```
            All the Gopher Servers in the World

    163. Cloud 9 Internet/
    164. Coalition for Networked Information/
    165. Coalition of School Networking (CoSN)/
    166. Coast Community College District/


  +-----------------------------------------------------------------+
  :                                                                 :
  : Search directory titles for hopkins                            :
  :                                                                 :
  :                                [Cancel ^G] [Accept - Enter] :
  :                                                                 :
  +-----------------------------------------------------------------+
    174. ComNet RWTH Aachen, (DE)/
    175. Common Knowledge: Pittsburgh/
    176. Communications Research Centre, Ottawa, CANADA/
    177. Communications Research Group, Nottingham University, (UK)/
    178. Communications for a Sustainable Future (Boulder, Colorado)/
    179. Comprehensive Epidemilogic Data Resource (CEDR)/
--> 180. Computational Biology (Welchlab - Johns Hopkins University)/
```

As the list of all Gopher servers grows ever longer, this kind of search grows more expensive. (In fact, some Gopher client programs have been known to run out of memory trying to display the list of all servers.) There is a global keyword index of Gopher site names to allow a user to quickly find a known site regardless of where it is located, without pulling down the list of all Gophers. This service is available on the central Michigan State University server. (Look under More About Gopher, then Search Gopherspace.) Gopher administrators may want to add pointers to this index.*

Special Web hints

World-Wide Web servers by their nature offer a great many embedded links. Over time it will be interesting to see whether users find the Web more navigable than Gopherspace. A few hints may make your journey easier:

---

* The service is located on gopher.msu.edu (port 70) under the selector 7/internet/others/ts.

- Mosaic and other browsers change the color of a link when you have selected that link at some point during a journey. You can exploit this as a sort of mark on the trail, reminding you that you've already visited a given way station.

- Use the "History" feature of Mosaic and other clients as another way to keep up with the points you have already visited.

- Use the "Hot List" feature to note Web documents of particular interest. You might find it especially useful to place your favorite Web starting points and indexes in your Hot List. This will make it easy for you to locate resources no matter where they reside.

- Many Web servers now offer a "Return to Front Page" option at the bottom of each page. If you get hopelessly tangled in a web, consider starting over again.

- More and more Web servers are incorporating title indexes, similar to those found on some Gopher servers, to allow you to find documents with keyword searches.

A master "catalog of catalogs"

As we have seen, Internet toolsmiths from around the world have undertaken a variety of cataloging efforts. One Web-based catalog offers pointers to this collection of catalogs. This will be a good place for you to visit periodically so that you can discover new catalogs as they come online. The catalog resides at the University of Geneva; point your Web client at the URL shown in Fig. 16.7.

Mailing lists

We saw in Chap. 7 some ways to search the list of LISTSERV-style mailing lists. There are a few other tactics for locating mailing lists of interest:

Dartmouth College maintains a list of LISTSERV and other mailing lists using other software. The list is available both on their LISTSERV and via their main Gopher service. The master file is laid out for processing by a computer program; Dartmouth offers programs to search the file for the Macintosh, the PC, for VAX VMS, and for VM/CMS.

To retrieve the human-readable list from Dartmouth, send the following e-mail:

```
To: listserv@dartcms1.dartmouth.edu
```

```
get listshrt package
```
[as the body of your message]

The Gopher folder with this package of files gives details on how to download the complete database and run the search programs. The Gopher service is `gopher.dartmouth.edu`, **port 70; the folder is** `List of Network Mailing Lists.`

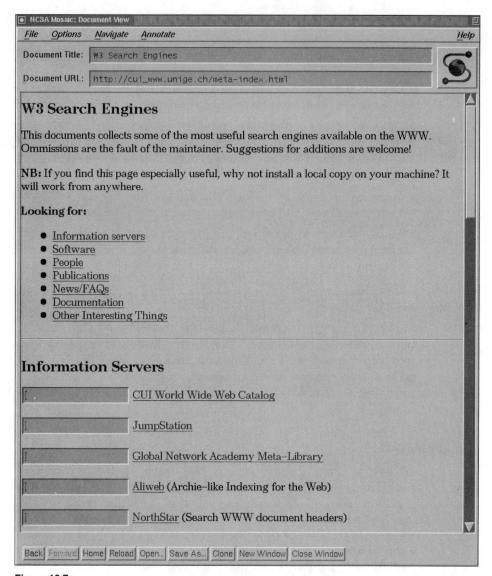

Figure 16.7

Marty Hoag of the University of North Dakota maintains a "list of lists" which he offers as a LISTSERV file. You can obtain a copy by sending the following e-mail:

```
To:  listserv@vm1.nodak.edu

get listsof lists    [as the body of your message]
```

After receiving the list by return e-mail, you can then browse the file locally. Note that the list is quite large.

Another "list of mailing lists" is posted periodically to the Usenet newsgroup `news.lists` under the title `Publicly Accessible Mailing Lists`. Currently contributed by Stephanie da Silva, this list is presented as a multipart posting. The list is quite comprehensive and covers a variety of mailing list processor technologies.

Another list of mailing lists is available on the Internet, and, for those who prefer printed catalogs over online files, as a book. The book is called *Directory of Electronic Journals, Newsletters, and Academic Discussion Lists.** It offers information on some 1400 mailing lists and electronic journals. You can retrieve the files via LISTSERV by sending the following mail:

```
To:  listserv@acadvm1.uottowa.ca

get ejournal1 directry     [as the body of your message]
get ejournal2 directry
```

To access the same information via Gopher, connect to the main server at the University of Maryland (`info.umd.edu`, port 70) then follow these menu items:

```
Educational Resources
    Reading Room
        Newsletters
            Directory of ENews
```

A comprehensive strategy

The successful Internet searcher will combine the various tools shown in the last section into a comprehensive search strategy. Just as a good reference librarian knows which items provide the most "bang for the buck" for particular kinds of searches, the Internet searcher will learn which tools are most effective.

It is best to treat Archie, Veronica, or any Internet search tool as a service that reveals *many* of the items you are looking for, but not necessarily exhaustively. The server may have missed a particular resource that you want, perhaps because the resource was added more recently than the last harvest of titles. Or, the information resource might have been down when the indexer

---

* *Directory of Electronic Journals, Newsletters, and Academic Discussion Lists* by Michael Strangelove, Diane Kovacs, and collaborators at Kent State University; edited by Ann Okerson, Association of Research Libraries (Washington, D.C.) 1993. ISSN 1057-1337.

tried to connect during that process. Or, the administrator might have taken steps to prevent indexing.*

If no one tool is exhaustive, then the Internet searcher has no choice but to use multiple tools. If you are relying on subject catalogs, be sure to search through more than one. Similarly, do not rely on Veronica alone for a search; that would limit the scope of your search to resources in Gopherspace. Be sure to use Web indexes such as the JumpStation as well.

Also note that tools like Archie and Veronica can lead to false hits. Due to the nature of their information-gathering task, such tools cannot reliably remove all old entries immediately. The indexer cannot drop a resource simply because it is not available during the update of the index; a given resource may disappear temporarily during an index scan, only to reappear online a few minutes later.

Of course, Internet search tools, like the Internet itself, are evolving rapidly. The Internet searcher will want to pay attention to such developments. Over time we can expect various Internet indexes to improve in many ways, with better user interfaces, faster and more powerful search engines, and better mechanisms to evolve for flagging both new and expired Internet resources. We can also expect to see integration of index tools, of delivery mechanisms such as Gopher and the World-Wide Web, or both. Such integration will ease the task of the Internet searcher.

FINDING PEOPLE

Just as there is no single kind of directory for resources on the Internet, there is no single directory of people on the Internet. This is one of the most frustrating experiences for new Internet users: They know that a friend or colleague does have Internet access at another institution, and they expect—quite reasonably—that it ought to be easy to look up their friend's Internet address. For instance, if you want to call someone by telephone, and you do not know the number, you can use the telephone to call Information and obtain the number, usually in less than a minute.

Similarly, information utilities like Prodigy offer comprehensive directories of their subscribers. You can quickly locate the e-mail address of a friend you know has an account on the same service. Although things ought to be that simple on the Internet, sometimes they are not. There are different technologies to choose from in building a directory service, and the Internet community remains fragmented as to which scheme will eventually dominate. In some cases you will be able to locate a person at another site quickly; in other cases

---

* Most Internet information providers who offer freely available services welcome the advent of indexing tools, but a few mavericks find them intrusive.

the search may take a while—and sometimes you will have to give up on an Internet lookup and revert to more conventional contact in order to obtain the e-mail address.

In the next few sections we will explore some of the common directory schemes and how you might use them. One approach would be to use each of the techniques shown below in turn while looking for the person in question. Another approach might be to go directly to the Gopher or World-Wide Web server offered by your friend's institution; the root menu may very well offer a direct pointer to their local directory service, or a gateway to same.

Because of the quite natural expectation that the Internet will make it as easy to look up someone as it is to send e-mail, many users overlook the obvious when trying to find a friend's e-mail request: call your friend on the telephone, or send a paper letter via the postal service, and ask. To make it even easier you can supply *your* address and have the friend write you first; the address in the From header should be usable when you address your reply.

Many users write to their own network administrator or Gopher manager or postmaster with questions like "How can I find my friend at the University of Southern North Dakota at Hoople?" Once you are armed with the tactics listed here, you will be about as well-equipped to do these searches as these information professionals. If you do send such queries to managers of Internet services, and you find their replies terse, imagine the number of similar queries they field daily from others in the same situation.

If all of your searching fails—including attempts at direct contact—and you know the name of the institution where your would-be contact is located, you might as a last resort send e-mail to the postmaster at that institution, who might be able to help you.

Many Gopher and World-Wide Web services offer pointers to the various kinds of global indexes on the Internet. Figure 16.8 is an example list of lists, from the Gopher server at Michigan State. We will discuss each of these services later in this chapter.

The University of Notre Dame has compiled a list of institutions that offer various directory schemes accessible via Gopher. Over 300 institutions are included in this list. The Notre Dame menu looks like Fig. 16.9. You can find a particular institution by selecting the geographic menu items, or you can select the "Search All the Directory Servers . . ." option, and type in a keyword. For instance, if you were looking for a server at the National University of Singapore, you might do a search for the keyword `singapore`.

Many institutions listed in the Notre Dame phone list use a very simple service referred to as CSO (after its place of invention, the Computer Services Organization at the University of Illinois). CSO is itself a client/server protocol; the client program often goes under the name ph, and the server program is often called `qi`. Each CSO server is configured to allow you to choose from a locally chosen set of fields (such as name, phone number, address, and other kinds of individual data). Gopher has understood how to handle CSO searches

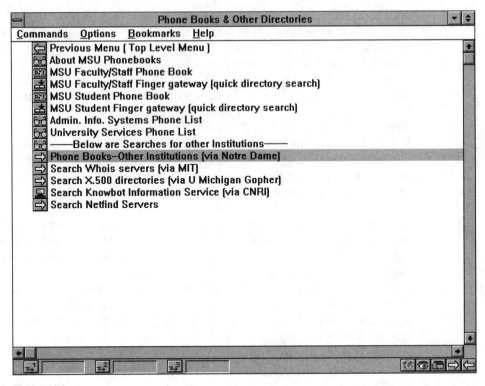

Figure 16.8

from its earliest days. If you are connected to a public Gopher client, and you select a CSO search, it will present you with the various fields that the corresponding site allows users to search.

Figure 16.10 depicts an example of a CSO search using the HGopher client and the CSO client that is packaged with HGopher. We are looking for Joel Cooper, who among other things manages the group that maintains this list of people directories. The small inset panel shows the query; the larger inset panel shows the response.

The CSO search protocol allows you to search across multiple fields at once. Exactly which fields are available for searching varies from site to site; some places offer only the field for the person's name; others allow all sorts of field searches. If you wanted to find all the journalism professors named Smith at the University of North Texas, you might submit this search:

```
+------------------------University of North Texas--------------------------+
:  name            smith                                                     :
:  department      journalism                                                :
:  title           professor                                                 :
:  office_phone                                                              :
```

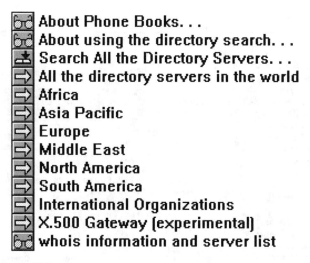

About Phone Books. . .
About using the directory search. . .
Search All the Directory Servers. . .
All the directory servers in the world
Africa
Asia Pacific
Europe
Middle East
North America
South America
International Organizations
X.500 Gateway (experimental)
whois information and server list

Figure 16.9

```
:   home_phone                                                      :
:   address                                                        :
:   office_address                                                 :
:   home_address                                                   :
:   permanent_address                                              :
:   email                                                          :
:   spouse                                                         :
:                                                                  :
:                                                                  :
:   [Switch Fields - TAB]              [Cancel ^G] [Accept - Enter] :
+------------------------------------------------------------------+
```

Some sites have opted to use WAIS databases for their people directories. Searches of these sites work well when accessed via WAIS or via this Gopher-mediated path.

X.500

We saw in Chap. 6 that an elaborate, sophisticated standard for electronic mail called X.400 is used by some organizations. In parallel, an elaborate, sophisticated standard for directories, called X.500, is also in use by some organizations. X.500 is especially popular in Europe, but is also used increasingly by organizations in North America. X.500 provides for a hierarchy from countries to organizations or localities (states, cities, or other jurisdictions) to departments to individuals; it is designed to be adequate as a scheme for building a directory of everyone on planet Earth. Besides being able to embrace the entire planet, X.500 offers the potential for addressing a short-

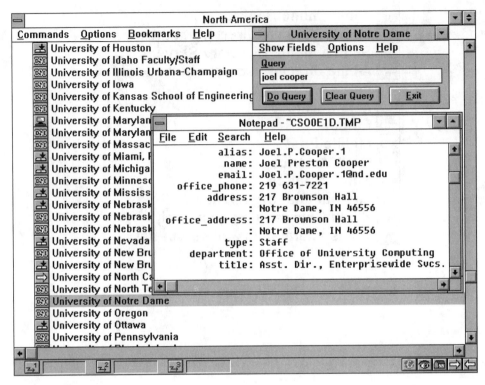

Figure 16.10

coming of many online people directories; too many such directories omit the departmental view of an institution, usually included in any sort of paper telephone directories.

Some believe that eventually the X.500 standard will be widely deployed, broadly understood, and used by the masses. In the meantime, a Gopher-to-X.500 gateway service offered at the University of Michigan allows users to make cursory use of X.500 without delving into its intricacies.* Upon selecting the gateway you see a list of countries; you can do a search at that level for an organization, or you can browse deeper and search for an individual.

Figure 16.11 is an example of the results of a search for Fabio Metitieri. We begin by knowing that he works for an organization called CSI-Piemonte in Italy. First we follow the Gopher-X.500 gateway menus until we find that organization. Then we can search that organization for his sur-

---

* The Gopher-to-X.500 gateway was implemented by Tim Howes. It is located on barbarian.rs.itd.umich.edu (port 7777) with a null selector. Other Gopher-to-X.500 gateways are run by an organization called SWITCH (gopher.switch.ch, port 7777) and by the Swedish University Network (hypatia.umdc.umu.se, port 7777)

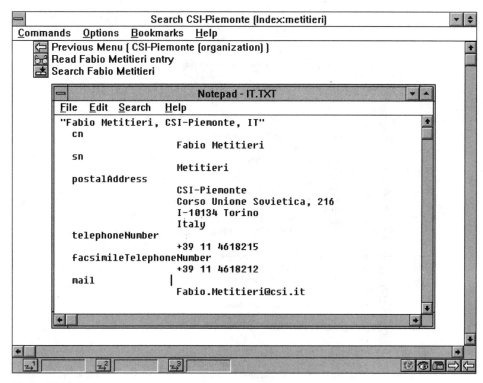

Figure 16.11

name. The entry associated with his surname offers the information shown in the figure.

Whois servers

A tool called Whois has long been used as a mechanism for scanning a centrally maintained database of Internet host names; we will see examples of how to plumb that central database later in this chapter. Many organizations have adopted the Whois program and protocol as a way of delivering people directories. A Gopher server located at the Massachusetts Institute of Technology offers a gateway that specializes in connecting to Whois servers. This Gopher server resides on the Gopher server at `sipb.mit.edu`, port 70. (Many Gophers contain a pointer to this service, including the Notre Dame list of directories shown in Fig. 16.9.*) The search interface is simple and straightforward. (See Fig. 16.12.)

---

* The selector string for the Gopher-to-Whois gateway at MIT is: `B:Internet whois servers`.

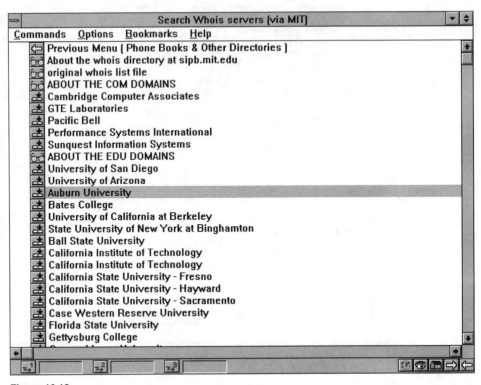

Figure 16.12

The MIT Gopher-to-Whois gateway offers you a chance to opt out of a search even after you fill in a selection; if you proceed, a document appears on your screen with the search results.

Whois is offered natively as a command on most Unix systems and under many other TCP/IP implementations. The typical form of the command is:

```
whois -h hostname personname
```

For instance,

```
whois -h whois.slac.stanford.edu "twain, mark"
```

The Usenet Posters database

One of the people indexes on the Internet may strike some as having a bit of a Big Brother feel to it. This is an automatically maintained index of the names and addresses of people who post to Usenet News. The index is maintained as a WAIS database at MIT; you can search it directly via WAIS, or indirectly via Gopher or WWW. The WAIS source is called:

```
usenet-addresses.src
```

If your WAIS client program doesn't know about this source, use the Directory of Servers to locate it. Or, use a Gopher or WWW gateway. For instance, to search this via Gopher, you might point your Gopher client at Michigan State University's server and then select:

```
Network and Database Resources/
      Internet Resources by Type/
            WAIS Servers/
                  WAIS sources via Gopher/
                        usenet-addresses.src <?>
```

If you choose to use a WAIS client for this sort of search, you might see the sort of screen shown in Fig. 16.13. In this case we are looking for Ed Vielmetti, a well-known Internet personality, and the vice president of an Internet service provider known as MSEN Inc.

As you can see, the database seems to hold several addresses for Ed. This could be because he actually has more than one e-mail address, due to having

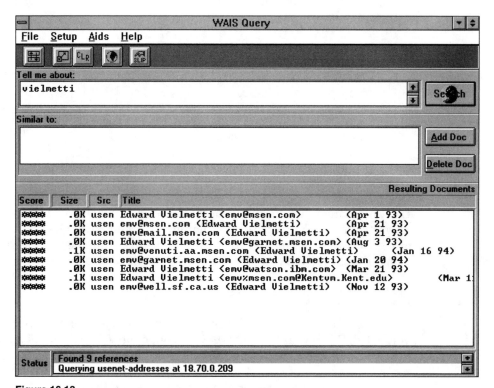

Figure 16.13

accounts on multiple systems. Or it might be because the database has been fooled into thinking there is more than one incarnation, as an artifact of gateways helping to deliver messages he has posted. Or there might actually be more than one person with that name who posts to Usenet from time to time. You therefore should exercise caution before concluding that an e-mail address found via this database corresponds to the person you were looking for.

The Finger command

The Finger command was originally intended to be a way to check on a colleague—typically who worked on the same Unix computer or network. Finger still exists on many systems, and not just Unix systems. It, too, carries with it some privacy concerns in that it may reveal more about an individual than he or she realizes is offered to the network at large. The Finger command has a very simple form:

```
finger person@host
```

For instance, if we want to learn more about Ed Vielmetti, we could do the following query, based on the information returned from our scan of the Usenet postings database:

```
finger vielmetti@garnet.msen.com
[garnet.msen.com]
Login: emv                          Name: Edward Vielmetti
Directory: /usr/msen/emv            Shell: /bin/bash
Office: Msen, 313-998-4562
Last login Sun Feb 6 12:43 (EST) on ttypb from irx1
Plan: content, content, content.
```

Netfind

The Netfind tool is one of the more elaborate attempts to develop a systematized mechanism for finding people on the Internet. Developed by Dr. Mike Schwartz at the University of Colorado, Netfind attempts to find people through a variety of internal strategies. There are a number of Netfind servers around the world. You can access the original server via Telnet:

```
telnet bruno.cs.colorado.edu
```

Because of its popularity, Netfind servers may reject your connection when overloaded. When that happens they will offer you a list of other servers to try. Once you connect to a Netfind server, you can then perform your search. Netfind tries a variety of schemes as it tries to hunt down your prey, and at times it will overwhelm you with more information than you want to see. The best tactic is to provide Netfind with enough specifics about your intended correspondent so that it can do the best matching. For instance, if you were looking for a Professor Turing in the mathematics department at the University of Colorado, you might try:

```
turing mathematics university colorado boulder
```

Sometimes Netfind will ask you to select among several site names so that it can narrow its search. One problem facing Netfind is that the explosion in Internet growth has caused so many hosts to be added as to strain its filtering algorithm. The program undergoes continuing improvement, however. For instance, as this book goes to press, Dr. Schwartz is implementing a scheme that allows a site to register the style of people directory service it uses locally. Thus, under this new scheme, the University of Natal can indicate that CSO is its people directory protocol, and the Centro de Supercomputacion de Galicia in Spain can indicate that its people directory is based on X.500. Armed with this information, Netinfo has the potential for knowing how to directly look for a particular person at a particular institution using the correct search protocol. It will take a while for all sites to register their preferred directory protocol; in the meantime, your best bet is to look for the institution using the various schemes listed previously.

The Knowbot Information Service

Another scheme for finding people is called the Knowbot Information Service, or simply Knowbot.* This service, offered by the Corporation for National Research Initiatives, is similar to Netfind in that it tries to use multiple techniques to find your elusive prey. You can reach the Knowbot service by various Gopher pointers (including the one shown above) or via Telnet:

```
telnet info.cnri.reston.va.us 185 [No password required]
```

FINDING PLACES

As you use the tools described earlier to find resources and people, in the process you often will find information about a place. If you scan the geographical listings of servers in the Gopher or World-Wide Web realms, you will find servers at specific locations. If you wanted to, you could connect to one of those servers and find its actual domain-style host name, but that is usually only nec-

---

* In some circles "knowbot" has caught on as a generic term for a knowledge robot—an automated agent that hunts for facts on your behalf. That was one of the senses the creators had in mind, but they did not intend the term to be generic; Knowbot is a trademark of CNRI.

essary if you want to record the resource in a local bookmark file.* In other cases, a published announcement of a new service will include a statement like:

> Acme Organization is proud to announce its new Gopher server. Point your clients to `gopher.acme.org`, port 70, and read about our altruistic mission.

If you want to connect to Acme's Gopher server, you do not have to worry about finding the host name; the announcement provides that information. Similarly, when you see an Internet e-mail address in a Usenet News article or a personal note, you need not learn any more about the exact location of the host in order to send e-mail to that address. Or, if you are looking for the Web server at the University of Erlangen-Nuremberg, browsing CERN's list of Web servers will get you there quickly. In other words, the mapping of geographic location to a specific Internet address simply is not an issue for the vast majority of Internet excursions.

Sometimes, however, it is useful to be able to find out various things about a network address as part of your search for information. For instance you may want to know what institution a host name belongs to. Conversely, you may know the name of the institution, and you want to find the main hosts at that institution. The ultimate repository of this information is the Domain Name System. In this section we will go over ways to plumb the DNS to find out more about a site. The steps shown here may appear somewhat obscure but in fact are only a primer in looking up Internet site information.

The WHOIS Database at InterNIC

The InterNIC maintains a Whois database that mirrors the host information in the Domain Name System, along with other kinds of information. This database can be the quickest way to find information about sites on the Internet. The InterNIC registration server can help. If your TCP/IP service supports the whois command, you can query the server by typing:

```
whois -h rs.internic.net <query>
```

For instance, if you want to find out about hosts at the University of Notre Dame, you might type:

```
whois -h rs.internic.net "University of Notre Dame"
```

The results might look like this:

---

* Furthermore, clients like Mosaic will record a hot list entry directly, without requiring you to transcribe information such as the host name.

```
University of Notre Dame (NET-NOTRE-DAME) NOTRE-DAME    129.74.0.0
University of Notre Dame (ND-DOM)                          ND.EDU
University of Notre Dame (BIND-ND) BIND.ND.EDU    129.74.250.100
University of Notre Dame (ODIN-ND) ODIN.CC.ND.EDU    129.74.4.18
University of Notre Dame (THOR-ND) THOR.CC.ND.EDU   129.74.35.173
```

This report reflects the information in the Domain Name System about Notre Dame. To obtain more information, you want details on the ND-DOM record. To get it, submit this query:

```
whois -h rs.internic.net nd-dom
```

The results might look like this

```
University of Notre Dame (ND-DOM)
   Notre Dame, IN 46556

   Domain Name: ND.EDU

   Administrative Contact:
      Wruck, James R.   (JRW39)  wruck@oucmail.cc.nd.edu
      (219) 239-5936
   Technical Contact, Zone Contact:
      Gulbranson, Roger  (RG12)  gulbranson.1@nd.edu
      (219) 239-7248

   Record last updated on 07-May-93.

   Domain servers in listed order:
   BIND.ND.EDU                  129.74.250.100
   IUGATE.UCS.INDIANA.EDU       129.79.1.9
```

Whois also likes to provide the following ominous message:

```
The InterNIC Registration Services Host ONLY contains Internet Information
(Networks, ASN's, Domains, and POC's).
Please use the whois server at nic.ddn.mil for MILNET Information.
```

This message is issued because many computers are still configured to point their Whois queries at the wrong server, predating the establishment of the InterNIC. (The nic.ddn.mil was the site for this database until April 1993.) If you have a Whois command properly configured on your system to point to the

InterNIC Whois server, you do not need to explicitly specify that server; for instance, you could simply type:

```
whois "University of Notre Dame"
```

You can connect to the InterNIC server via Telnet as well:

```
telnet rs.internic.net
whois
```

You will find a great deal of information on international hosts by mining the InterNIC Whois service, but there may be other databases with information on particular areas. For instance, a database with information on IP networks in Europe is offered by the RIPE organization. You can query this via Whois; for instance:

```
whois -h whois.ripe.net CERN
```

Telnet access to the same database, and other RIPE information, is also available:

```
telnet info.ripe.net

        RIPE Network Coordination Centre (NCC)

           Information Services Menu

    1 - About RIPE and the RIPE NCC
    2 - Browse through the NCC Document Store    (Gopher)
    3 - Keyword Search of the NCC Document Store (WAIS)
    4 - Search the RIPE Database                 (whois)
    5 - Browse through the NCC Document Store    (WWW)

    6 - HELP for mailing documents to the UK

    9 - Send Mail to the NCC
    q - Quit

Enter Selection:4
```

Netinfo (University of California at Berkeley)

A server offering several kinds of network lookup options resides the University of California, Berkeley. You can reach it via Telnet:

```
telnet netinfo.berkeley.edu 117
```

No login is required. Netinfo can perform several kinds of lookups on your behalf. First you tell Netinfo you want to look up some information about the Internet (it can also provide information on Bitnet and UUCP networks). Then you will be asked for an "argument"—that is, the item you want to look up. For instance, let's say you want to find out what host corresponds to the IP address 128.141.201.214. You would tell Netinfo to do a "reverse" lookup:

```
INTERNET - Name Server
Enter argument(s): 128.141.201.214
Connecting...
Getting directory.........


INTERNET - Name Server
  1)  HOST    - Search Internet host names for summary      [text]
  2)  REVERSE - Search Internet numbers for host names      [text]
  3)  ANY     - Search Internet names for any information    [text]
  4)  MX      - Search Internet names for mail exchangers    [text]
  5)  NS      - Search Internet names for nameservers        [text]
  6)  SOA     - Search Internet names for SOA information     [text]
  7)  How to search                                          [text]

Enter #=select p=previous page n ext page u=uplevel ?=help q=quit: 2
Connecting...
Getting text...


Name: www0.cern.ch
Address: 128.141.201.214
Aliases:
```

Some organizations do not run directly connected servers under a given name, but rather rely on proxy servers to forward e-mail on their behalf. This allows, for instance, Nadir Corporation to receive e-mail at that host name without actually running a server registered as nadir.com, with the assistance of an Internet service provider. The Internet provider acts as a proxy for Nadir Corporation, registering a so-called "mx" or "message exchange" record in the Domain Name System on their behalf. Option 1 in Netinfo will tell you that such a host has its e-mail handled by another site; option 4—the mx option—will provide more information about the proxy server.

nslookup

A tool that allows you to directly plumb the depths of the Domain Name System is known as nslookup. This tool may or may not be available to you, depending on what tools your system administrator or Internet service provider has made public. By using nslookup you can look for many of the kinds of information you can find in the InterNIC Whois database. With `nslookup`, however, you are look-ing directly into the Domain Name System, starting with records that can be provided by your local domain name server. You can extract a large quantity of information with this tool—even to the point of listing all the hosts known to a particular server. That is usually far more information than most people want; the tools shown above can be used to answer the vast majority of questions about Internet hosts. The documentation that comes with your TCP/IP software should tell more about this tool. Unix users may want to use the "man" page as a quick reference (i.e., by typing `man nslookup`).

E-mail servers

If your style of Internet access doesn't permit Telnet sessions, you might want to use an e-mail server that offers some ways to look up information in the Domain Name System.

You can also reach the Internic Whois server by sending e-mail to `mailserv@rs.internic.net`. The body of your e-mail message should contain the Whois search you want to be performed.

Another mail server, located in France, offers a window into the Domain Name System for e-mail users. To use this service send e-mail as shown in this example:

```
To: dns@grasp.insa-lyon.fr
Subject: [use any subject you wish]
addr msu.edu      Use addr to find the IP address for the host named.
name 35.8.2.61    Use name to find a host name given an IP address.
mx nyt.com        Use mx to find aliases registered
```

International postal and telephone code directories

Sometimes your search problem is not related to the geography of names and Internet addresses, but concerns other kinds of "address spaces." There are directories on the Internet that can help with these questions, as well. For instance, in our tour of the Internet in Chap. 2 we saw how to use the Geogra-phy Server at the University of Michigan.

There are other sorts of directories to address specific purposes. One exam-ple is ZIP codes: if you want to look up a ZIP code (postal code in the United States) you can use a WAIS database to do the search. The WAIS database `zip-codes.src` fills this role. As is the case with other WAIS databases, you can search this one with a WAIS client, or you can use a Gopher gateway to search the WAIS database, as with the previous example of the Usenet Posters addresses database.

Sometimes it is useful to find out what telephone area code corresponds with what location. Daniel O'Callaghan of the University of Melbourne set up this Gopher-based service; J. Q. Johnson of the University of Oregon has estab-

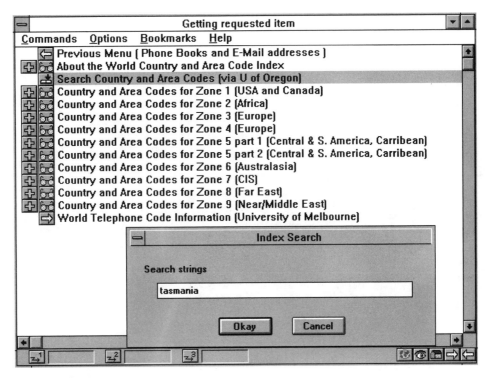

Figure 16.14

	+61-02	Australia	- Hobart [Tasmania]
	+61-03	Australia	- Launceston [Tasmania]
	+61-04	Australia	- Devonport [Tasmania]

Figure 16.15

lished a mirror.* The service, which can be found on `gopher.austin.unimelb.edu.au` (port 70) lets you search to see what area code corresponds to an area, or vice versa.† You perform the search by simply selecting the search item, and typing in the area code or place name. Alternatively, you can pull down the complete list for various zones around the planet. Figure 16.14 is an example of searching by place name.

The result of this search might look like Fig. 16.15.

---

* This is a good example of international cooperation as fostered by the Internet. One benefit of this kind of mirroring is better service for users and less load on international links; good network etiquette suggests that it is best to use the server that is closer to you.

† The Oregon mirror for this service resides on `gopher.uoregon.edu` (port 70) under the Reference menu. (The selector string is `1/Reference/Geographic & Travel Information/phones.`)

Mining the Internet:
A Librarian's Perspective*

Judith Lockard Matthews

GENERAL NOTES

There may well be no other profession with so much at stake in understanding, using, and contributing to the resources of the Internet as librarianship. Regardless of their environment, whether public, school, academic, private, or corporate, librarians are finding that the "library without walls" does indeed exist—and that the challenges and opportunities that the Internet presents are myriad and at times overwhelming. The very focus of the field—accessing information—involves not just locating existing information, but organizing and providing new information in ways that make it useable and therefore valuable. The Internet has opened a whole new world with regard to these activities. And perhaps most importantly, the Internet offers librarians a new means of distributing and thus sharing that information.

So how are librarians using the Internet? Let's look at some of the types of resources they use:

- Electronic mail
- General mailing lists/discussion groups

---

* Copyright © 1994 by Judith Lockard Matthews. All rights reserved.

- Specialized mailing lists/discussion groups
- Internet-accessible library catalogs and other resources
- Commercial databases
- Other free-access databases and electronic journals

E-MAIL AND MAILING LISTS

The predominant use of the Internet by librarians is, of course, for simple electronic mail.* E-mail is used heavily for in-house, work-related communications, especially in academic libraries. Librarians, then, can talk to their local peers but they can also communicate externally with colleagues and other professionals at distant locations.[†] For example, one librarian:

> . . . found an address for the National Agricultural Library, so I posted a question to them regarding average rents on farms in Washington, and whether or not rice can be cultivated here. Their response, complete with statistics, reached me five days later.[‡]

E-mail is really the common denominator of Internet use among librarians. Part of the reason for this is the simple reality that many have e-mail-only access to the Internet. Another reason is that e-mail is the most familiar use of computer networks in general. Over time, as librarians gain better Internet connectivity, we can expect a higher percentage to exploit other technologies.

Mailing lists take the building block of e-mail a step further and provide the most widespread and useful forum for librarians to exchange information. Mailing lists allow a simultaneous "mass mailing" of a message to often hundreds and sometimes thousands of subscribers. There are dozens of mailing lists dealing with specialized library topics that allow librarians to zero in on subjects of particular interest to them and to network with each other. These mailing lists are often international in scope. For instance, the ASTROLIB mailing list has as subscribers over 100 astronomy librarians from 22 countries around the world. This mailing list, like several others, is moderated in order to maximize its usefulness.

The ability for librarians (and others) to communicate in such specific forums expands the capacity for any one reference desk to include the knowl-

---

* See *The Internet and Special Librarians: Use, Training, and the Future,* by Sharyn J. Ladner and Hope N. Tillman. Washington, D.C.: Special Libraries Association, 1993. ISBN 0-9\87111-413-5. Ladner and Tillman have surveyed special librarians and other information professionals as to their various uses of the Internet.

[†] Karen Schneider, Electronic Resources Librarian at Newark Public Library, conducted a survey via several library-oriented mailing lists, and compiled a list, Internet Reference Success Stories. We recount some of these stories here, with permission.

[‡] Bonita Corliss, Seattle Public Library, Seattle, Washington.

edge and skills of other reference librarians whose primary focus lies in the same area. The patron receives the benefit: the collective expertise of, for instance, the global astronomy librarian community can be brought to bear on a given search. In a real sense, highly focused librarian mailing lists are fostering the creation of a global virtual reference service.

Some mailing lists deal with various aspects of librarianship:

PACS-L: public access computer systems forum (PACS-L@UHUPVM1). This mailing list deals with all computer systems made available by librarians to their patrons, including CD-ROM databases, computer-assisted instruction programs, expert systems, hypermedia programs, library microcomputer facilities, and local databases.

```
Address: listserv@uhupvm1.uh.edu*
```

ILL-L: interlibrary loan. This discussion group addresses policies, procedures, etc., for interlibrary loan.

```
listserv@vm1.spcs.umn.edu
```

CIRCPLUS: circulation and access services. A list for the discussion of issues relating to aspects of circulation in libraries, including stack maintenance and handling of reserve materials.

```
listserv@idbsu.idbsu.edu
```

LIBREF-L: discussion of library reference issues. A roundtable to facilitate discussion of reference librarianship issues such as staff training, evaluating reference services and resources, and the impact of electronic dissemination of information on reference activities and services.

```
listserv@kentvm.kent.edu
```

BIB-L: bibliographic instruction. A discussion list that focuses on effective ways to teach library patrons how to locate, understand and utilize library resources.

```
listserv@bingvmb.cc.binghamton.edu
```

INDEX-L: indexer's discussion group. A discussion group for indexers. (An "indexer" is a person who skims documents and assigns descriptive keywords that are used to index printed resources and online databases. The words used

---

* Except where noted, the mailing lists described in this chapter all use the LISTSERV mailing list software or programs that attempt to act as functional substitutes. To subscribe to one of these mailing lists, send e-mail to the address shown. The body of your message should include a subscription request with the name of the mailing list and your name, e.g.,

```
subscribe pacs-l Alison Lockard
```

as keywords usually are selected from a "controlled thesaurus" insuring uniformity of searching. Indexers do the behind-the-scenes work that makes it possible to search, for instance, the Criminal Justice Periodical Index.)

```
listserv@bingvmb.cc.binghamton.edu
```

Some library-oriented mailing lists focus on subject/discipline areas or types of libraries:

PAMNET: physics, astronomy and mathematics librarians discussion list (SLA-PAM).   This list was originally set up to facilitate communication among members of the Physics, Astronomy and Mathematics Division of the Special Libraries Association (SLA), but is open to non-SLA or -PAM Division members.
Send a subscription request to Maggie Johnson,

```
mjohnson@ukcc.uky.edu
```

BUSLIB-L: business libraries discussion list.   BUS-LIB-L provides a forum for dealing with all issues relating to the collection, storage, and dissemination of business information within a library setting regardless of format, including collection development, handling and weeding of materials, CD-ROM and online databases, user services, etc.

```
listserv@idbsu.idbsu.edu
```

MEDLIB-L: medical and health science libraries.   This list is an electronic conference dealing with practical and theoretical concerns relating to medical and health sciences libraries.

```
listserv@ubvm.cc.buffalo.edu
```

PUBLIB: public libraries.   This mailing list covers issues of importance to public libraries, including resources, staff and user training, reference service and resources, and public Internet access.

```
listserv@nysernet.org
```

GOVDOC-L: government documents.   A roundtable discussion among librarians and others interested in government document and other information issues such as the impact of electronic dissemination on access to information.

```
listserv@psuvm.psu.edu
```

CHMINF-L: chemical information sources.   This list serves as a forum for discussion of chemistry reference questions and the sources used to find information needed by chemists; news about existing reference sources; the appearance of new primary, secondary, or tertiary printed or computer-readable sources; prices and availability; search hints; and bibliographic instruction.

`listserv@iubvm.ucs.indiana.edu`

And still other library-oriented mailing lists address even more specialized topics:

SLAJOB: Special Libraries Association employment opportunities. A discussion group created by the SLA Student Chapter at the University of Indiana to announce position openings in special libraries. Internet-accessible mailing lists perform a very real role in helping libraries find staff, and librarians find new positions.

`listserv@iubvm.ucs.indiana.edu`

FEMINIST: ALA (American Library Association) social responsibility roundtable feminist task force

`listserv@mitvma.mit.edu`

PRO-CITE: the Personal Bibliographic Software discussion list. PRO-CITE is a software package used by librarians and researchers to build bibliographies on their personal computers. This mailing list discusses features of that software package.

`listserv@iubvm.ucs.indiana.edu`

FISC-L: fee-based information service centers in academic libraries. This electronic discussion forum deals with all issues related to starting and operating a fee-based information service in a library, including administrative and organizational issues, policies and procedures, marketing and public relations, or anything else relevant to this type of service.

`listserv@mitvma.mit.edu`

NOTIS-L: NOTIS library management software discussion list. NOTIS is a commercial library management software package marketed by a division of Ameritech Inc. and used by many of the larger research libraries in the United States and elsewhere. This mailing list is used by librarians and library systems staff to discuss its features and issues of common concern.

`listserv@uicvm.cc.uic.edu`

INTERNET-WIDE LIBRARIAN COLLABORATION: CASE STUDIES

Mailing lists which are very active and focused really set the stage for librarians to help each other as interactive reference "teams." This is especially true for lists which are aimed at a particular subject discipline. A librarian stumped by a reference question, for example, can place a query to colleagues on such a list and receive an answer (and often many answers) very quickly. In fact, a mailing list called STUMPERS-L is devoted to helping librarians work with one another to find answers to particularly intractable patron queries. For example:

```
Date: Tue, 01 Mar 1994 14:32:10 -0400 (EDT)
From: Terri Wear <twear@mail.ada.lib.id.us>
Subject: art term?
Sender: Terri Wear <twear@mail.ada.lib.id.us>
To: stumpers-list <stumpers-list@CRF.CUIS.EDU>
Errors-to: stumpers-1-error@CRF.CUIS.EDU
Reply-to: Terri Wear <twear@mail.ada.lib.id.us>
Message-id: <Pine.3.89.9403011420.C26928-0100000@mail.ada.lib.id.us>
MIME-version: 1.0
Content-type: TEXT/PLAIN; CHARSET=US-ASCII
Content-transfer-encoding: 7BIT

We need correct spelling for an art term that our patron believes is
pronounced breecolour, breacholor, bricholar? Patron believes it
means a sort of modern primitive art, i.e. using aircraft pieces to
build a sculpture, or making fishing poles out of sticks. Any ideas?
We've exhausted our limited art dictionaries/encyclopedias.

Terri Wear
twear@mail.ada.lib.id.us
10664 West Victory Road
Boise, ID  83709
```

A reply soon arrived:

```
Date: Tue, 01 Mar 1994 13:14:55 -0800 (PST)
From: Mary-Ellen Mort <memort@netcom.com>
Subject: Re: art term?
In-reply-to: <Pine.3.89.9403011420.C26928-0100000@mail.ada.lib.id.us>
To: Terri Wear <twear@mail.ada.lib.id.us>
Cc: stumpers-list <stumpers-list@CRF.CUIS.EDU>
Errors-to: stumpers-1-error@CRF.CUIS.EDU
Message-id: <Pine.3.85.9403011355.A8110-0100000@netcom2>
MIME-version: 1.0
Content-type: TEXT/PLAIN; charset=US-ASCII
Content-transfer-encoding: 7BIT
...

They Have a Word for It: A Lighthearted Lexicon of Untranslatable
Words & Phrases, Howard Rheingold (Tarcher, 1988):

Bricoleur (French): A person who constructs things by random messing
around without following an explicit plan. [noun]
```

A page or so elaborates on the term including:

"[Claude] Levi-Strauss, in describing the way 'primitive' cultures approach theory-building in their empirical disciplines, used the term bricolage as a model for the way all humans, 'primitive' or 'civilised,' build scientific theories by 'pottering around' with natural objects in various combinations."

Mary-Ellen Mort

Such cooperative problem solving among reference librarians is not limited to the Stumpers mailing list. Another librarian gives a similar example:

> When there was some question about the prudent practice of obtaining HIV testing for an adoptive infant born to an at-risk mother, I queried the NETNEWS [Usenet News] group sci.med.aids... Within a week, I received replies from all over the country, several from professionals working at specialized clinics, M.D.s, and the Pediatric AIDS Foundation. The information was invaluable and the patrons (in this case, we as parents and librarians) were greatly relieved.*

Or a much-needed missing page or even complete journal article might be faxed from one library to another:

```
Date:          Thu, 30 Dec 1993 14:24:57 -0500
Reply-To:      albyn@LPI.DNET.NASA.GOV
Sender:        SLA-PAM Special Libraries Association-Physics Astronomy
               Mathematics <SLA-PAM@UKCC.Bitnet>
From:          Carole Albyn <albyn@LPI.DNET.NASA.GOV>
Subject:       Nature issue missing/need art. asap
Comments: To: sla-pam@ukcc.uky.edu@EAST.DNET.NASA.GOV
To:            Multiple recipients of list SLA-PAM <SLA-PAM@UKCC.Bitnet>
```

We are missing our December 16 1993, v. 366 no. 6456 issue of Nature. We need an article entitled "Pulsars in motions" from it faxed this afternoon from anyone kind enough to do so. Our fax is (713) 486-2186.

Thanks in advance!

Carole Albyn, Lunar and Planetary Institute

Once again, the response was rapid:

```
From:          Carole Albyn <albyn@LPI.DNET.NASA.GOV>
Subject:       Nature article
Comments: To: sla-pam@ukcc.uky.edu@EAST.DNET.NASA.GOV
To:            Multiple recipients of list SLA-PAM <SLA-PAM@UKCC.Bitnet>
```

---

* Susan G. Miles, Central Michigan University, Mount Pleasant, Michigan.

```
Thanks Pam-netters I've had two responses in several minutes. I
believe we have the article that we need. Gosh that was quick work!
```

Albyn explains how the Internet allowed her to find a remote benefactor when local libraries happened to all lack the item in question:

> We tried local library connections to get the article for our scientist (who was desperate), but just couldn't get it. [A local university library] was closed due to holidays/intersession, [another's] issue was missing too, the public library didn't carry it at all. . . . Within several minutes of having it on the Net the article needed was faxed to me.

Library-oriented mailing lists might help a librarian locate the e-mail address of a particular researcher or expert. A cataloger might query others catalogers as to the handling of a particular library record. Or, a librarian might simply seek advice from others regarding a common library issue or problem. Still another might announce a library conference or new useful tool to information providers.

```
Date:      Fri, 21 Feb 1992 17:14:16 -0500
Sender:    "SLA-PAM Special Libraries Association-Physics Astronomy
           Mathematics" <SLA-PAM@UKCC.Bitnet>
From:      DAVID BIGWOOD 486-2134 <bigwood@LPI.DNET.NASA.GOV>
Subject:   LPI Databases
X-To:      sla-pam@ukcc.uky.edu@EAST.DNET.NASA.GOV
To:        "Judy Matthews" <MATTHEWS@MSUPA.Bitnet>

Folks,

The Lunar and Planetary Institute's databases are available on the Internet.
The LPI Center for Information and Research Services provides resources on
geology, geophysics, astronomy and astrophysics. Support services are
provided for other departments, such as publications, and computer.
Materials on these topics are available. The files may be accessed at
lpi.jsc.nasa.gov. Login as lpi. No password is required.

The available files are:

+ Journals - A catalog of our journal holdings.

+ New Arrivals - A file of our latest arrivals of books, documents and
journals.

+ Book Catalog - A catalog of our monograph and monographic series holdings.
A limited number of theses and documents which have been cataloged are
included.
```

```
+ Map Catalog - A start on cataloging our map collection. About 500
planetary maps are covered, most issued by NASA or the U.S.G.S. A
retrospective conversion is in process.


+ Lunar and Planetary Bibliography - A bibliography covering planetary
literature from 1980-. Earlier years will be added. All items in the
bibliography are at the LPI.
...


For comments and questions contact:
David Bigwood
bigwood@lpi.jsc.nasa.gov
```

We have seen that mailing lists can be used for reference assistance, peer discussion, resource-sharing, announcements, and problem solving; the uses are really as unlimited as the interests and needs of the subscribers. Mailing lists prove that there is strength in numbers as they provide librarians with the powerful resource of rapid, global peer communication. Examples of discussion list exchanges taken from PAMnet, the Special Libraries Association Physics-Astronomy-Math lists illustrate more of the possibilities just described. For instance:

```
Date:       Wed, 29 Sep 1993 09:19:22 -0600
Reply-To:   edward mays <emays@SOMNET.SANDIA.GOV>
Sender:     SLA-PAM Special Libraries Association-Physics Astronomy
            Mathematics <SLA-PAM@UKCC.Bitnet>
From:       edward mays <emays@SOMNET.SANDIA.GOV>
Subject:    Fireball over New South Wales-April 1993
X-To:       SLA-PAM@UKCC.UKY.EDU .
X-cc:       "Judy A. Geitgey" <jageitg@somnet.sandia.gov>
To:         Multiple recipients of list SLA-PAM <SLA-PAM@UKCC.Bitnet>


A researcher here at Sandia needs detailed information about a
fireball that appeared over the central part of New South Wales
on about April 16, 1993. The event is mentioned in the Sep. 11,
1993, issue of THE ECONOMIST: "...such a fireball blossomed over
the Australian town of Dubbo last April, and though it shook
things up a bit it did no damage." The quote is from an article
on impacts called "The Hard Rain."


Could someone suggest someone in Australia (or anywhere) to
connect for more information?


Thank you.
```

```
E. David Mays
Sandia National Laboratories
Technical Library, Org. 7144
PO Box 5800
Albuquerque, New Mexico 87185
(505) 292-9429
emays@somnet.sandia.gov
```

A response came back quickly, with both a suggestion as to whom to contact, and a list of relevant papers. Note that the original query came from someone in New Mexico; the reply came from a librarian at the University of California in San Diego, and the expert is based in New South Wales—at an institution with Internet access!

```
Date:       Wed, 29 Sep 1993 12:38:00 PDT
Reply-To:   Deborah Kegel <kegel%nowalls.ucsd.edu@SDSC.Bitnet>
Sender:     SLA-PAM Special Libraries Association-Physics Astronomy
            Mathematics <SLA-PAM@UKCC.Bitnet>
From:       Deborah Kegel <kegel%nowalls.ucsd.edu@SDSC.Bitnet>
Subject:    Re: Fireball over New South Wales-April 1993
X-To:       SLA-PAM@UKCC.Bitnet,
            emays%SOMNET.SANDIA.GOV%nowalls.ucsd.edu@Sdsc.Bitnet
To:         Multiple recipients of list SLA-PAM <SLA-PAM@UKCC.Bitnet>


I think the best source for the fireball over Dubbo would be to
contact RH McNaught at the Australian National University Mount
Stromlo/Siding Spring Observatory in New South Wales.

Telephone is 68-426262
fax is 68-422438
and email for the institution is:
   <userid>%MSO.ANU.OZ@UUNET.UU.NET
(There's also bitnet and SPAN addresses listed in the book
International Directory of Professional Astronomical Institutions
1990).

Here's a few of McNaught's papers - he publishes on meteors and
he's located in the right section of Australia near Dubbo.

Deborah Kegel

dkegel@ucsd.edu

Science & Eng Library
Univ Cal - San Diego
```

```
Author:        McNaught, R.
Affiliation:   Siding Spring Obs., Coonabarabran, NSW, Australia.
Title:         Wobbly ideas: photographs of 'spiralling' meteors.
Source:        The Astronomer, Jan. 1991, vol.27, (no.321):190. 0
references.
Author:        McNaught, R.H.
Affiliation:   UKESRU, Siding Spring Obs., Coonabarabran, NSW,
Australia.
Title:         Tamworth fireball.
Source:        The Astronomer, May 1989, vol.26, (no.301):11. 0
references.
Author:        MCNAUGHT RH (Reprint); GARRADD G.
Address:       SIDING SPRING OBSERV,COTTAGE 5, COONABARABRAN, NSW
2357, AUSTRALIA
Title:         ON GALAHS AND VORTICES.
Journal:       EMU, 1992 DEC, V92 DEC:248-249.
...
```

In one case, a librarian* needed to respond to a somewhat unusual request for a text. A patron wanted a physics text that was similar to another text, but the sought item needed to be written in a different language:

```
Date:          Tue, 26 Oct 1993 11:00:00 EST
Reply-To:      Judy Matthews <MATTHEWS@MSUPA.Bitnet>
Sender:        SLA-PAM Special Libraries Association-Physics Astronomy
               Mathematics <SLA-PAM@UKCC.Bitnet>
From:          Judy Matthews <MATTHEWS@MSUPA.Bitnet>
Subject:       Help
To:            Multiple recipients of list SLA-PAM <SLA-PAM@UKCC.Bitnet>


A faculty member has asked if I can locate a text,
written in German, that would be comparable to
"Classical Electrodynamics" by John David Jackson,
1975. Any suggestions or ideas on how I might
approach solving this? Thanks.


Judy Matthews
Physics-Astronomy Library
Michigan State University
E. Lansing, MI 48823


matthews@msupa.pa.msu.edu
```

---

* The author of this chapter, as it happens.

Several helpful replies soon arrived. For instance:

```
Date:    Wed, 27 Oct 93 09:18 PDT
To:      matthews@MSUPA.MSU.EDU
From:    Elaine Adams    <ECZ5EBA@MVS.OAC.UCLA.EDU>
Subject: (COPY)    Help


Judy:


Maybe Richard Becker & Fritz Sauter's Theorie der Elektrizitat, published by
Te ubner, Stuttgart will fill your request. The three volume set covers
electro-magnetic theory, magnetism and electricity. One of our professors
puts the set on reserve along with Jackson whenever he teaches the
electricity andmagnetism class. (I've always thought it was very odd to
put a German texton reserve for an undergraduate class, but the information
came in handy today!)


Hope that helps.


Elaine Adams
UCLA Physics Library
213 Kinsey Hall
Los Angeles, CA 90024
ecz5eba@mvs.oac.ucla.edu
```

Next, to the librarian's surprise, the author of the text in question replied:

```
Date:    Wed, 27 Oct 93 10:05:27 PDT
From:    jdj%theor3.hepnet@Lbl.Gov (NAME/JDJACKSON)
Message-Id: <931027100527.2022a783@Lbl.Gov>
Subject: More on German edition of Jackson's book
To:      matthews@msupa.msu.edu
X-ST-Vmsmail-To: LBL::"matthews@msupa.msu.edu"
X-ST-Vmsmail-Cc: JDJ


        Theoretical Physics, LBL (e-mail: jdj@theorm.lbl.gov), 27-OCT-1993


    Dear Ms. Matthews,
The German translation of my book, Klassische Elektrodynamik, is published
by Walter de Gruyter & Co., Berlin and New York. You can presumably find a
real address for ordering.


It occurred to me that the professor asking about a book of level
equivalent to my text might just be looking for a German passage on physics
```

for a German language exam! A German edition of Abraham and Becker or some article by Sommerfeld or Brillouin in Annalen der Physik in 1914 [refs. on p. 313 of Jackson] would serve that purpose just as well.

Dave Jackson

LIBRARY CATALOGS (OPACS)

Another of the most common reasons librarians access the Internet is to search other libraries' online catalogs, known as OPACS (Online Public Access Catalogs). A librarian might perform a known-item search to find out who owns a title, with the goal of patron referral to another library or for interlibrary loan purposes. A subject bibliographer might be curious to determine the strengths and weaknesses of her own or another library's collection and could perform subject or keyword searches to look at those holdings. A cataloger might search another university's catalog to see how a book or journal was cataloged by that institution. And when a library's online catalog crashes or cannot be accessed for some other reason, the fact that most libraries no longer have their old paper card catalogs on hand as backup can be less of a problem; call numbers, whether exact or just approximate, can usually be obtained by searching other catalogs that use the same classification system; patrons can then still be directed successfully to the right shelf locations. As one librarian illustrates this clever use of OPAC access:

> . . . I've been using the Boulder, Colorado public library OPAC via Hytelnet all morning to get approximate Dewey numbers for books. Our CLSI OPAC is down temporarily, and before we got Internet accounts our only resources was guessing or using old edition 19 Dewey Schedules.*

The advent of access to the Library of Congress over the Internet expanded the range of options available to all librarians with Internet access. The Library offers access to their catalog and to their copyright files, as well as a Gopher service known as Marvel (see Fig. 17.1). The Library of Congress system enables librarians to find information that otherwise would never be available in local collections. In this sense it is already fulfilling the function of a virtual library. For instance, one librarian at a public library used the LOCIS system to satisfy two patrons' search requests. Note in the second example her clever tactic of looking up the original legislation related to the program her patron wanted to learn about:

> A retired gentleman was looking for information on the Civilian Pilot Training Program, which he worked on during WWII. A search of our collection found a couple of paragraphs. I then searched the Library of Congress and New York State Library catalogs via the net and was able to identify a couple of books on the subject and obtain them via interlibrary loan.

---

* Frank Clover, Cumberland County Public Library, Fayetteville, North Carolina.

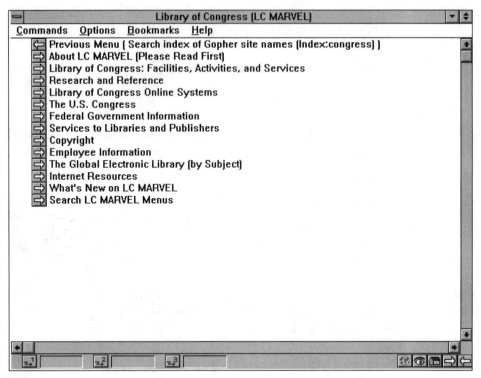

Figure 17.1

A patron requested information about the family medical leave act. I did a gopher search and located the statement that Clinton made when he signed the act. Then, via LOCIS, the online Library of Congress catalog, I found the bill and its sponsors, amendments, and so forth.

We do not have the space to carry hard copy of federal laws and regulations, and the Internet has helped with that.*

Here is another librarian's story of how Marvel was useful:

I had a patron who was looking for information in the Catalog of Federal Domestic Assistance. He was disabled and wanted to know if loans were available. The index to CFDA is miserable, but I found a gopher index available on LC MARVEL, the Library of Congress gopher. I used a simple boolean search ("handicapped and small business loans") to locate the precise programs the patron needed.†

Here is an example of how an online copyright search met a patron's needs:

A patron wanted to see if his ex-wife had copyrighted a story that they had written together (in happier days, I presume). I telnetted to marvel.loc.gov, the Library

---

* Meg Van Patten, Baldwinsville Public Library, Baldwinsville, New York.

† John Iliff, Pinellas Park, Florida.

of Congress gopher, and searched the copyright registration files. (A sample screen from the Library of Congress Gopher service is shown in Fig. 17.2.) The whole search took less than five minutes (half the time it took to do the original reference interview!)*

As these examples make clear, the ability to search other catalogs online expands both the resources and service capabilities of every library.

FREELY AVAILABLE INTERNET DATABASES

Librarians are learning to exploit the many freely available databases on the Internet. From electronic texts to biology databases to NASA spaceship launch information to the CIA World Data Book, freely available resources can prove useful for responding to many search requests. Here is an example of how the Geographic Name Server at the University of Michigan helped with one search:

A high school student needed the geographical coordinates of Glenville, Illinois for his math project. I used the Geographic Name Server which I accessed through tel-net to `martini.eecs.umich.edu 3000`. I left the printout on the desk for others

---

* Mary-Ellen Mort, Oakland, California.

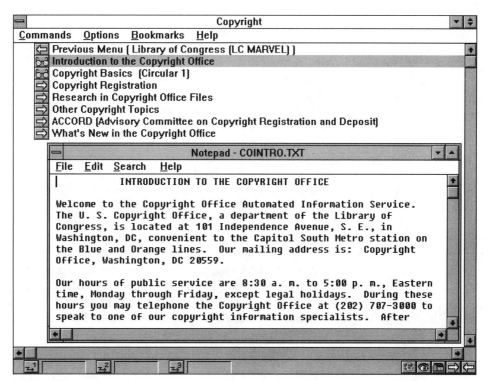

Figure 17.2

to use, since we often get a barrage of calls on the same topic when certain high school projects are assigned.

And here a database assisted another teacher:

A music teacher wanted the lyrics to a Guns N' Roses song so she could decide whether a student's request to include one of the band's songs in the [school's] music program was appropriate. I used a lyric server at [the University of Wisconsin–Platteville]. She received the lyrics and quickly decided that the song was definitely inappropriate.*

Another librarian details her success with freely available resources:

We get most of our current census information off Internet (by way of a gopher).

We have answered questions regarding biographies of the more obscure astronauts from telnetting to the NASA Spacelink.†

COMMERCIAL DATABASES: A COMPLEMENT TO INTERNET RESOURCES

As useful as Internet resources can be, it is still the case that commercial databases are essential for answering some search needs. Commercial databases can be used as complements to Internet searching. A prudent strategy is to attempt to resolve a search using freely available Internet resources, resorting to use of metered commercial databases as a last resort. This strategy can save considerable amounts of money.

The Internet can provide easier ways to access commercial databases that traditionally were accessed via long-distance telephone calls. Although each customer must still pay an access fee—usually at the cost of expensive connect-time charges—Internet access can be faster and more convenient.

If a library has subscriptions to a number of commercial databases, and those databases accept incoming Telnet sessions, it may be useful to create a menu of those databases in a local Gopher or World-Wide Web folder. Although most libraries require librarians to mediate searches of such commercial services—that is, end users are expected to work with a librarian to perform the search—putting all the titles together in one directory can be useful for the staff.

In some cases, commercial databases are accessible over the Internet and are open to an entire campus, with no per-use fees. Some libraries have set up shared access to such services over the campus network. A patron anywhere on campus can connect to the remote service, for instance, by selecting a title under Gopher. In situations where licenses only allow one access at a time from the campus, the Gopher server can be set up to enforce this limitation. Shared access in this form can be far more convenient for patrons; the traditional alternative has been to require them to physically visit a dedicated workstation.

---

* Brian Herman, Glenview Public Library, Glenview, Illinois.

† Kathy Petlewski, Plymouth District Library, Plymouth, Michigan.

One Internet-accessible library resource merits special notice: the Colorado Alliance of Research Libraries (CARL) operates a database service that allows searching of article indexes online. CARL also provides a service called UnCover that, for a fee, offers copying and delivery of materials of interest.* Copyright clearance is handled by CARL. Users can identify a relevant article and order it for immediate delivery via fax; payment arrangements include credit cards. CARL is a sort of hybrid service, with both freely available and for-fee components. It is a pioneering example of the kind of workload sharing across libraries that is likely to expand in the future.

Here is an example of how CARL UnCover provided useful answers for one librarian without need to resort to the for-pay service:

> A patron was looking for articles written by a botanist from the University of Florida. I work in a library with no specialized indices and only indirect access to Dialog or equivalent—what to do? I telnetted into UnCover at CARL, got titles to two papers by the botanist, and the patron was overjoyed.[†]

UNIVERSITY OF MICHIGAN SILS CLEARINGHOUSE—BUILDING AN ANNOTATED INTERNET RESOURCE GUIDE

It has always been the domain of librarians to classify, catalog, and make accessible information of all formats; information in a vacuum—without some system for access—is, after all, useless. So it is only natural and logical that librarians have a strong interest in taming the Internet jungle. One of the pioneering efforts to tame resources on the Internet was launched by Professor Joe Janes and Lou Rosenfeld of the School of Library and Information Studies at the University of Michigan. In the winter semester of 1993, Janes and Rosenfeld launched the Internet Resource Discovery project, a joint effort of the University of Michigan School of Information and Library Studies (SILS) and the university library. The goals of the project are:

- to provide students at the School of Information and Library Studies with an opportunity to increase their Internet skills and apply their knowledge to produce useful products, namely, guides to specific subject areas' Internet resources

- to provide the university library with these guides in order to help populate the subject branches of the library's gopher server . . .

- to benefit members of the Internet community who may wish to consult these guides for personal use or for assistance in building their own subject-oriented servers . . ."

---

* To reach CARL's service: `telnet pac.carl.org.` or `telnet database.carl.org`
[†] John Iliff, Pinellas Park, Florida.

The Clearinghouse search project began as an independent study course and was a major part of the course work during the fall 1993 semester. The instructors charged students to hunt for, evaluate, and enumerate Internet resources in chosen subject areas. The students divided into teams, each of which chose a specific subject area. This was one of the first organized attempts by librarians to build annotated Internet subject guides. The resulting resource guides produced by the students were then included in the Clearinghouse for Subject-Oriented Internet Resource Guides on the University of Michigan's ULibrary Gopher. The independent study course evolved into a regular SILS course known as "Internet: Resource Discovery and Organization" in the fall of 1993. A survey of these Internet explorers reveals some of the strengths and weaknesses they found in the various Internet information retrieval tools.

General observations from these searchers include the following suggestions:

- Obtain the latest tools. Client programs such as Mosaic and various Gopher and WAIS clients are evolving rapidly; new editions may have features, such as enhanced bookmarks, that make your searching easier.

- Know the limitations of your tools. "If you want to do a good, comprehensive search, it is crucial to learn what the limits are of the search tool. For example, with Archie, if your search returns the same number of hits as the search limit, then there are probably more resources available."* You can increase the number of hits, or narrow your search, to deal with this situation.

- Allow yourself enough time. One respondent said "[Plan] on devoting a lot of time to it because even though the possibilities are amazing, the path is rough."† Another observed that "This is a huge job and can only be accomplished during non-primetime hours."‡ (Many servers are overloaded during prime hours, and may deny access.)

- Define the scope of search carefully. One searcher advises: "Clearly define your subject. Then redefine it even more carefully." The large number of potential paths for information requires you to have a good concept of your target.

- Use existing resource lists and announcement mailing lists. "I love Internet lists. I like what Yanoff is doing. I really like Diane Kovacs' lists and found them to be extremely helpful. . . . I like Gleason Sackman's service too."§

- Be organized. As with any kind of research endeavor, you will need a way to organize your findings. "Use a convenient, flexible, organized collection method. We developed a database into which we could cut and paste as we went."¶

---

* Carol Briggs-Erickson.

† Gretchen Krug.

‡ Carol Briggs-Erickson.

§ Lisa R. Wood. (The guides Wood alludes to are described in Chap. 16.)

¶ Sheryl Cormicle.

- "Keep a list of interesting things you find, even if they don't pertain to your subject."*

- Persevere. "I think this type of exploration takes a lot of experimentation and learning by trial and error . . ."†

- "Look at what you can; make note of where you left off; re-execute the search later."‡

Some of the searchers had advice for dealing with people who are helping in your search:

- Connect with people. People will respond if they feel you will produce something of value to the Net community.

- "Be nice to everyone on the Net. Even if they flame you, you may need their help someday . . . Don't take flames to heart. If you did something wrong, learn from [the flames]; if you can't learn anything from the flame, the person was probably having a bad day (or just can't communicate with humans) . . ."§

- Employ people networks: "We found a good chunk of our stuff by making contacts and following up on leads from e-mail, Usenet, and mailing lists."¶

There were some specific comments on index tools. Most of the searchers had the most experience with Veronica. "Veronica is nice because it is a search tool. That seems obvious, but the size of the Internet requires a good search tool. . . . Yet I can see where Veronica is not sufficient for a thorough search of the expanse of the Internet."** ". . . I used Veronica a few times but I always felt like I was spinning my wheels."†† One searcher, whose topic area was film and video, found that Veronica was a good mechanism for finding resources, but that few were located: "The majority of information was not indexed by Veronica. Yet there was quite a bit of information that was. I found my Veronica searches to be high in precision but low in recall.‡‡ One searcher found the boolean search capability of Veronica to be lacking: "I just don't trust it . . . not enough information about where, what, and how it is searching. Also, the total fragmentation of the original context of the resource can be bewildering."§§ Another searcher also

---

* Wood.

† Krug.

‡Carol Briggs-Erickson.

§ Wood.

¶ Cormicle.

** Wood.

†† Catherine Kummer.

‡‡ Wood.

§§ Cormicle.

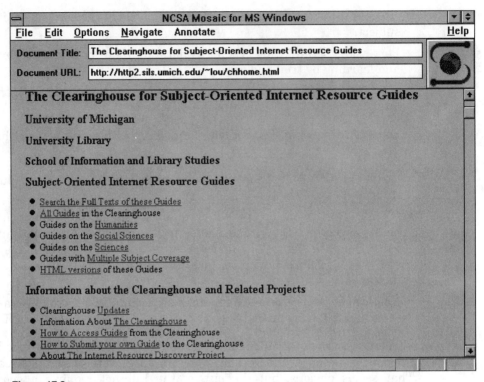

Figure 17.3

noted the problem of loss of context: "With Archie . . . there is no context; you don't know what you are looking at . . ."* "Archie was probably the least useful tool because the file names were so cryptic."†

Over time, of course, these tools are undergoing revision and enhancement. These observations reflect the experience of these graduate students as they used the tools to perform specific searches; your experience may vary as the tools improve. For instance, Bunyip Information Systems, the company that markets Archie, is working with the Internet community to deploy use of "IAFA templates," which will allow Internet information providers to provide descriptive titles and abstracts for their online resources.

The searchers notice problems with transient resources: ". . . there are many transient resources out there. Some were there when we started and were gone before the guide was finished. . . . I would keep trying off and on if I felt the database may prove to be valuable."‡ Another problem was false leads: "Mis-

---

* Wood.

† Kummer.

‡ Briggs-Erickson.

leading titles and perpetual 'under construction' status are also frustrating."* "Some of our Archie searches turned into false leads—the files were no longer on the server."† This experience should be noted by Internet information providers; you are doing a disservice when you place online promising folders that are bereft of useful information.

Today, the Clearinghouse offers resource guides compiled by SILS students and other contributors from around the Internet.

Figure 17.3 is the home page of the Clearinghouse, as rendered by Mosaic.

CONCLUSION

The experiences of librarians show that the Internet is an important resource in its own right, and that librarians and their patrons can benefit greatly from an organized approach to Internet searching. As more libraries gain Internet access, and as more librarians gain Internet search skills, these benefits will magnify.

---

* Cormicle.

† Kummer.

Electronic Publishing, Virtual Libraries, and the Internet

Benjamin Franklin would have loved the Internet. Consider his passion for communications technologies: he was an author and publisher of journals and almanacs; he was a founder and user of public lending libraries; he saw the mail as an important mass communications medium—not just a way for individuals to talk to one another. Transported to today's time, Franklin would no doubt enthusiastically embrace the Internet—as a purveyor of his own writings, as a publisher of others' texts, and probably as an Internet service provider. *Poor Richard's Almanac* and the *Saturday Evening Post* would be among the first electronic publications. We do not have Franklin as an advocate and creator of Internet publishing mechanisms, but we do have a number of talented individuals and visionary organizations leading the way toward electronic publishing. These groups include libraries, university presses, commercial publishers, and scholarly organizations. This chapter will explore the efforts of some of these electronic publishing pioneers, and the role the Internet will play in this exciting arena.

WHAT IS ELECTRONIC PUBLISHING?

For years, computers have been used to assist in the preparation of text for print publication. Whether a document is printed on a dot matrix printer, a laser printer, or a 1200-dot-per-inch typesetting machine, computer hardware and software are likely to play a major role in the preparation of printed matter. How does this relate to electronic publishing? In a nutshell, the idea of electronic publishing is to eliminate that last step of the process, physical printing. Instead, the document is captured in some sort of electronic form and distributed to remote recipients for viewing online or for printing at the user's site.

Electronic publishing is not just a theoretical concept in the Internet context. Already, serious scholarly journals are being offered to Internet readers in electronic form. Some of these e-journals follow a formal editing regimen that includes peer review. Publishers of newspapers and other popular periodicals are also finding ways to publish via the Internet.

Electronic publishing can offer some major advantages:

- In an age of information explosion, electronic publishing offers a way for scholars and other authors to disseminate their writings quickly. Potentially the editorial review process can be reduced to a fraction of the time required for many publications.

- As prices for print materials—in particular, scholarly journals—skyrocket, electronic distribution of information over the Internet offers the prospect for the scholarly disciplines to avoid the high costs of subscribing to commercial products.

Electronic publishing also faces challenges:

- The very ease with which one can create an electronic journal opens the prospect for a new flood of online material, much of which may be of questionable quality.

- Authors and publishers in the electronic medium face a bewildering set of format choices. Unless the reader is plugged into the same technology as the author, a document is useless, no matter how timely the material or how quickly it is made available.

- In the absence of adequate mechanisms to support individual subscriptions or pay-per-view access to materials over the Internet, publishers must devise new schemes for compensation of authors and their own coffers.

There is a distinction between electronic publishing and more conventional online databases. With online databases, the emphasis is upon searching and random access. The user is hunting for a particular piece of information across a vast database or set of databases. Electronic publishing seeks to deliver actual documents intended for more-or-less sequential reading. (The use of hypertext somewhat confounds the concept of sequential reading.) Documents to be read electronically have authors, editors, and definite titles, and often are delivered as parts of online magazines or electronic journals. Of course, there is some overlap between the area of electronic publishing and online databases; an example is the full-text database of *The New York Times* offered on the commercial Nexis database.

Despite the relative newness of electronic publishing, and despite these challenges, the Internet has already become an important medium over which electronic publishing is conducted.

ELECTRONIC PUBLISHING TECHNOLOGIES

Let's say you want to send a monograph you have written to a friend via the Internet. Assume your favorite word processor is Microsoft Word. Assume your friend uses PFS Write. If you send your document in Word's .DOC format to your friend, he or she will have a bit of a problem seeing what you wrote online, or printing it locally. The problem of formats extends to all examples of electronic publishing. Despite numerous attempts to devise "the" standard for electronic document interchange, the practical reality is that none of these standards is universally accepted.

As a result, many of the early efforts at deploying electronic journals over the Internet have adopted a least-common-denominator approach: text is delivered in flat ASCII form, which means that all the features that give richness to printed documents are lost: there are no bold headlines, no variations in fonts, and no photographs or diagrams.

The format of the document is not the only issue; means of access is also a concern. Many authors and publishers want to reach the broadest possible audience on the Internet, and that means delivering information to users with e-mail-only access. Consequently, LISTSERV and other mailing list processors have been popular for many pioneering e-journals. But these tools were really designed as discussion mechanisms, not ways to deliver documents. In particular, a list of back issues with readable titles must be offered as a separately maintained document. A tool like Gopher or World-Wide Web can offer vastly superior presentation of a collection of document titles. Some of the early e-journals are now also available via these methods.

Publishers and vendors of technology are not satisfied with the flat ASCII model of delivery, and are working toward broadly accepted alternatives. For years now some authors have supplied documents to their readers in PostScript form. Adobe Corporation's PostScript is the language most commonly used to drive laser printers. An author distributing a document in that form assumes that the reader will have ready access to a PostScript printer, or to an online viewing tool that will display the PostScript file on the user's screen.

By sending documents in PostScript form, an author can supply the features missing in flat ASCII files, including rich uses of multiple fonts including mathematical symbols, and diagrams and photographs. Unfortunately, although there is a rigorous standard for the PostScript language, various dialects have evolved, and these dialects are not portable. The result is that a recipient may send a file to the laser printer, only to find the file is utterly unprintable. The printer usually communicates its dissatisfaction via the useless semaphore of a blinking light. The author is unable to help, as the file prints perfectly fine on his or her printer. Even in cases where a document appears to print satisfactorily, often the printer does not have the same fonts installed as the author's word processor expected, and ill-fitting substitutes may occur.

In 1993, Adobe tried to address these problems by introducing a new Portable Document Format, and an Acrobat family of products capable of creating and displaying these files. Under the Acrobat model, the author of a document uses a special print driver to create a PDF file, or after the fact an author or publisher uses a tool called the Distiller to convert a PostScript file to PDF form. Acrobat has features designed to enhance portability; for instance it attempts to perform "intelligent font matching" so that a reader can view a document appropriately even if he or she lacks the particular software fonts used by the author. PostScript files can be quite large compared to their flat ASCII equivalents; PDF addresses this by using a more compact language and the compression of embedded images. Figure 18.1 summarizes the Acrobat family of tools:

Figure 18.2 is an example of what a file looks like as rendered by Acrobat. This is a sample page from a product of the New York Times Company called

Adobe Acrobat Software Family and the Portable Document Format

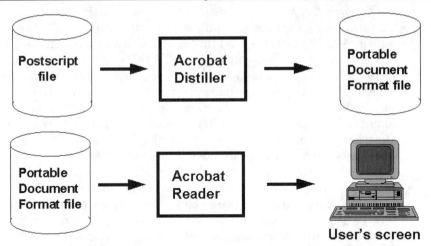

Acrobat Tools Summary:

Distiller: Converts Postscript into Portable Document Format
Reader: Displays PDF files at user's workstation
Exchange: Does Reader functions; also can serve as a print
                  driver to generate PDF difrectly from applications;
                  also supports embedded annotations
Composer: Builds searchable index of PDF files
Explorer: Plug-in addition for Reader/Exchange to search
                  indexes

Figure 18.1

TimesFax. TimesFax was originally developed by the Times as a brief (approximately eight-page) summary of the major articles in a given day's issue of the complete paper. The original TimesFax market was envisioned to be those aboard cruise ships and businesspeople overseas; the delivery medium is traditional facsimile. As of this writing, the Times is exploring the possibility of delivering TimesFax over the Internet using the Portable Document Format.

A tool like Acrobat offers the promise of delivering documents in their richest form, greatly advancing the possibilities for electronic publishing. But there are concerns: it takes a rather fast processor to scroll through such graphically rich documents. Unless one is using a state-of-the-art computer, paging through an electronic file with Acrobat is nowhere near as brisk as flipping pages of a printed document. Furthermore, the user of Acrobat must obtain the Acrobat Reader, which is a commercial product, and install the Reader, prior to viewing any PDF files. Although Adobe markets the Reader with volume pricing discounts, some organizations resist the idea of buying a proprietary tool and installing it on hundreds or thousands of computers.*

---

* This thinking could be a false economy; desktop laser printing is expensive, and online viewing might pay for the cost of a viewer.

Figure 18.2

Some advocates of Internet publishing see the HyperText Markup Language used in the World-Wide Web as a viable, and preferable, alternative to a proprietary solution like Acrobat. They argue that HTML can produce eminently readable documents, and that the networked hypertext orientation of HTML is better suited to Internet document delivery. Indeed, we have seen examples of the rich quality of display a browser like Mosaic can offer.

There are key differences between an approach like Acrobat and the HTML model. The main difference is one of philosophy: PDF allows an author to prepare a document that will be rendered on screen, or printed on paper, in a close approximation to the layout and appearance chosen by the author. In contrast, as we have seen, the Web follows a philosophy of allowing the reader to configure a browser such as Mosaic to present information according to personal preference. The following chart summarizes some of the differences between Acrobat and HTML.

Comparison of Online Publishing Technologies: PDF versus HTML

Feature	Portable Document Format	HyperText Markup Language
Origin	Adobe Corporation	World-Wide Web community (CERN, other institutions worldwide)
Base technology	Postscript printer language; JPEG still-image format	Standard Generalized Markup Language
Availability	Commercial	Public domain
Hypertext-capable?	Yes, supports internal hypertext links within documents; for instance, a table of contents could have links to the relevant pages	Yes, inherently hypertext-oriented; links in the form of Uniform Resource Locators point to other documents to retrieve
Authoring tools	Acrobat Distiller (given a PostScript file) or Exchange (used as a print driver in application such as MS-Word)	Text editors, with markup manually inserted, plus browser such as Mosaic for verification. [Various attempts at WYSIWYG editors underway]
Viewing software used by end-user workstations.	Acrobat Reader (or Exchange)	Mosaic (or other browser)
Who controls layout/presentation?	Generally, the author chooses layout, specific fonts, etc.; acrobat viewers can use "intelligent font matching" to simulate fonts that do not exist on a user's workstation	Generally, the user/author identifies the key elements of the document (headers, paragraphs, list entries) and the client program (browser) displays text according to various settings under user control

Basic unit transmitted over a network?	An entire PDF document (could be a page, a chapter, or a book)	A "page" including hypertext links; conceivably arbitrarily long, in practice usually no longer than a few screens of information

Acrobat is not the only commercial effort in the area of portable document technology. No Hands Software offers a tool known as Common Ground. Farallon Inc. also offers a similar tool, known as Replica; the Replica viewer is offered for Macintosh and Windows platforms, and is freely distributable. These products are marketed in a different fashion; the tools that allow users to read documents are given away at no charge, and the tools used to create the portable documents are sold to authors and publishers. As of this writing it is too early to tell whether one of these tools will achieve market dominance, or whether HTML or some other public domain alternative will become the Internet standard for electronic document delivery. (At time of publication, Adobe is rumored to plan to offer a freely distributed PDF viewer.)

Note that a tool called Ghostscript is used by many installations as a way to view PostScript files online. This tool, freely available under the Gnu license, generally is able to display PostScript files reasonably well despite the problem of dialects. A commercial product called Freedom of the Press provides the same function.

Besides PostScript and various portable document forms, there are some disciplines in which specialized formats are normally used for exchanging draft papers, and in some cases even e-journals. For instance, many mathematicians and scholars who use math in their work use a language called TeX, the brainchild of Stanford computer scientist Dr. Donald Knuth. TeX is a powerful language all its own, extremely adept at complex publishing tasks such as dealing with mathematical formulas. Users of TeX reach a level of fluency with the language such that some can read an article in that language and understand it. The more normal case is to convert the TeX "source code" into a language such as PostScript for local printing.

SGML AND ELECTRONIC PUBLISHING

We saw in Chap. 13 that the language of the World-Wide Web, HTML, is "SGML-complaint." In other words, HTML conforms to the older, more general standard known as the Standard Generalized Markup Language. SGML is an outgrowth of a language developed originally on mainframe computers under the name Generalized Markup Language. The purpose of SGML is to provide a mechanism for identifying the "elements" of a document. We saw examples of the sorts of elements one might tag with HTML—headlines, paragraph boundaries, links to other documents, etc.

But that is only one kind of markup that one might employ. One might also want to tag parts of a document for later textual analysis—for instance, whenever a proper noun is used, or whenever a piece of slang appears, or when a concept such as revolution or religion is mentioned in a certain way. Thus SGML allows multiple "views" of a document—one user might read a document sequentially, with the display of semantic tags suppressed; another user might ask the SGML browser to only display passages that relate to a particular concept as identified by the tags.

SGML is general enough to embrace all these different sorts of applications. SGML per se does not define the myriad kinds of element tags one might devise. Instead, SGML provides a framework so that an author, publisher, or scholar can define a set of tags suited to a particular application. For any particular application, the elements that make up a document are defined in a Document Type Definition, or DTD. Like any other SGML application, HTML has a DTD that defines the legal elements.

Besides allowing multiple views of a document, SGML has been defined as an object-oriented language for text. With SGML, text can be marked in such a way that it can be used by many different computer programs and processes. In fact, one of the goals of SGML is to provide a way for documents to be prepared for later reuse. The commercial word processing program of choice is subject to the whims of fashion; SGML has endured for many years and will continue to last. Authors and publishers either use special "authoring tools" that understand the elements of a given DTD, or they may employ translators that allow them to move from a word processing program or desktop publishing package to and from SGML.

Anyone who has ever programmed a computer is aware that a computer language is subject to errors in syntax. This is true for SGML; it is possible to compose an SGML document that contains errors. In such a case the document is said to not conform to the DTD. Commercial SGML products include a "parser" that validates the conformance of a given document. Note that in the particular case of HTML, client programs such as Mosaic, Cello, or Lynx explicitly do not take on the role of validating the language. Instead, they do the best job they can of rendering the document, and they leave it up to the author—and whatever parser tools that might be at his or her disposal—to validate each document.

Figure 18.3 is an example of a page of a book being prepared for publication using an SGML authoring tool from a company called Arbortext. Note the similarity between this example and the tags we saw in HTML. Later in this chapter we will discuss how some scholarly text-analysis endeavors benefit from SGML technology. (Example is shown courtesy of the copyright holder, Dr. Hal Varian.)

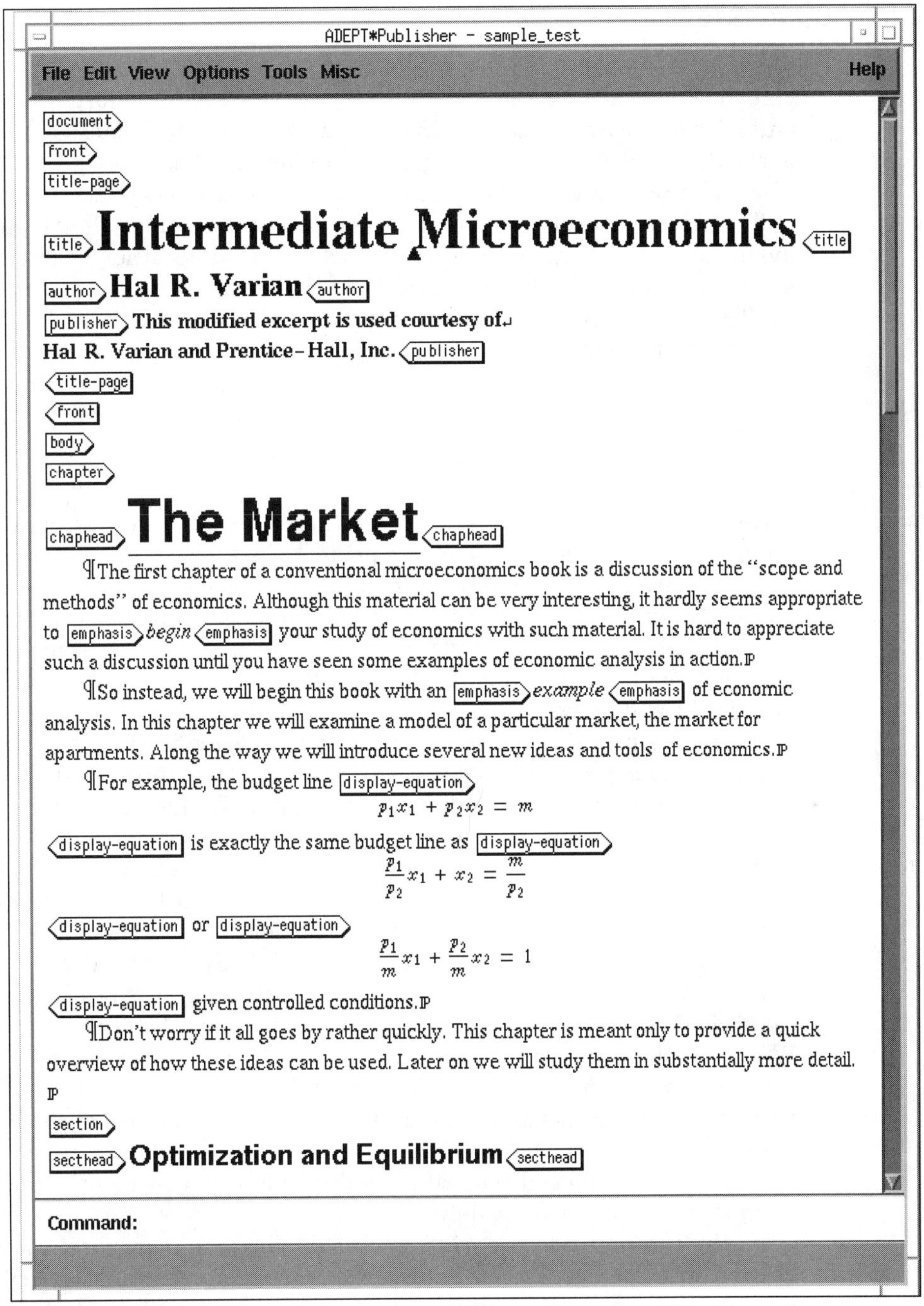

ADEPT*Publisher - sample_test

File Edit View Options Tools Misc   Help

document⟩
front⟩
title-page⟩

title⟩**Intermediate Microeconomics**⟨title

author⟩**Hal R. Varian** ⟨author

publisher⟩ **This modified excerpt is used courtesy of**
Hal R. Varian and Prentice–Hall, Inc. ⟨publisher
⟨title-page
⟨front
body⟩
chapter⟩

chaphead⟩ **The Market** ⟨chaphead

¶The first chapter of a conventional microeconomics book is a discussion of the "scope and methods" of economics. Although this material can be very interesting, it hardly seems appropriate to emphasis⟩ *begin* ⟨emphasis your study of economics with such material. It is hard to appreciate such a discussion until you have seen some examples of economic analysis in action.℗

¶So instead, we will begin this book with an emphasis⟩ *example* ⟨emphasis of economic analysis. In this chapter we will examine a model of a particular market, the market for apartments. Along the way we will introduce several new ideas and tools of economics.℗

¶For example, the budget line display-equation⟩
$$p_1 x_1 + p_2 x_2 = m$$

⟨display-equation is exactly the same budget line as display-equation⟩
$$\frac{p_1}{p_2} x_1 + x_2 = \frac{m}{p_2}$$

⟨display-equation or display-equation⟩
$$\frac{p_1}{m} x_1 + \frac{p_2}{m} x_2 = 1$$

⟨display-equation given controlled conditions.℗

¶Don't worry if it all goes by rather quickly. This chapter is meant only to provide a quick overview of how these ideas can be used. Later on we will study them in substantially more detail.
℗

section⟩
secthead⟩ **Optimization and Equilibrium** ⟨secthead

Command:

Figure 18.3

PIONEERING INTERNET
PUBLISHING EFFORTS

One of the earliest examples of an Internet publishing effort was the Project Gutenberg endeavor described in Chap. 2. Conceived by Professor Michael Hart of the Illinois Benedictine College, the Gutenberg effort has a goal of converting classical works into machine-readable form and making them available for online access via networks such as the Internet. Besides the Gopher pointer available at the University of Minnesota and many other Gophers, you can access the Gutenberg texts via FTP to this location: `mrcnext.cso.uiuc.edu`. A LISTSERV mailing list is devoted to discussion of this project; to subscribe, send the following e-mail:

```
To: listserv@vmd.cso.uiuc.edu
Subject: [use any subject you wish]
subscribe gutnberg Jane Doe
```

Another common early use of the Internet for a type of informal electronic publishing was the exchange of "preprints" of articles intended for print in traditional journals. This commonly took place between individuals on an ad hoc basis, and gradually has grown to reach a broader audience. Common formats include flat ASCII and PostScript. Distribution channels include e-mail, Usenet News, and anonymous FTP as well as more recent tools such as Gopher and World-Wide Web.

During the period of intense interest in cold fusion in 1989, the preprint process saw a flurry of activity as scientists worldwide announced studies either proving or disproving the findings of Ponds and Fleischman. Articles intended for paper journals such as *Physical Review Letters* were made available via FTP and announced in news groups such as `sci.physics` and in a special group named `alt.fusion` created for the subject. Readers at the University of Michigan and Carnegie-Mellon University were able to fetch articles directly over the Internet via their interinstitutional Andrew File System network.

The Cold Fusion example makes for an interesting case study as to whether rapid deployment of findings enhances or impedes the goal of good science. When corroborations and denunciations hit the network daily, one wonders if scholarship has been enhanced, or if it has turned into a feeding frenzy. Regardless of the merits of rapid electronic dissemination of articles in that case and in general, the existence of the network has made it impossible for discussion of an alleged scientific breakthrough to wait months and years for print journal articles to be delivered.

On the Internet, the preprint process has become more formalized and has become in some cases a major mode of exchange of scholarly writings. One example of this is the physics preprint archive maintained at Los Alamos National Laboratories. This archive has become so popular among some physicists so as to reduce their reliance on print journals. Having read a carefully written article in preprint form, a scientist may feel no need to review the final form of the article as published. The value of the Los Alamos archive was made clear when its creator, Paul Ginsburg, temporarily shut it down due to lack of adequate staff and computer resources: an outpouring of support and demands for restoration came (via e-mail) from around the world.*

You can access the Los Alamos physics preprint service, as well as other similar services, via a Gopher-based list offered at the University of Chicago. The server is `granta.uchicago.edu` (port 70) and the selector is `1/Preprints`. In addition to e-mail and Gopher access to their archives, Los Alamos is experimenting with the World-Wide Web as a delivery medium. Figure 18.4 shows what their home page looks like.

Electronic publishing has moved beyond the distribution of preprints to the creation of electronic journals—regularly-issued materials whose primary distribution channel is the Internet (or other networks). An early example of a serious electronic journal delivered via the Internet is the PACS Review. Founded in 1989 by Dr. Charles Bailey of the University of Houston, the PACS

---

* "E-mail Withdrawal Prompts Spasm," *Science,* vol. 262, October 8, 1993.

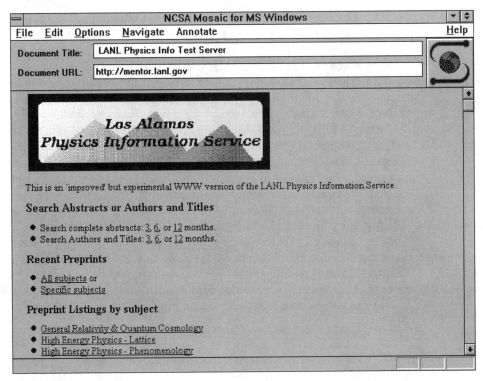

Figure 18.4

Review publishes articles concerning end-user computer systems in libraries. Articles published in the PACS Review undergo careful editorial and peer review. Initially, PACS Review was delivered via LISTSERV. In January 1994 the University of Houston libraries established their own Gopher server, which, among other things, houses archives of the PACS Review.*

The enthusiasm for electronic delivery of journals was demonstrated when the American Library Association offered a print edition of the PACS Review, causing at least one e-journal maven to denounce a paper edition of an e-journal as retrograde.

Another early example of an electronic journal was conceived and is edited by Dr. Steven Harnard, a cognitive scientist at Princeton University. His e-journal, Psycholoquy, was started in 1989. Dr. Harnad's goal was to provide a refereed forum for what he calls "scholarly skywriting." He believes that the process of writing itself can be enhanced through electronic publishing. He argues, "The prepublication phase of scientific inquiry, after all, is the one in which most of the cognitive work is done."† With electronic publishing, not only can the author and editor interact more quickly and effectively than via the traditional mechanism of mailing paper drafts back and forth; the author and the audience of readers can also interact. This interaction is important to the nurturing of the author's ideas; the author conveys his thinking and receives reaction at speeds much closer to the speed at which his mind concocts ideas in the first place. Dr. Harnad sees peer review as an important part of the process, ensuring high quality of original work.

Dave Rodgers, manager of electronic publishing efforts for the American Mathematical Society, has proposed a model for online publishing where the entire life cycle of a journal article is maintained in a comprehensive online system. From the germ of a concept for a proposed article to the editing cycle to the actual event of "publishing" to the letters to the editor, all transactions would be supported by this online system. If such a system were based on SGML, it could relatively easily support multiple views of a document. For instance, an author could see any or all of the comments of peer reviewers in context. Similarly, a reviewer could page through successive online drafts, ensuring that areas of concern have been rectified.

Many publishers and would-be publishers in academe see the World-Wide Web and Mosaic as the tools they have been looking for. At a November 1993 meeting of directors of university presses and members of the Association of Research Libraries, numerous speakers mentioned these tools as their choices for current or upcoming projects. Significantly, there was little mention of proprietary solutions as a means for broad distribution of electronic journals. This

---

* The Gopher server is located at info.lib.uh.edu (port 70; selector: 1/articles/e-journals/uhlibrary).

† Harnad, S. (1990), "Scholarly Skywriting and the Prepublication Continuum of Scientific Inquiry," *Psychological Science,* 1: 342-343.

could be because such tools were only recently deployed, or it could reflect a distaste for proprietary solutions given the advent of tools that are freely available for use by educational institutions.

One example of a relatively early e-journal that now offers a Web edition is PostModern Culture, an interdisciplinary journal with writings ranging from analytical to highly personalized essays. Like many e-journals, this periodical was delivered originally using LISTSERV. The Web edition includes a complete archive of back issues (see Fig. 18.5).

With a browser like Mosaic, scholars could use the World-Wide Web to disseminate research results in a far more graphic form. For instance, many researchers are using visualization to understand processes that cannot be seen by the human eye. The ability to include animation within a research paper could allow scholars to convey their thinking in ways that a paper journal could never approach. Figure 18.6 is an example of a screen offering visualizations of how molecules called buckyballs interact, as prepared by physicists and computer scientists at Michigan State University. Given access to Mosaic and a properly installed MPEG viewer on the local workstation, a reader anywhere on the Internet could browse these documents and could view one of the animations by simply clicking on the inline still image.

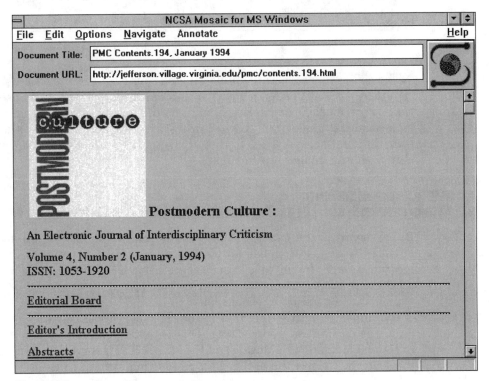

Figure 18.5

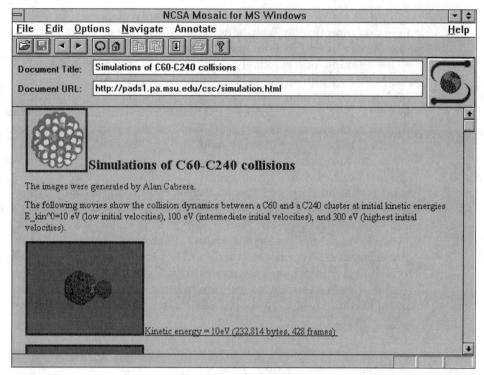

Figure 18.6

The ability to incorporate animation and sound into online documents opens countless possibilities for scholarly communication. One could envision applications for medical journals (animations of healthy versus diseased hearts, biomechanical models) to architectural journals (visualizations of a building from different perspectives) to rhetoric (sounds from a voice library with synchronized still images or film clips).

COMMERCIAL PUBLISHING
VIA THE INTERNET

By no means is the use of the Internet for online publishing limited to academic institutions. Commercial publishers are exploring ways to use the new medium as well. In one case, Novell corporation is using Mosaic to offer online access to reference manuals. Their Web home page shown in Figure 18.7 fully exploits the metaphor of a bookshelf.

You can select a title from this online bookshelf by placing the mouse cursor on a title of interest, and clicking. This is made possible thanks to a feature first implemented with Mosaic and the NCSA HTTP server. Known as ISMAP, the feature exploits the ability of a windowing system to associate a mouse

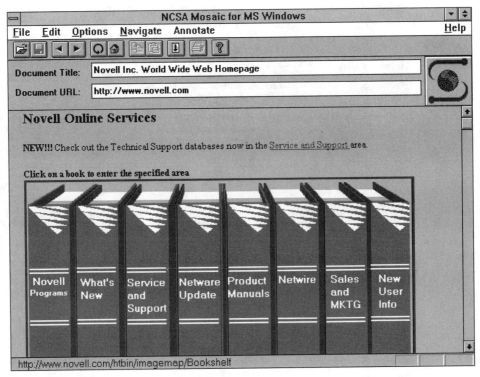

Figure 18.7

click with a spot on the screen. Mosaic communicates coordinate information to the server so that software on the server can determine which book the user selected. The Novell server extends the metaphor to show which book has been pulled off the shelf, and offers a table of contents. The user can click on a "chapter" within a book, or can select another book to open. (See Fig. 18.8.)

The publisher O'Reilly and Associates has embarked upon use of the Internet as a medium for delivering an online magazine about the Internet. The publisher has taken advantage of the relaxation of rules concerning advertising on the Internet; the magazine is distributed free of charge and includes online advertising. Known as *GNN Magazine* (for "Global Network Navigator"), this periodical includes articles about the Internet by various authors. Once again, the magazine is prepared for access via World-Wide Web. Figure 18.9 is an example of the home page of an issue of *GNN Magazine,* as rendered by Mosaic.

Newspapers and magazines are also beginning to explore Internet-mediated delivery. The American Cybercasting Corporation pioneered delivery of newspapers over the Internet, starting in early 1991. Typically, ACC offers subscriptions to a newspaper on a campuswide license. Many of the items offered are made available to locations that are not part of their normal circulation

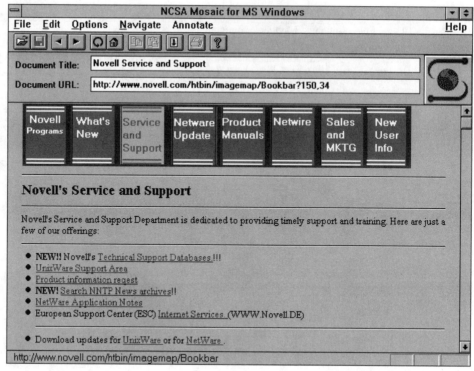

Figure 18.8

area so that the electronic sales do not undercut paper sales. Because all major newspapers are prepared using computer-based systems, it is usually relatively easy to capture full text for delivery in flat ASCII form. Popular magazines may find campus availability appealing because of the extension of markets and the fact that a flat ASCII version will not compete with the illustrated print edition for current subscribers. Titles available from ACC include:

News

Los Angeles Times

The Times of London

Moscow News

Washington Post

Washington Times

USA TODAY Decisionline

The Daily Telegraph (of London)

Jerusalem Post

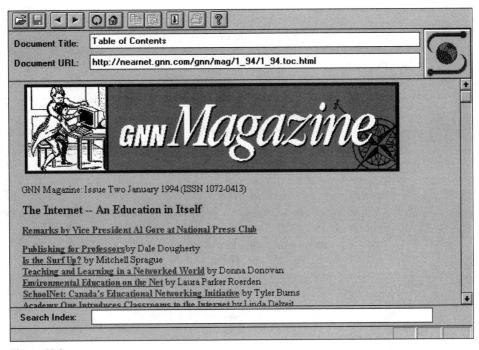

GNN Magazine: Issue Two January 1994 (ISSN 1072-0413)

The Internet -- An Education in Itself

Remarks by Vice President Al Gore at National Press Club

Publishing for Professors by Dale Dougherty
Is the Surf Up? by Mitchell Sprague
Teaching and Learning in a Networked World by Donna Donovan
Environmental Education on the Net by Laura Parker Roerden
SchoolNet: Canada's Educational Networking Initiative by Tyler Burns
Academy One Introduces Classrooms to the Internet by Linda Delzeit

Figure 18.9

Business
Associated Press Financial Data

Forbes

Investor's Business Daily

California Mangement Review

Engineering
Mechanical Engineering

Social science
Brookings Review

Foreign Policy

Imprimis

Insight on the News

The National Review

New Republic

Another vendor, Counterpoint Publishing, has established a medium for Internet readers to explore current issues of a large number of popular and specialty publications. Typically you will find one or two select articles from an issue, plus the complete table of contents. Also included for each title is information on how to subscribe. Figure 18.10 shows a sample of the titles offered by this service.

Several newspapers have established their own Gopher servers or dial-up bulletin boards as a way to supplement the print edition of the paper. One such pioneer is the *News and Observer* of Raleigh, North Carolina.* At least one newspaper, a weekly from Silicon Valley, sees the Web as the preferred mode of publication (see Fig. 18.11).

At least one book store has discovered the Internet as a way for potential customers to search for books and order them electronically. Book Stacks Unlimited accepts inbound access via Telnet to `books.com`. After a brief login process, you can look for books by author or title, browse book reviews, and order books using a credit card.

University presses are also beginning to use the Internet as a way to market, and in some cases, deliver their offerings. One of the leaders is the Mas-

---

* Their Gopher server is located at `merlin.nando.net` (port 70, null selector).

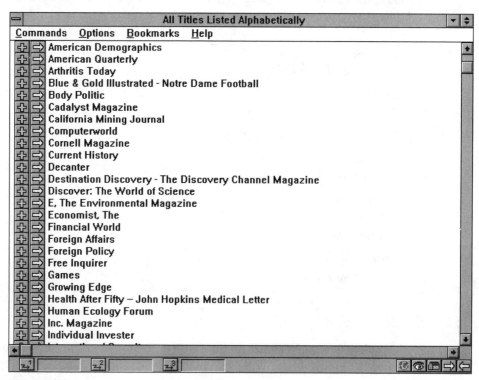

Figure 18.10

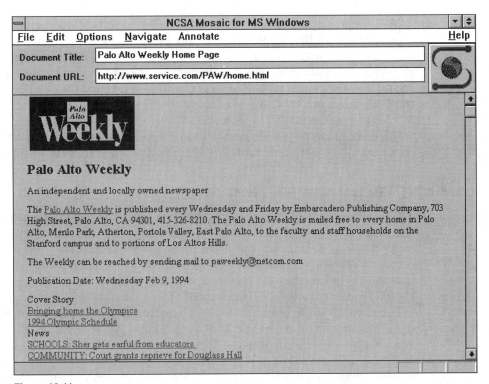

Figure 18.11

sachusetts Institute of Technology Press, which offers a catalog of titles, some sample jacket covers, and other useful information via MIT's Gopher.*

THE CAMPUS LICENSING MODEL VERSUS INDIVIDUAL SUBSCRIPTIONS

Several of the examples of commercial publications delivered over the Internet are offered on a campus licensing basis. This approach is appropriate for Internet delivery because mechanisms for charging on a per-reader subscription basis are still lacking in today's Internet. This model requires that someone decide on behalf of an organization that a license is worth acquiring on behalf of the entire organization (or perhaps a subgroup such as a department). Generally this model requires that access to the document be limited to readers whose IP addresses are known to be local. Readers are warned not to redistribute the material off-campus.

---

* Visit `gopher.mit.edu` (port 70) and select the title `MIT Press`.

Many scholarly e-journals are made available via the Internet at no charge. Publishers of traditional journals are beginning to explore ways to recover subscription fees for electronic versions. In some cases, proprietary schemes are being used to allow publishers and authors to recover fees for individual subscriptions. For instance, the Online Computer Library Center (OCLC) offers the *Online Journal of Current Clinical Trails* via the Internet. (Access is also available over Compuserve as well as direct dial-up into OCLC.) This service requires the user to install a proprietary viewing program called Guidon, and to obtain a password associated with his or her individual subscription.

COPYRIGHT AND THE REWARDS PROCESS

The problem of individual subscriptions brings up the general issue of the relationships among authors, editors, publishers, and readers. The purpose of copyright is to provide an incentive for the creative process, and to recognize certain ownership rights that belong to those who create documents in whatever form. The question is how—and whether—the traditional rewards process should translate to the electronic medium.

For popular publications, it seems clear that authors and artists will insist upon a remuneration process along traditional lines. Stephen King will not offer his latest thriller over the Internet for free access and redistribution.* Madonna will not set up a World-Wide Web server providing free access to her new multimedia album.† Authors and artists expect remuneration for their creative efforts.

Over time there will be more and more demand for support for individualized document orders on demand. This would in fact make it possible for a reader (or listener or viewer, as the case may be) to request a document—whether scholarly or popular—for Internet delivery, with payment going to the publisher and the author or performer. The Internet Engineering Task Force has several working groups that have discussed such mechanisms. The concept calls for an "Internet 900 number" that would allow readers to select documents for which a fee is charged, with billing to take place back to an account associated with the user.

As for the scholarly journal publication process, already some university presses, scholars, and librarians are asking whether this is a role for the commercial publisher in the electronic world. Prices of scholarly journals have risen dramatically in recent years; many libraries have seen double-digit price increases for several years running. The question arises: what is the role served by commercial publishers in scholarly communication? Dr. John Franks

---

* However, Mr. King has offered a short story freely on the Internet.

† However, Music Television's Adam Curry has established a World-Wide Web service, and has obtained permission from certain artists for Internet delivery of samples of their works. Point your Web client at http://www.mtv.com.

observes, "Not surprisingly it has occurred to some that the main thing required to turn a preprint data base into a true journal is a volunteer editor."* Many scholars feel that the rewards of scholarly publishing lie in areas such as pride in communicating new ideas to peers, promotion and tenure, etc. Financial rewards for scholarly writing, at least in journals, are seldom substantial. Internet-mediated delivery of e-journals could liberate scholars and their institutions from the commercial aspects of the publishing process—and could pose a serious threat to the revenue stream of commercial journal publishers.

Clearly, however, publishers of reference works and electronic books will be able to demand compensation for their investments. Anyone who has ever used a library for a research project knows that the credence one gives to a given source of information depends on the reputation of that source; individuals and libraries will pay for quality information. Whether information is to be delivered under campus licenses or individualized subscriptions, the Internet and its technologies are likely to be important in the emerging world of electronic publishing. The Encyclopedia Britannica has announced plans to make available an online edition; the initial version will be licensed to universities on a campus licensing basis, and the browsing tools will be Mosaic and WAIS. Given the framework WAIS provides for charging for information, endeavors such as this may lead to a realization of a practical information-on-demand service in the Internet context. Even after pay-per-view technology is in place, it is likely that many libraries and other organizations will continue to opt for campus or site licenses as an economical alternative.

DIGITAL DOCUMENT PROTECTION

As portable document transmission and display technologies improve, it will become increasingly easy for the unscrupulous reader to transfer digital copies of copyrighted materials to friends worldwide. Copyright protection techniques that rely on passwords for access will no longer be sufficient. Instead, there will be a need for technology that unlocks a given book or article for viewing by the particular reader. Public key cryptography technology, discussed in Chap. 19, may be brought to bear on this problem. With such schemes, an individual reader could use his or her personal digital "key" to read a document, but a digital copy sent to a friend would be useless. Indeed, under this scheme, a vendor could potentially make raw encrypted copies of a document freely available because the text would be useless without the key to unlock it.

Already some entrepreneurs are working on such schemes. A company called SoftLock Services offers a scheme whereby a user can unlock software (programs or data) on demand. The user or reader contacts SoftLock via tele-

---

* Franks, John, "The Impact of Electronic Publication on Scholarly Journals," *Notices of the American Mathematical Society,* vol. 40, no. 9, November 1993, pp. 1200–1202.

phone, dial-up, e-mail, or fax; provides credit card or other payment information; and receives a key in return.* Given an Internet authorization and accounting infrastructure, client programs such as Mosaic could perform such transactions on the user's behalf.

A related problem to the question of ensuring compensation for use of intellectual property is the question of verifying that an electronic document is in fact unaltered from the form in which it was originally published. It is trivial to use a text editor to alter a file fetched over the Internet; an unscrupulous archivist† could post the altered file with no notification and with the original author and title. One solution to this problem will be multiple document archives at trusted locations. Libraries may take on this role. If more than one trusted archive shows the same version of a document, readers will have confidence in its authenticity.

Here, too, software can be brought to bear on the problem. Public key encryption is one possible answer; an author can trust that a reader has a valid copy of a document because only the author is able to create that exact sequence of text. Another scheme, known as "hashing," performs a mathematical operation on each of the characters within a document, the result of which is a "hash" to be carried with the document and all online references to the document. Software can calculate the hash value for a purported true copy of the document, and compare the hash with the separately published value; if the hashes are identical, the document is authentic.‡

THE VIRTUAL LIBRARY

Thanks in part to the popular use of the term "virtual reality," the notion of a virtual library may convey an image of the library user putting on a virtual reality visor and gloves, walking into a virtual reference area or the virtual stacks, and manipulating virtual magazines and books rendered on-screen as three-dimensional, animated objects.

Certainly, that model will be implemented. But it is not the only model for a virtual library, and it misses a subtler, but vastly more important, connotation of the word "virtual." For years the concept of "virtual memory" has been a part of the computing lexicon. Simply put, virtual memory allows the user of a computer to pretend the machine has far more memory than is physically

---

* For information, send e-mail to introlong@softlock.com.

† The term "archivist" has a special meaning in library circles, with implications as to whether individual items are cataloged and how frequently they are accessed; here we use the term loosely to refer to the maintainer of an online archive, or repository, of digital documents.

‡ An excellent overview of digital protection technologies is: Graham, Peter S.: "Intellectual Preservation in the Electronic Environment," Proceedings of the 1992 Association for Library Collections and Technical Services, American Library Association Annual Conference, Arnold Hirshon, ed.

installed. This is accomplished by dedicating some of the machine's disk space to the task of extending the bank of apparently installed memory. The concept was first deployed in the late 1960s on mainframes, and made its way over time to minicomputers and now to personal computers. Your 80486 PC running MS-Windows, or your Macintosh running System 7, exploits virtual memory.

It is in this sense—the idea of extending a resource beyond what is physically installed—that the virtual library concept is most compelling. The traditional library invests a huge amount of capital—in the form of physical shelf space and budget for acquisitions—in order to meet the needs of its patrons. At any given instant, however, only a tiny fraction of the materials in a library is in use. The vast majority of books and space are, in a sense, lying fallow. When the next reader walks in and finds the book or journal that happens to meet a personal need, that particular item suddenly becomes valuable.

Not only do some items remain on the shelf, never to be used; the opposite situation also occurs frequently: one or more readers want access to a particular item, and that item has already been checked out by another patron. This is such a natural part of using a library that we are all quite accustomed to the process: we search the catalog and find what appears to be exactly the right book; but alas it is not on the shelf.

The traditional library has ways of dealing with the problem of highly desired items being in use. First, libraries limit the length of time an individual can use a particular item. Some libraries also institute a "recall" process whereby the patron currently holding an item desired by another patron is asked to return it. Libraries may also have a policy of trying to order additional copies of items that are particularly popular. Finally, libraries may have an interlibrary loan agreement with peer institutions. Through interlibrary loan, a reader can not only obtain an item when the local copy is in use; the reader may be able to gain access to a book or journal article that the local library never acquired in the first place. (Such arrangements include provisions for copyright clearance.)

The virtual library concept exploits the instant reproducibility of electronic materials to extend the scope of any given library's collection. It is not necessary for the local library to have all items that patrons might desire physically in its inventory. Instead, the library can electronically obtain a copy of the item *at the time the patron needs it*. The Japanese automotive industry pioneered a method of cost savings called "just-in-time" inventory control: parts are delivered to factories as needed, eliminating the need for costly stockpiles. In the library community, this concept is expressed as "just-in-time instead of just-in-case." It is a fundamental shift in the way a library fulfills its mission.

Inventor and author Raymond Kurzweil has lectured and written on this transition. He has identified two major advances in the delivery of large electronic documents—electronic books—that must take place before the virtual library model can develop:

- The technology must exist to deliver the electronic document in a form that serves as an acceptable alternative to the traditional print version it replaces.

- There must be a mechanism that rewards authors and publishers for their creative efforts.

Technology to allow the electronic document to replace the preacquired paper document does not necessarily imply online viewing of the document; the electronic copy could be delivered to the reader's location, where it is physically printed and carried away by the reader. This model is already in use under some interlibrary loan arrangements: rather than mailing a requested journal article to a patron at a cooperating institution, a copy of the article is sent via fax. In fact, the Internet has been used as a medium to support this mode of delivery: a project under the leadership of Ohio State University supports fax-over-Internet delivery of materials to the schools belonging to the midwest regional network CICNet. A project of the Research Libraries Group, known as Ariel, provides for fax-over-Internet delivery of documents to participating institutions nationwide.

This process works extremely well for transmission of relatively small amounts of information. For larger works, such as books, no reader would want to cope with hundreds of pages of loose paper for serious reading. One can envision technology that might provide on-site printing and binding of large volume materials, which may prove to be a viable alternative.

Another alternative to physical printing would be online display. Despite advances in display technology, the very best monitors, costing thousands of dollars, still do not approach the quality of the printed page. High-quality printing on high-quality paper has resolution and contrast characteristics unmatched by computer monitors. Moreover, high-resolution documents take a tremendous amount of disk space, and require high-end processing power to support rapid scrolling and paging.

Visionaries like Kurzweil see the inevitable march of technology providing answers to these problems. Magnetic and optical disk technologies continue to advance rapidly in terms of miniaturization, capacity, and cost. Display technology, such as active matrix liquid crystal displays, will offer higher resolution and lower power requirements. Processor power has been on a path of incredible improvement for many years: a given investment buys twice as much computing power as the same investment would have bought a year to 18 months earlier. Battery technology continues to improve.

This line of thinking argues that we will see notebook computers with sufficient computing power, display quality, storage capacity, and battery life to serve as a viable replacement to the printed book within a few years. At that time the electronic distribution component of the virtual library can become a reality.

The issue of compensation of authors for their creative efforts becomes even more important in an environment where an entire book can be downloaded to a hand-held digital display device, and when that technology becomes an accepted alternative to reading traditional bound paper books. The techniques for protection of documents discussed earlier must mature in order before authors will relinquish their works for distribution via the virtual library. When those technologies are in place, and when acceptable global catalogs are in place, libraries can cease the practice of ordering books for their inventory. Instead, when a patron wishes to obtain a particular title, an online order can be processed at the time of "check out."

Some skeptics wonder how this model leaves any room for the library at all. If the library has to pay for each use of the book, how can public library budgets afford to support free, individual check-out of books? Advocates of virtual libraries reply that in a pay-per-view world, the price of a title can be set far lower than in today's market, when the publisher hopes to recover value in proportion to the level of usage enjoyed by the institution. They argue that the just-in-time, virtual delivery model could actually stretch library book and periodical budgets to include access to far more titles; moreover, the titles acquired will be precisely those that patrons demand. Advocates argue that the digital future can even accommodate a form of online browsing at no charge, whereby the reader can skim a virtual copy and decide whether to acquire the particular item.

Those who love books may find the concept of a virtual library discomforting. No virtual library can offer the pleasure of browsing the stacks or of leafing through a book with handsome typefaces and superior paper and bindings. Even when portable display technology and intellectual property protection issues are resolved, will that be the death knell of books and magazines? This is not easy to predict, but few are claiming that printed materials will disappear within the next few decades. For most large, sequentially read works, books will remain the preferred medium.

In the near future, we can expect to see a range of archive alternatives for Internet information publishers. These might include:

- The author's own computer
- A departmental server, or a campus- or companywide server
- An archive established by an affinity group such as professional society
- An archive established and maintained by a library, or by a consortium of libraries

The idea of libraries running e-text archives fits well with the model of the virtual library. Libraries are looking to discover ways to share effort across institutions. This allows individual institutions to concentrate at what they do best. Some libraries become known for the strength of their collections. (Sometimes, it is surprising who shows what strengths; for instance, LaTrobe University in Bundoora, Australia prides itself on its collection of Canadian literature.) When it becomes as easy for a reader in Saskatoon to read items from that library as it is for a local reader, the richness of that collection will be available to a global audience of patrons.

Already the term "Virtual Library" has been adopted by some Internet information providers. In one sense, these nascent efforts could be seen as simple subject catalogs. In fact, they do meet the essential aspect of a virtual library—they offer a set of documents that are not physically located on their server, but rather are located anywhere on the global Internet. Some of the earliest virtual libraries include the Library of Congress's Marvel service, and North Carolina State University's Library Without Walls.

ORGANIZING AND CATALOGING INTERNET RESOURCES

If you walk into any modern research library, you would not even consider the prospect of sequentially browsing the shelves to find something. A building with 2 million books would take a lot of browsing before you found what you were looking for. Instead, you would make use of the online catalog. Modern online catalogs allow searching in the traditional ways—author's name, title, and subject—as well as keyword searching of the online abstracts. You narrow your search down to a short list of titles, you jot down the call numbers, and you head for the stacks.

When the quantity of resources on the Internet grows to a scale reaching or exceeding the sum total of the paper titles in all research libraries in existence, it will become at least as unthinkable to browse to find the document you are looking for. We will have to rely on a similar strategy for Internet searches as for bricks-and-mortar library searches: first you will perform a catalog search; then you will select among the titles that seem promising.

From the perspective of users, Internet navigation already is a serious concern. Organizing tools like Archie and Veronica are a beginning, but they are likely to prove inadequate over time. One of the reasons why library catalogs work well is that they are created with a great deal of human effort. At first glance it may seem appealing to try to shoehorn Internet cataloging into an existing scheme, such as the Dewey Decimal System or the Library of Congress system. But these systems really have a different goal than one wants in an Internet catalog: the call number system used in a conventional catalog is really a way to associate a specific shelf location with an entry in an index. The goal is merely to identify a unique spot on a shelf relative to other books. Neither Dewey nor LC numbering really attempts to create a rational ordering for all knowledge in which all logically related items are placed in adjacent spots in the catalog. Knowledge is a multidimensional web that cannot be represented in a simple, hierarchical cataloging scheme.

But this is not to say that the Internet could not benefit from the work of professional catalogers. Librarians who specialize in cataloging explain that their use of "controlled vocabularies" in the creation of catalogs is what helps build successful catalogs. An Internet catalog might have multiple keywords associated with a given title; users will hone their searches until they obtain a manageable list of candidate documents. Because professional catalogers assign descriptive keywords from generally accepted lists of descriptive terms, there is a measure of consistency in the cataloging of similar items. When a user does a subject search, related items show up in the online list, even if the call numbers are not adjacent.

Libraries already face the interesting question of deciding whether to list networked information resources in their online catalogs. Already some libraries have done so for selected e-journals. With the proliferation of networked resources, each library undertaking to catalog the Internet faces the same issues of what ought to be included in the virtual collection that confront Gopher administrators. Moreover, the effort involved in preparing a catalog record exceeds by a considerable margin the cost of adding a Gopher link. In fact, Martin Dillon, Director of Research at OCLC, has proposed a four-tier approach to cataloging Internet resources, with the effort expended proportional to the scholarly value of the item being cataloged. In brief, these levels are:

1. Cataloging is equivalent to that used for scholarly materials today.
2. "Brief record" cataloging as used by libraries for materials not of the highest rank.
3. Cataloging by automated means, supplemented by some human editing.
4. Catalog record is supplied by item's creator and collected automatically.

Should libraries undertake to catalog networked resources, they may wish to adopt a scheme such as Dillon proposes. Once a collection of documents reaches a certain size, readers must have a viable catalog in order to navigate the collection.

Libraries collectively will probably find it essential to form consortia and employ specialization to provide a much-needed division of labor in Internet cataloging. Rather than each library undertaking to catalog the entire Internet, networkwide cooperative cataloging efforts may evolve. Professional societies such as IEEE and the American Mathematical Society as well as professional library associations could serve as organizers of such efforts.

One challenge confronting anyone who tries to catalog Internet resources is the question of where one resource ends and another begins. A given server on the Internet could be considered a single resource, or it could be a respository of thousands of documents, each of which deserves cataloging. For instance, consider an electronic book archive on a Gopher server. For each book, subfolders are used to break the book into usable chunks. One book might be broken down into chapters; another into major sections, chapters, and parts of chapters. In neither case is there any agreed-upon pointer that defines that one entry is the actual start of the book. Gopher simply does not have the built-in structure necessary for an automated indexer, or for a human, to reliably define the beginning and end of an online document.

Members of the Internet Engineering Task Force have devised a scheme called IAFA (for "Internet Assigned Fields Authority") which may provide an answer for how resources are identified by Internet information providers for the sake of automated catalogers like Archie. An Internet resource provider who wants to have his or her resource cataloged would fill out an IAFA template and place the information online. This fits exactly with items 3 and 4 of Dillon's model. In cases were a title merits the labor-intensive effort of human cataloging, the IAFA records could serve as a starting point. Here is the beginning of the proposed IAFA template for documents:

```
Template-Type:              (any one of DOCUMENT, IMAGE or SOUND)
Category:
Title:
Author-Name:
Author-Organization-Name:
Author-Organization-Type:
Author-Work-Phone:
Author-Work-Fax:
Author-Work-Postal:
Author-Job-Title:
Author-Department:
Author-Email:
Author-Handle:
Author-Home-Phone:
Author-Home-Postal:
Author-Home-Fax:
Record-Last-Modified-Date:
Record-Last-Modified-Department:
Record-Last-Modified-Email:
```

Another IETF effort, the work to define standard Uniform Resource Identifiers, may yield both a scheme that fosters cataloging of Internet resources, as well as a standard mechanism to allow access to those resources. One goal of the URI effort is to define a Uniform Resource Name—roughly analogous to an International Standard Book Number—that could be "resolved" into a particular Uniform Resource Locator. As an analogy, consider how a customer might walk into a bookstore armed with the ISBN for a book on theoretical physics. A clerk looks up the book on the store's inventory computer, determines that the book is in stock, and helps the customer fetch the desired title from the shelf. Similarly, Internet users may someday be able to submit Uniform Resource Names to an automated service that locates copies of the work in question, and returns a list of Uniform Resource Locators—i.e., specific pointers to actual copies of the work online. A client program like Mosaic could automatically fetch a copy of the work from a nearby site.

Such mechanisms are not trivial to define. We have a pretty good idea of what we mean when we refer to titles of books. (Of course, even that can be murky; ask your book clerk for the Bible, and you will certainly be asked to clarify as to which edition.) With online resources, a standard resource identifier has to be able to point to ephemeral documents—"The current weather forecast for Austin Texas" or "today's *New York Times*." Although the answers are not yet in sight, it is clear we need something like the URI mechanism to make online publishing—and cataloging—workable.

As online library catalogs point to more and more Internet resources, the question arises: When does the catalog end, and the delivery of documents begin? Why not have "hot links" to online resources in the catalog itself? As early as November 1992, one library automation vendor, VTLS, was demonstrating a system capable of doing exactly that. Someday soon the catalog in your public library may be equally adept at showing you a path to a shelf location as it is at offering a Mosaic-like view of a document fetched across the Internet.

WHAT CONSTITUTES AN ELECTRONIC JOURNAL?

Just about anyone can declare an electronic serial to be an e-journal. By what standard do we decide whether to point to it in a library's catalog? Include all journals? Those that manage to produce two issues? Those that have been assigned International Standard Serial Numbers? Those that appear to be "scholarly"? Those that are peer-reviewed? Over time, librarians will probably have to apply the same sort of collection development procedures to online information as they do for their print holdings. Although most e-journals are currently delivered without a fee, there are costs to including substandard material—the human and machine costs of preparing and cataloging the material as well as the time the patron spends avoiding the chaff.

Some may believe that Internet-based publishing removes the need for discrete documents and journals. After all, why not just identify a resource as "the Gopher at Carnegie Mellon" or "the Web server at the Sorbonne" with the associated host names and ports? The answer lies in the need to be able to refer to particular issues of documents in order to continue discussion of the ideas contained therein. If documents on the Internet have no definite editions or realizations, but rather exist as part of an undifferentiated mass that can change at the whim of the author or editor, readers may find themselves trying to discuss moving targets.

So far, serious attempts at mounting e-journals have continued the practice of delivering regular issues, with some sort of editorial review process prior to the event of "publishing" online. Once publication occurs, the articles in a given issue are frozen; the author does not have the luxury of correcting errors in the online edition. These aspects of the traditional publishing process are essential for an Internet-based literature to develop.

Although most e-journals do follow the practice of having definite, numbered editions, the model of online publishing does offer certain liberating aspects. For instance, an e-journal offered at no charge is under no obligation to meet a particular printing schedule. Subscribers cannot complain that the periodical is late when they have no money at stake. If there are no advertisers, there is no pressure to publish. Of course, readers will expect that something called a "periodical" will arrive on a somewhat regular schedule; otherwise the journal will cease to be worth looking for.

Another liberating aspect of e-journals is that there need not be any pressure to "pad" an issue with a certain number of articles. A given issue of an e-journal could have only one article, or it could have many. Editors of print journals must live with a "feast or famine" cycle in which the number of good articles in the hopper seldom corresponds to the number of ad pages that have been sold.

Certain problems arise in the handling of online e-journals. For instance, with many sites capturing e-journals as published, and with all such local archives equally visible on the Internet, the question arises as to which archives are definitive. Already one prominent publisher of an e-journal archive has complained bitterly that out-of-date copies of experimental samples of the journal appeared in an archive. Those with a historical perspective might argue that old issues, no matter how experimental, are valid holdings for an archive; no print magazine is capable of demanding that a library toss out old issues that for whatever reason fail to measure up to current standards.

A related concern for the e-journal publisher is assuring that archives are complete. If a site offers to the Net an archive service purporting to include a particular journal without qualifying what is in the collection, the authors and editors associated with that journal will expect online compilation to be complete. Over time we can expect some online archives to develop a reputation as being more reliable than others; readers, authors, and publishers will flock to these superior archives.

Finally, at some point it will become necessary for e-text archives to adopt policies of collection development. As self-declared e-journals offered freely on the Internet proliferate, serious collections will have to exercise some judgment as to which items merit the human and computer resources of cataloging, and which items are no longer useful for retention in a collection.

INTERNET LITERATURE

One sign that the Internet has come into its own as a medium will be when we begin to see Internet works cited in general literature.* Brewster Kahle, the

---

* The latest edition of the *Chicago Manual of Style* includes guidelines for citing online materials. Some guidelines for electronic citation also appear in Kahle (see following footnote).

inventor of WAIS, argues that the ability for a reader to fetch a document cited in another document will be critical to the creation of literature on the Internet:

> B[ulletin] Board systems have not produced any astounding works of literature, I suggest, because it is difficult to reference older works. If older works were easy to find and reference, then people would be more inclined to make better entries. Better entries would get more references and be used more. No BBoard systems, that I know of, make this easy. Since editors, content searching, and archiving are all fundamental parts of the WAIS architecture, we stand a better chance of high-quality works being produced.*

SCHOLARLY TEXT ANALYSIS PROJECTS

Computers are widely used in the creation of print materials and in electronic journals. They are also increasingly being used to assist in the scholarly analysis of literature. Many of the efforts involved in such research find the Internet to be a natural medium to support research and dissemination of results.

Organizations involved in such efforts include:

- *The Text Encoding Initiative.*   This is a multinational cooperative effort to encode online texts such as classical writings; active organizations include Oxford University, the University of Chicago, the University of Virginia, and others. They have produced a set of TEI Guidelines, specifying rules for SGML markup for online e-texts.

- *Center for Electronic Texts in the Humanities (CETH).*   Based at Princeton, this organization seeks to advance scholarship in the humanities through the use of high-quality electronic texts. One CETH project calls for placing a comprehensive corpus of early works by women online.

- *The Electronic Text Center at the University of Virginia.*   This organization makes texts available for online research as part of their effort to extend Thomas Jefferson's vision of an "Academical Village" to the electronic realm. They are encoding a large body of writings in SGML, and have available on their campus search software that allows sophisticated searches; for instance following the flow of an idea across time, both in online full-text versions of classical works, and in online reference documents such as the *Oxford English Dictionary.*† (See Fig. 18.12.)

- *The ARTFL project.*   The American and French Research on the Treasury of the French Language (ARTFL) is a cooperative project established in 1981 by the Centre National de la Recherche Scientifique and the University of Chicago. Its objectives over the last several years have been to restructure

---

* Brewster Kahle, *Wide Area Information Server Concepts, Version 4, Draft,* 11/3/89 (from `ftp://wais.com`).

† Due to software licensing restrictions, access to the complete services of the Virginia center are limited to on-campus users. For more information, Telnet to `etext.lib.virginia.edu`, or point your Gopher client at `gopher.lib.virginia.edu` (port 70) and look under Electronic Text Center.

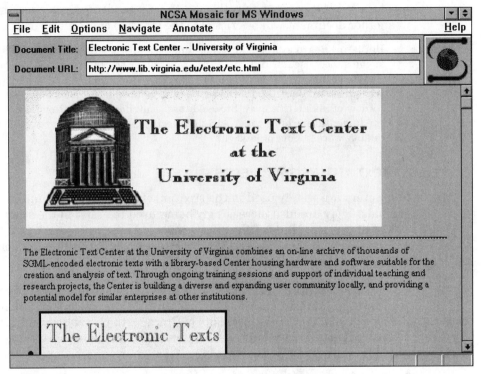

Figure 18.12

this database in such a way as to make it accessible to the research community, and to develop tools for its analysis. ARTFL began with a French project to use computers to assist in the creation of a dictionary of the French language; a large collection of French language texts was transcribed over a 20-year period.

Electronic text analysis projects are using the Internet to support collaboration and to publish information about their research.

WHERE TO FIND ELECTRONIC TEXTS AND JOURNALS

You can find more information about various collections of electronic journals and online texts at the following locations.

- Indiana University Library. Point your Gopher client to: `gopher.indiana.edu` (port 1067, selector `1/letrs/gopher`).

- CICNet Gopher. Point your Gopher client to: `gopher.cic.net` (port 70, selector `1/e-serials`).

# Chapter 19

Security and Privacy Issues

The most notorious incident involving Internet security was the attack of the Internet Worm. On Wednesday, November 2, 1988, Robert Morris Jr., a graduate student at Cornell University (and the son of a renowned security expert) unleashed a program whose purpose was to reveal a flaw in the Unix operating system, which is employed for many servers and client workstations at virtually every Internet site. The Worm was more injurious in its mode of attack than the author intended, and large numbers of sites experienced network, server, and client interruptions. The perpetrator was caught and eventually convicted under Federal law.*

Since that incident, stories about computer viruses and other modes of attack occasionally are covered by the popular press. In late 1993 a password-sniffing scheme was successfully used to compromise user accounts at an Internet service provider, Panix. As a result, user accounts were compromised at a number of other installations—those to which Panix subscribers also connected. Incidents such as as the Worm and the Panix break-in receive mass-media attention, but security and privacy concerns are a part of everyday life for Internet users. This chapter will explore some of the risks and challenges

---

* The story of how an Internet intruder was caught by a clever astronomer is related in *The Cuckoo's Egg: Inside the World of Computer Espionage,* by Clifford Stoll (Doubleday, New York, 1989, ISBN 0-385-24946-2). Stoll's book is mostly a detective story detailing how he caught someone repeatedly attacking a system he was responsible for; it also includes some general observations on security, and some specific information on the Internet Worm case.

in these areas, some of the steps you can take to protect yourself, and some of the technical solutions now in existence.

PASSWORD SECURITY: THE CORE OF PROTECTION

Virtually every computer service to which you log in employs a simple password protection scheme. Your account is assigned a unique user name and a password, both of which you must type in order to log in. Generally, the system administration staff will allow (and even encourage) you to change you own password; some systems employ automated processes that insist that you make such changes periodically.

One of the simplest ways that intruders compromise password security is by repetitively trying possible passwords against known valid user IDs. This process can be conducted via automated process; the intruder uses a computer program to attempt the break-in. One scheme, sometimes called "attack guessing," tries to determine a real password by seeing if any of a long list of candidate passwords in fact allows entry. Most systems will hang up a connection after several failed attempts to log in, but they may not detect repeated connections. Moreover, it is relatively common for Unix password files to be available to prying eyes. This is possible because these files are encrypted, so possession of the file does not equate to discovery of passwords. However, once a password file is in the hands of a would-be intruder, special "cracker" software will repetitively encrypt candidate passwords and try them against the encrypted form.*

There are some straightforward rules for account and password administration, but many users fail to take heed. If you follow these rules, the chances of your account being compromised are greatly reduced. If you fail to follow these rules, you are asking for trouble.

- Pick a password that does not relate in some obvious way to you. Do not use the name of your spouse, your child, or your pet. Do not use your initials, your telephone number, or the mascot of your alma mater. These pieces of information may be much more public than you realize.

- It is best to choose a word that is not a real word in any language. Some "attack guessing" schemes check to see if words out of standard dictionaries happen to match your password. A good approach is to pick the first letter of each word of a sentence that only you would devise.

---

* This is possible because the encryption algorithm used in Unix is public knowledge. The algorithm is said to be "one way"—an intruder cannot determine the original password even when the encrypted form is known. Thus, the intruder must employ repetitive attempts to match candidate words against the known encrypted password.

- Opt for a longer password over a short one. If your system allows eight character passwords, use all eight characters instead of three or four. Shorter passwords are more easily matched by cracker programs. If your system allows you to use mixed case letters as well as special characters, this can also make the password harder to crack. (It can also make the password harder to remember.)

- If you write a password down, put the paper copy in a secure place. Some guidelines suggest that you never write down a password, but the practical reality is that humans inevitably will do this.

- Do not reveal your password to anyone. A new generation of network con artist sometimes employs the scam of masquerading as a security expert trying to catch an intruder, if only you will assist by providing your password. Don't fall for it.

- Do not use the same password on multiple services. This rule is especially important, and especially often ignored. You cannot trust that all system administrators will protect your password. In particular, a dial-up bulletin board service run by a lone sysop out of his bedroom is not likely to have the same level of security as a major Internet service provider.* In the event of a major break-in, your password becomes the key to *all* the systems you have access to—unless you vary passwords used on different services.

- If you have any reason to believe a password has been compromised, change it immediately. Change passwords frequently in any event.

- Most systems will provide you with information as to the last time you logged in, as well as the last time someone attempted to log in, but failed. This is useful information—but the tendency is to let it scroll by unread. If you notice activity that doesn't correspond to your logins, change your password and contact your system administrator.

If you become an information provider running your own system, there are some special points to consider:

- Some computer operating systems are delivered with a set of "stock" initial passwords. Unless you change these passwords—all of them—you are exposed to a very simple attack from someone who has the manuals for the same system.

- When you are away from the system you administer, be very cautious about logging in over the Internet using secure passwords. An unscrupulous local administrator or user could be listening in. Consider isolating your everyday tasks, such as reading mail, on a user ID that has no special privileges.

---

* Of course, the vast majority of bulletin board operators run honest systems and are as concerned about security and privacy as you are. Alas, some major Internet service providers have had accounts compromised as well—all the more reason not to reuse passwords across multiple systems.

■ Many computer systems offer logging facilities that allow you to inspect patterns of use and abuse—for instance repeatedly failed login attempts. Use these tools to keep your eyes out for intruders. Use both the logging facilities of the native operating system and whatever tools you may install (e.g., Gopher or World-Wide Web servers).

■ Most corporate and campus networks have network administrators whose jobs include security. Ask your network administrator to audit your system setup to be sure it is secure. Also ask your network administrator to sign you up for local distribution of the Computer Emergency Response Team (CERT) mailing list. These reports detail specific weaknesses discovered in various flavors of various operating systems, and they tell system administrators how to work around these flaws while waiting for vendor responses.

■ If you install public client programs—programs that allow users to avail themselves of services without authentication—make sure the environment opened to these users is secure. Watch for openings in programs like `more` and `Telnet` that may allow users more privilege than you want to offer to users whose identity is not known.* Your local network administrator should be able to offer advice.

The basic mode of operation of Ethernet and other local area networks that employ shared media implies a certain inherent opportunity for intruders to "sniff" passwords. On large corporate and campus networks, this exposure can be isolated to departments or buildings through the use of routers. In some cases, where security of communications across a campus or wide-area link is essential, network administrators may acquire and install routers with built-in encryption capability. If you work on a campus or corporate network, and you are concerned about this aspect of security, ask your LAN or campus network administrator for details as to the level of exposure.

VIRUSES

Given the notoriety of the Internet Worm, how prevalent are such events? How often are viruses, worms, Trojan Horses, and other evil creatures inflicted upon innocent Internet users? It is impossible to appraise how much Internet transmission is a factor in the propagation of viruses. Any administrator of a microcomputer laboratory will tell you that the most common form of infection is the use of infected diskettes. Executable programs are often transmitted over the

---

* Specifically, some text editors and versions of `more` may make it easy for an anonymous user to create files and perform functions on the public client's workspace, leaving hazards for subsequent users. Look for a version of more (or a superior tool, `less`) that are known to be secure. Most versions of Telnet make it easy for a user to escape to a Telnet prompt; this makes it possible for the user to Telnet to an arbitrary host, which is frowned on in the case of anonymous users. Secure versions of such tools can be found in the archives for Internet delivery tools such as Gopher, via Archie searches, or by asking your local network administrator.

Internet, but the administrators of software repositories such as anonymous FTP sites usually screen their contributors and use antivirus software. Wherever you retrieve software from, antivirus software can provide peace of mind.

Just as well-known archive sites can generally be trusted, the converse rule is that unsolicited executable programs can be risky. As MIME and other standards make it easier to send executable programs to unsuspecting recipients, we can expect an increase in this form of attack. Even a PostScript file can contain commands that can write to your hard disk. If something arrives in your in-basket that you didn't ask for, think twice before executing it.

PRIVACY ON THE INTERNET

Suppose you walked into the corner video store one day, and you saw a sign that proclaimed to be a list of "Our Top 10 Renters, and the Names of the Videos They Like!" Suppose your name is number 1 on the list, and you are not especially proud of the video titles you have selected.

Or suppose the public library added a section to its online catalog listing the "hot 100 reference questions" and the names of all the patrons who asked each question.

Or suppose the local paper offers dial-up facsimile service, and one day an ad for the service lists your name and the titles you have fetched recently.

Surely all these invasions of privacy would be unthinkable. At a minimum, they would be a violation of trust with customers; in some cases, these actions might violate privacy laws. Yet very similar invasions of privacy are perpetrated by Internet information providers, wittingly or otherwise. Consider the log that was posted by one prominent Internet information provider.

```
Connections per Host
Host                              Number of Connections

freenet.Victoria.BC.CA                      35
lilt.loc.gov                                25
delphi.com                                  24
malachi.UCSC.EDU                            23
reverse.loc.gov                             17
tsp.spt.com                                 15
unicvm.uic.edu                              14
flag.loc.gov                                13
font.umd.edu                                13
nervm.nerdc.ufl.edu                         12
srbxy.delphi.com                            11
cougar.missouri.edu                         10
short.vcu.edu                               10
```

Because many users on today's Internet have their own workstations, the publishing of a fully qualified host name or IP address is sufficient to uniquely identify an individual. This invasion is not quite as dramatic as described above—after all, although individual addresses are shown, the log does not tie those titles to who asked for them. But the very fact that an individual connected to a service a number of times during a certain period could be used negatively; for instance, a boss might ask why the person was surfing the Internet at work.

Other Internet information providers are frequently arrogant in their attitude toward privacy. Anonymous FTP sites frequently proclaim to their users:

We log all activity. If you don't like this, go somewhere else.

In most cases, users do not have any reason to worry about what might be revealed in a log. Most logs do not reveal who fetched what title. Moreover, this might not be of concern. One might think "So I fetched the latest version of Cshow from an anonymous FTP site? Who cares if they reveal that?" If information providers want to keep track of usage, the thinking goes, isn't that their business?

Indeed, there are very good reasons why Internet information providers need to keep logs. These include:

- *Analyzing usage patterns.*   This allows the information provider to tailor the presentation of information to suit the user populace.

- *Analyzing index searches.*   This allows the information provider to find what items users are looking for that are not present, and over time to offer what customers need. It also allows those who create indexing tools such as Veronica to analyze how the search engine is used with the goal of improving the tool.*

- *Summarizing and analyzing usage across multiple servers.*   By pooling log data, information providers can divine an overall view of what users find worthwhile. It is possible, for instance, to take server logs from across the World-Wide Web and determine which categories of users find which titles the most useful—a sort of global Top 100 list.

- *Security.*   System administrators can employ usage logs to help isolate attacks on their systems.

These are all valid reasons to keep, and in some cases to share, log information. The library community, however, has long understood the need to protect patron confidentiality, and the Internet information provider community has yet to absorb this understanding into its collective consciousness. As more and more titles become available on the Internet, collections will come to resemble library collections. And there will be some titles that some patrons would

---

* For instance, the Veronica team has made arrangements with Veronica server administrators to share logs of queries so as to analyze the effectiveness of the system. The Veronica team is very careful to collect and distribute log information that masks the identity of users.

rather not have the world know they read. Internet providers need to consider points such as:

- How long should logs with specific user information be retained? What length of retention is required by security?

- When is it appropriate to share log information with other system administrators? What information is appropriate to share? Can a Gopher administrator sell a usage log to a magazine vendor?

- What information should be printed in logs that are made available in printed form for local distribution? What should be shown in log summaries made available for Internet retrieval? For instance, one rule of thumb might be that the least-significant token of each fully qualified host name should never be revealed. This could protect privacy of individuals, while yielding more useful log summaries.

Until understanding of these issues leads the information provider community to adopt some generally accepted rules, the Internet user would do well to realize that a system administrator may be watching his or her activity, and that others may learn about one's activity as well.

PRIVACY OF INTERNET E-MAIL

As we saw in Chap. 6, e-mail sent over the Internet traverses a number of relay stations on its path to delivery. We also saw that, occasionally, problems in addressing may cause e-mail to be lost along the way; in some cases such lost mail finds its way into the in-basket of a "postmaster." Unless the mail is encrypted in some fashion, it is entirely possible that the postmaster will see words that were intended only for the recipient's eyes.

It is also possible that in some cases an unscrupulous system administrator could trap e-mail. This could happen on the sender's host computer, on a machine somewhere along the path of delivery, or on the recipient's machine.

Finally, it is possible that e-mail might be subject to disclosure for legal reasons. This conceivably could occur under laws such as various Freedom of Information Acts, if the e-mail resides at any time on a system that belongs to a governmental organization subject to such laws. Or, a court order flowing from a criminal or civil investigation could lead to such disclosure.

There are also forms of inadvertent disclosure. A classic case arises when someone forwards mail to a third party, and the third party inadvertently replies to the original sender. This example's potential for embarrassment is magnified when the third party accidentally posts a reply to a mailing list, perhaps with thousands of subscribers. These incidents can take place due to slightly different interpretation of e-mail headers by various mail programs, and inattention on the part of the user. Extremely knowledgeable users are caught by these hazards from time to time.

In light of all these concerns, it seems that Internet mail is not very private. In fact, that is the proper conclusion to draw. Your best strategy when composing a message to be sent over the Internet is to ask yourself, "How injurious would it be if this message were posted publicly?" The percentage of Internet e-mail that is actually disclosed to parties other than intended recipients is probably extremely low, but the risk is real.

As the Internet is used increasingly for business transactions, the question arises as to whether to trust Internet e-mail for confidential information. For instance, should one be willing to mail a credit card number over the Internet? There is no absolute answer to the question. Certainly, the same con artists who live in other media will lurk on the Internet; one should not send a credit card number to any unknown vendor. If you choose to mail a credit card number to a reputable vendor, recognize the small but real chance that the information may be diverted. The level of your concern should not be excessive; no other mode of payment—telephone transactions, mail order, or handing a card to a waiter at a restaurant—is absolutely secure either.

The level of security and privacy experienced by Internet users can be greatly enhanced through digital encryption techniques. The remainder of this chapter describes some of the encryption techniques already in use on the Internet.*

ELECTRONIC MAIL AND ENCRYPTION ON THE INTERNET

With the growth of the Internet from a small, close-knit group of computer enthusiasts to a diverse community of hundreds of thousands of users, a need for protecting privacy has arisen. On today's Internet, any given user is apt to know—and be able to trust—only a small fraction of the other users. Furthermore, the Internet is now being used to conduct a wide variety of transactions. Some of these transactions would be considered confidential when conducted in a noncomputing environment.

Encryption is one of the most appealing means of increasing the confidentiality of computer-based information. Other means of providing security exist, such as configuring the operating system appropriately, keeping abreast of and installing security-related OS patches, and restricting physical access to the computer and/or network. However, often these options inconvenience users or require them to rely upon proper action on the part of their computer system manager. Furthermore, recent history has shown that traditional security measures are often inadequate defense against determined "crackers" or network snoopers.

---

* The sections of this chapter concerning Privacy Enhanced Mail and Kerberos were written by Mark Riordan.

Encryption, on the other hand, can be used by individual users to protect files and electronic communications from prying eyes with less reliance upon operating system security. Encryption can also be used in a variety of more specialized contexts, such as protecting transactions between network servers. This section, however, will focus on one of the most rapidly growing and user-visible uses of encryption: the encryption of electronic mail messages.

PRIVACY VERSUS AUTHENTICATION

Individuals interested in protecting their electronic mail messages may have two distinct needs. They may want privacy: the ability to hide the content of their messages from persons other than the intended recipient. Also, they may desire authentication: the ability to verify that a given message is really from the apparent sender. These two needs are distinct; a message like "From the boss: Send our customer list to XYZ Corp." need not be secret, but the recipient may well want to verify that the sender really was the boss.

Cryptographic technology can be used to address the need for authentication as well as the need for privacy. A *digital signature* of a message can be made by computing a check sum or hash function of the message (referred to in crypto-graphic circles as a *message digest*), and encrypting the result. The digital signature is transmitted along with the message, which itself may or may not be encrypted. The recipient then recalculates the message digest from the received message, and decrypts the encrypted version that accompanied the message. If the two match, the recipient knows that the sender knew the proper encryption key. Assuming that only authorized personnel know the encryption key, this means that the message was sent by an authorized individual.

INTERNET PRIVACY-ENHANCED MAIL

Use of encryption with e-mail requires that choices be made for the following:

- Encryption and authentication algorithms
- A means of communicating the encryption key to the correspondant
- A means of reformatting the ciphertext so it looks like an e-mail message

Given the large number of electronic mail users on the Internet, it is highly desirable that standards be adopted for all of these choices to ensure that messages encrypted by one user can easily be decrypted by the intended recipient. To this end, the Internet Engineering Task Force has issued a set of recommendations for standardizing the use of encryption with electronic mail. These proposed standards are collectively known as Internet Privacy-Enhanced Mail, or PEM. They are described in Internet Request for Comments (RFCs) numbered 1421 through 1424, available on many FTP sites as `rfc1421.txt` through `rfc1424.txt`.

The discussion that follows focuses on Internet PEM. However, because the issues addressed by Internet PEM apply to most environments and mail packages, the concepts are applicable to most e-mail encryption schemes.

Data encryption in Internet PEM

The data encryption algorithm chosen for Internet PEM is DES, the Data Encryption Standard approved by the U.S. National Bureau of Standards in 1977. DES is a traditional block encryption algorithm which enciphers 64 bits of data at a time. Encryption of an entire message requires that the message be broken into 64-bit chunks. Usually a *chaining* mode is used, in which the output from one 64-bit encryption is fed into the next, to further stymie unauthorized individuals attempting to read the message.

Despite early suspicion that DES might have been deliberately crippled by government-initiated modifications to its design, recent research results have tended to refute those beliefs. DES has withstood over 15 years of determined attacks by cryptanalysts worldwide. It is now generally believed that the primary shortcoming of DES is its modest key size of 56 bits, which may make exhaustive search of the 72×10^{15} possible DES keys practical in the near future with special-purpose equipment. This shortcoming can be overcome by encrypting a message multiple times with DES, but this option is not yet a part of the PEM standard. For most Internet applications, however, DES will be adequate for many years to come.

Public key cryptography and Internet PEM

Although Internet PEM allows for encryption of messages using only DES, in practice this option is rarely used. Instead, public key cryptography is used to supplement DES.

Public key cryptography, a fairly recent concept, is an encryption scheme in which messages are encrypted and decrypted with pairs of keys. One component of a user's keypair is used for encryption; the other is used for decryption. Thus, public key cryptography is sometimes referred to as *asymmetric* cryptography. This contrasts with traditional secret-key, or *symmetric* encryption schemes like DES, where the same key must be used both to encrypt and to decrypt. Though both halves of the keypair for a given user are computed at the same time, neither can be derived from the other.

This arrangement allows each correspondent to publish one-half of his keypair (the encryption key, public key, or *public component*), keeping secret only the decryption half, or *private component*. Users wishing to send a message to, say, Alice, simply consult a nonsecret directory of public components to find Alice's public key component. They encrypt their messages to Alice using her public key. Because only Alice knows her private component, only she can decrypt any of these messages to her. And none of the users corresponding with Alice need ever have first exchanged any secret information with her.

Each user needs keep secret only his or her own private component. Contrast this with traditional symmetric cryptography. In a group of N correspondents, each user must keep track of N-1 secret keys. Furthermore, the *total* number of secret keys required for traditional cryptography is (N)*(N-1)/2, much larger than the N keys required by public key cryptography. Thus, public key cryptography's value lies in improved key management, especially for large numbers of correspondents.

The public key encryption system used by most e-mail encryption systems—including Internet PEM—is the RSA (Rivest-Shamir-Adleman) public key algorithm. In practice, since RSA and other public key schemes are quite slow, a combination of RSA and the relatively fast DES algorithm is used in Internet PEM. An Internet PEM implementation generates a pseudo-random DES key, and encrypts the message using this one-time key. This DES key is encrypted using RSA, and the encrypted key is included with the message. The recipient's decryption program decrypts the DES key using RSA, and then decrypts the message using the DES key. Because the DES key is typically much shorter than the message, the result is an encryption process that is much faster than using RSA alone.

Key management in Internet PEM

For the value of public key cryptography to be realized, there must be an effective way for individual users to widely advertise their public key components. Furthermore, there must be a way to assure that a key purportedly belonging to a user really does belong to that user.

Internet PEM does not specify a standard means of disseminating public keys. Various implementations manage public keys in disk files, look them up over the network via specialized key servers, or even use the Unix `finger` program to obtain them from individual users' `.plan` files.

However, Internet PEM does address the issue of authenticating public keys. In Internet PEM, each public key is issued with a *certificate* which contains the name of the owner of the key, the name of the issuing agency, the public key itself, and a digital signature of the key, using the RSA key of the issuing agency. There may be many local issuing agencies, each of which holds a public key and a certificate issued by a higher-level issuing agency. At the highest level, there are a few well-known and trusted issuing agencies whose public keys are universally known.

A decryption program checking the validity of a user's public key examines the certificate for that key. The program checks to see whether the certificate's signature, affixed by the issuing agency, properly matches the contents of the certificate. If it does, the program knows that the public key is valid as far as that issuing agency is concerned. If there is some question regarding the issuing agency, the program examines the certificate for the public key of that agency. If the digital signature of that agency's certificate checks out, the program knows that that agency's key is valid as far as the next higher-level agency is concerned. This process continues until an agency is encountered which is trusted.

Internet PEM thus presupposes a hierarchy of trust, and agencies that essentially act as notaries public. Certificates and certificate-management services are sold by companies specializing in cryptographic services. This model is well-suited to large organizations with high security requirements. However, this formal trust model does not appeal to some private users and small organizations. Work is underway to cleanly extend the Internet PEM certificate model to situations in which there is no available universally recognized, well-trusted authority.

Message formatting in Internet PEM

The result of encryption with DES and most other modern encryption systems is a string of binary bytes. In general, "raw" encrypted messages cannot be successfully sent through electronic mail systems. Many mail systems, for instance, cannot transmit certain characters, or lines of text beyond a certain length. Internet PEM gets around potential mailer problems by recoding messages to a format acceptable to all mailers. An Internet PEM-compatible encryption program recodes blocks of three 8-bit bytes to four ASCII characters, and reformats these ASCII characters to lines of 64 characters in length. It also adds lines of text to the beginning of the message, specifying the identity of the sender, giving the value of the RSA-encrypted DES key, and so on. The result is a message over 33 percent longer than the original plaintext. The additional length is a small price to pay to guarantee that the encrypted message will survive its trip through mailers across the Internet.

This Internet PEM message recoding scheme is very similar to that used by the well-known Unix `uuencode` program. Unfortunately, the specific character encoding scheme used by `uuencode` was poorly chosen, and is not compatible with all mail systems. Thus, the Internet PEM recoding process differs in some details from that used by `uuencode`, and is not compatible with `uuencode`.

LEGAL ISSUES

Two legal issues apply to users of Internet PEM and related products in the United States. First, the United States places export controls on encryption technology. It is probably not legal to export PEM or similar encryption software outside the United States and Canada without an explicit license, or to give it to individuals who are not citizens or permanent residents of these two countries. Questions should be directed to the U.S. State Department's Office of Defense Trade Controls.

Secondly, the RSA and at least some other public key encryption algorithms are patented in the United States. The patents are held by Public Key Partners, a company closely associated with RSA Data Security, Inc. Inquiries can be made to RSA Data Security at (415)595-8782.

FREE E-MAIL ENCRYPTION
PROGRAMS AVAILABLE

Several programs designed for the encryption of electronic mail are available at no cost:

TIS/PEM. A complete implementation of Internet PEM for Unix systems. It is available in source code form from Trusted Information Systems, Inc., on the FTP site `ftp.tis.com`. The distribution includes nearly 10MB of C source code and documentation not only for the encryption program, but also for programs to create and sign certificates.

As a PEM implementation, TIS/PEM uses DES and RSA for encryption, using code licensed from RSA Data Security, Inc. It is used primarily in conjunction with the Rand MH mail program, but can be interfaced to other Unix mailers.

TIS/PEM is provided free for United States and Canada users with relatively few restrictions; the primary limitations are that users of TIS/PEM must not redistribute the software themselves and must not generate certificates for persons outside their organization.

TechMail-PEM. A complete implementation of Internet PEM for the Macintosh. It was written at the Massachusetts Institute of Technology under the direction of Jeffrey Shiller. TechMail-PEM contains both an Internet PEM encryption/authentication engine (using DES and RSA, as required by the RFCs), and a graphical mail program.

TechMail-PEM is distributed in executable form only, from `net-dist.mit.edu`. TechMail-PEM is free, but it includes technology licensed from RSA Data Security and is available for noncommercial use only.

PGP (Pretty Good Privacy). A general-purpose public key encryption program originally written by Philip Zimmermann, and subsequently enhanced by many others. PGP provides a unique "key ring" approach to key management, in which users build their own databases of public keys from keys signed by individuals they trust. For data encryption, PGP uses IDEA, a block key cipher designed in Switzerland and licensed from Ascom-Tech AG; for key exchange, RSA is used. PGP is not Internet PEM compliant.

PGP versions are available for MS-DOS, Unix, VMS, Amiga, Macintosh, and other operating systems. All are distributed with source code, and are available from a large number of FTP sites.

PGP is "guerrillaware" provided at no cost, but USA users should be aware that Public Key Partners, Inc. claims that the free version of PGP violates their patents. A commercial version of PGP is available from ViaCrypt.

RIPEM. A PEM-like public key encryption program written primarily by Mark Riordan, with a separate Macintosh version by Raymond Lau. Riordan's version, which runs on MS-DOS, Unix, Windows NT, and other operating systems, implements a subset of Internet PEM. Keys are obtained from network-based servers, from `finger`, or from local databases. Lau's version for the Macintosh adds nearly complete PEM support of certificates.

As a PEM subset, RIPEM uses DES for data encryption and RSA for key exchange. RIPEM also supports triple-key DES as a high-security extension to Internet PEM.

RIPEM is free of charge, but due to licensing arrangements with RSA Data Security, is available only for noncommercial use. The MS-DOS/Unix version is distributed with full source code; the Macintosh version is distributed as executable only. Both can be found on the FTP sites `ripem.msu.edu` and `rsa.com`.

The Usenet News group sci.crypt contains active—and often heated—discussions of cryptology-related issues. The PEM-DEV mailing list maintained by Trusted Information Systems, Inc. is a good source of information for developers of Internet PEM-compatible products. To join, send a mail message to `pem-dev-request@tis.com`. Finally, several FTP sites, including those mentioned above, contain information and programs related to cryptology. Use Archie to look for the keyword `crypt`.

Here is an example of how a message appears as encoded according to the PEM standard:

```
-----BEGIN PRIVACY-ENHANCED MESSAGE-----
Proc-Type: 4,ENCRYPTED
Content-Domain: RFC822
DEK-Info: DES-CBC,ED0FCABAFE134067
Originator-Certificate:
  MIIBpjCCAUICARYwDQYJKoZIhvcNAQECBQAwTTELMAkGA1UEBhMCVVMxIDAeBgNV
  BAoTF1JTQSBEYXRhIFN1Y3VyaXR5LCBJbmMuMRwwGgYDVQQLExNQZXJzb25hIEN1
  cnRpZm1jYXR1MB4XDTkzMDQxOTIwMDI1MFoXDTk1MDQxOTAwMDAwMFowZDELMAkG
  A1UEBhMCVVMxIDAeBgNVBAoTF1JTQSBEYXRhIFN1Y3VyaXR5LCBJbmMuMRwwGgYD
  VQQLExNQZXJzb25hIEN1cnRpZm1jYXR1MRUwEwYDVQQDEwxNYXJrIFJpcb3JkYW4w
  WTAKBgRVCAEBAgICBgNLADBIAkEy1Zc/H+pNFRQqHC4abJQV4gTzRuGoXmOFgdeP
  kDshmAB4dAa6qY8ypsLqDFmXfbEInjzwxz8weBHGRnTZwFcrMwIDAQABMAOGCSqG
  SIb3DQEBAgUAA08ABMavdfXztriNQZwk8Ma/YbMOd81sg/bASPXKi2FhmDn2WhdZ
  967PW+ZPYkCDnOJdUikP/41xvKuHhOPDNROvN+S1tgf0aFenF2m8/voX
Key-Info: RSA,
  HYDayJpaWvMCrtqWuzLkrjs+33cbF82yUqACkVyXABaav/qOmLDq9V+71IN2BcN5
  1qPNW5k/MrSWcpP6CJkKfqO=
MIC-Info: RSA-MD5,RSA,
  AwoGDQ1baDY6dja8j53JRfs1totWwjRe95+X+1zfJCaeJ6qap1PyORQw2qdQp95x
  nfsNICXzf6PojTNb/NAVZbUqHr/9agor
Recipient-ID-Asymmetric:
  ME0xCzAJBgNVBAYTA1VTMSAwHgYDVQQKExdSUOEgRGFOYSBTZWN1cm10eSwgSW5j
  LjEcMBoGA1UECxMTUGVyc29uYSBDZXJOaWZpY2F0ZQ==,18
Key-Info: RSA,
  ARhoGRjTcZ4Go+VdJTSC6mH61wArXAjGWkPsnFQ8JBVw8edLHHCOONZNzdTGYsrJ
  Nw2FDL8uLVqoWZXvnmFSQ+Q=
```

oXBRm+XQtB6SHdXua2173kAyeDv26P6jnYNOdPi/Wue3nJNZFOaqYOkNKbutGXhR
+bJzbxGj6EE6w1Ixqu8fCOXCIvmFQCmzOJBPxc1Au+ULAPudTyrBmJJKzqoJVh6a
-----END PRIVACY-ENHANCED MESSAGE-----

KERBEROS AUTHENTICATION

Providers of network-based services often need a way of ensuring the identity of their users. Kerberos is currently one of the most popular answers to this need.

Kerberos is a network-based authentication system. By *authentication,* we mean the act of determining, with a high degree of security, whether a user really is who he claims to be. Kerberos-based systems can also provide *authorization,* the act of determining whether a given validated user is allowed to access a given service such as interactive computing, printing, file service, and so on. However, authorization mechanisms in a Kerberos system are generally specific to the particular service in question, rather than embedded in Kerberos itself.

To an ordinary user, accessing a Kerberos-protected system typically looks just like logging into a system using traditional host-based security. The user is prompted for a username and password; if these check out, the user is automatically given permission to use the desired services as the need arises throughout the session.

Behind the scenes, however, Kerberos authentication is significantly more complex than, say, the traditional Unix approach of simply consulting a local /etc/passwd password file. Kerberos is a network-based service: a number of different computers may rely upon a single Kerberos system for authentication. Kerberos requires a number of different trusted server processes to be installed and advertised on the network. Computers using Kerberos for authentication must have special Kerberos-aware versions of programs like login and file server software installed on them.

Kerberos relies heavily upon the concept of a *ticket,* an encrypted packet of data passed amongst parts of the Kerberos system to communicate authentication information. The information in a ticket is encrypted with keys known only to the Kerberos servers and to *services,* which are programs like remote login or file server daemons that do the actual work desired by the user. Tickets also contain time stamps which cause them to expire after a period of time usually measuring several hours.

Conceptually, when a Kerberos-aware *client,* such as a login program, wishes to access a service, it submits a username and service name to Kerberos and asks for a ticket. Kerberos responds to the client by sending back a ticket containing encrypted information which would assure the remote service of the identity of the user. This ticket is itself further encrypted with the user's password. (This is possible because Kerberos knows the passwords of all the users in the Kerberos realm. This contrasts with most Unix systems, which store passwords only in one-way encrypted form.) The ticket is useless unless the client can decrypt it; the client does so after asking the user for the password. Note that the client never sends the password to Kerberos.

The client then sends a request to the service, along with the decrypted ticket. The service further decrypts the ticket using the key known only to it and Kerberos. If the ticket checks out, the service is allowed to perform the tasks requested by the client. If the client did not know the user's correct password, the ticket received by the service would be gibberish and would not be honored.

The Kerberos protocol is designed in such a way that sensitive information is never passed over the network in cleartext.* This important feature prevents unauthorized individuals from learning passwords by monitoring network traffic.

The actual details of the Kerberos protocol are quite complex and involve multiple session keys and multiple server programs within the Kerberos system. For a more complete description, consult the Kerberos documentation available via FTP to `athena-dist.mit.edu` in `/pub/kerberos/doc`.

FURTHER READING

The Usenet News group `comp.society.privacy` carries discussions that may be of interest. Also look in `news.answers` for periodic posting of extremely detailed Frequently Asked Question summaries on security and privacy.

---

* This is another way of saying that sensitive information is always encrypted if it must pass over the network. It is relatively easy for unscrupulous users to monitor traffic over broadcast networks such as Ethernet; the more networks your traffic traverses, the greater the exposure to such snooping.

Becoming an Internet Information Provider

One saying holds that "The power of the press is limited to those who own one." The explosion of desktop publishing alternatives would seem to extend the power of the press to many more people, but the question of distribution remains. The rapid decline in cost of computer hardware, and the exponential growth of the Internet and Internet-access options, combine to provide dramatically greater access to an online publishing medium that affords the opportunity for worldwide readership. The Internet can support publications of mass interest as well as those that appeal to a small, but definite, affinity group scattered around the globe.

Once you have spent some time cruising the Internet, you may be struck by the wide variations in the nature and quality of information that is online. Your reaction to some documents on the Net may be "I can offer documents that are more worthwhile than that." Good! That means you should become an Internet information provider.

Here are a few examples of individuals and groups who may want to publish via the Internet:

- Schools and school districts, sharing curricular information, student newspapers, and providing support for cooperative projects with sister schools across the nation or the globe.

- Individual authors of essays and scholarly or professional monographs. Already some pioneering individuals at some universities and corporations offer basic information about themselves in the form of online resumes. Figure 20.1 is an example.

- Artists, offering paintings, photographs, poetry, short stories, or book-length fiction.

- Performing artists, publishing, for instance, audio clips of rock or classical music.

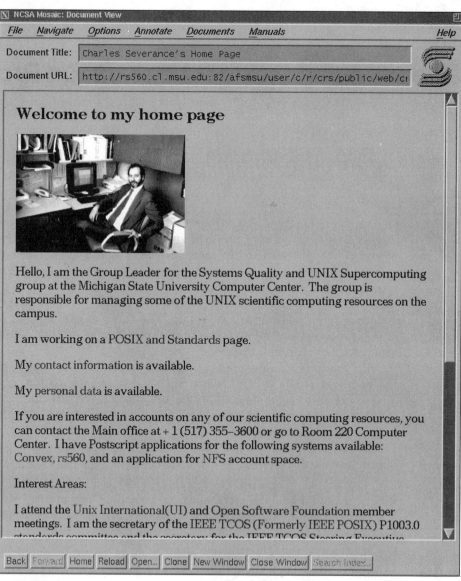

Figure 20.1

- Colleges and universities, offering information about their campuses, programs, and research.*

- Academic departments in universities, along with research agencies (both governmental and corporate), providing information about research activities, including overview as well as specific information.

- Corporations, offering employment information, general information about the company's products, "goodwill" publications, annual reports, etc. Service corporations could offer online brochures. Retail businesses could offer online catalogs and ordering services.

- Broadcast television and radio networks, providing information on upcoming programs, schedules, etc.

- Federal, state, and local governmental agencies, providing access to rules and regulations, forms, postal and telephone directories, travel information, etc. (See Fig. 20.2.) Civic organizations, convention bureaus, and chambers of commerce are also candidates.

- Foundations, offering information on grant opportunities.

---

* See Chap. 22.

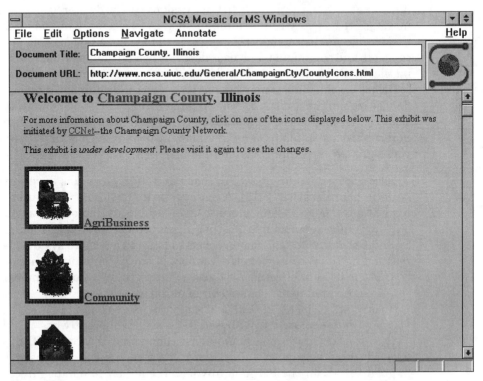

Figure 20.2

WHICH INTERNET INFORMATION
TOOL SHOULD I USE?

In order to become an Internet information provider, you will have to decide what information delivery tool or tools you want to use. The range of options for you as an Internet information provider is as broad as the types of information delivery technologies we have explored throughout this book.

The type of tool you want to use will depend on the kind of information you want to provide, and the nature of your audience.

Guidelines for choosing a tool

Mailing lists.   If your main goal is to foster discussion among an affinity group, a mailing list manager might be your best choice. For instance, if you have been named president of the American Association of Nematologists, you may find a mailing list a good way to support group discussion between annual conventions. Mailing lists can support both announcement-oriented information (from the organization to its members) and group discussion.

A LISTSERV-style mailing list can be the best choice of technology when your audience includes individuals who are dispersed geographically and across a variety of computer systems. As long as each individual has some sort of Internet e-mail access, the mailing list discussions can be delivered. The owner of the mailing list has very little training to do; users often are already familiar with their own e-mail systems, and merely need to learn a few mailing list processor concepts and commands. The user does not need to depart from his or her familiar electronic environment in order to join in group communications.

Before establishing a mailing list on a particular subject, it is a good idea to do a search to see if a similar mailing list already exists. You may want to join the existing list, or you may want to coordinate with the owner of the existing mailing list as to topic areas or names. You may also want to see if Usenet News groups exist that cover similar turf.

Bulletin boards.   Another way to reach an affinity group is to set up an online bulletin board service (BBS). A bulletin board system or computer conferencing system tends to foster more "conversationality" among its members than one normally sees in mailing list discussions. However, a bulletin board requires the user to "go" somewhere—to log into a remote system, rather than responding to postings from the comfort of one's own online mailbox. Bulletin boards can be very effective for those affinity groups whose members are sufficiently motivated to overcome a bit of online inertia.

If you want to install a BBS that supports users coming in over the Internet, you may choose to use a Unix-based BBS, which inherently has TCP/IP connectivity. Another option is a stand-alone commercial PC-based BBS, which has evolved into a very powerful system in its own right. As of this writing, commercial BBSes for the PC generally lack the ability to handle direct support of TCP/IP users, but there are ways to get around this problem; see the connectivity discussion below.* Another option is to run a BBS for the Macintosh; one such BBS, called FirstClass, supports dial-up as well as TCP/IP connections.

A special choice you might want to consider in the Unix realm is the Freeport software used for FreeNets around the country. This package is available for under $1000 and can be installed on a variety of Unix variants. If you want to establish a full-fledged FreeNet you will want to visit several established services via the Internet, and compare notes with other sites; running a FreeNet requires a dedicated volunteer organization. For more information, FTP to `nptn.org` or send e-mail to `freeport-info@po.cwru.edu`.

To read more about Unix BBS options, see the "Unix Compatible BBS Frequently Asked Questions" document, posted periodically to `comp.bbs.misc` and `news.answers`. For general information on BBS options, see various Usenet News groups under the `alt.bbs` and `comp.bbs` hierarchies.

Usenet news. You might decide that a Usenet News group is the best choice for your information. A Usenet News group is a somewhat different undertaking than a mailing list managed by LISTSERV or other mailing list processors. Usenet News is inherently different in its architecture and culture. With Usenet, group traffic is propagated around the world and retained at sites that offer News service for varying lengths of time. As an originating sponsor of a news group, you could set up an archive of that news group, but the archive exists outside of the Usenet realm (for instance, on a Gopher server). By contrast, with a LISTSERV mailing list, a log of back discussions is typically kept at the site that houses the mailing list, and standard search commands are well-defined.

Under Usenet, as with LISTSERV, there are moderated news groups, but membership in a news group is not a defined concept. A site can set up "local" news groups, which limits the scope of potential users to those people who have access to your local Usenet service—usually within your own company or campus. Local groups can be a useful discussion medium, especially if you want to reach members of your community who want to drift in and out of discussions at will. On the other hand, if you want to reach a very specific group of individuals who happen to be scattered geographically, a mailing list enables the sort of precise control over membership you want.† Also, a mailing list is more visible to its subscribers, forcing them to view new postings as they arrive via e-mail.‡

---

* Over time the vendors of commercial PC-based BBS packages will probably all add support for users connecting to the BBS over a Telnet session (or other TCP/IP connection). As of this writing, several vendors are working on such options. The TBBS product from eSoft may be one of the first systems with true TCP support.

† Or, a mailing list can be configured to allow membership of any new subscriber. Even in this case, the "membership" is far more defined than with Usenet; there is a definite list of subscribers, which can be reviewed by the mailing list owner and by others. Usenet News is broadcast to the global ether, and you do not know who your readers are.

‡ Some users find this aspect of mailing lists intrusive. They prefer Usenet discussions for that very reason: they can read the news group when they find it convenient, and avoid clutter in their mailboxes.

A global Usenet News group is less likely to be "yours" to control and shape. You have no control over the audience that subscribes to the group. It is possible for Usenet groups to be "moderated," which means that postings to the group are forwarded to a moderator for approval or rejection. This can bring focus to a news group even though the audience remains amorphous.

Global Usenet News groups outside of the `alt` hierarchy are created via a "Call for Votes" process. This process uses independent vote takers to ensure the validity of the vote. In order for a new group to be created, the results of the vote must reflect at least 100 more Yes votes than No votes, and at least twice as many Yes as No votes. The document "Usenet Newsgroup Creation Companion" by Ron Dippold describes the process in detail; this document is periodically posted to the Usenet group `news.answers`. To read more about choices in setting up an "alt" Usenet News group, see the document "So You Want to Create an Alt Newsgroup," by David Barr, also posted periodically to `news.answers`.

E-mail archive servers. If your goal is delivery of documents readily to the widest possible Internet audience, you could offer such documents via a mailing list manager, or you might install a special-purpose e-mail archive server. With a mailing list manager like LISTSERV, you can offer both discussion groups—i.e., true mailing lists—and stand-alone documents that can easily be retrieved by users via e-mail. Your users will have to fetch any stand-alone documents by explicitly mailing a request to the mailing list server under which the documents are stored. As the owner of a mailing list, you can update documents at will. LISTSERV will even allow your users to subscribe to Automatic File Distribution service, such that any stand-alone file will be automatically mailed to subscribers as updates are posted on the LISTSERV. There is more discussion of mailing list manager options later in this chapter.

There are numerous e-mail servers from which you might choose. The majority of these are designed to operate under Unix; the program is installed as a daemon that manages one or more archives. One of these servers, Almanac, is quite visible as the U.S. Department of Agriculture's tool of choice for information delivery. A document called "A Summary of Available Mail Archive Server Software" by Jonathan I. Kamens is posted periodically to the Usenet News groups `comp.mail.misc` and `news.answers`.

Finger servers. For short, simple informational documents, you may want to set up a Finger server. Finger, discussed in Chaps. 3 and 16, is a very simple command whose purpose was to provide information about an individual user. But you can set up special user IDs that correspond to particular pieces of information you want to deliver. For instance, suppose your company is registered as `tallmtn.ski.lodge.com`. Suppose you want to offer information on rates to prospective customers. You might set up a user ID under the name `rates`; your customers would issue the command:

```
finger rates@tallmtn.ski.lodge.com
```

To set up this very simple mode of information delivery, you simply create a user under the appropriate name and edit a file—usually named `plan` or `project`—which is to be delivered to anyone issuing the `finger` command to the specified address. Your operating system manual should give guidance on how to create a new user and set up Finger files appropriately.* You might want to set up multiple such user IDs for multiple purposes. For instance, it is common for an organization to set up an ID named `info` that accepts Finger probes for general information.

Anonymous FTP. If you want to offer collections of files to your users—especially if you want to offer a repository of binary files such as executable programs or large image files—you may want to set up an anonymous FTP service. Anonymous FTP is one of the basic protocols in the TCP/IP family, and it has been used for that purpose as long as the Internet has been online.

However, there are reasons to think twice before you settle on FTP as your main delivery mechanism. Over time, tools like Gopher and World-Wide Web are probably going to be more familiar to new users. In many cases, users may have access to Gopher (or even the Web) in a more accessible fashion than FTP. For instance, a microcomputer laboratory in a corporation information center, a university, or a public library, might offer Gopher as a menu option. Users would be able to move easily from one point to another in Gopherspace, clicking on documents of interest. Because Gopher and Web documents have titles instead of cryptic file names, collections can be endowed with much more descriptive names.

You may also find, as some archive services have found, that Gopher actually represents less load on your server than maintaining an FTP service does. This only is of concern if your service will have a large number of concurrent users.

There may still be times when you want to run an FTP service. The ability for a user to fetch a large collection of files via MGET may be a reason, for instance; that sort of service isn't easily offered via Gopher. If you do choose FTP as a delivery tool, see the overview of anonymous FTP setup later in this chapter.

Gopher. If you are going to offer a relatively large set of documents intended to be browsed by a broad audience, you may want to install a Gopher server. Users find Gopher accessible and intuitive, and Gopher is probably the most broadly used Internet document delivery tool at this point. Gopher has the advantage of requiring virtually no document preparation effort in many cases.

World-Wide Web. Or, you may want to choose to serve documents via a World-Wide Web. The Web can require somewhat more effort in document preparation, but the payoff can be far richer documents and support for far more elaborate interactions.

---

* The Finger program originated in Unix; see the appropriate `man` page or a Unix manual if you are running on a Unix server. Other operating systems also support this function either natively or with their TCP/IP package; see the appropriate manual.

WAIS. Finally, if you have a large collection of documents, and your users need to be able to sift among these documents for the particular documents of interest, WAIS may be the best tool for you to use.

Note: The choice of a particular technology does not exclude the use of others. It is common, for instance, to see Gopher paired with WAIS or FTP. In fact, if you want your service to be highly visible, it is a good idea to offer at least a shell of service in more than one arena. Let's say, for instance, you decide to offer a World-Wide Web service. You might also want to set up a Gopher service. That service could offer only a brief introductory note, pointing people in the direction of your Web server. This sort of cross-platform presence could greatly increase the "walk-in" traffic your service enjoys.

A good strategy for choosing a technology is to look around and see what others are doing. In particular, find someone who is offering similar documents, or who is in a similar situation to your own, and see how they choose to provide information. You may feel that their example shows they have taken the wrong approach, but the example of others can be instructive.

PROXY INFORMATION SERVICE PROVIDERS

In the world of books and magazines, few publishers are printers. Publishers concentrate on deciding what to print, in editing and preparing the material for printing, in marketing, and in distribution. They let someone else take on the responsibility of printing. This is not to say that physical printing is not important; it is simply a well-understood technology that is usually best managed by organizations who can concentrate on the technical details.*

In becoming an Internet information provider, one of your most important decisions is whether you want to install any tools at all, or whether you want to have someone else perform the task for you. In the simplest case, you can become an Internet information provider simply by becoming an active member of Usenet News groups and online mailing lists that interest you. This is a perfectly honorable way to make your views known; the only investment required of you is the time it takes to compose information. Many of the authors of Frequently Asked Questions documents have no interest in maintaining their own online service, but they do want to contribute documents to the Net. You can even specify in such documents the scope of allowable use—for instance, reserving copyright for any commercial use.

If your application does call for setting up a new online service, such as a Gopher server, another viable option is to have someone else manage the server for you. *You need not administer your own server—whether it be Gopher,*

---

* By contrast, most daily newspapers own their own printing plants. The analogy may be instructive; online publishers may indeed want to consider frequency of "publication" in deciding whether to do their own online "printing."

World-Wide Web, WAIS, or some other tool. Instead, you may choose to have someone else run your server for you. Possible choices include:

- If there is an existing server at your installation, you might choose to take advantage of it. The server might be a departmental Gopher or Web server, or perhaps one centrally located in your organization.

- Your Internet service provider might be willing to run a server for you, perhaps at a very attractive price. Both commercial Internet service companies and regional networks can be expected to offer such services. They might maintain the server at their location, registering it under your name. Locating the server on their premises can provide better backup and availability if your organization does not have a staffed computer room environment.

- A nearby community college or university might be willing to host a server for you. This option might be attractive to organizations such as individual schools, civic organizations, and county and city governments. Or, a group of schools might choose to locate a server centrally—say in the offices of the school district.

- A consultant or part-time employee might maintain a server on your premises for you.

Just as a book publisher is freed to concentrate on editorial, marketing, and distribution questions by hiring an outside printer, by selecting someone else to manage your service you free yourself from the technical details of server management. You do not have to worry about issues such as backup, operating system maintenance, hardware outages, server software maintenance, and so forth. Instead, you can concentrate on selecting and preparing documents to place online.

Here are questions to ask in forging a relationship with a proxy information service provider:

- Who is responsible for what aspects of document preparation? If the primary mode of delivery is the World-Wide Web, who has responsibility for creating the HTML form of the documents? What formats can you use to deliver new documents? (e.g., is flat ASCII suitable for viewing via Gopher expected, or can you mail a Word Perfect or Microsoft Word diskette?)

- How long will documents reside on the server? Who decides what old documents to prune? Is the decision based on age, or age and size?

- How often can documents be updated? Will the service manager set up automated processes to accept new versions of frequently changing documents? What mechanisms can you use to submit new documents online? (e.g., FTP, e-mail, or what?)

- Will the service bear the host name of the service provider, or your organization? Will the service appear as a separately registered server (e.g., your own

Gopher daemon) or will it appear as part of another service? Will standard port numbers be used?

- Who owns the documents posted on the server on your behalf? Are there any license or usage restrictions? Who is responsible for ensuring these restrictions are followed?

- If hardware is to be purchased as a part of setting up the service, who owns the hardware? Who is responsible for its maintenance?

- Where will the server physically reside?

- Who is responsible for backup? How often will backups be performed? Where will offsite backup tapes be kept?

- How important is security to this project? (For example, suppose a hacker broke in and destroyed all files online. Could your project survive the downtime? Could your project survive the loss of data between the last backup and the time of the attack?) What security steps are in place?

- What level of availability is guaranteed? (A quantified answer, in terms of number of outages per week, average duration of outage, and percentage of uptime, is best.) Who will staff the server? How many shifts are available?

- How fast is the Internet link between the location of the server and the Internet at large? How busy is that link now? How many users do you anticipate your service will attract? How many users does your service manager feel can be supported on available bandwidth? Will users at peak times be satisfied with response times?

- What is the duration of the agreement, and is there an escape option? How much warning must either party give before terminating the arrangement? What provisions are there for you to take over management of the service, should you decide to do so?

INFORMATION PROVIDER
CONNECTIVITY OPTIONS

Most modes of Internet information delivery will require that your server be directly connected to the Internet. If the server is located on your premises, that means your site must have true IP connectivity. One exception might be the case of certain e-mail or mailing list services; you might be able to use intermittent dial-up access as a viable option. Consult with your Internet service provider to see if this is a cost-effective choice. Other services, such as running a Gopher, Web, or WAIS service, generally demand true full-time access. You need to be able to serve documents or other information no matter when users connect to your service. If your readership is global, this is especially important; the sun never sets on the global Internet.

You may want to review the basic styles of Internet connectivity explained in Chap. 5. As a provider, your basic choices for connectivity are similar to those of any organization seeking to connect to the Internet. Your connectivity needs will vary in terms of services you offer.

If you elect to offer a service using a server that resides on your premises, you will want to be sure that you have the kind of connectivity your project demands. This includes both your connection to the Internet, and the network and network services you offer locally. If your organization has already registered a host domain in the Domain Name System, your network administrator can assign names for any new hosts on which you will run services.

If your organization does not have an Internet host domain assigned, and you want to establish a new Internet host domain—say, `tallmtn.com` or `benevolent.org`—you will need to register that domain before it can be used.* The InterNIC Registration Services group is charged with overseeing this process. You can find out more about the services of Registration Services by pointing your Gopher client to their server (`rs.internic.net`, port 70). That server offers general information as well as the "templates" for registering in various top-level domains. If you do not have access to Gopher, but you do have access via e-mail, an e-mail server can deliver Registration Services documents to you. Send e-mail of the following form:

```
To: mailserv@rs.internic.net
Subject: HELP
```

[body of message is ignored]

Note that in the United States new nodes are encouraged to register in the `us` domain where possible; that is, geographic host names are preferred. An example name is:

```
alpha.washington.la-unified.k12.ca.us
```

You will need to register your new name with the administrator of the appropriate top-level domain; see the "template" files offered at Registration Services (via Gopher or the mail server).

Your Internet service provider should be able to help you in registering a new node. In many cases he or she will contact the appropriate administrator of the top-level domain with the template filled out on your behalf. Although the process is not painful, your Internet service provider will have been through it before and can pursue your registration quickly.

Your organization may already provide the complete infrastructure you need as a new information provider. You may merely need to install some software on a server, and place that server on the local network; all other services may already be in place. However, it may be the case that you need to add one or more services beyond your server. For instance, your site may not provide any

---

* Recall the discussion of top-level domains in Chap. 3.

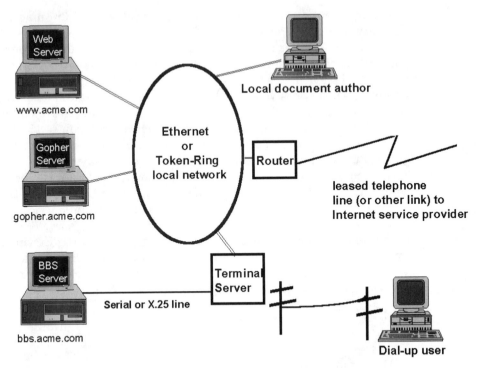

Figure 20.3

dial-up service to any users, and you want to accommodate that mode of access for certain users who have no other access. In that case, you might want to acquire a specialized piece of equipment known as a "terminal server." These boxes are really small computers with special versions of Unix; they are capable of talking to users dialing into modem pools and providing them with IP access to your local network. The user may invoke Telnet, or a menu option, to connect to a host on your network.*

In other cases, you may want to support access to a local service that does not accept TCP/IP (let alone inbound Telnet) connections. A classic example of such a service is a commercial bulletin board system. These systems have been tailored for the dial-up environment and, as of this writing, generally do not accept in-bound Telnet sessions. If you want to use this kind of software as part of your information providing mission, one way to provide connectivity is to use a serial line or an X.25 link into a Unix box that does have IP connectivity. Your terminal server, or another Unix box on your network, may be able to serve this role. From the point of view of the bulletin board system, the fact that your users are arriving at your site over the Internet is rendered invisible.

---

* Vendors of terminal servers include Xylogics, Livingston, Telebit, and numerous other firms.

BBS systems that can accommodate this sort of setup include Galacticomm's Major BBS.*

Figure 20.3 is meant to be illustrative. Note that it is not necessary to run multiple servers in order to become an Internet information provider! You may only need to offer one service to fulfill your mission. Furthermore, multiple services can be run on one computer—for instance, a Gopher server, a Web server, an FTP server, and a mailing list manager could all be run on one host computer. In fact, you can even decide to run different variants of servers on a single computer; for instance, some sites use both the Gn server and the Minnesota Gopher server on a single computer.†

As your service grows in popularity, its demands on your Internet connection will increase. Be sure you understand how much bandwidth your Internet service provider is willing to offer you. In some cases, even though you have a relatively high speed line, your provider may assume that you will not make full use of the available bandwidth at all times because that will tax the provider's capacity in general. Also be sure you understand your options for increasing line speed should growth dictate the need for an upgrade.

CHOOSING A HARDWARE AND OPERATING SYSTEM PLATFORM

If you do intend to manage your own online services, and if you need to acquire hardware toward that end, you may be pleasantly surprised at the hardware options open to you. Virtually all servers in common use are Unix workstations. The intense competition in the workstation market means you have a lot of choices, and the prices are extremely favorable.

Workstation vendors tend to market their hardware in two classes of configuration: server class and user class. In most cases, user-class machines will be more than adequate to handle roles as servers supporting Gopher, Web, or similar services. Vendors have been forced to offer extremely high computing power for user-class machines, and that horsepower can be applied to server applications, no matter what the marketing materials say. User-class workstations from vendors such as IBM, DEC, Sun, HP, and Apple have commonly been used by Internet document providers—in some cases with extremely large workloads.

---

* Be sure to distinguish access into the BBS versus other services, such as the ability to exchange Internet mail or Usenet News. These services do not imply the ability to support inbound Telnet sessions. If you are a BBS sysop and you want to provide Internet e-mail access to your users, you can do so via various options, including UUCP to a host with Internet connectivity. The Major BBS can handle this, as can the Wildcat BBS.

† Note that if you run multiple server software programs on a single computer, they cannot all use the same port. Thus if you run two Gopher server daemons on a single machine, only one of them can use the standard port (70); the others must use other ports (for example, 71, 7000).

Not surprisingly, faster machines can yield better performance. RISC-based architectures such as Sun SPARC, DEC Alpha, and the Power PC (Motorola, IBM, and Apple) should provide very capable servers at prices in the $5000 to $12,000 range. If you expect to serve a huge collection of documents to a very large number of users, you may want to consider the server-class machines that hardware vendors will try to sell you. Prices for such servers start around $15,000 and could easily reach $50,000 or even $100,000 or more.

If you expect your document collection to consume considerable disk space—and in the coming multimedia era, no disk is too small—try to obtain a server that can accept a SCSI* disk drive. SCSI disks are becoming available in very large capacities at favorable prices. As of early 1994, the cost of disk had fallen well below $1 per megabyte when purchased in sizes of 1 gigabyte or more. You may be able to save a great deal of money by buying as little of the workstation vendor's disk as possible, and using add-on SCSI disk for the bulk of your storage. Vendors of SCSI drives include Conner Peripherals, Fujitsu, Maxtor, Micropolis, and Seagate.

Having chosen large disk drives, be sure you have the capacity for backing that disk up. Options include 8mm, DAT, and other cartridge-tape formats. These formats typically can accommodate from 1 to 5 gigabytes on a single cartridge. In many cases this will be sufficient to back up your entire system on one cartridge—a luxurious situation in terms of simplicity of backup procedures.

Your system will also need to have standard components such as a monitor and keyboard. It will need cables to connect these components. It will also need to have TCP/IP software, and connectors for Ethernet or Token Ring as appropriate. Many workstations come with TCP/IP software and an Ethernet port as standard parts of the package; check with your vendor and your local network administrator to make sure you order all you need.

For the economy-minded, there are options for lowering the capital investment to the bare bones. One option is to use Intel-based hardware—i.e., IBM PC-compatibles running on an Intel processor or compatible CPU. You might want to buy an Intel 80486-class (or Pentium) PC as your server hardware. Very powerful computers can be had for under $2000. It would be possible to run a low-volume server on even older vintage hardware, but a 33-megahertz '486 is a good minimum if you can afford it.

The next question is what operating system to run on the machine. MS-DOS is not really intended to offer any sort of viable multitasking, but there is a software package called KA9Q that combines a pseudo multitasker with TCP/IP support, yielding the framework for a server solution. Many old data-processing hands would be uncomfortable with this as a platform for a production service, but there are some viable services running in this environment. Chapter 22 offers an example of how to set up a Gopher server under KA9Q.

---

* Small Computer System Interface—a standard interface.

Another option on Intel hardware is to run a flavor of Unix. Options here include the Intel version of SunSoft's Solaris product, or Berkeley Software Design's BSD/386 product (which despite the name runs on '486 and Pentium processors as well), the Santa Cruz Organization's SCO Unix, or Novell's UnixWare product. These options require you to reinstall one of this Unix variants as the primary operating system on the server.

If your budget is tight and your fortitude is high, you might choose to run a free Unix work-alike operating system called Linux. This is a complete Unix-like system for Intel hardware that you can actually obtain over the Internet. Management information system professionals who run "production" operations would shudder at the notion of running an operating system that is not supported by an established vendor,* but some information providers are running serious applications online under Linux. Although Linux lacks formal support, there is a worldwide network of Linux enthusiasts. To read more about Linux, see the Linux "Meta-FAQ" document periodically posted to news.answers. Another Unix workalike for Intel hardware is FreeBSD. See FAQ document available for anonymous FTP at freebsd.cdrom.com under the FAQ-386BSD directory.

OS/2 is another server option available to you for Intel-based hardware. OS/2 is IBM's multitasking operating system for the Intel architecture; although it has not enjoyed the commercial success of Microsoft Windows, it does have advantages in terms of robustness and multitasking capabilities. In Chap. 21 there is an example of setting up a Gopher server that runs on that platform.

Another server option that is becoming available is the Microsoft Windows NT platform, available on Intel and DEC Alpha platforms, and soon to be available for other hardware. Windows NT has TCP/IP support built into the operating system and may prove to be a very natural operating environment for Internet information services. Before that can happen, various server software packages will need to be "ported" to the NT platform.

On Apple hardware you can choose to run a server designed for the native System 7, or for an Apple flavor of Unix (A/UX). (As this book goes to press, trade journals report that Apple will discontinue support for A/UX in favor of another variant of Unix when PowerPC-based servers are announced.) Pricing of Macintosh hardware has become aggressive; a Power Mac could be a very cost-effective server. A pair of Gopher servers and at least one Web server are available for the native Mac environment; see the discussion later in this chapter.

Be sure that the system you buy has enough memory, and be sure you understand the options for expanding memory. A Gopher or Web server handling one or two users at a time might run comfortably on a machine with as little as 8 megabytes of memory. By contrast, if you have dozens of concurrent users you

---

* The author also shudders.

might need 64M, or 128M, or even more. Be especially aware of memory requirements if you intend to run a public client program, such as the "curses" client for Gopher, the Web client Lynx, Swais, Archie, or Netfind. Public client services such as these require users to log in to your system, and for dozens or hundreds of users the consumption of memory can be dramatic.

The best way to "size" a given system is to try to characterize your workload as accurately as possible, and find an existing site with a similar workload to see if the hardware configuration is adequate. Keep in mind that factors such as the amount of memory required for a given workload can also vary with the operating system and server software you choose; do not assume that another's experience will translate to different hardware and software.

A useful point to keep in mind about expansion: The distributed nature of many of these services enables you to split functions across multiple servers as growth in demand dictates. If you name and advertise your services with separate descriptive host names for each service, you will have maximum flexibility in moving services from one physical computer to another, or from one server package to another, as load on your computers or the need for new functionality dictates. For example, suppose your Gopher server includes a very popular menu—for instance, photographs of rock stars. Suppose the load generated by users accessing that menu alone equals the demand for the entire rest of the server. Assuming you want to continue serving the rock star documents, you could split off that menu onto a new computer of its own. If your users have been told to access that menu via the original address of the main Gopher server, you can avoid disruption by simply replacing the reference in the original server with a reference to the new, separate server. Your users will be none the wiser.

CASUAL VERSUS PRODUCTION SERVICE

For your service to achieve an Internet audience, you need to make sure that it is kept up to date and is generally available. It is best to try to keep the server up most of the time, minimizing downtime for maintenance. It is also a good idea to schedule downtime during off-hours (as determined by the location of your primary audience).

Be aware that hardware and software maintenance will require a recurring budget commitment. A standard rule of thumb is that 1 percent of initial investment per month should be set aside for maintenance. A hardware maintenance contract is essential for "mission critical" applications.

A production-quality online system must be periodically backed up in order to assure means of recovery in the event of hard-disk failure. It is best to think in terms of "when" a disk will fail, not "whether." The typical backup scheme dumps files to tape. On today's workstation-class servers, one can usually obtain a tape drive that can hold from several hundred megabytes to several gigabytes on one tape. Most production shops set up a schedule of daily and weekly backups. Daily dumps may be "change" or "incremental," containing only files that changed since the previous day; weekly dumps might be "full" dumps of the entire hard disk. If you have a tape drive capable of dumping the entire file system onto a single tape, you might find it more convenient to schedule a complete dump each day. On Unix systems, many administrators use built-in `dump` and `restore` programs, or the `tar` or `cpio` commands, as backup tools. Another option is to acquire a commercial backup program, which often will have superior features, such as a database to manage what files reside on which physical tape cartridges.

For a popular service you may find it useful to set up a test version of your server. If a test server computer is available you might use that machine; otherwise you can set up a separate daemon on your primary computer. You might use a test server as a staging area for new documents, offering document owners the chance to review postings as they will appear online before the document is placed on the "real" server.

If you will be doing the operating system administration on your system in addition to managing the server software, you will want to obtain vendor and other documentation on this aspect of your job. A good general text on Unix system administration is *Essential System Administration* by Aeleen Frisch.*

Performance tuning can become an important aspect of system administration. Modern multitasking computer systems can often be made to deliver better performance to your users by tuning various operating system controls. The result of such tuning is faster delivery of information to more users. Performance tuning experts offer general advice for all systems:

- Try to devise an objective benchmark of what you consider to be good performance. For instance, you expect your WAIS server to respond to 90 percent of its requests within less than 1 second. For production-quality services, try to get your management to commit to acquiring sufficient hardware and network resources to maintain your performance objective as the service grows.

- Keep track of how your system performs when it is performing well. Then, when it is performing badly, you will have a benchmark against which to compare. Most operating systems have performance monitoring numbers you can check periodically. You may want to automate a logging process that records these performance numbers at periodic intervals. Then, when a user complains "The Gopher server was impossibly slow at 10:00 a.m.," you can check your Gopher logs and your performance logs to see what the situation was.

- When tuning your system, change only one parameter at a time, and look at your performance measurements to see what effects ensue. If you change several settings at once, you may cancel good effects with bad—or you may fix things but not know why.

---

* O'Reilly and Associates, 1992, ISBN 0-937175-80-3.

■ All online computer services have one or more bottlenecks. Tuning is often a matter of solving one bottleneck, only to reveal another. If you are lucky, and your service grows popular, you may find you need to upgrade your server. Do not assume that you need to buy a new machine immediately; often an interim step, such as adding more memory, can be as effective and less costly.

The science of performance tuning varies from system to system, and within flavors of a given operating system.* A little bit of investment in this area can save you real money in hardware expenditures, so the effort can be worth your while.

NAMING YOUR SERVICE

You will need to assign a name to your service—both an Internet host name, and a friendly "title" visible to the Internet community. A convention that is common at a number of sites is to use the name of the service along with your site name. For instance, use gopher.msu.edu for a Gopher-based service, and wais.msu.edu for a campus WAIS server. Note that these host names need not be permanently assigned to specific computers. In fact, it is a good idea to name your services generically using aliases, and assign those aliases to particular hosts whose location can change. For instance, `gopher.msu.edu` might point to another host (say `burrow.cl.msu.edu`); someday you might move the Gopher server to another host (say `tunnel.cl.msu.edu`), but your users have all been told to configure their clients for the generic host.

The title for your service may be a simple outgrowth of your organization's name, such as "the Well Gopher" or simply "World Health Organization." You may want to choose a more general name for your service, especially if you expect to provide information via multiple platforms. The Bernoulli College of Aviation might call its service "The Bernoulli Airfoil" while offering documents using multiple tools—for instance, Gopher, WAIS, and a bulletin board. New administrators may want to review server names (listed in "All the Gopher servers in the world" at Minnesota and in CERN's list of "All Web servers") to see what sort of names others have chosen before picking their own. The title you choose will appear in global lists once you register your new service.

REGISTERING AND ANNOUNCING
YOUR SERVICE

Besides registering your host name in the Domain Name System, you also will want to register your service with the keepers of various directories of such services. The appropriate place to register varies by type of service:

---

* A general text on tuning Unix systems is *System Performance Tuning* by Mike Loukides (O'Reilly & Associates, 1991, ISBN 0-937175-60-9).

- Gopher administrators should announce new servers to the following addresses:

  gopher@ebone.net   (European servers)
  gopher@boombox.micro.umn.edu   (All other servers)

- To register a Web server or a new document, send e-mail to www-announce@ info.cern.ch.

- To register a new WAIS server, send e-mail to directory-of-servers @think.com.

- A new LISTSERV or other mailing list requires no formal registration process. (However, it is a good idea to check for names with similar topics or identical titles prior to creating your new mailing list.)

You will want to announce your service to appropriate mailing lists and Usenet News groups—both those specific to your type of service and those that cater to general announcements.

The announcement should include the name of the server as well as particular information on accessing it. For instance, for a Gopher server, the announcement should include the Internet address, its port number, and, if the service is a subfolder on an existing server, the selector string. The name can include labels such as "(experimental)" or "(under construction)" as appropriate.

Other places to which you may want to provide a general announcement include:

- comp.infosystems.announce: This Usenet News group is intended to be an umbrella location for announcing new services. Post your announcement to the local news group under that name, and the announcement will be forwarded to a moderator for posting to the news group within a few days. If you do not have Usenet access, send your announcement to infosys@msu.edu.

- newnir-1: This mailing list hosts information on new Networked Information Retrieval services. Send your submissions to newnir-1@itocsivm.csi.it.

- InterNIC Net Happenings: This mailing list, operated by Gleason Sackman in cooperation with InterNIC Information Services, is a place where new network resources as well as conference announcements, calls for papers, and so forth are announced. The address of the mailing list is:

  net-happenings@is.internic.net*

- NCSA What's New: This is a list of new services, sorted in reverse chronological order, offered at NCSA. Links are provided within the online announcement so readers can jump directly to the service using a tool like Mosaic. Most announcements are new Web services or documents. Send e-mail to the address currently listed online. Figure 20.4 shows what the NCSA What's New page looks like.

---

* Send announcements to the above address. To subscribe to this mailing list, send mail to listserv@is.internic.net with the message subscribe net-happenings Jane Doe as the body.

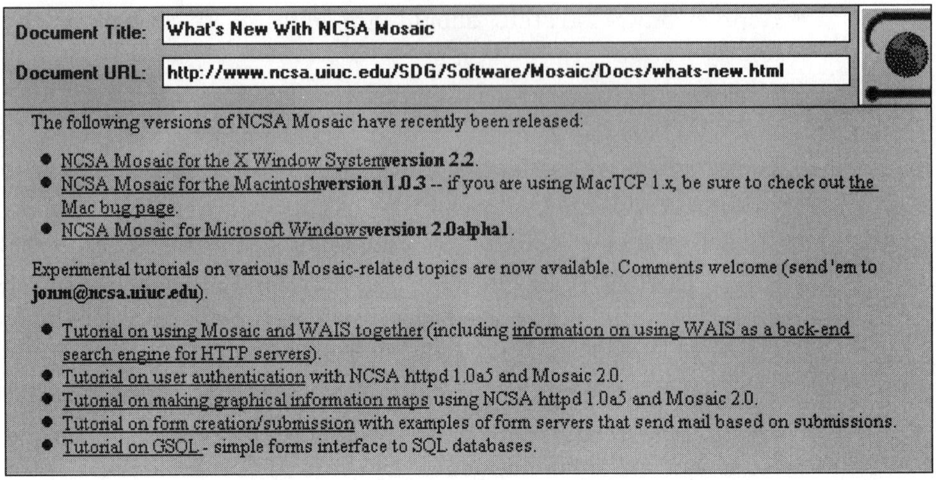

Document Title: What's New With NCSA Mosaic

Document URL: http://www.ncsa.uiuc.edu/SDG/Software/Mosaic/Docs/whats-new.html

The following versions of NCSA Mosaic have recently been released:

- NCSA Mosaic for the X Window System version 2.2.
- NCSA Mosaic for the Macintosh version 1.0.3 -- if you are using MacTCP 1.x, be sure to check out the Mac bug page.
- NCSA Mosaic for Microsoft Windows version 2.0alpha1.

Experimental tutorials on various Mosaic-related topics are now available. Comments welcome (send 'em to jonm@ncsa.uiuc.edu).

- Tutorial on using Mosaic and WAIS together (including information on using WAIS as a back-end search engine for HTTP servers).
- Tutorial on user authentication with NCSA httpd 1.0a5 and Mosaic 2.0.
- Tutorial on making graphical information maps using NCSA httpd 1.0a5 and Mosaic 2.0.
- Tutorial on form creation/submission with examples of form servers that send mail based on submissions.
- Tutorial on GSQL - simple forms interface to SQL databases.

Figure 20.4

Your announcement of a new service should strike a balance between completeness and conciseness. Tell your new readers what they need to know to connect to your service, what information you will provide, who are the likely authors of documents for the service, and how often updates can be expected. If your service is a mailing list or BBS, tell who can join and whether postings are moderated. If your service is an electronic journal, tell how editing takes place, where to send submissions for publication, and where the journal will be archived. In all cases, provide an e-mail address where readers can write for more information.

Setting up a mailing list

If you want to set up a LISTSERV or other mailing list, you should especially consider the idea of using an existing mailing list service for your new list. Most LISTSERV servers handle more than one mailing list, with the number of lists per server ranging from a handful to dozens or hundreds. The managers of these mailing lists are accustomed to working with information providers who may be located at remote installations. There are many examples of successful mailing lists that are managed by a list owner at a site far removed from the site that physically hosts the list service. You could contact an owner of an existing mailing list via e-mail to get in touch with its technical support person.

If you decide you do want to maintain your mailing list on a machine under your own control, consider the original package, LISTSERV. LISTSERV is the oldest of the mailing list managers, and is by far the most powerful and widely used. The current incarnation of LISTSERV runs on VM mainframes. The current vendor of LISTSERV, L-Soft International Inc., is working on versions of the tool for Unix and VMS; early releases for these platforms are expected as this book goes to press. For current information on LISTSERV, send e-mail to `sales@lsoft.com`.

If you want to run your own mailing list server, you can find such tools freely available for download on the Internet. Two of the most popular are the Unix ListProcessor by Anastasios Kotsikonas (available for anonymous FTP from `cs.bu.edu` under `/pub/listserv`)* and Majordomo (available at various FTP sites; use Archie to locate a copy near you).

Whatever mailing list manager you use, there is a risk of a large mailing list causing numerous problems with lost mail. It is a good idea to work with your network administrator and postmaster before establishing a large mailing list.

Appropriately enough, there is a mailing list for owners of LISTSERV mailing lists. To subscribe to it, send the following e-mail:

```
To: listserv@searn.sunet.se
Subject: [does not matter]

subscribe lstown-l Jane Doe
```

There is also a package of documents describing LISTSERV both for the user and the mailing list owner. Send mail to any LISTSERV server to retrieve a list of these files. For instance:

```
To: listserv@msu.edu
Subject: [does not matter]

index info
```

You will receive a list of files by return mail; send another message with the GET command to retrieve the files of interest.

A series of guides for mailing list owners written by Jim Gerland of the University of Buffalo is available. These guides include a generic mailing list owner document, a document by Lisa Covi containing tips for the mailing list owner, information on setting up a gateway between a mailing list and a Usenet News group, and more. To retrieve these files, send mail of the following form:

```
To: listserv@ubvm.cc.buffalo.edu
Subject: [does not matter]

get lsvowner $package
```

---

* The parent organization of Bitnet, CREN, acquired the rights to future versions of the Unix List Processor in early 1994. They intend to provide this tool to member organizations as well as licensing it for commercial use. Send e-mail to `info@listproc.net` for details. Versions of the tool prior to release 6.0c are expected to remain available at various FTP archive sites (including, as of this writing, `cs.bu.edu` under `/pub/listserv`).

Setting up anonymous FTP service

The typical anonymous FTP server is a Unix computer of some sort. A special daemon, `ftpd`, has the responsibility of handling incoming FTP connections and serving the files using the FTP protocol. Of course, the FTP daemon serves requests from users who have user IDs on the server system; the same daemon handles requests from anonymous users. Anonymous FTP usually involves setting up a user whose name is literally `ftp` or `anonymous`. The file hierarchy seen by users consists of subdirectories that belong to that user. Usually, files to be retrieved by users reside in a directory named `/pub` and its subdirectories. A special directory, called `/incoming`, is used to accept submissions from others around the Internet.

Setup of an anonymous FTP service requires authorization to create a new user on the computer where the service is to reside. Setup is usually as straightforward as adding the `ftp` user to the password file (usually `/etc/passwd`) using standard procedures for adding a new user, and changing a few permissions. The ftpd daemon is normally automatically started at system startup time under the inetd subsystem. See the `man` page for FTP, and your vendor's documentation on `ftpd` and `ftp`, for details appropriate to your system.

The maintainers of the anonymous FTP site at Washington University have developed an anonymous FTP server that provides features superior to the standard FTP daemon included with most Unix systems. Enhancements include support for logging of user transactions and automatic display of "README" files as a user enters each subdirectory. Many FTP archives rely on this tool. You can find the tool on their FTP archive, `wuarchive.wustl.edu`.

Gopher or Web?

The choice of whether to offer information via Gopher or the Web has all the marks of a religious dispute. We will not attempt to offer a definitive answer for the new information provider, but will instead offer five key points to consider:

1. Gopher is much more broadly deployed, and access to Gopher is also more broadly available. As mass-market information utilities become Internet service providers, they will probably offer Gopher gateways before they offer Web gateways. Quite simply, Gopher is more visible to the masses.*

2. Despite the advent of Gopher+, the Gopher protocol is inherently unable to deliver the same sort of mixed-media documents that HTML provides. If your audience has the right connectivity—that is, if your clients have access to Mosaic and run on relatively fast links—the Web offers the ability to deliver documents with the look of color magazine pages along with features such as

---

* As we saw in Chap. 13, the Lynx VT100 client can make the Web more accessible to the masses, minus of course the inline images.

sound, still images, and video, that one might expect on a CD ROM. All of these document types can be delivered via Gopher—*but as separate documents, not with narrative text and multimedia presented on a single page.*

3. Gopher+ offers the ability to support extended data types and fill-in-the-blank forms, but these features are available using HTTP/HTML clients and servers as well. Moreover, as we have seen in earlier chapters, there are ways to set up elaborate services such as locator maps using the Web.

4. Preparation of documents in the Hypertext Markup Language does require more effort. This requirement is not insurmountable, and HTML authoring tools will improve over time. But Gopher makes it trivially easy to offer many document types; document preparation for the Web does take more effort.

5. The Gopher philosophy tends to place a lot of functionality in the server; the Web design tends to encourage functionality in clients. For instance, when Gopher is used as a "front end" to WAIS databases, the user sees a Gopher search menu. By contrast, Mosaic has built-in WAIS client support, and the preferred mode of operation would be to have the user interact directly with the WAIS server. The Gopher model can support users running smaller, simpler clients; the Web model can be more efficient in terms of network utilization, and can put more power on the user's desktop.

Whether to use Gopher or the Web depends on what kinds of documents you want to serve, what kind of access your audience has, and how much effort you are willing to put into document preparation. As with other information-provider decisions, a good way to decide is to look at the efforts placed online already by other information providers. You may want to compare notes with a few to understand how well their choices have panned out.

Setting up a Gopher server

The original Gopher server is the Unix server from the University of Minnesota, referred to as gopherd. This server remains the prototypical Gopher server; it is the locus of most new development efforts, such as the deployment of Gopher+.

If you want to use the Minnesota Unix server, one point to consider is licensing. The University of Minnesota has adopted a policy of charging for use of its server for commercial applications. For the precise definition of whether your application will require a license fee, see the online documentation on Minnesota's server (under "Information About Gopher") or contact the Minnesota Gopher team at gopher@boombox.micro.umn.edu.

Setting up a Gopher server can be quite easy, and a couple of platforms can be especially easy. The Gopher server for the Macintosh from the University of Minnesota, Gopher Surfer, features drag-and-drop installation. Moreover, it is integrated with the WAIS-like search tool from Apple, AppleSearch, making it extremely easy for the information provider to index files. Also, through the use of software called Claris Extend, the Gopher Surfer can serve files such as collections of Microsoft Word or Excel documents to users who do not have those documents installed. Such files can be left on the server's disk in the native word processor or spreadsheet format, which can save a great deal of work on the part of the server administrator.

This server is an excellent choice for the information provider who does not want to spend a great deal of time setting up or maintaining a Gopher service. This server requires Mac TCP 2 or later. The AppleSearch tool is a proprietary product that must be purchased; it requires a 68040-class Macintosh such as the Quadra. You can run the AppleSearch tool on the same computer as the Gopher Surfer server, or you can choose to run the search engine on a separate machine. In either case, configuration is very simple.

For the Unix platform, an excellent choice is the Gn server, developed by Professor John Franks of Northwestern University. Gn offers the following features in its favor:

- It is easy to install on a wide variety of Unix hosts.

- Gn is freely available for commercial use.

- It supports use of WAIS for indexing of files, with a version of WAIS index code included with the software distribution. The WAIS package that is included offers boolean ("and" and "or") searching.

- Gn also includes a simple built-in indexing tool, with the ability to easily add a "Search All Menus" option to your service. This can be a valuable navigational aid for your users.

- Gn understands "structured" files. This is a feature pioneered in the Minnesota server, whereby, for instance, a Unix mailbox file is parsed into its component messages. As delivered to the user, those messages appear as separate titles in a folder. Gn extends this feature to support structuring as defined by the administrator. For instance, you can tell Gn to break a file up after a line of underscores or equal signs.

- Gn will allow you to store files on the server in compressed form. It will decompress these files "on the fly" before delivering them to your users. This can save you considerable server disk space. You simply inform Gn what compression tool to use via a configuration option.

- Gn offers the ability to limit delivery of files within a directory to specified IP addresses.

- There is excellent online documentation.

- Gn is a multiprotocol server; it "talks" the Gopher protocol to Gopher clients, and it delivers HTML documents to clients calling via HTTP (the Web protocol).

The ability of Gn to serve both Gopher and Web clients is a major advantage. This means that with a single server you can meet the needs of users calling from both realms. Developers of Gopher clients (including the University of Minnesota) have agreed to support the "i" document type* to be used for annotating Gopher menus. Gn can serve textual parts of a document using type "i" when talking to Gopher servers. When the document is delivered to Web users, the text and any embedded links are offered in standard HTML format. The result is that the same information is offered in a form both kinds of clients can accept.

The combination of ease of installation with the ability to serve Gopher and Web clients make Gn an outstanding choice for an initial server in the Unix environment. It also can be a useful "bridge" between Gopher and the Web for those information providers who decide to make this transition.

With Gn, you do lose some capabilities:

- Gn is not capable of supporting Gopher+ and probably never will be.

- Gn does not support connections to stand-alone WAIS databases; a search item on a Gn menu can use only the embedded WAIS search code (or the simple Gn indexer).

An example of setting up a Gn server is included in Chap. 21.

Because Gn uses a somewhat different structure for organizing the Gopher hierarchy than the Minnesota server uses, you will face some migration effort if you move from one to the other. However, migration of this sort can be done in stages, with both servers running at once during the process.

Numerous tools have been created that assist in managing Gopher servers. For example, tools that analyze logs, improve indexes, and extend support delivery of calendar-based information are available. Some of these tools can be retrieved from the University of Minnesota's FTP server. Others, particularly short Perl scripts, are posted by the authors on `comp.infosystems.gopher`. Thus, the discussion group is not only a source of accumulated wisdom; it also is a repository of helpful tools.

Various tools are available for anonymous FTP from the archives of the various creators and maintainers of server software (e.g., `boombox.micro.umn.edu` for Gopher; `info.cern.ch` for Web tools, and `wais.com` for WAIS tools).

A tool in particular you may want to look at is GO4GW, which is a generalized gateway package that is useful if you want to have your Gopher service deliver data that is managed by an external database such as Oracle. This tool is available on boombox.

Discussion on Gopher takes place on the Usenet News group `comp.infosystems.gopher`.

Librarians setting up Gopher services may want to subscribe to the LISTSERV mailing list `GO4LIB-L@ucsbvm.bitnet`; this mailing list covers numerous how-to questions and issues of particular interest to librarians.

---

* Pioneered by the University of Iowa's Panda developers.

Description of setting up a Gn server can be obtained online. The URL is:

`http://hopf.math.nwu.edu`

The University of Minnesota Gopher documentation can be found via their Gopher service, or by FTP to `boombox.micro.umn.edu`: Look in the `/pub/gopher/docs` directory for the Gopher Guide and for the Gopher Surfer guide.

The Gn Gopher server has a mailing list of its own. The list is highly focused on topics relating to Gn setup and administration. To subscribe to it, send mail to:

`majordomo@hmc.edu subscribe gn-maint-l`

Setting up a WAIS server

There is a basic choice as to WAIS servers: you can run the commercial product from WAIS Incorporated, or you can run the FreeWAIS tool from the Clearinghouse for Networked Information Discovery and Retrieval (CNIDR). A good path for getting started is to try out the FreeWAIS tool first and see if a WAIS server is the kind of tool you want to use. You may want to consider acquiring the commercial product in the interest of obtaining vendor support.

WAIS Inc. provides information about its products and about other clients and servers via anonymous FTP to `ftp.wais.com`, or via Gopher (`gopher.wais.com`, port 70).

Chapter 21 includes an example of setting up a FreeWAIS server.

Note that there is a distinction between running a stand-alone WAIS server, and using embedded WAIS indexing code in a Gopher server. In the former case, any user can query the server with a WAIS client. In the latter case, users are performing a search of a single database at a time using the search prompt provided by Gopher clients. When your database is supported as a stand-alone WAIS server, users with WAIS clients can include the database among several to be searched concurrently. Because that sort of concurrent use is one of the cornerstones of the WAIS design, you need to run stand-alone databases to fully participate in the WAIS world.

Note also that there are alternatives to WAIS for indexing servers, such as the example of running AppleSearch with a Gopher front end. For instance, the combination of AppleSearch and GopherSurfer on a PowerPC Macintosh could make for a very powerful network search engine with a relatively low hardware and software investment.

WAIS is discussed in the Usenet News group `comp.infosystems.wais`.

There are several WAIS-related mailing lists.

Setting up a World-Wide Web server

As is the case with Gopher, you have a choice of several servers for delivering Web documents. Examples include:

- *CERN's server.*   This is the original WWW server for Unix.

- *NCSA's HTTPd.*   This has been the server of choice for many state-of-the-art applications that work hand in glove with NCSA Mosaic.

- *Plexus.*   This is a server for Unix written in the interpretive language Perl.

- *MacHTTP.*   This server runs on the Macintosh operating system.* This server is designed for the Macintosh operating system (currently System 7) and it runs well on Quadra and Power PC class machines. As you might expect from a tool for the Macintosh, it is easy to install. Its demand for machine resources is small. The online documentation is quite complete.[†]

- *HTTP for Windows NT.*   Chris Adie of Edinburgh University has written a server for the Windows NT operating system. Available for FTP from `emwac.ed.ac.uk`, this tool is also easily installed: simply copy the files into the `/winnt/system32` directory and invoke `https -install`.

- *Gn.*   This is the multiprotocol Gopher/Web server discussed earlier.

The NCSA server is a good choice for information providers who want advanced functionality in a Unix server. Many of the advanced Web applications shown in this book were set up using this server. There is excellent documentation online at NCSA for using this server for the following sorts of applications[‡]:

- Running WAIS indexes with your Web service.

- Setting up graphical information maps similar to the weather maps shown in Chap. 13 and the Novell Reference Shelf shown in Chap. 18.

- Creating input forms for online questionnaires.

- Setting up authentication, whereby you can protect documents based on the user's IP address, or with specific user ID and password authentication. With Mosaic 2.0, passwords are blanked out on the user's screen as typed.

The Web project overview page at CERN is a good starting point for information at CERN, NCSA, and other key development sites. There you will find complete information on server choices currently available, in addition to client and HTML authoring documents. Its URL is:

```
http://info.cern.ch/hypertext/WWW/TheProject.html
```

---

* MacHTTP was written by Chuck Shotton of Health Science Center of the University of Texas at Houston.

[†] See `http://www.uth.tmc.edu/mac_info/machttp/readme.html`.

[‡] Currently, pointers to these documents appear on the NCSA "What's New with Mosaic?" page, a sample of which appeared earlier in this chapter.

CERN's page on becoming an information provider shown in Fig. 20.5 offers pointers to online documentation on servers, as well as to the tools document mentioned previously:

```
http://info.cern.ch/hypertext/WWW/Provider/Overview.html
```

A particular page you will want to look at is the Tools page at CERN. This document describes ancillary tools that you might use with your Web service, including tools for generating, editing, and maintaining HTML documents, log analysis tools, and "Web Wanderers" (i.e., robots that scan the Web for you). A number of authoring tools have been developed to assist information providers in preparing HTML documents. These tools allow you to edit your HTML in another environment, such as a word processor; the tool produces an HTML document that you can then install among other Web documents. An example of such a tool is shown in Chap. 21. You can read more about such tools by fetching this document:

```
http://info.cern.ch/hypertext/WWW/Tools/Overview.html
```

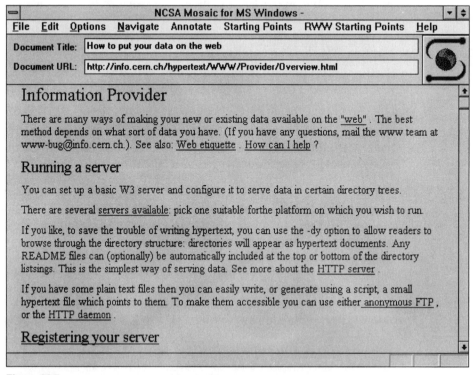

Figure 20.5

You can begin writing HTML documents without such tools, using a simple text editor. A good strategy is to find a document on the Web that has a similar layout to the one you want to write. Next, use Mosaic's Save As option (under the File menu) to save a copy of the document.* Be sure to save it in HTML format. Now, edit the document at will, substituting your own text and local document references. To check the validity of the document, periodically save it to disk, and use the "Open Local" option of Mosaic to see how it is rendered. On a windowing workstation, you can keep the raw text in one window, and Mosaic in another; simply invoke the Reload option in Mosaic as new versions are ready for inspection. (See Fig. 20.6).

The World-Wide Web is discussed in the Usenet News group comp.infosystems.www.

There is also a Web mailing list, where somewhat more arcane items are discussed; to join it, send e-mail to listproc@info.cern.ch with the body of your message including the subscription request (e.g., subscribe www-talk Jane Doe).

---

* Or, if you are running Mosaic on someone else's machine, use the Mail To option and send a copy to your e-mail address.

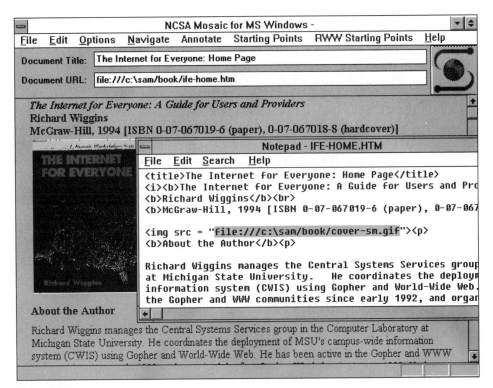

Figure 20.6

Preparing documents for
World-Wide Web delivery

The Web document language, HTML, is a way of marking up documents that generally conforms to the ISO standard 8879: "The Standard Generalized Markup Language (SGML)." It provides a way of encoding document structure with a minimum of presentation information. SGML provides a standard way of describing what the markup looks like.*

The description of the markup of elements used with a particular SGML-based encoding scheme is called a "Document Type Definition," or DTD. As HTML has evolved, the language as implemented and used has varied somewhat from the original DTD, but the basic concepts have held. The DTD for HTML is available on the Web as:

```
http://info.cern.ch/hypertext/WWW/MarkUp/HTML.dtd.html
```

As we saw in Chap. 13, HTML looks like plain text with tags attached. The tags are enclosed in angle brackets (<...>) and the names of the tags reflect the structure of the document. For instance, there are tags to enclose headings (<H1>This is a heading at level 1</H1>), the title of a document (<TITLE>The Title</TITLE>), lists (<OL> for an Ordered List), and so on.

Despite the efforts to encode only meaning in HTML, authors have requested some tags that define presentation. For instance, <B>text</B> places the word "text" in a bold font, if this is meaningful to the program interpreting the HTML (it might be a useful tag for a browser, but not for an automatic indexer).

The HTML language is very nearly locked as a standard. Design has already begun on another language, HTML+, which encodes more structure than HTML. Plans are also under way for style sheets, which give authors the ability to provide specific hints to browsers (along the lines of "use 12-point Roman for this," or "center that"). HTML is likely to remain supported for the forseeable future. Other languages may evolve that attempt to provide similar functionality.

Editing HTML. There are two basic ways to prepare HTML documents:

- Prepare the documents directly in HTML, either by hand or with the aid of a tool.

- Prepare the documents in some other form, and use a translator tool to convert to HTML.

A WYSIWYG (What You See Is What You Get) editor for HTML is included as a part of TkWWW, a family of Web-related tools provided as part of the X11

---

* Portions of the discussion on HTML document preparation include information written by Nathan Torkington.

library (see the `contrib` directory). If you do not have access to an X terminal, or if you do not care for this tool after trying it, you will want to explore other HTML preparation options. CERN provides a list of tools for Web information providers at this address:

`http://info.cern.ch/hypertext/WWW/Tools/Overview.html`

One option is to edit your document using a tool that can produce Rich Text Format (RTF) files. One such tool is Microsoft Word. You can then use an RTF to HTML converter, and if necessary edit the resulting file prior to delivering it on the Web. This tool, and others, are described in a summary available at:

`http://info.cern.ch/hypertext/WWW/Tools/Word_proc_filters.html`

There are also tools for converting special document formats, such as Unix man pages, Usenet FAQ files, and other specialized formats. They are described under:

`http://info.cern.ch/hypertext/WWW/Tools/Man_faq_filters.html`

You may have some files that you want to serve unaltered and unformatted. Examples might be computer programs. Plain ASCII can be turned into HTML by enclosing it in <PRE> ... </PRE> tags. This doesn't take advantage of the structure and presentation capabilities of HTML, however, and is only recommended for cases where this is truly the best way to present your information.

Barry Raveendran Greene of Johns Hopkins University has compiled a nicely organized collection of documents (including several of those mentioned in this chapter) on how to prepare HTML documents. The documents come from various sources, including CERN, NCSA, and various homes of Web pioneers. Figure 20.7 shows the starting page of this collection; note its URL.

Figure 20.8 is an example of an HTML editing tool, the HTML Assistant, which works under MS Windows.* This tool allows the HTML author to embed tags using the buttons depicted on the screen. For instance, you can use the mouse to select a section of text, then click on the `H1` button to cause that text to be tagged as a level 1 header.

Figure 20.9 shows what that document looks like as rendered by the Web client Cello.

Many Web information providers prepare their documents with a text editor and add the tags by hand. Another useful tactic is to begin with a similar document (whether written by you or someone else) and capture the HTML using Mosaic or another client; then you can use that document as an example, or even as a template which you edit by hand.

---

* HTML Assistant was written by Howard Harawitz; obtain it via FTP from `ftp.cs.dal.ca`.

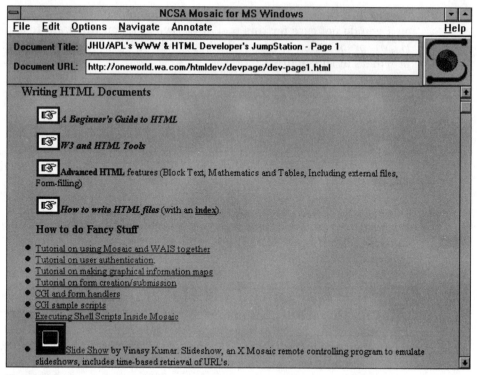

Figure 20.7

Note that Mosaic and other Web clients are designed to be tolerant of errors in documents. In general, Web clients will do the best they can when presented with bad HTML. Therefore, you cannot rely on the fact that Mosaic will display your document to verify that it is fully functional. You will need to look at the document as displayed and follow its internal links to ensure all is okay. A useful technique is to open a document you are "building" in one window using Mosaic, while editing the file in another window on your workstation. As you get a new iteration of your document ready for testing, save the file to disk in the editor, then hop back to the Mosaic window, and invoke the Reload option. In this way you can quickly view successive versions of your document as they would be seen by your users.

Avoid writing HTML that doesn't conform to the standard. HTML generally complies with the SGML standard, but some common extensions to the basic language deviate from the original HTML Document Type Definition. In the absence of widespread deployment of verification tools, you may have to rely on manual testing and inspection. Some HTML authors use an SGML parser to

---

* See the online Web documentation at CERN or NCSA to find a pointer to the original HTML DTD or to current renditions.

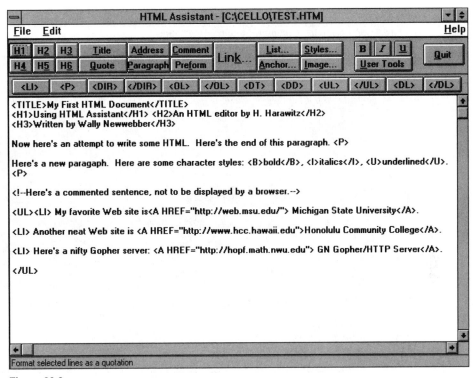

Figure 20.8

verify that their documents are valid, using the best DTD currently available.* This ensures that the readers of their documents will encounter documents that appear to the user as the author intended. Over time, the HTML standard should become solid, and a corresponding DTD should evolve. As mentioned in Chap. 18, there are commercial SGML products used in a variety of SGML-based endeavors outside the Web context. You can obtain a freely available SGML parser via anonymous FTP from `ftp.th-darmstadt.de` in the directory `/pub/text/sgml/sgmls/`.

There may be subtle differences in the ways browsers (clients) interpret various HTML tags, which may cause the same document to be displayed in different ways on different systems. Attempt to check the way your document appears on many different browsers. If you note a unique interpretation by one client, realize that if you rely on that unique interpretation, users of other browsers will not benefit. Use style sheets when they become available.

GATEWAY SERVICES

As a server administrator, you may also want to connect to a variety of other kinds of services that require gateway software external to the Gopher or Web server. In the Gopher realm, the Minnesota gopher server works well with a

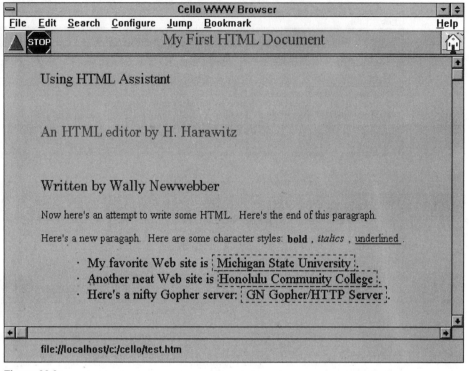

Figure 20.9

general gateway tool called go4gw. This tool can be found in the FTP and Gopher archives at Minnesota. As a matter of philosophy, the Web community tends to encourage direct interaction between the user's client program and any server of interest, but there are some examples of server-mediated gateway services. One of these is a Web-to-SQL gateway, allowing users to submit queries via Mosaic forms that are passed from the Web server to an SQL database. NCSA offers online documentation for such tools on their Web server.

Organizational and stylistic issues

If you are setting up a Gopher or Web service or an anonymous FTP service, organization is a key issue. You want your documents to be presented in a layout that users can navigate. There are no hard-and-fast rules for organization, but good general guidelines include:

- Strike a balance between depth and breadth of your document hierarchy. For instance, a Gopher menu with two dozen choices on the root menu will befuddle your users. Conversely, an anonymous FTP service that carries taxonomy to an extreme will frustrate users; avoid names like:

```
/pub/computers/microcomputers/ibmpc/msdos/utilities/graphics/screensavers
```

- Do not create folders in anticipation of upcoming items unless this is absolutely necessary. False leads and dead ends will turn off your users. Instead, offer flat files in a higher-level menu, and place those files in a subdirectory when you accumulate enough titles to warrant it.

- Use duplicate links judiciously. Too many occurrences of a link can cause all your folders to lose context.

Preparing HTML documents for delivery via the World-Wide Web requires more document preparation effort, and presents its own set of stylistic and organizational issues. Here are some general guidelines.

- Although it is tempting to include links of the form:

  For more information on lift rates at Tall Mountain, click **here,**

  some HTML authors suggest that this is poor style; rather than offering the link with the word "here," offer the link as a natural part of the text. For instance,

  We hope to see you soon at Tall Mountain. You may want to read more about our **lift ticket rates,** and **how to get here,** and **our lodge facilities.**

- Do not feel obliged to include a link at every conceivable point in a document. For instance, if you have offered a link to someone's personal page the first time his or her name appears in a document, do not add links every other time the name appears.

- Even though Web documents can point forward and backward to one another, try to have some sort of overall logical design of your Web structure. Draw a map to help lay out the flow of documents.

- Guard against creating islands in your Web structure—documents that have no obvious path from parent documents in your Web.

- Many Web documents now offer links back to the root of the server they belong to. Such a link might be labeled `Return to Home Page`. This can be very useful for people who land on a particular page via an index search. It also can be helpful for people who get tangled in your local web. You may want to include this sort of link as a matter of course in every document you post.

- Exercise restraint in your use of inline images. Use a stopwatch to time how long it takes for your typical user workstation to "paint" a screen using whatever client program they will use. Consider using small inline images that are links to larger versions of the same image; this common tactic will allow users to see each image in thumbnail without paying the cost of downloading several huge images.

- The imagemap tool (available from NCSA) allows you to offer icons that serve as "buttons" your users can select as a way to choose documents. If you use this support, also use the alt construct to offer a textual cue for users viewing the document via a nongraphical client such as Lynx. For example,

```
<a href="/overview.html"><img src=/icons/overview.gif alt=[Overview]"></a>.
```

- Follow the advice of established Web experts. For instance, Tim Berners-Lee, the main architect of the Web, has written a style guide with useful advice. See:

```
http://info.cern.ch/hypertext/WWW/Provider/Style/Overview.html
```

Serving your users in their native languages

Most vendors of computer systems are working to provide support for a variety of languages in their operating systems. Although many Internet document delivery tools have been designed by and for speakers of English, many servers are endowed with the ability to use a variety of character sets. Most servers and clients can support the Latin-1 (ISO 8859-1) character set, which provides accented characters needed in Romance languages. Other servers may support other character sets, many of which have corresponding ISO 8859 standards. For instance, the Minnesota Gopher server for the Macintosh is able to support a Japanese character set. Consult the documentation for the server you are using for details.

You need to consider what client software and what path into your service will be employed by any of your users who want non-English documents. For instance, their Unix terminal definitions, and the intervening path between the user and you, must support a "clean 8-bit data path" to allow 8-bit character sets to function properly. Similarly, you must use 8-bit editors and authoring tools. If you offer a public client service such as the curses Gopher client, you must use a version of curses that supports 8-bit characters. You will want to take special care to test clients and data paths to ensure that documents appear to users as you think they will.

Be sure you are indexed

As we saw in Chap. 16, there is a wide variety of Internet index tools, and more are coming online daily. If you want to reach the widest possible audience, you want to appear in these indexes. Check the various indexes associated with your type of service to be sure your documents and other resources are listed. Note that some of these services take as long as two weeks to index new servers or documents. If your server or documents you care about are not indexed, send mail to the maintainers of the indexing service and ask why.

Choose document titles that will help remote searchers find you. For instance, if you put a course catalog online, be sure the words "Course Catalog" appear in the title somewhere. If you choose a title that uses some cryptic service name, append a generally meaningful name in parentheses. For instance, if you have an arts calendar called "Artifacts," consider a document title such as "Artifacts (Arts Calendar for Greater Des Moines)."

Usage logs: setting up online logs

Usage logs can be a very useful way for you to gauge the quality of your service. They tell who is accessing which documents on your service (by IP address and time of day). Log analysis can help you pick better document titles, document content, and document organization.

Figure 20.10 is an example of the usage log for one week offered online by the main Gopher server at the University of Massachusetts. In addition to the information shown, the log also shows a bar graph depicting usage by time of day.*

Similar online logs are often provided by Web administrators. Tools to perform this function are available via the CERN page of Web tools (described

---

*This particular log uses an analyzer called GopherReport, written by Eric Katz at the National Center for Supercomputer Applications.

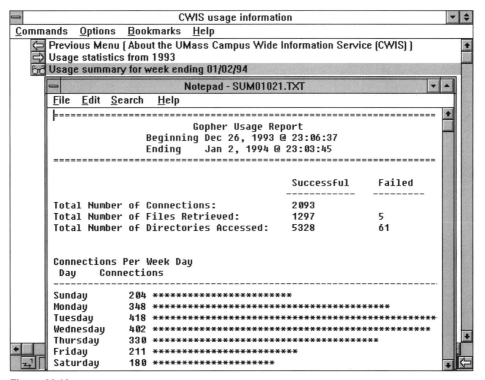

Figure 20.10

earlier). For instance, look for a tool known as `getsites`. Online traffic summaries are usually updated daily or weekly when an automated process summarizes the log information and creates a new online report. Some Web administrators even write custom programs that take up-to-the-minute log information and insert statistics into the HTML text for the home page—e.g., "This server has been accessed 12,345 times today."

Establishing Internet Information Services: Unix-Based Examples

Chapter 20 described the software choices available to a new Internet information provider. In this chapter we explore the steps required to actually set up specific server applications. Examples include:

- Installing the Gn server for Unix. This server is unique in its ability to serve both Gopher and Web clients, and therefore is a good choice for information providers who want to address the broadest base of users.

- Using the PERL language—an overview of a language that is extremely popular among Internet server administrators.

- Installing a WAIS server.

- Installing the World-Wide Web server from the National Center for Supercomputer Applications.

- Exploiting some advanced Web applications, such as interactive forms and maps.

SETTING UP A GN GOPHER SERVER*

In this section we'll walk through the process of creating a working Gopher server. Since it is smaller and easier to work with than the University of Minnesota's Unix server, we'll build the Gn server. Note, however, that the basic steps for building either server are very similar, differing largely in the specific layout of configuration files. You don't need to be a programmer to walk through the basic procedure outlined here. You will need to have access to, and know how to use, a text editor. For a few steps you will need write permission to various files which may not be accessible to ordinary users of your system. In the unlikely event things go wrong during the build phase, you may wish to obtain the assistance of someone who is a programmer.

A strategic note: You may find it best to start with a simple, sample Gopher layout for your data hierarchy when you first set up the server. This will allow you to concentrate on getting the server functioning, and to understand the basics of setting up a data directory under Gn. You can then fetch files from that sample hierarchy using Gopher and Web clients. Once you have this process under your belt, you might want to tackle serving HTML documents.

Obtaining the Gn Server Software

The first step is to find a place to work. One method which works is to create a directory for software packages, and subdirectory for each package. To create a directory, use the `mkdir` command. Use the `cd` command to change your working directory to the `packages` directory.

Both the Minnesota server and the Gn server are available by anonymous FTP. The Minnesota server is also available via Gopher. Note that the specific filenames shown here, which contain version numbers, will change as the servers are enhanced. Here is an example of obtaining the Gn server using anonymous FTP:

```
ftp ftp.acns.nwu.edu†
FTP Trying...Open
220 casbah.acns.nwu.edu FTP server (SunOS 4.1) ready.
 . . .
ftp> cd pub/gn
ftp> dir
 . . .
```

---

* The sections of this chapter describing Gn installation were written by Dennis Boone.

† The Gn server can also be downloaded via Gopher. Point your Gopher client to `hopf.math.nwu.edu` (port 70) and follow the menus to the server distribution; use your client's ability to save a file to disk. The file will be delivered in binary mode as is appropriate. You may also find the Gn server distribution on the University of Minnesota server FTP and Gopher services.

```
-rw-r--r--  1 379      20      2720   Feb 11 18:58  README
-rw-r--r--  1 379      20    107677   Feb  7 17:03  gn-1.19a.tar.gz
-rw-r--r--  1 379      20    132576   Feb 21 16:56  gn-2.01.tar.gz
-rw-r--r--  1 379      20      9536   Feb  4 03:41  srch.shar
  . . .
ftb> binary
200 Type set to I.
ftp> get gn-2.01.tar.gz
200 PORT command successful.
150 Opening BINARY mode data connection for gopher2.06.tar.Z (309474 bytes).
226 Transfer complete.
309474 bytes received in 8.498 seconds (35.56 Kbytes/s)
ftp> bye
221 Goodbye.
```

Building the Server

The Gn server comes packaged in a compressed `tar` file. The `.gz` suffix indicates compression the new Gnu `gzip` command. To extract the package, use the `zcat` command, and pipe its output (the now-uncompressed `tar` file) to the `tar` command like this:

```
gzip -cd gn-2.01.tar.gz | tar xvf -
```

The meanings of the `tar` options are:

x   Extract files

v   Produce a verbose listing of filenames and information

f   Extract from the file named in the next parameter (-)

-     Names the source file; in this case, standard input

The tar command should create a directory called `gn-2.01`, which contains several files. These files must now be compiled to produce the server. Use the `cd` command to change your working directory to `gn-2.01` (or whatever the directory name for your version is).

Next, you must configure the server. To do this, load the file `config.h` into your editor. There are five lines you need to consider. The first,

```
#define HOSTNAME           "gopher.msu.edu"
```

provides the server with the domain name of its host system. Many administrators choose to create an alias of `gopher` for their system (i.e., `gopher.acme.com` or `gopher.math.state.edu`). Other sites will likely create pointers to your information. Their pointers will break if you move your server to a new system with a different name. If you create an alias, you can take the alias with you to a new machine should it become necessary to move. Links using the alias name will continue to work. Establishing an alias name requires the cooperation of your domain administrator, who must add the name to the tables used by the domain name server.

Another compilation option gives a default human-readable title to your Gn service. This label will be used as the title of your service's home page for users who access the server via HTTP (the World-Wide Web protocol). To establish this title use a #define of the following form:

```
#define ROOT_MENU_NAME    "Michigan State University"
```

The files that you will serve to users will reside in a subdirectory of your Unix file system. The next statement tells the server where the top of your data tree resides:

```
#define ROOT_DIR          "/usr/local/gopher/gopher-data"
```

Later you will need to create this directory, unless it already exists. (If you are adding Gn service to an existing collection of information, you may elect to use the existing directory. It is possible for FTP and Gopher servers to share a common directory tree. If you are serving existing data using FTP, this is a quick way to get started with Gopher.) A word of caution is in order: Gopher's ability to retrieve files transparently using a variety of different protocols makes it an excellent choice for those users who need the information but don't need or want to understand the access technology. As a Gopher server administrator you are able to endow these files with friendly, human-readable titles. The techniques for doing this vary from server to server; we will see the Gn scheme later. If you choose to use Gopher to serve an existing FTP archive, consider adding friendly document titles; presenting raw Unix filenames instead of proper titles destroys a major advantage offered by Gopher.

A networked Unix system is like an apartment building: once you've found the right address you have to know at which door to knock. Unix "doors" are called TCP ports, and are labeled with numbers. Gopher traditionally lives at port 70. You are not obligated to run your server at that port, and if you are running more than one server on one computer, you certainly will have to run at least one of them somewhere else. Nevertheless, running your primary server at port 70 will make everyone's life easier, since most Gopher software knows that 70 is the default port. To configure GN for your port choice, change this statement:

```
#define DEFAULTPORT    "70"
```

If your system is short of disk space but has spare processing power, Gn can help you fit your information into the available space. If you use the compress command to reduce the size of your files, Gn will expand them on-the-fly as it delivers them to clients. The tradeoff here is that decompression requires some CPU processing time for each access by each user. The command Gn uses is configured in this statement:

```
#define DECOMPRESS        "/usr/bin/zcat"
```

Some systems have compress and uncompress, but don't have zcat. If you are working on one of these systems, try using this statement instead:

```
#define DECOMPRESS        "/usr/bin/uncompress -c"
```

Save these changes and exit the editor.

Next, load the file called "Makefile" into your editor. The top section of the file, shown below, contains a few lines you may need to change. If you do not have the GNU C compiler, your compiler is probably called cc, and you need to move the # character from the first "CC=" line to the second one. If your compiler is called something else, change "gcc" to that name.

On some systems, notably those derived from System V, you may need to link special libraries with the server. If you get error messages like "Undefined symbol", try moving the # character from the second "LIBS =" statement to the first one.

Move the # character from the first "INSTALL =" line to the second. The cp command works properly on most systems, while on many systems the install command behaves strangely or doesn't exist.

Finally, decide where you want to place the gn executable program. Change the "BINDIR =" line to point to the place you have chosen. Programs like Gn, which provide services to many users but are not a part of the operating system, are often placed in /usr/local/bin or /usr/local/etc.

```
#
#      Configurable Part.
#
#      Choice of Compiler.
#CC      = cc
CC       = gcc
#
#      Compiler Flags (-I.. *MUST* be included)
#
INCLUDES= -I.. -I../gn
CFLAGS    = $(INCLUDES)     # -DSYSV
#
#      Libraries to be included.
#
LIBS     =
#Use this with SysV
```

```
#LIBS    = -lsocket -lc
#
#    install program. SysV without GNU Utils - use cp
#
#INSTALL    = cp
INSTALL    = /usr/local/bin/install
#
#    Where to put the programs
#
BINDIR  = /usr/local/etc
```

Save these changes and exit the editor. Now, it's time to compile Gn. To do so, simply type:

```
make
```

and watch the fun:

```
$ make

Making gn

    (cd gn; make CC="gcc" CFLAGS="-I.. -I../gn" LIBS="" \
        INSTALL="/usr/local/bin/install" BINDIR="/usr/local/etc" )

    gcc -I.. -I../gn -c gn.c
    gcc -I.. -I../gn -c pselect.c
    gcc -I.. -I../gn -c init.c
    gcc -I.. -I../gn -c util.c
    gcc -I.. -I../gn -c acc.c
    gcc -I.. -I../gn -c csearch.c
    gcc -I.. -I../gn -c regcomp.c
    gcc -I.. -I../gn -c regfind.c
    gcc -I.. -I../gn -c send.c
    gcc -I.. -I../gn -c search.c
    gcc -I.. -I../gn -c sio.c
    gcc -I.. -I../gn -o gn gn.o pselect.o init.o \
                    util.o acc.o csearch.o regcomp.o \
                    regfind.o send.o search.o sio.o

Making mkcache

    (cd mkcache; make CC="gcc" CFLAGS="-I.. -I../gn " LIBS="" \
        INSTALL="/usr/local/bin/install" BINDIR="/usr/local/etc")

    gcc -I.. -I../gn -c mkcache.c
    gcc -I.. -I../gn -c init.c
```

```
gcc -I.. -I../gn -c form.c
gcc -I.. -I../gn -o mkcache mkcache.o init.o \
                        form.o ../gn/regfind.o \
                        ../gn/regcomp.o
```

```
Making uncache
```

```
(cd uncache; make CC="gcc" CFLAGS="-I.. -I../gn " LIBS="" \
    INSTALL="/usr/local/bin/install" BINDIR="/usr/local/etc")
```

```
gcc -I.. -I../gn -c uncache.c
gcc -I.. -I../gn -c init.c
gcc -I.. -I../gn -o uncache uncache.o init.o
```

Messages that aren't similar to the ones above probably indicate something went wrong. You might be able to ignore messages that begin "warning: . . ." but test carefully to make sure Gn is working properly. Error message like "Undefined symbol" mean that the system couldn't find certain important subroutines. See the note above on configuring the Makefile, which may solve this problem.

Installing the Gn Server

Now that you have built the Gn server, it's time to install it. Installing simply consists of copying the file to the appropriate directory. You'll need permission to write the executable into the directory you've chosen. You've already configured the Makefile to perform the installation for you, so all you need to do is type:

```
make install
```

and make will execute the appropriate commands.

Tell inetd About the Server

An important part of the Unix networking system is the superserver process called inetd. You can either run Gn under the control of inetd, or you can run Gn in a stand-alone fashion. You might choose to run Gn in a stand-alone fashion if you are running the service from a nonprivileged port (i.e., a port number greater than 1024) or for performance reasons. (The stand-alone server can perform better when your server is extremely busy.) To run the stand-alone version, see the online installation documentation discussion of sgn.

Inetd handles incoming connections on most TCP ports to which your server "listens." It uses two tables to determine, for any given port, what program should be run to service the connection. You need to edit these tables, which will require write permission to the files /etc/services and /etc/inetd.conf.

The file /etc/services describes the relationship between port numbers and service names. Edit this file and create the line

```
gn  70/tcp    gopher
```

Replace "70" with the value you placed in the "DEFAULTPORT" variable in the config.h file. This tells inetd (and other utilities) that port 70 is the "gn" service, and it might also be called "gopher".

The file /etc/inetd.conf tells inetd what program to run for each service it manages, what user ID to run the program under, and what command line arguments to pass to the program. Edit the file /etc/inetd.conf and insert the line

```
gn    stream   tcp nowait    nobody    /full/path/for/gn    gn
```

Replace "/full/path/for" with the value you placed in the "BINDIR =" statement in the Makefile.

After editing these files you must instruct the inetd process, which is always running, to read the changes. You will need to have root privileges to do this. Find the process ID number of the inetd process using this command:

```
ps aux | grep inetd
```

The resulting output should look something like this:

```
$ ps aux | grep inetd
root      4444  0.2  0.0  184  260      - S      Sep 05  2:46 /etc/inetd
boone    31399  0.0  0.0   84  140  pts/1 S    11:40:01  0:00 grep inetd
```

The second column contains the process number. In this case, the first line describes the inetd process. Its process number is 4444. To instruct this inetd process to reread the files, you would give the command:

```
kill -HUP 4444
```

Prepare the Gn Data Directory

Now that you have a server configured and installed, it's time to give it some information to serve. The first step is to create the root directory. If the directory you selected earlier already exists, skip this step. Use the mkdir command to create the directory you named in the ROOT_DIR variable in the config.h file. Above, we set this variable to:

```
#define ROOT_DIR                        "/usr/local/gopher/gopher-data"
```

so the appropriate command would be:

```
mkdir /usr/local/gopher/gopher-data
```

You will need write permission to the parent directory, in this case `/usr/local/gopher`.

Now place the files containing the information you want to publish into the Gopher data tree. This probably entails using the Unix command `cp` to copy the files from their current location. If you have any significant amount of information to present, you will probably want to organize it in a hierarchical scheme. To create directories for subcategories use the `mkdir` command.

Next, create a file in the Gn root directory, and each subdirectory, called `menu`.* This file describes the data in the directory which Gn will serve. Items not listed in this file will not be served. You can therefore hide items by not listing them here. Two lines in `menu` will describe the title and Gopher selector string for each file in the directory.

For example: Suppose you want to publish online information about plants and animals. Your Gn server will begin with information on various trees and birds. You will offer a file named `about.txt` in your Gn root directory; this file will describe the contents of your Gn server. The root directory also contains two subdirectories, called `trees` and `birds`. You place the following lines in the `menu` file:

```
Name=About this server
Path=0/about.txt

Name=Descriptions of trees
Path=1/trees

Name=Descriptions of birds
Path=1/birds
```

A user connecting to your server using the public Gopher client will see a root menu that looks like this[†]:

```
--> 1. About this server.
    2. Descriptions of trees/
    3. Descriptions of birds/
```

---

* Gn comes with a sample `menu` file in the distribution; see `/docs/sample.root.menu`.

[†] The Name and Path information in the menu file will be served to any Gopher client calling your Gn server. You may want to review the basic functioning of the Gopher protocol described in Chap. 12.

This simple menu has two document types, reflected as the first character in the Path field:

- Type 0 is the basic text file document type; it is used for the "about" file and for the descriptions of trees that appear under the /trees directory. Note that we chose file names ending in .txt for these text files; this was for emphasis only.
- Type 1 is the Gopher type that represents subdirectories. This document type is essential for offering a hierarchical menu structure.

When you set up documents in Gn, you will create Unix subdirectories that correspond to the tree structure you design for your server. Each one of these subdirectories will have its own menu file. You have descriptions for three different kinds of trees. You place the following lines in the file menu in the trees subdirectory:

```
Name=Birch
Path=0/trees/birch.txt

Name=Elm
Path=0/trees/elm.txt

Name=Oak
Path=0/trees/oak.txt
```

Leave a blank line between items. The "Name=" line must be first. It contains the descriptive name of the document or directory. The "Path=" line contains a type field (one or more characters) and a path from the Gn root directory to the file. Figure 21.1 shows how menu files define the documents you will serve.

Note that the basic Gopher protocol defined by the University of Minnesota calls for one-character type names. Gn supports all of the basic Gopher types, and also employs extended types of its own, denoted by 2- or 3-byte codes. These extended type codes are used internally by the Gn server to provide extended functions; although the extended codes appear in selector strings as defined by the Path= field, only the standard 1-byte types will be interpreted by Gopher client programs. Examples of types supported by the Gn server include*:

0Z	Compressed file, which gn will uncompress before delivery
1	Directory
1s	Directory which allows searches of all its contents

---

* See the Gn documentation for a complete list of Gn's extended type codes and their meaning.

Sample File Hierarchy for a Gn Server

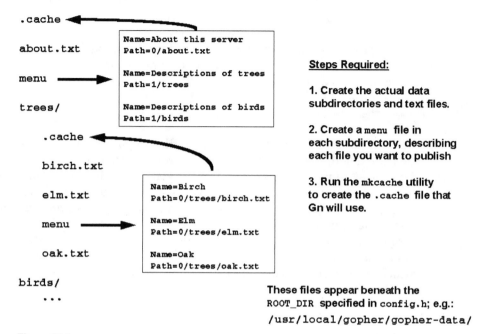

Steps Required:

1. Create the actual data subdirectories and text files.

2. Create a menu file in each subdirectory, describing each file you want to publish

3. Run the mkcache utility to create the .cache file that Gn will use.

These files appear beneath the ROOT_DIR specified in config.h; e.g.:

/usr/local/gopher/gopher-data/

Figure 21.1

7g   Search of a type "1s" directory

7m   Search of a file which contains multiple logical documents

7c   Search of all titles in the Gn data tree

One of the advantages of Gopher is its distributed nature—the ability for a server to point to documents that reside on other Gopher servers. You may wish to include such pointers in your server as well. To do so, you include links in your menu file pointing to those items on remote servers. A link consists of several lines in the menu file, including the Name= and Path= lines as described previously, and additional Type=, Host=, and Port= items.

For example, let's say your server is a repository for economic data for your state. The economics department at the University of Michigan has collected a list of economics-related gopher servers. You wish to provide a link to that list. You place the following line in a menu file:

```
Name=Economics-related Gopher servers (From University of Michigan)
Type=1
Host=gopher.econ.lsa.umich.edu
Port=70
Path=1/Other Gophers/Economics-related Gophers
```

Remember that many of the users of these links will be on computers besides yours, so you must provide fully qualified host names in your links. Many services on the Internet are willing to have other services include such pointers, but it never hurts to ask permission before doing so.

After you have constructed all of your menu files, the final step is to run the mkcache program. Use the cd command to change your current directory to the gn root directory, and type:

```
mkcache -r
```

The mkcache program will take the menu files in your gn data tree and convert each one to a file called .cache. The .cache file is in a format that is more efficient for gn to use, but less practical for you to edit by hand. You should run mkcache each time you add or remove files from your gn data tree, or if you change a menu file.* The first time you run mkcache, it is important to create .cache files throughout your gn data tree. This is done by using the -r option from the root of the gn data tree, as described above. Thereafter, when you make changes, it is acceptable to run mkcache in just the altered directory, without the -r option. (But, for completeness, you can always run mkcache -r from the root of your data tree whenever you see fit.)

Testing Your Gn Server

You should always test your server after adding or changing information in the tree, or when changing the menu files. Use your Gopher client to make sure that searches return all the matches you expect, that all files appear, no unexpected files appear, etc. If you have a variety of document types, be sure all can be fetched and viewed using Gopher clients. The first time you set up the server, you might also want to have some other users point their Gopher clients at it. If you have friends at remote sites, make sure they can access your server as well.

Gn as a World-Wide Web Server

In order to best serve users who connect to your server with clients like Mosaic, you will want to offer them documents marked up in HTML. By taking the time to construct HTML documents, you can provide your users with the richness of text with headlines and embedded graphics. There are two basic ways you can add HTML annotation to documents served by Gn:

---

* If you run your server on a port other than 70, you will want to specify the port number via the -p parameter to the mkcache command. See the man page for mkcache.

- You can include HTML markup in your `menu` files.

- You can prepare complete HTML documents and serve them, each in its entirety, by constructing pointers to the files in your `menu` files. These files will look very similar to the HTML files you would prepare for another Web server. (Note, however, that the Gn server is not intended to provide complete interoperability with other servers; if you migrate to another server, you will have to update parts of your data files.)

Because WWW links and text can be combined in arbitrary fashions, menus containing only links are rarely found in the WWW world. In contrast, the basic Gopher protocol did not define a mechanism for combining text with links on its menus. The type `"i"` extension, pioneered by the University of Iowa, is supported by most Gopher clients. This special document type allows you to offer a limited form of annotation to Gopher users, and Gn makes it possible for the annotation you add to its menu files to benefit your Gopher users.

When a user calls your Gn server using a Web client and asks for a menu file, Gn sends an HTML document that offers the items in that menu that you have set up for Web access. Special constructs that you may include in `menu` files allow you to take advantage of Gn's Web capabilities: the `Text=` and `httpText=` (and `endText=`) items, and the `GnLink=` item.

- Text found between `Text=` and `endText=` is placed into the HTML document generated when a WWW client calls. For Gopher client calls, the text is converted to type `"i"` items. HTML tags may be embedded in the text for WWW clients; these are stripped for Gopher clients.

- Text found between `httpText=` and `endText=` is served only to WWW clients.

You can create links to other WWW servers by placing HTML tags in text between `Text=` and `endText=` markers. For example, the economics data example mentioned previously could be represented in a menu file as follows:

```
Text=
  <A HREF="gopher://gopher.econ.lsa.umich.edu:70/11/Other Gophers/
  Economics-related Gophers"> Economics-related Gopher servers</A>
endText=
```

The `"gopher:"` says that the server at the other end of this link speaks the Gopher protocol. The `"//gopher.econ.lsa.umich.edu"` provides the name of the host where the server resides, and the `":70"` provides the port number on that host. The `"/1"` provides the document type that will be returned (in this case, type "1" for a directory). The string `"1/Other Gophers/Economics-related Gophers"` is the Gopher selector string; this will be sent to the specified Gopher server should the user select this item.

You can use the `Text=` construct to offer long paragraphs of annotation. They will be seen by users of Web clients such as Mosaic as normal HTML text, which is to say they will be word-wrapped so as to fit in the client window. When delivered to Gopher clients as type i data, the lines of annotation will be displayed as discrete lines of text as you entered them. Be sure to try out your menu files using a variety of client programs to make sure your users see what you want them to see.

Figure 21.2 shows how lines in a sample menu file correspond to a screen as rendered by Mosaic. In this case the sample screen is a page from the main Gn server at Northwestern University.

Besides offering HTML constructs in menu files, you can also serve entire HTML files using Gn. These files will have the `.html` suffix, and will contain markup of the same format we saw in Chap. 13—similar in form to the markup used in HTML documents served by any Web server. If you want to serve a document concerning weather to Web clients, you might create `weather.html` and describe it as follows in your menu file:

```
Name=Weather Information in HTML Format
Path=0/weather.html
```

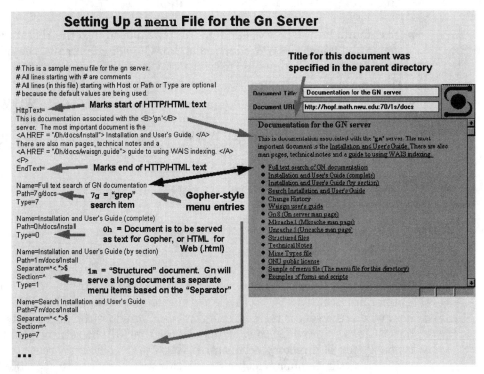

Figure 21.2

(This example applies to a document in your root menu; the path could include subdirectories as appropriate.)

If you have an audience of both Web and Gopher users, you can easily offer documents to both camps. You will want to prepare both an HTML version of the document and a plain text version of the document for your Gopher users. Gn allows you to define both documents in one menu item. For instance, you might have:

```
Name=Weather Information for both Web (HTML) and Gopher users
Path=0h/weather
```

The `0h` document type is a special flag to the Gn server. In this case, it says "I want to serve the file `weather` to my Gopher users and the file `weather.html` to my Web users." As server administrator, you will need to place both files in the data directory. One tactic for doing this is to prepare your HTML document first, and use Mosaic to save the file in "text-only" mode; the resulting file can be your starting point for your Gopher users.

Situations will arise in which you want to serve a given file or directory only to Gopher users or only to Web users. For instance, in the above example, you may want to supply Gopher menu items for links that are embedded in your `weather.html` file. But you do not want to serve those menu items to your Web users; that would be redundant. Gn offers special attributes—`GopherOnly` and `HttpOnly`—that you can associate with a menu entry to meet this need. For instance, suppose your HTML weather document has an in-line weather map. In this case you might include the following entry for a Gopher-only link:

```
Name=Current U.S. Weather Map
Path=0/maps/usweather.gif
Attribute=GopherOnly
```

Another attribute, `invisible`, allows you to store a file in a subdirectory but inhibit users seeing it when they reach the current menu. This is useful when you want to keep in-line images in the same directory as the HTML documents that reference them.

We've already discussed creating Gopher links to other Gopher items. If links to documents are specified using `Name=`, they will be presented to all clients as Gopher items. Gn servers are a special case, since they can provide HTML documents to WWW clients, and Gopher documents to Gopher clients. Presenting Gopher links to WWW clients would give those clients reduced functionality. Gn offers the `GnLink=` marker, used in place of the `Name=` marker, to provide a facility for presenting the appropriate type of link based on the type of the calling client. If you know the server at the other end of a link is a Gn server, you may wish to use the `GnLink=` marker. For example, the link to the Gn server operated by Gn author John Franks would be:

```
GnLink=John Franks' Gn server
Type=1
Host=hopf.math.nwu.edu
Port=70
Path=
```

When we configured Gn for this example, we used TCP port 70—the standard port for Gopher. Gn is smart enough to distinguish between Gopher and HTTP (Web) requests no matter what port the client calls. However, the standard port for the Web is port 80, and you may want to serve your Web clients by default on that port. Fortunately, it is easy to run two copies of Gn at once—you do not even have to duplicate the data tree! If you are running under inetd, simply run a second copy of Gn by adding another entry to /etc/services:

```
gn  80/tcp    www
```

Then add to /etc/inetd.conf:

```
http    stream   tcp nowait    nobody    /full/path/for/gn    gn
```

If you run more than one server process on one computer, you need to be sure that your .cache files point to the right port number. Use mkcache -p 80 to specify port 80, for instance; see the online documentation for mkcache for details.

You may want to add a special optional line to each menu file specifying who is responsible for that subdirectory. This feature is useful for Web clients with the ability to send mail to the named maintainer. If included, this Gn construct must appear as the first line in the menu file, in this form:

```
Maintainer=mailto:gnperson@host.edu
```

Menu files can also contain comments. Comment lines are for your benefit; they serve the same purpose as comment lines in computer programs. They are especially useful for complex menu files, such as those that contain HTML fragments. A comment line simply is a line beginning with a pound sign:

```
# A comment line begins with a pound sign (called a hash mark
# in the United Kingdom)
```

Online Gn Documentation

John Franks provides an excellent repository of online documentation for the Gn server. He makes use of the structured file feature of Gn to offer the installation manual both as a document suited for printing and sequential reading,

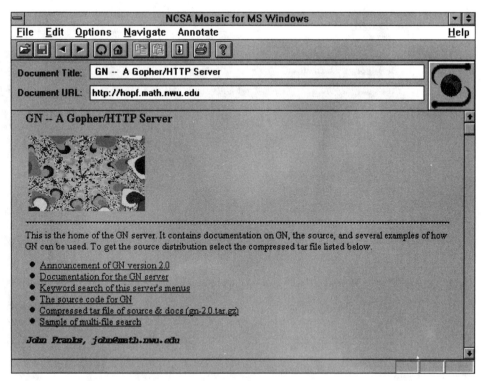

Figure 21.3

and divided into sections suitable for in-line reading as a hypertext document.*
Figure 21.3 shows how the Gn home page is rendered by Mosaic.†

The main documentation menu for the Gn server appears in Fig. 21.4. The
documentation even includes as an example a menu file for this menu itself. You
might want to retrieve and print a copy of the menu file as a useful example to
consult while you build your own Gn menus. If you intend to use Gn to serve
users with Web clients, you might also find it useful to point Mosaic at this documentation page and save the page as an HTML document. By comparing the
menu file with the HTML document, you will be able to understand how the Gn
server "wraps" the lines you prepare in the menu file with the necessary tagged
fields to contruct a complete HTML document suitable for Web users.

---

* Unfortunately, while there is excellent documentation about the Web online at CERN and at
NCSA, most of it is presented in a way that requires online navigation via the Web; their documentation is not as easy to print en masse as the Gn documentation.

† Naturally, because the Gn server is a multiprotocol server, you can read the online documentation using either a Gopher client or a Web client such as Mosaic. Point a Gopher client at
hopf.math.nwu.edu (port 70) or point your Web client at http://hopf.math.nwu.edu.

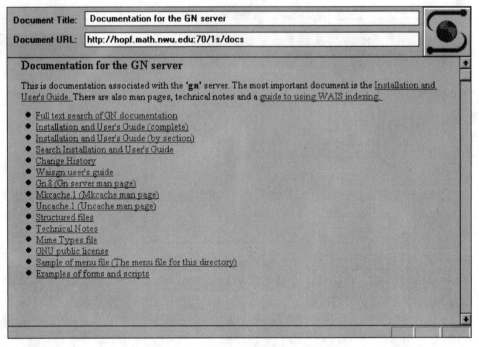

Figure 21.4

The online Gn documentation has complete information on other features of Gn, such as the ability to offer indexes to your documents (with either GnWAIS or with Gn's built-in indexer) and the ability to limit access to your Gn data hierarchy based on the user's IP address.

Once you have finished installing the Gn server and placing documents online, it is time to congratulate yourself: you've succeeded in become an Internet information provider. Now would be a good time to point your Gopher client to the University of Minnesota Gopher server and fill out the Gopher server registration form, which will cause your server to appear in the Minnesota registry of Gopher servers.

The Gn Server compared to the Minnesota Server

The Unix Gopher server from the University of Minnesota is the original Gopher server, and it is the most powerful. This server supports the Gopher+ protocol extensions, and it also has the ability to serve as a gateway to external FTP servers and external WAIS databases. You may want to use the Minnesota server if your main audience is Gopher-based and if you do not find the Gn server adequate. (You can, of course, run both servers, with some documents resident on one, and some on the other; the primary server could seamlessly point to the other one for those documents where appropriate.)

If you decide to run the Minnesota server, note that it uses a slightly different structure for describing documents in the Gopher hierarchy. Instead of a menu file with a line for each file, the Minnesota server uses subdirectories named .cap with files that provide titles (and optional display ordering information) for files resident on the local server, and a .links* file in each subdirectory to describe pointers to externally resident documents. If you do not provide a .cap file for a given document in the Gopher hierarchy, the Minnesota server will offer the file to clients anyhow—with the Unix file name in lieu of a title.

One of the reasons why Dr. Franks implemented Web functionality in the Gn server was to provide a bridge between the Gopher and Web realms. If you maintain an existing service with the Minnesota server, and you elect to migrate to the Gn server, you will need to translate your Gopher data tree to the Gn layout. The Gn software distribution includes a tool called uncache that will ease this transition; see the online Gn documentation for details.

If you want to run a public Gopher client—that is, if you want to be able to support users who do not have Gopher clients but who want to Telnet into your host—you may want to run the Minnesota "curses" client, regardless of which server you have chosen. Because all Gopher servers follow the same basic protocol, the public client will work with any Gopher server. Another alternative is to run a publicly accessible Lynx client service. Many sites are choosing this multiprotocol client as a way to provide access for their services, whether Gopher-based, Web-based, or both. Lynx provides most of the functionality of the Minnesota "curses" client, in addition to being able to negotiate Web-style hypertext.

A TOOL FOR SERVER ADMINISTRATORS: THE PERL LANGUAGE

Below is an example of the Perl language. Perl stands for Practical Extraction and Reporting Language. As its name indicates, Perl is able to easily consume and produce text in almost any format. It is therefore the tool of choice for many of the tasks of the Internet information server administrator—for massaging input files to be served, for analyzing server log information, and so forth. Perl is by no means the only language used for such utilities; the C language and the awk facility are often used for utilities supporting Unix-based servers.

---

* Actually, the Minnesota server assumes that any file whose name begins with a period contains link information; the file name .links is a common convention. The Gn server's use of a single menu file to describe both local documents and external links is a more straightforward design.

Notable characteristics of Perl include:

- Perl has many similarities to the programming language C, which is an essential component of life under the Unix operating system. However, unlike C, Perl is usually implemented as an "interpreted" language. This means that your program is not "compiled" into an efficient machine language program, but rather is interpreted "on the fly" as the program executes. On today's fast computers the performance penalty is not excessive, but you may want to recode frequently executed utilities in C for efficiency.

- Perl contains lots of punctuation. This makes it hard to read. Even advocates of Perl sometimes call it a "write-only" language—Perl makes it easy for programmers to get a lot of work done with a little bit of code, but it is not always easy for one to read another's Perl code.

- Perl has extensive support for regular expressions. These make it simple to locate interesting information amid other text.

- Arrays, lists, stacks, and queues are all essentially the same data structure, and Perl can manipulate them as such.

- Perl supports Unix system calls and makes it easy to perform networking tasks.

The following example is a relatively short Perl program. Its purpose is to move a file from a staging area in a server's anonymous FTP hierarchy into the home directory of the user invoking the command. Note that Perl programs often are considerably more complex than this one; a complete HTTP (World-Wide Web) server has been implemented in Perl.

```perl
#!/usr/local/bin/perl

    require "syslog.pl";

    $ENV{"PATH"} = "/bin:/usr/bin";

    &openlog("claim_incoming", "cons,pid", "user");

    ($user, $passwd, $uid, $gid, $quota, $comment, $gcos, $dir, $shell) =
        getpwuid($<);
    $grnam = getgrgid($gid);
    if (($user eq "drb") ||
        ($user eq "epl") ||
        ($user eq "mec") ||
        ($user eq "rww"))
    {
        opendir (D, "/home/ftp/incoming") || die
            "claim_incoming: unable to get list of files: $!";
```

```
@files = readdir(D);
closedir (D);
foreach $i (@files)
{
    foreach $j (@ARGV)
    {
        if ($i eq $j)
        {
            print "mv $i $dir\n";
            system ("/bin/mv", "/home/ftp/incoming/$i", $dir);
            print "chown $user.$grnam $dir/$i\n";
            system ("/bin/chown", "$user.$grnam", "$dir/$i");
            print "chmod 640 $dir/$i\n";
            system ("/bin/chmod", "644", "$dir/$i");
            &syslog("info", "$user got $i from ~ftp/incoming");
        }
    }
}
else
{
    &syslog("warning", "$user attempted to get @ARGV from ~ftp/incoming");
    exit (1);
}
```

A good text on the Perl language is *Programming Perl* by Larry Wall (the inventor of Perl) and Randal L. Schwartz (O'Reilly & Associates, 1992, ISBN 0-937175-64-1). You can also find considerable information about Perl in an FAQ periodically posted to the Usenet News group news.answers, including pointers to online documentation.

Managing a Unix WAIS System*

Perhaps the most daunting task for a newcomer to WAIS is the installation and use of the WAIS server. One portion of this discussion will focus on the issues involved in server startup and maintenance. A second section describes the use of the WAIS Text Indexer, another critical component of the WAIS system.

WAIS stands for Wide Area Information Servers. WAIS was designed by Brewster Kahle and colleagues at Thinking Machines, Inc. The original releases of WAIS were made through Thinking Machines in 1991 and 1992. WAIS was designed as an executive information system—a system that

---

* This section was written by Jim Fullton of the Clearinghouse for Networked Information Discovery and Retrieval.

allows users with no knowledge of the details of the system and no advanced information-searching skills to locate critical documents within a very large collection of potentially similar information. This model requires both a distributed information dissemination mechanism and a data location system.

The dissemination mechanism, which is frequently referred to as the protocol engine, is based on the 1988 version of the Z39.50 standard. The data location system is a text-searching engine that makes use of a concept known as relevance feedback, described in Chap. 15.

Several changes are occurring in the WAIS world. The most important is the migration of WAIS from Z39.50-1988 to Z39.50-1992, which is the current official standard. WAIS is also moving away from an automatic dependence on free text-searching systems.

WAIS is available from several sources. The Clearinghouse for Networked Information Discovery and Retrieval (CNIDR) provides support for the non-commercial versions of WAIS (freeWAIS), while a variety of companies provide commercial versions of Z39.50-92 conformant-text and data-searching systems. WAIS, Inc. provides a commercial version of the 1988 compliant version of WAIS, with a vastly improved text-searching system. WAIS, Inc. is also developing a line of WAIS products based on Z39.50-92. In March 1994, CNIDR announced a new tool, ZDIST, that implements the 1992 standard of Z39.50. Note that this new tool is not interoperable with the current generation of WAIS clients, which support the 1988 standard.

The Function of the WAIS Server

Before learning to use the WAIS Server, you must first understand what it does. The server is the publisher's link to the outside world. It provides the mechanism for WAIS clients to interact with various information searching engines, such as the WAIS text search engine. There is frequently a bit of misunderstanding surrounding the server—it's commonly confused with the search engine. Why is this? In the freely available versions, it's because the WAIS server and text searching engines are so tightly integrated with each other. When you install the WAIS server, you automatically get the WAIS text search engine. Don't let this confuse you—they occupy separate places in the WAIS system.

The server provides everything needed to accept network connections from WAIS clients and pass the queries generated by those clients to the appropriate search engine. All the user needs to do is set it up properly.

The indexer prepares the text information for access by the WAIS text search engine. If you use a WAIS server that doesn't rely upon the built-in text searching engine, you don't need the indexer. Instead, there will be a separate set of instructions on how to prepare your data for access under WAIS.

Compiling FreeWAIS

The first step in the process is to locate and compile the freeWAIS source distribution. You can get it by anonymous FTP from ftp.cnidr.org, sunsite.unc.edu, wais.com, or many other sites. When retrieving the free-WAIS distribution, be sure to use the binary option under FTP.

After the FTP session, you will have a file called freeWAIS-x.x.tar.Z. (The x.x will be replaced with the current version number.) This is a compressed tar file. You must uncompress this file and use the tar program to extract the programs.

```
uncompress freeWAIS-x.x.tar.Z
tar -xvf freeWAIS-x.x.tar
```

These procedures will create a directory called freeWAIS-x.x and populate it with the freeWAIS source code.

Move (cd) into that directory and edit the Makefile. You will have to set the TOP variable to the full pathname of the current directory. For instance, a starting path for a user named Fullton might be:

```
/home/users/fullton/freeWAIS-0.2
```

You will see quite a few options in the Makefile. Almost all of these apply to the indexer. This Makefile fragment shows a possible configuration for a site. The meanings of the various options are discussed below.

```
RELEASE = freeWAIS-0.2

RM = /bin/rm -f
AR = ar

# on SGIs set this to true
RANLIB = ranlib
#RANLIB = true

# on IBM RS6000 this should be c89.
CC = gcc
#CC = gcc

# set this for your site. This syntax only works in SunOS
# for other UNIX-like OS's set this to this directory.
#TOP:sh = pwd
# or fill in the blank for other OS's
#TOP = ?
#comment-me:
#@echo You must set "\$$(TOP)" to point to the freeWAIS src directory
```

```
TOP = /home/users/fullton/freeWAIS-0.2
```

TOP points to the top-level of the freeWAIS distribution.

```
SUPDIR = $(TOP)/ir

# compiler specific stuff
#
# for old BSD add -DBSD
# for newer BSD that needs to use <sys/dir.h>, add -DBSD43
# for System V add -DSYSV
# for XENIX add -M3e -Zi
# USG for Unix Dirent in lib
# for SGIs running IRIX 4.0.1, add -cckr
#
```

For most machines, the default will work.

```
# For a little better security in the server, add -DSECURE_SERVER
# this sets the server user id to -u argument after startup.
# for relevance feedback in the search engine, add DRELEVANCE_FEEDBACK
#
#   dgg additions
# LITERAL == waisserver, search for "literal strings"
# BOOLEANS == waisserver, search with boolean AND, NOT operators
# PARTIALWORD == waisserver, search for partial words, hum* matches human,
hummingbird, …
# BIO == waisindex, waisserver changes including symbol indexing & search & bio
data formats
#
# -DUSE_SYSLOG if you want logging to be done with syslog rather than
# fprintf
#
# -DNEED_VSYSLOG if your C library does not have a vsyslog () function
#   in it (and you defined USE_SYSLOG)
#
# -DDUMPCORE will force the waisserver to dump the core when aborting
#   otherwise the core will not be dumped
#
# -DEND_MERGE if you want to merge the index files at the end of an
#  index process otherwise they are merged as we go along
```

This can save a lot of temporary disk space.

```
#
# -DSTEM_WORDS to stem words during indexing and queries
#
```

```
# Note - the default Porter Stemmer removes trailing e's from words -
# variable becomes variabl - this can impact the use of literals in
#searches!!!!!!!!!!!
```

Do be careful using the stemmer. The use of a stemmer can improve the quality of your search, as well as decrease the size of your index, but it will adversely impact literal searches.

```
#
# -DLIST_STEMS to show stemmed words in server log and indexer output
#
# -DSTELAR enables NASA STELAR additions - of interest only to NASA.
#

CFLAGS = -g -I$(SUPDIR) -DSECURE_SERVER -DRELEVANCE_FEEDBACK -DUSG -DBOOLEANS
-DPARTIALWORD -DLITERAL -DSTELAR
MFLAGS = -k

MAKE = make $(MFLAGS)
```

Then, type `make` and it should compile in a few minutes.

WAIS SERVER INSTALLATION

There are several different ways to install the WAIS server. While you can always remove the WAIS server from the system, running it under `inetd` is the best method for a permanent installation, as it requires a bit less maintenance. There is a performance tradeoff between running in `inetd` versus stand-alone: when a new connection is accepted through `inetd`, a new copy of the `waisserver` program must be loaded into memory and executed, which can take a small amount of time as the disk is accessed. When the server is running as a stand-alone process it merely duplicates itself in memory for each connection.

If you don't have root access, and can't get it, you must run the WAIS server as a process under your account. You must also choose a port that it can operate on. The normal port for WAIS is 210, but that port can only be used by a process executed by root. You must choose a port number greater than 1024. Try something like 5000 or 8000. You must then determine where the data directory resides. This is easy if you created the information bases yourself—it's wherever you put the data. Then, decide where you want the server logs to go. Logs can become quite large, so be sure you have plenty of disk space. You must also make sure that you have permission to write files in that area.

Now you must start the server. Assuming you have already compiled everything, you will find the server in the `bin` directory in the freeWAIS distribution.

It's called `waisserver`. Now you need the port and directory information we discussed above. Start the `waisserver` like this:

```
bin/waisserver -d (path for the data) -p (port number) -e
(logfile) &
```

The `waisserver` will now answer queries!

Installing the `waisserver` to run under `inetd` is equally easy. You must edit `/etc/services` and `/etc/inetd.conf`. Add this line to `/etc/services`:

```
z3950       210/tcp        wais
```

and add this line to `/etc/inetd.conf`:

```
z3950 stream tcp nowait   (path to bin)/waisserver waisserver.d -d
        (path for the data) -p (port number) -e (logfile)
```

Some systems may require you to enter the account name in this line. It's safe to use another line in `inetd.conf` as an example—just be sure to maintain the `stream tcp nowait` parts. Remember—you must log in as root to edit the above files!

Now, restart `inetd`, and the `waisserver` will automatically answer queries on port 210.

There are several other options that may be used in conjunction with the `waisserver` command:

```
Usage: ./waisserver [-p [port_number]] [-s] [-d directory] [-u user] [-v]
-p [port] listen to the port. If the port is supplied, then
    that tcp_port number is used. If it is not supplied
    then the Z39.50 port (210) is used.
-d directory: means to use the directory as the source of databases.
    Defaults to the current directory.
-e [file]: set log output to file, or /dev/null if not specified.
-l log_level: set log level. 0 means log nothing,
    10 [the default] means log everything.
-s means listen to standard I/O for queries. This is the default
-u user: if started as root, setuid to user after startup.
-v prints the version.
```

Using the WAIS Indexer

The indexer has many options, some of which are quite confusing. The following listing of options should explain things bit.

```
Usage: ./waisindex [-d index_filename]
        [-a] /*adding to an existing index, otherwise it erases
the index */
```

If you have already indexed a large collection of information and just want to add additional documents to it, use the -a option. It's frequently easier to just reindex the entire database, but this can be useful when you want to add a set of data with a different type to a currently existing database. (*Note:* if you are trying to index something dynamic, like network news, the -a option can be less useful than you might think. This option does nothing to preserve the actual documents, so if the documents disappear the server will simply point the user to nonexistent data.)

```
[-r] /* recursively index subdirectories */
```

The -r option allows you to index all of the files in a subdirectory, or hierarchy of subdirectories, rather than requiring each filename to be entered on the command line. For example, if you have 25,000 files in a directory, use the -r option and provide the directory name on the command line. The contents of the directory will be indexed.

```
[-mem mbytes] /* number of megabytes to run this in */
```

The indexer runs faster if you have a lot of memory. If you don't have a lot of memory and specify too large a number for the indexer, it will run very slowly. For a dedicated system, it's probably all right to specify at least half of the available memory.

```
[-register] /* registers the database with the directory of
    servers.                        This should be done with care. */
```

WAIS makes use of a "directory of servers" to allow users to find interesting databases to search. Using the -register option allows you to enter a description of your database and have a descriptive data structure (called a .src file) e-mailed automatically to the directories of servers at Thinking Machines and CNIDR.

```
[-export] /* uses short dbname and port 210 */
```

The -export option causes the full name of your machine and the port number to be entered into the .src file. Be sure to use this when you use the -register option.

```
[-e [file]] /* set log output to file, or /dev/null if not specified */
```

The WAIS indexer generates a lot of descriptive output, such as log messages. The -e option lets you tell the server where to write that information. If you specify -e without a file, the output is discarded. If you don't specify the -e flag, the output goes to standard output (usually the screen).

```
[-1 log_level] /* set log level. 0 means log nothing,
                          10 [the default] means log everything */
```

How much information can you stand?

```
[-v] /* print the version of the software */
```

```
[-stdin] /* read file names from stdin */
```

Unix gurus sometimes like to pass file names to the indexer from other programs, or from files. This option permits that

```
[-pos | -nopos] /* include (don't include - default) word position
information /*
    [-nopairs | -pairs] /* don't include (include - default) word pairs */
```

These two rather arcane options enable the storage of word position information in the index. Some servers can use that information to improve the quality of the searches.

```
[-nocat] /* inhibit creation of catalog /*
```

By default, the indexer creates a "catalog" of documents in the index. This catalog can be retrieved and viewed by users, particularly if a search returns no hits. It's useful to turn this off if you have many documents in your database, as the resulting catalog can be quite large.

```
[-contents] /* Index the contents: this is good for types that
                    inhibit the indexing of the contents (like gif). /*
[-nocontents] /* Index only the filename, not the contents /*
```

"Contents" flags allow the user to override the default indexing characteristics of the indexer type. It's not useful to index the information within a GIF file, so by default only the name of the file is indexed. If for some reason you wished to index the contents of a GIF file, you could override the default behavior of the GIF indexing type by using the -contents flag.

```
[-keywords "<string>"] /* Keywords to index for each document. */
[-keyword_file <filename>] /* File of keywords to index. */
```

The -keywords and -keywords_file options allow the user to specify a list or file of words to index into each document, regardless of whether they already occur in the document. For example, if I am indexing a collection of documents on cheese-making and wish the word "cyclotron" to result in a hit for each one, I can use the `-keywords "cyclotron"` option to ensure that. This can be useful in conjunction with the `-a` option to selectively add keywords to particular documents without modifying the document itself.

```
[-T type] /* type becomes the "TYPE" of the document. */
```

"Typing" is one of the more complex WAIS issues. Each document has one or more "types" associated with it. Let's say you have a document in TEXT format. When the client retrieves it, the client needs to know to use a TEXT viewer to display it to the user. If the data happens to be a GIF file, the client needs to know to use a GIF viewer for presentation. Each indexing format (below) associates a particular type with each data object, depending on the object. The `-T` option allows the user to override that predefined type.

```
[-M type,type] /* for multi-type documents. */
```

It is possible to have more than one document associated with a headline. Let's say you have a document in both TEXT and PostScript. You want the user to be able to retrieve either. Using the `-M` option allows you to do this. There are several important details, though. The data file must have an extension that is the typename in capital letters. Consider the documents `outline.TEXT` and `outline.PS`. `outline.TEXT` is plain text, while `outline.PS` is the same thing in PostScript. The option `-M  TEXT,PS` will cause the `outline.TEXT` file to be indexed, and the user will be given a choice of TEXT or PS for the formats when a retrieval is requested.

The remaining options define the data format to the indexer. Basically, the indexer needs to be able to extract a headline from each document, and know the start and end of the document. It's possible to have more than one "document" in a single file.

The most commonly used type is probably `"first_line"`. This type tells the indexer that the first line of a file is the headline, and the rest is text. It's possible to add new types, but you need to be a programmer to do it.

```
[-t   /* format of the file. if none then each file is a document */
         text /* simple text files, this is the default */
      | bibtex /* BibTeX / LaTeX format */
      | bio /* biology abstract format */
      | cmapp /* CM applications from Hypercard */
      | dash /* entries separated by a row of dashes */
      | dvi /* dvi format */         | emacsinfo /* the GNU documentation system
*/
      | first_line /* first line of file is headline */
      | filename /* uses the filename part of the path for the title */
```

```
| ftp /* special type for FTP files. First line of file is headline */
| gif /* gif files, only indexes the filename */
| irg /* internet resource guide */
| jargon /* Jargon File 2.9.8 format*/
| mail_digest /* standard internet mail digest format */
| mail_or_rmail /* mail or rmail or both */
| medline /* medline format */
| mh_bboard /* MH bulletin board format */
| netnews /* netnews format */
| nhyp /* ?:? hyper text format, Polytechnic of Central London */
| one_line /* each line is a document */
| para /* paragraphs separated by blank lines */
| pict /* pict files, only indexes the filename */
| ps /* postscript format */
| refer /* refer format */
| rn /* netnews saved by the [rt]?rn newsreader */
| server /* server structures for the dir of servers */
| tiff /* tiff files, only indexes the filename */
| URL what-to-trim what-to-add /* URL */
| AAS_abstract /* AAS abstracts using AAS LaTeX macros */
| listserv_digest /* standard internet mail digest format */
| stelar /* stelar abstracts - third line is h1 */
  ] filename filename ...
```

Once you have completed these steps, your WAIS server is ready for production. Installing a WAIS server is actually a fairly simple task; don't be discouraged by the abundance of options that are presented by the indexer—it's a sign of the flexibility of the WAIS system for information publishing on the Internet.

INSTALLING A WORLD-WIDE WEB (HTTP) SERVER

There are two basic aspects to serving a set of documents over the Internet: preparing the documents in the proper format, and setting up the server. In the case of the World-Wide Web, basic document preparation requires somewhat more work than is the case with Gopher. In many cases, a Web server has less work to do than a Gopher server, and actual installation of the server is relatively straightforward. On the other hand, preparing HTML documents entails somewhat more work than placing files on a Gopher server may involve. See the discussion of HTML document preparation in Chap. 20.

As we gave seen, the Gn server is an excellent way to serve both Gopher and Web clients. Gn also offers some of the advanced functionality of Web-only servers; however, if you want to be able to handle the most elaborate applications, you may need a more powerful server. The NCSA httpd server is a good choice because its developers, co-located with the developers of Mosaic, have been able to engineer enhancements on server and client side at the same time.

httpd is a well-written package, and installation of the package is generally "clean" on a variety of platforms. NCSA offers the source code for httpd, and it also offers executable binary versions of the package for several popular platforms. Although many Unix system administrators prefer to build packages from source code where possible, the binary alternative is attractive because it requires less initial effort.

You can obtain excellent online documentation for the httpd server—via the Web, of course. Figure 21.5 depicts the top-level page that begins that documentation. You can retrieve the installation package from NCSA via FTP to ftp.ncsa.uiuc.edu (look under /Mosaic/ncsa_httpd). Besides the server packages themselves, you will find a single large tar file with a package of httpd documents; these files are basically a bundling of the documents online at NCSA in HTML form, and you will probably find it more convenient simply to read them using Mosaic over the Internet, printing parts as appropriate.*

The main httpd documentation page shown in Fig. 21.5 points to installation instructions for the server. The URL for that document is:

```
http://hoohoo.ncsa.uiuc.edu/docs/setup/Install.html
```

This document offers specific advice on the phases of bringing httpd online. Each of the main bulleted items shown is a link into extensive online documentation for the steps required to build a server and place it in operation. You will want to consult this online documentation for complete information and for any recent updates. Here is a summary of the major steps involved in bringing up httpd:

Downloading the HTTP server.   If you choose to download a binary version of the program—i.e., the program in executable form, already compiled—NCSA's online text provides pointers. If NCSA does not offer an executable binary for your computer (or operating system level), or if you prefer to work from source code, this section provides guidance on how to build the system. If you have ever installed a source package on a Unix system, such as the Gn example above, the process is quite similar. In the case of httpd, you need to observe the installation note and set a BSD configuration flag as appropriate for your system before building the executable.

You will need to pick or create a subdirectory that will serve as home for the httpd server, and download the server package into that directory using either anonymous FTP or a client like Mosaic to fetch it over the Web. Let's assume your home will be:

```
/usr/local/etc/
```

---

* You might prefer to have a single installation document suitable for placing in a three-ring binder for offline sequential reading. Some server developers feel, however, that online documents are easier to maintain, especially for a rapidly changing public domain package like HTTPD.

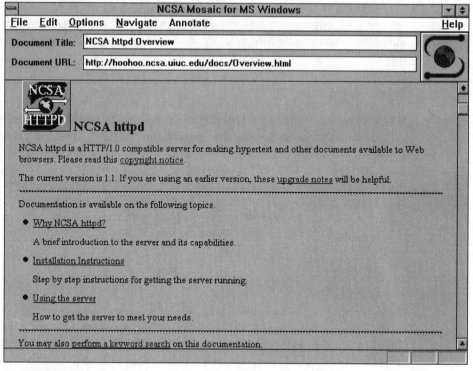

Figure 21.5

When installation is finished you will have installed the following into this directory:

Subdirectory or name	Purpose
httpd	A home for the httpd executable binary.
conf/	The configuration files for the server.
logs/	A home for the log files produced by the server during normal operations.
support/	A home for various support programs used with httpd.
cgi-bin/	A home for the executable scripts to be used with the Common Gateway Interface (CGI), the mechanism that provides a framework for advanced functions such as locator maps.

Once you have the file in the target directory, use the tar command to break out the components of the distribution file, e.g.,

```
tar xf ncsa_httpd1.1.tar
```

Configuring the HTTP server. To configure the NCSA `httpd`, you will edit a series of configuration files. The software distribution package includes initial versions of these files, which you can use as a template. First you must configure the server itself, providing basic information such as the mode of operation and the TCP port number you want to use.

Configuration option	Meaning
ServerType	Whether the server runs under `inetd` or stand-alone.
Port	The TCP Port number. (Use 80 for the standard port, which requires running under `inetd`, or running `httpd` from the root user if stand-alone.)
User	Specifies the user name for daughter processes if the server is running stand-alone mode.
Group	Specifies the group ID used if server runs stand-alone.
ServerAdmin	Defines the e-mail address of the server administrator (you!).
ServerRoot	Specifies the location of `httpd`—the place in the directory hierarchy where the server executable will reside. The default is `/usr/local/etc/httpd`.
ServerName	Specifies the domain-style host name of the host the server is running on—e.g., `www.msu.edu`. This is needed for some specific situations on some systems.
TimeOut	How long the server should wait for a client to start a query or accept information; specified in seconds, with a default or 1200.
ErrorLog	Where `httpd` should log errors. Default: `logs/error_log` (underneath the directory specified by `ServerRoot`).
TransferLog	Where `httpd` should log errors. Default: `logs/access_log`.
PidFile	For stand-alone servers, specifies where the daemon process ID (pid) is to be logged. Default `logs/httpd.pid`.
AccessConfig	Tells where your access configuration file is. Default: `conf/access.conf`.
ResourceConfig	Tells where your resource configuration file is. Default: `conf/srm.conf`.
TypesConfig	Tells where your types configuration file is. This file defines for `httpd` the associations between file extensions and MIME content types. Default: `conf/types.conf`.
IndentityCheck	Whether to log remote user names in `access_log`. Defaults to "off."

Configuring resources (documents and executable scripts). Once you have defined the server's basic configuration, you need to configure the way documents and scripts are handled. Once again, you can use a template file included in the server distribution as a starting point. Your resource configuration file will be called `srm.conf` by default.

Configuration option	Meaning
DocumentRoot	The subdirectory where the server will find the documents you wish to serve.
UserDir	`httpd` supports "user directories"—a way to ease publishing of documents by individuals who have permission to place files on the host running the `httpd` server. This option tells where `httpd` should look for files, relative to each user's home directory.

Configuration option	Meaning
DirectoryIndex	The name of a file that will serve as the index for documents in your server's document hierarchy. The default is index.html. (If index.html does not appear in a given directory, httpd will generate an index based on the files that are present if a client calls for the Uniform Resource Locator of that directory.)
AccessFileName	The name of the access control file that will be found in each directory of the document hierarchy. Default: .htaccess.
AddType	Defines association between file extensions and MIME-style content types, overriding information in the TypeConfig file.
AddEncoding	Defines encoding scheme for types added via AddType.
DefaultType	The file type httpd should assume if no explicit association based on file extension applies. The default is text/html.
Redirect	A way to allow your server to point users to another URL (possibly on another host) for a given document. You can have as many Redirect statements as you wish in the configuration file.
Alias	A way to tell httpd to look for a document or directory in another place on your server.
ScriptAlias	Tells httpd to look for scripts in a different location on your server. Works with CGI scripts (the newer, preferred scheme).
OldScriptAlias	Tells httpd to look for scripts in a different location on your server. Works with old-style server scripts (not the preferred scheme).
FancyIndexing	If set to on, tells httpd to include icons and file sizes when serving a directory index to a client. Default is off.
DefaultIcon	Specifies an icon to serve for a given document type.
ReadmeName	The name of a "read me" file you might place in each subdirectory of your document hierachy, with a general description of the directory.
AddDescription	Specifies a textual description to be automatically generated for a given file or file extentionsion; this description is included when httpd generates an index.
AddIcon	Specifies an icon httpd should supply for a given file type.
IndexIgnore	Specifies files (as partial file names) to be ignored when HTTP generates an index.

Note: Many of these configuration options exist to help manage situations where users point their clients at a given directory in your document tree, instead of fetching documents explicitly pointed to by other documents you prepare. When this happens, httpd builds an index of the directory for you, and serves that index to the client. In most cases you will want to prepare HTML documents that serve as complete menus for your document hierarchy, and you will not need to concern yourself with supporting undirected probes into your server. You will want to be sure to provide an index.html file for the root of your document hierarchy.

You will want to consider whether to exploit the following features initially or later in your use of this server.

- *Access Control.* NCSA httpd provides several options for controlling access to particular document subdirectories. You can specify Host Filtering, which limits access to documents based on the caller's Internet domain, or you can use User Authentication features of Mosaic to perform user name/password authentication before a document will be delivered. These features provide you with powerful control over access to your documents. When initially installing your server, you probably want to make documents generally available. When you want to limit documents, see the Access Control section of the online NCSA documents.

- *Selecting scripts.* Choosing executable scripts that perform commonly desired functions (such as scripts to tell the date and time), to interface to a CSO server via forms, to set up locator maps, etc., `httpd` comes with a suite of such scripts intended to be used as examples or templates for building your own scripts. You need not install any of these scripts in order to start using `httpd` to serve documents on the Web.

Moving into place. At this stage you move the `httpd` executable binary file, the configuration files, the log files, the script files, and the support program files to the subdirectories you have chosen for these respective parts. You need to ensure that the user under which `httpd` runs has permission to write into the subdirectory that holds the log files.

Starting the server. Now you are ready to set up your server to start automatically when the host computer is started. The appropriate steps depend on whether the server will run stand-alone or not.

- If the server will be controlled by `inetd`, you need to edit `/etc/services` to include a statement for the `httpd` process. For example,

```
http 80/tcp
```

This example shows use of TCP port 80, the standard HTTP port.
Define the server as an inetd process with the following statement:

```
httpd stream  tcp nowait  nobody  /usr/local/etc/httpd/httpd  httpd
```

You can restart the `inetd` process in the current session using the steps shown for installing a Gn server. In the future, when the server hardware is rebooted, `httpd` will start automatically.

- If the server will run stand-alone, you need to invoke the server program as a command. To do so, simply type `httpd` (or `/usr/local/etc/httpd/httpd` if you are currently in another directory).*

If you are running the server stand-alone, and you want to use a TCP port of 1024 or less, you will need to run with root permission. *This is generally*

---

* Note that the `httpd` command accepts command-line options to override the defaults for the ServerRoot and the Server Configuration file. These options allow you to move between different configurations for testing of new setups. See the online documentation for details.

not advisable for security reasons; consider running under `inetd` *if you are using a privileged port (such as the default of port 80).* If you run the server under root privileges you may want to configure your system to start the `httpd` process automatically upon system startup; see your operating system manual for details.

After all of these steps are complete, it is time for you to try your skills at creating HTML documents. You start by building a "home page"—the page that is delivered to clients if they send a request to your host without specifying a path in the Uniform Resource Locator. For instance, assume your server's domain-style host name is `www.nadir.com`, and a user performs an "Open URL" function with the following:

```
http://www.nadir.com/
```

This translates into a request for the index file for the root menu of your service. Assuming you left the `DirectoryIndex` configuration option with its default value, your server will look in the document directory, whose location was specified by the `DocumentRoot` option for a file called `index.html`. Therefore, in the default case you need to create a file called `index.html` and place it in `/usr/webdata` or whatever location `DocumentRoot` specifies.

The explicit address for your home page would be:

```
http://www.nadir.com/index.html
```

If your server's port number differs from the default of 80, you will need to tell users to specify a URL with the appropriate number. For instance, if you chose port 1234:

```
http://www.nadir.com:1234/index.html
```

By default your server will look for files as defined by Alias and ScriptAlias, and UserDir options. For initial document preparation you need not exploit these features; read the online documentation for more information on how to do so later.

Within the `index.html` document, you can embed references to other documents that reside on your local document hierarchy, or that reside elsewhere on the Web. For instance, if you add a subdirectory called `trees` with a description of a number of types of trees, you might refer your users to a file called

```
http://www.nadir.com/trees/elm.html
```

Of course, any reference to a document on your server demands that you create that document in the appropriate spot in your `DocumentRoot` hierarchy. Otherwise, your users will be informed that the referenced file does not exist when they try to select it.

Not all of your files will be HTML documents. For instance, if you provide in-line images, they will reside as separate files (typically in GIF or XBM format) with appropriate file extensions. Normally your users will see these files only by fetching an HTML document you have prepared that references them.

ADVANCED WEB SERVICES

NCSA and collaborators from the Web community have pioneered several advanced applications operating under httpd and Mosaic. These advanced applications are now based on the Common Gateway Interface (CGI), which specifies the rules for interaction between your Web server and an external program or script you prepare to meet a specific need. Other servers, such as Gn, offer similar functionality in similar ways. CGI is explained in the following document:

```
http://www.ncsa.uiuc.edu/cgi/intro.html
```

Examples of advanced applications include:

Control over the delivery of documents based. You can control document access based on password protection or the user's IP address. For online documentation, see documents beginning at

```
http://hoohoo.ncsa.uiuc.edu/docs/info/Security.html
```

Fill-in form support. Under this application a user is presented with a form with fill-in blanks; the user's input is fed to an executable script you specify. See:

```
http://www.ncsa.uiuc.edu/SDG/Software/Mosaic/Docs/fill-out-forms/
    overview.html
```

There are two ways in which forms are handled between Mosaic and httpd: Method=Get and Method=Post. The Get method causes Mosaic to append the information the user types at the end of the URL it sends to the server. The Post method causes Mosaic to send the information as a separate data block; your CGI program will receive the form input on the standard input stream, with the environment variable CONTENT_LENGTH set to the number of bytes of data. The Post method is the newer scheme and it is preferred.

Imagemap support. This application allows information providers to determine which spot on the user's screen has been selected with a mouse click, so that a server script can respond appropriately. There are two ways in which this feature is invoked:

Sample HTML for a Fill-In Form

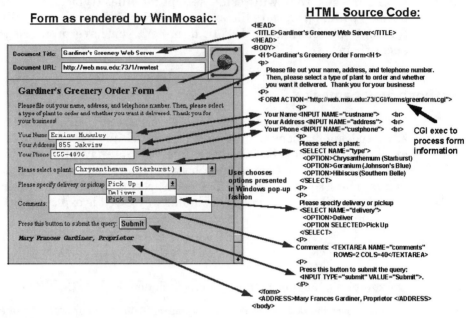

Figure 21.6

- *As a graphical menu option mechanism.* For example, the Web-based reference shelf prepared by Novell and shown in Chap. 18 uses this scheme. When a user clicks on an area that corresponds to a book, the coordinates of the click are returned to the server, and a special `imagemap` script determines the correspondence of the coordinates to a particular polygon. This tells the server script which Web page to deliver next—the one corresponding to the book the user selected.

- *As a way to interact with a script that understands what to do with coordinate information.* For instance, if you have an application that understands three-dimensional objects and will rotate them based on the user's choice of perspective, you could feed the coordinates from a user's click to that application, and you could send the results back to the user in the form of a graphical image drawn from the new perspective.

An NCSA tutorial on interactive map applications appears at:

```
http://wintermute.ncsa.uiuc.edu:8080/map-tutorial/image-maps.html
```

Note that these advanced features are not exclusively implemented in NCSA `httpd`; you may be able to exploit them in other servers. For instance, Gn is capable of supporting forms and maps scripts.* For a demonstration of how Gn handles these advanced features, see:

```
http://hopf.math.nwu.edu:70/1/docs/examples
```

Figure 21.6 is an example of the source code for a fill-in form served by Gn, showing how the elements of the form correspond to the screen as rendered by Mosaic.

---

* Note, however, that Gn's scheme for handling CGI scripts is slightly different than that of NCSA HTTPD, so scripts will require changes if moved from one server to the other. See the respective online documentation for the Common Gateway Interface and scripts.

Establishing Internet Information Services: Non-Unix Examples

This chapter continues our examples of managing Internet information servers, with examples of setting up services on non-Unix platforms. Examples include:

- Installing the GopherSurfer application for the Macintosh—a server that requires minimal installation effort—virtually a "plug and play" server application.

- Installing a Gopher server for OS/2.

- Installing the KA9Q Gopher server—a tool that allows the MS-DOS user to deliver documents via Gopher.

SETTING UP A GOPHER SERVICE: THE GOPHERSURFER SERVER

In the realm of Unix server tools, the Gn Gopher server is relatively easy to install and maintain. If you seek a server that is even easier to install, consider the Macintosh server from the University of Minnesota. Known as Gopher-Surfer, this package is designed for the Macintosh environment running the standard Mac operating system (System 7 or later).

The GopherSurfer distribution package resides with other Gopher server packages available for FTP from `boombox.micro.umn.edu`. You will need to have a Macintosh that has been assigned a permanent IP address and is running the Mac TCP implementation of TCP/IP.

Before running the GopherSurfer package, you will need to enable the Macintosh Thread Manager. To do this you simply drag the Thread Manager to the System folder.

Setup and file administration under the Gopher server are accomplished entirely through configuration dialog boxes. There is no need to edit or create any external files. The documentation that comes with GopherSurfer is extremely readable and the required installation steps are easy to follow. GopherSurfer is endowed with the Gopher+ enhancements that allow serving of a wide variety of file types in addition to supporting interactive features such as forms input.

Figure 22.1 is an example of the configuration menu for GopherSurfer.

The screen in Figure 22.2 shows GopherSurfer makes it easy for the information provider to specify an information source for the server to offer to Gopher users.

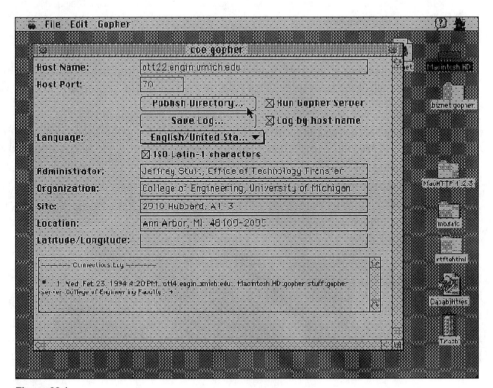

Figure 22.1

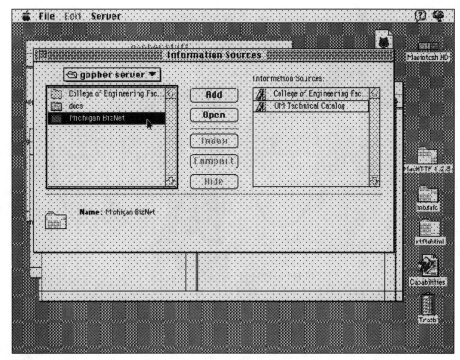

Figure 22.2

GopherSurfer works hand-in-glove with Apple's commercial indexing tool, AppleSearch (see Fig. 22.3). AppleSearch requires a 68040-based Macintosh.* The GopherSurfer application can run on the same computer as the Apple-Search package, or GopherSurfer can reside on a different machine, communicating with the AppleSearch server over an AppleTalk network. From the point of view of Gopher clients, the AppleSearch-resident databases will appear as search items.

GopherSurfer provides an option in its Gopher menu that allows you to log onto the AppleSearch database, whether local or remote (see Fig. 22.4).

SETTING UP A GOPHER
SERVER UNDER OS/2

The OS/2 Gopher Server, GoServe, was developed by Mike Cowlishaw† at the IBM United Kingdom Laboratories, in Hursley, England. It runs under OS/2

---

* AppleSearch has been announced for the PowerPC as well.

† This section of text was written by David Singer of IBM's Almaden Research Laboratory. The author of GoServe, Mike Cowlishaw, is best known as the inventor of a popular computer language, Rexx. Rexx is an interpreted language somewhat analogous to Perl. Utilities written for a GoServe service are normally written in Rexx—as is GoServe itself.

Gopher Surfer / AppleSearch Server Options

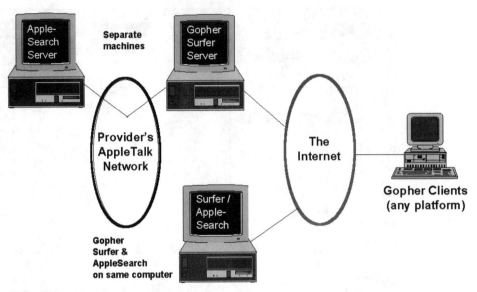

Figure 22.3

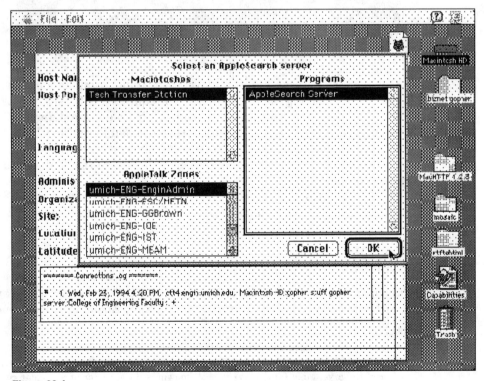

Figure 22.4

Version 2.x and requires the IBM TCP/IP for OS/2 product, version 1.2.1 or later. If you are using version 1.2.1 of TCP/IP, you must apply at least the April, 1993 CSD (Corrective Service Diskette, which is IBMese for "fix").

Unlike the Unix Gopher servers, you do not need to compile GoServe; you do, however, need to write (or modify) a Rexx program which gives your server its personality. This program is called the "filter"; a sample filter is provided with the GoServe package, but you will probably want to change it to suit your environment better.

Planning for GoServe

The GoServe code itself and your "filter" must reside in the same directory; for the purpose of this example, we'll assume that you will put them in D:\GOSERVE. The data which you want to serve out can be anywhere on your system (including directories you mount from servers via NFS, LAN Requestor, or any other network operating system); it is easiest if all the data resides in a single directory and its subdirectories, but this is not required. For this example, we'll start by putting all the data into the F:\PUBLIC directory and some subdirectories.

You must also choose which port you wish to use for your server. The standard port for Gopher is port 70; you may use any port, but you are limited to ports numbered 999 or less unless your GoServe directory is on a drive formatted for the High Performance File System (HPFS), which allows for names which don't fit the DOS "8.3" pattern. In this example, we'll use port 70.

Obtaining the Code

You can obtain the server via FTP from `software.watson.ibm.com` in `/pub/os2/ews/goserv.zip`, or via Gopher from `index.almaden.ibm.com` in the "OS/2 Gopher" menu. Updates to the server will usually be available first on `index.almaden.ibm.com`.

You can obtain CSDs to TCP/IP from software.watson.ibm.com, in the `/pub/tcpip/os2` directory; look for files of the form `tcpipcsd.package`.

Unpacking GoServe

Once you have obtained the code, use PKUNZIP (or any compatible program) to unpack it. Goserv.zip will expand into six files:

`goserve.exe`	the actual executable program
`gofilter.70s`	the sample filter
`goserve.doc`	documentation for the program
`gosmenu.cmd`	a tool to help create menu files
`goserve.abs`	a brief description of the program
`license.txt`	terms and conditions for using the program

Adapting the Filter

The first thing to do is to adapt the filter to your environment. At the very least, this requires editing the filter to point to the root of your data tree (F:\PUBLIC in our case), and changing the name so that the extension matches the port number you'll be using (70).

Here's the sample GoFilter.70S file provided with the package:

```
/* Sample minimal GoServe filter program */

parse arg source, selector, selector2                    /* Get arguments */
parse var source server port transaction who .           /* Often useful */

say who':' selector                              /* [show filter running] */

drive='d:'                                                 /* Data drive */
dir=drive'\godata'port'\' /* Data root directory (e.g. "d:\godata70\") */

/* This very simple filter just builds the full path name of a file from */
/* the selector and returns that. Note we do not put the full path in    */
/* menus, as this could allow clients to access all files on the server  */
/* machine, which is rarely desirable.                                   */

if selector='' then selector='mainmenu.'port          /* 'startup' case */
return 'File name' dir''selector
--------------------------------------------------------------------------

To make it work in our sample environment, we have to change the two
assignment statements (fifth and sixth non-blank lines) to point to our
data directory, like this:

--------------------------------------------------------------------------
drive='F:'                                                 /* Data drive */
dir=drive'\public\'          /* Data root directory (we use "F:\public\") */
```

We have to save the file as `"GoFilter.70"` in the D:\GOSERVE directory.

Building a GoServe Menu File

We also need to create an initial menu file, f:\public\mainmenu.70; this file is served when a client sends a null line, asking for this server's root menu. There are many ways of creating this file; the easiest is probably to use the "gosmenu" command supplied with GoServe. Use your favorite editor to create a file named f:\public\main.men, as follows.

The first line of this file is a required comment:

```
; your.host.name 70
```

Change "`your.host.name`" to your host name in the previous line.

Any line which does not begin with a blank in column 1 becomes a line in the menu. The first character is the Gopher type (for example, "0" for plain text file). The rest of the line is the actual Gopher menu line, except that the semi-colon is used as a tab, and the hostname and port are filled in based on the specifications in the first line of the file.

```
0 Input file to GOSMENU, used to create this menu.;main.men
0 Actual main menu file, as a text file.;mainmenu.70
1 Recursive pointer to this menu;mainmenu.70
1 University of Minnesota root Gopher server;;gopher.micro.umn.edu;70
```

Add more lines to this file to make more files visible on the menu. For example, if you have an "About this Gopher Server" file named `F:\PUBLIC\ABOUT.ME`, you'd add this line to the file:

```
0 About this Gopher Server;about.me
```

Then run `gosmenu` to create the actual menu file, `f:\public\mainmenu.70`, like this:

```
d:\goserve\gosmenu F:\public\main.men F:\public\mainmenu.70
```

Starting the Server

To start the server, all you have to do is open an OS/2 window, change your current directory to the `D:\GOSERVE` directory, and issue the `GOSERVE` command.

If something is wrong, the server will display a message box explaining the problem; when you press the "OK" button, the server will terminate. Otherwise, the server will display a window showing its current status. You can control the server using the menu bar on this window.

If you want more information than the server displays in the window, you will need to run another program, `PMPRINTF` (also written by Mike Cowlishaw, and also available through the IBM Employee-Written Software program). You can get `PMPRINTF` via Gopher from `index.almaden.ibm.com` on the "OS/2 Gopher Client and Server" menu (look for `PMPRTF`), or via FTP from `software.watson.ibm.com`, in `/pub/os2/ews/pmprtf.zip`. Obtain the file, use `PKUNZIP` (or a compatible program) to unpack it, and issue "`START PMPRINTF`". This will bring up a scrolling window into which the Gopher server will write progress reports and error messages.

You can specify the "DIAG" option when you start GoServe to get more information written to the PMPRINTF window.

More about the Filter

It is the filter's job to take the selector string sent by a client and return a string which GoServe itself uses to decide exactly what to send back in response to this request. The filter is passed three pieces of information:

- The "source," which is a four-token string, containing:

  This system's IP address

  A sequential transaction number

  The port number of this Gopher server

  The client's IP address

- The "selector," which is the string passed by the client up but not including a tab

- The "extra," which is any data sent by the client after the first tab (this is used for searches and as part of the Gopher+ protocol)

The filter returns a string, which consists of a prefix, optional modifiers, and a value. The prefix can be:

- STRING. In this case the string is returned to the client. The string may include CR-LF (carriage return/line feed) pairs; GoServe appends a final CR-LF.

- FILE [modifiers] NAME. In this case the value is the name of the file to be returned to the client. The possible modifiers are:

  BINARY tells GoServe to send the file back exactly as it appears on disk. If BINARY is not specified, GoServe will strip a trailing Ctrl-Z, and will append .<CR><LF> to BINARY for a binary file.

  ERASE tells GoServe to erase the file if it is successfully transmitted.

- CONTROL. See the documentation for the possible values.

Advanced Features of GoServe

So far, we have a working OS/2 Gopher server up and running; it serves to calling clients any information in the F:\PUBLIC directory and its subdirectories, though only those items in the menu file are easily found by a client.

There are several things that you might want to do to enhance the server, either to provide greater security or to add function. We'll accomplish our goals by modifying the filter program; no changes are required to GoServe itself. We'll look at three:

- Generating information dynamically
- Remote control of GoServe
- Restricting client access to those files explicitly mentioned in menus

It is easy to allow the filter to dynamically build information to return to a client; that information can either be generated entirely by the filter, or the filter can call another program (which can be written in languages other than Rexx) which can write a file whose contents will eventually be returned to the client.

We'll change the simple filter above to recognize two special selectors:

!now   returns the current time

!dir   returns a directory listing of the current directory

This filter also uses the filename to decide whether a file should be served as binary or not; files with extensions of .TXT and .DOC are considered nonbinary, while all other files are considered binary.

The changes are at the bottom of the listing:

```
/* Sample GoServe filter program */

parse arg source, selector, selector2              /* Get arguments */
parse var source server port transaction who .        /* Often useful */
say who':' selector                          /* [show filter running] */

drive='F:'                                          /* Data drive */
dir=drive'\public\'        /* Data root directory (we use "F:\public\") */

/* This very simple filter just builds the full path name of a file from */
/* the selector and returns that. Note we do not put the full path in    */
/* menus, as this could allow clients to access all files on the server  */
/* machine, which is rarely desirable.                                   */

if selector='' then selector='mainmenu.'port          /* 'startup' case */
if selector='!now' then return 'STRING' 'It is' time() 'on' date()'.'
if selector='!dir' then
   do
   'DIR >' transaction'.DIR'
   return 'File ERASE name' transaction'.DIR'
   end

/* We must have a filename; use the extension to decide if it's binary.  */

nonbinary = '.DOC .TXT'
ext = translate(right(selector,4))
```

```
if pos(ext, nonbinary) = 0 then
  return 'FILE BINARY NAME' dir || selector
else
  return 'FILE NAME' dir || selector
```

Remote Control of GoServe

The filter can ask GoServe to perform certain tasks (such as archiving its audit file, or resetting its internal counters). You may not want to open up these functions to the entire Internet; this example shows how you can allow only users in your own local network to perform control functions. We'll allow anyone to send a request for statistics; we'll only allow users on the local network (defined, for the purpose of this example, as hosts whose IP addresses differ from this machine's only in the last octet) to request a directory listing.

```
/* Sample GoServe filter program with remote control */


parse arg source, selector, selector2                /* Get arguments */
parse var source server port transaction who .       /* Often useful */


say who':' selector                           /* [show filter running] */


drive='F:'                                          /* Data drive */
dir=drive'\public\'          /* Data root directory (we use "F:\public\") */

/* This very simple filter just builds the full path name of a file from */
/* the selector and returns that.  Note we do not put the full path in   */
/* menus, as this could allow clients to access all files on the server  */
/* machine, which is rarely desirable.                                   */

if selector='' then selector='mainmenu.'port       /* 'startup' case */
if selector='!now' then return 'STRING' 'It is' time() 'on' date()'.'
if selector='!stat' then return 'CONTROL STATISTICS'
if selector='!dir' then
  do
  /* Let's limit this to our local group */
  mynet = subword(translate(server,' ','.'),1,3)
  requestnet = subword(translate(who,' ','.'),1,3)
  if (mynet <> requestnet) then
    return 'STRING Sorry!'
  /* OK, the request is approved; do it. */
  'DIR >' transaction'.DIR'
  return 'File ERASE name' transaction'.DIR'
  end
```

```
/* We must have a filename; use the extension to decide if it's binary.  */

nonbinary = '.DOC .TXT'
ext = translate(right(selector,4))

if pos(ext, nonbinary) = 0 then
  return 'FILE BINARY NAME' dir || selector
else
  return 'FILE NAME' dir || selector
```

Restricting Clients Under GoServe

The simple filter shown above allows clients to access any files in the F:\PUB-LIC directory, or any of its subdirectories. In many cases, this is acceptable; however, you may prefer to limit clients to *only* those files which you explicitly choose to publish. To do this, you need to compare the selector string sent by the client to the contents of the menus you make available. To make this easier, we'll assume certain conventions apply:

- The selector string is the actual filename (relative to the F:\PUBLIC directory—so if the file is F:\PUBLIC\SECRET\STUFF, the selector will be SECRET\STUFF).

- Each directory has one and only one menu, and it is named MENU.portnumber (in our case, MENU.70).

This filter also uses the Gopher type in the menu to decide whether to serve a file as binary or not.

```
/* GoServe Filter with enhanced security */

parse arg source, selector, selector2              /* Get arguments */
parse var source server port transaction who .      /* Often useful */

selector = translate(selector)
say who':' selector                                /* [show filter running] */

drive='f:'                                                  /* Data drive */
dir=drive'\'public'\'                              /* Data root directory */

/* This filter ensures that the file being requested is in the menu of   */
/* the appropriate directory.  If not, an error string is returned.       */


/* Handle the simple case of a request for the root menu: */
if selector='' then
  return 'FILE NAME' dir || 'menu.'port
```

```
/* Convert backslashes into slashes for convenience: */
selector = translate(selector,'/','\')

/* Some clients send '/' as a root menu request. Be kind to them. */
if selector='/' then
  return 'FILE NAME' dir || 'menu.'port

/* This is a more complicated selector.  Parse out any directory
   specification, then check that directory's menu file to be sure
   the requested file is listed. */

tailpos = lastpos('/', selector) + 1
if tailpos=1 then
  do
  dirpart = ''
  tail = translate(selector)
  end
else
  parse upper var selector dirpart =(tailpos) tail

/* If the requested file is named MENU.70, we have to look in its
   parent directory, not this one. */
if tail='MENU.70' then
  do
  tailpos = lastpos('/', substr(dirpart,1,length(dirpart)-1)) + 1
  if tailpos=1 then
    dirpart = ''
  else
    parse upper var dirpart dirpart =(tailpos) .
  end

/* Ensure that the Rexx SysFileSearch routine is loaded: */
call RxFuncAdd 'SysFileSearch', 'RexxUtil', 'SysFileSearch'

/* And search the menu file to be sure that no one's pulling a fast one. */
call SysFileSearch tail, dir || dirpart || 'MENU.' || port, 'HITS.'
if rc<>0 then
  return 'STRING 3Sorry,' selector 'is not available.' || '09'x || ,
         '09'x || 'error.host' || '09'x || '70'

/* Now, make sure that the filename actually is in the filename, not in
   the description. */

ok = 0
do i = 1 to hits.0 until ok
  parse upper var hits.i type +1 . '09'x test '09'x .
  ok = (translate(test,'/','\') = selector)
```

```
      if ok then
        isbinary = (0 <> pos(type, '459'))      /* Binary types */
   end

   /* Now, if "ok" is true, we can serve out the file; if not, send out
      an error. */

   if ok then
     if binary then
       return 'FILE BINARY NAME' selector
     else
       return 'FILE NAME' selector
   else
     return 'STRING 3Sorry,' selector 'is not available.' || '09'x || ,
            '09'x || 'error.host' || '09'x || '70'
```

These examples show how you can use Rexx to implement specific functions as a GoServe administrator.

SETTING UP THE KA9Q GOPHER SERVER

KA9Q is a PC-based, multitasking network operating system that was originally written by Phil Karn* to supply Internet services to ham radio operators. Since then it has been modified and has had services added by many people.

The KA9Q Gopher server is an inexpensive,[†] powerful Gopher server platform that runs on a 286 or higher PC. It supports the following features:

- Multiple simultaneous connections

- Three different search engines to search text files or dbaseIII files

- Full support for the basic Gopher protocol (non Gopher+)

- Extensive log file that can be automatically mailed to the Gopher administrator

- A choice of manual or automatic indexing of Gopher information

KA9Q comes in many different versions that supply different services. This description is for the version maintained by Ashok Aiyar[‡] and accessible via FTP from boombox.micro.umn.edu in the /pub/gopher/PC_server/ka9q direc-

---

* "KA9Q" is the ham radio call sign owned by Phil Karn. KA9Q is copyright Phil Karn <karn@qualcomm.com>. The software is free for noncommercial and educational use; $50.00 a copy for commercial use.

† The Gopher server code was written by Chris McNeil <cmcneil@mta.ca> and enhanced by Peter Crawshaw <pcrawshaw@mta.ca> and Chris McNeil.

‡ This version of KA9Q is maintained by Ashok Aiyer <ashok@biochemistry.cwru.edu>. Certain examples in this section are by Ashok Aiyer.

tory. KA9Q is used primarily to support a large variety of TCP/IP based servers running on a single PC. In addition to the Gopher server, this version of KA9Q supports:

- *POP2/POP3 mail servers.*   Mail servers that support the Post Office protocol versions 2 and 3. They work with many popular PC- and Mac-based mail clients, such as POPMail for the Mac and PC from the University of Minnesota, and the Mac- and Windows-based versions of Eudora from Qualcomm.
- *FTP Server.*   File transfer protocol server.
- *Finger Server.*   Get information on users using the Finger Protocol.
- *CSO server.*   Two CSO-type servers are supplied. Use the CSO protocol to set up online curable phone books.

KA9Q Installation Steps

This version of KA9Q requires at least a 80286-based PC with a network card that supports the packet driver specification. This description will describe how to set up the Gopher server. The documentation you receive with the program will describe how to set up other servers.

1. FTP the required files from `boombox.micro.umn.edu`.
2. Create the following directories:

`\NOS`	The executable and its configuration file (autoexec.nos) goes here.
`\NOS\SPOOL`	Log files are created here.
`\GOPHER`	The root of the Gopher system.
`\NOS\SPOOL\HELP`	The help files go here (if desired).
`\NOS\SPOOL\MAIL`	Mail messages go here.
`\NOS\SPOOL\MQUEUE`	Outgoing mail work files.
`\NOS\SPOOL\RQUEUE`	Isn't used.
`\NOS\SPOOL\TEMP`	Temporary files get created here.
`\NOS\FINGER`	Users' Finger files can go here.
`\NOS\SPOOL\rewrite`	Mail rewrite rules.
`\PUBLIC`	Anonymous FTP root directory.

3. Install the packet driver that comes with your network card.
4. Create an `autoexec.nos` file in the `\nos` directory.
5. Put the information that you want available via Gopher in the `\gopher` directory. (*Note:* Information can reside on multiple drives but each drive *must* have a `\gopher` directory.)
6. Start up the KA9Q program.

Creating the autoexec.nos File

The `autoexec.nos` file is an ASCII file. The easiest way to get KA9Q up and running is to edit the supplied `autoexec.nos` file. An example file follows; note comment lines beginning with number symbol (#):

```
# AUTOEXEC.NOS for (CWRU/BIOC v1.92 - axa12) NOS
# configured by Ashok Aiyar.
# If using Bootp
#
attach packet 0x60 pk0 5 1500  # packet driver at 0x60, 5 buffers, MTU=1500)
ifconfig pk0 broadcast 255.255.255.255
bootp pk0
host name biochemistry.cwru.edu
domain suffix cwru.edu.
domain verbose on
domain translate off        # don't turn name translation on
domain cache size 20
domain cache wait 300
domain retry 1
domain maxwait 90
#
```

Notes: (1) For bootp to work, you must initially set a broadcast address of 255.255.255.255—the correct value is received from the BOOTP server. (2) I have to specify a full host name as the name received from our BOOTP server is just "biochemistry." Several others have also reported a problem with the node name received during BOOTP, and I am working on a fix. Also a domain suffix is not provided by the BOOTP server, and hence is entered here.

Configuring NOS without using BOOTP

```
# AUTOEXEC.NOS for (CWRU/BIOC v1.92 - axa12) NOS
# configured by Ashok Aiyar.
#
# basic host configuration
hostname biochemistry.cwru.edu
ip address 129.22.152.44
domain suffix cwru.edu.
#
# domain nameserver (DNS) configuration
domain addserver 129.22.4.1 # secondary nameserver
domain addserver 129.22.4.3 # primary nameserver
domain verbose on
domain translate off  # don't turn name translation on
domain cache size 20
domain cache wait 300
domain retry 1
domain maxwait 90
```

```
#
# host interface configuration - Cabletron card with packet driver
attach packet 0x60 pk0 5 1500 # packet driver at 0x60, 5 buffers,
  MTU=1500
ifconfig pk0 ipaddr 129.22.152.44 netmask 255.255.0.0 broadcast
  129.22.255.255
route add default pk0 129.22.1.1
route add 129.22.0.0/16 pk0
#

Section 2 -- The rest of AUTOEXEC.NOS - whether you use BOOTP or not

# configuring memory parameters
watch on
watchdog on
memory thresh 7168
memory efficient yes
memory ibufsize 3072
memory nibufs 10
#
# TCP/IP parameters
ip rtimer 60
ip ttl 255
tcp window 2048
tcp mss 1460
tcp irtt 10000
#
# unattended operation
attended off
mbox maxmsg 100   # each user can store upto 100 messages
mbox expert on
mbox password "password"   # password for remote sysop operation
#
# let's maintain a log!
log \nos\spool\net.log
#
# telnet client accept echo request from remote server
echo accept
#
# SMTP parameters
smtp batch no
smtp gateway po.cwru.edu
smtp maxclients 40
smtp mode route
smtp quiet yes
smtp timer 60
smtp t4 120
smtp usemx yes
```

```
# smtp server checks to see if there is any mail to send every 60
# seconds. If a particular host/connection is down, then the
# "smtp t4" command causes the mail to be sent via the defined smtp
# gateway after a defined period of time in seconds (120 seconds)
# "smtp usemx" causes MX records to be used while sending.
#
# remote reset/exit/kick parameters
start remote
remote -s password
# If the server appears to be stuck and you want to kick/restart it,
# from a remote site using Ka9Q, the command would be
# "remote -k password biochemistry.cwru.edu kick|reset|exit"
#
# FTP client/server - binary transfer mode
ftype image
#
# start the servers
start ftp
start smtp
start echo
start discard
start pop2
start pop3
start finger
start cso
#
# map the keyboard
source c:\nos\config.kbd
#
# lock the console
lock password "password"   # password to unlock console with
lock   # console gets locked automatically
```

KA9Q Gopher Server Setup

To manually set up your server to make information available you create item description files named `ginfo` in each directory under the `\gopher` root directory. The KA9Q server uses the basic Gopher document types defined in the Gopher RFC. The syntax of the `ginfo` file corresponds to the standard item descriptor that the server will deliver to client programs according to the Gopher protocol:

```
<type><display string>TAB<transfer type><file name>TAB<host name>TAB<port>
```

The following is a sample `ginfo` file in a sample `c:\gopher` directory. Tabs are denoted by #. It is important to use a text editor that does not convert tabs to whitespace as tabs are an integral part of the protocol; also, the last line *must* be terminated with a <CR><LF>.

```
0About this Gopher#0g:/about.TXT#gopher.mta.ca#70
0FYI on Gopher#0g:/gopher.rfc#gopher.mta.ca#70
1Mount Allison Information System#1f:/info#gopher.mta.ca#70
1Canadian Weather Forecasts#1g:/weather#gopher.mta.ca#70
2Mount Allison Staff Phone Book##gopher.mta.ca#70
2Mount Allison Student Phone Book##gopher.mta.ca#105
1Other Gophers#1_other_gophers ac.dal.ca#70
1Mount Allison ACI Gopher#aci.mta.ca#70
```

dbaseIII items are type p and are entered as below:

```
1<description>#<p><drive><file name>#hostname#port

ie 1My sample dbase#pc:/test/mydb.dbf#gopher.mta.ca#70
```

Text search items are entered as below.

```
7Sample Text Search#7c:/text/#gopher.mta.ca#70
7Sample Selective Text Search#7c:/text/*.doc#gopher.mta.ca#70
```

In the first example all text files in `c:\gopher\test` directory are searched. In the second only files with the `.doc` extension are searched.

Figure 22.5 is an example of a typical Gopher screen as served by the KA9Q server to the HGopher client:

Using the mkginfo Utility to Create ginfo Files

To ease in the maintaining of the Gopher server you can create `ginfo` files by the use of the `mkginfo` utility program. To run it, change to the directory you want a `ginfo` file in and type `mkginfo <gopher server name>` where the Gopher server name is the official host name of the Gopher server. That is,

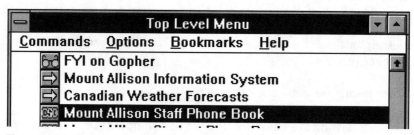

Figure 22.5

```
cd c:\gopher\test
mkginfo gopher.mta.ca
```

This creates a usable `ginfo` file in the test directory. You can than go in and edit the display strings to be whatever you want them to be. If you have only text files with the `.txt` extension you can start each file with a `GINDEX:` line as follows.
GINDEX:<description you wish displayed to the client>. That is,

```
GINDEX:About this Gopher
```

`About this Gopher` is what the client sees for this item description.

Automatic indexing

If you don't create `ginfo` files the Gopher server will create Gopher indexes on the fly for you. Each time you connect to a directory, the server will look in the directory and send your client a Gopher index.

This has the advantage of being maintenance-free as you never have to maintain Gopher `ginfo` files. The displayed index is always up to date. The disadvantage is that the display string is just the file name (which may be fairly cryptic in some cases).

Figure 22.6 is an example of what a client sees when the server creates an index on the fly.

It is interesting to note that if there is a dbaseIII file in the directory it will create a search item automatically. It will show up as a directory, but if you click on it you will get a list of fields in the database. They will show up as search items. To a client it appears as shown in Fig. 22.7.

Note: The Gopher server does not use the dbase index file. Only the `.dbf` file. Memo fields in the file are ignored.

Setting up the CSO Name Servers

This version of KA9Q has two CSO-type name servers. One runs on port 70 and one on port 105. To set up the information databases, create a dbaseIII file for each server. Name one file `cso.dbf` and the other `cso1.dbf`, place these files in the `\nos` directory and create a pointer to them in your main `ginfo` file.

Figure 22.6

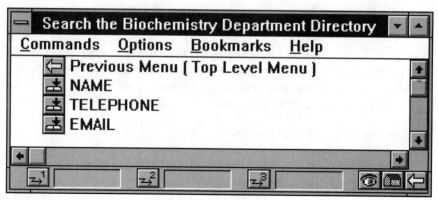

Figure 22.7

You must manually edit a `ginfo` file to add your CSO entries. The entries look as follows:

```
2Mount Allison Staff Phone Book##gopher.mta.ca#70
2Mount Allison Student Phone Book##gopher.mta.ca#105
```

Figure 22.8 is a typical CSO-type query.
Figure 22.9 shows the results.

The Gopher Log File

To automatically mail the Gopher log file to the Gopher administrator add a line as follows to your `autoexec.nos`:

```
at time "sendgopherlog user@hostname"
```

For example:

```
at 0600 "sendgopherlog cmcneil@test.mta.ca"
```

This will mail the Gopher log to `cmcneil` at 6 a.m. each morning.

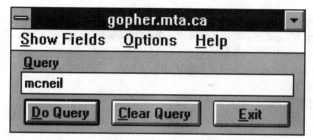

Figure 22.8

```
╔══════════════════════════════════════════════════════════════╗
║  ▬          Notepad - ~CSO1820.TMP                    ▼  ▲   ║
╠══════════════════════════════════════════════════════════════╣
║  File   Edit   Search   Help                                 ║
╟──────────────────────────────────────────────────────────────╢
║                    NAME: McNeil, Chris                   ▲   ║
║                  OFFICE: 2473                                ║
║                    HOME: 536-2246                            ║
║              DEPARTMENT: Computing Services             ▼   ║
╚══════════════════════════════════════════════════════════════╝
```

Figure 22.9

KA9Q Security Considerations:
Other Details

Any file in a \gopher directory or subdirectory is accessible by anyone who can connect to your server. For this reason *never* put information in the \gopher tree that is not meant to be accessible.

Additional security is available by use of the IP filtering capabilities of this version of KA9Q.

KA9Q does not use EMS/XMS, but can use as much conventional memory as you can provide. MS-DOS 5.0 provides features for freeing low conventional memory under the names HIMEM.SYS and EMM386.EXE; see Help Memmaker for details. Here is an example config.sys file:

```
device=c:\dos\himem.sys
device=c:\dos\emm386.exe i=a000-b7ff noems i=e000-f7ff
dos=high,umb
devicehigh=c:\dos\setver.exe
files=30
buffers=10
stacks=0,0
shell=c:\dos\command.com /e:256 /p /f
```

All TSRs* in AUTOEXEC.BAT are also loaded into upper memory. The only TSRs used are:

Smartdrv

TCP/IP packet driver

ANSI driver — VT102.COM (screen manager)

Doskey

---

* A "TSR" is a "Terminate and Stay Resident" program. Such programs, which perform one or another utility function, remain installed in memory for the duration of a computer session.

Building a Campus-Wide Information System

Universities revolve around knowledge—its discovery, dissemination and preservation. In order to achieve its knowledge mission, a university also must disseminate information about itself. Historically such information was presented in a variety of print media—from campus maps to the course catalog to the library catalog to the faculty and student telephone books to newspapers and newsletters.

The deployment of campus computer networks, combined with the evolution of tools like Gopher and World-Wide Web, have made it possible for universities to make available online versions of documents traditionally offered in paper form. The term "campus-wide information system" or CWIS refers to a system that brings together online documents and ways to access campus computing resources under a single comprehensive umbrella.

A well-designed and carefully constructed CWIS can be a very useful tool in helping a university document itself. But CWISes do not exist in a vacuum; virtually every major university is now connected to the Internet, and in recent years Internet connectivity has extended to many smaller universities, colleges, and community colleges. (Indeed, the early 1990s have seen some secondary schools connect to the Internet.) With so many schools on the Internet, and with access for the public at large becoming more prevalent, a CWIS becomes not only useful for a campus's existing community; it becomes a valuable way for prospective members of the community to learn more about an institution. A university that does not see fit to establish a CWIS for its existing community may find itself at a disadvantage competing with other schools for faculty, staff, and students.

The CWIS is also visible to those who seek to collaborate with the university—peer institutions that might enter into joint projects, smaller institutions that may view the university as a provider of some services, or agencies that are evaluating whether or not to grant funds. A university may find that the costs involved in creating a solid CWIS are justified by the image projected to these constituencies.

The term "campus-wide information system" generally evokes the image of a school, and this chapter will focus mainly on CWISes in the education context. However, the notion of creating a centralized service that brings together documents and other computer services need not apply only to educational institutions. Businesses and governments would do well to consider the CWIS concept to build online information centers, whether serving a specific campus or the entire institution.

The most important aspect of the CWIS is the notion of gathering together information about the campus into a single location. The providers of that information can be as varied as all the departments on a campus, but for the CWIS to be effective, those seeking information should be able to find it by connecting to a single well-known service.

ORIGINS OF THE CWIS CONCEPT

Although hundreds of campus-wide information systems have flourished in the last few years, many deployed using client-server, network-oriented software, the original CWISes were mainframe based. Cornell University is generally credited with deploying the first campus-wide information system. The tool was known as CUINFO. It was offered on Cornell's general-purpose academic IBM mainframe running the VM/CMS operating system. The original CUINFO system was created by Steve Worona.* CUINFO began service on October 10, 1982. Cornell had broad campus connectivity to its mainframes, and it encouraged widespread access to the mainframes by faculty, staff, and students. With so many users visiting this central service, the mainframe was a natural choice for deploying a centralized information system.

CUINFO grew into a very complete campus-wide information service. A glimpse of its topical breadth is obvious when you glance at its main menu from 1985:

---

* Many others contributed to the CUINFO effort; one other key developer was Paul Adams.

```
          CUINFO - Cornell University Information

Title      Contents                     Title      Contents
--------   --------------------------   --------   --------------------------
ABROAD     Information on Study Aboard   HOUSING    On- and Off-Campus Housing
ACADEMIC   From Academic Offices/Depts  LIBRARIES  Schedules for all Libraries
ATHLETICS  Schedules, Facilities, etc.  MOVIES     Cornell Cinema Schedule
BUS        Bus Schedules                MUSIC      Concerts, Folk Music, etc.
CALENDAR   Academic Calendar            OEO        Office of Equal Opportunity
CAREERNET  Alumni Career Advising Prog  PERSONNEL  Univ. Personnel Services
CCS        Computer Services Info       PRELIMS    Schedule of Fall Prelims
CHRONICLE  This Week's Headlines        RELIGION   Religious Services & Groups
COLLOQ     Colloquia, Seminars, etc.    RESTS      Off-Campus Restaurants
CONNECTION The Cornell Connection       ROSTER     Courses—Fall Term, 1985
DINING     Campus Eateries              SEO        Student Employment Office
DIRECT     Staff & Student Directories  SUPPORT    Student Support Services
FINAID     Financial Aid Office         THEATRE    Campus Theatrical Events
HEALTH     University Health Services   UPDATES    Recent CUINFO Updates


    Please select a title. (Blank line to exit.)
```

One of the most popular items on CUINFO was a sort of online advice column called Dear Uncle Ezra, which provided answers to problems unique to members of a campus community. Here is an example of Uncle Ezra wisdom, circa 1986.*

```
Dear Uncle Ezra...September, 1986

---------------------------- Page 1 of 82 -----------------------
DEAR UNCLE                              9/26/86
    I AM FAILING EVERYTHING. I NEED SERIOUS HELP.
                                SINCERELY,
                                JOHN DOE


Dear John,                              9/30/86
    Happily, help is available. The best place to start is at the
Learning Skills Center, 357 Olin Hall, 255-6310. They have tutors,
tests, time management techniques, and study skills assistance.
Other services can be found under "ACADEMIC" and "PERSONAL" in
another part of SOS for specific problems.
                                Uncle Ezra
```

---

* Back issues of Uncle Ezra are archived on the current Gopher-based implementation of CUINFO at Cornell (gopherl.cit.cornell.edu, port 70).

CUINFO grew in terms of its functionality and the breadth and depth of documents online. Over time, several other universities adopted the CUINFO software to serve the same function. Examples include Penn State, the University of Arkansas, and the WVNET network in West Virginia.

Other pioneering CWIS sites include:

- *Iowa State University,* whose CWIS was inaugurated in January 1984. The underlying software technology was a mainframe database tool called SPIRES, an acronym for Stanford Public Information Retrieval System. (Developed at Stanford University, SPIRES was a popular database tool for IBM mainframes, and was used in some ways as a sort of CWIS at Stanford.) The Iowa State CWIS was called Cynet. Some of its early documents included a course catalog with a search capability, allowing, for instance, students to quickly find all junior-level English classes, or all classes that meet on Mondays at 8:00 a.m. Cynet was used heavily by Iowa State recruiters as they visited high schools around the state.*

- *Lehigh University,* which deployed a CWIS under the Music mainframe operating system in 1986. The Lehigh effort was undertaken as part of a joint study with IBM and McGill University. (One of the developers of the Lehigh system, Timothy J. Foley, wrote his dissertation on the subject of CWIS development.)

- *Virginia Tech,* which implemented its "Policy Display System" on an IBM mainframe as well, with production commencing on July 1, 1986. (Implementors of the Virginia Tech system included Bruce B. Harper and Wayland Winstead.)

Another mainframe-based CWIS was developed at Princeton University, which deployed a system known as Princeton News Network.† Also initially developed for VM/CMS, PNN went into production in December 1988. PNN evolved into a multiplatform system, with data served from the mainframe and from a Unix host. Eventually Princeton developed Unix and Macintosh clients for PNN. The PNN software was adopted for use by other early CWIS campuses, such as Northwestern, Arizona State, and the University of Alabama. Eventually over 100 sites licensed PNN (though some may not have placed it in production).

The pioneer mainframe CWIS sites have moved to tools like Gopher and World-Wide Web for their CWIS platforms. Cornell replaced CUINFO with a Gopher version in November 1993. Princeton decommissioned PNN in favor of

---

* Cynet was the brainchild of David Boylan (then Dean of Engineering), and was implemented by Mike Bernard, George Covert, and John Hauck.

† The designer and chief evangelist for PNN was Howard Strauss. The main developer was Tom True.

Gopher in January 1994. The mainframe sites were looking for replacements more oriented to the client/server, open-network model. In fact, Steve Worona, now an assistant to the Vice President for Information Technologies at Cornell, says that Cornell nearly undertook designing their own protocol that would allow them to move their pioneering CUINFO mainframe campus information service to a network/workstation environment, "but then we found out about Gopher, and it was exactly what we were looking for."

Today it is fashionable to dismiss mainframes as dinosaurs—relics to be disposed of as quickly as possible. Still, it is important to realize that many of today's newer CWISes, while sporting fancy graphics and perhaps multimedia documents, probably are not as complete in their coverage of their campuses as the pioneering mainframe systems were.* CUINFO had more breadth and depth of documents online in their CWIS in 1986 than many sites have today using more modern tools. As Worona has been known to say, "An information system is 90 percent information and 10 percent system." Builders of CWISes would be wise to realize that getting the technology in place is only a part of the battle.

Even though the advent of the graphics-capable CWIS does not guarantee greater completeness of information, it does afford opportunities for documents to become more readable than flat ASCII text rendered in a typewriter font with no images. Universities are already beginning to exploit networked multimedia as a way to describe their campuses. For example, the University of Illinois has placed online via the World-Wide Web a lovely brochure describing much about the campus with accompanying images. A glance at this online brochure gives an idea of the potential for presenting a CWIS with richly embedded graphics. Figure 23.1 shows the beginning of the brochure as rendered by Mosaic.

As Internet connectivity for the masses improves, more campuses will want to offer such online brochures, even including audio and moving images. It will always be important, however, to tell the story completely in text so that those without access to multimedia facilities will continue to be able to read the information you want to convey.

CHOOSING A PLATFORM

Just as any general Internet information provider must choose a hardware and software environment for the server, so must you as a CWIS administrator. Gopher and World-Wide Web are overwhelmingly popular software packages for CWISes. You must also choose a hardware platform. The analysis of hardware and software options outlined in Chap. 20 applies to you as a CWIS coordinator.

---

* And of course the mainframe can speak the newer protocols, as is proven by clients and servers for Gopher on MVS and VM/CMS platforms.

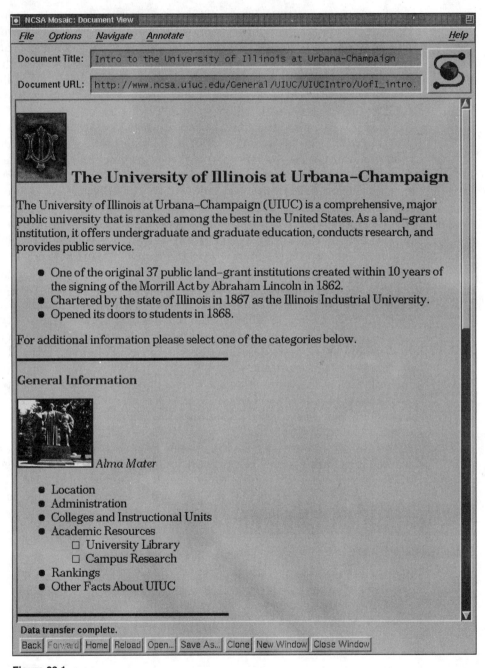

Figure 23.1

There are, however, special software options for the CWIS administrator. Specialized software is available intended specifically for the CWIS application. One example is Techinfo, developed by the Massachusetts Institute of Technology and in use there and at several other sites as their CWIS. Techinfo was desgined in 1989 and supports users with Techinfo client software and via a rich VT100 public client. Techinfo is available freely for other sites who wish to use it. To read more about Techinfo you can connect to the MIT service via Telnet (to `techinfo.mut.edu`; login is automatic).*

Another site with a CWIS using unique technology is the University of California at Berkeley, whose Infocal system is the first CWIS based on an interoperable implementation of the Z39.50 protocol. To try this system, Telnet to `infocal.berkeley.edu`.

Another option to consider is a commercial product called VTX, marketed by Digital Equipment Corporation. VTX is in use at thousands of sites worldwide. With the first version deployed in 1984, VTX was one of the first commercial client/server products. Today VTX is used by many businesses as *companywide* information services. A license fee is paid for the server, and client software is freely available. Clients are available for DEC's Ultrix platform, and for Windows. Clients can connect over Decnet as well as TCP/IP. VTX is multilingual; nine languages are supported. VTX supports indexes with exact-word, phrase, and boolean searches.

VTX is integrated with DEC's office automation product, All-in-One. This means, for instance, that users can easily grab VTX-owned documents and mail them to other users; information providers can also exploit this integration, for instance posting a calendar from All-in-One to VTX. Sites that already have a DEC-based computing environment may be especially interested in VTX as an option.

The CWIS at North Carolina State University uses VTX; the example sessions connecting to NCSU shown in Chap. 2 show how VTX looks to the VT100 user.

Most CWIS software options make it possible for you to use more than one server computer if you so choose. For instance, your main Gopher server might point to other Gopher servers, either in your facility or elsewhere on campus, for specific documents or even specific folders. Exercise this option with discretion. Carried to an extreme, you might rely on dozens of separate servers, perhaps residing on the desktops of those who own or prepare a given document. This is appealing in terms of the distribution of control, but this model brings with it the significant chance that parts of your CWIS document structure will be inaccessible at any given time. Suppose a workstation with a

---

* Besides developing the Techinfo software, MIT has implemented a very complete CWIS, which serves as a good example for other CWIS administrators, whether or not the software is of interest.

particular document goes down, and that workstation is behind the locked door of an employee who is on vacation. Getting the data back on line may be difficult.

By contrast, a centralized server often can be located in a computer room that is staffed by operators who can restart the server in the event of outages, log problem reports, perform regular disk backups, and so forth. You may want to identify what parts of the CWIS are "mission-critical" information, and have a policy that such information must reside in the central server. With the right automated support tools (discussed later) you can make it as easy for your providers to post to the central server as it would be for them to maintain their documents on their own machines.

In general, a server offering Gopher or Web documents requires relatively little computing horsepower. Note that if you run a public client, such as the "curses" Gopher client or Lynx, you may find that the public client is consuming considerable resources. You will want to plan how powerful a server to use with your intended uses in mind.

Many campuses have found it useful to use a dedicated computer for their CWIS service. This has certain advantages: for instance, downtime for upgrades can be minimized, scheduled for a time when CWIS users are not likely to be online. The CWIS will not be subjected to CPU bottlenecks caused by other unrelated tasks—and it will not cause such disruptions, either. This is not to say that a dedicated workstation is essential for a CWIS; many sites run on shared machines quite happily.

Many campuses have multiple Gopher or Web servers. If you are the central CWIS administrator, you will face this as a fact of life. In many cases this is appropriate for the college or department involved; they may possess the technical expertise necessary, and they may have a volume of documents and a rate of change in the online information that justify their own servers. A central CWIS should include pointers to such departmental servers (assuming they want the servers to be accessible to the outside world). You will also want to select specific documents located on the departmental servers that may be of campuswide interest, and include pointers to these documents in the CWIS.

Although you should not discourage departmental servers, beware of fragmenting information across too many servers. To take the example of the course catalog again, imagine each department maintaining its own course list in its own format. Students would find navigation among such a setup difficult at best. In such cases, department-specific information is still best placed in the CWIS in a consistent format. Of course, departments may want to supplement such information on their own servers; for instance, the biology department might post announcements of new or one-time courses on its own server, with the official course descriptions and schedules delivered in the central listings. Departmental servers might include items such as departmental meeting minutes, schedules for departmental seminars, homework assignments for courses, prepublication journal articles, etc.

THE ROOT MENU AND THE ORGANIZATION OF DOCUMENTS

Deciding what titles to include in the root menu (or initial screen, or home page) of your CWIS can be surprisingly problematic. It is hard to organize all of the information about a campus (perhaps also including pointers to the larger Internet) in a concise manner.

One school of thought holds that the initial menu should be concise and very general in its titles. Here is an example of a relatively terse menu that has received considerable praise since its introduction:

```
       University of California - Santa Cruz, InfoSlug System

        1.  About UCSC InfoSlug/
  -->   2.  Index to the InfoSlug Menu Tree <?>
        3.  The Academic Divisions/
        4.  The Campus/
        5.  The Classroom/
        6.  The Community/
        7.  The Computer Center/
        8.  The Library/
        9.  The Researcher/
       10.  The Student Center/
       11.  The World/
```

Others may feel that a longer list of initial choices, with more explanatory text, is more useful:

- Despite the broad categories, navigation still is not obvious. Is an online plastics database under the Researcher or under the Library? Is the course catalog under Academic Divisions or under the Classroom? Longer titles—especially as annotated in a World-Wide Web CWIS—might offer more clues.

- Some services, such as an online telephone book, might be used very frequently. Placing such items in the root menu means fewer keystrokes for users.

The question of how broad and how verbose a root menu should be cannot be resolved to the satisfaction of all CWIS administrators; different people have different opinions on the matter. The mode of presentation of the root menu may affect your decision; the two-column presentation offered by CUINFO and by NCSU's CWIS seems to hold more initial choices better than a single-column display does. As a CWIS implementor you should at least be aware of the basic distinction, and you might want to spend some time exploring existing CWISes to see which ones you feel are most effective.

No matter how carefully you design your system, you may inadvertently make parts of it hard to navigate. You may find it useful to ask some testers not part of the menu design team to report on their first trips through the CWIS. They may be able to suggest improvements. Of course, you will not be able to please all customers no matter how valiant your efforts, but real user experience can be useful.

One challenge facing all CWIS administrators is that every information provider on campus believes his or her document deserves placement on the root menu. This can be a good argument for a brief root menu with no direct pointers to text documents: the information provider cannot complain as easily with no similar documents in the root menu as examples.

As you build your CWIS, some areas in your information hierarchy will inevitably be less fully developed than others. It is tempting to implement the entire envisioned document structure, then fill in the folders as documents become available. This can lead to empty folders and blind alleys. Your users may be happier if you flesh out the tree structure only as documents become available to populate those folders.

TYPES OF INFORMATION TO OFFER

Here are some of the broad categories of information you may want to include in your CWIS:

- *General information about the university.* Brief history, photographs of campus, campus maps, parking information, visitor information (main sights, places to eat)

- *Academics.* Catalogs, calendars, enrollment procedures, academic advising, closed class list; noncredit course information; adult and night classes; online connection to the enrollment database

- *Housing.* Residence halls, local housing options

- *Alumni information.* How to join association, events

- *Health.* Student health center, medical/clinical center; advisory brochures, counseling options, radiation/biological/chemical safety procedures

- *Employment.* Faculty, staff, student (on-campus as well as placement services)

- *Libraries.* Services, hours, locations, gateways to catalog and to online research-oriented databases; connections via online forms or e-mail for services such as interlibrary loan

- *Campus computing information.* Services offered, gateways to e-mail services for students and faculty/staff, host services

- *People directories.* Faculty/staff and student phone books online, e-mail directories (if separate)

- *University ordinances.* Bylaws, rules, policies, procedures

- *Handicapper information.* Building accessibility, facilities (talking PCs, TDDs, etc)

- *Transportation.* Campus bus lines, local transportation information, getting to campus by train or airplane

- *Events.* Seminars, plays, movies, concerts—by date, by type of event, by venue

- *Weather.* Local weather, pointers to other weather servers

- *Classified advertisement services.* Student ride lines, items for sale

- *Campus purchasing services.* Catalogs and forms; connection to online purchasing system

- *Town/gown relations.* Community information

- *Outreach programs.* University outreach/extension services and facilities information

- *Computer resources.* Pointers to information resources on the larger Internet

This list is not meant to be exhaustive. As is true for menu design, you will want to look at other CWISes so as to benefit from others' choices as to what information to provide.

DOCUMENTING THE DOCUMENTS

Many CWIS administrators establish a policy of thoroughly documenting the documents they place online. Information to be included with each document may include:

- The name of the author/owner of the document

- The e-mail address to write for further information or corrections

- The date the document was last updated

- The expiration date

- Any special information about the document, such as copyright information, official/unofficial status, restrictions on reuse, limitations on off-campus use

Some software platforms may provide more facilities for recording this sort of "meta information" than others. For instance, the Gopher+ standard was defined in part so as to provide named fields to hold these pieces of information. Over time we can expect Gopher+ clients that display these fields, either all the time or upon request for a chosen document. If the CWIS platform you have selected does not provide specific fields for these items, you may want to establish a style sheet that calls for the information to be included with each document, for instance, following all other text. If you have selected World-Wide Web as your platform, you might use hyperlinks for this purpose; the name of the author might be a selectable item, pointing to an online resume. In fact, the `address` tag is intended to provide a standard way to insert the e-mail address of the document's owner; in practice it is often included at the end of each document.

Your users will also find it useful for there to be a document in each basic area of the CWIS explaining who is responsible for that set of documents. For instance, in a Gopher-based CWIS, you might include an "About" file in each major folder, and include a standard paragraph that details what campus unit provided the information, how often it will be updated, etc. If your CWIS software does not support meta-information fields, you might use "About" files to save the effort of documenting each individual file.

In a Gopher-based CWIS you may want to use the ability to explicitly order the items in a folder so as to present them in a logical sequence. Details of this feature vary from server to server, but all provide a way to override alphabetic numbering.

Sometimes in a hierarchical menu system like Gopher you may have a folder with items that could be logically grouped into subsections, but you want the entire list to appear as a single menu. One trick used by some administrators is to use special characters in titles to provide visual separation on the screen. For instance, a menu of seminar titles might look like this:

```
              Client software for the Gopher System

         1.   About Gopher clients in general
         2.   Gopher information from U Minnesota
         3.   ----------- MS-DOS Clients -------------
         4.   PC Gopher III
   --> 5.     U Texas "Curses" Client
         6.   ---------- MS-Windows Clients -------------
         7.   HGopher
         8.   WinGopher
         9.   ---------- Macintosh Clients -------------
        10.   TurboGopher
```

The titles with dashed lines are pseudo documents, used simply as separators. Normally you would not expect users to select the separator titles. In fact they might all point to the same physical file, which simply would include a line to the effect "This document is a separator in the menu; see the titles following the current one." Or, you could use type "i", the Gopher annotation type now supported by most clients.

Of course, such shenanigans would not be necessary in an HTML (World-Wide Web) document. You would simply use headers or list structures to visually separate the logical groupings of items.

SPECIALIZED DOCUMENTS

Chapter 20 gave some examples of how information providers offer online usage statistics. Some CWISes post usage statistics online for readers to peruse. In particular, this allows campus information providers to see which documents are the most popular. Some sites merely provide a summary report. Other sites augment reports with a folder offering direct links to the ten most popular titles in the CWIS. Still other sites may offer online graphs showing usage. In most cases, these usage statistics are updated daily or weekly; some World-Wide Web services report utilization up to the minute.* Online usage logs should not include any information that shows specific activity by fully qualified domain name of the client, so as to protect user privacy.

The CWIS can serve as a useful feedback mechanism. You can include a simple mechanism to allow users to leave comments. One approach is to publish an e-mail address for comments. A typical approach is to use a common mailbox address and use your server's mail forwarding capabilities to have copies of comments sent automatically to your CWIS team. A typical address might be of the form `comments@gopher.msu.edu`.

A useful supplement to an e-mail comments address is an online Guest Book. This is a simple Telnet application that allows users to jot down comments. It can be gratifying as a CWIS administrator to receive comments from one's campus community and from all over the world. Software that can serve as a Gopher Guest Book is available on Minnesota's archive.†

Some CWIS administrators include a folder for reporting suggestions and the administrator's responses online in the CWIS itself. This has two benefits: your community sees that you respond to suggestions, and redundant suggestions are minimized.

Another useful specialized document is a list of recent updates. Such a list can take two forms: it could be an automated list generated from a script, or it can be a manually-updated list with a little bit of commentary describing new folders or documents. Some CWISes offer both. Depending on your CWIS software, the list might include hot links to the resources themselves. Your users may find the list of recent updates a useful way to stay abreast of new documents.

A CWIS will need to include complete information on the CWIS software, such as where to obtain client software. In the case of Gopher and World-Wide Web you can point to other online documents across the Internet, as well as providing specific local information.

PROVIDING NAVIGATION AIDS

Your users will be able to better navigate the network of information you weave if you provide a document that gives some understanding of the overall

---

* A paraphrase of an accountant's rule comes to mind here: it is a good idea not to spend more resources reporting on CWIS utilization than the information is worth. A weekly or monthly summary of usage will suffice in most cases.

† Guest Book software was written by Dennis Boone of Michigan State University.

plan. This can take the form of general explanation of how documents fall into main categories. If your CWIS is Gopher-based, you may want to prepare a "road map" that shows the lay of the land. An example of such a map appears in Chapter 16; you can produce a similar map using a tool called Gophertree.*

Another useful navigation aid is an index of all the titles in your CWIS. For Gopher CWISes, you might consider a tool called ts/tb.† It is also possible to build such an index with some custom programming and with WAIS as your search engine. Such an index will be most useful if the index itself is extremely visible, perhaps in the root menu (as is the case with the InfoSlug Gopher menu shown earlier).

THE CWIS POLICY COMMITTEE

Depending on how computing services are governed on your campus, you may want to form (or have formed) a committee to advise on the formation of the CWIS, and perhaps even to help in the design of its layout. A committee can provide valuable insights during formation of the CWIS, especially if the members are drawn from diverse constituencies on campus. It's especially advisable to include representatives from the library, from the public relations area, and from other areas involved with traditional means of disseminating information.

Of course, everyone has had a bad experience with committees, and if your CWIS is designed by committee, you run the risk of being told that's exactly what it looks like. It is important that the CWIS committee allow the CWIS administrator to continue to experiment with adjustments to the layout of the document structure, in light of feedback from users and new information to be posted.

Besides assisting in the formation of the CWIS, the policy committee can advise on issues such as what kinds of documents are to be included, and what kinds of users will be encouraged or discouraged. For instance the committee may decide that parts of the CWIS are to be labeled as official university information, and may specify policies for approvals for posting in those areas. Other parts of the CWIS might be free of those strictures.

PROMOTING THE CWIS

A big part of building a CWIS is evangelism. Although much of the campus will instantly agree that such a comprehensive central information service is a good idea, getting information providers to provide, and users to use, can be a challenge. Examples of evangelism include:

---

* Gophertree was written by Dennis Boone. It is available on the FTP archive at boombox.micro. umn.edu.

† This index tool was also written by Dennis Boone.

- Short courses on how to use the CWIS

- Specialized presentations to departments as to how they can become information providers

- Articles in newsletters and campus newspapers

- How-to information in the campus telephone directory; i.e., a page describing what the CWIS is and how to connect to it

- Print brochures*

- Easy access to the CWIS in campus microcomputer laboratories

A special challenge is deploying client software around the campus. To encourage users to install client software, you can emphasize the advantages—better user interface, better access to information—in all the forums listed above. Make sure the telephone help-line staff are familiar with client options. Consider putting up local copies of the client software for access via anonymous FTP, with the clients preconfigured to connect to your CWIS.

Many users may have workstations that lack sufficient resources (memory, disk space, CPU horsepower) to adequately run the appropriate client program. Others may have the ability but lack the inclination. In order to serve such users you may want to run a public client (such as Lynx or the public Gopher client). The public client can also make it easy for your campus community to tap into the CWIS from off-campus.

One strategy for promoting your CWIS (or any online service on the Internet) is to give it a proper name. Examples of such names include InfoSlug at the University of California - Santa Cruz; GopherBlue at the University of Michigan; and KUfacts at the University of Kansas. A catchy name can serve as a useful "handle" so that the name of the CWIS comes readily to mind. Moreover, your CWIS name can refer to your entire campus-wide information *system,* even if parts of it are implemented across technologies. For instance, KUfacts can refer to both Gopher and World-Wide Web views of the integrated service at Kansas.

ENCOURAGING CAMPUS INFORMATION PROVIDERS

In order to populate your CWIS with useful information from around the campus, you will need to "sell" your potential information providers on the value of using the CWIS. They need to see how online publishing will assist them in their missions. Again you might think of yourself as an evangelist, pleading

---

* It is ironic to use a print brochure to promote an online system, but this can be an effective approach.

your case rationally but with religious fervor. Some of the advantages that you might tout include:

- The ability to reach a broad audience, including others outside the campus community. For example, if your campus has an events center, putting a calendar of upcoming major events online may help their ticket sales.

- Potential for quick updates for frequently changing information.

- Opportunity to provide an online archive of information for historical review.

Direct evangelism of information providers can include telephone calls or e-mail to them when new documents are announced or old ones are updated. As you work with a new provider, you will often find that, like many other users, they have not yet installed client software on their workstations. You may want to allocate some staff time to the special task of helping information providers get client software installed and configured. By providing them with a better view of the CWIS, you encourage them to contribute their documents as well.

One way to assist new providers is to prepare a document describing their options for posting information on the CWIS. Explain the formats you can accept, how to convert documents from popular word processor formats (such as Word Perfect or Microsoft Word), any policy guidelines, etc. Place this how-to document online on the CWIS as well as making it available in print form.

In general, it is not advisable to post information without contacting the "owner" of the document on campus. Although you may feel that information already provided to the public in print form is fair game for online posting, some information providers may have specific concerns about online distribution. You should identify the owner(s) of documents and be sure they approve the posting on the CWIS first.

You will want to establish guidelines as to how large a quantity of information you are willing to post at no charge. Some campus providers may come to you with huge databases they wish to add to the CWIS, which may strain your available disk resources. With disk prices falling, reasonable charging can recover such costs. (On the other hand it is desirable to avoid charging if possible for "reasonably small" documents in order to encourage all providers.)

At some points your evangelism may be too successful: a flood of documents may appear at once from providers who all expect fast posting. Take comfort in this sign of success.

AUTOMATING DOCUMENT POSTING

By allowing automated posting of documents in the CWIS, you make it easy for your providers and for yourself. Automation is most important for documents that change frequently and that can be prepared by the provider in a "CWIS-ready" format easily. It is not advisable to provide direct access to the file system of your CWIS server; this makes it too easy for posting errors to take place, sometimes with extreme consequences. Instead, you want to provide a scheme whereby an automated process picks up documents sent to a staging area and places the documents in appropriate spots. You can take several approaches in the automation process.

A common approach to automating the posting of documents submitted by information providers is to provide a staging area into which the users can FTP their submissions. You might allocate a special user ID that corresponds to each online document (or set of documents). The provider transfers a new version of the document into the staging area. In the common case of a Unix-based server, a `cron` job checks each staging area periodically to see if new submissions are present. If so, the document is automatically posted into the appropriate spot in the file system. Scripts to perform this sort of trick are often written in Perl.

Alternatively, you may want to set up a mechanism that accepts documents from your information providers via e-mail. Some providers may be more comfortable with e-mail as their means of submission. Again, scripts to perform this type of updating are often written in Perl. Some public-domain tools, such as a program named `deliver`, can help you automate this process; deliver parses incoming e-mail message headers, splitting off files and running scripts as appropriate.

It is a good idea for your automated scripts to send an e-mail note back to the information provider for each posting received. This lets the provider know that an update is about to take place. This is especially important if you choose an e-mail-based automated posting option, because it is relatively easy for a nefarious user to forge such postings. If you mail a note back to the presumed information provider, and if your automated process defers actual posting to the CWIS for a few hours, you will have the opportunity to interrupt a pending bogus posting. The `deliver` tool allows such automated reminders.*

Tools like `deliver` are commonly available for anonymous FTP; use Archie to locate a copy near you. You can also look for tools in the archive for your specific CWIS platform. For instance, Gopher administrators may want to use tools available on the `boombox.micro.umn.edu` archive; in particular, look under the directory `/pub/gopher/Unix/GopherTools`.

If your campus has deployed a networkwide file system, you may be able to use that system to help providers deliver documents for posting on the CWIS. For instance, the University of Notre Dame has made such use of the Andrew File System. Information providers are able to update documents located in areas allocated to the individual user under AFS; AFS permissions preclude a provider from writing outside the designated areas. Additionally the Notre Dame system allows authorized users to submit documents via e-mail. Figure 23.2 depicts how the Notre Dame system works.

---

* `Deliver` can be located at anonymous FTP sites through Archie.

Gopher Architecture at Notre Dame

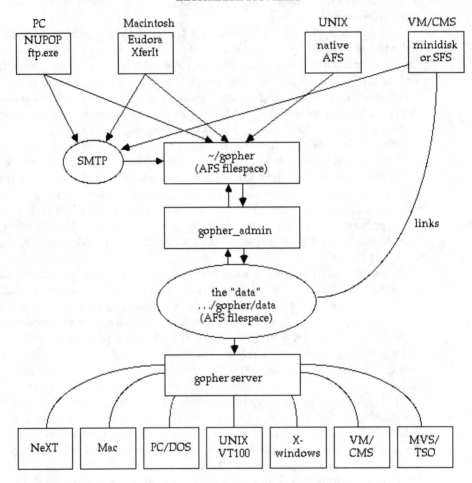

Figure 23.2 (*Courtesy of Joel Cooper, assistant director of the Office of University Computing at Notre Dame*)

While automation can greatly ease your burden as CWIS administrator, it is axiomatic that no automated system runs smoothly in all cases. You will want to review recent postings periodically to ensure that various automated posting scripts are doing their jobs. From time to time your scripts will need tuning in order to repair problems. Commercial products such as VTX may require less use of customized scripts; eventually, we might expect to see commercially supported Gopher or Web servers that provide built-in tools that address many of the database sides of running a CWIS.

REPLACING PRINT DOCUMENTS

One estimate holds that 10 percent of the cost of running a university is related to printing. Even if accurate, that figure no doubt overstates the amount of money that could be saved by moving to online publication; there are certain fixed costs that continue no matter how a document is "published," and online publishing, while inexpensive, is not free.

Nonetheless, online publishing of documents does provide opportunities for saving money as well as saving trees. Most CWIS administrators do not set as a goal the elimination of print editions of particular documents. Instead, the primary goal is getting versions of those documents online. Once the concept of online delivery has been proved, the owners of documents will in some cases come forward, proposing that the online version become the only means of delivery. Early candidate documents might be those that are expensive to publish and are amenable to online delivery. An example might be a manual of business procedures—the sort of document that is large, referred to only occasionally, but keenly sought when an individual needs to know a particular piece of information. Online publication can be superior to the print edition in such a case; the paper version tends not to be updated as frequently as it should, and it tends to be located somewhere far away from the person who wants it at any given instant.

CWIS administrators and their information providers would not want to move a given document to exclusive online delivery without careful consideration. Has access to the CWIS reached a broad enough audience to justify removal? You do not want to stop paper publication if you will lose a large part of your audience.

Also, be sure that the CWIS is not the only location of some vital piece of information. A classic example is the telephone directory: you do not want the CWIS to be the only repository of this information. For instance, you may need to be able to look up the phone number of a member of the CWIS team when the server is down!

Cases in which you and your information providers have decided to use the CWIS as the exclusive means of distributing a document may present a golden marketing opportunity. For instance, one university decided to provide the list of team schedules in the intramural basketball league only on the CWIS; no paper schedules would be handed out. Student use of the CWIS increased dramatically. Of course, such a scheme can only succeed if access to the CWIS is well-deployed, both via dial-up and campus computer labs.

PUBLIC KIOSKS

Most campuses offer information booths or displays that contain maps and printed guides to campus. In some cases you may want to consider installing public kiosks that can access the CWIS as a way to provide more complete and more up-to-date information.

Such kiosks need to be in a secure area. You may want to designate machines in a staffed microcomputer laboratory as CWIS terminals. In less secure areas you may want to anchor the workstation securely in a physical cabinet. Some CWIS administrators have opted to set up touch-screen terminals, so as to minimize problems of accidental or malicious rebooting of the kiosk terminal.

For greatest security, some sites have begun to use "boot ROMs" in PC-compatible machines to force the workstation to bootstrap load over the network. The workstation may not even have a local hard disk in this sort of environment. A system image including startup commands is downloaded over the network. This makes it extremely difficult for a malicious browser to reboot the machine and damage its software configuration.

You may want to restrict the documents that can be viewed in the kiosk. If your kiosk is capable of showing Usenet News articles, for instance, you may find the display dominated by people who are reading various news groups, making the kiosk unavailable to visitors who need to learn about campus. There are various approaches to follow. You might create a custom server that has pointers to those documents that you want to deliver on the CWIS, for instance. Some clients will allow you to specify a parameter that serves as a starting point; for instance, some Gopher clients let you specify an initial selector string, which could correspond to a part of the Gopher hierarchy suitable for the CWIS users.

Setting up this sort of kiosk can require a fair amount of custom work, both in building the physical kiosk and in setting up software. Standard tools such as Gopher clients are developed primarily for the desktop market, not for the specialized kiosk application. But some CWIS administrators have found the effort worthwhile. In the long run we may see commercial products offered that address this need.

EXPLOITING EXISTING ONLINE DATABASES

Any campus that has not embarked upon building a CWIS probably already has some information available online in one form or another. If you are responsible for establishing a CWIS from square one, you will want to take advantage of such online information where feasible. Gopher, World-Wide Web, and other tools will generally allow you to provide Telnet access to external hosts; simply by putting pointers into existing services (assuming they accept inbound Telnets) you can begin to organize such resources.

Note, however, that having the user invoke a number of separate Telnet-accessible services can interrupt the smooth delivery of information you can offer with native documents. Most Gopher clients, for instance, issue a warning when you exit to a Telnet process; also, most clients present the required login information to the user in a dialog box, and the user is required to type in login information. This is not as easy on the user as clicking on a document and having it appear on the screen.

Furthermore, one of the basic ideas of a CWIS is to present information in a common form. A myriad of separate external host services, perhaps each with its own search language, is exactly what we are trying to move away from in building a CWIS. The goal with the CWIS is to make information accessible in a comprehensive, central repository. The more documents you can offer in the native format, the better. When weighing whether to use an external search tool, ask yourself what the typical mode of access to the document will be— what kind of searches will the typical user want to perform?

Consider the university course catalog as an example. Suppose your campus has an existing course catalog browsing facility online, and the question is whether to use that tool, or to export the information to be loaded as documents in your new Gopher service. An external search engine might be able to present the catalog with more sophisticated search capabilities than a tool like Gopher can offer. Your users, however, are likely to want to browse the catalog as much or more than they want to search it. If the catalog is organized into a logical hierarchy, students and others will be able to quickly zoom in on the information they want. Moreover, the titles in the catalog will appear in Gopherspace indexes such as Veronica; if the course catalog is buried in an external search mechanism, the course titles will be invisible to Internet indexing tools.

Figure 23.3 is an example showing how a catalog might be presented in Gopher, from the University of Minnesota.

In some cases, existing external databases may be so large, or the search processes so elaborate, that the only viable option is to offer Telnet access to the existing services. Examples might include the library catalog and various large databases provided with proprietary search software. The external search engines will be superior to the Gopher or Web browsing model in such cases. Fortunately there are ways to provide inbound Telnet access to most such services, even if they are mainframe resident, if the host of the external database has a TCP/IP connection to the campus network.

A particular issue is what sort of telephone lookup software is offered on the campus network. Choices include:

- A WHOIS database
- QI/PH (respectively, the server and client for the CSO telephone protocol devised at the University of Illinois)
- X.500
- Use of the index facility native to the CWIS software; e.g., a Gopher index that returns a document for each individual (or perhaps one document for each unique surname)

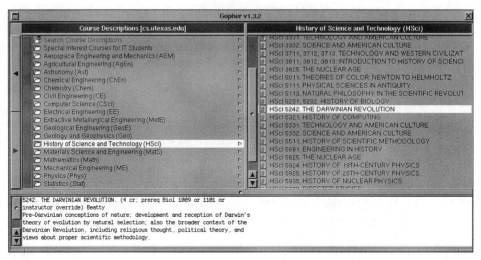

Figure 23.3

The strategy of using an index in the native CWIS can be surprisingly effective; the user types in a surname and quickly hones in on specific choices. Other mechanisms require the use of gateways, or, in the case of QI/PH, the launching of a separate client program on behalf of the user. The choice of which of these technologies to use will depend on the general computing and networking strategies on the campus; i.e., the decision may not rest with the CWIS administrator. Whoever makes the choice of what technology to use may find it helpful to see what similar institutions have selected.

SECURITY CONCERNS

More and more copyrighted and licensed materials are appearing on campus networks. Where possible you may want to add pointers to these resources via the CWIS. Note, however, that the terms of your licenses will typically restrict the sort of access you may provide. In some cases a resource is licensed for campuswide use; in other cases access is limited to a department; in still other cases an item, such as a CD-ROM, is licensed for nonnetworked single-user delivery. As a CWIS administrator you will want to work with your information providers to ensure that any items you point to are in fact available for distribution to a campuswide or worldwide audience.

Several CWIS servers provide for IP-address limitations on incoming users, either for the entire server's document base, or on a folder-by-folder basis. This can allow you to limit access to documents served by the CWIS to the campus community. You will need to be sure that the server does not accept the IP address of terminal servers accepting anonymous dial-up users if the vendor of a licensed resource is concerned about local or long-distance telephone users tapping into the resource.

In cases where online resources must be limited to the campus community, often the external database will have a built-in authorization check, often asking the reader to enter a student number or staff ID number. If the resource is available on a host that is Internet-visible, such authorization is essential. In some cases your information providers may rely upon the IP address of the user to verify that a person is on campus. This can open an inadvertent back door if the CWIS points to it. For instance, suppose you list such a resource in your Gopher-based CWIS. From the point of view of the machine serving the information, the Gopher server is on campus, so it passes the IP address test. But if you are running a public "curses" client on that server, and if it accepts incoming users from around the Internet, then all of those users will appear to be local.

Another back door can be inadvertently opened if someone else on campus runs a server that accepts dial-up or inbound Telnet users. If the other person's server points to a resource whose access is offered on a campus-only basis by your CWIS server, the locality test can be passed for users who are not local. As CWIS administrator you will have to work with the other server administrator to resolve the problem.

Any authorization scheme that relies on IP addresses opens up the possibility of back doors. An example of another back door can affect Gopher-based CWISes. Because the Gopher can act as a proxy client for FTP services, it will open an FTP session on behalf of a client who requests a file restricted to campus-only access. Thus your Gopher server can open up access to files that a campus FTP administrator believes are limited to on-campus delivery. In fact, if a user is willing to construct the appropriate "FTP:" selector string, your server can be tricked into FTPing files from servers to which it has no document pointers! As CWIS administrator you will want to work with campus FTP administrators so that they are aware of this issue. The mechanics of this security hole are depicted in Fig. 23.4.

If you run a public client, you will want to be careful to avoid some specific security problems. If your public client can launch a Telnet session, a user can, under certain circumstances, escape to a Telnet prompt and subsequently can "open" a connection anywhere on the Internet. This can potentially enable the anonymous user to attack remote hosts. A version of Telnet called `telnot` can be found on various FTP archives; this tool closes the hole. There are also security problems with the standard `more` text browser under Unix; a tool called `less` solves some of these, as well as providing additional features. Use Archie to locate current copies of these tools.

THE CWIS AND THE HANDICAPPED

A campus-wide information system can be very helpful for members of the campus community who are challenged by visual, hearing, or physical impair-

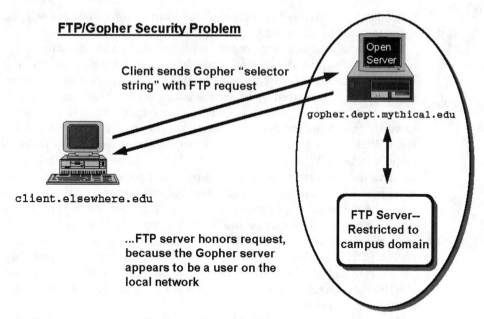

Figure 23.4

ments. Information that previously was available only in printed form, for instance, becomes accessible to the blind. Consider the experience of Michael Hudson, a staff member at the Office of Handicapper Services at Michigan State University:

> I wanted to drop a quick line and tell you how much Gopher means to me. I discovered Gopher about two months ago and cannot believe how much information is out there. I have found the new Veronica option very helpful as it allows me to build a directory of items that are specific to my interest. This is undoubtedly a great service for anyone who finds it. However, for me it is unbelievable. I am legally blind and I have always said that the most difficult aspect of blindness is the lack of readily available information. Gopher has the ability to change all of that. For the first time, I feel like I can easily and independently access important campus and worldwide information. . . . I use a speech synthesizer and a PC compatible computer to access the Gopher system.

The "talker" technology Hudson refers to is available in relatively inexpensive forms; audio cards such as the Soundblaster for the PC come equipped with software that is able to pronounce common words (and spell the words it cannot pronounce). Special-purpose hardware and software may be even better equipped to meet such needs.

It is hard to overstate how great an advantage this can afford. Consider, for example, the ability to easily read campus newspapers and newsletters once they are available on the CWIS. Although there exist reading machines that can scan such materials optically—performing the text-to-audio function fairly effectively—use of these systems can be cumbersome with print matter in the form of newspapers. By placing the machine-readable version of the newspaper available online, your CWIS extends this information resource to the visually impaired in a consistently usable form.

Note that the graphical user interface is antithetical to the use of such tools. A blind user obviously does not benefit from pull-down menus navigated by use of the mouse. On the contrary, a talker works well with software such as the Gopher curses client. The user can become adept at navigating menus by using a consistent number of strokes of the cursor key.*

Similarly, those with hearing impairments may find a CWIS quite useful. However, if, as multimedia tools become more common, you as a CWIS administrator begin exploiting the potential for audio narration, you should bear in mind that exclusive reliance on audio may disenfranchise part of your audience. With a little more effort, the text script associated with audio documents can be made available online alongside the audio selections—the equivalent of closed captioning on television.

THE CWIS AS HISTORICAL ARCHIVE

When you add documents to the CWIS, you are capturing a snapshot about some slice of the campus history. Once you've placed a document online, it is quite easy to set up a corresponding archive of that document. Such an archive can serve as a useful repository for an online historical record.

Here are some examples of how an archive might be useful:

- The student newspaper might be the only periodic record of campus life. On many campuses the faculty and staff grumble about the quality of reporting in the student paper, but such a record is far better than no record at all.

- Similarly, the faculty-staff newsletter can serve as a record of when events transpired, and the university's official perspective on policies and happenings.

- A calendar of events may seem obsolete the instant the last date on the calendar passes. But a "past events" archive could have surprising uses later on. A list of what performers appeared at the campus performing arts center, for instance, could be useful both for historical and for marketing purposes.

- Back issues of the official university academic programs description could be extremely useful for long-term students, for employers considering job appli-

---

* VT100 clients such as Lynx may allow visually impaired users to navigate through complex Web documents using similar strategies. This is an area that merits further study. Where the sighted user can skim large amounts of text annotations relatively quickly, the talker technology may need enhancements to assist in intelligent skimming of hypertext documents.

cants who attended your university, or for curriculum committees considering program changes.

Disk is cheap. When in doubt, archive. You can prune an archive you later decide is useless: by contrast, it's much harder to construct an archive retrospectively.

THE CWIS MAILING LIST

A very active and productive mailing list hosts discussions of CWIS administration issues. It is called CWIS-L and is hosted at Michigan State University. To subscribe send e-mail to:

```
listserv@msu.edu
```

Your message should include in the body a subscription request of the form:

```
subscribe cwis-1 John Doe
```

You may find archived discussions of this mailing list particularly useful, as other CWIS administrators have faced similar issues. To see the index of log files, send the following e-mail to listserv@msu.edu:

```
index cwis-1
```

Internet Information Provider Profiles

A definition of an "Internet information consumer" would be reasonably straightforward to concoct; the term would refer to someone who has some sort of access to the Internet and uses it to obtain information. We could quibble as to what constitutes "information" but otherwise the meaning is fairly obvious. Defining "Internet information provider" would be a little trickier. Would this include someone who posts frequently to Usenet News groups? Someone who occasionally contributes to a little-known mailing list? Someone who puts a file up for anonymous FTP? Someone who once sent e-mail from Compuserve to a friend on the Internet? In some sense, all of these examples represent people who've used the Internet as a medium for delivering information.

For the purposes of our discussion, the definition must be a bit narrower. An information provider on the Internet is someone who regularly delivers information to an audience. The audience need not be massive to be significant; a few dozen scholars from around the world who share an interest in a particular subject area could be a substantial audience. The provider may have felt a calling to start delivering information via the Internet, or the provider's job may inherently have led to the Internet as an online publishing medium.

We offer these profiles in order to show that Internet information providers are real human beings, not monolithic institutions. Just as the Internet can hide geography, at times it can obscure authorship. In many cases, the inspiration of a single person was all it took to bring a resource to the Internet, and these cases have provided some of the most interesting, exciting, useful, or scholarly resources to date.

Besides showing that Internet information providers have human faces, we also hope to inspire others to the same calling. Obviously, one valuable feature of the Internet is the capability for a consumer to search huge information resources spanning worldwide distances. But consumers should also think of themselves as potential providers. As Internet information tools evolve, and as workstations become more powerful, it becomes viable for virtually every consumer to become a provider at some level:

- A university graduate student or faculty member might keep a description of research interests and recent papers online for others to peruse.

- A scientist studying a relatively narrow subject area in a business or government research laboratory might start an electronic journal in order to communicate with colleagues around the world.

- A graphic artist might put a set of samples—images and descriptions—online for potential clients around the world to review (with, of course, a complete online résumé).

- An aspiring musician might do likewise, with audio samples awaiting an Internet-savvy record company president.

- A bureaucrat in a government agency might encourage his management to publish that agency's information via the Internet—or better yet he or she would just get a Gopher or WWW server in production.

Most of our examples represent individuals who were among the pioneering Internet information providers. Generally the level of computer expertise is high, but in some cases the pioneers rely on colleagues or staff members to handle the technical issues. In any event the profiles reveal a bit about what inspired these providers, and what challenges and opportunities they see for Internet information delivery.

KEVIN HUGHES

Kevin Hughes was one of the first publishers of multimedia documents using the Web and Mosaic. He started a World-Wide Web service for Honolulu Community College in May of 1993. Although that was his first Internet service, he quickly became a leader in providing a graphically oriented, campus-wide information system. Currently he is employed by Enterprise Integration Technologies, a firm in the Silicon Valley.

Hughes is modest about his efforts: "I never thought of myself as a provider, but I had always believed in sharing information and helping others to get wired, so I suppose I just fell into the job naturally. In a way, I am changing my dreams and ideas into reality." He encourages others to do likewise: "The important thing is that one simply has to decide to do it. I had been lurking on the Net for years until I discovered the Web. I knew right away it was a Good

Thing and that I could translate my visions more readily through it than anything else."

Hughes' Web service has been popular from the start: "In the first 30 days of operation, our HTTP server received traffic from nearly 1000 hosts and had over 15,000 requests. We had visitors from the Media Lab, AT&T, Sony, Nippon Telephone & Telegraph . . . they just kept coming!" His announcement that on-campus movies were available brought even higher levels of access (see Fig. 24.1).

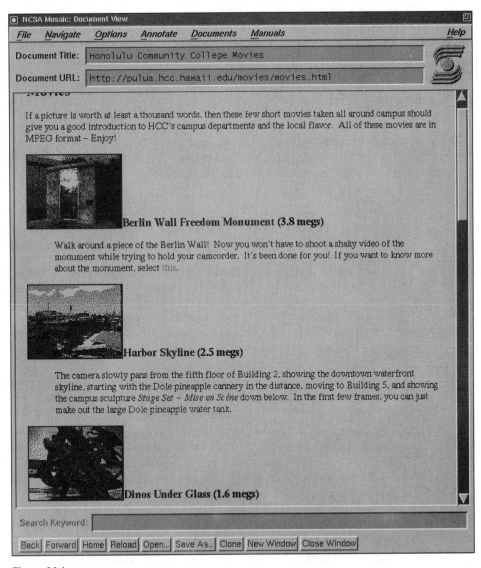

Figure 24.1

Hughes is ambitious in his list of wishes for network technology: "For instance, I'd like 30 frames-per-second, resizable, searchable, stereo audio movies. I'd like interactive hypermedia editing and page layout. I'd like to see support for Japanese characters, interactive forms, intelligent Webspace searches, collaborative software, and virtual reality environments." He realizes how ambitious these dreams are: "But I know I can act spoiled, and be picky, because one day it will happen, in one form or another. And that technology won't be fair, and I won't be satisfied, until the day that everyone has true, full access to it. Perhaps I'll never be satisfied!"

Because of the nature of the material Hughes posted while at HCC, copyright was not an impediment. However, he was careful to obtain permission from those he photographed before placing their images on the Net. Because he recorded the audio and shot the video for his online movies, he did not need to secure those rights. As for text, he either obtained permissions or wrote the text himself. Hughes does feel that the quality of information offered via the Internet will be limited in some cases until there are mechanisms for compensating authors.

Perhaps not surprisingly, this Internet innovator is young: he was 21 at the time he started his Web service. He sees the Net as an important factor for today's youth to embrace:

> Those of my generation are going to be the movers and shakers of the Internet tomorrow. People will have to start paying more attention to them and give them what they need to fulfill their dreams. I can't speak for everyone, but people my age are probably more globally oriented, computer-literate, technologically saturated, media-savvy, and more in debt than any previous generation. Those who can make a difference must help make sure that this does not become a society of haves, who have all the network access, and have-nots, who can do nothing more but operate their Nintendos. If you don't work for the future, the future won't work for you.

MICHAEL MEALLING

Another Campus-Wide Information System resides at the Georgia Institute of Technology, under the stewardship of Michael Mealling. Mealling has served as a Unix network administrator at Georgia Tech since 1991. He describes himself as a "net.hog." Mealling was one of the early adopters of Gopher, and eventually came to manage 10 different Gopher servers. He also became an early advocate for Mosaic and WWW, arguing in early 1993 that the Web was the superior mechanism for delivering documents, and that Gopher servers were appropriate for those organizations that did not have the motivation or expertise to prepare HTML documents.

Mealling believes that the availability of charging mechanisms for Internet delivery of documents will cause the quality of information delivered to improve. He argues, however, that freely offered documents can and will coexist alongside commercial products. He prefers for information to be freely available where possible: "This is why I personally like to live in the realm of free information. I don't mind pushing around copyrighted stuff but I prefer all of my info providers to be as open as possible."

Mealling is active in the Internet Engineering Task Force efforts to define Uniform Resource Identifiers as a standard mechanism for identifying and transporting documents across the Internet. He dreams of the day when Internet publishing tools will be a part of everyone's operating system environment: "Long term I can't wait until MacOS comes with a desktop that has a hard drive icon, a trashcan, and a printing press icon so that *everyone* can publish simply by dropping a file into that folder. And the publishing scheme is truly *open* so that MS-DOS, MacOS, Unix, VMS, VM, MVS, AmigaDOS, MULTICS, OS400, CP/M, NOS, AppleDOS 3.3, users will be able to participate."

Figure 24.2 depicts the Georgia Tech home page.

CHARLES BAILEY

Charles Bailey is the Assistant Director for Systems at the University of Houston Libraries. He has served in systems-related positions at several other libraries. The author of several papers on library automation and electronic

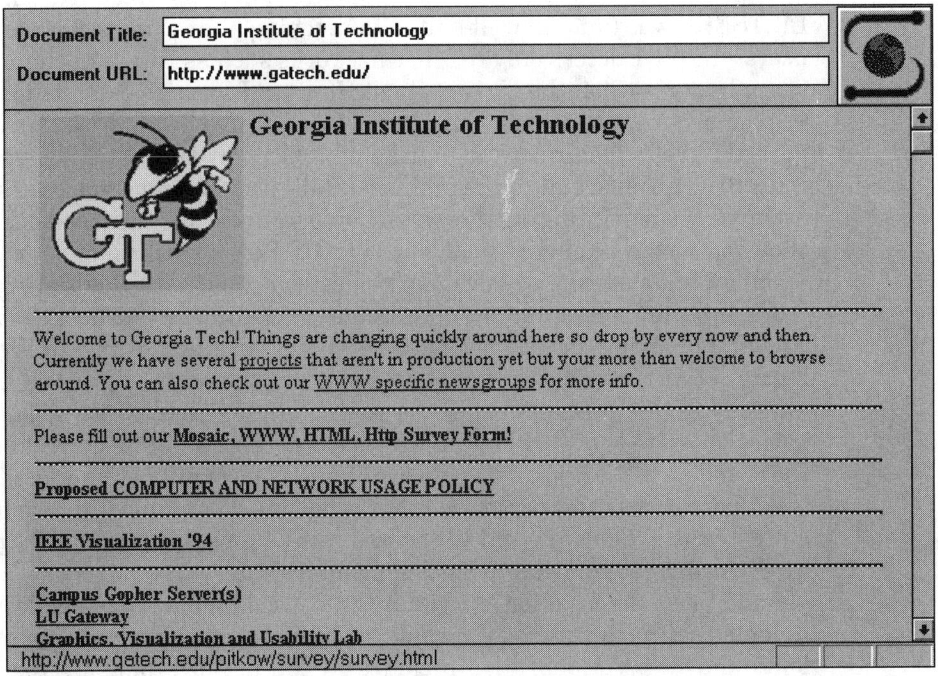

Figure 24.2

publishing, Bailey received Apple Computer's Network Citizen award in 1992, and the Library and Information Technology Association's Library "Hi-Tech" award in 1993. Bailey has been a serious user of the Internet since 1987.

In 1989, Bailey established a moderated LISTSERV mailing list called PACS-L. The purpose of that mailing list is to foster discussion of online pub-lic-access services in libraries, such as the online catalogs that are accessible over the Internet. Also in 1989, Bailey founded PACS Review, a pioneering electronic journal, whose charter was to cover many of the same issues. He remains its editor-in-chief. In 1990, along with Dana Rooks, he established Public-Access Computer Systems News, an electronic newsletter.

PACS Review contains articles that have been selected by the editors as well as a section for peer-reviewed articles selected through a double-blind process (the reviewer and the author do not know the other's name). One of Bailey's goals in establishing PACS Review was to test the viability of network-based electronic journals.

Given the specialized nature of his offerings, Bailey's online documents are popular. PACS-L has over 6500 subscribers in 56 countries. Many more readers may access the mailing list via various gateways. LISTSERV technology has served his goals well; even the PACS Review is distributed through that medium. At the time when Bailey started his journal, Gopher and the Web were still years from deployment; anonymous FTP would have been his only main-stream delivery method. By using standard e-mail as its delivery mechanism, LISTSERV was (and is) well-suited to reaching a far-flung audience, including users who have access only to other networks such as Bitnet or commercial ser-vices. In early 1994, the University of Houston Libraries established their own Gopher service, and issues of the PACS Review are now archived there. At least part of Bailey's inspiration in setting up a Gopher-based archive was to retain control over the format of the archives; Bailey had found some online e-journal archives disappointing in the way they organized his materials. Figure 24.3 shows what the Gopher version of the PACS Review looks like.

Bailey finds editing of a scholarly electronic journal to be time-consuming. Work includes screening of submissions, recruiting of authors, evaluation of drafts, managing of the peer-review process, and editing of final drafts. Because PACS Review is offered on a slightly irregular schedule, based on the quantity of incoming material, the workload presented by these sundry tasks varies. Despite the workload, Bailey says he would not hesitate to undertake these endeavors if he had it to do over again. He says, "Like many librarians, I feel that the existing paper-oriented scholarly communication system is in a state of crisis. Scholars and librarians can help reinvent scholarly publishing by exploring network-based electronic publishing."

Bailey sees the need for "a ubiquitous method for distributing electronic doc-uments that have at least the same sophistication as printed documents (e.g., fonts and illustrations)." He includes in the list of promising tools Acrobat, Gopher+, and MIME.

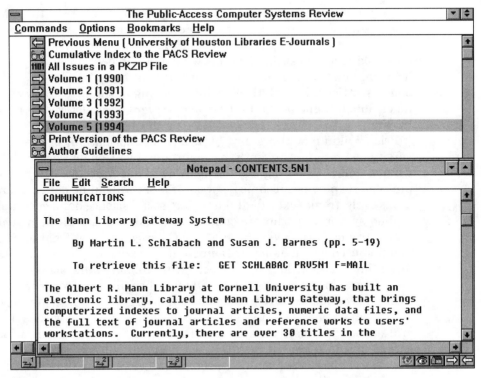

Figure 24.3

The PACS Review is copyrighted, and the University of Houston retains the right to republish its contents. The contents are made freely available to anyone on the Internet (or other networks). Individual authors, however, retain copyright to their articles, and can reuse the material elsewhere.

Bailey worries about privatization of the Internet: "Academic and other noncommercial Internet users need to be vigilant as the network infrastructure is privatized. Many Internet users and information providers enjoy subsidized access to the network. If universities and other nonprofit institutions could no longer afford to provide this kind of subsidized access due to unfavorable changes in network fee structures, the network culture could change dramatically."

JOHN PRICE-WILKIN

John Price-Wilkin has been active in Internet information delivery since 1988, when he was a beta tester for the new Internet access to the ARTFL French literature database. In 1989 he began providing an electronic text service at the University of Michigan. One of his earliest projects was making available the *Oxford English Dictionary* to members of the UM campus community. For that project, he made use of commercial software packages called Pat and Lector running on a Unix workstation. Because of the computer platform, these applications were accessible via Internet protocols, but licensing restrictions precluded general Internet access other than for demonstrations. In early 1992, while working at the University of Michigan, he established one of the first Gopher servers administered in an academic library.

Price-Wilkin now is systems librarian for information services at the University of Virginia. Currently he maintains two Gopher servers for the university, and is exploring the use of World-Wide Web technology for various projects. He provides technical support for several online data centers—in the areas of electronic texts, digital imaging, social science data, geographic information systems, and multimedia. Price-Wilkin assists in the distribution of an electronic journal, *The Bryn Mawr Classical Review.* That journal, edited and produced by Dr. James O'Donnell, is an example of how the Internet can foster information delivery projects with collaborators across institutional and geographic barriers. Price-Wilkin is heavily involved with the use of SGML for online text archives such as the Virginia e-text center. He sees the Web as an advance in Internet document delivery, but he wishes it were general enough to accept an arbitrary Document Type Definition, which would enable him to serve his SGML-based documents to anyone on the Web. He says "I'm happy about many aspects of the technology I'm using; I'm deeply dissatisfied with others."

For Price-Wilkin, content is as important an issue as technology:

> Despite my dissatisfaction with the tools, the bigger issue we face is building the body of canonical resources. As information providers come to understand the need to represent structure in text, and the layered relationship of SGML, DSSL, and page display languages like PostScript, tools will become widely available. We'll still lack large bodies of available SGML-encoded texts, however, and our ability to take advantage of that structural nature we've come to understand will be hampered.

Asked how many hours he spends on the Internet in a given week, Price-Wilkin's response is "frightening question." He believes that others should exploit the Internet as an information delivery medium, but, "I'd never encourage someone to do it in isolation from a professional background or interest. That is, I see the strongest need for services coming from subject specialists and traditional information providers."

He sees a problem with some of the uses of network technology for information delivery: "The path of least resistance drives the activities of most technologists, creating toy collections that have little future value. Compromises that affect the usefulness and even integrity of the data only postpone critical issues that are represented in standards movements and the development of information delivery protocols."

DAVID SEAMAN

David Seaman also works at the University of Virginia, where he heads its Electronic Text Center. Under his direction, the Center has been providing information to the Internet community since August 1992. The Center offers information both via Gopher and World-Wide Web. Their main service is the provision of thousands of on-line full texts marked up in SGML. They use software called Pat (from a vendor called OpenText) to search and display the electronic texts. Users can access the collection using an X Window application called PatMotif, or a VT100 client called Patty. Documents are marked up in SGML so as to allow a variety of different ways of viewing the text. Gopher and the Web are becoming important access methods as well. For instance, a hypertext archive of British poetry is online (see Fig. 24.4).

Many of the texts offered by the Center cannot be offered for general Internet access, due to licensing restrictions on the Pat search software and in some cases on the texts themselves; full access is provided to members of the Uni-

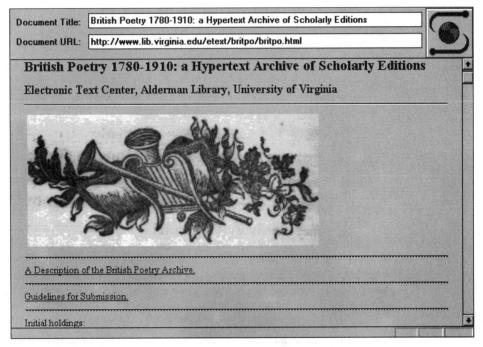

Figure 24.4

versity of Virginia campus community. Remote access to those parts of the collection that are freely available has been popular; over 1600 individuals used the materials in 1993. Seaman uses the Internet for training in use of the e-text archives, and to answer user questions.

Seaman sees wider use of SGML as a natural extension of the kind of uses his center has explored. He anticipates that publishers will offer greater access to SGML-encoded versions of texts for campus site licenses. Copyright is a concern for him, as restrictions necessarily limit the delivery of documents to a narrower audience than he would prefer. Although he feels that "pay as you read" charging schemes will be helpful in promoting access to documents over the Internet, he feels "a fair proportion of the services that I imagine as being limited by the lack of chargeback mechanisms are ones that I am very happy to do without." Seaman feels that the privatization of parts of the Internet is inevitable "and can be to our advantage if the services, in-house access, and tools develop at a greater rate. What does worry me is that the current humanities user community has such a small voice in the development of the Net, and in the description, cataloging, and structuring of data services on the Net."

SUSAN HOCKEY

Susan Hockey is another example of that rare breed of people who combine high levels of computer expertise with a desire to support use of computing technology in the humanities. She began using computers in 1969 when she wrote her first Fortran program on an Atlas computer, which she proclaims was the first-ever computer that performed paging. She spent 16 years at Oxford University, managing projects such as the development of the Oxford Concordance Program, a major research tool in the humanities. Hockey now heads the Center for Electronic Texts in the Humanities (CETH), a joint project of Rutgers University and Princeton University. Their mission is to advance scholarship in the humanities by the use of high-quality electronic resources.

CETH has developed an Inventory of Machine-Readable Texts in the Humanities, which is available to users of the Research Libraries Information Network. CETH has been working to build a corpus of humanities texts, such as a collection of writings of early women authors in the English language, for use by the scholarly community. Like others in the e-text community, Hockey sees SGML as a key tool for supporting the kind of research scholars need to undertake. SGML tagging allows those who are marking up a document to identify specific usages in a way that concepts can be traced across time; for instance, as spellings change slightly. Hockey plans to use the facilities of the Text Encoding Initiative's SGML implementation, "which was designed to deal with the many and varied characteristics of scholarly texts in the humanities." Hockey sees both marked-up text and the original documents as important to scholarship: "At a later stage we plan to incorporate images as well as text so that users can search on the encoded text and retrieve an image of the text or manuscript if they wish."*

Hockey had originally conceived of using CD ROM as the distribution medium of choice, but now sees the Internet as the best way to make many collections available to scholars worldwide. She is concerned about the authenticity of online archives:

> We would also like to see mechanisms for authenticating data so that users can have some assurance of quality in the texts we hold. By quality we mean error-free—as far as possible—with uniform encoding which addresses scholarly needs, and from a reliable source which is well-documented. We also consider stability and continued maintenance of the resources to be crucial for our long-term development plans and this could have some implications for ownership issues.

As of this writing CETH does not yet offer core materials via the Internet, but they do sponsor a LISTSERV mailing list (`ceth@pucc.princeton.edu`) for discussion of their projects. Information on CETH is also available via Gopher (see Fig. 24.5).

Hockey's current research includes how to catalog and document electronic texts in the humanities, as well as evaluation of SGML-based client-server software in light of current Text Encoding Initiative guidelines.

PETER FLYNN

Peter Flynn has been working with computers since he helped build an analog computer in high school in the late 1960s. He is active in several computing organizations, serving as an officer in the TeX user group and in the Irish Computer Society. He ran the first gateway between the Irish academic network and the outside world starting in 1984. Flynn hosts various Internet services:

- An Acronym Server (send `help` to `freetext@iruccvac.ucc.ie` for details)
- Over a dozen mailing lists
- A Web service as part of the Thesaurus Linguarum Hiberniae, a text database of Irish literature dating as far back as 600 A.D.

---

* Another scholar using computers to make texts available to his peers, Dr. Kevin Kiernan of the University of Kentucky, has already found empirically that provision of images can be useful to scholarship. For instance, he has made scanned images of original text from Beowulf, and discovered that the scanned versions offer the individual scholar the opportunity to note handwritten changes that may be subject to alternative interpretations. When one scholar prepares a machine-readable version of a document, only his or her interpretation of ambiguously written passages will prevail.

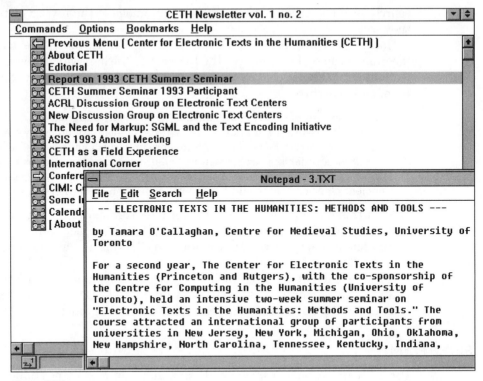

Figure 24.5

The building of the TLH archive is a 10-year project, aimed at students and researchers in Celtic Studies, Linguistics, Folklore, History, Geography, and any subject relating to Ireland. Figure 24.6 is an example of a document from the archive.

Flynn is happy with technology such as SGML and the Web tools, and would welcome more people contributing their services via the Web. Flynn sees open technologies as critical for success in this sort of online publishing. He believes therefore that a proprietary solution like Acrobat's Portable Document Format is not a good alternative to SGML and HTML; besides being proprietary, he feels Acrobat "is barking up the wrong tree, concentrating way too much on display format when the key to successful document handling is *structure.*"

Copyright is an issue for Flynn in his role of Internet publisher: many of the TLH texts will require copyright permission. Copyright owners have in many cases agreed to online publication if the print edition of their works is no longer in the current catalog. Only copyright-free texts will be made generally available, though Flynn would like to offer access to copyrighted materials under a scheme that offers secure individual authorization that is acceptable to the

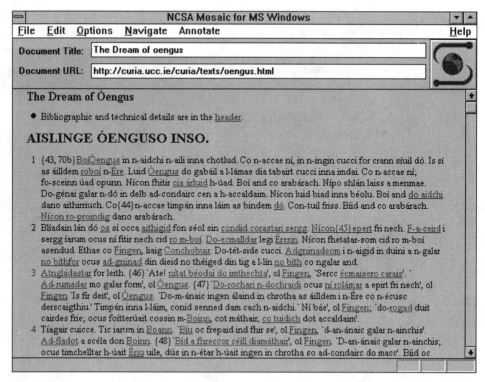

Figure 24.6

holders of copyright. He sees the advent of per-individual chargeback schemes as potentially helpful to efforts such as his, but he also worries that "it may encourage charging unnecessarily by avaricious institutions who fail to understand the cooperative nature of networking."

ARCHIE WARNOCK

A paper-tape terminal connected to a remote time-shared computer was Archie Warnock's window into the world of computing during his high school days in the late 1960s. His odyssey carried him to DEC PDP-11 minicomputers, to VAXes, to personal computers, and finally to Unix machines. Today an 80486-based PC running the Linux version of Unix graces his desktop. Warnock works for Hughes STX at NASA's Goddard Space Flight Center, doing science support work. He says he spends at least 40 hours a week on the Net: "It's my job to stay current and look for new ideas that might be used in making information available online. Not a bad deal . . ."

Figure 24.7 shows the Web home page Warnock uses to offer documentation of his project's services.

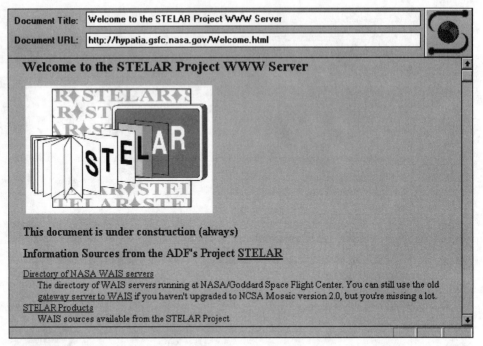

Figure 24.7

Warnock is responsible for a WAIS database that holds over 75,000 abstracts of articles from astronomical journals. His office supports a number of other WAIS databases as well. The service went online in October 1992, and handles in excess of 10,000 queries per month. Figure 24.8 shows an example of a WAIS query looking for abstracts of articles that relate experiments carried out on Skylab.*

Warnock says that since these databases have been in place, relatively little maintenance effort has been necessary—ensuring the databases are current, the servers are running normally, and so forth. Currently he is concentrating on finding information to place online, and ways to automate the process of posting information. He credits Jim Fullton (who works at CNIDR, the home of Free WAIS) with encouraging the use of a WAIS database. Warnock says, "WAIS has now given us the capability to make information available to a wide cross-section of the user community with an absolute minimum of software development and with a very small staff. It's been extremely resource efficient."

For Warnock, the combination of the display capabilities of Mosaic with the search capabilities of WAIS is important: "I believe that by merging query and

---

* Skylab was the United States' first space station, deployed in the mid-1970s.

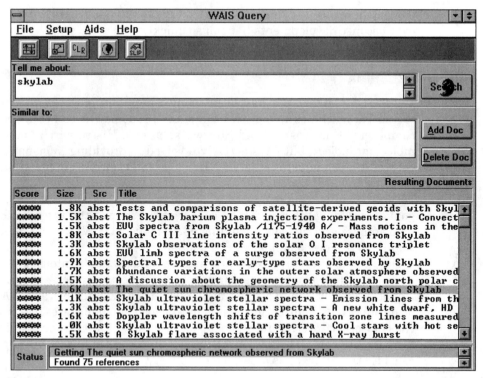

Figure 24.8

discovery capabilities of WAIS with the retrieval and display capabilities of WWW and Mosaic, we're on the verge of a revolution in on-line services. I'm looking down the road at using WWW as the tool for true electronic publishing—scientific journals and the like." Copyright is a serious issue for the kinds of services he provides:

> We can't give complete, unrestricted access to the materials we want to place online without undercutting the commercial service that provides them. And if we *did* undercut them, there would be no source for the information. . . . The fact of the matter is that it costs money to make many types of information available. Publishers require funds to pay editors and to maintain hardware and all the other things that go into the process, and they have to get those funds from somewhere.

Warnock believes the future of Internet information publishing is bright, but he is uncertain as to what direction it may take, given the rapid advances made possible by tools like WAIS in only a few years. He says, "The moral, for development projects, is that you have to be flexible, and make it possible to incorporate new technologies and new philosophies as part of the dynamic development process. And you have to stay current—it's more critical now than ever because developments happen so quickly."

HIROSHI MIZUSHIMA

Dr. Hiroshi Mizushima has been using computers since high school, from "primitive machines to big host computers," but now uses MS-DOS personal computers, Macintoshes, and Sun workstations. His research background is molecular biology, but he is actively involved in providing information via the Internet on behalf of his employer, the National Cancer Center Research Institute, located in Tokyo.

Dr. Mizushima implemented a Gopher server in February 1993, with the goal of providing information on cancer research over the Internet. He is also using other delivery tools, including anonymous FTP, WAIS, and mailing lists. Figure 24.9 shows a sample of his Gopher service.

Documents offered by NCC are freely available to all Internet users. As of June 1993 their Gopher was handling 500 requests per day—the most active Gopher server in Japan at the time. Thus far, copyright is not an issue for him, as he offers only information that is free of such encumbrances. He is willing to consider other Internet technologies but he finds that Gopher is adequate for his current goals. Dr. Mizushima urges others with information to provide to consider the Internet as a method of delivery.

PETER SCOTT

One of the best-known catalogs of Internet resources is Peter Scott's Hytelnet database.* This database is a compilation of services such as online library catalogs offered as a database and as software that will run under MS-DOS or under Unix. The name "Hytelnet" is a hybrid of "hypertext" and "Telnet." There are Gopher and Web versions of the Hytelnet database as well. Scott released the first version of Hytelnet in 1990. Scott's "day job" is manager of small systems in the systems department of the University of Saskatchewan in Saskatoon, Canada. Scott has had full access to the Internet since 1989.

Hytelnet is Scott's main Internet-related labor of love. He says, "I was inspired to create Hytelnet because, at the time, I thought that Internet users would like to have an electronic version of paper directories." Scott spends fifty to sixty hours per week on the Internet, either reading and writing e-mail, or updating information for Hytelnet.

Scott sees privatization of the Internet as a risk, limiting access to those who can pay. He says "Information should be available to everyone at no cost."

---

* See the discussion of Hytelnet and other tools for finding resources in Chap. 16.

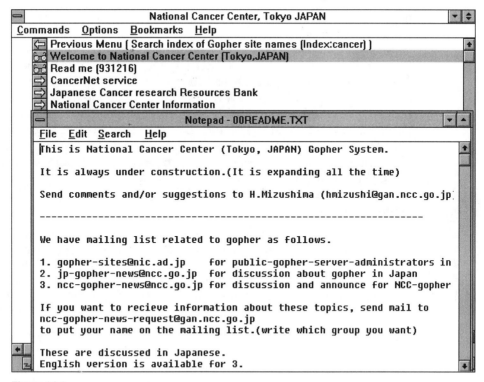

Figure 24.9

One problem Scott encounters from time to time is sites that run old versions of his database for public access. When he chances upon such sites, he urges them to upgrade. (That problem is an inherent risk for a database whose entire contents are distributed as a package.)

ANNE O'DONNELL

Anne O'Donnell grew up on a computer terminal with a paper tape reader, and, she says, as a bad typist, fell victim to hard-to-correct typographical errors. An infinite loop in one of her first programs led her to promise never to work with computers. Her experience with programming Fortran in college did not inspire her to pursue computing, but her first job as a seismic analyst included some Fortran programming, and she came to enjoy working with computers. She moved into programming in earnest, and eventually took a job as a physical scientist with the National Oceanic and Atmospheric Administration (NOAA). Her current desktop machine is a Sun workstation.

O'Donnell's experience with the Internet dates back to ARPANET days. Her current main service involves providing access to NOAA datasets over the

Internet. The original application supporting users was a custom application implemented in the database language RDBMS and accessible via Telnet; during the last year, she has worked to provide access to these datasets via WAIS. Because many of her users will not be able to install WAIS clients on their workstations, she also has chosen to implement a Gopher server as a "front end" to the WAIS datasets. WWW is another option for access to the datasets.

The NOAA user community is hard to describe. Users include scientists, teachers, resource managers, etc. Lawyers and insurance companies use NOAA information to determine historical weather data. Analysis of logs shows that users come in from all over the world, and from various organizations. O'Donnell finds that the service requires relatively little upkeep. She sees standard tools as providing an advantage for the user as well as the information provider:

> To put up more specialized software, it needs to be tested, tested, and tested with users so that it is relatively easy to use. The user interface to our database is somewhat difficult because of the software package we are using. We have to provide manuals to users to help them use the software. But at least they can eventually find what they want. . . . I think Gopher, WAIS, and WWW will be easier for our users and also easier for us to maintain. I would suggest that others look at these software packages.

NOAA's Gopher is available at `gopher.esdim.noaa.gov`; their Web service resides at `www.esdim.noaa.gov`.

O'Donnell sees a need for more powerful search options: "I'd like to see more done with WAIS—"fielded" searches, i.e., search only parts of the text for certain words. For example, the user could request data collected in Colorado versus seeing "hits" on data because the main contributor happens to live in Colorado. I'd like a more intuitive WAIS client so that users don't need to be helped through using it the first time."

Copyright is not a concern for O'Donnell; all of the NOAA datasets are freely available for all users.

Like many other information providers, O'Donnell is concerned about the Internet's future: "I do worry about privatization of the Internet, both from the point of view of our user community—I think we'll lose lots of users—but also from the point of view of my office being able to keep up with what's going on in the Internet world."

ED VIELMETTI

Although the other information providers profiled in this chapter are technically savvy, their focus lies in the providing of information, not access to the Internet per se. Ed Vielmetti is unusual in that he wears both hats. He is a well-known "net personality" who has contributed WAIS databases, the creation of new Usenet News groups, many postings of helpful advice on those news groups and in other forums, and archives of useful software. In addition,

Vielmetti is the vice president of an Internet service provider known as MSEN, located in Ann Arbor, Michigan.

Vielmetti's first use of computers took place over a 300-bit-per-second modem; he connected to a computer at Northern Michigan University while a high school student in that region. While in college at the University of Michigan, he received an Apple II computer as a gift from his parents, and he was hooked. In 1985 Vielmetti obtained a Zenith MS-DOS computer, and began looking for software for it. He decided to start an online archive of the best of public domain software, and he housed that archive on the mainframe computer at the university. The Simtel20 archive, maintained by Keith Peterson, was online, and Vielmetti used the then-slow Internet link from the university to obtain and examine new packages for possible inclusion in the archive.

Vielmetti compiled one of the first lists of anonymous FTP sites, "back in the days before Archie, when there was no real way of finding out where files were to be gotten from, you just knew because someone had told you. I went through some of my saved-up mail announcing stuff, collated the sites with a brief description of what was on them, and sent it out." The year was 1986.

When that project became unwieldy, Vielmetti found another volunteer to take it over. Then he moved onto another project, building a Usenet News group called `comp.archives`. He says `comp.archives` was a lot of fun: "I wrote some code to filter through the whole Usenet News group stream, to read all the articles, and to try to guess which ones were announcements of new programs.* At its peak I was re-posting updates of 30 announcements in a day." Eventually he found another volunteer to take over that project.

Vielmetti was one of the founders of Msen in 1991. "Having graduated from the university and leaving a university job . . . there was no obvious way to keep an Internet connection." Because he was accustomed to T1 speeds, a dial-up service was not adequate. So he and some partners founded an Internet service provider. "We started Msen with the idea that the network was too hard to learn about, too hard to use once you had found it, and too hard and too expensive to connect to. So we decided to try to do something about it, and offer our own network service."

During a consulting stint with the regional network CICNet, Vielmetti began exploring how to use Gopher and WAIS to ease access to information. Currently Msen offers a variety of services to its users, including a Gopher server that is also available for Internet access. One of the most popular services on the Msen Gopher is the Online Career Center, an Internet-based market that serves employers and job seekers alike; employers can post "help wanted" advertisements, and those seeking positions can post their resumes online (see Fig. 24.10).

---

* This, no doubt, is one of the earliest practical applications of an information agent or information filter for a serious data-gathering endeavor on the Internet.

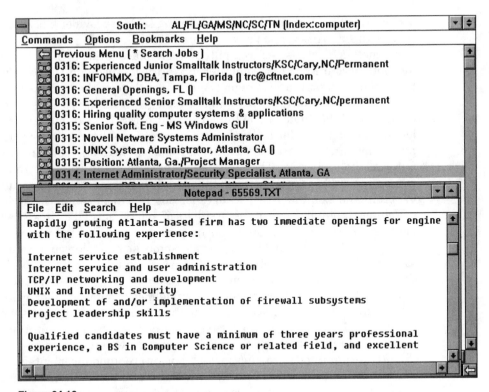

Figure 24.10

Not only has the Online Career Center proved a popular Internet service, it has also served as an interesting example of a self-fulfilling prophecy: When *New York Times* reporter John Markoff wrote that some Internet service outages were causing people to "stop and gawk on the information highway," causing further traffic jams, he cited the Online Career Center on the Msen Gopher as one of the busy services on the Internet. The load on Msen's Gopher doubled that day.

Vielmetti sees bandwidth as a big part of the challenge of providing superior information delivery:

> The biggest problem is these stupid analog modems that are between me and the people I'm trying to serve. I will be glad for the day when the last of them is retired, just like we retired the acoustic coupler, and when there is reasonable digital service (like ISDN) to the home. Not only will it mean more bandwidth—and the newer cool Internet stuff like Mosaic can use that bandwidth, I assure you—but it will also be the end of endless finger-pointing between us and the telephone company over whether a particular long piece of copper is good enough.

In Vielmetti's opinion, an important part of history flows through the Internet every day. "Stale copies of data are, well, part of the historical record. There's so little real history of the Internet that's accessible in any meaningful way, and as a result the odd scraps of e-mail from ten to twenty years ago attain 'relic' status." Still, he sees the need for archives to be selective: "There is a lot of crud out there on the nets, probably as bad as my first experience of looking through disk after disk of little PC utilities to change the color of the screen. You deal with it by throwing out the crud and talking about the good stuff."

The Future of the Internet

The early 1990s have seen a confluence of Internet-related trends:

- Dramatic growth in the size of the Internet, within the count of Internet hosts growing at a rate exceeding five percent *per month*

- The deployment of protocols such as Gopher and World-Wide Web, and client programs such as Mosaic, that represent a sea change in how a user looks for and retrieves documents over the Internet

- An explosion of interest in the "information highway" concept, with politicians, telecommunications companies, and the entertainment industry all promising brave new worlds of information delivery

It is perhaps folly to hazard guesses as to the future in an environment of such ferment and upheaval. Nonetheless, in this chapter we will gaze into the crystal ball.

WHICH INFORMATION DELIVERY TOOL WILL PREVAIL?

Gopher, World-Wide Web, and WAIS have attained a status of the holy trinity of Internet information delivery tools. It is useful to compare the relative levels of usage of these tools. The chart in Fig. 25.1 is based on sample data gathered by the Merit Network as part of their management of the NSFnet

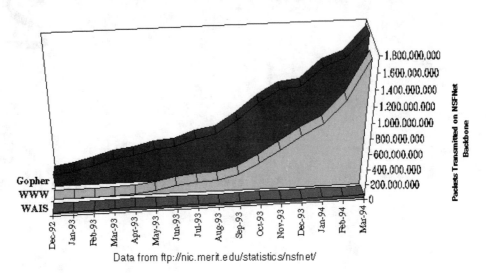

Internet Information Retrieval Tool Usage Trends

Data from ftp://nic.merit.edu/statistics/nsfnet/

Figure 25.1

backbone. It compares the number of packets transferred for each of these three services.

Note several caveats in interpreting this data:

- The data is based on packets transmitted, not on number of user transactions. Because the World-Wide Web tends to deliver long documents with large in-line images, this tends to overstate the number of Web transactions; a given Gopher menu might be 2000 bytes in size, whereas a Web home page might be 20,000 or 200,000 bytes.*

- Transmission of large quantities of data is not necessarily indicative of effective information delivery. Theoretically, a WAIS search might allow a user to quickly locate a particular piece of information, whereas the Gopher or Web user might spend hours browsing titles and running up the packet meter.

- These numbers measure data transferred over the NSFnet backbone; they therefore do not reflect usage when the user and the server reside on a non-U.S. network or between two points in the United States that do not require NSFnet links.

---

* Data for bytes transmitted are also available; packets transmitted are shown in order to reflect actual load on the network. A chart of bytes transmitted would show roughly similar relative levels of usage.

- These numbers reflect usage on the standard IANA-assigned ports. If, for instance, a Gopher server runs on port 1070, that usage is not shown. Moreover, it is common to run WAIS databases "behind" Gopher servers. Such configurations will give credit to the Gopher server instead of the WAIS server if the former delivers the data over the backbone.

- This chart should be considered in context. For the last month shown, Gopher represented about 2.5 percent of the traffic on the backbone, placing it number 9 among identified applications. By contrast, the number 1 application, FTP data delivery, accounted for 21 percent of the packets (and 41 percent of the bytes) delivered. The tried-and-true FTP protocol is still delivering the bulk of data over the Internet.

Despite these caveats, we can see definite patterns in this data. Gopher and the Web have experienced explosive growth in the amount of information they deliver, and there is no reason to suspect these trends will abate. WAIS, by contrast, has experienced a roughly static level of usage for over a year.

The number of Gopher and Web servers has grown dramatically; from early 1993 to early 1994, the number of Gopher servers quadrupled, and the number of Web servers increased by a factor of 14. As this book goes to press, there are over 1400 registered Gopher servers, with over 6500 "discovered" during Veronica index runs. There are over 1200 Web servers. There are about 125 WAIS servers, representing over 490 WAIS "sources." Of course, these numbers are not directly comparable. Just as the Library of Congress holds more books than a small public library, it could be the case that a given WAIS server holds more data than several Gopher servers. Nonetheless, it is clear that both in terms of data delivered and in terms of servers online, Gopher and the Web are clearly outstripping WAIS.

Where will these trends lead us? It seems likely that over time either the Gopher community will adopt HTML—effectively ending the distinction between Gopher and the Web—or the Web will eventually overtake Gopher as the primary Internet browsing and document delivery tool. That day could be a long way off, however: many users who have slow access to the Internet—and many others who have fast access but who do not like to wait 20 seconds for a home page to appear on screen—prefer Gopher over the Web. Gopher has a definite role to play, at least for the next few years.

As for WAIS, there may be a resurgence of interest in that tool, or in other tools that implement the Z39.50 standard. In today's Internet much of the activity of navigation takes place through browsing, and through recording of interesting topics in local hot lists or bookmarks. This model is adequate for casual searching with a relatively small universe of documents—especially when users are willing to accept the fact that they never discover many documents of interest. As we saw in Chap. 14, tools like Veronica can ameliorate the search problem somewhat—but Veronica is a title search tool, unable to give insight into the contents of documents. The WAIS concept may prove an essential mechanism for sifting among extremely large collections of documents.

Whether it is WAIS or some other index tool, we will probably reach a point where the normal mode of Internet navigation involves consulting an index as the first step. It is possible to navigate through the collection in a used bookstore or in a small public library by browsing the shelves. It would be unthinkable to try to browse the shelves of a large research library with 3 million volumes. Instead, one always consults the catalog when performing any sort of serious search. An online catalog allows a user to identify a list of candidate documents, chosen based on an understanding of the content of each document. Whether such a tool comes from the Archie developers, the WAIS developers, a consortium of libraries, or some other community, we will need such a tool to support serious, purposeful searching of an Internet with millions of documents and other resources.

A STANDARD BOOK NUMBER FOR THE INTERNET

This book, like all other books from established publishers, has an International Standard Book Number, or ISBN. Periodicals are similarly assigned International Standard Serial Numbers (ISSNs). These are standard "handles" one can use in ordering books, in searching library catalogs, etc.

The Internet needs similar standard names for documents and online resources. The Uniform Resource Locator created for use in the World-Wide Web is a start along these lines. It is a standard way to name a particular document on a particular server.

The Internet Engineering Task Force is working to establish a general standard for a Uniform Resource Identifier that would build upon the URL concept. Under the URI umbrella one would also find Uniform Resource Names, which are roughly analogous to ISBNs. An ISBN identifies a particular title, but does not tell you where you will find copies of the title. For that information you have to interrogate your local library or book store. In the Internet context, the URI engineers envision a global, distributed directory service, analogous to the Domain Name System, that will provide you (or your client program) with a list of URLs that correspond to a given URI. In other words, you tell the service you are looking for a copy of Moby Dick, and the service gives you a list of places where you might find it. Your client, being intelligent, picks a place that is accessible over a short-haul, uncongested link, and you have gained access to your chosen resource.

This scenario sounds sensible in theory, but the devil is in the details of designing a working system. One issue is how URNs will be assigned, and what constitutes a work whose content is "equivalent" to another version. For instance, if a publisher offers an image file in TIFF format, and an archive site offers a copy in JPG format, are the two documents equivalent, therefore meriting the same URN? Who will make this decision? One school of thought argues that only the publisher can answer that question—but what is the mechanism by which the answer will be promulgated?

The problem of equivalence extends to any document that can take multiple forms. Should the flat ASCII version of a monograph have the same URN as the PostScript version? Certainly not, say some: the PostScript version may contain graphics and formatting that make the two inherently different. Certainly so, say others: the content of the text is what is important.

A similar thorny question is one of how to handle time-specific titles. One would want to be able to say to a client, "Get me the current weather forecast" or "Fetch me a copy of today's *Washington Post*." If an archive site has not yet received the "current" version of the document you seek, you may get stale data. In any event, the URN for the "current" version of a document will necessarily point to different URLs over time, complicating the delivery process.

Although the task force working on these issues faces daunting questions, their work will no doubt eventually bear fruit. A workable URI scheme will have many advantages:

- Indexing of documents will be enhanced.

- It will be easier for users to include citations in documents they write, without fear that particular copies of the cited documents will disappear. Just as a paper can refer to *Time* magazine by volume and number, without concern as to whether it is archived at a particular library, a future online paper can refer to a particular number of an online journal, without the author worrying about which archive site holds a copy.

- It will be easier to develop technology to support caching of documents, promoting more efficient use of Internet communications links. (See discussion of caching later in this chapter.)

DYNAMIC DOCUMENTS

Print documents are inherently static: A great deal of work may go into document preparation, but once the document is printed, the moving finger has writ. Most online documents are similarly static: An author prepares the text, and it remains as written until a subsequent update phase.

Online document delivery offers the possibility for documents to be updated "on the fly" using automated processes. This could be as simple as a weather server inserting the current local temperature in the text of an explanation of how to use the server. Ever-more elaborate schemes can be envisioned, whereby HTML becomes a dynamic rather than a static medium. For example, researchers at the University of Minnesota offer an interactive geometry service. (See Fig. 25.2.) This server, for instance, allows users to ask for 3-D rendering to be redrawn from the perspective of the user's choice.

Another example of delivery of dynamic information via the Web is offered at Stanford University. A group there has set up a virtual environment that tests

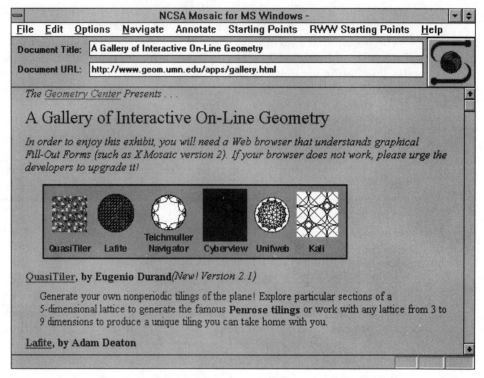

Figure 25.2

one's ability to solve problems relating to the space shuttle. The user interacts with a virtual system and is given different results based on choices made, as shown in Fig. 25.3.

In a sense, these developments are nothing profound; they are merely an example of interactive computing. But these efforts go far beyond the traditional interactive computing model, presenting the user with documents that exhibit all the richness that a client like Mosaic can display on the screen, and allowing user interaction via custom form screens and locator maps. Such user interfaces make the traditional VT100 or 3270 full-screen terminal appear to be a distant relic.

HTML+ AND ADVANCED HYPERMEDIA

As elaborate as documents can be with a client like Mosaic rendering HTML, there is room for still richer modes of presentation. One effort, under rigorous discussion in the World-Wide Web community, is the development of HTML+. Spearheaded by Dave Raggett, an employee of Hewlett-Packard in the United

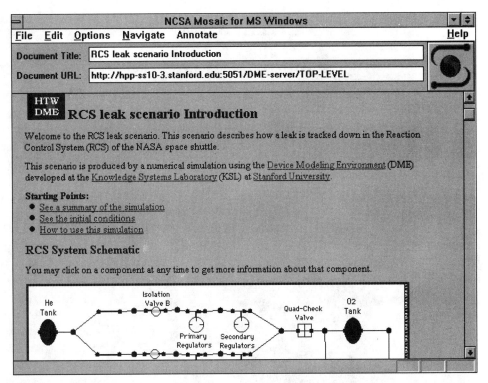

Figure 25.3

Kingdom, HTML+ is a successor to HTML intended to offer documents with even greater functionality. As the community discusses the extended language, Raggett implements the features in a client program he has developed. Figure 25.4 is an example screen as rendered by his client.

One simple distinction between HTML+ and HTML is the ability of text to "wrap" around embedded images. Compare this screen to every Mosaic example shown in this book—none of them shows this form of wrapping, because it is not a defined feature of HTML. This relatively simple enhancement has sparked intense debate in the Web community. One line of argument holds that this sort of precise control over layout does not belong in HTML, or in any SGML-compliant system. When precise layout is required, goes the reasoning, the publisher should use a tool that is intended for that purpose—PostScript, Acrobat, or other alternatives. If HTML becomes burdened with such features, the job of authoring will become needlessly complex, and clients and servers will become cumbersome.

HTML+ advocates argue that we must progress beyond HTML, so that documents on screen can take on all the attributes of elaborate printed text, while continuing to offer modes of interaction only possible in an online medium.

Figure 25.4

They propose other extensions, such as support for embedded tabular information, with table elements presented in discrete cells no matter the display terminal. They also argue that the Web needs to be able to deliver mathematical symbols for display on client terminals, because a great deal of scientific information must be expressed in mathematical terms.

Whether multimedia documents are delivered via HTML or HTML+, one aspect of the future of multimedia pertains more to inspiration than technology: in the first year after Mosaic was deployed, there has been a veritable race to see who can deliver the most elaborate information via the Web. The question is: what is the depth of commitment to multimedia authoring? We see much breadth of involvement, across individuals and institutions; when networked multimedia is broadly understood—when it is "old hat"—will the commitment continue?

If the depth of commitment is shallow, we may well see an Internet full of elaborate multimedia experiments that offer relatively little content. Or, we may see authors retrench from multimedia, while still making good use of the hypertext aspects of the Web. In any event, the deployment of effective authoring tools will be welcomed by all Web document authors.

ENHANCED TOOLS FOR THE INFORMATION PROVIDER

Besides improved tools for authoring documents for the Web (and other media) we can also look forward to improvements in the servers used to deliver information. There is no reason why a server should be hard to install; the Minnesota GopherSurfer product is proof. Over time we may see server software—on many platforms—that is highly functional yet easy to install. Indeed, there is no reason why an operating system cannot come prepackaged with server functionality. Take heed, Microsoft; you should ship Windows NT with a working Gopher server as part of the system.

In addition to ease of installation, there is the question of managing data. A Gopher or Web administrator has much more to do than place data online: often the data needs conversion or massaging for presentation; old data must be expired or updated periodically; licensed data must be served only to those authorized; document utilization patterns must be analyzed.

A commercial server product could address all of these needs, as well as providing support of a vendor. Such a product might provide automation for the document submission and update process, send notices to document owners that documents need updating, warn the administrator of unusual client activity, produce preformatted usage logs, etc. After the first generation of server administrators grows weary of routine maintenance tasks, there could be a considerable market for such a product.

SMARTER CLIENTS; BETTER NAVIGATION TOOLS

As powerful as Internet clients have become, one can imagine further improvements. For instance, suppose your client is able to notice aspects of your Internet cruising behavior—which documents are your favorite selections, which documents have links that you select often, which documents take a long time to display, which index search tools you use a lot, and so forth. A client could enhance your navigation by adapting to your behavior.

Another level of tool would make it easier for Internet users to deal with information overload. This class of tool is often mentioned as a way to cope with a barrage of incoming e-mail. Several research projects have been undertaken to provide tools to help; one example is the Information Lens project at MIT. This sort of tool attempts to recognize which items of incoming mail are critical (note from your boss) and which can be dispensed with (a flame from a malcontent on a news group). Tools that address this problem are beginning to find their way into commercial products.

The search for a simple yet powerful tool that enhances navigation is analogous to the search for a unified field theory: many Internet engineers would love to solve the problem. Ultimately the task is the same as the general problem of how to provide a user interface that combines ease of use with the ability to fetch particular pieces of information from a chaotic universe of data. The next few years will certainly see improvements in navigation tools, both in the Internet and the broader context.

THE DIAL-UP ACCESS PROBLEM

In order to experience Internet resources in their richest depth, you must have a direct IP connection to the Internet; this is a basic assumption on the part of authors of client applications like NCSA Mosaic. As we saw in Chap. 5, IP dial-up users can use SLIP or PPP protocols to obtain true IP connectivity; however, this option has problems:

- SLIP and PPP are cumbersome to set up in many cases.
- SLIP and PPP each impose overhead that lowers effective bandwidth; the loss is perceptible when downloading large files over a relatively slow modem link. (PPP is somewhat more efficient than SLIP but still adds overhead.)
- Problems with SLIP and PPP connections require more skilled diagnostic effort to resolve than do conventional dial-up modes.
- Many Internet service providers charge steep premiums for SLIP or PPP access

Contributing to the woes of the dial-up IP user is the large array of vendors involved, as seen in Fig. 25.5. As a dial-up user, you may acquire parts from a large number of different suppliers. Your computer and its operating system may count for one or two vendors; another vendor may supply the modem; the telephone service represents one or two more service providers; your Internet service provider will usually be a different company; the terminal server employed by the service provider was probably made by still another party. Furthermore, your TCP/IP software package likely comes from yet another vendor, and your client programs may come from several vendors.

In theory, all of these disparate pieces are supposed to fit together thanks to standards. In practice, actual functioning is often less than ideal. When there are problems, the user may be bounced back and forth among the various vendors.

The Dial-up Connectivity Conundrum: Multiple Vendors

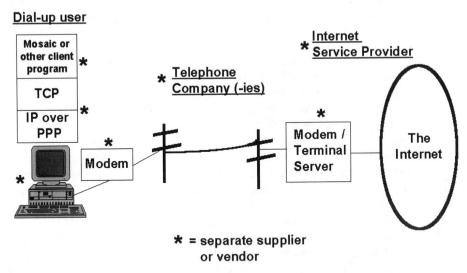

Figure 25.5

Are there solutions to this conundrum? Happily the answer is "yes." Favorable trends include:

- TCP/IP software packages in general, and PPP support in particular, are becoming easier to install.

- TCP/IP may come installed on your operating system. Windows NT, for instance, comes with TCP/IP support built in. Most workstation implementations of Unix have always included TCP/IP. If such systems have PPP ready to use for dial-up, the user's burden is lightened.

- Some vendors are integrating TCP/IP with other components. Notis Systems Inc. is said to plan to offer a functional version of their WinGopher product with a TCP/IP package ready to install.

- Internet service providers may begin to offer ready-to-install TCP/IP packages that are known to work well in the service provider's environment. O'Reilly and Associates has announced an "Internet in a Box" package, for instance.

- Better documentation and packaging of TCP/IP products may come in noncommercial forms as well. For instance, the staff of Merit Inc. (the organization in Michigan that operates Michnet and managed the NSFnet backbone during its period of explosive usage growth) has been active in preparing easy-to-install PPP access for Macintosh and other users.* Even an individual benefactor can help: N. Dean Pentcheff of the University of South Carolina has built a DOS Internet Kit including public domain TCP/IP code and instructions for installation by the SLIP (dial-up) user as well as the directly attached user.†

For TCP/IP to prosper in the dial-up environment, these trends must bear fruit, or an alternative to IP must be provided for the dial-up user. Such an alternative would have to offer the power of client programs like Mosaic in order to yield the same rich access directly connected users have come to expect. In a mass-market environment, installation of such tools must be the model of simplicity. Surveys have shown that a large proportion of owners of video cassette recorders do not understand the steps required to program these devices—and PPP setup can be more complicated. For the mass market, installation of the Internet-access tool must be as simple as putting a floppy in a drive and running an automated installation program.

One TCP/IP vendor, NetManage, markets a version of its Chameleon TCP/IP product for MS-Windows that is specifically tailored for dial-up users. They tout ease of installation as a primary selling point. They include with this Internet Chameleon product scripts that are preconfigured for use with a set of specific Internet service providers. They also bundle with their product a Gopher client, so that the beginning user need not acquire and install a Gopher client over the network. This combination of ease-of-installation and bundling of tools could make startup for the new dial-up user much more palatable. Figure 25.6 is an example screen showing Chameleon in action, with a Gopher client and a fetched image dominating the screen, and with various other Internet tools available at the click of an icon.

SIMPLIFIED DIAL-UP APPLICATIONS: THE PIPELINE MODEL

Attacking the same problem from the perspective of an Internet service provider is a software offering from a company called the Pipeline. This relatively new service provider is the brainchild of author James Gleick, known for his book on fractal theory and his biography of Richard Feynman. Gleick saw a need for a simple user appliance that provides a new kind of window into the Internet—one that presents the different Internet services and tools in a coherent package.

---

* Point your Gopher at nic.merit.edu (port 70) and look in the informational files as well as the Merit Software Archives gateway. (You will obviously need to do this via a service that provides you with Internet access, for instance at your office or via a commercial Internet provider that offers Gopher service.)

† FTP to tbone.biol.scarolina.edu, and look in /pub/kit.

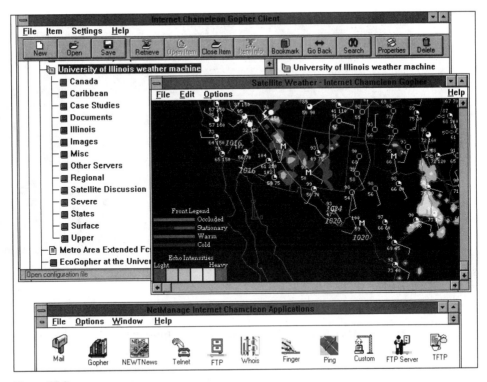

Figure 25.6

The Pipeline offers an MS-Windows graphical interface. Like the user package for America Online or CompuServe's CIM, it is easy to install—put a floppy in its drive, and tell the Program Manager to run a Setup program.*

Figure 25.7 shows the main menu on the Pipeline. Note that a variety of Internet functions are shown, including e-mail, Usenet News, a Talk tool, and online help. Popular initial documents from the Gopher realm are offered, including paths into other Gophers.

The Pipeline offers built-in help at the touch of another icon, as shown in Fig. 25.8.

The Pipeline uses icons and structural elements on the screen to depict various Internet services in a fashion appropriate to the service. For instance, the Pipeline presents the Usenet News hierarchy using folders to represent the

---

* A demonstration version of the Pipeline program is available for download over the Internet, for instance for those who have Internet access at work and who want to obtain an Internet access tool for home use. Point your Gopher client at `gopher.pipeline.com` (port 70), or use FTP to access `ftp.pipeline.com`, or send e-mail to `info@pipeline.com`.

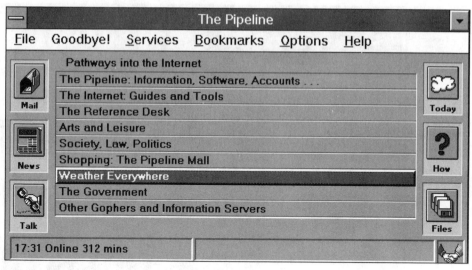

Figure 25.7

various parts of the tree. You can use the mouse to select folders of interest and thereby move into different discussion areas. (See Fig. 25.9.)

In addition to making these services available in an easy-to-install, easy-to-use package, the Pipeline service offers a form of multitasking services. A user can start a download of a file, then resume the interactive session, reading mail and so forth, at the same time. The Pipeline client program communicates with the server over a protocol that gives priority to the interactive messages,

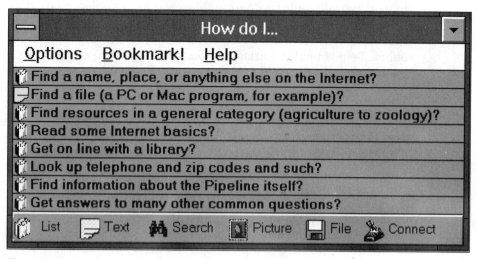

Figure 25.8

essentially allowing the file transfer to take place in the background. Users of conventional dial-up services would find this feature most appealing; rather than watching a meter slowly turn as a large file downloads, the user can move on to other online tasks.

MASS-MARKET INFORMATION UTILITY
ACCESS TO THE INTERNET

In the United States, millions of customers have connected to mass-market information utilities such as Prodigy and Compuserve. While those two firms offer Internet e-mail gateways, two of their competitors, Delphi and America Online (AOL), have staked claims as Internet service providers, the former with gateways to Gopher, FTP, and Usenet, the latter promising advanced Internet connectivity.

The America Online model, to be deployed as this book goes to press, could be an exciting development. The AOL package for MS-Windows offers a graph-

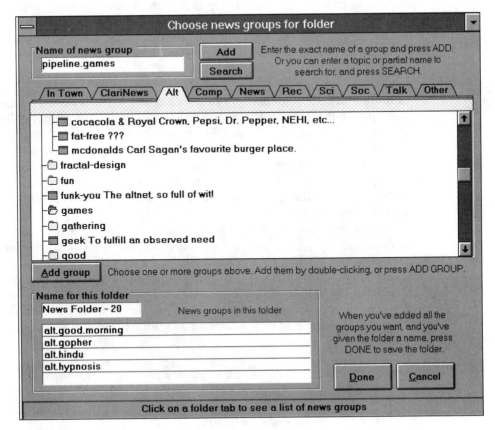

Figure 25.9

ical user interface, but with all graphic icons resident locally on the user's machine; there is no delay painting screen options while such icons are downloaded over a telephone line. AOL has been able to market itself effectively by distributing the AOL client package in a ready-to-install form via mass mailings and magazine bundling. Obviously, such a package cannot impose installation burdens or the mass distribution will be a wasted investment.

The model could provide the underpinnings of an easy-to-install, easy-to-use, efficient window into Internet services. The question is what kind of services AOL and its competitors will present to users. Like Delphi before it, AOL promises to offer Gopher services. Their plans include a sophisticated caching server, which would alleviate the burden that a mass market of users might place on popular Gopher sites, while providing better performance to the user community.

The question is what Internet services AOL and its competitors will offer. For instance, will a user be able to run something that looks like a Gopher client, click on a photograph or a sound, and have the file downloaded and displayed appropriately? Will AOL and its competitors offer World-Wide Web access via their standard interface? Although applications such as Mosaic were designed to run over TCP/IP, there is no inherent reason why they must.* A service provider could implement a client program that is able to communicate with an intermediate server under the control of the service provider, causing HTML documents to be delivered to the user's workstations. The utility would bundle Mosaic-like functionality in their standard client program. This scenario might look like Fig. 25.10.

A mass-market utility is likely to offer a ready-to-run client package, which has built into it all the functionality the service wants to support. This opens the possibility of not requiring PPP at all; the vendor might choose its own protocol for communication between the client's machine and the service provider's server. The precise mechanics of the dialog between this intermediate server and the user are not critical; the key issue is exporting the richness of services like the Web to a user who lives on the other end of a telephone connection.

The price that users might pay for such an arrangement is the inability to run standard client programs, such as Mosaic or their favorite Gopher client, via the mass-market information utility. By contrast, with PPP access, a user can install any standard Internet client program and it will work over a modem connection exactly as it would via a direct connection. In exchange for loss of ability to run whatever client one wishes, the user gains an easy-to-install package, all of which is supported by the information utility. It would even be possible for

---

* For instance, as a proof of concept, Eric Kasten, a programmer at Michigan State University, has demonstrated that Mosaic running under the Linux operating system can export its user interface to a remote X Window terminal over a conventional serial dial-up connection. This can be accomplished with a program known as term, a program whose purpose is to make Unix shells, commands, etc. be accessible over a serial link.

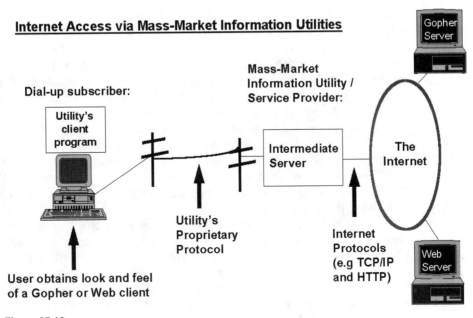

Internet Access via Mass-Market Information Utilities

Figure 25.10

the utility to automatically download updates to the client program; this is one of the successful features of the Prodigy information service.

NEW BACKBONES; NEW CONNECTION SCHEMES

The creation of the NSFnet backbone is one of the most important events in the history of the Internet. It enabled the spectacular growth of the Internet that continues to this day. Having succeeded so thoroughly, the NSF now proposes to bow out of the business of providing the backbone of the U.S. information infrastructure. They have devised a new scheme, under which a multiplicity of national backbones would be deployed. In a sense, the NSFnet itself would retreat to its original purpose of serving the needs of scientists running super-computer applications; the new backbone, to be called vBNS,* would operate at a significantly higher speed (155 megabits per second, replacing the current 45-megabits-per-second links). In parallel to this network would be a variety of commercial and government backbones, operating in an environment of competition as well as cooperation.

---

* Very High Speed Backbone Network Service.

The new plan calls for NSF to provide funding of regional networks, leaving it up to them to connect to national backbone services. Over a five-year period, NSF plans to reduce those subsidies to zero. NSF calls for the creation of Network Access Points (NAPs), which will allow interconnection of regional networks, the vBNS, and foreign networks. In response to the NSF plans, one consortium of regional networks, CoRen, has already formed. Contracts for the new NSF scheme are to be announced in mid-1994.

Not only are changes coming at the backbone level. Options for connecting LANs to Internet service providers will also change over the next few years. Alternatives to traditional, leased lines are finally coming into their own. ISDN, talked about for many years, is finally being deployed in the United States. Other alternatives to leased lines, such as Frame Relay and SMDS, are also being deployed.

Newer LAN/WAN connection technologies offer the prospect of carrying a mixture of traditional data with real-time information such as voice telephone calls and image data, all over standard digital telephone services. One important technology in this area is Asynchronous Transfer Mode (ATM), which has been designed by the international telephony community. ATM transmits data in "cells" containing 48 bytes of data and 5 bytes of header information. ATM is designed to transmit time-critical data, such as real-time voice, intermingled with other kinds of information for which delivery times are less critical.

A REPLACEMENT FOR IP

The "IP" part of TCP/IP was designed under the assumption that perhaps a few thousand hosts would be attached to a network. With over 2 million hosts now IP-accessible, IP is approaching its design limit.

One problem IP faces is the consumption of address space. Due to the way IP addresses are segmented into classes of networks, much of the address space is "wasted." In particular, addresses for Class B networks are largely used up. Just as the telephone industry in North America has been able to "free" some new area codes (by relaxing the rule that an area code must have a "0" or a "1" in the middle) the Internet community has adopted a scheme, called Classless Internet Domain Routing (CIDR) that will preserve addresses by abandoning the old class rules. CIDR is expected to provide relief until the late 1990s, when a new scheme is required.

The IETF is working on the successor to the IP protocol. There are several contendors. One is called "TUBA," which embraces an OSI standard called CLNP; another is called IP version 4. While differing in design philosophy and features, both schemes sport considerably larger address space. Some engineers believe that a successor to IP needs to be designed to handle the ultimate load imaginable—say, 10 devices for every person on the planet Earth, with room for growth in population as well as devices.

PAYING FOR BANDWIDTH

There is a widespread perception that the infrastructure of the Internet in the United States is funded by massive amounts of Federal dollars. While it is true that Federal funding, largely through the National Science Foundation, has helped build important parts of that infrastructure, the sum total of such investments works out to at most a few dollars per user per year.

Recall the concept of the Internet as a "network of networks." Much of the cost of the Internet infrastructure is borne by the regional networks and their constituent organizations. The capital investments that fund construction and upgrading of corporate or campus networks may dwarf the annual expenditures required to link those networks together. You cannot appraise the cost of all roads and bridges in the United States by measuring the expenditures on the interstate highway system—and in the case of the Internet, the proportion of money spent for the national infrastructure is probably lower.

Even though the current investment in national networking is relatively low, a true national information infrastructure will not come so cheaply. The demands of multimedia applications will far outstrip the capacity of current local, regional, and national networks. Consider that Internet Relay Chat accounts for 2.5 percent of the packets transmitted on the NSFnet backbone. But today's IRC is entirely a text medium—generally speaking, the data transmitted is limited by the aggregate typing speed of the participants.* Now imagine IRC transformed into a multimedia mode of communication—with real-time audio and full-motion video. A single transmitting station could chew up the bandwidth of a T1 telephone line—and because the "chatter" is retransmitted to all recipients, this could translate into consumption of 100 percent of a number of network links. Now multiply that level of bandwidth consumption by thousands of existing users, and assume a trend that brings in new users. It is easy to see how the data highway would quickly become overloaded.

This scenario is not far-fetched. Vendors are selling low-cost workstations endowed with sound and still-image capabilities today. Vendors of high-end workstations are beginning to include cameras as well as microphones with the equipment. All it will take to transform such a workstation into a videophone, or even a sophisticated real-time video conferencing system, is standardization on software.

Nor is the multimedia explosion limited to real-time communication. Multimedia e-mail will flourish as more e-mail packages embrace the MIME standard. There is no reason why MIME-capable Usenet News readers cannot be deployed, transforming that global discussion venue into a global forum for sounds, images, and video. And as we have seen clearly, the World-Wide Web

---

* As of January 1994 IRC accounted for over 140 billion bytes per month on the NSFnet backbone. That implies that either a lot of people are chatting, or a moderate number of people are doing a huge amount of chatting.

and clients like Mosaic make it possible for readers to fetch rich multimedia documents on demand.

In this context of explosive bandwidth demands, it is inevitable that we will see changes in the way that we pay for the Internet. Today, the links between corporate or campus networks are traditionally leased telephone lines. The NSFnet backbone links are also simple leased telephone lines; currently they operate at T3 rates, or 45 megabits per second. Traditional leased lines will continue to make sense for some applications, but in many cases, other options will become more attractive. For instance, consider the case of a college campus that has a large medical school and a population of students who mostly commute. During the daytime, the medical school may be busy shipping or fetching real-time medical images, and the student population may be sending and receiving e-mail, browsing remote libraries, and fetching software files from remote repositories. At certain times during the day, usage of the campus's Internet link may drop to very low levels; at night, it may virtually disappear.

If that campus decided to acquire a communications link to its Internet service provider adequate to handle its peak load levels, it could easily need several T1 lines—perhaps a T3 line. But a during slack periods, the "excess" bandwidth of the lines would be wasted. In effect, the college would rent capacity that would never be used.

New communications technologies such as ATM, and new billing options from telecommunications vendors, will provide ways in which an organization with such "bursty" demands can buy the *average* capacity it needs, rather than the *peak* capacity. The telecommunications vendor agrees to provide a "committed service level" of bandwidth that meets the consumer's average needs. Users would be able to consume bandwidth in excess of the average at those times when their demand is high. Pricing might call for "excess" consumption to be paid for based on usage levels—number of cells transmitted, for instance. The advantage of this scheme to the consumer is that the organization need only buy what it typically needs, while retaining the flexibility to consume more bandwidth as required.

Extending the logic of this sort of model to the entire Internet, two economics professors at the University of Michigan, Hal Varian and Jeff Mackie-Mason, have proposed that generally bandwidth on the Internet should be priced on a usage-sensitive basis.* They propose a scheme whereby bandwidth is priced through a sort of real-time bidding process, where prices are bid up during periods of congestion, and fall during slack times. Their thesis is that the marginal cost of of sending a packet over a network is virtually nil when the network is not busy; by contrast, the cost is extremely high when the network is congested. Therefore, they argue, a pricing scheme should reward usage that can be deferred to off-peak times, and should reflect the high cost of sending

---

* Their writings on the subject, along with other economics texts, can be found on gopher.econ. lsa.umich.edu (port 70).

packets at times of congestion.* Low-volume, low-priority packets, such as those associated with e-mail, would travel across the Internet at virtually no cost. High-volume, high-priority information would cost much more, especially during times of congestion.

Just as toll roads are anathema to many drivers, schemes such as this do not sit well with many of those who have been associated with the construction of the Internet to date. They note that, at least as generally deployed in many settings in the United States, the Internet provides remarkably democratic access, and that access does not bring with it per-usage fees. For instance, a scientist at a research institute collaborating via an international Internet link with a colleague doing similar research need not worry about the meter running during every file transfer.

Advocates of per-usage pricing argue that, however noble the current mode of operation seems, it is not the most efficient way to allocate scarce resources. Universities do not provide unlimited, free long-distance telephone calls to their students; when Internet communications tools become a viable substitute for the telephone, why should the university provide subsidies for "long distance" calls in the form of payments to the Internet service provider? Moreover, given scarce resources, how can the current system choose between competing applications? Who decides if limited bandwidth should be used for undergraduates playing a real-time war game, as opposed to transmission of a video feed of a heart surgery in progress to a consulting physician across the globe? Advocates of usage charging argue that it is impossible to decide between such dissimilar uses administratively—e.g., forbidding game-playing during certain times of day—and that by making charges reflect real costs, an organization can best promote overall efficiency.

Furthermore, advocates of per-usage pricing argue that it is not valid to assume that aggregate bills would be higher under their schemes. For one thing, by paying average instead of peak prices, the basic bandwidth bill will probably be lower. It should be cheaper to buy the equivalent of $\frac{1}{10}$ of a T1 link, with the right to use twice a T1 worth of bandwidth for a specified premium. Also, the potential bandwidth offered by fiber-optic technologies is staggering, and there is every sign there will be competition in the market, keeping prices low. Moreover, if there were cases where it remained more economical to acquire fixed-bandwidth leased lines, there is no reason why vendors could not continue to market such flat-rate services.

Finally, those who advocate usage-sensitive pricing point out that the costs need not be borne by each end user in proportion to usage. For instance, a university might choose to offer a certain quota of Internet usage to each student as a part of a benefit package financed by student fees. The quota might be set high enough to allow essentially unlimited e-mail transfer along with a large

---

* Deferral to off-peak times does not necessarily imply waiting for hours; congestion might clear after only a few minutes or even a few seconds.

chunk of bandwidth for other uses. Although the university would itself face varying costs from student to student, it need not reflect all of those variations to each consumer.

Opponents of usage-sensitive pricing see other problems. Imposing an accounting system on TCP/IP or any other networking scheme has its own costs. Some TCP/IP experts worry that an accounting scheme could cost more to implement than any aggregate benefits that would accrue. Per-packet advocates reply that a scheme could use statistical sampling to minimize the costs of accounting.

The debate over how to charge for bandwidth will be one of the more interesting battles of the next few years. Those who live in countries that already impose per-packet pricing may find it curious to see such battles waged in the United States, where citizens and politicians often decline to consider the experiences of other nations.

PAYING FOR INFORMATION

If paying for bandwidth is a thorny issue, paying for content is perhaps even more so. In many cases visionaries see the Internet as a way for information providers and consumers to be liberated from the tyranny of the intermediary—the publishers. In fact we will probably see a mix of schemes for compensating authors and publishers as varied as the kinds of publications. There is a wide range of authors, publishers, and readers of information. Many categories come to mind:

- From narrowly focused to extremely general topic areas
- From local in scope to global
- From a narrow affinity group to a broad heterogeneous readership
- From mass entertainment to arcane scholarly material
- From fleeting durability to enduring classics

With many different categories of documents, and with similar diversity in readership, many models of Internet publication will probably ensue:

- Freely available documents with no advertising
- Freely available documents with "sponsorship" à la public radio
- Documents available freely, with large amounts of incorporated advertising
- Documents available via individual subscription
- Documents available on a campus- or site-subscription basis

This variety of models can accommodate different ways of rewarding authors and publishers for their intellectual property and distribution efforts. Of course, there can be competition across some of these areas; if a commercial publisher of a scholarly journal charges rapacious prices for an online version delivered via the Internet, members of the community may well cancel their subscriptions and start their own freely available journal.

Besides models for delivery of discrete documents, we will also need new models for delivery of information from online databases. The maintainers of most quality databases will only provide useful, complete, accurate data given the incentive of cost recovery. In the past, vendors such as Mead and Dialog have relied on direct billing based on dial-up usage of their services. The Internet needs an effective "Internet 900 number" scheme that will allow users to retrieve needed information from commercial information providers. This mode of delivery is sometimes called payment "by the sip." It could greatly enhance the process of locating information: users could rely on a mix of freely available and for-pay services.*

This is another area where WAIS in particular, and Z39.50 in general, could be very useful. If you as a user do not have an account with a particular information service, currently you must open such an account to perform a search. Given the right charging mechanisms, you should be able, at your option, to search across a wide range of for-pay services, with payment due to your Internet service provider, and with no need for you to sign up for each and every disparate service.

CHALLENGING THE FAX AND EXPRESS COURIER SERVICES

Facsimile technology has a fascinating history. It was conceived in the early 1800s, was patented in 1843, and saw its first widespread use as a way to transmit images for newspapers in the 1920s. In the 1960s facsimile was adopted by business as a means for document transmission. In the late 1980s and early 1990s, the availability of cheap fax machines and inexpensive fax options for personal computers transformed the fax into a commonplace tool. Today it is estimated that one-fourth of all business telephone calls carry a fax transmission. This translates to a huge investment in facsimile transmission.

The fax is extremely popular, yet it rests on obsolete technology. It persists because it supplies a universally understood standard document transfer mechanism. Already there are efforts to use the Internet to carry facsimile information:

■ The Research Libraries Group has a project called Ariel that supports interlibrary document transfer using the Internet. The regional network CICNet has conducted similar project using technology developed at Ohio State.

---

* This is a logical extension of the model used by CompuServe and its ilk, which distinguish between basic and surcharged services.

- In 1993 two Internet luminaries, Marshall Rose and Carl Malamud, announced "An Experiment in Remote Printing" under which the Internet would be used to carry facsimile-type documents to large organizations.*

- Commercial organizations offer services to bridge the gap between the Internet and the fax world. For instance, one company, Faxinet, sells a service that translates e-mail messages to facsimile form for delivery to recipients' fax machines.†

If both parties to a fax transfer have Internet access, and if both parties could agree upon document format, the use of fax protocols or devices could be avoided altogether. Developments such as the Portable Document Format from Adobe and the MIME e-mail standard could usher in an era in which Internet mail substantially encroaches upon fax document delivery. Overnight delivery services could also eventually find their services facing electronic competition.

TRAFFIC JAMS ON THE DATA HIGHWAY‡

In the absence of mechanisms to fund improvements of the speed of Internet links and the capacity of Internet servers, we can expect to see various forms of traffic jams. In fact, such situations are already commonplace. It is common for Archie servers to be overloaded during daytime hours. Many anonymous FTP sites limit access to a certain number of simultaneous users. Similar overloaded conditions arise at one time or another with most popular Internet services.

There are various clever schemes that Internet information providers have devised to cope with overloaded conditions. An anonymous FTP service in Finland throttles the amount of information delivered to each user based on individual consumption and the overall bandwidth available. A recent enhancement to the Veronica menu offered at the University of Nevada at Reno tries to list those Veronica servers that are offering the best response to users.

Other steps that may prove important in conserving Internet bandwidth are improved mirroring and caching. Consider the case of a single bird watcher in Vancouver who selects documents from the Web server for the Australian National Botanic Gardens. A typical page with numerous images might be 40 kilobytes or larger. Now suppose that 10,000 bird lovers in Vancouver fetch these pages after watching a television report on a bird nearing extinction. Because of the way Internet clients connect directly to their servers, no matter how remote, it might be the case that 400 megabytes of data will be transmitted across busy international links to service the needs

---

* Send e-mail to `tpc-faq@town.hall.org` for more information.

† Call 617-522-8102.

‡ This extension of the Data Highway metaphor is so popular that it has been used twice for different articles in the *New York Times;* we cannot improve on this title.

of the 10,000 users. But most of that information is static—if the network were smarter, it could deliver each 40-kilobyte page only once to some relay station in British Columbia, which in turn forward the pages as requested to the individual readers.

That process, in a nutshell, is the way a caching server might work. Caching technology is used in all sorts of computer applications, including in the memory and disk subsystems of most modern microcomputers. Caching is simply a scheme whereby frequently accessed information is kept handy, for quick delivery when new demands for it arise.

In the Internet context, caching would require some additional complexity in the way information is fetched. Rather than immediately hopping to the remote server, your client program might have its request satisfied by some nearby intermediate server. That server would have the responsibility for discerning if a locally cached copy of the information were in fact identical to the document you were looking for. A caching server that delivers yesterday's headlines when you ask for today's would be of no use.

There are numerous examples of waste in the way information is delivered on today's Internet. Every user in Europe who fetches the list of all Gophers in North America from the Minnesota server might as well get that information from a server in Europe. In the absence of effective caching tools, we will probably see more sites establish mirror services. Mirrors require cooperative agreements and manual setup effort, but they can pay off in terms of saved bandwidth and better service to users.

These approaches are helpful, but they do not solve the problem of how to upgrade popular Internet services in proportion to the demand for their services. In the long run, some sort of scheme that compensates service providers is probably the only method that will ensure growth of services in proportion to demand.*

THE INTERNET AS THE PROTOTYPE FOR THE INFORMATION SUPERHIGHWAY

In the United States, it seems 1993 was the year when the masses heard the term "Information Superhighway," and 1994 and beyond are the years in which we will see if government and business can deliver on the promises made. Already one major deal between a regional telephone company (Bell Atlantic) and a major cable TV company (TCI) has collapsed. It seems certain that more courtships—and more spurned romances—are in the offing.

---

* Of course, even in the for-profit sector, growth in demand for network services can sometimes be so explosive as to outstrip the ability of the provider to keep pace. For instance, over a period of a few months in early 1994, the information utility America Online saw its subscriber base double in size. This resulted in occasional access problems. However, in this context, new subscribers imply a new revenue stream that can pay for necessary enhancements to the provider's network and server capacity.

The vision one holds of the information superhighway depends on the background one brings to the question. If the starting point is telephony, the emphasis is on interpersonal communication, and being able to call who you want when you want. If the starting point is cable television, the emphasis is likely to be on full-motion video plus audio delivered for entertainment purposes. Even if one particular courtship has failed, the merging of these two visions of a superhighway has an inevitable logic to it: telephony enhances cable television by adding the element of two-way interpersonal communication, and service on demand. Cable television brings to telephony the ability to deliver wide-bandwidth multimedia information (and entertainment).

These industries also carry some negative baggage: telephone companies have not always been noted for their rapid adoption and deployment of new technologies their customers demand. Cable television companies have not always been noted for their responsiveness to individual customer problems. Will the telephone company that spent ten years deploying ISDN be quick to deploy new Internet technologies? Will the cable company that cannot remove snow from channel 17 respond when their domain name service is down?

The results could be staggering:

- Multimedia one-to-one electronic mail on a mass scale
- Multimedia many-to-many communications, à la Usenet News and Internet Relay Chat, on a mass scale; games on the multiuser Internet MUD model transformed into high-bandwidth multimedia experiences
- Video-on-demand services, whereby viewers select movies of choice delivered by video servers that house thousands of available titles

Those who come to the information superhighway debate from an Internet background see challenges as well:

- How do we ensure universal access to the data highway?
- How do we provide adequate bandwidth and server resources to meet the needs of a mass audience?
- How do we preserve the sense of free access to resources from near and far?
- How do we keep the Internet in particular, and the broader international information infrastructure in general, from degenerating into a mere extension of global entertainment empires?

Alas, a search of Internet information resources reveals no server offering definitive answers.

Cornucopia of Resources

No print catalog can cover more than a fraction of the Internet's myriad resources. This chapter offers a listing of some of the online documents and online resources that are representative of resources on the Internet. The items listed are not necessarily the most current or the most comprehensive in a given category. Use Internet subject guides and the other search strategies outlined in Chap. 16 to find more resources as they come online in these and other categories.

The resources described in this chapter are available via a variety of Internet technologies. In many cases, information providers use more than one technology, or move from one technology to another over time. You may find that some of these services offer pointers to their other modes of delivery; for instance, an FTP archive may be supplemented or replaced by a Gopher or World-Wide Web server. Once again, online indexes can help you locate any of these services that might have moved to new pastures.

You may want to review the relevant chapter for a given technology to refresh your understanding of how to use it for a given resource. Here are some notes particular to the types of services listed:

FTP. We provide the host name and the path name where the file is located. You should be able to connect to the host, log in as "anonymous" or "FTP", and obtain the file via the Get command. Be sure to use "text" or "binary" mode as appropriate.

LISTSERV and other mailing lists.   We list sufficient information for you to subscribe to the mailing list. You may want to use LISTSERV or other tools' capacity to review archives of prior discussions, or you may find such archives online elsewhere (say, on a Gopher or FTP server).

Gopher.   We list the name of the server, the port number, and the selector string.* These three items should be sufficient to allow you to point your Gopher client at the service, using the "Open Gopher" or "File/New" option, or using the client's bookmark option.

If you cruise Gopherspace by using Telnet to access a public client, you may not be able to invoke an Open Gopher function. In this case, use the List of Gophers found at Minnesota and on most servers to locate the site by name, then follow their menu options to get to the data. *Note:* Usually the selector string can be used as a hint as to the title paths to follow as you traverse the hierarchy.

World-Wide Web.   We provide the Uniform Resource Locator (URL) for each title. You should be able to insert this exact URL into the "Open URL" dialog box with a client like Mosaic. With Lynx, the VT100-style client, you should be able to type "g" then type in the URL. (*Exception:* if you are using Telnet to reach a public Lynx client, the ability to specify a URL will probably be disabled. In this case you will want to use Web site lists or catalogs to traverse the Web until you find the document in question.)

Mosaic and other clients should be able to accept URLs that correspond to Gopher and FTP services as well. For example,

`gopher.msu.edu` **(port 70) selector** `1/libraries`

becomes

`gopher://gopher.msu.edu:70/11/libraries`

(Note that the Gopher document type, in this case "1," is normally "doubled" when the Gopher specification is turned into a URL. The reason is an artifact of the different retrieval scheme of Gopher and the Web.)

AEROSPACE

- **NASA Spacelink:** An online gold mine of information and images related to NASA, popular in the educational community, from Marshall Space Flight Center in Alabama.

  Telnet: `spacelink.msfc.nasa.gov`, **log in as** `newuser`

- **Master Index of NASA Web pages:** via Goddard Space Flight Center:

  Web: `http://hypatia.gsfc.nasa.gov:80/NASA_homepage.html`

---

* Note that some Gopher clients refer to the "selector" as the "path." The meaning is identical.

AGRICULTURE

- **Agricultural Genome Gopher and World Wide Web:**   Almost all of the information contained on these servers is from the USDA Plant Genome Program. This includes information about maps, loci, probes, references, germplasm, and related data.

  Gopher: `probe.nalusda.gov` (port 70)
      selector = null

  WWW: `http://probe.nalusda.gov:8000/index.html`

- **Almanac Users' Guide-Extension Service, USDA(ES):**   An information server designed to answer request received through electronic mail. It delivers autogenerated, multimedia documents to network users through electronic mail and accepts document submissions. Almanac allows you to get reports, newsletters, journals, articles, sounds, and graphics images. To obtain help file, e-mail to: `almanac@esusda.gov` with `send guide` as body of message.

- **Journal of Extension:**   A peer-reviewed journal for the Cooperative Extension Service includes articles ranging from agricultural issues to adult education to family issues.

  Gopher: `wissago.uwex.edu` (port 70)
      selector = `1/joe`

ARCHITECTURE

- **Architecture Image Library (Johns Hopkins University):**   This directory contains images and indexes of contemporary architecture, organized into subdirectories by architect(s).

  Gopher: `gopher.hs.jhu.edu` (port 70)
      selector = `1/Images/Architecture`

- **Laboratorium voor architectuur (LaVA):** An electronic platform for discussing architecture and computer-aided architecture. Faculty of Architecture, Building and Planning, Eindhoven University of Technology, The Netherlands.

  Gopher: `gopher.tue.nl` (port 70)
      selector = `1/TUE-CIS/Bouwkunde/OASE`

ARTS

- **Miscellaneous Art Resources:** Collections of art resources from around the Internet.

  Gopher: `riceinfo.rice.edu` (port 70)
      selector = `0/Subject/Arts`

  WWW: `http://www.einet.net/galaxy/Arts-and-Humanities/Visual-Arts.html`

- **FineArt Forum:** A seven-year-old publication serving the art and technology community.

  WWW: http://www.msstate.edu/Fineart_Online/home.html

ASTRONOMY

- **American Astronomical Society:** Contains information on the Society, meeting schedules, meeting abstracts (in HTML), staff directory and an HTML version of the AAS Job Register.

  WWW: http://blackhole.aas.org/AAS-homepage.html

- **Astronomical Internet Resources:** Contains pointers to potentially relevant resources available via Internet.

  WWW: http://stsci.edu/net-resources.html

- **National Radio Astronomy Observatory:** Contains all papers received 1986 forward plus unpublished ones dating back to 1978 and the ST Scl file has everything received in the last couple of years, along with all papers received since 1982 and not yet published. For information on database contents, contact either: library@nrao.edu or library@stsci.edu

BIOLOGY

- **ANU Bioinformatics**

  FTP: life.anu.edu.au

  Gopher: life.anu.edu.au (port 70)
        selector = null

  WWW: http://life.anu/edu/au:80/

- **Biodiversity and Biological Collections Gopher:** Contains information of interest to systematists and other biologists of the organismic kind.

  Gopher: huh.harvard.edu (port 70)
        selector = null

- **Biodiversity WWW (World-Wide Web), Australian National Botanic Gardens**

  WWW: http://155.187.10.12:80/index.html

- **Conservation Ecology:** A peer-reviewed journal.

  WWW: http://journal.biology.carleton.ca/

- **ExPASy World-Wide Web (WWW) molecular biology server:** This server is dedicated to the analysis of protein and nucleic acid sequences as well as 2-D PAGE. It allows you to browse through a number of database such as SWISS-PROT, SWISS-2DPAGE, PROSITE, REBASE, EMBL, PDB,

FLYBASE and OMIM and get information on software packages for molecular biology.

WWW: http://expasy.hcuge.ch/

- **Flora Online:** An electronic botanical journal for systematics and biogeography.

  Gopher: huh.harvard.edu (port 70)
      selector = 1/newsletters/flora.online

- **Johns Hopkins University BioInformatics Web Server:** Contains some interesting biological databases, electronic publications for biology, a section to help you with your software needs, and of course links to other Web servers.

  WWW: http://www.gdb.org/hopkins.html

- **Microbial Germplasm Database:** A database of microorganisms (~40,000) and other reproducible genetic elements that are maintained in research-oriented culture collections.

  Gopher: ava.bcc.orst.edu (port 70)
      selector = 1/mgd

- **North American Benthological Society (NABS):** Available in searchable form over the Internet via the University of Notre Dame Gopher server.

  Gopher: gopher.nd.edu (port 70)
      selector = 1/Notre Dame Academic and Research Data/
          Aquatic Biology

- **Pacific Rim Biodiversity Catalog and Index:** Information from nearly 200 natural history institutions throughout the world concerning the taxonomic, geographic and temporal composition of their Pacific Rim zoological and paleontological holdings.

  Gopher: ucmp1.Berkeley.edu (port 70)
      selector = 1/Pacrim

BULLETIN BOARD SYSTEMS

- **Mother of All BBSes:** An attempt to build a single index of all Internet-accessible bulletin boards.

  Web: http://www.cs.colorado.edu/homes/
      mcbryan/public_html/bb/summary.html

BUSINESS

- **CommerceNet:** A Silicon-Valley based consortium led by Enterprise Integration Technologies, CommerceNet works to make the Internet usable by businesses and their customers.

  WWW: http://www.commerce.net

- **Internet Business Journal**

  Gopher: gopher.fonorola.net (port 70)

        selector = 1/Internet Business Journal

- **NASDAQ Financial Executive Journal:** A joint project of the Legal Information Institute at Cornell Law School and the NASDAQ Stock Market.

  WWW: http://www.law.cornell.edu/nasdaq/nasdtoc.html

- **Securities & Exchange Commission EDGAR database:** A service of the Internet Town Hall, offering access to electronic company filings. See the introductory document via Gopher to learn about other modes of access.

  Gopher: gopher.town.hall.org (port 70)

        selector = 1/edgar

- **World Bank Public Information Center**

  Gopher: ftp.worldbank.org (port 70)

        selector = null

CARTOGRAPHY

- **Xerox PARC PubWeb Server:** An HTTP server that accepts requests for map renderings and returns an HTML document including an inline GIF image of the requested map.

  WWW: http://pubweb.parc.xerox.com:80/

CENSUS STATISTICS

- **Statistics Canada:** Online statistics about Canada, from the official government body, in English and in French.

  Gopher: gopher.census.gov (port 70)

        selector = null

- **United States Bureau of Census**

  Gopher: gopher.census.gov (port 70)

        selector = null

CHEMISTRY

- **American Chemical Society Gopher:** Contains supplementary material pages from the Journal of the American Chemical Society from the beginning of 1993.

  Gopher: acsinfo.acs.org (port 70)

        selector = null

- **Periodic Table of the Elements**

    Gopher: `ucsbuxa.ucsb.edu` (port 70)
    selector = `1/.Sciences/.Chemistry/.periodic.table`

COMMUNICATIONS

- **Computer Communications Newsletter:** Features article summaries on new-generation computer and communications technologies from over 100 trade magazines and research journals; key U.S. and international daily newspapers, news weeklies, and business magazines; and, over 100 Internet mailing lists and USENET groups.

    LISTSERV: Email to `listserv@ucsd.edu` (Leave the "Subject" line blank.) In the body of the message, type:
    `SUBSCRIBE HOTT-LIST` (do not include first or last names)

- **Comserve:** The electronic information service for scholars and students interested in human communication studies (communication, journalism, mass communication rhetoric, speech, social linguistics, ethnomethodology, etc.). To access Comserve, send an electronic mail message to: `comserve@vm.ecs.rpi.edu` with "send comserve helpfile" as body of message.

COMPUTATIONAL SCIENCE

- **Computation Sciences from ICTP-Trieste (Italy)**

    Gopher: `gopher.ictp.trieste.it` (port 70)
    selector = `1/ictp/computing`

COMPUTER SCIENCE

- **Association for Computing Machinery:** Founded in 1947, ACM is the largest and oldest educational and scientific computing organization in the world today.

    Gopher: `gopher.acm.org` (port 70)
    selector = null

- **Computer Literacy Project from University of Tasmania**

    Gopher: `info.utas.edu.au` (port 70)
    selector = `1/Departments/Education/Computer Literacy Project`

- **Computer Science Technical Reports:** A list of sites that appear to distribute technical reports.

    WWW: `http://www.vifp.monash.edu.au/techreports/`

- **CPU: Working in the Computer Industry**

  Online subscriptions to CPU are available at no cost by e-mailing `list-serv@cpsr.org` with a blank subject and a single line in the body of the message: `SUBSCRIBE CPSR-CPU` <your first name> <your last name>

- **IEEE Computer Society:** IEEE Computer Society is a world-renowned source of information relating to all aspects of computer science and engineering, including the publication of periodicals and newsletters, sponsoring conferences, workshops and symposiums, and the development of standards.

  Gopher: `info.computer.org` (port 70)
       selector = null

- **Journal of Artificial Intelligence Research (JAIR)**

  For more information about the journal, send electronic mail to `jair@cs.cmu.edu` with the subject "autorespond" and the message body `"help"`.

- **Kluwer ftp server:** Offers comprehensive information on Kluwer's Electrical Engineering & Computer Science journals.

  FTP: `world.std.com`
      login: `anonymous`
      directory = `Kluwer/journals`

- **Siggraph Online:** Maintained for ACM SIGGRAPH by volunteers as a service to the active computer graphics community.

  FTP: `siggraph.org`
      login: `anonymous`

- **Theory and Formal Methods, Dept. of Computing, Imperial College, U.K.:** Contains papers and software written by members of the section as well as an extensive collection of papers and bibliographical data obtained from colleagues working in similar areas throughout the world.

  Gopher: `theory.doc.ic.ac.uk` (port 70)
      selector = null

- **Worldwide Newsletter:** A list of University/Academic Computing Newsletters.

  Gopher: `gopher.uga.edu`
      selector = `1/UGA Departments/Computing & Networking/Newsletters/Worldwide Newsletters`

COMPUTER

- **Anthony's X Icon Library:** A collection of small bitmaps for both programming and X application icons.

  FTP: `export.lcs.mit.edu`
      login: `anonymous`
      directory = `contrib/AIcons/`

CRIME

- **FBI UNABOM Task Force:** FBI Gopher.

    FTP: naic.nasa.gov
    login: anonymous
    directory = /files/fbi

    Gopher: naic.nasa.gov (port 70)
    selector = 1/government-resources/fbi

    WWW: http://naic.nasa.gov/fbi/FBI_homepage.html

CULTURE

See the variety of groups under the soc.culture hierarchy in Usenet News for ongoing discussions of comparative culture. The quality and subject matter can be uneven, but many discussions include participants from around the world, offering an international perspective on comparative culture.

DIRECTORIES

- **German Zip-code Conversion:** To convert the old German Zip codes into the new ones.

    WWW: http://www.uni-frankfurt.de/plz/plzrequest.html

DISASTERS

- **Emergency Preparedness Information eXchange (EPIX):** To facilitate the exchange of ideas and information among Canadian and international public and private sector organizations about the prevention of, preparation for, recovery from and/or mitigation of risk associated with natural and sociotechnological disasters.

    Gopher: disaster.cprost.sfu.ca (port 5555)
    selector = null

ECONOMICS

- **Economic Conversion Information Exchange**

    Gopher: sunny.stat-usa.gov (port 70)
    selector = 1/DEFCON

- **EGopher:** Provides an electronic forum for owners of Gopher servers on the Internet and coordinators of other network information services targeted at the area of economics.

    LISTSERV: please send a MAIL message to:
    LISTSERV@SHSU.Bitnet stating in the text of the MAIL:
    SUBSCRIBE EGopher "Your Real Name in Quotes"

- **University of Michigan Economics Gopher/Web server:** A gopher at the Department of Economics, University of Michigan. See the paper "Economics of the Internet."

  Gopher: `alfred.econ.lsa.umich.edu` (port 70)
  selector = null

EDUCATION

- **Consortium for School Networking (CoSN)**

  Gopher: `cosn.org` (port 70)
  selector = null

- **ERIC Clearinghouse on Assessment and Evaluation (ERIC/AE):** Information about educational and psychological testing.

  Gopher: `vmsgopher.cua.edu` (port 70)
  selector = `lgopher_root_eric_ae:[000000]`

- **Florida Tech Education Gopher**

  Gopher: `sci-ed.fit.edu` (port 70)
  selector = null

- **IBM ACIS Higher Education Information Server (IKE):** A gopher-based server offering IBM information, application software, and a bulletin board for IBM users in the higher-education community.

  Gopher: `ike.engr.washington.edu` (port 70)
  selector = null

- **Internet Resource Directory for Educators**

  FTP: `tcet.unt.edu`
  login: anonymous
  directory = `pub/telecomputing-info/IRD`

- **Texas Studies Gopher:** An Internet gopher server designed to provide instructional resources and information about Texas's natural and cultural history and the Texas environment.

  Gopher: `chico.rice.edu` (port 1170)
  selector = null

- **U.S. Department of Education (ED)**

  Gopher: `gopher.ed.gov` (port 70)
  selector = null

- **CICNet K-12 Gopher:** A general collection of documents and pointers to online services of interest to teachers and others in K–12 education. To help educators incorporate Internet resources into their lesson plans, the server also includes summaries of several "Internet in the classroom" projects.

Gopher: gopher.cic.net (port 70)
  selector = 1/cicnet-gophers/k12-gopher

EMPLOYMENT

- **Online Career Center:** A nonprofit employer association that provides its members with effective, economical employment advertising, outplacement services and online communications.

  Gopher: garnet.msen.com (port 9062)
    selector = null

- **Academe This Week:** An online version of the American journal *The Chronicle of Higher Education,* including its complete job listings.

  Gopher: chronicle.merit.edu (port 70)
    selector = 1/.ads

ENVIRONMENT

- **EnviroGopher**

  Gopher: envirolink.org (port 70)
    selector = null

- **Global Change Master Directory (GCMD)**

  Telnet: 128.183.36.23
    login: NSSDC

- **USA Environmental Protection Agency**

  Gopher: futures.wic.epa.gov (port 70)
    selector = null

ETHNIC STUDIES

- **INDIANnet Census Information and Computer Network Center:** National computer network to provide civic information useful to American Indian and Alaskan natives.

  FTP: pines.hsu.edu
    login: anonymous

  LISTSERV: email to listserv@spruce.hsu.edu
      In the message area of your e-mail,
      include the command:
      sub indiannet-1 "your name"

- **Jewishnt at BGUVM:** A discussion forum on all things concerning the establishment of the Global Jewish Information Network.

> **LISTSERV:** Email to `listserv@bguvm.bgu.ac.il`
> In the message area of your e-mail,
> include the command:
> `sub jewishnut`your full name

- **Jewish Studies Judaica eJOURNAL:** The world's largest online journal devoted to ongoing research and current events in Jewish Studies. For subscription information, contact one of our two e-mail addresseses: `JEWSTUD-IES@israel.nysernet.org` or `H-JUDAIC@uicvm.uic.edu`

GENEALOGY

- **ROOTS-L:** A discussion list where those who have interest in genealogy may communicate via e-mail messages in hopes of finding more family history information.

  > **LISTSERV:** Email to `listserv@vm1.nodak.edu` with a message of the form:
  > `subscribe` firstname lastname

GEOGRAPHY

- **GeoGopher**

  Gopher: `dillon.geo.ep.utexas.edu` (port 70)
       selector = null

- **Geographic Name Server**

  Telnet: `martini.eecs.umich.edu` (port 3000)

- **Oklahoma Geological Survey Observatory:** Collects 176 Mb of real-time continuous seismic data, geomagnetic data, and earth tide (*sic*) recordings per day.

  FTP: `leonard.okgeosurvey1.gov`
       login: `anonymous`

  Gopher: `wealaka.okgeosurvey1.gov` (port 70)
       selector = null

GRANTS AND SCHOLARSHIPS

- **Miscellaneous Grant & Scholarship Directories:** A collection of grant opportunities listings (mostly U.S. federal grants) from around the Internet.

  Gopher: `riceinfo.rice.edu` (port 70)
       selector = `0/Subject/Grants`

HANDICAPPER INFORMATION

- **Information Technology and Disabilities:** A new, quarterly electronic journal devoted to all aspects of computer use by persons with disabilities.

LISTSERV: E-mail to `listserv@sjuvm.stjohns.edu`
In the message area of your e-mail, include the command:
`sub itd-jnl` firstname lastname

- **Deaf Gopher:** Resources of interest to the hearing impaired, from Michigan State University.

  Gopher: `gopher.msu.edu` (port 70)
  selector = `0/dept/deaf`

HEALTH

- **HEALTHLINE:** From University of Montana student health services.

  Gopher: `selway.umt.edu` (port 700)
  selector = null

- **National Library of Medicine:** The world's largest research library in a single scientific and professional field.

  Gopher: `gopher.nlm.nih.gov` (port 70)
  selector = null

- **NUS-NCI CancerNet**

  Gopher: `biomed.nus.sg` (port 70)
  selector = `1/NUS-NCI-CancerNet`
  WWW: `http://biomed.nus.sg:80/`

HISTORY

- **Historical Text Archive:** Complete historical texts, via Mississippi State University.

  Gopher: `ucsbuxa.ucsb.edu` (port 70)
  Selector: `1/.Social/.History/.Archives`

- **Online Modern History Review:** Designed to satisfy the needs of the modern scholar who wants convenient and immediate access to the latest historical research.

  Telnet: `freenet.victoria.bc.ca`

- **Today's Events in History**

  Gopher: `cs6400.mcc.ac.uk` (port 70)
  Selector: `1/misc/today`

INTERNET

- **DIMUND Document Information Server:** A repository for Document Understanding information and resources.

> **Gopher:** `dimund.umd.edu` (port 70)
>   selector = null

- **EDUPAGE:** A summary of some of the week's news items on information technology, provided as a service by EDUCOM, a consortium of leading colleges and universities seeking to transform education through the use of information technology. To subscribe to EDUPAGE, send a note to `edupage@educom.edu` with your name, institution name and e-mail address

- **FTP of Hypertext Presentation on E-journals:** A hypertext resource to explain what e-journals are (over 175 sample issues, most in their entirety), where e-journals can be located (e.g., CICNet's gopher archive of electronic journals), and how to get them (documentation on gopher, SGML, TeX, etc.).

> **FTP:** `oak.oakland.edu`
>   directory = `pub/msdos/hypertext`, to get the files:
>   `MONTANAO.ZIP` Hypertext gopher and ejournal samples 1 of 3
>   `MONTANAB.ZIP` Hypertext gopher and ejournal samples 2 of 3
>   `MONTANAC.ZIP` Hypertext gopher and ejournal samples 3 of 3

- **HYTELNET Gopher:** Designed to assist users in reaching all of the INTERNET-accessible libraries, Free-nets, CWISs, BBSs, and other information sites by Telnet.

> **Gopher:** `liberty.uc.wlu.edu` (port 70)
>   selector = `1/internet/hyteinet`

- **Information Infrastructure Task Force (IITF):** A computer bulletin-board system to provide public access to IITF and other National Information Infrastructure- (NII-) related documents, including IITF schedules, committee reports, and minutes of meetings.

> **Gopher:** `iitf.doc.gov` (port 70)
>   selector = null

- **InterNIC Gopher and WWW servers:** A wealth of official information from the tripartite InterNIC. See especially the Web server for its rich collection of graphics.

> **Gopher:** `gopher.internic.net` (port 70)
> **WWW:** `http://www.internic.net`

- **Internet Monthly Report**

> **FTP:** `venera.isi.edu`
>   login: `anonymous`
>   directory = `in-notes/imr/imryymm.txt`
>   or by sending an e-mail message to "`rfc-info@ISI.EDU`" with
>   the message body "`help: ways_to_get_imrs`"

- **LISTSERV Database:** A searchable database based on Dartmouth's list of listserv groups.

Telnet: `infotrax.rpi.edu`
> type LIS at prompt

- **Network Training Materials Gopher:** An experimental gopher server set up to promote and encourage network training.

Gopher: `trainmat.ncl.ac.uk` (port 70)
> selector = null

INTERNATIONAL RELATIONS

- **Russia-American World-Wide Web Server:** A common base of information about issues affecting relations between our countries, and by providing a common "meeting place" where folks can find and communicate with each other.

WWW: `http://solar.rtd.utk.edu/friends/home.html`

JOURNALISM

- **The Journalism List:** Identifies and describes briefly a number of resources specifically targeted to, or valuable for, journalists. For a copy of the list, send e-mail to John S. Makulowich at `verbwork@access.digex.net`.

- **Voice of America's International News and English Broadcasts:** Includes the texts, in English, of radio reports prepared by VOA staff correspondents, contract news reporters ("stringers"), and feature and documentary writers.

FTP: `ftp.voa.gov`
> login: `anonymous`

Gopher: `gopher.voa.gov` (port 70)

LAW

- **California Legislative Information:** Included are the state constitution, senate and assembly bills, the California code and statutes, and miscellaneous directories and guides to the legislative process and the legislature.

Gopher: `gopher.ucsc.edu` (port 70)
> selector = 1/The Community/Guide to Government—U.S., State and Local/California Legislative Information

- **Federal Communications Law Journal:** Published by the Indiana University School of Law at Bloomington and the Federal Communications Bar Association.

WWW: `http://www.law.indiana.edu:80/fclj/fclj.html`

LIBRARIES AND LIBRARY SCIENCE

- **BALT-INFO:** An electronic user's network using existing INTERNET resources to connect Baltic area librarians and information specialists in Lithuania, Latvia, and Estonia with their counterparts in the west. For information send e-mail to Dawn Mann at `mannd@rferl.org`

- **BIBLIO-France:** Established in France to serve the French library community.

  LISTSERV: E-mail to `listserv@univ-rennes1.fr`
             `subscribe biblio-fr` firstname lastname

- **CARL UNCOVER:** Information.

  FTP: `ftp.lib.berkeley.edu`

- **College & Research Libraries NewsNet:** An abridged electronic edition of C & RL News accessible on the Internet through the Gopher server at the University of Illinois at Chicago.

  Gopher: `gopher.uic.edu` (port 70)
          selector = `1/library/crl`

- **Current Cites:** Information Systems Instruction & Support from the University of California, Berkeley.

  FTP: `ftp.lib.berkeley.edu`
      directory = /pub/Current.Cites

- **Library and Information Technology Association (LITA)**

  LISTSERV: E-mail to `listserv@dartmouth.edu`
            `subscribe litanews` firstname lastname

- **Library of Congress Marvel:** A global information system combining the vast collection of information available at and about LC with the many electronic resources accessible through the Internet.

  Gopher: `marvel.loc.gov` (port 70)
      selector = null

- **National Archives Audiovisual Information**

  FTP: `ftp.cu.nih.gov`
      login: `anonymous`
      directory = `NARA_AUDIOVISUAL`

- **NCSU's "Library Without Walls":** Modeled after a physical library and includes several different areas.

  Gopher: `dewey.lib.ncsu.edu` (port 70)
      selector = `1/library`

- **Public-Access Computer Systems (PACS) News:** An electronic library journal dealing with computer systems in libraries, covering topics such as campus-wide information systems, CD-ROM LANs, document delivery systems, electronic publishing, expert systems, hypermedia and multimedia systems, locally mounted databases, microcomputer labs, network-based information resources, and online catalogs.

Gopher: `info.lib.uh.edu` (port 70)

      selector = `1/articles/e-journals/uhlibrary/pacsnews`

LITERATURE

- **BRYN MAWR Medieval Review** (BMMR): Timely reviews of current work in all areas of medieval studies.

  LISTSERV: Email to `listserv@cc.brynmawr.edu`

        `subscribe BMR-L` firstname lastname

- **Electronic Antiquity:** An electronic journal covering classical antiquity; and **DIDASKALIA: Ancient Theater Today:** Timely dissemination of news relevant to those who work on ancient theater and its modern incarnations. Both offered by the University of Tasmania.

  Gopher: `info.utas.edu.au` (port 70)

        selector = `1/Publications/`

- **E-Text Archives:** A general archive of electronic texts from around the world.

  Gopher: `etext.archive.umich.edu` (port 70)

        selector = null

- **Project Gutenberg Newsetter**

  LISTSERV: E-mail to `listserv@vmd.cso.uiuc.edu`

        `sub gutnberg your name`

MATHEMATICS

- **Electronic Journal of Differential Equations (EJDE):** Electronic journal dealing with all aspects of differential equations.

  FTP: `ejde.math.swt.edu`

      login: `anonymous`

  Gopher: `ejde.math.unt.edu` (port 70)

        selector = null

- **Electronic Transactions on Numerical Analysis (ETNA):** An electronic journal for the publication of significant new and important developments in numerical analysis and scientific computing. Send e-mail to `etna@mcs.kent.edu`, subject should be `"ETNA registration"`

■ **Euromath Center at the University of Copenhagen**

Gopher: gopher.euromath.dk **(port 70)**
      selector = 1/Euromath

MEDICINE AND LIFE SCIENCES

■ **Life Sciences Collection, University of Michigan Library Gopher:**
Collections of documents on genetics, cancer, AIDS, National Institutes of
Health, etc. Includes pointer to the Center for Disease Control's *Morbidity
and Mortality Weekly.*

Gopher: una.hh.lib.umich.edu **(port 70)**
      selector = 1/science/lifesci

MILITARY

■ **Navy News Service (NAVNEWS):** Official news and information about
fleet operations and exercises, personnel policies, budget actions, and more.
Send e-mail to navnews@nctamslant.navy.mil. Please include your Internet
e-mail address in the text of your message.

MOVIES

■ **National Film Preservation Board Registry** Via the Library of
Congress.

Gopher: marvel.loc.gov **(port 70)**
      selector: 1/research/reading.rooms/motion.picture/nfpb

MUSIC

■ **Compact Disc Connection:** A searchable, online database of over 70,00
CD titles. You can search by artist, title, song, catalog number, etc.

Telnet: 157.151.0.5
      login: cdc

■ **Early Music:** Archives of EARLYM-L & rec.music.early.

Gopher: olymp.wu-wien.ac.at **(port 70)**
      selector = 1/.earlym-1

■ **Ethnomusicology Research Digest**

Gopher: gopher.cic.net **(port 70)**
      selector = 1/e-serials/alphabetic/e/ethnomusicology-research-
      digest

NEWS AND MEDIA

- **French Language Press Review:** Summaries of French language news as summarized by the French Embassy and posted by Georgetown University; Gopher archive maintained at Michigan State University.

  Gopher: gopher.msu.edu (port 70)
  selector = 1/news/news/general/french_language

PALEONTOLOGY

- **University of California Museum of Paleontology:** A Web server rich in graphics.

  WWW: http://ucmp1.berkeley.edu/

PATENTS

- **Internet Town Hall Patent Database:** A full-text recent patent database. Browse via their Gopher; follow instructions online there for WAIS access.

  Gopher: town.hall.org (port 70)
  selector = 1/patent

PERSONAL FINANCE

- **Building A Home Buyers' Educational Program Guidebook:** Designed to be a resource for the development and implementation of home buyer education programs.

  FTP: cce.cornell.edu
  directory = /pub/home-buyers-guide

PHILOSOPHY

- **American Philosophical Association Gopher**

  FTP: mrcnext.cso.uiuc.edu
  Gopher: apa.oxy.edu (port 70)
  selector = null

PHYSICS

- **LANL Physics Information Service:** Information service for nuclear and particle physics.

  Gopher: gopher.lanl.gov (port 70)
  selector = null

POLITICS AND GOVERNMENT

- **FedWorld Electronic Marketplace:** Connect to more than 100 government-operated bulletin boards and online systems.

  Telnet: `fedworld.gov` and follow login prompts.

  FTP: `ftp.fedworld.gov`

- **Library of Congress Information System (LOCIS):** Contains bills and resolutions introduced to the U.S. Congress.

  Telnet: `locis.loc.gov`

- **National Performance Review:** "From Red Tape to Results."

  FTP: `FTP.CU.NIH.GOV`
     login: `anonymous`
     directory = `/USDOC-OBA-INFO`

- **Supreme Court Opinions on Internet**

  FTP: `ftp.cwru.edu`
     login: `anonymous`
     directory = `/hermes`

- **United Nations Development Programme**

  Gopher: `nywork1.undp.org` (port 70)
     selector = null

- **United Nations Justice Network (UNCJIN):** A worldwide network to enhance dissemination and the exchange of information concerning criminal justice and crime-prevention issues.

  Gopher: `UACSC2.ALBANY.EDU` (port 70)
     selector = `1/newman`

- **White House Daily News**

  To receive daily news releases from the White House, send a message to: `almanac@esusda.gov`
  In the body of the message enter: subscribe `wh-summary`

- **White House Electronic Publications:** Frequently asked questions.

  WWW: `http://www.acns.nwu.edu/us.gov.online.html`

PRIVACY

- **A Citizen's Guide to Using the Freedom of Information Act**

  Gopher: `eryx.syr.edu` (port 70)
     selector = `1/Citizen's Guide`

- **Electronic Communications Privacy Act:** Document related to e-mail privacy.

FTP: ftp.eff.org
   login: anonymous
   directory = /pub/CAF/law/

PUBLISHING

- **Electronic Newsstand**
- **Online Bookstore**
  - **O'Reilly & Associates:** Catalog of books and software.

    Gopher: gopher.???? (port 70)
       selector = null
  - **Prentice-Hall Gopher:** Catalog of books and software.

    Gopher: gopher.prenhall.com (port 70)
       selector = null
  - **Princeton University Press Gopher**

    Gopher: gopher.pupress.princeton.edu (port 70)
       selector = null
  - **Massachusetts Institute of Technology Press Gopher**

    Gopher: gopher.????????????? (port 70)
       selector = null

RELIGION

- **Buddhist Journal:** An electronic journal serving the global Buddhist community. Send e-mail to dharma@netcom.com stating that you would like to subscribe to GASSHO.
- **Vatican Exhibit on World-Wide Web**

  WWW: http://www.ncsa.uiuc.edu/SDG/Experimental/
     vatican.exhibit/Vatican.exhibit.html

SCHOLARLY AND PROFESSIONAL ASSOCIATIONS

- **University of Waterloo Scholarly Society Catalog:** A folder on the Gopher server maintained by the UW Library that offers pointers to online resources of numerous scholarly societies.

  Gopher: uwinfo.uwaterloo.ca (port 70)
     selector = 1/servers/campus/scholars

SCIENCE (GENERAL)

- **THE SCIENTIST:** A biweekly newspaper for scientists and the research community.

  FTP: ds.internic.net
  login: anonymous
  directory = /pub/the-scientist

SEISMOLOGY

- **Quakeline:** The database of the National Center for Earthquake Engineering Research (NCEER), contains bibliographic information on the subjects of earthquakes, earthquake engineering, natural hazards mitigation, and related topics.

  Telnet: ubvm.cc.buffalo.edu
  select BISON from the NETMENU

SPACE

- **NASA's Project STELAR:** Provides access to a number of online databases and services of interest to the astronomical community.

  WWW: http://hypatia.gsfc.nasa.gov:80/
  STELAR_homepage.html

- **Rennes University Space Photos**

  FTP: ftp.cicb.fr
  login: anonymous
  directory = /pub/Images/ASTRO

- **Space Science Overview on World-Wide Web**

  WWW: http://info.cern.ch/Space/Overview.html

STATISTICS

- **Journal of Statistics Education**

  E-mail to archive@jse.stat.ncsu.edu
  subscribe jse-announce FirstName LastName

SYSTEMS SCIENCE

- **Complexity International:** A Hypermedia Journal of Complex Systems Research.

  FTP: life.anu.edu.au
  login: anonymous
  directory = /pub/complex systems/ci

Gopher: life.anu.edu.au (port 70)
       selector = 1/complex_systems/ci
WWW: http://life.anu.edu.au:80/ci/ci.html

TRAVEL

- **Travel Archive:** Travel information from the Usenet News group rec.travel.

  FTP: ftp.cc.umanitoba.ca
      login: anonymous
      directory = /rec-travel

- **US State Department Travel Advisories**

  FTP: ftp.stolaf.edu
      login: anonymous
      directory = /pub/travel-advisories
  Gopher: gopher.stolaf.edu (port 70)
         selector = 1/Internet Resources/US-State-Department-
         Travel-Advisories

VEGETARIANISM

- **Vegetarian Newsletter**

  LISTSERV: listserv@vtvm2.cc.vt.edu
         send sub granola firstname lastname

- **Vegetarian Restaurants**

  FTP: rtfm.mit.edu
      directory = pub/usenet/news.answers/vegetarian/guide

VIDEO ARCHIVES

- **MPEG Movie Archive:** See Fig. 26.1.

WEATHER

- **Flood Information:** Information concerning flood activities in the state of Illinois since July 1993.

  Gopher: ilces.ag.uiuc.edu (port 70)
      selector = 1/Flood-Information

- **Meteorological Data Available over the Internet:** A guide to various sources of meteorological, oceanographic, and geophysical data.

  FTP: vmd.cso.uiuc.edu
      login: anonymous

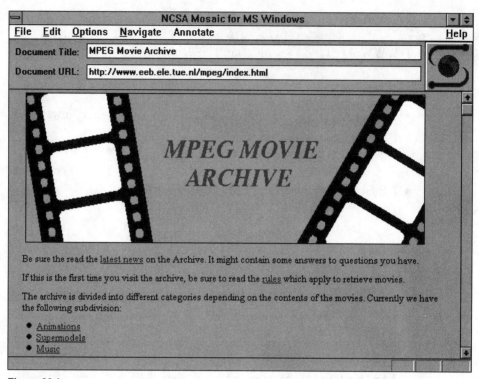

Figure 26.1

- **METEOSAT Images of European Weather**

  Gopher: gopher.uni-bayreuth.de (port 70)
  selector = 1/Service/Meteosat

- **United Kingdom Weather Maps**

  WWW: http://web.nexor.co.uk/places/satelite.html

- **University of Illinois Department of Atmospheric Sciences Weather Machine**

  Gopher: wx.atmos.uiuc.edu (port 70)
  selector = null

- **University of Michigan Weather Underground**

  Telnet: madlab.sprl.umich.edu (port 3000)

ZOOLOGY

- **Mammal Species of the World:** A taxonomy online at the Smithsonian Institution

Gopher: `nmnhgoph.si.edu` (port 70)
       selector = `1/.vertebrate`

- **Zoology Directory, Stanford University**

Gopher: `genome-gopher.stanford.edu` (port 70)
       selector = `/topic/zoological`

Epilogue

Peter Lyman

University Librarian
The University of Southern California

YOUR DRIVER'S LICENSE
FOR THE INFORMATION HIGHWAY

This book is not about computers or computer networks, it is about navigating the Internet. To navigate—this is a book about activity, the craft of exploring the global reference room—*that* is the Internet. The single most distinctive fact about the Internet is that it is the first communications medium designed specifically for person-to-person exchange of information on a global scale. And this book is your driver's license for navigating the Internet.

The map showing Internet access in countries across the world (illustrated in Chap. 1) inevitably changes the way we will think about the future of information and libraries. Politicians tell us that "the information highway" is a tool for economic competition between nations, but it's too late, the Internet is already a global communications web which is building citizen-to-citizen relationships across nations. This web is not simply an impressive technical achievement, although it is that, but this technology has become the basis of a global culture dedicated to the sharing of information without economic or political barriers.

The Internet is often defined as a network of networks, connecting well over 20 million people, and growing at a rate of 10 percent a month or more. As of December 1993, the Internet was estimated to contain 22,000 different networks supporting at least 2 million host computers in 69 countries; there are a lot more now. Although it evolved from the ARPANET and NSFnet (both American government research networks), today it is more like a social movement, a medium of communication built and paid for by those who use it. The "nodes" on the network are identified by type and country. Types include education (.edu), government (.gov), organizations (.org), and many more—all these tacitly American. But today the Internet has become international, and the suffix of an Internet address is likely to be Australia (.au) or Swiss (.ch).

Although it is democratic, it is certainly not representative. The Internet has no government, although the Internet Society has created itself ex post facto as a forum for discussion and resolution of issues regarding the organization and management of something that has grown in an organic manner. To join the Internet Society, send electronic mail to "isoc@isoc.org".

The Internet is democratic in another sense. Like fax, it transcends the efforts of government postal and telegraph offices to control access to information. James Billington, the Librarian of Congress, recently told me that the materials in the Library's exhibit on the secret archives of the Soviet Union were confiscated by the Conservatives in the Russian Parliament when they were returned to Russia. But the Library of Congress, in cooperation with the University of Virginia, places images and texts from its exhibits on the Internet. Billington reports that the exhibition has been downloaded to Internet nodes all over Russia.

Ultimately there are no secrets on the net; secrets are no longer possible. Hackers are a kind of inverse secret police, breaking through all technical barriers to access imprisoned information. Unfortunately, like secret police, the ends often do not justify the means. Just as the printing press ultimately gave rise to the idea of freedom of the press, with attendant rights and duties, very soon we must define a code of rights (and duties) on the net. (*Note:* Steven Gilbert, Frank Connolly, and I attempted to do this in our paper for the Office of Technology Assessment, "A Bill of Rights for Electronic Citizens," which was published on the net, and printed in the *Educom Bulletin* (1991). The Electronic Frontier Foundation, Inc., 238 Main St., Cambridge, MA 02142—or eff@eff.org), whose newsletter is distributed on the net, was founded by Mitch Kapor to report, analyze, and advocate policies about these issues.

As a technology, the Internet thus far has been defined by three universal applications, running under TCP/IP (Transmission Control Protocol/Internet Protocol). SMTP, or electronic mail as it is known to mere mortals, is a very distinctive medium for the exchange of personal messages. FTP, file transfer protocol, provides the ability to exchange files of information, which essentially provides the ability to have access to multimedia information worldwide, instantaneously and at virtually no cost. And Telnet, the ability to use programs on computers anywhere on the Internet, has become the basis of networked publishing. In recent years Gopher and World-Wide Web have become equally important. Naturally the use of each of these applications is subject to the permission of the owner, but a distinct feature of Internet culture is that permission is often given to someone named "public." On this technical foundation have been built the first important tools for navigating information on a global scale: Gopher and Mosaic.

This is the Internet—a global medium for communication created by millions of participants, which transcends nations, corporations, and governments, yet uses their resources. It is less than this, and more. It is less in that it was largely created by scientists and engineers, and its applications, culture, and language reflect their information cultures. Yet it is more—today it is used by hundreds of thousands of people who can use SMPT, FTP, and Telnet without having a clue what those acronyms might mean. At some point there was a metamorphosis, and a computer technology became the defining communications medium of the twenty-first century so far, which the very first inhabitants of the twenty-first century call *cyberspace*.

The political sociology of technology

When I met Richard Wiggins, we both worked at Michigan State University. I was a faculty member, teaching political philosophy, and assistant director of academic computing. He was in charge of the operating system of a new IBM mainframe, which I needed to learn about. We were discussing an arcane point of VM design when Richard taught me the most important fact I've ever learned about computers. As a philosophy major, I had studied logic; in our culture, the computer not only has the prestige as the logical artifact, it is virtually a symbol of rationality. Thus by training and cultural inclination I made the mistake of assuming that computer systems were logical, perhaps rational. Richard quickly corrected my mistake: computer systems have histories, not structures. To understand them, one needs to understand the people who designed them, the problems they faced, the mistakes they made, the bugs they discovered, and the fixes they invented. The computer operates by logic, but it is not logical. It is human, all too human.

The cultural values which are currently embedded in this technology (which mark its origins but are in no sense fundamental to it) and the human frailty of computers is why I began doing research in the field. I had been studying anger in social movements, since social movements often use angry rhetoric to mobilize political power. There came a time in the mid-1970s when angry social movements no longer wanted white male social scientists studying them. When I asked my friends for ideas about where I could study anger, they all replied, "Go to the computer center!" And, in fact, the computer center is a very good place to study anger, and rage. The machine, which has great cultural prestige for being a "brain," does not obey us. And we become angry, even enraged. What nonengineers do not realize is that even engineers feel enraged at computers. That is why we give commands to computers, as if to a dog or a slave. This is why we have control keys, to force the computer to obey when it is bad.

And when it won't obey, there are break keys. The break key is ambiguous: does it mean "I'll break you!" or "you're broken"? I favor the latter interpretation, since only machines can be broken, not people. And we get angry at broken machines because then we have to pay attention to them, when their proper place is to become tacit, tools which disappear from our attention while we think about the task at hand. And the ultimate weapon provided to us is the escape key, in which we wake up from a bad dream. Or, the ultimate act of bad faith: rather than reason with it, we simply kill it. Turn it off. Pull the plug. It's only a movie. Tomorrow is another day.

As Sherry Turkle has pointed out in *The Second Self,* the most annoying characteristic of the computer is that it is our culture's mirror on rationality, the artifact with which we contemplate human nature. The image of the computer performs the function which the image of the wild child provided for the Enlightenment; we see ourselves more clearly in our opposites. Ultimately, this cybernetic language of command and control fails to solve the philosophical contradiction we face between the ultimate logical brain and a machine which disobeys us. This language is an artifact of a particular culture—the engineer's culture which created the Internet, a culture which was focused on "the man/machine interface." For example, when we are called "users," our relationship to technology suggests dependence. To my ear, the term "user" suggests drug dependency (but technologists insist this is a problem with my ear, not their inventions).

It is not the relation to the machine which is fundamental, it is the relationship between humans using machines to communicate with each other. Just as Nolan Bushnell, a designer of computer-based robots, once called "stand-alone computers" paraplegic, computers without network communications might be defined as autistic.

The Internet has a far different structure, since it is about connections between computers which are used as a media for human communication, not human/machine relations. Thus the Internet is a social medium which makes possible a whole new array of communications, rather like the printing press made possible pamphlets and books. When we think about the Gutenberg revolution, we don't think about movable type (which, in any case, was invented in Korea before Gutenberg invented it), we think about books or pamphlets. And although books and pamphlets were the most important object of trade, they are only artifacts that enable a society collectively to create, preserve, and use knowledge in a very successful way. By analogy, the Internet is not about computers (the printing press), or SMTP and FTP and Telnet and Gopher (libraries, bookstores, books, pamphlets, newspapers), it is about the way we create, preserve, and use knowledge. We are inventing new forms of knowledge on the Internet, and new forms of knowledge will make possible new forms of society that we cannot even guess about today. But I'll guess about them a little later. (As a matter of professional ethics I must report that technology forecasts are almost always wrong.)

I like the term "navigation" because, while it implies substantial technical skills, it is more like a skilled performance than an act of logic; navigation requires continuous judgment, and the purpose of navigation is not technology—technology is a mere means for exploration. More fundamental than technical skill, navigating the Internet requires curiosity and determination. This is an important pedagogical point in using this book: network navigational skills are learned by practice, and it is much more important to learn from mistakes than to avoid making mistakes in the first place. Navigating the net is more like learning to drive than solving a mathematical problem.

How did the transition from the mainframe to the network, from cybernetic command and control to communication, come to be? Initially the ARPANET was a technology for the exchange of information between government and defense contractors. The NSFnet improved upon the system, to enable scientists to use distant supercomputers; yet last year MERIT research showed that among scientists, two-thirds of the use of NSFnet was for communication, not computation. Scientists used NSFnet to find each other (name look-up) and to exchange papers and information; in essence, the Internet was their library, but a library focused upon the creation of knowledge by a scholarly community, as well as for its publication and preservation. This only reminds us that the applications that define the Internet are more tools for information management than for computation.

Like written letters, electronic mail is a written communication, subject to the normal lexical and rhetorical rules which we use to say things in writing. Electronic mail is fast and personal, like talking on the telephone, but the telephone is synchronous (someone has to be there to answer before you can talk), while e-mail is asynchronous (they can pick up the message and answer later). E-mail is something new, both telephone and writing, yet neither. This has created problems, like flaming, a tendency to emotional excess in e-mail communications. Because it is interactive, like a conversation, our emotions get involved, but unlike a conversation we can't use nonverbal communications to provide emphasis without giving offense. But in e-mail we exaggerate for emphasis. Often it turns into flaming, uncontrolled emotional statements. This is several problems in one: we need new rhetorical rules for the medium; we need ethical norms for the medium; perhaps we need italics and boldface for graphic expression of emphasis. Be warned: electronic mail cannot be used for resolving conflicts, it is best for the communication of information, and if used for problem-solving it requires a positive social relationship.

Yet the problem of flaming is a clue to the nature of this new medium, and is no different from the problems we face in using any medium of communication. Would you send a love letter by fax? or in a business letter format, printed and with traditional business salutations? There is a fundamental relationship between the content of a message and the social relationship within which it is appropriately sent. Each medium of communication has strengths and weaknesses which shape the nature of the messages we would send. The appropriate use of electronic mail is still emerging as the Internet connects diverse social groups. Flaming, for example, was not seen as an important problem when e-mail was used only within technical groups, which share a common language and culture (that is, essentially a male group in which violent language is generally assumed to be playful, as in a game). The fact that flaming is now defined as a problem is a reflection of the growing social and cultural diversity among users of the network.

Similarly, FTP is important not simply because it is a way to exchange documents, although no one in the world need wait for the latest research in physics. It is important because it is a new mode of publication. And Telnet is important. You don't have to own a specialized computer, or be near one, to use it from your desktop. Gopher has become the first client-server application to join the top five Internet programs, and in the future information-finding and exchange applications are likely to define the Internet. WAIS is particularly interesting; since the distinctive information problem of modernity is "information anxiety," there is too much information and we don't know how to select from all the sources which saturate everyday life (television, radio, computers, print).

Thus, quantitative improvements in technology have made possible qualitative changes in the sociology of the network, and changed the network from a computational resource to a global medium for the creation and publication of information. Karl Wittfogel once theorized (in a book called *Oriental Despotism*) that throughout history the technology of transportation limited the size of empire; the speed with which messages (and other scarce resources) were transmitted was a finite limit on the extent of political coordination that was possible. The relationship between distance and time is changed if a book can be sent around the world in seconds. The Internet abolishes some of the inequalities that stem from distance; it abolishes the political geography of knowledge. For this reason, countries like Australia, which have suffered from geographical distance from the information markets of the world, have been the most advanced in formulating government policies to apply network technologies to problems of education and economic competition.

Of course, the network does not abolish other important sources of inequality, like access to wealth, education, health care, and so forth. It may well magnify them if we do not define a right to information as a basic empowerment for every human being. And yet, information is closely related to wealth in modern economies; the *Wall Street Journal* recently reported that 40 percent of American export income was based upon intellectual property. And from an international perspective, access to information may be one of the most important resources in health care, economic development, and education. The relationship between information and wealth has had the consequence of framing the discussion of the information highway legislation as a commercial question. A critical moment in the future of the Internet occurred when the National Information Infrastructure legislation was placed in the domain of the Congressional commerce committees rather than in the education committees. Yet, in time, it might well be framed as a foreign policy question, in which the network is defined as a medium for economic development and health care in the third world.

The network as the new printing press

The invention of the network is like the invention of the printing press in several senses.

First, we are still very early in the evolution of this invention. It took nearly a century for the printing press to be used for purposes other than imitating handmade manuscripts; the information on the network today is still largely designed in imitation of printed documents. Scholars in a number of disciplines have developed software for electronic journals which are essentially experiments in creating new kinds of information environments on the network and, implicitly, new kinds of social relationships among scholars. An electronic journal called Psycholoquy states a research problem, which becomes a forum for intense scientific debate (which much more closely resembles the scholarly process than the neat formats of printed journal articles). The Online Mendelian Inheritance in Man (OMIM) is a database containing worldwide scientific research on the human genome, a field changing so fast that printed information is almost always out of date; the online journal is time-stamped when it is printed, because in the modern world the value of information is often related to its timeliness. These experiments suggest one possible future of the network, a medium for the creation and exchange of information by groups of people (who may be located around the world) in media crafted specifically for certain kinds of content.

Second, the printing press was important not only because it made books, but because the books made possible new kinds of organizations, like libraries, scientific disciplines, and, ultimately, democratic societies based upon an educated citizenry. We still do not know what kinds of organizations might be built upon the Internet. But consider the example of the credit card: each of us is free to roam the world largely without cash, because there is an international digital network which can read our credit cards and establish credit nearly anywhere. Or consider modern stock markets, in which financial instruments can be traded 24 hours a day around the world because computer networks keep track of the information. What kinds of artistic, scientific, and educational environments might be built using the same technology?

Third, as with the early days of the printing press, much of the information on the network is published locally with very little quality control. We have yet to invent the electronic equivalent of publishers, who provide investment, quality control, marketing, and pricing. It is likely that the entertainment and telecommunications industries will provide the first models for network publishing, but it is important to remember that much of the innovation that has driven the American economy came from independent inventors, not large corporations.

Described as an "information highway," we think of the Internet as a medium of transportation; described as something we "navigate," it is a place for exploration. Terms like "user" and "information highway" and even "navigation" implicitly define the Internet as technology, and this, while valid, fundamentally misses the point. It's a little like calling the reader of a book a user of the printing press, although for that matter the book format itself was an invention (the codex) and a technology, but one so familiar we don't recognize it as such. The Internet must be defined, initially but fundamentally, as a new medium for communication which is still being invented.

To put this point in another way, while we indeed "use" technology in order to read texts on the computer, the term *user* is not itself a very rich description of what we do. To use richer terms, provisionally borrowed from our experience in another medium for communication: on the Internet we are readers, perhaps authors, sometimes publishers. The Internet consists of texts of different kinds; ultimately reading is the interface between human and computers, although this point is often ignored. We read texts on the screen; we give commands using words. Granted, these texts are often organized differently; back to the future, we "scroll" through texts as if they are precodex papyrus. Or they are organized in an almost wholly new kind of library, in databases or spreadsheets or hypertext, distributed around the globe.

On the other hand, the term *user* illuminates an important difference in the kind of artifact with which we communicate in print and on the Internet: we read a book, because printed objects become a tacit part of our bodies, disappearing from the mind's eye; but the artifact with which we read on the Internet is a computer, which cannot ever entirely disappear from view. The "computer" (whose name no longer describes its function very well, although it does describe its technical operations) cannot disappear from our awareness because it is the essence of the machine not to have an essence, but to continuously allow us to redefine its function, to make choices. In this sense we are always authors on the Internet, because the passive surrender to the text that enables reading to create worlds of imagination is not ultimately possible. There is always an element of participation and construction in the texts we read on the net. This is why computers, however logical, have the power to disobey.

But publishing on the net is qualitatively different from print publishing. For the first time in any medium, all texts are potentially global. Just as the extent of empire was limited by its means of transportation, so the extent of science, letters, and arts has been tacitly limited by the means of distribution of print. The world of knowledge can be navigated almost instantaneously. This technical feat has immense sociological consequences. For the first time, intellectual communities can form without respect to the limits of distance. In political terms, for the first time there is no such thing as exile. The concept of nation itself will change, since migrant ethnic communities can participate in the intellectual cultures of their nation of origin no matter how far away.

The technology of print—the press and the codex and paper—changed history because it made modern science possible. When science was published it was made public and subject to criticism, and it was made cumulative. Both of these developments irreversibly separated knowledge from religion. Print made nations possible, by publishing in national languages, thus creating a literature and a cultural identity; the foundation of national libraries almost always occurs as a founding act of a new nation. Print made democracy possible, giving people the information they needed to participate in government.

The public library has been one of the foundations of American democracy: Benjamin Franklin founded the first public library and was one of the founders of the Constitution; Andrew Carnegie founded public libraries across the nation, which supported the schools and small businesses. Today, the Internet has become a library built by readers. In 1992, OCLC research estimated that the Internet, Bitnet, and Usenet together contained 3.1 million FTP files, 337 library catalogs, 111 Listserv sites with uncounted lists, 3275 conferences, 26 electronic journals, 72 newsletters, 16 digests, and 3794 newsgroups. The 1994 *Directory of Electronic Journals, Newsletters and Academic Discussion Lists* published by the Association of Research Libraries includes 440 electronic journals and 1800 scholarly lists and newsletters. However, at least this much information was freely distributed around the world. More important, anyone who wished to become a publisher has become one; this is a library created by the producers of information.

On the other hand, not every collection of information is a library. The term "collection" implies a principle of selection, which reflects the information and knowledge needs of a community. Every library defines a community. In this library, information about UNIX outnumbers information about eunuchs about 10 billion to one. Judged by its content, thus far this is a library for people who use data, not knowledge, and for people who are more likely to use the net to look things up than browse or read a long narrative. But it is rapidly becoming more intellectually diverse. We know the technology of the Internet, and are beginning to map the library, but we do not yet know the sociology: who uses the Internet? This is a technology created by and for engineers. Most of them have access to the Internet, which is funded by grants or employers; most of them live in a world in which knowledge appears to be free, because they create knowledge and their access to copyrighted knowledge is subsidized. From an anthropological point of view, they are part of a gift economy, in which the exchange of information is the way social relationships are established and nurtured. Right now, the Internet is a tribal culture in a world governed by markets. Not for long.

Any human activity which, while founded on government subsidy, is now growing 10 percent monthly with only very tiny government subsidy and now includes millions of members worldwide might also be called an international market. The enforcement of copyright would radically increase the quality of information on the Internet. The means to track the use of copyrighted information and charge for it is not technically impossible; it was just very low priority to the tribe that created this village.

Thus, the next great policy issue in the evolution of the Internet is to define the domain: Is this an "information highway," essentially an economic activity dominated by private corporations? Or is it "electronic citizenship," essentially a political activity governed by the public interest? This is not a simple question. Copyright itself is an attempt to balance between the right to knowledge, defined in the U.S. Constitution as "progress in the sciences and useful arts," and economic incentives to encourage invention and publication. The copyright laws are compromises between private property and public good. There are other mechanisms which might be used: the net might be a private activity regulated like cable TV or broadcasting, with some portion of revenue or activity dedicated to the public good; or the net might be governed by a public corporation. The point is, the net is too important not to be the subject of a policy debate. Invented by technologists, it is now used by citizens but may soon be dominated by giant corporations selling entertainment. This book tells you how to qualify for net citizenship, but you need to participate in its governance.

What kinds of citizenship and politics are potentially made possible by the Internet? Listen to the voice of Ithiel de Sola Pool: "The regulation of electronic communication is not entailed in its technology but is a reaction to it. Computers, telephones, radio, and satellites are technologies of freedom, as much as was the printing press."* Ithiel de Sola Pool is one of the most important scholars in the field of technical innovation; later in his book he makes a crucial point for legislators, "so too with electronic publication networks, a normative system must grow out of actual patterns of work. The law may then lend support to these norms."† Our polity now faces a very important question: What is the proper balance between the right to innovation or free speech and the need for regulation in order to promote key industries or to protect intellectual property?

Finally, the net has changed the definition of the computer from computation to a means for the invention of new arts, meaning the term "arts" in the broadest possible sense. For the first time since the eighteenth century, there is a renaissance in the way we visualize information, and like the Renaissance, this is an age in which entirely new forms of knowledge are being created.

Historically, knowledge was identical to the format in which it was published; the ideas in this book are inseparable from the book commodity itself. The author has defined its form, and the readers must (more or less) conform to the limits of that form; the title "author" is related to "authority" in this sense. But in digital formats, the reader can decide how knowledge should be structured and viewed. In a spreadsheet, data can be looked at in a grid, or as a pie chart, or as a bar chart, or as a scattergram. An equation can be seen as a formula, or as a three-dimensional color graphic. Literacy from now on gives the reader a choice, the format of knowledge must conform to the reader's needs, and there is intellectual freedom and tolerance in this.

Similarly, entirely new forms of representation of knowledge are being created. Computer graphics create animations, which are so familiar in television commercials and films we accept them as real. Popular music includes a great variety of synthesized sounds. We have the tools to build entirely new kinds of literature.

---

* Ithiel de Sola Pool, Technologies of Freedom, Harvard University Press 1983, p. 229.

† Ibid., p. 249.

In this sense, the digital library on the network is an entirely new phenomenon. It does not replace print; by and large it cannot compete with the rhetorical and lexical formats optimized by print and developed for print, But it will create entirely new kinds of texts, of knowledge, of literature, of libraries, and nations.

History has changed. Columbus is still right; the earth is round. But the world is cyberspace. This book is the Ellis Island for a new world; you will be given a new name (eight characters only in your user name), but after that you'll be a citizen of a new global village.

Installing Mosaic for Microsoft Windows

NCSA offers freely available versions of Mosaic for MS-Windows, for the Macintosh and for the X Window interface under Unix. The software is freely available for retrieval via anonymous FTP. See the NCSA license terms for information about commercial use of Mosaic. As this book goes to press, several companies have licensed Mosaic for commercial packaging and distribution. If you have acquired a commercial copy of Mosaic, see the documentation that comes with that version. Commercial packages of Mosaic should be considerably easier to install than the freely available version, especially when packaged with TCP/IP software.

This appendix describes how to install the Windows version of NCSA Mosaic. In order to run this software, you will need to have a direct connection to the Internet, or your TCP/IP software will need to simulate such a direct connection using PPP or the equivalent. (See Chap. 5.) Your TCP/IP package will need to comply with the Winsock standard. Fortunately, virtually all commercial TCP/IP packages for Windows do offer support for this standard. If you are not sure whether your TCP/IP product supports Winsock, consult the documentation. (Another sign of Winsock support is the presence of a `WINSOCK.DLL` file on your hard disk.)

Before you start installation, it is a good idea to close all open Windows applications. This will protect you from losing information if something crashes.

As of version 2, Mosaic for Windows is a 32-bit application. This means that Mosaic will require special support code for 32-bit applications. Mosaic isn't the only such application; many other programs now require 32-bit support. Windows 3.1 does not come with 32-bit application support, but Microsoft offers a 32-bit add-on that is freely available over the Internet. (Versions of Windows after 3.1 will probably have 32-bit support built in.) To see if you have installed this 32-bit support code on your system, look for a /WINDOWS/SYS-TEM/WIN32S directory. If that directory is present and has files in it, you probably have 32-bit support. If the directory is not present, you will need to add this support before you can run Mosaic under Windows. You can obtain a copy of the 32-bit package from NCSA via FTP. The following sample session shows how:

```
C:\mkdir win32s
C:\WIN32S>ftp ftp.ncsa.uiuc.edu
FTP Software PC/TCP File Transfer Program Version 2.2 07/06/93 17:24
Copyright (c) 1986-1993 by FTP Software, Inc. All rights reserved.
FTP Trying...Open
220 zaphod FTP server (Version 6.23 Thu Apr 8 06:37:40 CDT 1993) ready.
Userid for logging in on zaphod.ncsa.uiuc.edu (rww)? ftp
331 Guest login ok, send e-mail address as password.
Password for logging in as ftp on zaphod.ncsa.uiuc.edu? wiggins@msu.edu
230- it was last modified on Sat Sep 12 18:30:42 1992 - 602 days ago
230-Please read the file README.FIRST
230- it was last modified on Sun Oct 3 17:45:17 1993 - 217 days ago
230-Please read the file README_Dialin
230- it was last modified on Wed Sep 2 14:21:17 1992 - 612 days ago
230 Guest login ok, access restrictions apply.
ftp:zaphod.ncsa.uiuc.edu> cd /PC/Mosaic
257 "/PC/Mosaic" is current directory.
ftp:zaphod.ncsa.uiuc.edu> dir
drwxrwxr-x 2 9396     wsstaff      512 May  8 06:07 old
-rwxrwxr-x 1 12984    wsstaff     4300 Apr 25 14:08 readme.now
-rwxrwxr-x 1 12984    wsstaff     3599 Mar 19 14:51 slip.txt
drwxrwxr-x 3 9396     wsstaff      512 May  8 06:06 sockets
drwxrwxr-x 2 12984    wsstaff      512 May  8 06:07 source
drwxrwxr-x 2 12984    wsstaff      512 May  8 06:07 util
drwxrwxr-x 2 9396     wsstaff      512 May  8 06:06 viewers
-rwxrwxr-x 1 12984    wsstaff   748572 Apr  7 17:02 win32s.zip
-rwxrwxr-x 1 12984    wsstaff   263431 Apr 25 14:03 wmos20a4.zip
drwxrwxr-x 2 12984    wsstaff      512 May  8 06:06 zip
Transferred 900 bytes in 1 seconds (7200 bits/sec, 900 bytes/sec)
226 Transfer complete.
ftp:zaphod.ncsa.uiuc.edu> get win32s.zip
local file (default win32s.zip):
Transferred 751316 bytes in 32 seconds (187829 bits/sec, 23478 bytes/sec)
226 Transfer complete.
ftp:zaphod.ncsa.uiuc.edu> binary
200 Type set to I.
```

```
ftp:zaphod.ncsa.uiuc.edu> get win32s.zip
local file (default win32s.zip): [Hit Enter to select the default]
Transferred 748572 bytes in 31 seconds (193179 bits/sec, 24147 bytes/sec)
226 Transfer complete.
ftp:zaphod.ncsa.uiuc.edu> quit
```

Both WIN32S and the other tools provided with Mosaic are delivered in PKZIP format. You will need a copy of the PKUNZIP Shareware utility to unpackage them. (PKUNZIP is available at many anonymous FTP sites; use Archie to locate a copy if you don't have one.)

To unpackage WIN32S, type this command:

```
pkunzip win32s.zip
```

Currently NCSA embeds WIN32S with another ZIP file and a Readme file. Take a look at the Readme file online (or print it), and then unpack the inner ZIP file. For instance,

```
pkunzip win32s11.zip
```

A number of files will be unpacked onto your hard disk. Now you want to run the Windows Setup program. If you are not already running Windows, start it up. Go to the Program Manager, and pull down the File menu. Select Run. You want to run the Setup program in the WIN32S directory as shown in Fig. A.1. The Setup program will install both the 32-bit support and a program called FreeCell that will allow you to verify installation. As a part of the Setup process you'll be asked to restart Windows.

Once you have WIN32S installed, you can now install Mosaic. First, you will want to create a subdirectory to hold the ZIP file. Then you will want to fetch the file from NCSA:

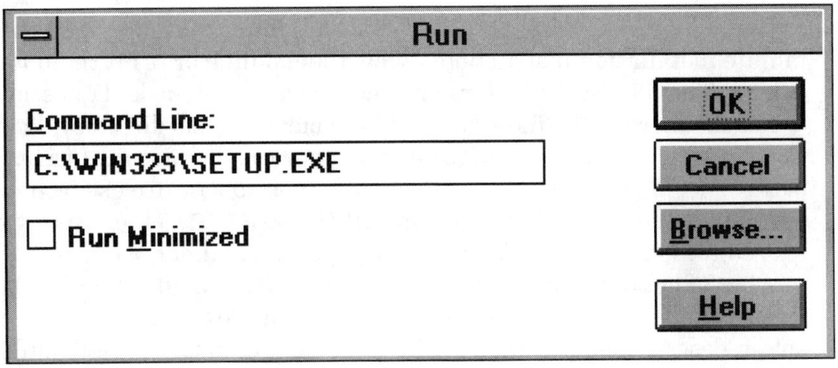

Figure A.1

```
C:\mkdir mosaic
C:\cd mosaic
C:\MOSAIC>ftp ftp.ncsa.uiuc.edu
Userid for logging in on zaphod.ncsa.uiuc.edu (rww)? ftp
331 Guest login ok, send e-mail address as password.
Password for logging in as ftp on zaphod.ncsa.uiuc.edu? wiggins@msu.edu
ftp:zaphod.ncsa.uiuc.edu>cd /PC/Mosaic
ftp:zaphod.ncsa.uiuc.edu> get wmos20a4.zip
local file (default wmos20a4.zip): [Hit Enter to select the default]
Transferred 263431 bytes in 14 seconds (150532 bits/sec, 18816 bytes/sec)
226 Transfer complete.
ftp:zaphod.ncsa.uiuc.edu>quit
```

Now you can unpack Mosaic:

```
C:\MOSAIC>pkunzip wmos20a4


PKUNZIP (R)        FAST!        Extract Utility        Version 2.04g 02-01-93
Copr. 1989-1993 PKWARE Inc. All Rights Reserved. Shareware Version
PKUNZIP Reg. U.S. Pat. and Tm. Off.


_ 80486 CPU detected.
_ XMS version 2.00 detected.
_ DPMI version 0.90 detected.

Searching ZIP: WMOS20A4.ZIP
   Inflating: FAQ.TXT
   Inflating: INSTALL.TXT
   Inflating: INSTALL.WRI
   Inflating: MOSAIC.INI
   Inflating: README.NOW
   Inflating: UPDATE.TXT
   Inflating: MOSAIC.EXE
```

The INSTALL.TXT and README.NOW files are important; they provide up-to-the-minute installation instructions. View them online or print them for the latest details. The file FAQ.TXT offers answers to frequently-asked questions.

You should copy the file MOSAIC.INI to your \WINDOWS directory. This initialization file will control the configuration of your copy of Mosaic. Leave the original MOSAIC.INI file in the \MOSAIC directory for possible future use; you may want to revert to it sometime. Now you can edit the MOSAIC.INI file, using your favorite text editor (such as the Notepad editor available under Windows). There are a number of options you can change in the MOSAIC.INI file, which is laid out in a format similar to other Windows initialization files. Take a look at the various option descriptions provided in the Readme file; most of the default values for these options are reasonable, so you can start off with the file as delivered.

One item you will want to edit is the Home Page= line. This specifies the name of the Web server you want to connect to by default. You can start by connecting to NCSA, as the file is configured to do, but you will do yourself and NCSA a favor if you change this line to point to a local Web server; the NCSA server is quite busy. You should also specify the domain-style host name of your local Usenet News and mail servers.

By itself, Mosaic can display text and inline images on your screen. In order to show you full-screen renditions of still images, or to display movies, or to play audio documents, Mosaic will rely on the services of external viewing tools. The [Viewers] section of the MOSAIC.INI file specifies the name and location on your hard disk of each of these tools. Do not edit the sections of the file labeled User Menu or Hot List; Mosaic offers a Menu Editor under its Navigate menu item that allows you to edit this information from within Mosaic itself.

While updating MOSAIC.INI, you will also need to specify the name and location of your Telnet program, which varies from one implementation of TCP/IP to another. For instance, if you use PC/TCP from FTP Software Inc., you might specify the following statement in MOSAIC.INI:

```
telnet="c:\pctcp\tn.exe"
```

Several viewers are available from NCSA's FTP archive. For example, NCSA offers a package called Lview as a suggested viewer for GIF and JPG still images. If you have installed that file per the NCSA MOSAIC.INI file, you will place it in:

```
C:\WINDOWS\APPS\LVIEW
```

For instance, suppose you want to fetch the Lview tool so you can view still image files. First, create the appropriate directory, then fetch the file:

```
C:\mkdir \windows\apps\lview
C:\cd mkdir \windows\apps\lview
C:\WINDOWS\APPS\LVIEW>ftp ftp.ncsa.uiuc.edu
Userid for logging in on zaphod.ncsa.uiuc.edu (rww)? ftp
331 Guest login ok, send e-mail address as password.
Password for logging in as ftp on zaphod.ncsa.uiuc.edu? wiggins@msu.edu
ftp:zaphod.ncsa.uiuc.edu>
ftp:zaphod.ncsa.uiuc.edu> cd /PC/Mosaic/viewers
250 CWD command successful.
ftp:zaphod.ncsa.uiuc.edu> dir
total 2711
-rw-r--r--  1 root     1            461 May  8 06:06 .index
-rwxr-xr-x  1 12984    wsstaff  1192261 Apr 13 16:42 gs261exe.zip
-rwxr-xr-x  1 12984    wsstaff   174939 Apr 13 16:42 gsview10.zip
-rwxr-xr-x  1 12984    wsstaff     2554 Nov 28 03:24 lview.txt
-rwxr-xr-x  1 12984    wsstaff   224269 Apr 25 14:11 lview31.zip
```

```
-rwxr-xr-x  1 12984    wsstaff      6781 Apr 18 03:12 mpegw32e.txt
-rwxr-xr-x  1 12984    wsstaff    921020 Apr 18 03:12 mpegw32e.zip
-rwxr-xr-x  1 12984    wsstaff       979 Apr 13 16:45 readme.1st
-rwxr-xr-x  1 12984    wsstaff     21236 Mar 19 14:53 speak.exe
-rwxr-xr-x  1 12984    wsstaff      8339 Apr 25 14:12 wham.txt
-rwxr-xr-x  1 12984    wsstaff    138130 Apr 25 14:13 wham131.zip
-rwxr-xr-x  1 12984    wsstaff      1047 Apr  4 15:27 wplany.doc
-rwxr-xr-x  1 12984    wsstaff     19123 Mar 27 22:24 wplny09b.zip
ftp:zaphod.ncsa.uiuc.edu> binary
ftp:zaphod.ncsa.uiuc.edu> get lview31.zip
```

You may want to fetch and install viewing tools at the same time you obtain Mosaic itself. Each tool will require unpacking from its ZIP file, and installation in the Program Manager.

Once you have Mosaic and the viewers you need in place, it's time to tell Windows about these tools. To do so, in Program Manager you will select File, then New, then Program Item, then the full path of each viewer you want to install. Use the Browse option to help you locate each tool. Type in a Description for each; this will appear underneath the tool's icon in Windows. You will also want to specify a Working Directory where the tool can store files it creates. See Fig. A.2.

Besides installing the viewing tools you will want to use, you need to install Mosaic itself. Once again, under Program Manager, select File, then New, then Program Item, then enter the full path name where Mosaic is located for the Command Line box. Also specify a Working Directory and a Description as in Fig. A.3.

Now, you are ready to run Mosaic. Simply click on the icon as it appears in Windows (under Main or the applications window that was active when you installed the icon). Mosaic should begin running. If you specified Autoload

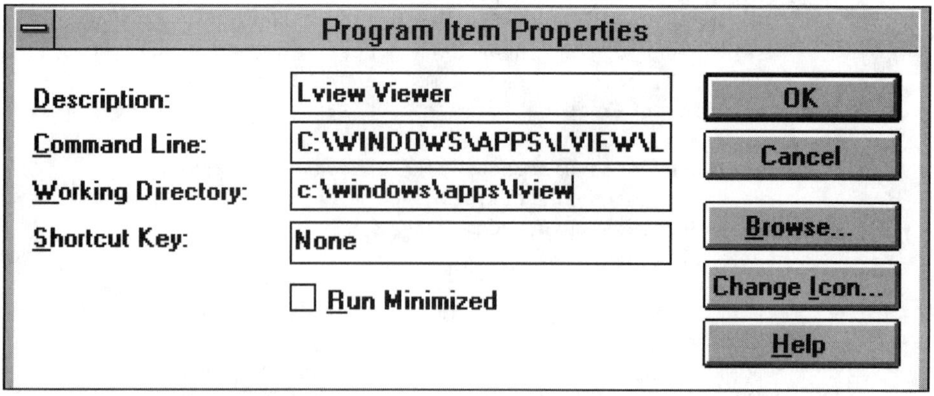

Program Item Properties

Description:	Lview Viewer
Command Line:	C:\WINDOWS\APPS\LVIEW\L
Working Directory:	c:\windows\apps\lview
Shortcut Key:	None

☐ **Run Minimized**

OK   Cancel   Browse...   Change Icon...   Help

Figure A.2

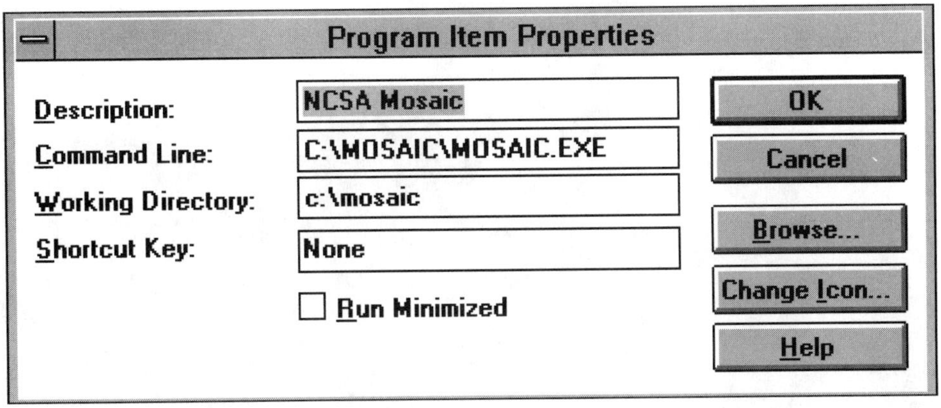

Program Item Properties		
Description:	**NCSA Mosaic**	**OK**
Command Line:	**C:\MOSAIC\MOSAIC.EXE**	**Cancel**
Working Directory:	**c:\mosaic**	
Shortcut Key:	**None**	**B**rowse...
	☐ **R**un Minimized	**Change** **I**con...
		Help

Figure A.3

Home Page = Yes, when Mosaic starts it will connect to the Home Page specified in your MOSAIC.INI file and display it for you.

Windows Mosaic differs slightly from its namesakes on other platforms. You will want to explore its options for managing User Menus and Hot Lists as ways to set up your own collections of favorite Internet resources.

If Mosaic does not run properly, you will want to recheck the installation steps to make sure you did them all correctly. If this appears to be the case, and Mosaic still won't work right, contact your network support personnel or your Internet service provider support staff for help.

Directory of Internet Service Providers

This appendix offers an abbreviated list of Internet service providers. This marketplace is in extreme flux; any directory of service providers in print form is by definition obsolete. Therefore you will want to consult the online directories of service providers listed in Chap. 5 in order to obtain an up-to-the-minute list of providers that are local to you. Most of those online directories can be retrieved via services that offer Internet e-mail.

Before you contact prospective providers, make a list of the services you want. For instance, do you want to use a 14.4-kilobit modem—or perhaps a 28.8-kilobit modem? Do you want PPP access so you can run Mosaic? What services do you want—e-mail, Gopher, World-Wide Web, Usenet News, anonymous FTP, Internet Relay Chat? See if any items on your list cost extra.

A special class of dial-up service that is becoming popular in the United States is 800, or toll-free, service. Typically, you sign up for the service with a credit card number, which is billed an hourly fee for your usage. This can be very useful if you travel a lot; dialing long distance to your home Internet service provider can be very expensive. Some of the 800-number services offer hourly rates well below $10 per hour; you may be able to obtain long-distance Internet access at rates that compete favorably with conventional long-distance fees. Be sure you understand all the fees involved before you sign up.

If you wish to obtain a permanent connection so that you can become an Internet information provider, review the alternatives in Chap. 5 and discuss them with your prospective service provider. Remember, many service providers will, for a fee, serve as your proxy, running a Gopher, World-Wide Web, or other service on your behalf. In many cases you will be able to edit your data while they manage the server software.

Many of the mass-market information utilities will offer more complete Internet services over time. Such mass-market utilities often offer trial packages bundled in computer magazines or provided with new computers, modems, or communications packages. You may find the mass-market utility offers all the Internet access services you desire; if not, you can use the services to access up-to-date information on other service providers. As this book goes to press, America Online and Delphi Internet offer Gopher service that will allow you to easily connect to the InterNIC Gopher and retrieve their online listings of other service providers. You might also post a query to the Usenet News group alt.internet.access.wanted. Also, be sure to explore local access alternatives such as nearby universities, FreeNets, and computer clubs.

For each service provider shown, the information provided includes: *Name; postal address; telephone number; e-mail address; comments on services offered or service areas.*

UNITED STATES SERVICE PROVIDERS

Advanced Network & Services (ANS); 2901 Hubbard Road, Ann Arbor, MI 48105; 313-663-7610; info@ans.net. A major backbone provider in the United States that also offers dial-up and leased-line access.

Alternet; UUNET Technologies, 3110 Fairview Park Dr., Suite 570, Falls Church, VA 22040; 703-204-8000; alternet-info@uunet.uu.net. A major provider of dial-up and leased-line services.

America Online (AOL); 8619 Westwood Center Drive, Vienna, VA 22182; 800-827-6364; postmaster@aol.com. Mass-market utility offering Internet services such as e-mail, Gopher, and Usenet News.

a2i Communications; 1211 Park Avenue, Suite 202, San Jose, CA 95132; [voice number unknown]; info@rahul.net. A California-based dial-up provider.

BARRNET (Bay Area Regional Research Network); Information, 115 Pine Hall, Stanford University, Stanford CA 94305; 415-725-1790; info@barrnet.net. The regional network in northern California.

Big Sky Telegraph; Western Montana College, P.O. Box 11, Dillon MT 59725; 406-683-7338. A low-cost dial-up provider associated with various bulletin board systems and the educational community.

CERFnet (California Educational and Research Federation Network); P.O. Box 85608, San Diego, CA 92186; 619-455-3900; help@cerf.net. A California educational network that has branched into 800-number dial-up service nationwide in the United States in addition to a variety of leased-line services. Also offers some international access.

CICNet; 2901 Hubbard Drive, Ann Arbor, MI 48105; 313-998-6102; `info@cic.net`. A regional network serving the midwestern United States that also offers nationwide 800-number access.

Colorado Supernet; Colorado School of Mines, 1500 Illinois, Golden, CO 80401; 303-273-3471; `info@csn.org`. A statewide network in Colorado.

Delphi Internet; 1030 Cambridge Avenue, Cambridge, MA 02138; 800-695-4005; `info@delphi.com`. A long-standing information utility that has branched into Internet services.

Digital Express (Digex); 6006 Greenbelt Road, Suite 228, Greenbelt, MD 20770; 301-220-2070; `info@digex.com`. A Washington, D.C. based service with local access in the D.C. area as well as Orange, California.

HoloNet; 46 Shattuck Square, Suite 11, Berkeley, CA 94704; 510-704-0160; `info@iat.mailer.net`. Local Internet access in 1000 cities across the United States, Canada, and Mexico.

MichNet; MichNet Information, c/o Merit Network, 2901 Hubbard, Pod G, Ann Arbor, MI 48105; 313-764-9430; `info@merit.edu`; a regional network offering dial-up access to 90 percent of the populace of Michigan. MichNet is operated by Merit, which has had important roles in the management of the NSFnet.

MSEN; 628 Brooks Street, Ann Arbor, MI 48103; 313-998-4562; `info@msen.com`. A pioneering commercial provider of dial-up service in southeast Michigan, known for its Gopher service and its hosting of the Online Career Center database.

NEARnet; 10 Moulton Street, Cambridge, MA 02138; 617-873-8730; `nearnet-staff@nic.near.net`. The New England regional network.

Netcom Online Communications Services; 4000 Moorepark Ave., Suite 209, San Jose, CA 95117; 408-544-8649; `ruthann@netcom.com`. A popular California-based provider.

NYSERNet; 200 Elwood Davis Road, Suite 103, Liverpool NY 13088; 315-453-2912; `info@nysernet.org`. The regional network in New York State.

Panix; [postal address unknown]; 212-877-4854; `alexis@panix.com`. A New York City-based public access Unix service that offers many Internet services.

Performance Systems International (PSI); 11800 Sunrise Valley Drive, Reston, VA 22091; 703-620-6651; `info@psi.com`. A major provider with "points of presence" in many U.S. cities, PSI offers leased-line and dial-up services.

The Pipeline; 150 Broadway, Suite 1710, New York, NY 10038; 212-267-3636; `info@pipeline.com`. New York City-based service offering an easy-to-install graphical user interface for Windows users—some non-N.Y. users find this interface so useful that they connect to the Pipeline over the Internet after connecting to a local Internet provider in their area.

SURAnet; 1353 Computer Science Center, 8400 Baltimore Boulevard, College Park, MD 20740; 301-982-4600, info@sura.net. Regional provider in southeast United States.

THEnet; Office of Telecommunications Services, Service Bldg. Room 319, Austin, TX 78712; 512-471-2444; info@nic.the.net. The regional network in Texas.

The Well; 27 Gate Five Road, Sausalito, CA 94965; 415-332-4335; info@well.sf.ca.us. An online service in the San Francisco bay area that offers Internet services as well as running locally oriented bulletin boards and Gopher documents.

AUSTRALIA

AARNet; AARNet Support, GPO Box 1142, Canberra ACT 2601, Australia; 61-6-249-3385; aarnet@aarnet.edu.au. The Australian national academic network.

CANADA

BCnet; British Columbia Internet Network, Room 419, 6356 Agricultural Road, University of British Columbia, Vancouver, B.C., Canada V6T1W5; 604-822-3932.

CA*net; CA*net Information Centre, Computing Services, University of Toronto, 4 Bancroft Avenue, Room 116, Toronto, Ontario Canada M5S 1A1; 416-978-6620; info@CAnet.ca. A national research and academic network.

EUROPE

EUnet; EUnet Network Operations Center, Kruislan 409, 1098 SJ Amsterdam; 31-20-592-5109; info@eu.net. An umbrella organization representing European networks.

NETHERLANDS

SURFnet; P.O. Box 19035, NL-3501 DA Utrecht, The Netherlands; 31-30-310290; info@surfnet.nl. A Dutch provider of TCP/IP and X.25 services for academic and research communities.

NORDIC COUNTRIES

NORDUnet; UNI-C, DTH Building 305, DK-2800 Lyngby, Denmark; 45-45-93-83-55; Peter.Villemoes@uni-c.dk. A collaborative effort of the national research networks in the Nordic countries.

UNITED KINGDOM

Demon Internet Services; 42 Hendon Lane, London N31TT, England; 44-81-349-0063; internet@demon.co.uk. An early and major Internet provider in the United Kingdom.

Pipex; Unipalm Ltd., 216 Cambridge Science Park, Cambridge CB4 4WA, England; 44-223-424616; pipex@pipex.net. A commercial Internet provider.

SWITZERLAND

SWITCH; Limmatquai 138, CH-8001 Zurich, Switzerland; 41-1-261-8188; postmaster@switch.ch. The Swiss academic and research network.

Internet Country Codes

The two-character country codes used in the Internet Domain Name System are drawn from an international standard, ISO 3166. In today's world, political boundaries can change frequently; you may want to consult online versions of this list for up-to-date information. (Use Archie or Veronica and search for "country codes" to find a current edition.)

Country	Code
AFGHANISTAN	AF
ALBANIA	AL
ALGERIA	DZ
AMERICAN SAMOA	AS
ANDORRA	AD
ANGOLA	AO
ANGUILLA	AI
ANTARCTICA	AQ
ANTIGUA AND BARBUDA	AG
ARGENTINA	AR
ARMENIA	AM
ARUBA	AW
AUSTRALIA	AU
AUSTRIA	AT
AZERBAIJAN	AZ
BAHAMAS	BS

BAHRAIN	BH
BANGLADESH	BD
BARBADOS	BB
BELARUS	BY
BELGIUM	BE
BELIZE	BZ
BENIN	BJ
BERMUDA	BM
BHUTAN	BT
BOLIVIA	BO
BOSNIA HERCEGOVINA	BA
BOTSWANA	BW
BOUVET ISLAND	BV
BRAZIL	BR
BRITISH INDIAN OCEAN TERRITORY	IO
BRUNEI DARUSSALAM	BN
BULGARIA	BG
BURKINA FASO	BF
BURUNDI	BI
BYELORUSSIAN SSR	BY
CAMBODIA	KH
CAMEROON	CM
CANADA	CA
CAPE VERDE	CV
CAYMAN ISLANDS	KY
CENTRAL AFRICAN REPUBLIC	CF
CHAD	TD
CHILE	CL
CHINA	CN
CHRISTMAS ISLAND	CX
COCOS (KEELING) ISLANDS	CC
COLOMBIA	CO
COMOROS	KM
CONGO	CG
COOK ISLANDS	CK
COSTA RICA	CR
COTE D'IVOIRE	CI
CROATIA (local name: Hrvatska)	HR
CUBA	CU
CYPRUS	CY
CZECHOSLOVAKIA	CS
DENMARK	DK
DJIBOUTI	DJ
DOMINICA	DM
DOMINICAN REPUBLIC	DO
EAST TIMOR	TP
ECUADOR	EC
EGYPT	EG

EL SALVADOR	SV
EQUATORIAL GUINEA	GQ
ESTONIA	EE
ETHIOPIA	ET
FALKLAND ISLANDS (MALVINAS)	FK
FAROE ISLANDS	FO
FIJI	FJ
FINLAND	FI
FRANCE	FR
FRENCH GUIANA	GF
FRENCH POLYNESIA	PF
FRENCH SOUTHERN TERRITORIES	TF
GABON	GA
GAMBIA	GM
GEORGIA	GE
GERMANY	DE
GHANA	GH
GIBRALTAR	GI
GREECE	GR
GREENLAND	GL
GRENADA	GD
GUADELOUPE	GP
GUAM	GU
GUATEMALA	GT
GUINEA	GN
GUINEA-BISSAU	GW
GUYANA	GY
HAITI	HT
HEARD AND MC DONALD ISLANDS	HM
HONDURAS	HN
HONG KONG	HK
HUNGARY	HU
ICELAND	IS
INDIA	IN
INDONESIA	ID
IRAN (ISLAMIC REPUBLIC OF)	IR
IRAQ	IQ
IRELAND	IE
ISRAEL	IL
ITALY	IT
JAMAICA	JM
JAPAN	JP
JORDAN	JO
KAZAKHSTAN	KZ
KENYA	KE
KIRIBATI	KI
KOREA, DEMOCRATIC PEOPLE'S REPUBLIC OF	KP
KOREA, REPUBLIC OF	KR

KUWAIT	KW
KYRGYZSTAN	KG
LAO PEOPLE'S DEMOCRATIC REPUBLIC	LA
LATVIA	LV
LEBANON	LB
LESOTHO	LS
LIBERIA	LR
LIBYAN ARAB JAMAHIRIYA	LY
LIECHTENSTEIN	LI
LITHUANIA	LT
LUXEMBOURG	LU
MACAU	MO
MADAGASCAR	MG
MALAWI	MW
MALAYSIA	MY
MALDIVES	MV
MALI	ML
MALTA	MT
MARSHALL ISLANDS	MH
MARTINIQUE	MQ
MAURITANIA	MR
MAURITIUS	MU
MEXICO	MX
MICRONESIA	FM
MOLDOVA, REPUBLIC OF	MD
MONACO	MC
MONGOLIA	MN
MONTSERRAT	MS
MOROCCO	MA
MOZAMBIQUE	MZ
MYANMAR	MM
NAMIBIA	NA
NAURU	NR
NEPAL	NP
NETHERLANDS	NL
NETHERLANDS ANTILLES	AN
NEUTRAL ZONE	NT
NEW CALEDONIA	NC
NEW ZEALAND	NZ
NICARAGUA	NI
NIGER	NE
NIGERIA	NG
NIUE	NU
NORFOLK ISLAND	NF
NORTHERN MARIANA ISLANDS	MP
NORWAY	NO
OMAN	OM
PAKISTAN	PK

PALAU	PW
PANAMA	PA
PAPUA NEW GUINEA	PG
PARAGUAY	PY
PERU	PE
PHILIPPINES	PH
PITCAIRN	PN
POLAND	PL
PORTUGAL	PT
PUERTO RICO	PR
QATAR	QA
REUNION	RE
ROMANIA	RO
RUSSIAN FEDERATION	RU
RWANDA	RW
SAINT KITTS AND NEVIS	KN
SAINT LUCIA	LC
SAINT VINCENT AND THE GRENADINES	VC
SAMOA	WS
SAN MARINO	SM
SAO TOME AND PRINCIPE	ST
SAUDI ARABIA	SA
SENEGAL	SN
SEYCHELLES	SC
SIERRA LEONE	SL
SINGAPORE	SG
SLOVENIA	SI
SOLOMON ISLANDS	SB
SOMALIA	SO
SOUTH AFRICA	ZA
SPAIN	ES
SRI LANKA	LK
ST. HELENA	SH
ST. PIERRE AND MIQUELON	PM
SUDAN	SD
SURINAME	SR
SVALBARD AND JAN MAYEN ISLANDS	SJ
SWAZILAND	SZ
SWEDEN	SE
SWITZERLAND	CH
SYRIAN ARAB REPUBLIC	SY
TAIWAN, PROVINCE OF CHINA	TW
TAJIKISTAN	TJ
TANZANIA, UNITED REPUBLIC OF	TZ
THAILAND	TH
TOGO	TG
TOKELAU	TK
TONGA	TO

TRINIDAD AND TOBAGO	TT
TUNISIA	TN
TURKEY	TR
TURKMENISTAN	TM
TURKS AND CAICOS ISLANDS	TC
TUVALU	TV
UGANDA	UG
UKRAINIAN SSR	UA
UNITED ARAB EMIRATES	AE
UNITED KINGDOM	GB
UNITED STATES	US
UNITED STATES MINOR OUTLYING ISLANDS	UM
URUGUAY	UY
USSR	SU
UZBEKISTAN	UZ
VANUATU	VU
VATICAN CITY STATE (HOLY SEE)	VA
VENEZUELA	VE
VIET NAM	VN
VIRGIN ISLANDS (BRITISH)	VG
VIRGIN ISLANDS (U.S.)	VI
WALLIS AND FUTUNA ISLANDS	WF
WESTERN SAHARA	EH
YEMEN, REPUBLIC OF	YE
YUGOSLAVIA	YU
ZAIRE	ZR
ZAMBIA	ZM
ZIMBABWE	ZW

Glossary

ACK   Acknowledgment. As a part of a communications protocol, an ACK is simply a positive signal that information was received, or that a requested negotiation is accepted. Compare NAK.

Acrobat   A family of tools from Adobe Corporation that allows publishers to translate Postscript files into a Portable Document Format, and users to view them on common computer platforms. Because Postscript comes in many dialects and with many dependencies on specific environments, portability is a problem. Acrobat makes files portable, and makes it possible for users to view files online, not just print them.

Address Resolution Protocol (ARP)   This Internet protocol makes it possible for TCP/IP to run over a low-level networking standard; ARP translates IP addresses to the physical addresses of hardware adapters. ARP is commonly used when TCP/IP runs over Ethernet networks. The ARP process is invoked by TCP/IP software transparently on behalf of the user.

Anonymous FTP   Anonymous FTP servers allow users to retrieve files without the need for assigned user IDs (literally the word "anonymous" is used as the login ID). This service is offered by many sites on the Internet. See **Archie.**

API   Applications Programming Interface. An API tells a programmer specifically how his or her program should interface to some sort of system service. As a user you generally don't worry about APIs, but in some cases you may have to find software that conforms to an API your TCP/IP package supports; e.g., you want a Gopher client program that can work with the Winsock API.

Archie   A network service that allows users to discover which anonymous FTP sites house particular files of interest. Developed at McGill University (and now Bunyip Information Systems), future versions of Archie will allow searching for resources by abstract, author name, and other criteria; Archie will become even more important as a tool for finding Internet resources.

ASCII file   A file encoded in the 128-character ASCII (American Standard Code for Information Interchange) character set. The term "flat ASCII file" is often used to refer to a simple text file, with no embedded special formatting codes or binary data. In FTP transfers, "text" and "ASCII" are synonymous.

Asynchronous Transfer Mode (ATM)   ATM is a relatively new communications medium that is suitable for high-speed links (such as fiber optics) and fast switching. ATM moves data in 53-byte "cells" (quite small compared to packet sizes for other media such as Ethernet). ATM is the first low-level media standard that's suitable for local area networks as well as wide area networks.

authoring tool   Software (and perhaps hardware) to facilitate creation of online documents, especially hypertext or multimedia documents.

backbone   In a hierarchically organized network, the top level of the network, with the main arteries that feed smaller subnetworks.

baseband   A cable medium that carries only one "channel" of information. Ethernet was conceived as a baseband medium, and is still most commonly deployed in that fashion (though sometimes it is carried as a single channel on a broadband medium).

Binary file   Binary files consist of streams of bytes whose meaning is defined by some external format standard; the contents are generally unrecognizable when viewed as text. For example, executable computer programs are binary files. In FTP transfers, a binary file is specified by "bin" or "image" settings.

BIND   Berkeley Internet Domain Software. This computer software, originally developed for Berkeley UNIX, is commonly used by **name servers** as they perform Domain Name System functions.

bridge   A device used to connect segments of a local area network together. Bridges operate at the "media access layer," forwarding, for instance, Ethernet datagrams across segments of a network. See **router.**

broadband   A cable medium that carries more than one "channel" of information.

browser   A tool that allows a user to "browse"—skim, read, or scan—a file. Some browsers are as powerful as text editors in their ability to search for text within a file, but they lack the ability to change the file. The word "pager" is sometimes used instead. In the World-Wide Web community "browser" is sometimes used to refer to the client software that allows users to "browse" documents on the Web.

CCITT   An acronym for an international standards body whose title (translated from French) was International Telephone and Telegraph Consultative Committee. CCITT is responsible for the official standards such as X.25 and X.400. CCITT's parent organization, the International Telecommunications Union, has renamed the CCITT as ITU-T.

CD-ROM   Compact Disk-Read Only Memory. The use of digital Compact Disks to deliver large collections of software or documents. A single CD-ROM disk can hold several hundred megabytes of data. CD-ROMs are often used to deliver.

Client/Server   A model for distributing computing transactions between client software, residing on a user's workstation, and server software, residing on a host computer. The host could be a UNIX workstation, a mainframe, or some other type of computer. The client handles most of the information presentation functions, and the server handles most of the database functions. A protocol specifies how the two should communicate. The client/server model is growing in popularity as workstations and networks grow in power and capacity.

cracker   Someone who tries to break into computer systems using unauthorized approaches. This term is supplanting "hacker," allowing that term to retain its venerable connotations.

CSO   A protocol that allows client/server searching of simple databases such as phone books. Named after the Computing Services Organization at the University of Illinois, the CSO protocol enjoys widespread usage in the Gopher community, despite more elaborate standards for such "white pages" services. (Sometimes called "CCSO.")

Curses A software feature under UNIX that allows a programmer to support full-screen terminal sessions. Said to be a play on words referring to the cursor keys.

CWIS Campus-Wide Information System. An information system that offers integrated access to information pertaining to a campus; originally referred to such systems at colleges and universities; now used at other schools and institutions. A CWIS contains documents (e.g., course schedules, lists of current events, and academic job openings) and connections to other computer systems (e.g., online library catalog). CWISes began on mainframes and are now commonly implemented under the client/server model. Gopher and WWW are commonly used for CWISes; other CWISes may use different technologies (for instance, the TechInfo software from MIT).

datagram A unit of data to be transferred over a network; a message to be sent over a TCP connection is transmitted in one or more IP datagrams. A datagram is similar to a telegram in that it has in its headers specific addressing information that allows it to be routed across the Internet all the way to its destination.

DTD Document Type Definition. A DTD defines the structure of a particular set of markup codes to be used for a particular set of documents in the SGML world. For instance, there is a DTD defining the Hypertext Markup Language used in the World-Wide Web.

e-mail Electronic mail. A system supporting creation of messages to be conveyed within a computer system or across networks for delivery to individuals or groups.

FAQ Frequently Asked Question. Documents that list such questions and their answers are referred to as FAQs. Much of the documentation in the Usenet world resides in FAQ files (in many cases periodically posted to the group `news.answers`.)

Firewall A means of protecting a site on the Internet that has heightened security or privacy concerns. Sites behind firewalls may not be accessible (or even visible) using standard tools.

FreeNet One of a number of community-oriented bulletin-board systems around the world. The original FreeNet was established in Cleveland Ohio at Case Western Reserve University. The concept has spread worldwide. Many FreeNets are accessible via the Internet as well as local dial-up.

FTP File Transfer Protocol. A standard protocol for sending files from one computer to another on TCP/IP networks, such as the Internet. This is also the command the user usually types to start an FTP session; "FTP" is sometimes used as a verb, e.g., "FTP this file from msdos.archive.umich.edu."

FQDN Fully Qualified Domain Name. A domain name that is specified completely, such as mugwump.cl.msu.edu. A fully qualified name uniquely specifies a host on the global Internet.

full-duplex A communications link that is able to transmit data in both directions simultaneously.

gateway A service that translates messages between differing protocols or formats; e.g., a Gopher server can act as a gateway to a WAIS database, or a gateway might allow Internet-style (SMTP) mail to go to an X.400 network. (In early ARPANET/Internet usage, "gateway" was used to mean a "router." This usage has been abandoned.)

GIF Graphics Interchange Format. A still-image file format promoted by CompuServe. Software to view GIF images is commonly available for most computing environments in the form of public domain, shareware, or commercial products.

GNU Acronym for GNU is Not Unix. A project to deliver Unix operating system clones and related tools as freely available software; the Gn Gopher server and the PostScript viewing utility Ghostscript are examples of tools offered under the Gnu license.

Gopher A hierarchical menu system for delivering documents over the Internet. Conceived at the University of Minnesota, Gopher is characterized by relative simplicity of design and ease of implementation. Gopher follows the client/server model but also embraces the concept of a public client, allowing access for users who have not installed specialized software.

Gopherspace All documents and all openly accessible Gopher servers, seen as a collection. Because Gophers are connected to one another, one can jump from server to server, either at the root level, or directly deep into another Gopher's hierarchy.

hacker A term used originally to refer to a programmer who spends long hours refining a computer program or system to enhance its function or performance; this connotation implies veneration. A more popular connotation of "hacker" is more negative, often implying someone who attempts to break into computer systems. (See **cracker.**)

half-duplex A communications link that can transmit information in both directions, but only one direction at a time; the link must be "turned around" for data to switch direction.

home page The initial page on a World-Wide Web (HTTP) server. More loosely, the root document describing an organization (or individual) offered via the Web.

HTML The Hypertext Markup Language used to describe documents to be delivered via the World-Wide Web. HTML allows a document to contain links to another document, giving WWW its hypertext (and hypermedia) capabilities.

HTML+ A proposed successor to HTML, offering richer presentation options, such as the ability to describe tabular information or text that is intended to "wrap" around a graphic. HTML+ is expected to be a superset of HTML; that is, a client that can handle HTML+ documents will be able to handle HTML documents.

hypertext A scheme for supporting embedded links within documents. While browsing a document with hypertext links, a user can select one of those links and quickly move to the document it points to. Popularized by the HyperCard Macintosh program.

hypermedia A multimedia system that incorporates hypertext-style links embedded within documents. Many CD-ROM systems offer hypermedia documents. Given a client such as NCSA Mosaic and a set of image and sound players, the World-Wide Web becomes a networked hypermedia environment.

HYTELNET A hypertext database of Internet systems, such as online catalogs and CWISes. The PC version of the program is available from Peter Scott at the University of Saskatchewan. The Unix and VMS versions can make Internet connections to listed systems; the PC version cannot.

IANA Internet Assigned Numbers Authority. Internet protocol writers must agree upon standard values for fields used within the protocols. IANA is the organization that registers these standard numbers. For instance, IANA assigned TCP port 70 to Gopher. IANA also registers other "assigned numbers" such as MIME content types.

IETF   Internet Engineering Task Force. IETF devises new and updated protocols to be used on the Internet. It is an informal body composed of Working Groups that carry on discussions over the Internet and in periodic meetings.

internet   Any network of networks. (Note lowercase *i*.)

Internet   The global network of networks based on the TCP/IP protocol family that evolved from the ARPANET. (Note capital *I*.)

Internet information provider   A person or organization that "publishes" information for others to read via the Internet. The information provider might run a network server (such as a Gopher server, an e-mail server, or a World-Wide Web server) or the information provider might rely upon a proxy server to physically host the information.

Internet service provider   A company or other organization that offers access to the Internet for individuals or other organizations. Styles of access offered by Internet service providers vary dramatically, from e-mail only to simple dial-up to direct-connection-type services.

inverse multiplexing   The process of using more than one physical communications path to carry a single channel of communications. For instance, ISDN telephone service typically offers two 64 kilobit/second channels; with hardware and software to perform inverse multiplexing, one can combine these two channels for an effective rate of 128 kilobits/second.

IP address   A unique number assigned to a computer on a TCP/IP network. Conventions have been set up to assign IP numbers in a systematic fashion across the Internet. Whether a machine is a large server or a small PC, if it is to be on the Internet, it must have an assigned IP address. IP addresses look like "35.8.2.61." There are always four numeric values, separated by periods, in IP addresses.

JFIF   JPEG File Interchange Format. A name sometimes applied to image files that implement the **JPEG** compression scheme.

JPEG   Joint Photographic Experts Group. A still-image file format that allows efficient compression. The JPEG compression scheme is "lossy"; it does not preserve all of the data, but it can yield significant space savings with little perceptible loss. JPEG viewers are relatively slow compared to GIF viewers.

local area network (LAN)   A network that covers a relatively small geographic area, such as an office, a floor of a building, or an entire building. In some cases a network that serves a small campus might be considered a LAN.

lossy compression   A compression scheme that does not guarantee preservation of all the bits of information in the original data. JPEG, for instance, is a lossy image compression scheme. The user selects a quality factor during compression that determines the amount of loss. This term can be misleading; the quality of a compressed JPEG image can be perfectly satisfactory despite the loss of information.

man pages   Unix systems support a `man` command, which is a way to view pages from the Unix reference manual online. Software packages intended for installation under Unix often include the appropriate man pages for installation along with the executable programs.

MIME   Multipurpose Internet Mail Extensions. Initially, an extension of Internet mail standards to allow binary data to be embedded in Internet (RFC 822) mail. Since its introduction in 1992, MIME has been implemented on several computer platforms (often under the name "Metamail"), and it is increasingly viewed as the appropriate standard for packaging multimedia information to be moved across dissimilar computing environments, whether sent via e-mail or otherwise.

mirror   A service that replicates another service. For instance, a site may "mirror" another site's Gopher or FTP offerings. Sites agree to serve as mirrors of popular or unique network resources in the interest of network efficiency and reliable service.

Mosaic   A multipurpose client program developed by the National Center for Supercomputing Applications. Mosaic acts as a client for multiple Internet services, including Gopher, WAIS, WWW, Usenet News, and FTP. Initially implemented on Unix systems supporting X Window and Motif. Versions of Mosaic are available for the Macintosh and Microsoft Windows as well.

MPEG   A cousin of **JPEG,** MPEG is a standard for files containing moving images (and, optionally, sound in the MPEG-2 variant).

multiplex   To carry more than one stream of information or channel over a communications medium. For instance, a broadband coaxial cable or a fiber-optics cable almost always carries multiple channels of data.

name server   A computer that looks up information in the Domain Names System on behalf of a client. When you connect to a host on the Internet by specifying a Domain Name, the software on your computer queries a local name server, which either provides your computer with the IP address for you (if it is responsible for the address you seek), or it tells your computer to look for the address at another name server elsewhere.

Net, the   A generic label for the world of online information, sometimes used to refer to the Internet, sometimes used even more broadly. "I found an answer to my Windows problem on the Net today" might refer to getting an answer via Usenet News or a mailing list. "It's on the Net" might mean a document is available via Gopher or World-Wide Web, or a program is available for anonymous FTP.

NIC   Network Information Center. Various forms of NICs have existed over the years in support of the Internet. Currently, the most visible NIC is the InterNIC, an NSF-funded venture that provides services to the Internet at large. Details of InterNIC services are available from the InterNIC Gopher (`is.internic.net`, port 70).

NIC   Network Interface Card. A general term for the interface card one plugs into a computer in order to connect it to a local area network. Well over 100 vendors sell such interface cards for IBM PC clones alone; many computers come with a built-in network interface.

NNTP   Network News Transmission Protocol. The protocol used to deliver **Usenet News.**

packet   A chunk of data to be delivered over a network. This term is used rather broadly, and is applied to data units at the Ethernet layer, the IP layer, or in other networking contexts.

packet switching network   A network that moves packets as independently routed units; a given packet need not follow the same path as others with the same starting and ending points.

pager   a utility program that allows a user to "page" through a file. In the Unix world, the built-in tool "more" is commonly used as a pager. An improved tool called "less" allows the user to page forward and backward in a file. See **browser.**

PH   The client program that allows searching of a CSO-style telephone book.

platform   A particular hardware and software environment. Examples: MS-DOS on an 80486 personal computer, Unix on a Sun SPARCstation, System 7 on a Macintosh Powerbook 180.

PostScript   A printer description language from Adobe. PostScript is the dominant format used for desktop publishing. Documents in PostScript format are commonly shared across the Internet and printed on laser printers after retrieval from a remote archive.

PPP   Point-to-Point Protocol. A relatively new protocol that provides for TCP/IP to be carried over a variety of point-to-point connections. In particular, PPP allows dial-up telephone users to connect to the Internet as if they were directly attached users. With PPP (or similar functionality) a user can use Internet client software, such as a Gopher client, in a dial-up session. Without PPP, the user must dial into a host or public client service via a conventional terminal session (usually VT 100).

PEM   Privacy Enhanced Mail. A proposed standard mechanism for encrypting e-mail on the Internet.

provider   This term is used in two senses: (1) as a service provider; i.e., an organization that offers Internet access to individuals or organizations, and (2) as an information provider; i.e., an individual or organization using the Internet as a vehicle for delivering information to others.

public client   A service to which one can connect, typically via Telnet, offering some of the features of a client program one would install on a workstation. A public client can make it possible to access a service that otherwise might be inaccessible, but usually at a cost of losing functions (such as graphics).

QI   Query Interpreter. The server that answers queries from a CSO-style telephone client such as PH.

RFC   Request for Comments. Documents that define both proposed and adopted Internet protocol standards. RFCs are numbered in an ordinal fashion.

resolver   Software on a client computer that connects to the Domain Name System in order to "resolve" a domain-style host name into an IP address.

resource discovery   The process of locating documents or services of value on a computer network. This term is used in two connotations: purposeful searches, where the user knows what the goal of the search is, and serendipitous discovery, where the user encounters useful or interesting resources while browsing.

router   A computer that determines where to forward packets intended for a remote network; routers are the devices that connect local area networks and wide area networks, creating an internet. At a minumum, a router used on the Internet knows how to route IP packets; some routers operate as "multiprotocol routers," handling, for instance, IP as well as Netware IPX at once. A router is distinguished from a **bridge** by the kind of work each does. Bridges operate at a lower level, the "media control layer" (for instance, Ethernet).

selector string   A string of characters that is associated with an item in a Gopher menu; the selector is delivered to the Gopher client program along with the title for the document and the address and TCP port of the server. When a user chooses a title, the client passes the selector string to the server, which is how the server knows what file to send back. The contents of the selector string are irrelevant to the client. Sometimes referred to as "path."

SGML   Standard Generalized Markup Language. SGML is a scheme (and an ISO standard) for describing structural information embedded within a document. SGML is popular in scholarly and electronic publishing as a way to provide multiple views of a document and to foster document reuse. An SGML-compliant set of structures called HTML is used by World-Wide Web.

SLIP   Serial Line IP. A protocol that allows users to connect to the Internet over dial-up telephone connections with TCP/IP service over the phone line. Being supplanted by PPP.

SMTP   Simple Mail Transfer Protocol. A protocol for sending e-mail messages between computers on TCP/IP networks, such as the Internet. The user does not run a program named SMTP; instead, various e-mail packages know how to utilize this protocol.

snail mail   Conventional delivery of paper mail, i.e., by the postal service; the term emphasizes the contrast with **e-mail.**

surfing   Browsing the Net more or less at random, hopping from document to document, and from host to host, as whim dictates. Surfing was enabled by the deployment of tools like Gopher, which make such navigation trivially easy. Cf "channel surfing" on cable systems with dozens of channels.

sysop   System Operator. Used typically in the bulletin board system community to refer to the manager of the BBS. In the Internet community, the term "system manager" or "system administrator" is used to refer to those who manage computer systems; "network managers" manage networks; and "moderators" or "list owners" manage network mailing lists.

system administrator   A person, usually with a computer programming background, who administers the operating system and key applications programs on a computer system. Equivalent to "system programmer" as used in mainframe circles.

TCP/IP   Transmission Control Protocol/Internet Protocol. Technically, TCP and IP are separate protocols; together they allow computers on the Internet to communicate by providing a reliable way for bytes to be delivered in order over a network connection. Connections are made to TCP "ports," allowing multiple connections per machine. A port is described by a number (e.g., Gopher servers typically use port 70).

Telnet   The protocol used over TCP/IP for remote-terminal sessions. Usually implemented as a command of the same name.

TN3270   A variant of Telnet that allows TCP/IP connections to IBM mainframes that utilize the IBM 3270 terminal conventions.

Trojan Horse   A type of hostile attack software, whereby the hostile program masquerades as an innocent system. For example: a computer program presents a login screen as if you have reached a known host over the network, when in fact you are connected to the attacker's system.

Uniform Resource Identifier An umbrella term for standards that describe Internet resources in a uniform way. The IETF is considering a Uniform Resource Locator, which will be a standard way to name a particular document on a particular network server. Another proposed standard, the Uniform Resource Number, will be a unique number (analogous to an ISBN) assigned to a document or resource regardless of its location. Another form of URI may address electronic citations.

Uniform Resource Locator (URL) A name that uniquely identifies a document or service on the Internet. URLs were defined and deployed in the World-Wide Web community; the Uniform Resource Identifier standards will incorporate URLs.

union list A list comprising the "union" of two or more lists. Libraries often use this term when they combine, for instance, multiple catalogs into a single, complete catalog; the resulting union list shows all holdings from all of the catalogs. "Union lists" of Internet resources are beginning to appear.

Usenet News A distributed discussion list system, much of whose traffic is carried over the Internet. Usenet News services consist of news "feeds" typically provided by one or more servers on a campus network, and news "readers" (i.e., client software that communicates with the server over a news delivery protocol known as NNTP).

VAN Value Added Network. Denotes a computer network that offers services beyond those of a simple data communications pipe, such as electronic mail, mailing list services, and access to tools like Gopher, the World-Wide Web, and WAIS.

Veronica A service that provides an Internet-wide index of Gopher document titles. Developed at the University of Nevada, Veronica servers periodically poll all the Gopher servers they can connect to and build a title index that can, in turn, be pointed to as a standard Gopher index.

virtual library An online collection of electronic books and journals, organized systematically for access over a network. Usually connotes the notion of providing access to the union of the online collections of several separate library entities, so that the combined collection is available to the patrons of each constituent library.

VT 100 The dominant communications protocol for full-screen terminal sessions. The VT 100 standard was defined by the Digital Equipment Corporation in the 1970s. Most terminal emulation software packages (e.g., Kermit and PROCOMM) implement VT 100 or its descendants (VT 220, VT 320).

v.fast (Pronounced "vee dot fast.") A slang term for the next generation of modems, able to send data at a base speed of 28,000 bits per second.

V.32/V.32 bis A pair of related international standards for modems that communicate at a data rate of 14,400 bits per second. Many of today's popular modems combine these standards with V.42 and V.42 bis features, providing error-free transmission of data at effective rates up to 57,600 bits per second.

V.42 An international standard for error detection and correction in modem transmissions.

V.42 bis An international standard for data compression in modem communications.

WAIS Wide Area Information Servers. Based on an extension of the Z39.50-1988 standard, WAIS allows searches of documents on one or more WAIS servers. Originally promulgated by Thinking Machines Corporation, WAIS is now offered in a commercial version (by WAIS, Inc.) and a public domain version (by the Clearinghouse for Networked Information Discovery and Retrieval). The WAIS search engine is commonly used by Gopher servers. An index document under the Unix Gopher server can point to a stand-alone WAIS server.

white pages   A directory service that is organized the same way as telephone book white pages; i.e., indexed by the name of the person, place, or resource you want to look up.

Whois   A relatively simple protocol (and related software) for searching "white pages" directory information on the Internet. Whois is used as a way to search the registry of Internet hosts maintained by the InterNIC; it is also the tool of choice for publishing directory information at a number of Internet sites.

Whois++   A proposed standard for providing a relatively simple, but powerful, integrated directory service for locating people, places, and resources on the Internet, extending on the model of Whois.

wide area network   A network that covers a large geographical area, perhaps as large as a state, a nation, or even an international area.

World-Wide Web   A network-based hypertext document delivery system. Developed at CERN in Switzerland, WWW is growing in popularity. As a hypertext system, WWW supports links to other documents within a given document; by comparison, Gopher does not.

xbm   An X Window bitmap file; an image file format used commonly in the X community.

X Window   A standard that allows a graphical user interface to be manipulated over a TCP/IP network, X Window comes from the Massachusetts Institute of Technology and the X consortium. Contrary to what one might expect in client/server nomenclature, an X server runs at a user's workstation, allowing an X client at a remote computer to manipulate the user's screen and accept commands from the user. Many sophisticated graphical applications are initially deployed under X Window. Sometimes referred to simply as "X." Technically, X by itself is simply the protocol; a "window manager" such as Motif is required to make X useful.

X.25   A communications protocol widely used as public and private data networks were built in the 1970s and 1980s. X.25 is still used for point-to-point links in many networks.

X.400   A standard for addressing and interchange of e-mail; the addressing scheme is hierarchical, highly generalizable, and virtually impenetrable to the human eye.

X.500   A hierarchical, distributed directory scheme for looking up information about organizations and individuals. X.500 is general enough in its design so as to theoretically be able to hold information about all organizations and individuals in all countries on the planet. X.500 was designed to complement X.400.

yellow pages   A directory service that is organized the same way as telephone book yellow pages; i.e., organized into categories of services.

Z39.50   A NISO standard defining a client/server model for searching bibliographic and other databases. There are 1988 and 1992 versions of Z39.50. WAIS follows the Z39.50 protocol, as do some other implementations of client/server search tools.

Z39.58   A NISO standard describing a Common Command Language for online catalogs. The theory is that a user moving from one catalog to another should be able to type the same commands on various systems.

Index

ABOUT THE AUTHOR

Rich Wiggins manages the Central Systems Service group in the Computer Laboratory at Michigan State University. He coordinates the deployment of MSU's campus-wide information system (CWIS) using Gopher and World-Wide Web. He has been active in the Gopher and WWW communities since early 1992, and organized the first Gopher Workshop in August 1992. He began working with computer networks in 1979 as a consultant helping users of the Merit network. Previously, he has contributed to a book on the VM/CMS operating system and to *Computer Language* magazine. He moderates the Usernet News group comp.infosystems.announce.

ABOUT THE SERIES

The J. Ranade Workstation Series is McGraw-Hill's primary vehicle for providing workstation professionals with timely concepts, solutions, and applications. Jay Ranade is also Series Editor in Chief of the J. Ranade IBM and DEC Series and Series Advisor to the McGraw-Hill Series on Computer Communications.

Jay Ranade, Series Editor in Chief and best-selling computer author, is a Senior Systems Architect and Assistant V. P. at Merrill Lynch.